D1089112

MIAMI-DADE COLLEGE LIBRARY

Historic Documents
of 2009

Heather Kerrigan, Editor

Includes Cumulative Index, 2005–2009

CQ PRESS

A Division of SAGE
Washington, D.C.

MIAMI DADE COLLEGE LIBRARY

CQ Press
2300 N Street, NW, Suite 800
Washington, DC 20037

Phone: 202-729-1900; toll-free, 1-866-4CQ-PRESS (1-866-427-7737)

Web: www.cqpress.com

Copyright © 2011 by CQ Press, a division of SAGE. CQ Press is a registered trademark of Congressional Quarterly Inc.

All rights reserved. No part of this publication may be reproduced or transmitted in any form or by any means, electronic or mechanical, including photocopy, recording, or any information storage and retrieval system, without permission in writing from the publisher.

Permissions for copyrighted material appear on page 673, which is to be considered an extension of the copyright page.

Sponsoring and Development Editor: Andrew Boney
Volume Editor: Heather Kerrigan
Contributors: Hilary Ewing, Linda Fecteau, Melissa Feinberg, Heather Kerrigan, Roger K. Smith
Copy Editor: Debbie K. Hardin
Production Editor: Emily Bakely
Cover Designer: Malcolm McGaughy, McGaughy Design
Cover Photos: AP Images
Composition: C&M Digitals (P) Ltd.
Indexer: Julia Petrakis

⊛ The paper used in this publication exceeds the requirements of the American National Standard for Information Sciences—Permanence of Paper for Printed Library Materials, ANSI Z39.48-1992.

Printed and bound in the United States of America

14   13   12   11   10   1   2   3   4   5

The Library of Congress cataloged the first issue of this title as follows:
Historic documents. 1972–
Washington. Congressional Quarterly Inc.

1. United States—Politics and government—1945—Yearbooks.
2. World politics—1945—Yearbooks. I. Congressional Quarterly Inc.
E839.5H57   917.3´03´9205   72-97888

ISSN 0892-080X
ISBN 978-1-60426-998-7

Contents

JANUARY

FEBRUARY

MARCH

APRIL

AUGUST

SEPTEMBER

OCTOBER

NOVEMBER

Thematic Table of Contents

GOVERNMENT AND POLITICS

HEALTH AND SOCIAL SERVICES

INTERNATIONAL AFFAIRS
Africa

INTERNATIONAL AFFAIRS
Asia

INTERNATIONAL AFFAIRS
Europe

INTERNATIONAL AFFAIRS
Latin America and the Caribbean

INTERNATIONAL AFFAIRS
Middle East

INTERNATIONAL AFFAIRS
Russia and Former Soviet Republics

INTERNATIONAL AFFAIRS
Global Issues

NATIONAL SECURITY AND TERRORISM

RIGHTS, RESPONSIBILITIES, AND JUSTICE

List of Document Sources

CONGRESS

EXECUTIVE DEPARTMENTS AND AGENCIES

INTERNATIONAL NONGOVERNMENTAL ORGANIZATIONS

JUDICIARY

NON-U.S. GOVERNMENTS

U.S. NONGOVERNMENTAL ORGANIZATIONS

U.S. STATE AND LOCAL GOVERNMENTS

WHITE HOUSE AND THE PRESIDENT

Preface

A continuing economic crisis around the world; the inauguration of President Barack Obama; a contentious battle over national health care reform; political turmoil in Guinea-Bissau and Honduras; a landmark election in Japan; the confirmation of the first Hispanic Supreme Court justice; and significant Supreme Court rulings on elections, DNA testing, and searches in schools are just a few of the topics of national and international importance chosen for discussion in *Historic Documents of 2009*. This edition marks the thirty-eighth volume of a CQ Press project that began with *Historic Documents of 1972*. This series allows students, librarians, journalists, scholars, and others to research and understand the most important domestic and foreign issues and events of the year through primary source documents. To aid research, many of the lengthy documents written for specialized audiences have been excerpted to highlight the most important sections. The official statements, news conferences, speeches, special studies, and court decisions presented here should be of lasting public and academic interest.

Historic Documents of 2009 opens with an "Overview of 2009," a sweeping narrative of the key events and issues of the year which provides context for the documents that follow. The balance of the book is organized chronologically, with each article comprising an introduction entitled "Document in Context" and one or more related documents on a specific event, issue, or topic. The introductions provide context and an account of further developments during the year. A thematic table of contents (page xv) and a list of documents organized by source (page xix) follow the standard table of contents and assist readers in locating events and documents.

As events, issues, and consequences become more complex and far-reaching, these introductions and documents yield important information and deepen understanding about the world's increasing interconnectedness. As memories of current events fade, these selections will continue to further understanding of the events and issues that have shaped the lives of people around the world.

How to Use This Book

Each of the 70 entries in this edition consists of two parts: a comprehensive introduction followed by one or more primary source documents. The articles are arranged in chronological order by month. Articles with multiple documents are ordered according to the date of the first document. There are several ways to find events and documents of interest:

By date: If the approximate date of an event or document is known, browse through the titles for that month in the table of contents. Alternatively, browse the monthly tables of contents that appear at the beginning of each month's articles.

By theme: To find a particular topic or subject area, browse the thematic table of contents.

By document type or source: To find a particular type of document or document source, such as the White House or Congress, review the list of document sources.

By index: The five-year index allows researchers to locate references to specific events or documents as well as entries on the same or related subjects. The index in this volume covers the years 2005–2009. A separate volume, *Historic Documents Index, 1972–2005,* may also be useful.

Each article begins with a section entitled "Document in Context." This feature provides historical and intellectual contexts for the documents that follow. Documents are reproduced with the spelling, capitalization, and punctuation of the original or official copy. Ellipsis points indicate textual omissions (unless they were present in the documents themselves indicating pauses in speech), and brackets are used for editorial insertions within documents for text clarification. Other excerpting exceptions are presented in brackets preceding the document text. The excerpting of Supreme Court opinions has been done somewhat differently than other documents. In-text references to laws and other cases have been removed to improve the readability of opinions. In those documents, readers will only find ellipses used when sections of narrative text have been removed. Full citations appear at the end of each document. If a document is not available on the Internet, a print citation is provided. For further reading on a particular topic consult the "Other Historic Documents of Interest" section at the end of each article. These provide cross-references for related articles in this edition of *Historic Documents* as well as in previous editions. References to articles from past volumes include the year and page number for easy retrieval.

Overview of 2009

The year 2009 brought significant change to Washington, with the swearing in of a new president, the installation of a new cabinet, the confirmation of a new Supreme Court justice, and the announcement of new domestic and international policy goals. President Barack Obama came to office optimistic yet facing incredible economic challenges and two wars abroad. His campaign promise to enact major health care reform met with strong opposition in parts of the country and in Congress, despite Democratic control of the House and Senate. In what many considered a premature decision, President Obama was awarded the Nobel Peace Prize after less than one year in office. The president traveled abroad extensively, at one point attending the UN climate change summit, a meeting that produced few new agreements for capping carbon emissions.

Around the world, many nations continued to feel the effects of recession. Industrialized nations implemented government spending programs to provide a necessary infusion of funds to put people back to work, while developing nations scrambled to make up for aid lost when the recession hit and wealthier nations were no longer able to provide help. North Korea's and Iran's governments continued building a nuclear arsenal in 2009, seemingly unfazed by UN sanctions. Japan elected a new government, and in Africa and South America various nations experienced regime change, some through peaceful measures and others through coups and assassinations.

GLOBAL ECONOMIC CRISIS

The economic crisis that began in 2007 continued into its third year in 2009, again dominating headlines. U.S. unemployment rose from 7.6 percent in January to 10 percent in December; in Michigan, unemployment hit its highest level in twenty-five years, at 15.4 percent, largely because of the closure of multiple car-manufacturing plants. Across the country, as an increasing number of citizens found themselves unemployed, states and localities had their social services stretched to the breaking point. Decreased tax revenue meant less money for social services, and states and cities scrambled to make up for lost revenue by increasing taxes and fees.

To help shore up the economy and close billion-dollar budget gaps by infusing more money into state and local governments, Congress passed the American Recovery and Reinvestment Act of 2009 (ARRA) in February. The act, which carried a more than $700 billion price tag, was intended to create and preserve jobs, increase funding for infrastructure and energy efficiency, expand social benefits to those most in need, and help families through tax cuts.

The ARRA was one of the largest government spending projects since World War II and followed on the heels of the George W. Bush administration's Economic Stimulus Act of 2008. Newly elected president Obama made it an early goal of his presidency to see that the ARRA was passed by Congress. In the House of Representatives, the bill was easily passed, thanks to the Democratic majority, but in the Senate, it faced more resistance, as Democrats were still struggling to capture the elusive sixty-seat majority. The argument in both houses of Congress rested on how much the program would cost and what the ultimate benefit would be. Republicans argued that the costs would far outweigh the number of jobs created, thus adding to the deficit, while Democrats, citing Mark Zandi, chief economist and cofounder of Moody's Economy .com, said the jobless rate would be 2 percent higher without the government infusion of funds.

On February 4, 2009, the Congressional Budget Office (CBO) released a report on the stimulus package, giving its independent assessment of how the program would benefit Americans. According to the CBO, the plan would initially increase employment and the U.S. gross domestic product (GDP), but by 2019, the overall GDP would decrease, largely because of declining productivity and business investment, not because of unemployment. In a letter dated February 11, 2009, the CBO indicated that there was great debate among economists about how well the plan would actually work. Most economists agreed, however, that success would rest largely on whether jobs were created at a high enough rate. The White House estimated that the program would create or save 3.5 million jobs in 2009 and 2010.

Zandi estimated that if the stimulus worked as expected, by the end of the year, monthly job losses would be closer to 250,000 per month, down from the 500,000 per month at the time the stimulus passed. Although this was not a perfect test—because there was no way to predict with absolute accuracy whether the economy would turn itself around or, if it did, whether the infusion of funds was responsible—by the end of the year, the Bureau of Labor Statistics announced in its monthly report that in November the economy had lost 11,000 jobs, the lowest number in two years.

By late 2009, the economy was beginning to show signs of improvement. In September, chair of the Federal Reserve Board Ben Bernanke announced that the recession had ended. However, Bernanke warned that economic troubles were not over yet. Regardless of the amount of improvement shown, the White House reminded Americans that there was still work left to be done. At the end of 2009, the outlook on long-term employment remained grim.

The United States was by no means alone in facing a third year of recession. Many large, industrialized nations around the world continued to feel the effects of the downturn, and many developing nations, dependent on aid from the industrialized countries, suffered as well. Some nations implemented stimulus plans or helped to bail out failing banks as the United States had done. To aid nations worldwide, in April the Group of 20 (G-20) pledged $1.1 trillion to the International Monetary Fund (IMF) and other international financial organizations.

Health Care

Likely the most contentious issue in politics in 2009 was health care reform. President Obama came into office promising to reform the nation's health care and health insurance systems to ensure fair and affordable coverage for all Americans. Shortly after his inauguration, Obama called on Congress to put together a proposal for reform and pass it before the end of 2009. Republicans in both houses, along with a small number of Democrats, put up heavy resistance to the bill, which constantly evolved as it made its way through five congressional committees to reach the House and Senate floors. During the August congressional recess, senators and representatives returned to their home districts and called town hall meetings with citizens to discuss plans for health care reform. The heated debates that ensued during these meetings, at which some attendees compared the government's health care plans to socialism, dominated news coverage. Despite the airing of grievances, opinion polls throughout 2009 continued to show that a majority of Americans supported health care reform.

President Obama's objective in calling for health care reform was to provide health insurance coverage to tens of millions of Americans without it, prevent insurance companies from denying coverage for preexisting conditions or imposing caps on annual or lifetime claims, and contain the cost, which had risen at a rate higher than that of inflation for many years. The plan would require Americans to carry health insurance, in the same way drivers are required to have car insurance. Anyone who chose not to purchase insurance, and did not receive it from his or her employer, would be charged a fine. For those unable to afford health insurance, subsidies would be offered to help defray the cost of premiums, and the income limit for Medicaid qualification would be raised. In addition, young adults would be able to remain on their parents' coverage well into their twenties.

Early on, the Obama administration rejected the idea of single-payer government-run insurance like that offered in Canada, but President Obama was a supporter of a public option, an early point of contention in the House and Senate and among voters. The public option would allow citizens to purchase group health insurance through the federal government. Obama argued that the public option would infuse competition into the health insurance market that would help bring down costs. As the year progressed, however, the president increasingly backed away from the idea of a public option.

In an effort to refocus the debate, President Obama spoke before a joint session of Congress on September 9, during which he called on leaders of both parties to work together to reach a compromise. The president also used his speech to clarify what he characterized as false information being used to scare voters away from health care reform, including the threat of death panels (which were touted by the opposition as deciding who would receive life-saving care and who would not), and the question of whether illegal immigrants would be insured. President Obama's plan, and those in Congress, ensured that no person illegally in the United States would receive government-sponsored health coverage.

In the House, it was likely that health care reform would pass, given the comfortable Democratic majority. However, Democrats still needed to scramble to ensure enough votes for passage when the bill came up for a vote. Republicans in the House criticized the Democrats for wanting to pass health reform no matter what it took or what was included in the bill. Some Democrats criticized the bill, saying that it was too weak and industry friendly. Another heated issue was abortion and whether government-subsidized insurance plans would be required to cover them. Rep. Bart Stupak, D-Mich., a socially conservative Democrat, attached an amendment preventing government options from covering abortions. Liberal Democrats argued that this restricted reproductive rights. The Stupak amendment remained in the health care bill that came to a vote on the floor on November 7. The reform bill barely passed, by a vote of 220–215, with thirty-nine Democrats and all but one Republican voting in opposition.

In the Senate, however, the situation played out much differently. Sixty votes were needed to avoid a filibuster, and although Democrats briefly held a sixty-seat majority, the death of Sen. Edward Kennedy, D-Mass., who had devoted considerable effort in the Senate to health care reform, left Democrats one vote short of a filibuster-proof majority. Regardless of the number of seats held by Democrats in Congress, getting the entire party to vote for health care reform proved to be a challenge. When Senate Democrats learned they would garner no support from Republicans, they were forced to rethink their strategy and focus on crafting legislation that would at least attract all the members of their own party.

Republicans in the Senate stepped up their criticism of what they dubbed "Obamacare" and prepared to filibuster any legislation that came to the floor, especially if it contained a public option. Other Republicans took action to thwart health care reform, including former Republican vice-presidential candidate Sarah Palin, who said that what she considered the government takeover of health care would create the aforementioned "death panels" that would ration end-of-life care. Although her claim was erroneous, it was spread by anti–health-care reform groups and Republican pundits around the country. An up-and-coming national movement, the Tea Party (with TEA standing for *taxed enough already*), used health care reform as a platform to air their concerns about excessive government spending, waste, and intrusion.

Various alternatives to the public option were debated in the Senate, including a network of nonprofit insurance cooperatives or an option for earlier buy-in to Medicare. However, none of the options attracted sixty senators. Majority Leader Harry Reid, D-Nev., originally announced that the legislation would retain the public option, but after Sen. Joe Lieberman, I-Conn., said he would not support such a bill, Democrats were forced to cater to his interests and remove the option. Democrats also needed to work to gain support from Sen. Ben Nelson, D-Neb., who took issue with abortion funding. To appease Nelson, the Democrats reached a deal that would place restrictions on abortion funding and would exempt Nebraska from paying to expand Medicaid. The Senate bill came to a vote on December 24 and passed 60–39. The differing provisions in the House and Senate bills would need to be merged in conference committee, meaning the health care debate would continue into 2010.

SUPREME COURT DECISIONS

The U.S. Supreme Court welcomed a new justice, Sonia Sotomayor, and handed down significant rulings on civil rights, judicial recusal, voting rights, and the rights of prisoners. Sotomayor, the first Hispanic justice in the Court's history, replaced retiring justice David Souter. Sotomayor faced tough questioning before the Senate Judiciary Committee, which focused a good amount of attention on a comment previously made by the justice in which she explained that "a wise Latina woman with the richness of her experiences would more often than not reach a better conclusion than a white male who hasn't lived that life."

One issue on the Supreme Court's 2009 docket involved whether judges should remove themselves from a trial if they have received campaign funds from someone involved in the case. On June 2, 2009, the Court took up judicial recusal for the first time, and voted 5-4 in *Caperton v. A.T. Massey Coal Company* that the Due Process Clause of the Fourteenth Amendment had been violated by a West Virginia supreme court justice who had refused to step down from a case that involved a campaign donor. The justices writing for the majority overturned a decision that the judge was not required to recuse himself. According to the Supreme Court majority, although there was no proof of bias, the "probability of actual bias on the part of the judge . . . [was] too high to be constitutionally tolerable."

The Court took up the issue of state's rights in *District Attorney's Office for the Third Judicial District v. Osborne,* in which a prisoner sought access to the DNA evidence that had been used against him at trial in an effort to run additional tests that he claimed would prove his innocence. The Court ruled 5-4 that it could not overturn state decisions, which in this particular case would mean the petitioner would have to abide by state law in the jurisdiction in which he had been convicted.

In *Northwest Austin Municipal Utility District Number One v. Holder et al.,* the Court took up the issue of the 1965 Voting Rights Act. Voting nearly unanimously, and avoiding constitutional issues, the Court questioned whether the Voting Rights Act was still necessary after more than four decades had passed.

The constitutionality of strip searches of students was on the Court's docket for 2009 after an underage student in Pennsylvania was forced to take her clothes off and pull her underwear aside on suspicion that she was carrying prescription-strength painkillers with the intent to give them to students. This was not the first time the Court had taken up the issue of student's rights while on school property, most often finding that students lose some constitutional privacy rights but retain others. In this instance, the Court ruled 8-1 in *Safford v. Redding* that the student's privacy rights had been violated because the school had no reasonable proof that she had been carrying prescription-strength painkillers.

In one of the most highly publicized cases of 2009, the Court took up the issue of the Civil Rights Act as it pertained to hiring. In *Ricci v. DeStefano,* white firefighters in New Haven, Connecticut, sued the city over a promotional exam that was administered but later thrown out after no African American scored high enough to qualify for a promotion. The white firefighters claimed reverse discrimination. New Haven, on the other hand, said that it was trying to follow federal law that looks suspiciously on promotional exams that disadvantage minorities. In this case, the Court ruled 5-4 that the white firefighters had been discriminated against by New Haven, which was held in violation of Title VII of the Civil Rights Act.

Foreign Affairs

In early 2009, African issues were high on the international radar, beginning on March 2, 2009, when Guinea-Bissau's democratically elected president, João Bernardo Vieira, was killed during a clash between two rival factions. The head of the nation's military had been killed hours earlier. The immediate concern was that a coup had taken place that would threaten democracy in the small African nation. Although the government of Guinea-Bissau announced that there had been no coup, international observers worried that the new president would be unable to maintain control.

Only two days after the death of Vieira, the International Criminal Court (ICC), located in The Hague, The Netherlands, charged Sudan's president, Omar al-Bashir, with war crimes and crimes against humanity. The ICC issued a warrant for Bashir's arrest and called on member nations, and Sudanese, to turn him in. The ICC's charges stemmed mainly from violence in Darfur, where, during the previous six years, nearly 300,000 people had died, some from starvation and others during combat. Bashir showed no signs of backing down, and the Sudanese constitution gave the president immunity from criminal prosecution.

North Korea continued its nuclear program in 2009, announcing in May that it had conducted its second test in three years. Initial reports indicated that the blast was as strong as those in Japan during World War II, when atomic bombs were dropped, but later investigations concluded that although the test was twenty times larger than North Korea's first test in 2006, it fell far short of the levels from Hiroshima and Nagasaki. International leaders immediately condemned the action and called for increased sanctions and pressure. Japan, South Korea, the United States, China, and Russia had been holding talks with North Korea on its nuclear program since 2003 in an effort to halt the production and use of nuclear weapons, but progress had been slow, and the nuclear test in May and an earlier long-range missile test in April had put a damper on future talks.

Iran made news in 2009 for continued development of its nuclear program and its June 2009 presidential elections. President Mahmoud Ahmadinejad won re-election, but alleged fraud fueled protests across the country. The protests in Iran set off international speculation that the regime was beginning to fall apart. According to reports, opposition election observers had been barred from entering various polling locations; Web sites featuring Ahmadinejad's opponent, Mir Hossein Mousavi, were blocked; and various polling locations ran out of ballots or were unable to match the number of eligible voters with the number of votes cast. In addition, immediate election results gave Ahmadinejad a consistent percentage of the vote across the country, and victory in Mousavi's home region.

Immediately after election results were announced, supporters of the opposition took to the streets, burning buses and chanting "Death to the Dictator." Police used batons and tear gas to disperse the crowds, and nearly 1,000 Iranians were arrested. Protestors were warned that they risked being beaten, jailed, or even killed. After the nation's Guardian Council certified the election results, a court was set up to try protestors; many were forced to tape confessions in which they admitted to participating in a Western-backed plot to overthrow Ahmadinejad's government.

After the election crisis, Iran issued a statement to various Western nations indicating that it wanted to meet to discuss nuclear programs in other countries, but not Iran's program. Representatives from the United States, United Kingdom, China, Germany, France, and Russia met with Iranian leaders in October to discuss providing Iran enriched uranium for the purpose of fuel production, a proposal Iran initially indicated it would accept but that it later rejected. By the end of 2009, talks between Iran and the six nations had broken down.

In South America, the president of Honduras, Manuel Zelaya, was overthrown in a military-backed coup. The conflict initially erupted over Zelaya's proposal for a referendum on whether Honduras should hold an assembly to reform the nation's constitution. Opponents saw this as a move to ensure his re-election. Zelaya returned to Honduras in September to work toward a compromise possibly involving his reinstatement as president.

In Japan, citizens found themselves with the third prime minister in as many years, as Taro Aso, who took office in September 2008, resigned in August after his party was handily defeated in parliamentary elections. For the second time since the 1950s, the Liberal Democratic Party lost power. Analysts said the defeat of the Liberal Democrats could mark the end of that party's virtually unchallenged rule. Yukio Hatoyama, leader of the Democratic Party, was chosen by parliament as the new prime minister. High on Hatoyama's agenda was ensuring that Japan realign itself with the rest of Asia and distance the nation from unpopular American programs, such as the war in Iraq. Another point of contention for Hatoyama was the unpopular presence of American troops at Okinawa.

Newly elected President Obama traveled to more countries in his first year in office than any previous first-year president. One issue Obama had been advocating at home and abroad in 2009 was taking action against climate change, and in December, he attended the UN-sponsored climate change summit in Copenhagen. During the meetings, the United States attempted negotiations with China, a major holdout on agreeing to carbon emissions caps, and with developing nations that were unwilling to cut back on production to cap emissions. In the end, the summit produced little more than an agreement recognizing the danger of climate change. The United States said it would continue to work toward global agreements regarding climate change into 2010.

WARS IN IRAQ AND AFGHANISTAN

Two challenges facing the new president when he entered office were the wars in Iraq and Afghanistan. Public sentiment had long ago soured on both conflicts, but Obama had the difficult task of deciding whether to decrease or increase troops in both countries, a decision he promised not to politicize.

In February, Obama announced that an official timeline for withdrawal from Iraq had been agreed on. President Obama's plan, announced six years after the United States entered Iraq, was to bring approximately 100,000 troops home from Iraq by August 2010, while 50,000 troops would stay until 2011. Those remaining would continue to train Iraqi security forces and ensure the continued stabilization of the country.

During his presidential campaign, Obama had promised to bring troops home from Iraq within sixteen months of his inauguration. The eventual withdrawal plan he chose after consulting with military advisors would have most troops leave the country in nineteen months and would allow him to shift more units to Afghanistan, where the situation was increasingly deteriorating as extremists continued to regain a foothold in the country.

In December, after facing extensive criticism for taking too much time to make a decision on Afghanistan, President Obama announced that he would increase the number of troops there by 30,000. This marked the second troop increase since Obama took office in January 2009. During his announcement at West Point, Obama said that he had consulted the top military officials in the region, all of whom requested that more troops be deployed to ensure increased stability for the fledgling government in Afghanistan.

The troop increase was politically risky for Obama, who drew criticism from his own party over the $30 billion price tag at a time when the United States faced a serious economic crisis. Republicans, on the other hand, were generally supportive of the move to invest more resources in Afghanistan but encouraged the president not to set a timeline for withdrawal. President Obama said that he planned to begin withdrawing troops from Afghanistan by summer 2011.

Shortly before President Obama made the decision to increase the number of troops in Afghanistan, Hamid Karzai, Afghanistan's first democratically elected president, had been re-elected to a second term in office in an election plagued by fraud. Karzai was initially declared the winner in August, but an investigation found that many votes had been cast illegally. A recount showed that Karzai had not received the 50 percent necessary to win the election, so a runoff was scheduled for November. Shortly before the runoff,

Karzai's opponent dropped out of the race, citing the inability of election board members to remain impartial because they were appointed by Karzai. With no opponent, Karzai was declared the winner by default. Obama took the opportunity of Karzai's questionable election to encourage the leader to rid his government of corruption and shift his focus instead to building a stronger nation and partnering with neighboring countries to deny the Taliban safe haven.

—Heather Kerrigan

January

The Foreign Intelligence Surveillance Court Declares Warrantless Wiretapping Legal

JANUARY 15, 2009

On January 15, 2009, the Foreign Intelligence Surveillance Court (FISC) released a decision it first made in August 2008, stating that telecommunications companies must assist the federal government by intercepting phone calls and e-mails made by or coming to American citizens suspected of being terrorists. The ruling resulted from a case that involved a telecommunications company that refused to comply with a federal mandate stating that it must assist the U.S. government by intercepting calls and e-mails from U.S. citizens who were thought to be spies or terrorists.

The court ruling was another segment of a long string of arguments over whether the administration of President George W. Bush was overstepping its authority by allowing warrantless wiretaps of U.S. citizens after the September 11, 2001, terrorist attacks.

The Foreign Intelligence Surveillance Act Before and After September 11, 2001

Before the terrorist attacks of September 11, 2001, the National Security Agency (NSA) was permitted by statute to wiretap conversations outside of the United States, but was required to obtain a warrant from the surveillance court if it intended to tap into any calls made inside the United States. The 1978 Foreign Intelligence Surveillance Act (FISA), which created the Foreign Intelligence Surveillance Court, was established to determine when surveillance could be used in the United States as an effort to protect national security. Under that law, the Justice Department could apply for a warrant to wiretap an individual within the United States or another country, and the warrant was generally granted as long as the person being wiretapped was considered a foreign spy or terrorist. The act also allowed emergency surveillance of up to twenty-four hours without a warrant, as long as a judge was notified and a subsequent application was filed.

After September 11, 2001, the Bush administration secretly authorized the NSA to tap calls originating in or going to the United States as long as one person on the call was thought to be a member of a terrorist organization. Under the Bush policy, no warrants were required because the administration claimed that in the interest of national security, obtaining warrants before wiretapping could be too time-consuming when terrorist activity was thought to be involved.

The Bush Plan Comes to Light

The *New York Times* broke the story of Bush's wiretapping policy, and his administration, possibly fearing public backlash, admitted that it was true. Bush said that although warrantless wiretaps were outside the realm of what the FISC would allow, as president of the United States, he had the constitutional responsibility to gather foreign intelligence for the purpose of national security through any means necessary, which included directing people to conduct warrantless wiretaps. Therefore, the president claimed, as commander in chief, a duty enshrined in the Constitution that could not be taken away by Congress, FISA could not be used to stop him from carrying out these duties. "If al Qaeda or their associates are making calls into the United States or out of the United States," the president said, "we want to know what they're saying."

Further, the Bush administration said that FISA allows for warrantless wiretaps that are authorized by another statute, including the Authorization for Use of Military Force, passed by Congress on September 14, 2001. This authorization, concerning Iraq, made no specific mention of warrantless wiretaps, but the Bush administration argued that the necessary protections outlined in the authorization could include such surveillance, as long as it could be proven that the surveillance was being carried out in the interest of national security.

After Bush's plan came to light, public outcry—and a congressional House majority won by Democrats in the 2006 midterm elections—led many legislators to seek wiretap reform. In an effort to crack down on the president's warrantless wiretaps, in 2007 Congress passed the Protect America Act (PAA), which gave the NSA the authority to wiretap, without a warrant, communications of those believed to be terrorists that at some point pass through the United States. This law was replaced in 2008 by the FISA Amendments, which shielded telecommunications companies from lawsuits brought by its customers who had been wiretapped at the request of the federal government and added additional protections to the warrantless wiretapping of those "reasonably believed" to be inside the United States.

Argument over Surveillance

When Bush's plan became public, Democrats and Republicans in Congress responded with outrage but offered different suggestions on how to deal with the surveillance and wiretapping situation. Sens. Mike DeWine, R-Ohio, and Arlen Specter, R-Pa., wanted to bring the NSA surveillance program under a congressional committee or the FISC. Democrats, on the other hand, said that bringing the program into a committee would legalize an illegal activity.

Civil liberties groups expressed great dismay over the Bush surveillance policy, arguing that judicial oversight is necessary to prevent abuse of a wiretapping system. The claim by many groups was that without such judicial oversight, the government could be monitoring protest groups without cause. After passage of the PAA of 2007 and FISA Amendments of 2008, these civil liberties groups believed they would not prevail in Congress, so the American Civil Liberties Union and other civil liberties groups filed lawsuits for journalists and lawyers who worried that because they sometimes communicate with people who could be monitored, their calls could be tapped. These groups maintained that there was no reason to conduct a full-blown wiretap without a warrant because under the PAA, and later the FISA Amendments, the Bush administration had the ability, if pressed for time, to obtain a wiretapping warrant within seventy-two hours of beginning the wiretap, or, if war is declared, to wiretap for fifteen days before being required to alert Congress. This, they said, should resolve the president's argument that he did not have enough time to apply for a warrant before wiretapping because of how quickly terrorists can appear and disappear.

BUSH VERSUS THE CONGRESSIONAL RESEARCH SERVICE

The Congressional Research Service (CRS), which produces nonpartisan reports for Congress on a wide array of issues, listed many reasons why the president had over-stepped his constitutional powers. Bush argued that as commander in chief, Article II of the Constitution gave him "all necessary authority," which could include warrantless wire-taps, to protect the United States from attacks. The CRS said that such broad powers contradict what Congress was trying to establish in 1978 with FISA, which required the president to obtain a warrant from the FISC first.

Bush also argued that the September 14, 2001, congressional resolution allowed him to "use all necessary and appropriate force" against those who conducted the September 11, 2001, terrorist attacks, and the administration maintained that such "necessary and appropriate force" included monitoring communications as an essential part of waging war. The Justice Department agreed with the president, noting that monitoring communications goes back to George Washington's administration. The CRS argued that surveillance is important but "it is not clear that the collection of intelligence constitutes a use of force" authorized by the September 14 resolution.

Another Bush administration argument stemmed from the 2004 case of *Hamdi v. Rumsfeld,* in which the Supreme Court ruled that the September 14, 2001, resolution allowed for the arrest and detention of American citizens on a foreign battlefield, something that is generally illegal unless Congress authorizes it. President Bush said that this ruling meant that the congressional resolution gave him the ability to conduct any activity considered essential to waging a war. The CRS responded that the ruling only covered detention, and that it would be a stretch to say that it also covered surveillance.

The final argument raised by the Bush administration centered on the 1978 FISA legislation, in which the president is given a fifteen-day grace period to seek a warrant during war time and also provides an exception to requirements "where authorized by statute." President Bush maintained the September 14 congressional resolution fit the "where authorized" exemption, whereas the CRS said FISA is a reflection of Congress's belief that it can regulate the president's use of warrantless surveillance.

COURT RULING

As noted earlier, the case tried by the FISC was first brought in 2007 when an unnamed telecommunications company complained that the government's wiretaps without warrants were in violation of the constitutional rights of the customers using the company's phone and Internet service. The company also claimed that if warrantless wiretaps were allowed, the president had too much power that was unchecked by the legislative or judicial branch. "By placing discretion entirely in the hands of the executive branch without prior judicial involvement," the company argued, "the procedures cede to that branch overly broad power that invites abuse." In response to this claim in its ruling, the court wrote, "[T]his is little more than a lament about the risk that government officials will not operate in good faith. . . . That sort of risk exists even when a warrant is required."

In this case, the FISC was looking specifically at the provisions of the PAA, which expanded the president's ability to conduct warrantless wiretaps. By the time the case had been decided, this act had already been overturned by Congress. However, the court still found that the Bush administration's warrantless wiretapping plan had sufficient safeguards to protect ordinary American citizens and that it stood up to constitutional privacy standards.

In its decision, the FISC became the first to say that the Fourth Amendment statute requiring warrants does not apply to collection of foreign intelligence when a U.S. citizen is involved. The court wrote that such telecommunications companies as the one that brought this case must cooperate with the government in an effort to find and intercept calls and e-mails made by American citizens if they are suspected of being terrorists or spies for other countries. Bruce Selya, the chief judge in the case, wrote, "[O]ur decision recognizes that where the government has instituted several layers of serviceable safeguards to protect individuals against unwarranted harms and to minimize incidental intrusions, its efforts to protect national security should not be frustrated by the courts."

The ruling never addressed whether the president was committing an illegal act when he ordered warrantless wiretaps without congressional approval. While conservatives celebrated the ruling, which was released just days before the end of the Bush administration, legal experts maintained that the ruling would have little effect on future situations because the law in this case had been superseded by new legislation. The Justice Department reported that it was "pleased with this ruling."

—Heather Kerrigan

Following is the United States Foreign Intelligence Surveillance Court of Review opinion on warrantless wiretapping, in which the court, on August 22, 2008, ruled that in some circumstances warrantless wiretaps were legal. The heavily redacted opinion was not released until January 15, 2009.

United States Foreign Intelligence Surveillance Court on Warrantless Wiretaps

DOCUMENT

Made Public January 15, 2009

United States Foreign Intelligence Surveillance Court of Review

No. 08–01

In re: Directives [redacted text]* pursuant to section 105B of the Foreign Intelligence Surveillance Act.

[redacted text]
Petitioner, Appellant.

On petition for review of a decision of the United States Foreign Intelligence Surveillance Court

[Hon. Reggie B. Walton, *U.S. District Judge*]

Before
Selya, *Chief Judge,*
Winter and Arnold, *Senior Circuit Judges.*

. . .

*The text and footnotes that have been redacted from this opinion contain classified information

August 22, 2008

SELYA, *Chief Judge.* This petition for review stems from directives issued to the petitioner [redacted text] pursuant to a now-expired set of amendments to the Foreign Intelligence Surveillance Act of 1978 (FISA). . . . Among other things, those amendments, known as the Protect America Act of 2007 (PAA) . . . authorized the United States to direct communications service providers to assist it in acquiring foreign intelligence when those acquisitions targeted third persons (such as the service provider's customers) reasonably believed to be located outside the United States. Having received [redacted text] such directives, the petitioner challenged their legality before the Foreign Intelligence Surveillance Court (FISC). When that court found the directives lawful and compelled obedience to them, the petitioner brought this petition for review.

As framed, the petition presents matters of both first impression and constitutional significance. At its most elemental level, the petition requires us to weigh the nation's security interests against the Fourth Amendment privacy interests of United States persons.

After a careful calibration of this balance and consideration of the myriad of legal issues presented, we affirm the lower court's determination that the directives at issue are lawful and that compliance with them is obligatory.

I. THE STATUTORY FRAMEWORK

On August 5, 2007, Congress enacted the PAA . . . as a measured expansion of FISA's scope. Subject to certain conditions, the PAA allowed the government to conduct warrantless foreign intelligence surveillance on targets (including United States persons) "reasonably believed" to be located outside the United States. . . . This proviso is of critical importance here.

Under the new statute, the Director of National Intelligence (DNI) and the Attorney General (AG) were permitted to authorize, for periods of up to one year, "the acquisition of foreign intelligence information concerning persons reasonably believed to be outside the United States" if they determined that the acquisition met five specified criteria. . . . These criteria included (i) that reasonable procedures were in place to ensure that the targeted person was reasonably believed to be located outside the United States; (ii) that the acquisitions did not constitute electronic surveillance; (iii) that the surveillance would involve the assistance of a communications service provider; (iv) that a significant purpose of the surveillance was to obtain foreign intelligence information; and (v) that minimization procedures in place met the requirements of 50 U.S.C. § 1801 (h). . . . Except in limited circumstances (not relevant here), this multi-part determination was required to be made in the form of a written certification "supported as appropriate by affidavit of appropriate officials in the national security field." . . . Pursuant to this authorization, the DNI and the AG were allowed to issue directives to "person[s]"—a term that includes agents of communications service providers—delineating the assistance needed to acquire the information. . . .

The PAA was a stopgap measure. By its terms, it sunset on February 16, 2008. Following a lengthy interregnum, the lapsed provisions were repealed on July 10, 2008, through the instrumentality of the FISA Amendments Act of 2008. . . . But because the certifications and directives involved in the instant case were issued during the short shelf life of the PAA, they remained in effect. . . . We therefore assess the validity of the actions at issue here through the prism of the PAA.

[redacted text] . . .

[Section II, containing background information on the case and laws at issue, has been omitted.]

III. ANALYSIS

[Section A, containing discussion of standing determinations de novo, has been omitted.]

B. The Fourth Amendment Challenge.

We turn now to the petitioner's Fourth Amendment arguments. In the Fourth Amendment context, federal appellate courts review findings of fact for clear error and legal conclusions (including determinations about the ultimate constitutionality of government searches and seizures) de novo. . . . We therefore review de novo the FISC's conclusion that the surveillances carried out pursuant to the directives are lawful.

The petitioner's remonstrance has two main branches. First, it asserts that the government, in issuing the directives, had to abide by the requirements attendant to the Warrant Clause of the Fourth Amendment. Second, it argues that even if a foreign intelligence exception to the warrant requirements exists and excuses compliance with the Warrant Clause, the surveillances mandated by the directives are unreasonable and, therefore, violate the Fourth Amendment. The petitioner limits each of its claims to the harm that may be inflicted upon United States persons.

1. *The Nature of the Challenge.* As a threshold matter, the petitioner asserts that its Fourth Amendment arguments add up to a facial challenge to the PAA. The government contests this characterization, asserting that the petitioner presents only an as-applied challenge. We agree with the government.

A facial challenge asks a court to consider the constitutionality of a statute without factual development centered around a particular application. . . . Here, however, there *is* a particularized record and the statute—the PAA—has been applied to the petitioner in a specific setting. So viewed, they go past the question of whether the PAA is valid on its face—a question that would be answered by deciding whether *any* application of the statute passed constitutional muster . . .—and ask instead whether this specific application offends the Constitution. As such, the petitioner's challenge falls outside the normal circumference of a facial challenge. . . .

We therefore deem the petitioner's challenge an as-applied challenge and limit our analysis accordingly. This means that, to succeed, the petitioner must prove more than a theoretical risk that the PAA could on certain facts yield unconstitutional applications. Instead, it must persuade us that the PAA is unconstitutional as implemented here.

2. *The Foreign Intelligence Exception.* The recurrent theme permeating the petitioner's arguments is the notion that there is no foreign intelligence exception to the Fourth Amendment's Warrant Clause. The FISC rejected this notion, positing that our decision in *In re Sealed Case* confirmed the existence of a foreign intelligence exception to the warrant requirement. . . .

. . . Applying principles derived from the special needs cases, we conclude that this type of foreign intelligence surveillance possesses characteristics that qualify it for such an exception.

For one thing, the purpose behind the surveillances ordered pursuant to the directives goes well beyond any garden-variety law enforcement objective. It involves the acquisition from overseas foreign agents of foreign intelligence to help protect national security. Moreover, this is the sort of situation in which the government's interest is particularly intense.

The petitioner has a fallback position. Even if there is a narrow foreign intelligence exception, it asseverates, a definition of that exception should require the foreign intelligence purpose to be the primary purpose of the surveillance. For that proposition, it cites the Fourth Circuit's decision in *United States* v. *Truong Dinh Hung.* . . . That dog will not hunt.

The court previously has upheld as reasonable under the Fourth Amendment the Patriot Act's substitution of "a significant purpose" for the talismanic phrase "primary purpose." . . . As we explained there, the Fourth Circuit's "primary purpose" language— from which the pre-Patriot Act interpretation of "purpose" derived—drew an "unstable, unrealistic, and confusing" line between foreign intelligence purposes and criminal investigation purposes. . . . A surveillance with a foreign intelligence purpose often will have some ancillary criminal-law purpose. . . . The prevention or apprehension of terrorism suspects, for instance, is inextricably intertwined with the national security concerns that are at the core of foreign intelligence collection. . . . In our view the more appropriate consideration is the programmatic purpose of the surveillances and whether—as in the special needs cases—that programmatic purpose involves some legitimate objective beyond ordinary crime control. . . .

Under this analysis, the surveillances authorized by the directives easily pass muster. Their stated purpose centers on garnering foreign intelligence. There is no indication that the collections of information are primarily related to ordinary criminal-law enforcement purposes. Without something more than a purely speculative set of imaginings, we cannot infer that the purpose of the directives (and, thus, of the surveillances) is other than their stated purpose. . . .

We add, moreover, that there is a high degree of probability that requiring a warrant would hinder the government's ability to collect time-sensitive information and, thus, would impede the vital national security interests that are at stake. . . . [redacted text] Compulsory compliance with the warrant requirement would introduce an element of delay, thus frustrating the government's ability to collect information in a timely manner. [redacted text]

For these reasons, we hold that a foreign intelligence exception to the Fourth Amendment's warrant requirement exists when surveillance is conducted to obtain foreign intelligence for national security purposes and is directed against foreign powers or agents of foreign powers reasonably believed to be located outside the United States.

3. *Reasonableness.* This holding does not grant the government carte blanche: even though the foreign intelligence exception applies in a given case, governmental action intruding on individual privacy interests must comport with the Fourth Amendment's reasonableness requirement. . . . Thus, the question here reduces to whether the PAA, as applied through the directives, constitutes a sufficiently reasonable exercise of governmental power to satisfy the Fourth Amendment.

We begin with bedrock. The Fourth Amendment protects the right "to be secure . . . against unreasonable searches and seizures." U.S. Const. amend. IV. To determine the reasonableness of a particular governmental action, an inquiring court must consider the totality of the circumstances. . . . This mode of approach takes into account the nature of the government intrusion and how the intrusion is implemented. . . . The more important the government's interest, the greater the intrusion that may be constitutionally tolerated. . . .

The totality of the circumstances model requires the court to balance the interests at stake. . . . If the protections that are in place for individual privacy interests are sufficient in light of the governmental interest at stake, the constitutional scales will tilt in favor of upholding the government's actions. If, however, those protections are insufficient to alleviate the risks of government error and abuse, the scales will tip toward a finding of unconstitutionality.

Here, the relevant governmental interest—the interest in national security—is of the highest order of magnitude. . . . Consequently, we must determine whether the protections afforded to the privacy rights of targeted persons are reasonable in light of this important interest.

At the outset, we dispose of two straw men—arguments based on a misreading of our prior decision in *Sealed Case.* First, the petitioner notes that we found relevant six factors contributing to the protection of individual privacy in the face of a governmental intrusion for national security purposes . . . (contemplating prior judicial review, presence or absence of probable cause, particularity, necessity, duration, and minimization). On that exiguous basis, it reasons that our decision there requires a more rigorous standard for gauging reasonableness.

This is a mistaken judgment. In *Sealed Case,* we did not formulate a rigid six-factor test for reasonableness. That would be at odds with the totality of the circumstances test that must guide an analysis in the precincts patrolled by the Fourth Amendment. We merely indicated that the six enumerated factors were relevant under the circumstances of that case.

Second, the petitioner asserts that our *Sealed Case* decision stands for the proposition that, in order to gain constitutional approval, the PAA procedures must contain protections equivalent to the three principal warrant requirements: prior judicial review, probable cause, and particularity. That is incorrect. What we said there—and reiterate today—is that the more a set of procedures resembles those associated with the traditional warrant requirements, the more easily it can be determined that those procedures are within constitutional bounds. . . . We therefore decline the petitioner's invitation to reincorporate into the foreign intelligence exception the same warrant requirements that we already have held inapplicable. . . .

Having placed *Sealed Case* into perspective, we turn to the petitioner's contention that the totality of the circumstances demands a finding of unreasonableness here. That contention boils down to the idea that the protections afforded under the PAA are insufficiently analogous to the protections deemed adequate in *Sealed Case* because the PAA lacks (i) a particularity requirement, (ii) a prior judicial review requirement for determining probable cause that a target is a foreign power or an agent of a foreign power, and (iii) any plausible proxies for the omitted protections. For good measure, the petitioner suggests that the PAA's lack of either a necessity requirement or a reasonable durational limit diminishes the overall reasonableness of surveillances conducted pursuant thereto.

The government rejoins that the PAA, as applied here, constitutes reasonable governmental action. It emphasizes both the protections spelled out in the PAA itself and those mandated under the certifications and directives. . . .

The record supports the government. Notwithstanding the parade of horribles trotted out by the petitioner, it has presented no evidence of any actual harm, any egregious risk of error, or any broad potential for abuse in the circumstances of the instant case. Thus, assessing the intrusions at issue in light of the governmental interest at stake and the panoply of protections that are in place, we discern no principled basis for invalidating the PAA as applied here. . . .

The petitioner suggests that, by placing discretion entirely in the hands of the Executive Branch without prior judicial involvement, the procedures cede to that Branch overly broad power that invites abuse. But this is little more than a lament about the risk that government officials will not operate in good faith. That sort of risk exists even when a warrant is required. In the absence of a showing of fraud or other misconduct by the affiant, the prosecutor, or the judge, a presumption of regularity traditionally attaches to the obtaining of a warrant. . . .

Similarly, the fact that there is some potential for error is not a sufficient reason to invalidate the surveillances. [redacted text] . . .

It is also significant that effective minimization procedures are in place. These procedures serve as an additional backstop against identification errors as well as a means of reducing the impact of incidental intrusions into the privacy of non-targeted United States persons. . . .

The petitioner's concern with incidental collections is overblown. It is settled beyond peradventure that incidental collections occurring as a result of constitutionally permissible acquisitions do not render those acquisitions unlawful. . . . The government assures us that it does not maintain a database of incidentally collected information from non-targeted United States persons, and there is no evidence to the contrary. On these facts, incidentally collected communications of non-targeted United States persons do not violate the Fourth Amendment. . . .

IV. Conclusion

Our government is tasked with protecting an interest of utmost significance to the nation—the safety and security of its people. But the Constitution is the cornerstone of our freedoms, and government cannot unilaterally sacrifice constitutional rights on the altar of national security. Thus, in carrying out its national security mission, the government must simultaneously fulfill its constitutional responsibility to provide reasonable protections for the privacy of United States persons. The judiciary's duty is to hold that delicate balance steady and true.

We believe that our decision to uphold the PAA as applied in this case comports with that solemn obligation. In that regard, we caution that our decision does not constitute an endorsement of broad-based indiscriminate executive power. Rather, our decision recognizes that where the government has instituted several layers of serviceable safeguards to protect individuals against unwarranted harms and to minimize incidental intrusions, its efforts to protect national security should not be frustrated by the courts. This is such a case.

We need go no further. The decision granting the government's motion to compel is affirmed; the petition for review is denied and dismissed; and the motion for a stay is denied as moot.

So Ordered.

SOURCE: U.S. Federal Judiciary. "In Re: Directives [redacted text] Pursuant to Section 105B of the Foreign Intelligence Surveillance Act." August 22, 2008. www.uscourts.gov/newsroom/2009/FISCR_Opinion .pdf?WT.cg_n=FISCROpinion_WhatsNew_homepage.

OTHER HISTORIC DOCUMENTS OF INTEREST

FROM PREVIOUS *HISTORIC DOCUMENTS*

Roland Burris and Al Franken Seated During Dynamic Year in U.S. Senate

JANUARY 15 AND JUNE 30, 2009

In 2009, the U.S. Senate faced multiple changes, including the lengthy election and appointment processes of two Democratic senators, the death of longtime senator Edward Kennedy, D-Mass., and the switch in party from Republican to Democrat by Sen. Arlen Specter of Pennsylvania. The major concern was how the balance of power would shift after all of these changes. Democrats were hoping to reach the elusive sixty-seat filibuster-proof majority that would give them almost ensured success in passing important legislation before them, including health care reform. The hardest-fought Senate seat battles in 2009 included the rejection and later acceptance of Roland Burris as a senator from Illinois and the long legal battles that led to Al Franken's confirmation as Minnesota's junior senator.

ROLAND BURRIS'S CONFIRMATION

When Roland Burris, a former Illinois comptroller and attorney general, was appointed on December 30, 2008, by Illinois governor Rod Blagojevich to fill the Senate seat left vacant by Barack Obama after his election as president, the Democratic leadership in Congress immediately refused to seat Burris. Governor Blagojevich had been arrested on December 9, 2008, by federal authorities on corruption charges alleging an attempt to sell the vacant Senate seat for personal financial gain. Democrats argued that the Constitution gave them the authority to decide who should and should not be seated, stating from the beginning that they would use that argument to refuse any appointment by the disgraced Blagojevich.

The Democratic leadership based their argument on the way in which Burris was chosen, not his qualifications. "This is not about Mr. Burris," said Senate leaders. "It is about the integrity of a governor accused of attempting to sell this United States Senate seat." Jim Manley, spokesperson for the Senate leadership, said, "We are not making a judgment about the qualifications of the appointee, but about whether the appointment itself was tainted by fraud. We believe we are entitled to do that. This is like judging the integrity of an election, free from fraud and corruption."

Burris, however, said that he would appear at the Senate to present his credentials when senators were sworn in for the new term. "The governor has the constitutional and statutory authority to make the appointment. We are certainly going to make contact with the leadership of the Senate to let them know that the governor of Illinois has made a legal appointment and that I am currently the junior senator for the state of Illinois," he said.

On January 5, 2009, the secretary of the U.S. Senate, Nancy Erickson, rejected Burris's certification of appointment. She stated that Burris had not met the qualifications of

Senate Rule 2, which requires an appointment to be signed by both a governor and a secretary of state.

In response to Erickson's decision, the Illinois Supreme Court ruled on January 9, 2009, that to be seated as a senator Burris need only receive the signature of the governor. The court also ruled that the Senate certification form was simply a recommendation and that the appointment registration form filed by the Illinois secretary of state should serve as proof that Burris's appointment was valid. The state supreme court noted in its decision that "no explanation has been given as to how any rule of the Senate, whether it be formal or merely a matter of tradition, could supersede the authority to fill vacancies conferred on the states by the federal constitution."

Burris obtained a certified copy of his appointment registration and delivered it to Erickson. On January 12, 2009, Erickson announced that the registration provided by Burris was proof that his appointment was valid. The Senate leadership agreed to seat Burris, and he was sworn in by Vice President Dick Cheney on January 15, 2009.

In early February, Burris filed a sworn affidavit with the Illinois House of Representatives committee that was conducting Blagojevich's impeachment trial. In it, he stated that Blagojevich had requested Burris's assistance in fundraising before appointing him to the Senate seat; this was not what Burris had told the House in earlier testimony. The Illinois House considered a perjury investigation, but by the end of 2009, no investigation had begun. On November 20, 2009, however, the U.S. Senate Ethics Committee released a letter to Burris, saying, "The Committee found that you should have known that you were providing incorrect, inconsistent, misleading, or incomplete information to the public, Senate and those conducting legitimate inquiries into your appointment to the Senate."

AL FRANKEN WINS IN MINNESOTA'S SENATE RACE

In Minnesota, Democrat Al Franken, an author, comedian, and former liberal radio show host, and Republican Norm Coleman, one of the state's two U.S. senators, went head to head in the November 2008 election. When the results came in on November 4, 2008, of the three million ballots cast for the Senate seat, Coleman looked to be ahead by about 700 votes. However, when the official results were tallied on November 18, Coleman was ahead by a mere 215 votes, which, by Minnesota law, meant an automatic recount was required. Two months later, on January 5, 2009, the election was reversed, and Franken was declared the winner, by 225 votes.

In response to the recount that certified Franken as the winner, the Coleman campaign announced that it would file a lawsuit for another recount. "The Coleman campaign has consistently and continually fought to have every validly cast vote counted, and for the integrity of Minnesota's election system, we will not stop now. The Minnesota Supreme Court has made sure that an election contest will need to be filled quickly to ensure that an accurate and valid recount can be achieved." In its request for another recount, the Coleman campaign focused on the 654 rejected absentee ballots, 150 ballots from Democratic areas of the state that Coleman claimed were double-counted in Franken's favor, larger numbers of ballots in some precincts after the election than were originally counted, and 130 ballots lost after election night that were still supposedly included in the recount tally.

On April 13, 2009, a three-person panel in Minnesota ruled Franken the winner, and the Coleman campaign vowed again to appeal the decision. "More than 4,400 Minnesotans remain wrongly disenfranchised by this court's order . . . [W]e must appeal to the Minnesota Supreme Court so that no voter is left behind," said Ben Ginsberg, Coleman's attorney.

More than two months later, on June 30, 2009, the Minnesota Supreme Court declared in a 5–0 ruling that Franken was the winner of the Senate race by 312 votes. In his victory speech, Franken commented on being the final seat needed for a Democratic filibuster-proof majority. "I know there's been a lot of talk about the fact that when I'm sworn in I'll be the 60th member of the Democratic caucus. But that's not how I see it. The way I see it, I'm not going to Washington to be the 60th Democratic senator. I'm going to Washington to be the second senator from the state of Minnesota and that's how I'm going to do this job."

Franken's first task as senator was to join the confirmation hearing of Supreme Court justice nominee Sonia Sotomayor as a member of the Senate Judiciary Committee. He began his line of questioning, one week after being confirmed as a senator, connecting Sotomayor's earlier mentioned interest in watching "Perry Mason" as a young child, to her "determination to defy the odds." As soon as Franken mentioned the television show during the hearing, questions were raised as to whether he planned to be serious in his new role or whether he would continue to draw on his background as a comedian. Franken, however, reported that he did not think that his questions, which included judicial activism and net neutrality, were funny. "I thought it was more of a human moment than a humorous moment. It was about getting to know her as a human being."

Guy-Uriel Charles, a professor at Duke University, read the situation differently. "Obviously, the risk is that he won't be taken seriously, that he will be viewed as a clown. But, oddly enough, it seems that if he played it as a straight man, without any humor, he would have been taken less seriously."

SENATE CHALLENGES REMAIN

Even though they had the necessary sixty-seat filibuster-proof majority in the Senate, Democrats had difficulty passing what some considered the most important legislation of the year—health care reform legislation pushed by President Obama. Health care reform was a hard-fought issue for Senator Kennedy during his long tenure in the Senate. After he died on August 25, 2009, many Democrats encouraged their colleagues in both the House and Senate to pass the health care reform bill in his memory. "Ted Kennedy's dream of quality health care for all Americans will be made real this year," said Speaker of the House Nancy Pelosi. After the House of Representatives passed its version of the bill 220–215, with only one Republican voting in its favor, Senate Democrats, having recently lost their sixty-seat majority, worked day and night up until Christmas Eve to get a bill passed. The last time the Senate voted on Christmas Eve was in 1895. Early on December 24, 2009, by a vote of 60–39, senators passed a health care bill along party lines (with two independents joining the Democrats), giving it the necessary push to go into conference committee. The outcome of the vote came down to the last minute, with Majority Leader Harry Reid, D-Nev., giving concessions to Sen. Ben Nelson, D-Neb., to secure his vote.

—Heather Kerrigan

Following is a January 15, 2009, press release from Sen. Harry Reid, D-Nev., on the appointment of Roland Burris as Illinois's junior senator; the Minnesota Supreme Court's decision of June 30, 2009, declaring Al Franken winner of the November 4, 2008, Senate election; and a June 30, 2009, press release from Sen. Harry Reid, D-Nev., on the Minnesota Supreme Court decision to declare Al Franken winner in the Minnesota U.S. Senate race.

Senate Majority Leader Harry Reid's Remarks on Appointment of Roland Burris

January 15, 2009

There are many paths to the United States Senate. It is fair to say that the path that brought our new colleague from Illinois to us was unique.

Whatever complications surrounded his appointment, we made it clear from the beginning—both publicly and privately—that our concern was never with him.

I didn't have the pleasure of meeting Senator Burris until last week. I found him to be engaging, gracious and firm in his commitment to become a good and effective United States Senator.

Given the uncertainty around his appointment, all of his statements and actions—again, both publicly and privately—reflected a strong character that will serve him well as he begins his service to the people of Illinois.

Senator Burris, on behalf of all Senators, we welcome you as a colleague and a friend.

SOURCE: Sen. Harry Reid. "Reid Statement on Roland Burris." January 15, 2009. http://democrats.senate .gov/newsroom/record.cfm?id=306753&.

Minnesota Supreme Court Declares Al Franken Winner of Senate Seat

June 30, 2009

State of Minnesota
In Supreme Court

A09–697

Cullen Sheehan and Norm Coleman, contestants, Appellants, *v.* Al Franken, contestee, Respondent.	Ramsey County In the Matter of the Contest of General Election held on November 4, 2008, for the purpose of electing a United States Senator from the State of Minnesota,

Filed June 30, 2009

Syllabus

1. Appellants did not establish that, by requiring proof that statutory absentee voting standards were satisfied before counting a rejected absentee ballot, the trial court's decision constituted a post-election change in standards that violates substantive due process.

2. Appellants did not prove that either the trial court or local election officials violated the constitutional guarantee of equal protection.

3. The trial court did not abuse its discretion when it excluded additional evidence.

4. Inspection of ballots under Minn. Stat. § 209.06 (2008) is available only on a showing that the requesting party cannot properly be prepared for trial without an inspection. Because appellants made no such showing here, the trial court did not err in denying inspection.

5. The trial court did not err when it included in the final election tally the election day returns of a precinct in which some ballots were lost before the manual recount.

Affirmed.

Opinion

Per Curiam

Appellants, incumbent Republican United States Senator Norm Coleman and Cullen Sheehan, filed a notice of election contest under Minn. Stat. § 209.021 (2008), challenging the State Canvassing Board's certification that Democratic-Farmer-Labor challenger Al Franken was entitled to receive a certificate of election as United States Senator following the November 4, 2008 general election. . . .

[Background on the case has been omitted.]

The State Canvassing Board's certification is prima facie evidence that Franken, the contestee, has been elected to the office. Coleman, the contestant, bears the burden of proof in the trial to show that the Board's certification was in error. On appeal, we give the trial court's findings of fact in an election contest the same weight as a trial court's findings of fact in any civil action and will not set aside those findings unless Coleman demonstrates that they are clearly erroneous. But we review a trial court's conclusions of law de novo.

Appellants raise essentially five issues: (1) whether the trial court violated Coleman's right to substantive due process by requiring strict, rather than only substantial, compliance with the statutory requirements for absentee voting; (2) whether Coleman's right to equal protection of the laws was violated, either by differences among jurisdictions in their application of the statutory requirements for absentee voting or by the court's rulings on the statutory requirements for absentee voting; (3) whether the court erred in excluding certain evidence; (4) whether the court erred in declining to order inspections of ballots and other election materials for precincts in which Coleman alleges that ballots may have been double-counted during the manual recount; and (5) whether the court erred by including in the final vote tally the election day returns from one Minneapolis precinct in which some ballots were lost before the manual recount.

I.

We turn first to the question of whether Coleman's right to substantive due process under the United States Constitution has been violated. Whether Coleman's right to substantive due process was violated is a question of law, which we review de novo.

During trial, the court identified, in an order issued February 13, 2009, ten categories of rejected absentee ballots that would not be considered legally cast as a matter of law because the ballots failed to comply with one or more of the statutory requirements for voting by absentee ballot. . . .

The United States Supreme Court has limited the reach of substantive due process to ensure that wrongs addressed are truly of a constitutional magnitude. We have noted that "courts are, 'reluctant to expand the concept of substantive due process because guideposts for responsible decisionmaking in this unchartered area are scarce and open-ended.'" . . .

Although we have not previously considered substantive due process in the context of an election dispute, we agree with the federal courts and adopt the federal rule to determine whether a substantive due process violation has occurred in an election. To prevail on a claim that a change in election standards violated substantive due process, the contestant must show a change that is patently and fundamentally unfair. In other words, the contestant must show likely reliance by the voters on an existing election procedure and a change in that procedure that results in significant disenfranchisement of the voters. Under this standard, in order to sustain a substantive due process violation, Coleman must prove as a threshold matter that the post-election change about which he complains—the trial court's adherence to a strict compliance standard—changed the procedures on which the voters relied on election day. . . .

[A discussion of Minnesota election law has been omitted.]

We conclude that our existing case law requires strict compliance by voters with the requirements for absentee voting. Thus, we reject Coleman's argument that only substantial compliance by voters is required. Having rejected this argument, we also conclude that the trial court's February 13 order requiring strict compliance with the statutory requirements for absentee voting was not a deviation from our well-established precedent.

Because strict compliance with the statutory requirements for absentee voting is, and has always been, required, there is no basis on which voters could have reasonably believed that anything less than strict compliance would suffice. Furthermore, Coleman does not cite, and after review of the record we have not found, any evidence in the record that election officials required only substantial compliance in any past election or any official pronouncements that only substantial compliance would be required in the November 4, 2008 election. Nor does Coleman point us to the testimony of any voter who neglected to comply with the statutory requirements for absentee voting in reliance on either past practice or official assurances that strict compliance was not required. Indeed, Coleman's counsel acknowledged during oral argument that Coleman cannot claim that any voters changed their behavior based on the alleged substantial compliance standard.

For all of these reasons, we hold that Coleman has not proven that the trial court's February 13 order violated substantive due process.

II.

We next examine Coleman's argument that the constitutional guarantee of equal protection was violated in this case. Coleman's equal protection argument is two-fold. First, he argues that the differing application and implementation by election officials of the statutory requirements for absentee voting violated equal protection. Essentially, Coleman contends that similarly situated absentee ballots were treated differently depending on the jurisdiction in which they were cast and that this disparate treatment violated equal protection. Second, Coleman contends that equal protection was violated when the trial court adhered to the statutory requirements for acceptance of absentee ballots, in contrast to the practices of local jurisdictions during the election.

Both parts of Coleman's equal protection argument depend on his assertion that differential application, either by election officials or by the trial court, of the statutory requirements for absentee voting violates equal protection. But equal protection is not violated every time public officials apply facially neutral state laws differently. The United States Supreme Court has held that "an erroneous or mistaken performance of [a] statutory duty, although a violation of the statute, is not without more a denial of the equal protection of the laws." The Court then explained that the "more" that is required for a violation of equal protection is intentional or purposeful discrimination. . . .

[Past court decisions have been omitted.]

We conclude that the standard applied in *Snowden* and *Draganosky* is the proper standard to apply in this case. Accordingly, in order to prevail on his equal protection claim of disparate application of a facially neutral statute, Coleman was required to prove either that local jurisdictions' differences in application or the trial court's application of the requirements for absentee voting was the product of intentional discrimination. Coleman neither claims nor produced any evidence that the differing treatment of absentee ballots among jurisdictions during the election was the result of intentional or purposeful discrimination against individuals or classes. Nor does Coleman claim that the trial court's February 13 order, establishing certain categories of ballots as not legally cast, was the product of an intent to discriminate against any individual or class. . . .

Coleman makes the additional argument that the non-uniform application of the statutory standards for absentee voting nevertheless brings this case within the ambit of the United States Supreme Court's decision in *Bush v. Gore,* 531 U.S. 98 (2000) (per curiam). . . .

[Background on the Bush case has been omitted.]

. . . we conclude that Coleman has not proven that either election officials or the trial court violated his right to equal protection.

III.

Coleman next contends that the trial court improperly excluded (1) evidence of absentee ballots accepted on election day and in the manual recount that would not satisfy the standards established by the trial court, and (2) evidence of disparities among jurisdictions in their application of the statutory standards governing absentee ballots. . . .

A.

. . . We conclude that the trial court ruled correctly that Minnesota law provides no remedy for wrongly accepted absentee ballot return envelopes once those envelopes have been opened and the ballots inside deposited in the ballot box. Accordingly, we conclude that the court did not abuse its discretion in excluding the evidence.

B.

Coleman also argues on appeal that the trial court improperly precluded him from introducing additional evidence of "local officials' widely differing practices for accepting absentee ballots" on election day. Coleman made an offer of proof of the evidence he sought to introduce. We conclude the court did not abuse its discretion in excluding this evidence.

As we have explained, in order to prevail on his equal protection claim, Coleman was required to prove intentional or purposeful discrimination on the part of either local election officials or the trial court. But Coleman does not contend that the additional evidence he sought to introduce would have proven intentional or purposeful discrimination on the part of any election officials or the trial court. We therefore conclude that in excluding this evidence, the court did not abuse its discretion.

IV.

Coleman also claims that the trial court erred in denying his petition for inspection of ballots for certain precincts in which he alleges that double-counting of ballots occurred. The trial court concluded that Coleman had not met his burden to show that an inspection was needed to prepare for trial, noting Coleman's concession at the hearing on the petition that he would be able to prove his case without an inspection, by calling election judges as witnesses and by subpoenaing voter rolls and ballots. The court also concluded that inspections under Minn. Stat. § 209.06 (2008) are limited to the ballots themselves and do not include voter rolls or other election materials sought by Coleman. Finally, the court noted that the parties had already reviewed the ballots during the manual recount. . . .

[Minnesota law has been omitted.]

Coleman argues that he had an absolute right to inspection under section 209.06 and that the trial court had no discretion to deny his petition. Coleman contends that the denial of the inspection foreclosed his ability to gather information to fully present his case of double-counting of unmarked duplicate ballots during the manual recount. Coleman's claim that the statute provides an absolute right to an inspection is contrary to our ruling in *Christenson v. Allen,* 264 Minn. 395, 119 N.W.2d 35 (1963). In *Christenson,* we said that under the plain language of section 209.06, an inspection is allowed only upon a showing that an inspection is needed to prepare for trial of the election contest.

Coleman conceded at the hearing on the petition for inspection, and does not dispute here, that he could prove his claim of double-counting by subpoenaing the ballots and election materials and by subpoenaing witnesses to testify. This concession negates any claim that he made the required showing of necessity and any contention that he was prevented from proving his case by denial of the inspection. Coleman called no witnesses with direct knowledge of the handling of duplicate ballots in the relevant precincts, but he did introduce at trial voter rosters, envelopes from accepted absentee ballots, copies of ballots challenged during the manual recount, and machine tapes from the identified precincts in which he alleges double-counting of absentee ballots occurred. On appeal, Coleman has identified nothing additional that an inspection of ballots under section 209.06 would have produced. We therefore hold that the trial court did not abuse its discretion in denying the petition for inspection.

V.

Finally, Coleman contends that the trial court erred when it ruled that missing ballots from Minneapolis Ward 3, Precinct 1, were properly included in the State Canvassing Board's January 5, 2009 certification of legally cast votes. During the manual recount, election officials could locate only four of the five envelopes of ballots from Minneapolis Ward 3, Precinct 1. Voting machine tapes showed a total of 2,028 ballots cast and counted in the precinct on election day, but only 1,896 ballots from the precinct were available for the recount, a difference of 132 ballots. The State Canvassing Board determined that an envelope of ballots had been lost and, rather than certify only 1,896 votes in the recount, accepted the election day returns for that precinct. . . .

Coleman articulates no compelling reason why that same principle should not apply here. The ballots are missing, but Coleman introduced no evidence of foul play or misconduct, and the election day precinct returns are available to give effect to those votes. We hold that the trial court did not err in ruling that the election day precinct returns for Minneapolis Ward 3, Precinct 1, were properly included in the tally of legally cast votes.

VI.

For all of the foregoing reasons, we affirm the decision of the trial court that Al Franken received the highest number of votes legally cast and is entitled under Minn. Stat. § 204C.40 (2008) to receive the certificate of election as United States Senator from the State of Minnesota.

Affirmed.

SOURCE: Minnesota Supreme Court. *Coleman v. Franken*. A09–697. June 30, 2009. www.lawlibrary.state .mn.us/archive/supct/0906/OPA090697–0630.pdf.

Senate Majority Leader Harry Reid on Election of Al Franken

June 30, 2009

I congratulate Senator-elect Al Franken, the next Senator from the state of Minnesota.

The people of Minnesota will now finally get the brilliant and hardworking new senator they elected in November and the full representation they deserve. After all the votes have been counted and recounted, the Minnesota Supreme Court has made the final determination that Minnesotans have chosen Al Franken to help their state and our country get back on track.

The Senate looks forward to welcoming Senator-elect Franken as soon as possible. He will play a crucial role as we work to strengthen our economy, ensure all Americans can access and afford quality health care, make our country more energy independent, confirm the President's outstanding nominee to the Supreme Court, and tackle the many other challenges we face.

I once again encourage Governor Pawlenty to respect the votes of his constituents and the decisions of his state's highest court. He should put politics aside, follow his state's laws and finally sign the certificate that will bring this episode to an end.

Source: Sen. Harry Reid. "Reid Statement on Senator-Elect Al Franken." June 30, 2009. http://demo crats.senate.gov/newsroom/record.cfm?id=315226&.

OTHER HISTORIC DOCUMENTS OF INTEREST

FROM THIS VOLUME

FROM PREVIOUS *HISTORIC DOCUMENTS*

Barack Obama Sworn in as President of the United States

JANUARY 20, 2009

After a hard-fought, nearly two-year presidential primary and election cycle, Barack Obama, a Democratic first-term U.S. senator from Illinois, defeated opponent Sen. John McCain, R-Ariz., on November 2, 2008, and became the first African American president of the United States. Obama's inauguration was highly anticipated not only in the United States but around the world. As January 20, 2009, drew closer, Washington, D.C., braced for an expected two million visitors to the city and on the National Mall to witness the historic event.

INAUGURATION CROWDS

More than one and a half million people packed the National Mall between the Capitol and the Washington Monument on January 20, 2009, to witness the swearing in of the nation's first African American president. Analysts watching the crowds said that it was clear that African Americans were more prevalent at this inauguration than they had been in the past. As part of its election coverage, CNN interviewed those coming to the National Mall to witness the event, and in their accounts African American attendees compared Obama's inauguration to other defining moments in American history. "This is America happening," Evadey Minott of Brooklyn, New York, told CNN. "It was prophesied by [Rev. Martin Luther] King that we would have a day when everyone would come together. This is that day. I am excited. I am joyful. It brings tears to my eyes." Others spoke of how Obama's inauguration was another step in the history of African American struggle. L. J. Caldwell from Somerset, New Jersey, said, "When you think back, Malcolm [X] fought. Then we come a little further, Rosa Parks sat. Then come up a little further, and Martin [King Jr.] spoke. Then today, President Obama ran, and we won." Patrick Bragg of Bethesda, Maryland, saw the inauguration as a coming together of all people and all races. "I've been sitting here thinking—it's really beautiful. This is what I would consider the true representation of all of America. Obama gives everyone space at the table."

It was not just U.S. citizens who attended the inauguration on the National Mall: People came from around the world to witness the event, which many saw as a turning point in the relationship between the United States and the rest of the world. Simon Ginty of England told CNN, "This is an international moment as well as an American moment. I'm excited to see how Obama changes things. I imagine things are gonna be on the up." "This is a world event," Susan Butler from Canada told CNN. Fatima Cone, who came from Ivory Coast, said that Obama's inauguration wasn't just about the struggle of African Americans in the United States. "The fight is the same for all blacks," she said to CNN. "It's the same story. It's the same fight wherever you come from."

The Washington, D.C., transit system tried to prepare for the crowds, but according to the Washington Metropolitan Area Transit Authority, it was taking people hours to get on to subway trains both coming to the inauguration and leaving. Once attendees arrived, they faced massive security operations and checkpoints set up to filter people coming on to the National Mall and the nearby parade route; the security lines were often slow. Because of the sizeable crowds, some areas of the National Mall were shut down at 9 A.M., three hours before Obama was set to take the oath of office. Tickets for seats at the U.S. Capitol were nearly impossible to obtain, but many people who got the tickets were turned away at security gates because of the chaos caused by the crowds. This drove many would-be inauguration attendees into local bars and restaurants to watch the festivities on television.

Obama's Inaugural Speech

Standing next to his wife, Michelle, and their daughters, Malia and Sasha, at noon on January 20, 2009, Obama took the presidential oath of office to become the nation's forty-fourth president. After the oath, Obama addressed those watching from the National Mall and those around the country and the world. He struck a somber yet optimistic tone while talking about the state of the country and the challenges facing it. "That we are in the midst of crisis is now well understood. Our nation is at war against a far-reaching network of violence and hatred. Our economy is badly weakened. . . . Homes have been lost, jobs shed, businesses shuttered. Our health care is too costly, our schools fail too many. . . ." He also spoke to his opponents, saying, "There are some who question the scale of our ambitions, who suggest that our system cannot tolerate too many big plans." "Their memories are short," he said, "for they have forgotten what this country has already done. . . . What the cynics fail to understand is that the ground has shifted beneath them, that the stale political arguments that have consumed us for so long no longer apply."

Obama hinted at the work to be done on the economy, asking Americans to come together to confront and then move past "our collective failure to make hard choices," and also spoke of his plan to leave Iraq responsibly and hand it over to its people. He called on those around the world, many of whom may have been put off by previous administrations, to look for a way forward and a path to peace with the United States. He pledged to combat global corruption and help the people of suffering nations.

Obama also spoke about the change his presidency represented, saying that sixty years ago, his father "might not have been served at a local restaurant." The African American community rejoiced over the election of Obama, and came out in droves to attend his inauguration, but Obama, the forty-seven-year-old son of a white woman from Kansas and a black father from Africa, rarely brought up race during his speech. However, the new president, in a gesture symbolic of the historic nature of his election, took the oath of office on the same Bible Abraham Lincoln used when he was first sworn into office in 1891.

After the ceremony concluded and Obama had bid farewell to former president George W. Bush and former first lady Laura Bush, the new president went to the Capitol, where he signed papers to nominate his cabinet and attended a lunch at the U.S. Capitol with members of Congress.

In his speech to lawmakers over lunch, President Obama revisited the theme he introduced in his inaugural address of the difficulty involved in overcoming challenges and once again noted his optimism that they would be met. In addition, President Obama called on Democrats and Republicans to come together "with a sense of purpose and civility and urgency." He told them, "It doesn't mean we're going to agree on everything. . . . And I assure you our administration will make mistakes."

Despite frigid temperatures, President Obama and the first lady exited the presidential limousine twice during the 1.7-mile parade route from the Capitol to the White House to wave to the crowds.

Obama's Cabinet

The president submitted his cabinet nominations before the beginning of the inaugural luncheon, and after lunch, the Senate reconvened and by unanimous consent confirmed seven of Obama's choices. Steven Chu was appointed secretary of energy; Arne Duncan, former chief executive officer of Chicago Public Schools, was appointed secretary of education; Janet Napolitano, then Arizona's governor, became secretary of homeland security; Peter Orszag was appointed secretary of the Office of Management and Budget; Ken Salazar was appointed secretary of the interior; Eric Shinseki was appointed secretary of veterans affairs; and Tom Vilsak, the former governor of Iowa, was appointed secretary of agriculture.

Although the seven had been confirmed, it still left many seats open, including secretary of state, for which Obama nominated his one-time Democratic presidential primary opponent, former first lady Sen. Hillary Rodham Clinton, D-N.Y. The Senate had been set to vote on Clinton's confirmation the day of the inauguration, but Republicans delayed the vote until January 21, 2009, because of the stated concern that foreign donors to the charitable foundation headed by her husband, former president Bill Clinton, would represent a conflict of interest. On January 21, 2009, Hillary Rodham Clinton was confirmed as secretary of state.

Although confirmation of these eight cabinet positions presented relatively little trouble in the Senate, other cabinet positions would prove trying. Filling the secretary of commerce position was the most challenging. President Obama first nominated New Mexico's Democratic governor, Bill Richardson, who later withdrew his nomination because his state administration was the subject of a federal corruption probe. Sen. Judd Gregg, R-N.H., was President Obama's second nominee, but Gregg later withdrew his nomination over disagreements with the president's fiscal policy. A third nominee reportedly dropped out before being officially announced, and President Obama moved on to his fourth pick, former governor Gary Locke, D-Wash., who was confirmed by the Senate. Eric Holder, who was confirmed as attorney general, had his confirmation held up by the Senate Judiciary Committee as members delved into Holder's views over Bush administration policies of detention and interrogation methods of suspected enemy combatants. Former senator Tom Daschle, D-S.D., who was nominated by President Obama to be secretary of health and human services, withdrew his nomination in early February 2009 because of questions regarding unpaid back taxes.

Roberts's Mistake

While post-inauguration celebrations took place around the world, constitutional scholars and others pointed out that Chief Justice John Roberts had misspoken while administering the oath of office, flubbing the precise wording at one point and at another point not allowing the president time to repeat the oath. Although the Constitution made certain that Obama became president at noon on January 20, 2009, to quiet dissenters, including conservative Fox News anchor Chris Wallace, who said, "We're wondering here whether or not Barack Obama is in fact the president of the United States," Roberts administered the oath again at 7:35 P.M. on January 21, 2009, in the Map Room of the White House. The Constitution lays out the oath as "I do solemnly swear (or affirm) that I will faithfully execute the Office of President of the United States. . . ." Chief Justice Roberts said instead, "that I will execute the office of president to the United States faithfully."

Although Roberts did not publically comment on the mistake, Obama was jovial about it, telling members of the press in attendance at the second oath, "The bad news for the [press] pool is there's 12 more [inaugural] balls."

—Heather Kerrigan

Following is the text of the speech given by Barack Obama upon his inauguration as president of the United States on January 20, 2009.

DOCUMENT   *Barack Obama's Inaugural Address*

January 20, 2009

My fellow citizens, I stand here today humbled by the task before us, grateful for the trust you have bestowed, mindful of the sacrifices borne by our ancestors. I thank President Bush for his service to our Nation, as well as the generosity and cooperation he has shown throughout this transition.

Forty-four Americans have now taken the Presidential oath. The words have been spoken during rising tides of prosperity and the still waters of peace. Yet every so often, the oath is taken amidst gathering clouds and raging storms. At these moments, America has carried on not simply because of the skill or vision of those in high office, but because we the people have remained faithful to the ideals of our forbearers and true to our founding documents.

So it has been; so it must be with this generation of Americans. That we are in the midst of crisis is now well understood. Our Nation is at war against a far-reaching network of violence and hatred. Our economy is badly weakened, a consequence of greed and irresponsibility on the part of some, but also our collective failure to make hard choices and prepare the Nation for a new age. Homes have been lost, jobs shed, businesses shuttered. Our health care is too costly. Our schools fail too many. And each day brings further evidence that the ways we use energy strengthen our adversaries and threaten our planet.

These are the indicators of crisis, subject to data and statistics. Less measurable but no less profound is a sapping of confidence across our land, a nagging fear that America's decline is inevitable, that the next generation must lower its sights. Today I say to you that the challenges we face are real. They are serious, and they are many. They will not be met easily or in a short span of time. But know this, America: They will be met.

On this day, we gather because we have chosen hope over fear, unity of purpose over conflict and discord. On this day, we come to proclaim an end to the petty grievances and false promises, the recriminations and worn-out dogmas that for far too long have strangled our politics.

We remain a young nation, but in the words of Scripture, the time has come to set aside childish things. The time has come to reaffirm our enduring spirit, to choose our better history, to carry forward that precious gift, that noble idea passed on from generation to generation: the God-given promise that all are equal, all are free, and all deserve a chance to pursue their full measure of happiness.

In reaffirming the greatness of our Nation, we understand that greatness is never a given. It must be earned. Our journey has never been one of shortcuts or settling for less. It has not been the path for the fainthearted, for those who prefer leisure over work or seek only the pleasures of riches and fame. Rather, it has been the risk-takers, the doers, the makers of things—some celebrated, but more often men and women obscure in their labor—who have carried us up the long, rugged path toward prosperity and freedom.

For us, they packed up their few worldly possessions and traveled across oceans in search of a new life. For us, they toiled in sweatshops and settled the West, endured the lash of the whip, and plowed the hard Earth. For us, they fought and died in places like Concord and Gettysburg, Normandy and Khe Sanh.

Time and again, these men and women struggled and sacrificed and worked 'til their hands were raw so that we might live a better life. They saw America as bigger than the sum of our individual ambitions, greater than all the differences of birth or wealth or faction.

This is the journey we continue today. We remain the most prosperous, powerful nation on Earth. Our workers are no less productive than when this crisis began. Our minds are no less inventive. Our goods and services no less needed than they were last week or last month or last year. Our capacity remains undiminished. But our time of standing pat, of protecting narrow interests and putting off unpleasant decisions, that time has surely passed. Starting today, we must pick ourselves up, dust ourselves off, and begin again the work of remaking America.

For everywhere we look, there is work to be done. The state of the economy calls for action, bold and swift, and we will act not only to create new jobs but to lay a new foundation for growth. We will build the roads and bridges, the electric grids and digital lines that feed our commerce and bind us together. We will restore science to its rightful place and wield technology's wonders to raise health care's quality and lower its cost. We will harness the sun and the winds and the soil to fuel our cars and run our factories. And we will transform our schools and colleges and universities to meet the demands of a new age. All this we can do. All this we will do.

Now, there are some who question the scale of our ambitions, who suggest that our system cannot tolerate too many big plans. Their memories are short, for they have forgotten what this country has already done, what free men and women can achieve when imagination is joined to common purpose and necessity to courage.

What the cynics fail to understand is that the ground has shifted beneath them; that the stale political arguments that have consumed us for so long no longer apply. The question we ask today is not whether our Government is too big or too small, but whether it works; whether it helps families find jobs at a decent wage, care they can afford, a retirement that is dignified. Where the answer is yes, we intend to move forward. Where the answer is no, programs will end. And those of us who manage the public's dollars will be held to account to spend wisely, reform bad habits, and do our business in the light of day, because only then can we restore the vital trust between a people and their government.

Nor is the question before us whether the market is a force for good or ill. Its power to generate wealth and expand freedom is unmatched. But this crisis has reminded us that without a watchful eye, the market can spin out of control. The Nation cannot prosper long when it favors only the prosperous. The success of our economy has always depended not just on the size of our gross domestic product, but on the reach of our prosperity, on our ability to extend opportunity to every willing heart, not out of charity, but because it is the surest route to our common good.

As for our common defense, we reject as false the choice between our safety and our ideals. Our Founding Fathers, faced with perils that we can scarcely imagine, drafted a charter to assure the rule of law and the rights of man, a charter expanded by the blood of generations. Those ideals still light the world, and we will not give them up for expedience's sake. And so to all the other peoples and governments who are watching today, from the grandest capitals to the small village where my father was born, know that America is a friend of each nation and every man, woman, and child who seeks a future of peace and dignity, and we are ready to lead once more.

Recall that earlier generations faced down fascism and communism not just with missiles and tanks but with sturdy alliances and enduring convictions. They understood that our power alone cannot protect us, nor does it entitle us to do as we please. Instead, they knew that our power grows through its prudent use. Our security emanates from the justness of our cause, the force of our example, the tempering qualities of humility and restraint.

We are the keepers of this legacy. Guided by these principles once more, we can meet those new threats that demand even greater effort, even greater cooperation and understanding between nations. We will begin to responsibly leave Iraq to its people and forge a hard-earned peace in Afghanistan. With old friends and former foes, we will work tirelessly to lessen the nuclear threat and roll back the specter of a warming planet. We will not apologize for our way of life, nor will we waver in its defense. And for those who seek to advance their aims by inducing terror and slaughtering innocents, we say to you now that our spirit is stronger and cannot be broken. You cannot outlast us, and we will defeat you.

For we know that our patchwork heritage is a strength, not a weakness. We are a nation of Christians and Muslims, Jews and Hindus and nonbelievers. We are shaped by every language and culture, drawn from every end of this Earth. And because we have tasted the bitter swill of civil war and segregation and emerged from that dark chapter stronger and more united, we cannot help but believe that the old hatreds shall someday pass; that the lines of tribe shall soon dissolve; that as the world grows smaller, our common humanity shall reveal itself; and that America must play its role in ushering in a new era of peace.

To the Muslim world, we seek a new way forward based on mutual interest and mutual respect. To those leaders around the globe who seek to sow conflict or blame their society's ills on the West, know that your people will judge you on what you can build, not what you destroy. To those who cling to power through corruption and deceit and the silencing of dissent, know that you are on the wrong side of history, but that we will extend a hand if you are willing to unclench your fist.

To the people of poor nations, we pledge to work alongside you to make your farms flourish and let clean waters flow, to nourish starved bodies and feed hungry minds. And to those nations like ours that enjoy relative plenty, we say we can no longer afford indifference to suffering outside our borders, nor can we consume the world's resources without regard to effect, for the world has changed, and we must change with it.

As we consider the road that unfolds before us, we remember with humble gratitude those brave Americans who, at this very hour, patrol far-off deserts and distant mountains. They have something to tell us today, just as the fallen heroes who lie in Arlington whisper through the ages. We honor them not only because they are guardians of our liberty, but because they embody the spirit of service, a willingness to find meaning in something greater than themselves. And yet at this moment—a moment that will define a generation—it is precisely this spirit that must inhabit us all.

For as much as Government can do and must do, it is ultimately the faith and determination of the American people upon which this Nation relies. It is the kindness to take in a stranger when the levees break, the selflessness of workers who would rather cut their hours than see a friend lose their job, which sees us through our darkest hours. It is the firefighter's courage to storm a stairway filled with smoke, but also a parent's willingness to nurture a child, that finally decides our fate.

Our challenges may be new. The instruments with which we meet them may be new. But those values upon which our success depends—honesty and hard work, courage and fair play, tolerance and curiosity, loyalty and patriotism—these things are old. These things are true. They have been the quiet force of progress throughout our history. What is demanded then is a return to these truths. What is required of us now is a new era of responsibility, a recognition on the part of every American that we have duties to ourselves, our Nation, and the world. Duties that we do not grudgingly accept but, rather, seize gladly, firm in the knowledge that there is nothing so satisfying to the spirit, so defining of our character, than giving our all to a difficult task.

This is the price and the promise of citizenship. This is the source of our confidence—the knowledge that God calls on us to shape an uncertain destiny. This is the meaning of our liberty and our creed; why men and women and children of every race and every faith can join in celebration across this magnificent Mall, and why a man whose father less than 60 years ago might not have been served at a local restaurant can now stand before you to take a most sacred oath.

So let us mark this day with remembrance of who we are and how far we have traveled. In the year of America's birth, in the coldest of months, a small band of patriots huddled by dying campfires on the shores of an icy river. The Capital was abandoned. The enemy was advancing. The snow was stained with blood. At a moment when the outcome of our Revolution was most in doubt, the Father of our Nation ordered these words be read to the people:

"Let it be told to the future world . . . that in the depth of winter, when nothing but hope and virtue could survive . . . that the city and the country, alarmed at one common danger, came forth to meet [it]."

America, in the face of our common dangers, in this winter of our hardship, let us remember these timeless words. With hope and virtue, let us brave once more the icy currents and endure what storms may come. Let it be said by our children's children that when we were tested, we refused to let this journey end; that we did not turn back, nor did we falter. And with eyes fixed on the horizon and God's grace upon us, we carried forth that great gift of freedom and delivered it safely to future generations.

Thank you. God bless you, and God bless the United States of America.

SOURCE: U.S. Executive Office of the President. "Inaugural Address." *Daily Compilation of Presidential Documents* 2009, no. 00001 (January 20, 2009). www.gpo.gov/fdsys/pkg/DCPD-200900001/pdf/DCPD-200900001.pdf.

OTHER HISTORIC DOCUMENTS OF INTEREST

FROM THIS VOLUME

- President Obama's Address Before a Joint Session of Congress and Republican Response, p. 81

FROM PREVIOUS *HISTORIC DOCUMENTS*

- 2008 Presidential Election Victory and Concession Speeches, *2008,* p. 519
- Senators Obama and McCain in the Final Presidential Debate, *2008,* p. 497
- 2008 Democratic and Republican Presidential Primaries, *2008,* p. 8

President Obama Calls for the Closure of Detention Facilities at Guantánamo Bay

JANUARY 22 AND DECEMBER 15, 2009

On January 22, 2009, after only two days in office, President Barack Obama issued Executive Order 13492 calling for the closure of the Guantánamo Bay detention center within one year and a suspension of all proceedings in the military commission system. The order marked a significant departure from former president George W. Bush's detention policies and prosecutions, which were heavily criticized by human rights groups and the international community. Obama's order initiated a lengthy and at times contentious review of past practices and raised questions about where the remaining detainees would be sent and how they could be brought to justice.

CREATING A DETENTION PROGRAM

President Bush opened the detention center at U.S. Naval Station Guantánamo Bay, Cuba, shortly after the September 11, 2001, terrorist attacks. The facility was intended to house "unlawful combatants" or individuals suspected of having ties to organizations such as al-Qaida and the Taliban. Over the course of its seven-year existence, the facility had held approximately 800 detainees of varying nationalities. Justice Department lawyers had advised the Bush administration that those held at Guantánamo Bay would be beyond the jurisdiction of domestic courts, a declaration that immediately drew criticism. In a Military Order in November 2001, President Bush established a new military commission system to prosecute the Guantánamo detainees. The order was highly controversial and sparked a rigorous debate over what rights should be afforded to suspected terrorists, as military commissions typically require defendants to forgo some of the rights they would enjoy in civilian courts, including the right to habeas corpus. Human rights organizations, such as Amnesty International and Human Rights Watch, were sharply critical of the fairness of the commissions, claiming any proceedings would amount to no more than "show trials" and contending that the United States would not consent to any American facing a similar trial in a foreign country. Such organizations also decried the living conditions at Guantánamo and alleged that guards and interrogators at the facility had abused and tortured detainees. The U.S. Supreme Court did not rule until June 12, 2008, that the Military Commissions Act, legislation providing congressional authorization of the military commission system, was unconstitutional and that Guantánamo prisoners had a right to habeas corpus.

By the end of the Bush administration, the federal government had moved more than 500 detainees from Guantánamo Bay by releasing them to their home countries or transferring them to a third country, leaving 245 at the facility. Approximately sixty additional detainees had been cleared for release, but the U.S. government had not yet been able to find a third country willing to take them. Another 80 detainees fell into what was referred to as the "preventive detention" category, meaning there was little evidence against them, but intelligence officials insisted they were too dangerous to release.

Obama's Promise

During the 2008 presidential campaign, then-senator Barack Obama promised that if elected, he would close the detention center at Guantánamo Bay. On January 22, 2009, the newly inaugurated president took a major step toward honoring that promise by signing Executive Order 13492. The order called for the detention center to be closed within one year and suspended all current and pending proceedings before military commissions until a full review of that system could be completed. It officially extended all protections afforded by the Geneva Conventions to detainees and called on the secretary of defense to review the "conditions of detention" at Guantánamo to ensure full compliance with those provisions. In addition, the order directed the Central Intelligence Agency (CIA) to shut down whatever remained of its network of secret prisons, where detainees may have been held for months or years before transfer to Guantánamo, and required all intelligence officials and government agencies to abide by the U.S. Army Field Manual when interrogating suspected terrorists. It declared that any detainees remaining at Guantánamo at the time of closure "shall be returned to their home country, released, transferred to a third country or transferred to another United States detention facility in a manner consistent with law and the national security and foreign policy interests of the United States."

Mixed Reactions

Reaction to President Obama's order was swift and varied. In testimony before Congress, Admiral Dennis Blair, then nominee for the position of director of national intelligence, described the detention center as "a rallying cry for terrorist recruitment" and said, "The guiding principles for closing the center should be protecting our national security, respecting the Geneva Conventions and the rule of law, and respecting the existing institutions of justice in this country." Human rights organizations also expressed their support. Andrew Romero, executive director of the American Civil Liberties Union, proclaimed the order had "reaffirmed American values and is a ray of light after eight long, dark years." However, Republican leaders argued that closing the center would be a threat to national security and pointed to reports that some recently released detainees had since rejoined al-Qaida or other terrorist organizations.

To facilitate the detention center's closure, President Obama requested that Congress authorize $80 million in funding in its supplemental appropriations bills. In early May 2009, the Senate Appropriations Committee voted to include $50 million in its supplemental bill, but stipulated the funding would only become available once the president had submitted a detailed plan for closing the facility and relocating the detainees. However, on May 20, 2009, the full Senate voted nearly unanimously to strip all funding for the Guantánamo closure from the bill. Meanwhile, the House omitted any funding for Obama's request in its legislation, leaving him to try to move forward without sufficient funding.

DETERMINING WHERE THE DETAINEES WOULD GO

Perhaps the biggest question raised by Obama's order was where the detainees would be relocated once Guantánamo closed. One possibility was to repatriate those who had been cleared for release or transfer them to a third country. Many speculated that European countries would provide the safest relocation options, as their judicial systems would ensure detainees' protection and humane treatment. Although France, Italy, Portugal, and Spain expressed a willingness to help, other European countries, particularly Germany, were hesitant, demanding assurances that the detainees no longer posed any threat and a reasonable justification for why they should accept these individuals when the United States would not. Britain had already taken fourteen former detainees and refused to take anymore. The Obama administration also initiated talks with Saudi Arabia and Yemen to discuss sending 100 Yemeni detainees to detention centers in Saudi Arabia. By December 2009, only the tiny island of Palau had agreed to help, temporarily resettling seventeen Uighur detainees from northwestern China who may have faced torture or unfair trials upon returning to their home country.

For those detainees who would either face some form of trial or be held indefinitely, the question remained whether they could be transferred to domestic prisons. The issue soon pitted the need for job creation in a struggling economy against national security concerns, as two rural midwestern towns proposed relocating detainees to their ailing prisons. Citizens of Standish, Michigan, offered that town's maximum security prison, which was scheduled to close and eliminate nearly 300 jobs unless new prisoners were brought in. But Rep. Peter Hoekstra, R-Mich., led a vocal opposition against the proposal, and the Standish prison closed on October 31, 2009. A similar debate developed in Thomson, Illinois, in early November. Town leaders suggested the government purchase the nearly empty, maximum security Thomson Correctional Facility, located approximately 150 miles west of Chicago. The proposal received strong backing from Sen. Richard Durbin, D-Ill., and Democratic governor Pat Quinn, who claimed it could bring nearly 3,000 jobs and up to $1 billion over four years to the area. Opponents such as Rep. Mark Kirk, R-Ill., countered that such a move would make Illinois and the Chicago metropolitan area "ground zero for Jihadist terrorist plots, recruitment and radicalization." Still others claimed detainees would be able to recruit other inmates to terrorism. On December 15, 2009, the Obama administration decided to purchase the Illinois facility to "house a limited number of detainees from Guantánamo," as well as federal inmates transferred from overcrowded prisons. In a letter to Governor Quinn, administration officials offered assurances that "Federal inmates will have no opportunity to interact with Guantanamo detainees" as they would be kept in separate sections of the prison, and that federal departments and agencies would "work closely with state and local law enforcement authorities to identify and mitigate any risks" associated with maintaining the facility's security.

FACING JUSTICE

The Obama administration also faced the question of how to prosecute the remaining detainees if not through the military commissions system. Options included trying detainees in federal court, using the military courts martial system, revising the military commissions system to make such trials less controversial, or creating an entirely new national security court system. Ahmed Ghailani, accused of participating in the 1998 bombings at U.S. embassies in Tanzania and Kenya, would be the first detainee to appear before a federal court. On June 9, 2009, he pled not guilty to all charges and will be tried in federal court in September 2010.

Then, on November 13, 2009, Attorney General Eric Holder announced that alleged September 11 mastermind Khalid Sheikh Mohammed and four other detainees suspected of being involved in the 2001 terrorist attacks would be sent to New York to face trial in a federal court, located blocks from where the World Trade Center towers once stood. Holder said prosecutors would seek the death penalty in each case and declared, "We need not cower in the face of this enemy. Our institutions are strong. Our infrastructure is sturdy. Our resolve is firm, and our people are ready." The announcement sparked immediate opposition and outrage. The CIA expressed concerns that questions raised during a trial might expose sensitive information about U.S. intelligence-gathering techniques and expressed worry that the fact that Mohammed had been waterboarded more than 180 times in 2003 might jeopardize the case against him, given the disparate views on whether information gained during waterboarding can be considered reliable. Others, particularly leaders in the Republican party, claimed a trial in federal court would give Mohammed a platform from which to spread his jihadist views and smear the United States, as he could not be denied the right to testify. The trial will not occur until late 2010, because formal charges have not been filed against most of the five detainees in question.

A Lingering Challenge

In an interview with NBC News on November 18, 2009, President Obama acknowledged for the first time in public that the Guantánamo Bay detention center would not close by his self-imposed mid-January deadline, but he also said he expects the facility will close sometime in 2010. This admission further underscored the many challenges and obstacles Obama must face before his executive order can be fulfilled.

—Linda Fecteau

> *Following is the executive order signed by President Barack Obama on January 22, 2009, directing the prompt closure of the Guantánamo Bay detention facilities and a December 15, 2009, letter from federal officials to Illinois governor Pat Quinn concerning the purchase of the Thomson Correctional Center to house, in part, detainees from Guantánamo Bay.*

DOCUMENT

Obama Signs Executive Order Calling for the Closure of Guantánamo Bay

January 22, 2009

By the authority vested in me as President by the Constitution and the laws of the United States of America, in order to effect the appropriate disposition of individuals currently detained by the Department of Defense at the Guantánamo Bay Naval Base (Guantánamo) and promptly to close detention facilities at Guantánamo, consistent with the national security and foreign policy interests of the United States and the interests of justice, I hereby order as follows:

Section 1. Definitions. As used in this order:

(a) "Common Article 3" means Article 3 of each of the Geneva Conventions.

(b) "Geneva Conventions" means:

(i) the Convention for the Amelioration of the Condition of the Wounded and Sick in Armed Forces in the Field, August 12, 1949 (6 UST 3114);

(ii) the Convention for the Amelioration of the Condition of Wounded, Sick and Shipwrecked Members of Armed Forces at Sea, August 12, 1949 (6 UST 3217);

(iii) the Convention Relative to the Treatment of Prisoners of War, August 12, 1949 (6 UST 3316); and

(iv) the Convention Relative to the Protection of Civilian Persons in Time of War, August 12, 1949 (6 UST 3516).

(c) "Individuals currently detained at Guantánamo" and "individuals covered by this order" mean individuals currently detained by the Department of Defense in facilities at the Guantánamo Bay Naval Base whom the Department of Defense has ever determined to be, or treated as, enemy combatants.

Sec. 2. Findings.

(a) Over the past 7 years, approximately 800 individuals whom the Department of Defense has ever determined to be, or treated as, enemy combatants have been detained at Guantánamo. The Federal Government has moved more than 500 such detainees from Guantánamo, either by returning them to their home country or by releasing or transferring them to a third country. The Department of Defense has determined that a number of the individuals currently detained at Guantánamo are eligible for such transfer or release.

(b) Some individuals currently detained at Guantánamo have been there for more than 6 years, and most have been detained for at least 4 years. In view of the significant concerns raised by these detentions, both within the United States and internationally, prompt and appropriate disposition of the individuals currently detained at Guantánamo and closure of the facilities in which they are detained would further the national security and foreign policy interests of the United States and the interests of justice. Merely closing the facilities without promptly determining the appropriate disposition of the individuals detained would not adequately serve those interests. To the extent practicable, the prompt and appropriate disposition of the individuals detained at Guantánamo should precede the closure of the detention facilities at Guantánamo.

(c) The individuals currently detained at Guantánamo have the constitutional privilege of the writ of habeas corpus. Most of those individuals have filed petitions for a writ of habeas corpus in Federal court challenging the lawfulness of their detention.

(d) It is in the interests of the United States that the executive branch undertake a prompt and thorough review of the factual and legal bases for the continued detention of all individuals currently held at Guantánamo, and of whether their continued detention is in the national security and foreign policy interests of the United States and in the interests of justice. The unusual circumstances associated with detentions at Guantánamo require a comprehensive interagency review.

(e) New diplomatic efforts may result in an appropriate disposition of a substantial number of individuals currently detained at Guantánamo.

(f) Some individuals currently detained at Guantánamo may have committed offenses for which they should be prosecuted. It is in the interests of the United States to review whether and how any such individuals can and should be prosecuted.

(g) It is in the interests of the United States that the executive branch conduct a prompt and thorough review of the circumstances of the individuals currently detained at Guantánamo who have been charged with offenses before military commissions pursuant to the Military Commissions Act of 2006, Public Law 109–366, as well as of the military commission process more generally.

Sec. 3. Closure of Detention Facilities at Guantánamo. The detention facilities at Guantánamo for individuals covered by this order shall be closed as soon as practicable, and no later than 1 year from the date of this order. If any individuals covered by this order remain in detention at Guantánamo at the time of closure of those detention facilities, they shall be returned to their home country, released, transferred to a third country, or transferred to another United States detention facility in a manner consistent with law and the national security and foreign policy interests of the United States.

Sec. 4. Immediate Review of All Guantánamo Detentions.

(a) *Scope and Timing of Review.* A review of the status of each individual currently detained at Guantánamo (Review) shall commence immediately.

(b) *Review Participants.* The Review shall be conducted with the full cooperation and participation of the following officials:

(1) the Attorney General, who shall coordinate the Review;

(2) the Secretary of Defense;

(3) the Secretary of State;

(4) the Secretary of Homeland Security;

(5) the Director of National Intelligence;

(6) the Chairman of the Joint Chiefs of Staff; and

(7) other officers or full-time or permanent part-time employees of the United States, including employees with intelligence, counterterrorism, military, and legal expertise, as determined by the Attorney General, with the concurrence of the head of the department or agency concerned.

(c) *Operation of Review.* The duties of the Review participants shall include the following:

(1) *Consolidation of Detainee Information.* The Attorney General shall, to the extent reasonably practicable, and in coordination with the other Review participants, assemble all information in the possession of the Federal Government that pertains to any individual currently detained at Guantánamo and that is relevant to determining the proper disposition of any such individual. All executive branch departments and agencies shall promptly comply with any request of the Attorney General to provide information in their possession or control pertaining to any such individual. The Attorney General may seek further information relevant to the Review from any source.

(2) *Determination of Transfer.* The Review shall determine, on a rolling basis and as promptly as possible with respect to the individuals currently detained at Guantánamo, whether it is possible to transfer or release the individuals consistent with the national security and foreign policy interests of the United States and, if so, whether and how the Secretary of Defense may effect their transfer

or release. The Secretary of Defense, the Secretary of State, and, as appropriate, other Review participants shall work to effect promptly the release or transfer of all individuals for whom release or transfer is possible.

(3) *Determination of Prosecution.* In accordance with United States law, the cases of individuals detained at Guantánamo not approved for release or transfer shall be evaluated to determine whether the Federal Government should seek to prosecute the detained individuals for any offenses they may have committed, including whether it is feasible to prosecute such individuals before a court established pursuant to Article III of the United States Constitution, and the Review participants shall in turn take the necessary and appropriate steps based on such determinations.

(4) *Determination of Other Disposition.* With respect to any individuals currently detained at Guantánamo whose disposition is not achieved under paragraphs (2) or (3) of this subsection, the Review shall select lawful means, consistent with the national security and foreign policy interests of the United States and the interests of justice, for the disposition of such individuals. The appropriate authorities shall promptly implement such dispositions.

(5) *Consideration of Issues Relating to Transfer to the United States.* The Review shall identify and consider legal, logistical, and security issues relating to the potential transfer of individuals currently detained at Guantánamo to facilities within the United States, and the Review participants shall work with the Congress on any legislation that may be appropriate.

Sec. 5. Diplomatic Efforts. The Secretary of State shall expeditiously pursue and direct such negotiations and diplomatic efforts with foreign governments as are necessary and appropriate to implement this order.

Sec. 6. Humane Standards of Confinement. No individual currently detained at Guantánamo shall be held in the custody or under the effective control of any officer, employee, or other agent of the United States Government, or at a facility owned, operated, or controlled by a department or agency of the United States, except in conformity with all applicable laws governing the conditions of such confinement, including Common Article 3 of the Geneva Conventions. The Secretary of Defense shall immediately undertake a review of the conditions of detention at Guantánamo to ensure full compliance with this directive. Such review shall be completed within 30 days and any necessary corrections shall be implemented immediately thereafter.

Sec. 7. Military Commissions. The Secretary of Defense shall immediately take steps sufficient to ensure that during the pendency of the Review described in section 4 of this order, no charges are sworn, or referred to a military commission under the Military Commissions Act of 2006 and the Rules for Military Commissions, and that all proceedings of such military commissions to which charges have been referred but in which no judgment has been rendered, and all proceedings pending in the United States Court of Military Commission Review, are halted.

Sec. 8. General Provisions.

(a) Nothing in this order shall prejudice the authority of the Secretary of Defense to determine the disposition of any detainees not covered by this order.

(b) This order shall be implemented consistent with applicable law and subject to the availability of appropriations.

(c) This order is not intended to, and does not, create any right or benefit, substantive or procedural, enforceable at law or in equity by any party against the United States, its departments, agencies, or entities, its officers, employees, or agents, or any other person.

BARACK OBAMA
The White House
January 22, 2009

Source: U.S. Executive Office of the President. "Executive Order 13492—Review and Disposition of Individuals Detained at the Guantánamo Bay Naval Base and Closure of Detention Facilities." *Daily Compilation of Presidential Documents* 2009, no. 00005 (January 22, 2009). www.gpo.gov/fdsys/pkg DCPD-200900005/pdf/DCPD-200900005.pdf.

Letter from Federal Officials to Illinois Governor Detailing Decision to Purchase Thomson Correctional Facility to House Guantánamo Detainees

December 15, 2009

The Honorable Pat Quinn
Governor of Illinois
Chicago, Illinois 60601

Dear Governor Quinn:

On January 22, 2009, President Obama issued Executive Order 13492, directing the closure of the detention center at Guantanamo. A key purpose of this Order was to protect our national security and help our troops by removing a deadly recruiting tool from the hands of al-Qa'ida. This should not be a political or partisan issue. This action is supported by the nation's highest military and civilian leaders who prosecuted the war against al-Qa'ida under the previous administration and continue to do so today. It is also supported by five previous Secretaries of State who served in both Democratic and Republican administrations, including those of Presidents Nixon, Ford, George H. W. Bush, Clinton, and George W. Bush.

On November 12, 2009, you wrote to Defense Secretary Robert Gates and Attorney General Eric Holder proposing that the Federal Government work with the State of Illinois to acquire the Thomson Correctional Center to house Federal inmates and a limited number of detainees from Guantanamo Bay, Cuba. We appreciate the leadership and assistance you and Senator Dick Durbin have provided during our evaluation of this proposal. We also would like to thank Thomson Village President Jerry "Duke" Hebeler and the people of Thomson and the surrounding region for their support and hospitality.

We write to inform you that the President has directed, with our unanimous support, that the Federal Government proceed with the acquisition of the facility in Thomson. Not only will this help address the urgent overcrowding problem at our nation's Federal prisons, but it will also help achieve our goal of closing the detention center at Guantanamo in a timely, secure, and lawful manner.

Executive Order 13492 directed us to close the detention facility at Guantanamo Bay and to conduct a review of the most secure and efficient way to adjudicate each of the Guantanamo detainee cases. This is part of the President's aggressive posture in the fight against al-Qa'ida that uses all instruments of our national power, including: keeping the pressure on al-Qa'ida and its leadership globally; strengthening homeland security and increasing cooperation and intelligence sharing among Federal agencies and between the Federal Government and state and local authorities; recognizing our values as a critical piece of our battle against our enemies; prosecuting detainees in Federal courts, which have safely and securely prosecuted terrorists for many years; trying detainees for violations of the law of war in military commissions, which were reformed by bipartisan legislation signed by the President in October; and transferring detainees to their home countries or third countries that agree to accept them, when consistent with our national security interests and humane treatment policies.

As the President has made clear, we will need to continue to detain some individuals currently held at the Guantanamo Bay detention facility. To securely house these detainees, Federal agencies plan to work with you and other state officials to acquire the nearly vacant maximum security facility in Thomson, Illinois. This facility will serve dual purposes. First, the Department of Justice will acquire this facility primarily to house Federal inmates. The Bureau of Prisons has a pressing need for more bed space in light of current crowded conditions. Second, the Defense Department will operate part of the facility to house a limited number of detainees from Guantanamo. The two parts of the facility will be managed separately, and Federal inmates will have no opportunity to interact with Guantanamo detainees.

The security of the facility and the surrounding region is our paramount concern. The facility was built in 2001 to maximum security specifications, and after acquisition it will be enhanced to exceed perimeter security standards at the nation's only "supermax" prison in Florence, Colorado, where there has never been an escape or external attack. Federal departments and agencies, including the Departments of Homeland Security, Justice, and Defense, will work closely with state and local law enforcement authorities to identify and mitigate any risks, including sharing information through the state's "fusion center" and working with the Federal Joint Terrorism Task Force.

The President has no intention of releasing any detainees in the United States. Current law effectively bars the release of the Guantanamo detainees on U.S. soil, and the Federal Government has broad authority under current law to detain individuals during removal proceedings and pending the execution of final removal orders.

Federal officials also have consulted with local, county, and state law enforcement authorities to begin the process of identifying additional resources they may require to handle the increased population of Federal inmates and detainees. We are pleased that Illinois law enforcement authorities endorsed this plan in a letter to the Secretary of Defense and the Attorney General dated December 2, 2009. We also note that more than 30 villages, towns, cities, counties, chambers of commerce, and other community and business organizations have sent letters, approved resolutions, or otherwise expressed their support for this plan. We are greatly encouraged by this support, and we commit to working with local authorities closely as this process moves forward.

There are many steps still to be taken and many requirements still to be met, but we look forward to working with you to complete the Federal acquisition of the facility in Thomson.

Sincerely,

Hillary Rodham Clinton
Secretary of State

Robert M. Gates
Secretary of Defense

Eric H. Holder, Jr.
Attorney General

Janet Napolitano
Secretary of Homeland Security

Dennis C. Blair
Director of National Intelligence

Source: U.S. Executive Office of the President. "Letter to Governor Quinn." December 15, 2009. www .whitehouse.gov/sites/default/files/091215-letter-governor-quinn.pdf.

OTHER HISTORIC DOCUMENTS OF INTEREST

FROM THIS VOLUME

FROM PREVIOUS *HISTORIC DOCUMENTS*

President Obama Signs the American Recovery and Reinvestment Act of 2009

JANUARY 28 AND FEBRUARY 17, 2009

On February 17, 2009, President Barack Obama signed the much anticipated American Recovery and Reinvestment Act of 2009 (ARRA) at the Denver Museum of Nature and Science. "Today does not mark the end of our economic troubles," he said. "But it does mark the beginning of the end—the beginning of what we need to do to create jobs for Americans scrambling in the wake of layoffs; to provide relief for families worried they won't be able to pay next month's bills; and to set our economy on a firmer foundation."

As the president signed the bill, the United States was facing what seemed to be an unstoppable economic downturn. Nearly two and a half million homeowners faced fore-closure in 2008, up 81 percent compared with 2007 figures. The national unemployment rate stood at 7.6 percent, up nearly one half of a percent since December 2008.

The ARRA, which represented one of the largest government spending projects since the World War II era, was enacted to make investments in infrastructure and energy efficiency, while also helping families with tax cuts and increased social benefits.

THE AMERICAN RECOVERY AND REINVESTMENT ACT OF 2009 IN CONGRESS

The ARRA followed on the heels of the George W. Bush administration's Economic Stimulus Act of 2008 and the Emergency Economic Stabilization Act of 2008. In the Senate, passage of a stimulus plan was expected to be difficult, because Democrats did not hold the necessary sixty seats needed to pass the legislation themselves. They would have to pull support from across the aisle. On January 6, 2009, Senate Majority Leader Harry Reid, D-Nev., introduced the Senate's version of the ARRA.

The ARRA was first introduced in the U.S. House of Representatives on January 26, 2009, by Rep. David Obey, D-Wis., with the Senate version of the bill adopted as an amendment. In the House, Democrats held a majority of the seats and knew they could easily pass the legislation. The debate, however, was often heated, with criticism coming from the Republican side of the aisle over inflation of the federal deficit, increased gov-ernment spending, and a lack of evidence of clear benefits. Rep. C.W. (Bill) Young, R-Fla., lamented,

How many jobs will these new programs create? How would the money be spent? Who would receive the money? These are all questions I would have

asked if our Appropriations Committee, which has the responsibility of overseeing discretionary spending, had ever held a single hearing on these programs.
The truth is, none of our subcommittees ever held a hearing on any of the
programs in this bill. This legislation was drafted by a small handful of members with little if any input from Republican members of this House.

Rep. Steny Hoyer, D-Md., defended the bill, saying that according to analysis by
Mark Zandi, chief economist and cofounder of Moody's Economy.com, the jobless rate
would be 2 percent higher without the government infusion of funds. The House vote on
January 28, 2009, split along party lines, with no Republicans voting for the bill and only
11 Democrats voting against it.

The differences between the House and Senate versions of the ARRA, worked out in
conference committee, included a sizable discrepancy in spending. The original Senate
bill had proposed $827 billion in recovery spending, whereas the final House measure
that was signed by the president requested only $787 billion. The Senate included in its
version more money allocated toward health care, green energy, a home buyer's credit,
and new Social Security payments for the elderly; the House version proposed more
spending on education, infrastructure, and increased aid to citizens who are unemployed
or low-income earners. In conference committee, the Senate's version of the bill was
added to the House version as an amendment. When the combined bill went before the
Senate, the vote, on February 10, 2009, was 61–37, with only three Republicans voting in
favor of the ARRA.

Specifics of the American Recovery and Reinvestment Act of 2009

The intent of the ARRA was to create and preserve jobs in an effort to promote economic recovery; assist those most affected by the recession; increase economic efficiency
with advances in science, health, and technology; invest in infrastructure, including the
environment and transportation, in an effort to provide long-term benefits; and to help
stabilize the budgets in states and localities to ensure that social services were not
reduced.

The funds included $288 billion for tax cuts, $237 billion of which went to individuals, including payroll tax credits; a one-year extension of exceptions to the alternative
minimum tax; a child tax credit; a college tax credit; a first-time home buyer credit; a halt
to taxes on the first $2,400 a person receives in unemployment benefits; and a home
energy credit. Tax cuts for companies totaled $51 billion. The health care industry
received $147.7 billion in the bill, some of which went to Medicaid and some to offset the
costs of the Consolidated Omnibus Budget Reconciliation Act (COBRA) insurance for
those who are unemployed. Health care funds also went toward funding advances in
health information technology, medical research, medical care for members of the military and their families, and money to the Veterans Health Administration and Indian
reservations for health care purposes. Education received an allocation of more than $90
billion, including money to prevent teacher layoffs, increase technology in the schools,
increase teacher salaries, increase financial aid available for higher education, analyze
student performance, and build new or modernize existing schools. The unemployed,
retired, and low-income earners received $82.5 billion under the ARRA, which included
an extension of unemployment benefits, increased welfare payments, assistance for

employment services and food banks, and a one-time payment to Social Security recipients. Infrastructure projects received a total of $80.9 billion, to be used for highway and bridge construction, rail and other mass transportation projects, drinking water improvements, and the modernization and creation of "green" government fleet vehicles and government facilities. A portion of the funds for infrastructure were also slated for bringing broadband and wireless Internet access to rural and urban areas around the country. Energy, a big portion of the ARRA, received $61.3 billion, much of which went toward the construction of an electric smart grid, which can save users energy, reduce costs, and increase how efficiently energy is delivered. The energy investments were also to be used to fund green technology research and training and help state and local governments looking to buy more energy-efficient vehicles. The ARRA also set aside funds for housing, scientific research, state block grants to stem state budget cuts, police forces, port and transit security, and fire protection.

PRESIDENT OBAMA CALLS FOR INCREASED TRANSPARENCY

"What I am signing is a balanced plan with a mix of tax cuts and investments. It is a plan that's been put together without earmarks or the usual pork barrel spending. And it is a plan that will be implemented with an unprecedented level of transparency and accountability," Obama said upon signing the bill. "And we expect you, the American people, to hold us accountable for the results. That is why we have created Recovery.gov—so every American can go online and see how their money is being spent."

The Web site created by the Obama administration to increase citizen approval for his economic recovery plan was to include specific dollar amounts and tracking of the stimulus, as well as an indication of where the money was being spent on a state-by-state basis. However, an article in the *Washington Post* from May 21, 2009, noted, "[T]hree months after the bill was signed, Recovery.gov offers little beyond news releases, general breakdowns of spending and acronym-laden spreadsheets and timelines." According to the *Post,* Recovery.org, a privately run site tracking ARRA spending to give businesses information they need to submit bids for government contracts, "is actually providing detailed information about how the $787 billion in stimulus is being spent." The government quickly promised a redesign of the federally run site.

DETERMINING IF THE AMERICAN RECOVERY AND REINVESTMENT ACT OF 2009 IS WORKING

The Congressional Budget Office (CBO) released a report on the stimulus package on February 4, 2009, that stated that the plan would initially increase employment and the gross domestic product (GDP), but by 2019, the GDP of the United States will have decreased between one-tenth and one-third of a percentage point, caused largely by decreased productivity and business investment. According to a February 11, 2009, letter from CBO director Douglas Elmendorf, there is disagreement among economists about how well the stimulus plan will actually work. An updated report released by the CBO in March 2009 noted that the predicted decrease in GDP will be caused by low wages and worker productivity, not increased unemployment.

To find out if the ARRA is working, the Obama administration and American citizens must determine how to judge the progress of the initiatives. Economists believe an increase in the number of jobs and a decrease in unemployment would be the most conclusive proof of the act's success. President Obama agrees. A week before signing the bill he said, "That's bottom-line number one, because if people are working, then they've got enough confidence to make purchases, to make investments. Businesses start seeing that consumers are out there with a little more confidence, and they start making investments, which means they start hiring workers. So step number one, job creation." The White House expects 3.5 million jobs to be created or saved in 2009 and 2010 by ARRA investments.

Zandi agreed with the White House. "A key benchmark will be this fall. If stimulus is working as expected, then monthly job losses should be closer to 250,000 per month, down from over 500,000 currently." Zandi cautioned, however, that this is not a perfect test because we will never know how many jobs the economy *would* have lost or created without the ARRA. The November 2009 jobs report, however, showed that November job loss stood at only 11,000, the lowest point in two years.

Other economists argued that the level of discretionary spending by consumers will help determine how well the ARRA is working. When people feel better about their personal economic situation, so the argument goes, they will begin making purchases outside of basic necessities.

When signing the bill, President Obama managed expectations about how quickly the stimulus plan would begin working. "None of this will be easy. The road to recovery will not be straight. We will make progress, and there may be some slippage along the way." But, he said, "We have begun the essential work of keeping the American dream alive in our time." Comments by Zandi indicate that he believes that the stimulus package alone will not get the economy back on its feet. "A financial stability plan and a foreclosure mitigation plan must also be implemented," Zandi said.

Obama closed the speech delivered during the signing of the ARRA on a hopeful, forward-looking note. "Our American story is not—and has never been—about things coming easy," the president said. "It's about rising to the moment when the moment is hard, converting crisis into opportunity, and seeing to it that we emerge from whatever trials we face stronger than we were before."

—Heather Kerrigan

Following is a floor speech in support of H.R. 1, the American Recovery and Reinvestment Act of 2009, by Rep. Steny Hoyer, D-Md., and a statement in opposition to H.R. 1 by Rep. C.W. (Bill) Young, R-Fla., both made on January 28, 2009, along with a statement by President Barack Obama upon signing the American Recovery and Reinvestment Act of 2009 on February 17, 2009.

Rep. Steny Hoyer, D-Md., in Support of the American Recovery and Reinvestment Act

DOCUMENT

January 28, 2009

. . . Over a year ago, it appeared to us that the economic program adopted in 2001 and 2003 was not working. . . . We had the worst 8 years of job production that we've had in any administration since Herbert Hoover. And as a result of the failure to produce jobs, our country was in great distress and our people were challenged and at risk.

And so the administration and the Democratic leadership of the Congress and the Republican leadership of the Congress sat down at the table together and came up with a program to stimulate the economy, about $160 billion. And we worked together in a bipartisan fashion. It was a Republican President, but a Democratic-led Congress—in fact, agreed to the administration's increase in that program, as you recall, because we had suggested $100 billion—and we worked in a bipartisan fashion.

And then in September, some months later, Secretary Paulson, the Republican Secretary of the Treasury, came to us, met with the leadership, and said we have a crisis. Indeed, we had invited him down because we thought that there was real trouble. He said we have a crisis, we need to act, and we need to act immediately. A Democratic-led Congress responded to Secretary Paulson and said, we'll work with you. We'll work with you because our country needs a joint response. And we did that.

And when that legislation came to the floor, very frankly, a majority of Democrats supported the Republican administration's request; a majority of his party in this House did not. We now have a Democratic administration and a Democratic-led Congress, and I'm hopeful that we'll have bipartisan work continuing to meet this crisis caused, from my perspective, by the failure of policies that we've been pursuing economically over the last 8 years. . . .

As you know, we're dealing with one of the worst economic climates in memory: 2.6 million jobs last year; the worst housing market since the Great Depression; financial turmoil that has threatened the savings and retirement of millions. That's the context in which this administration is taking office.

As we move to confront this crisis, we welcome the criticism of our Republican friends and others. But let's put that criticism in some context, again, not for a partisan sense but for a sense of instruction of the perception of what worked and what did not. I would suggest that, frankly, much of what I have heard from my Republican colleagues over the last 20 years in terms of what would work and what would not work was inaccurate.

Let's remember President Bush's saying, "My administration remains focused on economic growth that will create more jobs." Let's remember how the minority party reacted to the Clinton economic plan in 1993. Newt Gingrich said of that plan that it would lead to "a job-killing recession." A leader of the Republican Party made that observation. He was dead, flat, 100 percent wrong. In fact, we created 22 point some odd million jobs in those 8 years, an average of 256,000 per month. This administration has averaged less than 40. You need 100 to stay even.

John Boehner, the Republican leader, said at that point in time, "The message is loud and clear, cut spending first and shrink the size of this Federal Government," in opposing the economic program.

In reality, the Democratic plan led to unprecedented economic growth. We all know that. The 1990s were the best economic period of time statistically that we have had in this country in the service of anybody in this Congress including the Reagan years.

Let's remember how Republicans reacted to [the] Budget Reconciliation Act in 1990 when George Bush the first was President of the United States. Tom DeLay said, "The Democratic package will destroy our economy." Now, the Democratic package was, of course, an accommodation made between President Bush; Dick Darman, head of OMB; and ourselves. In reality, that program, opposed overwhelmingly by Republicans, reduced the budget deficit by approximately $482 billion.

. . . Today, I hope that our Republican colleagues will put that history aside and join with us to pass this bill and try to help restore our prosperity. . . .

The American Recovery and Reinvestment Act is projected to create or save 3 to 4 million jobs. What does it do? I know Mr. Obey has said this, but let me repeat it. Tax relief, $275 billion to working Americans and to small businesses. States will be helped. Policemen, teachers won't have to be laid off so that we can keep our communities safe and our children educated. Core investments in infrastructure. I know we'd like to do more in infrastructure. The sad news is it's tough to spend it quickly in the infrastructure field. We need to do more. We will do more.

Protecting vulnerable populations. People are in food lines historically long. People are unemployed in historic numbers. States are stretched with their Medicaid assistance to people who need health care.

In energy, we have all talked about energy independence. We had a big debate last year about energy independence and how to get there. This bill deals with energy independence and creating jobs in the course of getting to energy independence.

Health care, we all know John McCain talked about it in his campaign. Barack Obama talked about it in his campaign. Everybody knows that if we don't get soon to health care reform and health care progress, we won't be able to afford the kind of health care that Americans need and want accessible to them and their families.

Education, training, we're not going to be competitive in this world if we don't make sure our children are well educated. We're pricing young people and their families out of an education. We can't afford to do that or we won't compete with the Japanese, the Chinese, the Germans, the Indians, and others.

Mark Zandi, a former economic adviser to Senator McCain's presidential election, found that "the jobless rate will be more than 2 percentage points lower by the end of 2010 than without the fiscal stimulus."

I'm sure almost every Member of the House could find something that he or she thinks should not be in here. I know I could. I know others could. Some people want more in, some people want less in. But, frankly, most of the economists I have talked to think this is about the right mix. It may not be specifically what each wants but about the right mix between tax cuts and spending.

This legislation is a result of an honest, urgent effort to include the best ideas from economic experts from across the spectrum as well as both sides of the aisle. It's an effort that cannot become weighed down by bipartisanship or parochial interests. There are no earmarks in this bill. Overall, this plan contains what is widely viewed as the right mix of spending and tax cuts to spur our economy. It will include tax relief for 95 percent of working families; tax cuts for job-creating small businesses; projects to put Americans to work renewing our crumbling roads and bridges; and nutrition, unemployment, and health care assistance to those families who are being hit hardest by this recession.

This administration inherited the situation in which we find ourselves. The Democratic leadership tried to work with the Bush administration to get us out of it. Hopefully, we will continue to do that in a bipartisan fashion.

The Congressional Budget Office estimates that two-thirds of the recovery funds will be spent in the first 18 months, which means an immediate jolt to our economy. And we will continue working with President Obama to increase that number.

The CBO also estimates that if we pass this bill, by the end of next year, America will have up to 3.6 million more jobs, 3.6 million more Americans working and being able to support their families.

Besides creating jobs immediately, we will invest in new energy technology, upgrade our schools with 21 Century classrooms, and computerize health records to reduce costs and improve care.

All of those are investments that promise growth and savings in the years to come to ensure that our Nation does not slip back after bringing us out of recession, which is what this is designed to do. We don't want it to slip back. So we have medium-term investment as well as short-term investment.

Finally, we have included in the recovery plan unprecedented levels of accountability and transparency so we and our constituents will know that their tax dollars are being spent on getting us out of a rescission [*sic*], not siphoned off to the politically connected. So there will be no earmarks or pet projects in this bill. The new Accountability and Transparency Board will be working to keep waste and fraud far away from this bill. And all of the plan's details, all, will be published online so that we and our constituents can track the success of these efforts to turn our economy back into the productive engine that it's been in the past.

I close the way I started. We worked in a bipartisan fashion with the Bush administration. When they saw a crisis, we responded. The majority of our Members supported the programs suggested, promoted by the Bush administration. We did so because we believed it was in the best interest of our country. We move on this bill because we believe it's in the best interest of our country.

So I ask all of us, Democrats and Republicans, but people who care about their country, their constituents, our families and our children, to join together. Lyndon Johnson said once, "It's not difficult to do the right thing; it's difficult to know what the right thing is." We have worked together over the last months to try to come up with as close to the right thing as we can.

We urge all of the Members on this floor to vote for America, its people, its economic health. Support this legislation.

SOURCE: Rep. Steny Hoyer. "American Recovery and Reinvestment Act of 2009." *Congressional Record* 2009, 155, pt. H620, H624–H625. www.gpo.gov/fdsys/pkg/CREC-2009-01-28/pdf/CREC-2009-01-28-pt1-PgH620.pdf.

DOCUMENT

Rep. C.W. (Bill) Young, R-Fla., in Opposition to the American Recovery and Reinvestment Act

January 28, 2009

Mr. Chair, I rise to express my concerns about H.R. 1, the American Recovery and Reinvestment Act of 2009. They are concerns about its cost, estimated at more than $1.1 trillion; its ability to really create jobs [and] stimulate our economy; and about the procedure with which it was written and brought before this House.

The Congressional Budget Office estimates the cost of this legislation at $815 billion. But that is before we factor in the cost of the interest payments—totaling $347 billion over the next 10 years—that Americans will incur to finance this, the largest spending bill every [sic] brought before Congress.

And what do we get for our "investment"? Nobody knows how many jobs, if any, this legislation will create. The Congressional Budget Office estimates that only 15 percent of the spending in this bill will even take place between now and the end of the fiscal year on September 30th. The agency further estimates that by the end of the next fiscal year on September 30, 2010, that just half of the funds provided in this legislation will be expended. One can only wonder how this legislation, with the intended goal of creating sustainable jobs, can do so with such a slow obligation of funds.

Instead, this legislation puts our nation on the hook by creating 32 new programs totaling some $137 billion. This includes a $79 billion State Fiscal Stabilization Fund at the Department of Education which the State of Florida I represent and our public schools and their students will not even qualify for because of the complicated formula under which the funds will be given to the states.

How many jobs will these new programs create? How would the money be spent? Who would receive the money? These are all questions I would have asked if our Appropriations Committee, which has the responsibility of overseeing discretionary spending, had ever held a single hearing on these programs. The truth is, none of our subcommittees ever held a hearing on any of the programs in this bill. This legislation was drafted by a small handful of members with little if any input from Republican members of this House.

President Obama met with the Republican members of the House Tuesday to ask for bipartisan support for this stimulus legislation. Instead, I sense there is bipartisan opposition to the process under which we consider this legislation. Democrats and Republicans alike are on record as saying we should slow down the process and do it right.

We need only look back four months ago to the way in which the House and Senate handled the $700 billion financial bailout to see what happens when we act in haste, with little deliberation, and virtually no input from the members of Congress. We wind up with wasteful federal programs, managed by government bureaucrats, with little or no oversight, and with few if any positive results.

Last year, we considered legislation to help individual homeowners with their mortgages. I supported that bill, because it tried to help people keep their homes. Last October, we considered legislation to bailout the financial industry and financial executives. I voted against that legislation twice because it was a $700 billion mistake that did not help people. Now we are on the verge of repeating that mistake with a new $815 billion bailout that likewise does little to help people get back on their feet and find work.

Mr. Chair, no one in this chamber would deny that our nation faces unprecedented economic challenges in the days and months ahead. Many of my colleagues in this House who oppose this legislation want to provide help to get Americans back to work. But we want to do it the right way without driving our nation further into the economic doldrums and passing the debt on to our children and our grandchildren.

We also want to do so in a fiscally responsible manner. The Congressional Budget Office, in its analysis of this legislation, concluded that "federal agencies, along with states and other recipients of that funding, would find it difficult to properly manage and oversee a rapid expansion of existing programs so as to expend the added funds as quickly as they expend the resources provided for their ongoing programs."

Let us heed the calling of the American people last November 4th. They asked us to put the elections and politics behind us and start working together to solve America's problems. President Obama came to Congress this week to ask for our help. But we cannot help if we do not have any input. We cannot help if we have no committee hearings. We cannot help if our subcommittees do not have a hand in writing this legislation. And we cannot help if we have little opportunity to amend this bill when it is brought before the House. No legislation is perfect, let alone one that will spend $815 billion and create 32 new programs.

Mr. Chair, let us vote down this legislation to send it back to the committees and signal that the American people demand a thoughtful and deliberative process in deciding how to spend their hard earned dollars. This is their money, not ours, and we have the responsibility to be good stewards of it.

Source: Rep. C.W. (Bill) Young. "American Recovery and Reinvestment Act of 2009." *Congressional Record* 2009, 155, pt. H620, H631–H632. www.gpo.gov/fdsys/pkg/CREC-2009-01-28/pdf/CREC-2009-01-28-pt1-PgH620.pdf.

Obama on Signing the American Recovery and Reinvestment Act

February 17, 2009

Today I have signed into law H.R. 1, the "American Recovery and Reinvestment Act of 2009." The Act provides a direct fiscal boost to help lift our Nation from the greatest economic crisis in our lifetimes and lay the foundation for further growth. This recovery plan will help to save or create as many as three to four million jobs by the end of 2010, the vast majority of them in the private sector. It will make the most significant investment in America's roads, bridges, mass transit, and other infrastructure since the construction of the interstate highway system. It will make investments to foster reform in education, double renewable energy while fostering efficiency in the use of our energy, and improve quality while bringing down costs in healthcare. Middle-class families will get tax cuts and the most vulnerable will get the largest increase in assistance in decades.

The situation we face could not be more serious. We have inherited an economic crisis as deep and as dire as any since the Great Depression. Economists from across the spectrum have warned that failure to act quickly would lead to the disappearance of millions of more jobs and national unemployment rates that could be in the double digits. I want to thank the Congress for coming together around this hard-fought compromise. No one policy or program will solve the challenges we face right now, nor will this crisis recede in a short period of time. However, with this Act we begin the process of restoring the economy and making America a stronger and more prosperous Nation.

My Administration will initiate new, far-reaching measures to help ensure that every dollar spent in this historic legislation is spent wisely and for its intended purpose. The Federal Government will be held to new standards of transparency and accountability. The legislation includes no earmarks. An oversight board will be charged with monitoring our progress as part of an unprecedented effort to root out waste and inefficiency. This board will be advised by experts—not just Government experts, not just politicians, but also citizens with years of expertise in management, economics, and accounting.

So much depends on what we do at this moment. This is not about the future of my Administration. This effort is about the future of our families and communities, our economy and our country. We are going to move forward carefully and transparently and as effectively as possible because so much is on the line. That is what we have already begun to do—drafting this plan with a level of openness for which the American people have asked and that this situation demands.

BARACK OBAMA
The White House,
February 17, 2009

SOURCE: U.S. Executive Office of the President. "Statement on Signing the American Recovery and Reinvestment Act of 2009." *Daily Compilation of Presidential Documents* 2009, no. 00088 (February 17, 2009). www.gpo.gov/fdsys/pkg/DCPD-200900088/pdf/DCPD-200900088.pdf.

OTHER HISTORIC DOCUMENTS OF INTEREST

FROM THIS VOLUME

FROM PREVIOUS *HISTORIC DOCUMENTS*

February

Iceland Elects Its First Female and Openly Gay Prime Minister

FEBRUARY 4, 2009

In fall 2008, Iceland found itself mired in a financial crisis that gave rise to significant social unrest. As first the economy and then the government failed, Iceland turned to Minister of Social Affairs and Social Security Johanna Sigurdardottir for new leadership, selecting her to serve as the country's first female prime minister and the world's first openly gay national leader. Sigurdardottir had become well known for her reaction to a lost bid to become chair of the country's Social Democratic party in 1994, predicting, "My time will come." Yet she could not have predicted the exact circumstances that would propel her to the prime minister's office.

AN ECONOMIC CRISIS

Iceland had benefited from a fairly stable economy since gaining its full independence from Denmark in 1994. By 2008, it had risen to prominence as one of the world's wealthiest nations, boasting one of the highest gross domestic products (GDP) per capita and ranking third out of 182 countries in the United Nations Human Development Index.

In 2001, the government of Prime Minister Geir Haarde and the Central Bank of Iceland moved to deregulate commercial banks during a period of significant economic growth, enabling them to take greater risks in the international market—risks that generated multimillion-dollar debts. When the banks tried to refinance in October 2008, they were unable to because of the sheer volume of their debt. The government stepped in to nationalize the country's three largest banks and save them from complete collapse, but acted too late to prevent the failure of the country's entire financial system. In the weeks immediately following the banking crisis, property values dropped by more than a third, unemployment soared to 10 percent, rampant inflation sent food prices skyrocketing 73 percent, and the value of Iceland's currency, the krona, plunged. The government negotiated a loan package worth approximately $2.1 billion with the International Monetary Fund (IMF) to stave off further damage, and Finland, Sweden, Norway, and Denmark pledged an additional $2.5 billion in loans, but job losses continued and prices remained high.

During this time, many Icelanders grew angry with the government and the "business elites," claiming their incompetency had led to the nation's economic downfall. "The Icelandic public fear that their country has virtually been stolen by the globetrotting business elite that spent more time rubbing shoulders with high society than giving back to the society that enabled them to live this privileged life," wrote the *Guardian*'s Eirikur

Bergmann. Icelanders began demonstrating peacefully in late October 2008, but tensions escalated in January 2009. When the Althingi, Iceland's parliament, resumed its session on January 20, 2009, members were greeted by more than 2,000 angry protestors who surrounded the building and demanded a new election. Members of the Althingi initially sought to outlast the protest and blockaded themselves inside the parliament building. Demonstrators broke windows, banged on pots and pans, and hurled eggs and yogurt at the building. The demonstration lasted all night and into the next morning, setting off a wave of other protests throughout Reykjavik for the next five days. At one event, police used tear gas for the first time in nearly fifty years to disperse a crowd of several hundred people, but even this action failed to discourage the protestors.

THE GOVERNMENT RESIGNS

Several prominent officials resigned their posts in the days following the protests, including Minister of Commerce Bjorgvin Sigurdsson. "The anger and distrust of the people is too deep for me to be able to gain their faith again," he said. On January 26, 2009, Prime Minister Haarde announced that the coalition between his right-wing Independence party and the center-left Social Democratic Alliance had come to an end and delivered the government's resignation to President Olafur Ragnar Grimsson, making Iceland the first country to change its government as a direct result of the global financial crisis. (Because Iceland's president serves independently of parliament as head of state, with very limited political powers, Grimsson was to remain in office during the transition.) In his statement before the Althingi, Haarde said, "The demand by the Social Democratic Alliance that it take over the office of Prime Minister was not part of the coalition platform we agreed upon and is unacceptable." The president requested that the outgoing government remain in office until a new government was formed and called on the leaders of the Social Democratic Alliance and the leftist, environmentally focused Left-Green Movement to discuss the formation of a new minority coalition government, claiming those two parties had the best chance of working together effectively. After several days of negotiations led by Foreign Minister Ingibjorg Gisladottir, the parties agreed to the president's proposal. The Social Democratic Alliance proposed Sigurdardottir to lead the new coalition government as prime minister until the next election, scheduled to take place on April 25, 2009.

"SAINT JOHANNA"

At the time of her selection, Johanna Sigurdardottir was one of Iceland's most popular politicians with an approval rating of approximately 73 percent. She was also Iceland's longest-serving member of parliament, having first been elected in 1978. Sigurdardottir is credited with a number of policies that expanded housing opportunities for the poor, protected the rights of the handicapped and the elderly, and strengthened the social welfare system during her two stints as minister of social affairs and social security, earning her the nickname "Saint Johanna." She was also a member of the Althingi's Presidium, a governing body that helps set the legislative agenda, and served on numerous committees, including those on foreign affairs, industry, constitutional affairs, and economy and trade.

Some attribute Sigurdardottir's popularity to the resonance of her humble beginnings with Iceland's middle class. Born in 1942, she studied commerce in high school but did not go on to receive a college degree. After high school, she became a flight attendant for Loftleidir Airlines, now known as Icelandair, and served as a union organizer. She also worked in the office of a box factory before being elected to the Althingi. Even as she rose through the ranks of the government, Sigurdardottir declined some of the benefits of higher office, including the official limousine and driver provided to all ministers, choosing to drive her Mitsubishi to work instead.

Sigurdardottir, openly gay, lived with her partner of six years, Jonina Leosdottir. However, this fact seemed to matter little to Icelanders. "Being gay is not an issue in Iceland," said Frosti Jonsson, the chair of Iceland's gay and lesbian association. "There are so many openly gay prominent figures in both the public and private sector here that it doesn't affect who we select for our highest offices. Our minds are focused on what counts, which is the current situation in the country."

A New Government

Sigurdardottir was sworn in as prime minister on February 1, 2009. In a speech before the Althingi several days later, she called for reconciliation between the public and the government, stating, "We have to learn from the mistakes which have brought us to where we are today." She promised to overhaul the country's financial and regulatory systems, starting with a change in leadership of the Central Bank and "an examination of the connections between the country's business sector, its economy and its politics." Sigurdardottir also said the government would implement new programs to stimulate domestic and foreign investment, create new jobs, and provide expanded opportunities for public participation in shaping the structure of government.

Sigurdardottir's appointment was greeted with mixed reactions from her fellow politicians. "She is a senior parliamentarian, she is respected and loved by all of Iceland," said Environment Minister Thorunn Sveinbjarnardottir. Yet opponents claimed her leftist politics would not be able to turn the economy around. "Johanna is a very good woman—but she likes spending, she is a tax raiser," said former prime minister Haarde. Most did not expect her to remain in office beyond the April election, as it was widely speculated that her party would not fare well at the polls.

However, the Social Democratic Alliance garnered nearly 30 percent of the vote, securing twenty seats in the Althingi. The Left-Green Movement won sixteen seats—enough to allow them to appoint the prime minister, thus enabling Sigurdardottir to retain her post.

Iceland on the Mend

Since the April 2009 election, Sigurdardottir has continued pursuing her platform of financial reforms. She appointed a new governor and deputy governor of the Central Bank in June as well as a new board for the Financial Supervisory Authority. Iceland has also made significant progress in meeting the requirements of the Economic Recovery Program established by the IMF as a condition for the $10 million loan, which include restructuring the banking system and paying off outstanding loans owed to other Nordic countries. On July 17, 2009, the Althingi voted to approve a plan for Iceland to apply for full European Union (EU) membership in hopes that it would further stabilize the economy. The vote marked a major reversal in policy, as the government had previously chosen to remain outside of the EU to protect Iceland's fishing grounds from other European fleets.

MIAMI DADE ᶜᶜ   ᴸᴵᴮᴿᴬᴿY

Despite the progress it has made, Iceland still has plenty of work to do. The Directorate of Labor announced that the country's unemployment rate remained at approximately 7 percent in September 2009. The IMF had forecast that Iceland's economy would shrink by a total of nearly 9 percent by the end of 2009—GDP fell by 6.3 percent—and further projected that the contraction would continue in 2010. It remains to be seen whether Sigurdardottir can continue leading her country out of its economic quagmire.

—Linda Fecteau

Following is a speech by Iceland's first female prime minister, Johanna Sigurdardottir, on the platform of her new government, given February 4, 2009.

Iceland's New Prime Minister Speaks on Government's Platform

February 4, 2009

Mr. Speaker, fellow Icelanders.

It can have escaped no one that our country is passing through a deep economic downturn. Within a very brief period, the government has had to act responsibly and determinedly, to keep the wheels of business and industry turning and to reinforce the security net for the nation's households and families. Nations in our part of the world have enjoyed the greatest success when they have managed to combine social responsibility with utilising the advantages of the market, to benefit public interests rather than individual interests. We have to learn from the mistakes which have brought us to where we are today.

The collapse of the Icelandic financial system has resulted in public turmoil, in protests fuelled by justified anger and, not least, a heightened need for involvement and action. It is my hope that the social unrest we have experienced is now behind us and that we are on the path towards reconciliation. The environment created by the difficult economic situation has fostered fertile social debate. Discussion has been heated, producing a wide variety of ideas and demands for changing the structure of our society. Public involvement has been more extensive than previously known in Iceland.

We have heard the views of a great number of people. In my opinion, it is important for us, as politicians, to find ways to enable as many people as possible to make their voices heard. We must not be so limited by the restraints of party politics that we lose touch with the public. No politician wants to lose touch with those people he or she is serving. Our work requires us to maintain close good contact with the public who elected us to work on its behalf. I am convinced that the tumult of recent months has touched all of us and left a lasting impression. The government which has now taken office was created under highly exceptional circumstances. Public demands for change have had effect and the government will make every effort to channel these voices and the demands made into effective action through its own acts and working practices.

The new coalition of the Social Democratic Alliance and the Left-Green Movement prioritises the following changes for the sake of democracy and greater social justice: Changes to the constitution which will enshrine national ownership of the country's natural resources, provide for public referenda and a special constitutional assembly, which will open a new chapter in public participation in shaping the structure of government. Furthermore, preparations will get underway on drafting a code of ethics for the Ministerial Offices; legal provisions on the responsibility of ministers, making this comparable to that in neighbouring countries; and new rules on the appointment of District and Supreme Court Judges.

Electoral laws will be amended to make it possible to vote for individual candidates in national elections, ideally so that these can be implemented in upcoming elections.

All of these changes are intended to increase democracy and the involvement of the general public, as well as to remove all sorts of discrimination which have been criticised. They are clear indications that the demands made by the public in the debate of recent weeks have reached the ears of the authorities and are now being put into practice by the government.

Fellow Icelanders.

The past few months have been difficult for all of us. Many people have lost their assets and their jobs, some companies have gone bankrupt while others continue in low gear. All of us need to join hands in an effort to get business and industry moving again, to put the wheels of the economy in motion to improve the situation of businesses, and that of households no less.

In an effort to fight the corruption in our society, we cannot avoid an examination of the connections between the country's business sector, its economy and its politics. Let us begin this process at once, and in unison. But our actions must be fair and ethical, honouring the basic principle that no one is guilty until proven to be so according to law and proper procedure. We must honour the rights of each individual and take care to ensure that in setting things straight we do not embark on any type of witch hunt. We enjoy the rule of law in this country and neither the government nor members of the Althingi intend to circumvent its basic principles. I would like to emphasize that here this evening.

On the other hand, it is crucial that we succeed in reviving the confidence of the general public in Iceland in its government and economy. Furthermore, we need to regain the respect of others and improve Icelanders' reputation abroad. No country can prosper without good relations with other nations. There is a direct connection between our image and reputation abroad and the resurrection of the domestic economy. Our financial and regulatory systems need an overhaul. They have failed to achieve their purpose and in so doing have lost their credibility, both towards the wider world and the domestic community.

This is unacceptable, because such parties who do not enjoy the trust of others cannot perform their key roles in the reconstruction. We must face this fact. We politicians are no exception here, which is why it is important to hold elections this spring, giving the politicians a chance to put their case to and receive the verdict of the electorate.

The new government has already set this process in motion and has submitted a bill to [the] Althingi amending the Act on the Central Bank of Iceland. The Board and executive of the Financial Supervisory Authority have resigned and it is important that a new board be appointed for the Authority as soon as possible. The government has requested that the executive of the Central Bank of Iceland step aside as well. The commercial banks have undergone extensive changes, and this process is far from complete.

One of the government's most important priorities is to ensure that financial institutions have the necessary strength to support the revival of business and industry. In accordance with the economic recovery programme agreed by the International Monetary Fund (IMF) and the government, we are now doing our best to reconstruct the financial system. The programme is proceeding according to schedule and the government will ensure that co-operation with [the] IMF is effective and secure.

The government places emphasis on working concertedly and rapidly to complete the valuation of assets of both the old and the new banks. This has taken more time than anticipated. Once the work is concluded, it will be possible to refinance the banks. Every effort will be made to set the economy in motion again as soon as possible. Companies are struggling with greater difficulties than ever before, including enormous indebtedness, dropping demand and income, an unstable currency and high interest rates.

Clearly, in such circumstances, the banks must proceed with caution. They must at the same time shoulder responsibility for showing discipline towards businesses while participating in economic recovery efforts. The anticipated rapid slowing of inflation should create the premises to cut the policy rate and improve the business environment. Conditions need to be created to enable the relaxing of currency controls and lowering of interest rates as expeditiously as possible.

I expect the government to provide more details of its plans for financial system reconstruction as soon as next week, together with various important measures in this connection. A committee at work under the direction of the Prime Minister's office, led by Swedish expert Mats Josepsson, will present its first proposals to the government at the end of this week. The objective is to foster the development of healthy financial activities, directed primarily at serving the needs of customers. This should lay the foundation for improving the situation of households and corporates.

A core tenet of the new government's efforts is to ensure responsible management of economic and monetary affairs. With regard to fiscal matters, the preliminary outlines of the repayment schedule for coming quarters need to be fixed and preparations begun on government budgets for the coming years. The Bill of Legislation introduced in the Althingi to amend the Central Bank Act provides for the establishment of a special Monetary Policy Committee. This committee will make decisions on the use of the Bank's monetary policy control mechanisms. Such a committee could play a key role in formulating currency and monetary policy in Iceland in coming quarters. The committee is to include external experts, foreign or domestic, with the aim of adding to the credibility of the monetary policy pursued.

Fellow Icelanders.

The unemployment figures in this country are far too high at the moment and, unfortunately, are bound to increase further. These figures represent thousands of individuals: mothers, fathers and children. Whole families are affected by the downturn we are currently experiencing. It is painful to think that the perilous business ventures of a few have already resulted in the unemployment of over 13,000 people.

We have to respond with actions to create jobs and preserve those already existing. We will make a concerted effort to find ways of stimulating investment by domestic and foreign parties, creating new private sector jobs. The government will soon present its programme of public works and tenders. Various measures have already been taken by public authorities in labour market matters and to encourage innovation.

The Housing Financing Fund's authorisations to grant loans for housing maintenance will be increased and full repayment made of VAT on labour at the construction location of such projects. We know that major developers are simply waiting to begin work. It is up to us to help this happen as soon as possible. With the same end in mind, we are determined to expand the lending capacity of the Institute of Regional Development.

In all these important undertakings we will promote consultation with the social partners. We will take concerted action in response to the financial difficulties facing households in the country in close consultation with stakeholders. A welfare monitoring group, composed of various parties, will be established to follow the consequences of the banks' collapse and make proposals for actions. Here we can learn from the bitter experience in Finland.

The government has already introduced a bill on debt restructuring, a new option in Iceland, and one I have been attempting to launch for a long time. In the coming weeks additional bills will be introduced to improve the legal situation of individuals facing temporary payment difficulties. The Insolvency Act will be amended to improve debtors' legal position. Until now too much emphasis has been placed on the legal rights of creditors in the case of bankruptcy.

Laws will be adopted on private pension savings granting fund members a temporary authorisation to withdraw their private pension savings to meet pressing financial needs.

Fellow Icelanders.

I have listed here the substance of the principal items comprising the platform of the government now at the helm. This cabinet is a minority coalition of the Social Democratic Alliance and the Left-Green Movement, supported by the Progressive Party. Although it will hold office for only a brief period, it is in many ways unique. For the first time, an equal number of women and men comprise the government in Iceland; this is only the third time such has happened in the world. In addition, two new ministers were invited to join as external professionals, i.e. ministers who have not until now been involved in politics. These two ministers will steer ministries which are very important in the reconstruction ahead, and will play a key role in restoring public confidence. Under these circumstances I think this was the correct decision. I ask everyone to bear in mind that this government will be extremely short-lived, allotted a mere 82 days to carry out important tasks, task[s] of vital significance to the nation.

I am very satisfied with the responsibility which the members of the Left-Green Movement, the Progressive Party and the Social Democratic Alliance here in the Althingi have shown in enabling this governmental co-operation, thereby resolving the cabinet crisis which had developed. Taking on the major tasks awaiting us definitely calls for courage and determination. I am encouraged by the fact that the parties supporting the government are ready to accept this responsibility, with elections just around the corner. I would also like to thank the members of the Independence party for their contribution to the last government and especially the former Prime Minister, Geir H. Haarde. I know that I speak for the entire nation in wishing him a speedy recovery.

Furthermore, I would like to take this opportunity to remind parliamentarians of our responsibility in the present circumstances. There is good reason to request especially that the entire parliament work together to expedite the progress of measures intended to mitigate the impact of the banks' collapse on business and industry, households and families. I urge parliament to show consideration for the government given these circumstances. I also promise that we will do our best to work and consult with other parliamentarians in the coming weeks. Our co-operation is essential for the nation—and we must not fail in this respect.

I also address my words to the nation. If ever there was a need for Icelanders [to] stand together and support one another, it is now. We have to reinforce society's safety net. All of us must be alert: the trade unions and the national government, municipalities, the church, the Red Cross and other NGOs and charitable organisations who often work miracles in this regard.

But we must also roll up our sleeves and begin the task of building a new welfare society. We have to be alert to new business opportunities, create the ground for start-up companies to take root in, and give companies already operating the leeway to increase their speed and need for labour. I urge all of business and industry to join forces with us—and to show consideration for the fact that there is much that needs rebuilding.

Fellow Icelanders.

Determination rather than fear is what we need. We have to take on those projects and tasks that have been left in abeyance during the years of plenty. Everyone who can do so must make a contribution, because only by so doing can we speedily work our way out of these difficulties.

This government could be described as based on an agreement on a new beginning—new values. There has been a paradigm shift in the public attitude in this country. A consensus has developed on values differing from those which have been in the spotlight in recent years. A consensus has developed on our shared responsibility: we are all in the same boat.

The government which is now commencing its first working week is a liberal welfare government, representing a broad spectrum of opinion. A government which intends to rebuild, to create stability, and to defend the basic services of our welfare system.

I would like to express my thanks for the many greetings and messages of encouragement from individuals and organisations in Iceland and from leaders of other countries, which my government and I have received in the past few days. Foreign colleagues have expressed their understanding of our situation in telephone conversations, which is a source of great encouragement.

I hope it will be the epitaph of this government to be deemed the forerunner of a new era in Icelandic society, where democracy and the influence of the individual citizen acquire real meaning. This is and should be the government of the people of this country.

SOURCE: Office of the Prime Minister of Iceland. "Platform of the Government—Report from the Prime Minister." February 4, 2009. http://eng.forsaetisraduneyti.is/news-and-articles/nr/3387.

OTHER HISTORIC DOCUMENTS OF INTEREST

FROM THIS VOLUME

FROM PREVIOUS HISTORIC DOCUMENTS

President Obama Calls for Executive Pay Cap

FEBRUARY 4, 2009

In February 2009, the Obama administration announced that it was seeking to impose a $500,000 cap on the salaries of top executives working at companies that received bailout funds from the federal government. The administration also sought to stop bonuses other than typical stock dividends from being paid out to these employees and placed additional restrictions on types of stocks as well. The move to strictly regulate executive pay came amid public outcry over news of extravagant pay packages at companies whose weakened finances had necessitated federal bailout money.

OBAMA'S PLAN V. BUSH'S PLAN

President Barack Obama called for the pay cap on February 4, 2009. He said his decision was "only the beginning of a long-term effort" to change the way banks pay their employees. The president called the Wall Street bankers "shameful" for the $20 billion in bonuses paid out, while across the country, people were losing their jobs and homes as the economy collapsed. "If the taxpayers are helping you," President Obama said in an NBC *Nightly News* interview, "then you have certain responsibilities to not be living high on the hog." Sen. Claire McCaskill, D-Mo., used stronger terms when she called for a $400,000 pay cap, calling Wall Street executives "a bunch of idiots" who were "kicking sand in the face of the American taxpayer."

President Obama's executive pay plan, created by Treasury Secretary Timothy Geithner, sought to close the executive pay loophole the Bush administration had created in the Emergency Economic Stabilization Act of 2008 that in effect exempted all companies from a salary cap. As the legislation was originally written, any bank receiving bailout funds was supposed to have salary restrictions put in place by the government, but they were not strictly enforced. In addition, the top five executives at any company that received bailout funds could not receive a rich severance package, or "golden parachute," and the company could not deduct from taxes any pay over $500,000. Any company that received emergency funds was required to reduce the size of bonuses to the top fifty executives by 40 percent. The Bush plan also tried to limit pay by asking the Securities and Exchange Commission to develop new rules that would require large companies to disclose any compensation given to executives that was not tied to job performance. A recent study by Equilar, a compensation research firm, found that although the Bush administration attempted to put a cap on pay, little to nothing had changed because of these efforts.

Before the Emergency Economic Stabilization Act of 2008 was signed, Bush pushed Congress to make a one-sentence change to the legislation that meant salary caps would only apply to firms that received bailout money by auctioning off their troubled assets to the federal government. At the time Congress approved and inserted the change into the legislation, the Bush administration had not used the auction procedures to allocate any of the $335 billion that had thus far been committed to the bailout plan nor did it plan to use the auction in the future. This meant that any company that had received bailout funds had no salary restrictions.

Under President Obama's plan, the salary limits would apply only to those financial institutions accepting the remaining Troubled Asset Relief Program (TARP) funds, valued at $350 billion. The plan did not apply to the 350 companies that had already received bailout funds through TARP. President Obama's plan limited executive compensation and bonuses at the companies receiving the second stage of bailout funds to $500,000. Under the new pay cap, no company receiving the TARP funds would be allowed to give their highest wage earners a bonus more than one-third of his or her salary. Lawrence H. Summers, the director of the National Economic Council, wrote to Congress that the plan would require that "executive compensation above a specified threshold amount be paid in restricted stock or similar form that cannot be liquidated or sold until the government has been repaid." In addition to the pay cap and stock restrictions, a nonbinding shareholder vote was required for approval of executive compensation goals, and company boards were required to approve nonessential spending, such as on parties, private planes, and executive retreats. President Obama's plan also required that if any of the top twenty-five executives at companies receiving the second stage of TARP funds were found to be using deceptive practices or lying on financial statements, the compensation, bonuses, and stock incentives would be taken away. Golden parachutes (generous payment given to executives who sever ties with a company) for the top ten executives at each of these companies were disallowed, and the next twenty-five executives in line were slated to get one year's pay in the event that he or she left the company—still significantly less than the typical golden parachute awarded. Once companies paid back the government's money, they would no longer be restricted by these salary and incentive pay caps.

It was believed that the salary cap would make banks think twice about asking for additional government funds and would motivate them to repay the government quickly. According to David Viniar, chief financial officer at Goldman Sachs, his company was hoping to repay the government as quickly as possible to "be under less scrutiny and under less pressure."

Although many of the companies receiving some of the federal government's $700 billion in bailout funds were deemed safe from bankruptcy, five that were on the brink of bankruptcy—Citigroup, Bank of America, AIG, General Motors, and Chrysler—all had executives who had earned well over $500,000 per year in the past. For example, Bank of America's chief executive, Kenneth Lewis, made $20 million in 2007, with $5.75 million of that allocated as salary and bonuses. General Motors' chief executive, Richard Wagoner, made $14.4 million, with a bulk of it in stock, options, and noncash benefits, plus a $1.6 million salary. At Citigroup, the chief executive made $3.1 million.

President Obama found support on both sides of the aisle in Congress for his plan to cap pay. Christopher Dodd, D-Conn., chair of the Senate Banking Committee, said, "There is absolutely no reason why hard-working American taxpayers should be financing, directly or indirectly, excessive compensation for corporate executives whose decisions, in many cases, have crippled their firms and weakened the broader economy." There was agreement from Republicans in Congress as well. John Boehner, R-Ohio, the House minority leader, said, "If anyone is looking for the taxpayer to help bail their company out, these types of executive pay caps are appropriate."

Obama's irritation with the executives at companies accepting bailout money from the government was apparent. "For top executives to award themselves these kinds of compensation packages in the midst of this economic crisis is not only in bad taste, it's a bad strategy, and I will not tolerate it as president." He continued by saying that such excessive pay is "exactly the kind of disregard for the costs and consequences of their actions that brought about this crisis—a culture of narrow self-interest and short-term gain at the expense of everything else." He explained that what made him and most Americans angry was that top executives were being awarded for failure with money they received from taxpayers.

The president cautioned that his desire for pay caps was not meant to stop American success. "This is America. We don't disparage wealth. We don't begrudge anybody for achieving success. And we believe that success should be rewarded. But what gets people upset—and rightfully so—are executives being rewarded for failure. Especially when those rewards are subsidized by U.S. taxpayers."

Holes in the Plan and Possible Consequences

Although President Obama's plan put forth rules that were tougher than any that had been introduced previously, there were still some loopholes. The pay cap only applied to large companies relying on the government to bail them out, and there was no restriction on the size of stock incentives, which often account for a large portion of an executive's annual pay; the government had to be paid back the loaned money before any executive at a given company would be allowed to cash in the stocks. For any company that did not require "exceptional financial recovery assistance," such as the amount of bailout money given to AIG or Citigroup, as long as the company put its executive pay policies and stock awards to a shareholder vote, the $500,000 cap would not apply.

Bankers and economists pointed to possible unintended consequences from President Obama's plan. Some economic analysts expected to see a brain drain at the upper levels of the companies affected by the pay cap, and this loss of institutional knowledge could put some firms at risk. Another risk might arise from an inability to hold on to top performers and to hire top performers at a competitive rate. According to compensation consultant Alan Johnson, as quoted in *USA Today*, "The unintended consequence is you end up killing the institution you tried to save. You drive away the good people." According to James Reda, founder and managing director of James F. Reda & Associates, there are only a handful of companies that pay their top executives $500,000 or less per year. "It would be really tough to get people to staff," he said. "I don't think this will work." On the other hand, there are those who believe the pay caps will affect a broader range of financial firms, creating a new pay structure on Wall Street that could include a decrease in cash bonuses and an increase in company stock awarded to long-term employees.

Some, like Nell Minow of the Corporate Library, a company that tracks executive pay and the governance of private companies, believe the pay cap only scratches the surface of the larger underlying problem, which is the corporate board structure. Minow said the best way for a company to survive into the future is to strengthen its board, ensuring that those serving as directors receive a majority of votes at annual shareholder meetings, rather than just seating the person who is in the best interest of the company's structure.

THE SALARY CAP TAKES EFFECT

In June 2009, President Obama appointed Kenneth Feinberg as "pay czar" at the Department of the Treasury. In this position, Feinberg was to ensure that companies receiving federal bailout funds properly follow the executive compensation rules laid out by the president.

In October 2009, Feinberg cut the pay of the top twenty-five executives at the seven companies receiving bailout funds by nearly 90 percent from 2008 salary levels. In December 2009, Feinberg instituted the $500,000 pay cap on the 2009 compensation packages for executives at AIG, Citigroup, General Motors, and GMAC. The rules only covered the 26th through 100th highest paid employees at the company. Those making less than $500,000 were kept on at normal salaries to allow the company to function properly and to continue to attract top talent. "These negotiations with these companies have been very cordial, very constructive," said Feinberg. "There's been some disagreements but I think there's general acceptance that the process has worked out very well." Although Feinberg said the negotiations had been going well, many top executives threatened to quit if he followed through with his proposals, but no one did. Twelve companies receiving bailout funds were deemed "exceptional cases" and were not required to adhere to the $500,000 cap, after lobbying by the Treasury Department and Federal Reserve, which indicated that these companies were in need of keeping their pay structure to retain talent.

—Heather Kerrigan

Following is a speech by President Barack Obama calling for caps on executive pay, delivered on February 4, 2009.

President Obama on Executive Pay Caps

Thank you, Tim [Geithner], for your hard work on this issue and on the economic recovery.

The economic crisis we face is unlike any we've seen in our lifetime. It's a crisis of falling confidence and rising debt, of widely distributed risk and narrowly concentrated reward, a crisis written in the fine print of subprime mortgages, on the ledger lines of once mighty financial institutions, and on the pink slips that have upended the lives of so many people across this country and cost the economy 2.6 million jobs last year alone.

We know that even if we do everything that we should, this crisis was years in the making, and it will take more than weeks or months to turn things around.

But make no mistake: A failure to act, and act now, will turn crisis into a catastrophe and guarantee a longer recession, a less robust recovery, and a more uncertain future. Millions more jobs will be lost. More businesses will be shuttered. More dreams will be deferred.

And that's why I feel such a sense of urgency about the economic recovery and reinvestment plan that is before Congress today. With it, we can save or create more than 3 million jobs, doing things that will strengthen our country for years to come. It's not merely a prescription for short-term spending, it's a strategy for long-term economic growth in areas like renewable energy and health care and education.

Now, in the past few days, I've heard criticisms that this plan is somehow wanting, and these criticisms echo the very same failed economic theories that led us into this crisis in the first place: the notion that tax cuts alone will solve all our problems; that we can ignore fundamental challenges like energy independence and the high cost of health care; that we can somehow deal with this in a piecemeal fashion and still expect our economy and our country to thrive.

I reject those theories, and so did the American people when they went to the polls in November and voted resoundingly for change. So I urge Members of Congress to act without delay. No plan is perfect, and we should work to make it stronger. No one is more committed to making it stronger than me. But let's not make the perfect the enemy of the essential. Let's show people all over the country who are looking for leadership in this difficult time that we are equal to the task.

At the same time, we know that this recovery and reinvestment plan is only the first part of what we need to do to restore prosperity and secure our future. We also need a strong and viable financial system to keep credit flowing to businesses and families alike. And my administration will do whatever it takes to restore our financial system. Our recovery depends on it. And so in the next week, Secretary Geithner will release a new strategy to get credit moving again, a strategy that will reflect some of the lessons of past mistakes while laying the foundation of the future.

But in order to restore trust in our financial system, we're going to have to do more than just put forward our plans. In order to restore trust, we've got to make certain that taxpayer funds are not subsidizing excessive compensation packages on Wall Street.

We all need to take responsibility. And this includes executives at major financial firms who turned to the American people, hat in hand, when they were in trouble, even as they paid themselves customary, lavish bonuses. As I said last week, this is the height of irresponsibility; it's shameful. And that's exactly the kind of disregard of the costs and consequences of their actions that brought about this crisis: a culture of narrow self-interest and short-term gain at the expense of everything else.

This is America. We don't disparage wealth. We don't begrudge anybody for achieving success. And we certainly believe that success should be rewarded. But what gets people upset, and rightfully so, are executives being rewarded for failure, especially when those rewards are subsidized by U.S. taxpayers, many of whom are having a tough time themselves.

For top executives to award themselves these kinds of compensation packages in the midst of this economic crisis isn't just bad taste, it's bad strategy, and I will not tolerate it as President. We're going to be demanding some restraint in exchange for

Federal aid, so that when firms seek new Federal dollars, we won't find them up to the same old tricks.

As part of the reforms we're announcing today, top executives at firms receiving extraordinary help from U.S. taxpayers will have their compensation capped at $500,000, a fraction of the salaries that have been reported recently. And if these executives receive any additional compensation, it will come in the form of stock that can't be paid up until taxpayers are paid back for their assistance.

Companies receiving Federal aid are going to have to disclose publicly all the perks and luxuries bestowed upon senior executives and provide an explanation to the taxpayers and to shareholders as to why these expenses are justified. And we're putting a stop to these kinds of massive severance packages we've all read about with disgust; we're taking the air out of golden parachutes.

We're asking these firms to take responsibility, to recognize the nature of this crisis and their role in it. We believe that what we've laid out should be viewed as fair and embraced as basic common sense.

And finally, these guidelines we're putting in place are only the beginning of a long-term effort. We're going to examine the ways in which the means and manner of executive compensation have contributed to a reckless culture and a quarter-by-quarter mentality that in turn helped to wreak havoc in our financial system. We're going to be taking a look at broader reforms so that executives are compensated for sound risk management and rewarded for growth measured over years, not just days or weeks.

We all have to pull together and take our share of responsibility. That's true here in Washington; that's true on Wall Street. The American people are carrying a huge burden as a result of this economic crisis, bearing the brunt of its effects as well as the cost of extraordinary measures we're taking to address them. The American people expect and demand that we pursue policies that reflect the reality of this crisis and that will prevent these kinds of crises from occurring again in the future.

Thank you very much.

SOURCE: U.S. Executive Office of the President. "Remarks on the National Economy." *Daily Compilation of Presidential Documents* 2009, no. 000057 (February 4, 2009). www.gpo.gov/fdsys/pkg/DCPD-200900057/html/DCPD-200900057.htm.

OTHER HISTORIC DOCUMENTS OF INTEREST

FROM PREVIOUS *HISTORIC DOCUMENTS*

DOCUMENT IN CONTEXT

Special Court Finds Vaccines Do Not Cause Autism

FEBRUARY 12, 2009

On February 12, 2009, a special federal court ruled in a series of cases regarding a possible link between the combined vaccine for measles, mumps, and rubella (MMR) and autism. In each case, the court found no evidence to suggest that the MMR vaccine causes autism, meaning that thousands of families with autistic children are not entitled to compensation from companies that manufacture the vaccines. This decision marks a turning point in an international movement that sought to link vaccines to autism.

AUTISM

Autism is a developmental disorder that affects 1 in every 110 children in the United States. Effects of autism can include impaired communication and social skills. At this time, no specific cause of autism has been identified, although scientists believe that a number of factors, including genetics and viral infections or toxins to which a fetus is exposed, may be contributing factors.

The number of children being diagnosed with autism is on the rise, but, as scientific studies denying the link between autism and the MMR vaccine have often pointed out, the rate of MMR vaccines is *not* increasing. Researchers have also noted that the age at which autism is diagnosed is the same for children who have and have not received the MMR vaccine. Some scientists believe that autism begins in infancy, but, depending on how mild the symptoms are, can go unnoticed until the child is a toddler. One explanation for the rise in the number of children being diagnosed with autism is that there is now a widely accepted and known definition of the disorder, therefore opening it up to broader application to more children. The number of health professionals who specialize in identifying and treating autism is also on the rise, leading to a higher rate of diagnosis.

The MMR vaccine–autism link gained traction after a British study approximately ten years ago reported that the measles portion of the MMR caused intestinal inflammation that could eventually lead to autism. Other researchers, however, have not been able to replicate this finding. Scientific studies have long indicated that the MMR vaccine and autism are not linked, and federal and state health officials have warned parents who are nervous that by not vaccinating their children they are putting them at greater risk.

Vaccines work when an individual is administered a dead or weakened form of the virus or bacteria that causes the disease in question. The body "learns" how to fight off the virus by producing the appropriate antibodies. If a child is then later exposed to a disease for which he or she has already received a vaccine, the body recognizes the virus and is able to quickly produce the same antibodies to fight it off before it becomes a serious problem. According to the National Center for Health Statistics, approximately 1 in every 12 children in the United States today does not receive the MMR vaccine, in large part in response to the fear that the vaccine and autism are linked. As noted earlier, because the symptoms of autism are generally first visible around the same time a child receives the MMR vaccine, parents and some health professionals have concluded that the two circumstances are related. In addition, although early forms of the MMR vaccine did not contain thimerosal, a mercury-containing compound used as a preservative, other vaccines administered to young children at the same time did contain the compound, and there was some belief that an interaction between the MMR vaccine and a mercury-containing vaccine could be hazardous. Concerned parents raised the possibility that mercury exposure from the vaccine could be the cause of autism in children. Scientists were never able to make this connection, however. In 2004, the U.S. National Academies' Institute of Medicine concluded that although mercury is a neurotoxin, the levels present in childhood vaccines through the addition of thimerosal was not enough to cause any neurological disorder, including autism. Nevertheless, thimerosal began being removed from childhood vaccines in 1999 in an effort to reduce the amount of lifetime mercury exposure to children.

The question of the vaccine–autism connection was highly publicized when politicians and celebrities voiced their concerns in the media in the first decade of the twenty-first century. Robert Kennedy Jr. wrote in a 2005 *Rolling Stone* article that there was a "government cover-up of a mercury/autism scandal." Rep. Dan Burton, R.-Ind., said in 2007, "I believe, as do many credible scientists and researchers, that the clear correlation between the dramatic rise in the number of autism cases, and the rapid expansion of the childhood vaccination schedule during that 20-year period, points to the mercury-based preservative thimerosal—routinely used in pediatric vaccines during the period—as a contributing factor to our country's literal epidemic of autism. In fact, I firmly believe my own grandson became autistic after receiving nine shots"

COURT CASES

The special court that ruled in this case was originally established in 1986 by Congress as part of the National Vaccine Injury Compensation Program, which sought to provide compensation when the occasional person suffered a serious side effect or death caused by a vaccine. Under the federal program, those who are found to have injuries related to a vaccine are entitled to more than $1 million in damages, with estate awards limited to $250,000. The special court was established under the legislation to hear cases and provide an alternative to suing vaccine makers directly, which could put manufacturers out of business and thus caused a serious health crisis in the United States. Instead, Congress has those afflicted from vaccines prove their case to a "special master." The special masters, as the judges are called in these cases, are appointed by the U.S. Court of Federal Claims to serve four-year terms. The special masters oversee the collection of information related to cases that come before the court and render a final decision on whether the evidence presented is conclusive in showing that a vaccine may have caused serious injury. No juries are involved in cases heard by this court.

To seek compensation from the National Vaccine Injury Compensation Program, one must file a case with the U.S. district court where the injury or death occurred or where the person on whose behalf the case is being filed lives or lived. To receive a monetary award, the complainant in the case must have received one of the vaccines covered by the program, such as diphtheria, polio, tetanus, whooping cough, and the MMR. To receive a monetary award, a person must prove that he or she was injured or had a previous injury aggravated, or his or her representative must prove that the person was killed by one of the covered vaccines. In the case of injury, the person must be able to prove that the injury lasted for more than one year and that more than $1,000 in expenses was incurred due to the injury. Anyone previously compensated in another form for injury, or any previously compensated representative of an individual who died, is not eligible to receive an award.

The award amount decided on by the special masters can be paid out for medical expenses, lost wages, death benefits, and pain and suffering. The acceptance of an award means that the person bringing the suit will seek no further compensation for damages.

In 2002, the Office of Special Masters began to conduct meetings with attorneys for all the families bringing cases to the court regarding the link between the MMR, thimerosal, and autism. After those meetings, the Office of Special Masters decided to take a two-stage approach to the cases. First, they would look into the general issue of whether vaccines can be linked to autism or other childhood developmental disorders and what factors lead to the development of autism. Second, they would take what they found and apply it to test cases.

The court created a litigation steering committee to divide all the families bringing autism cases to the Office of Special Masters into one of three categories: those who claim that the MMR vaccine combined with thimerosal-containing vaccines can cause autism; those who believe thimerosal-containing vaccines can cause autism without being combined with other vaccines; and those who believe MMR vaccines, without thimerosal, can cause autism. In the first three test cases, brought by the Cedillo, Snyder, and Hazlehurst families, the rulings were related only to whether the MMR vaccine, in combination with a thimerosal-containing vaccine, could cause autism.

The special masters began hearing cases related to the MMR vaccines in 2007. The first three decisions drew on 5,000 pages of transcripts, 939 medical articles, and 50 reports written by experts in the field. In total, the three rulings were 650 pages long. The three different special masters who handled the cases released findings that were similar to each other and that reached the same conclusion: In each case, the parents had to prove that it was more likely than not that their child's autism was caused by the MMR or other vaccines that contained thimerosal, and in each case the special master concluded that there was no link.

According to Dr. Max Wiznitzer, an autism specialist who was an expert witness for the government, "The cases focused on several core questions. . . . Can thimerosal-containing vaccines cause immune dysfunction? Did immune dysfunction allow the measles virus contained in the MMR vaccine to persist in the body, and did the vaccine-strain measles cause the children to develop gastrointestinal and central nervous system (CNS) problems, including autism?"

On the issue of thimerosal, the expert witnesses for the plaintiffs testified that mercury in high doses can be toxic to humans. The government's witnesses countered that ethyl mercury, the substance found in thimerosal, does not have the same chemical makeup as methyl mercury, from which the plaintiffs' experts were drawing evidence.

Ethyl mercury, in such small amounts, the government said, does not damage the immune system of children.

In the first case, special master George L. Hastings ruled on the charges brought by Theresa and Michael Cedillo of Yuma, Arizona, and called the evidence brought by the two parents "very wrong." "Unfortunately, the Cedillos have been misled by physicians who are guilty, in my view, of gross medical misjudgment," Hastings wrote in his findings. The Cedillo case involved their daughter, Michelle, who became sick one week after receiving her MMR vaccine; nearly 13 years later, she had lost most of her vision and required constant care because of the advanced state of her autism.

In the second case, special master Denise Vowell heard evidence brought by Kathryn and Joseph Snyder of Port Orange, Florida, who claimed that the MMR vaccine caused their son a pervasive developmental disorder. In her ruling, Vowell wrote, "The evidence presented was both voluminous and extraordinarily complex." But, she said, her conclusion was that autism experts "were far more qualified, better supported by the weight of scientific evidence research and authority, and simply more persuasive on nearly every point."

In the third case, Patricia Campbell-Smith ruled in the case brought by Rolf and Angela Hazlehurst of Jackson, Tennessee, who claimed that the MMR vaccine caused their son to develop regressive autism. Campbell-Smith wrote in her ruling that although she was touched, as a parent, by what had happened to the Hazlehurst's son, the plaintiff's evidence was not sufficiently conclusive.

Attorneys for the parents whose cases were tried by the three special masters have said that they will appeal, which they can do through the U.S. Court of Federal Claims. If the decision at the U.S. Court of Federal Claims proves unsatisfactory, the attorneys can bring the case before the U.S. Court of Appeals for the Federal Circuit, from where parties in the case can appeal to the U.S. Supreme Court. The Supreme Court has heard at least one case that first originated in the Office of Special Masters, dealing with encephalopathy, or brain dysfunction. In *Shalala v. Whitecotten,* in 1995, the court determined that because of the child's abnormally small head, encephalopathy existed before the child received a vaccine.

Aftermath

In a statement following the court's ruling, the U.S. Department of Health and Human Services (HHS) reported that it will continue to support research "to better understand the cause of autistic disorders and develop more effective methods of treatment." However, the HHS noted, "the medical and scientific communities . . . have found no association between vaccines and autism. . . . Hopefully, the determination by the Special Masters will help reassure parents that vaccines do not cause autism."

Autism Speaks, an autism research and advocacy group, responded to the ruling by encouraging families with autistic children to continue to seek answers. "While large scale studies have not shown a link between vaccines and autism, there are lingering legitimate questions about the safety of vaccines that must be addressed. Our families deserve nothing less than an exhaustive search using a rigorous scientific approach."

Some have called the denial by doctors, pharmaceutical companies, and others of a link between vaccines and autism a conspiracy, and it remains to be seen whether such critics will accept the special court's ruling on the three cases or take it as more evidence of a conspiracy.

Doctors will now face the challenge of explaining to parents what the special court's decision means, what the evidence has shown, and how they should proceed with the vaccination schedule for children.

The Office of Special Masters only has the ability to make legal decisions, not scientific interpretations of the health care matters at hand. With thousands of cases yet to be heard by the court, many of which deal with autism, it is unclear if, presented with different evidence, the court will rule consistently in denying the link between autism and vaccines.

—Heather Kerrigan

Following are excerpts from three separate cases, Cedillo v. Secretary of Health and Human Services, Snyder v. Secretary of Health and Human Services, *and* Hazlehurst v. Secretary of Health and Human Services, *in which the Office of Special Masters ruled that there is not sufficient evidence to conclude that vaccinations cause autism; each case was filed February 12, 2009.*

Cedillo v. Secretary of Health and Human Services

February 12, 2009

[Footnotes and parenthetical notations have been omitted.]

In the United States Court of Federal Claims

Office of Special Masters

No. 98–916V

Theresa Cedillo and Michael Cedillo, as parents and natural guardians of Michelle Cedillo, Petitioners *v.* Secretary of Health and Human Services, Respondent.	Vaccine Act Entitlement; Causation-in-fact; MMR/Autism Causation Issue; MMR/Gastrointestinal Dysfunction Causation Issue; Thimerosal/Immune Damage Causation Issue.

(Filed February 12, 2009)

Ronald Homer and Sylvia Chin-Caplan, Boston, Massachusetts, for petitioners.

Vincent Matanoski and Lynn Ricciardella, U.S. Department of Justice, Washington, D.C., for respondent.

DECISION

Hastings, Special Master.

    This is an action in which the petitioners, Michael and Theresa Cedillo, seek an award under the National Vaccine Injury Compensation Program on account of several conditions, including autism and chronic gastrointestinal symptoms, which afflict their daughter, Michelle Cedillo. I conclude that the petitioners have *not* demonstrated that they are entitled to an award on Michelle's behalf. I will set forth the reasons for that conclusion in detail below. However, at this point I will briefly summarize the reasons for my conclusion.

    The petitioners in this case have advanced a causation theory that has several parts, including contentions (1) that thimerosal-containing vaccines can cause immune dysfunction, (2) that the MMR vaccine can cause autism, and (3) that the MMR vaccine can cause chronic gastrointestinal dysfunction. However, as to each of those issues, I concluded that the evidence was overwhelmingly contrary to the petitioners' contentions. The expert witnesses presented by the respondent were far better qualified, far more experienced, and far more persuasive than the petitioners' experts, concerning most of the key points. The numerous medical studies concerning these issues, performed by medical scientists worldwide, have come down strongly against the petitioners' contentions. Considering all of the evidence, I found that the petitioners have *failed* to demonstrate that thimerosal-containing vaccines can contribute to causing immune dysfunction, or that the MMR vaccine can contribute to causing either autism or gastrointestinal dysfunction. I further conclude that while Michelle Cedillo has tragically suffered from autism and other severe conditions, the petitioners have also failed to demonstrate that her vaccinations played any role at all in causing those problems. . . .

[Section I, detailing the law behind the decision in the case, has been omitted.]

[Section II, detailing the facts in the case, has been omitted.]

[Section III, containing the procedural history of the case and controversy involving autism and vaccines, has been omitted.]

[Section IV, detailing the issues to be decided during the case, has been omitted.]

V. PETITIONERS HAVE NOT DEMONSTRATED EITHER THAT THIMEROSAL-CONTAINING VACCINES *CAN* HARM INFANT IMMUNE SYSTEMS IN GENERAL, OR THAT SUCH VACCINES *DID* HARM MICHELLE'S IMMUNE SYSTEM

The first part of petitioners' overall causation theory is their contention that thimerosal-containing vaccines damaged Michelle's immune system, thereby making it possible for the vaccine strain measles virus to persist within Michelle's body.

    First, as noted above, I observe that I find this portion of petitioners' theory to be essentially *unnecessary* to the rest of their causation argument. That is, if petitioners were able to persuade me that the vaccine-strain measles virus *did* likely persist in Michelle's body and cause damage to either (or both) her brain or gut, I *would* compensate such damage. It would not matter *why* the vaccine-strain measles virus was able to persist. Therefore, resolution of this part of petitioners' theory is not strictly necessary for resolution of this case. However, as explained above, this case was designated as a "test case," to *provide guidance* for the other pending autism cases. Therefore, I will evaluate this contention of the petitioners, and explain why I find that the evidence in the record does *not* support either the proposition that thimerosal-containing vaccines *can* damage immune systems *in general,* or the proposition that such vaccines *did* damage *Michelle's own* immune system.

A. The evidence does not support the general proposition that thimerosal-containing vaccines can damage infants' immune systems. . . .

B. Petitioners have not demonstrated that thimerosal-containing vaccines harmed *Michelle's own* immune system. . . .

VI. The Unigenetics Testing That Purported to Find Evidence of Persisting Measles Virus in The Intestinal Tissue of Michelle and Others was Not Reliable . . .

[The description of the testing by Unigenetics and further history of the case has been omitted.]

VII. Petitioners Have Not Demonstrated That the MMR Vaccine *Can* Cause Autism in General, or That an MMR Vaccination *Did* Cause Michelle's Autism

A. Summary of petitioners' theory

The next step in petitioners' theory is that the vaccine-strain measles virus, persisting in Michelle's body, damaged her brain, thereby causing her autism. In this regard, they rely primarily on the testimony of Dr. Marcel Kinsbourne, who has substantial credentials as a pediatric neurologist. Dr. Kinsbourne accepts the accuracy of the testing of the gut biopsy of Michelle discussed above, as a demonstration that the vaccine-strain measles virus persisted and replicated in her body. He opined that the persisting virus invaded Michelle's brain, prompting a response of her immune system, and that the inflammation produced by that response disorganized certain critical circuits in her brain, thereby causing the autism.

In support of this theory, Dr. Kinsbourne opined that autism is a neurological disorder, the product of defective brain circuitry. He explained that the measles virus, in its "wild" non-vaccine form, has been found in the past to cause a number of neurologic disorders. . . . He opined that since Michelle has experienced both chronic gastrointestinal problems and the chronic neurologic disorder known as autism, the most reasonable conclusion is that a *single* causative agent—*i.e.,* the vaccine-strain measles virus—is the cause of *both* chronic conditions.

In Michelle's case, Dr. Kinsbourne also found the *timing* of the onset of Michelle's chronic intestinal symptoms and her symptoms of autism to be quite important. He opined that Michelle was a normally developing infant up until the time of her MMR vaccination on December 20, 1995, when she was about 16 months old. . . . He stated that Michelle began to suffer diarrhea "within two weeks" of the vaccination, which he viewed as the onset of her chronic gastrointestinal problems. He also stated that Michelle's first symptoms of neurologic dysfunction, which later were recognized to be symptoms of *autism,* began *abruptly* during the period of fever that began one week after that vaccination. . . .

Finally, Dr. Kinsbourne also seemed to find it important that Michelle's autism falls, in his opinion, into the category of "regressive autism." Regressive autism is a form of autism in which the child does not merely fail to develop normally, but actually *loses* skills in language and related areas, usually sometime during the second year of life. This aspect of Dr. Kinsbourne's testimony seemed to indicate his view that the MMR vaccine is likely to play a causative role *specifically* in cases of *regressive autism,* as opposed to autistic cases in which the child does not experience regression. And the petitioners' briefs also indicate that the petitioners' causation theory in this case is specifically targeted to cases of *regressive* autism, as opposed to other cases of autism.

B. Reasons for rejecting petitioners' general theory

After a complete analysis of the record, I conclude that I must reject both petitioners' *general theory* concerning the causation of autism, and their contention that the measles virus substantially contributed to *Michelle's own* autism. Petitioners have failed to demonstrate that it is "more probable than not" either that the MMR vaccine *can* cause or contribute to autism in general, or that a MMR vaccination *did* cause or contribute to Michelle's autism. In this Part B of Section VII of this Decision, I will discuss petitioners' and Dr. Kinsbourne's *general* theory that the measles virus can cause or contribute to autism. Thereafter, in Part C, I will discuss the issue of the *specific* causation of Michelle's own autism. . . .

[Further discussion has been omitted.]

C. Reasons for rejecting the claim that the MMR vaccine substantially contributed to *Michelle Cedillo's* autism

I must also reject the claim that the MMR vaccine substantially contributed to *Michelle Cedillo's* autism, for several reasons set forth below.

1. I have rejected the petitioners' "general causation" theory.
. . . Thus, since the petitioners have failed to demonstrate any validity to their *general causation* theory, it follows inescapably that they have also failed to demonstrate that the autism of *Michelle Cedillo herself* was caused by her MMR vaccination.

2. Petitioners' theory depends upon the existence of a reliable laboratory test finding of persisting measles virus, which does not exist in Michelle's case.
. . . Therefore, petitioners' and Dr. Kinsbourne's conclusion that the MMR vaccine substantially contributed to *Michelle's* autism must be rejected for that reason alone.

3. Dr. Kinsbourne relied upon incorrect assumptions concerning the timing of Michelle's autism symptoms.
Dr. Kinsbourne also made it clear that, in offering his causation opinion in Michelle's case, he relied upon the certain assumptions concerning the *timing* of the onset of

Michelle's symptoms of autism. . . . However, upon a complete analysis of the record, I conclude that these assumptions of Dr. Kinsbourne were *not* correct. To the contrary, the evidence shows that (1) Michelle exhibited symptoms of autism *prior* to her MMR vaccination, and (2) Michelle did *not* experience an abrupt onset of autism symptoms shortly after her MMR vaccination. . . .

4. No evidence of brain inflammation

Dr. Kinsbourne's hypothesis, as previously noted, is that the persisting vaccine-strain measles virus invaded cells in Michelle's brain, prompting an immune system response, and that the *inflammation* produced by that response disorganized critical circuits in her brain, thereby causing the autism. Petitioners, however, failed to supply any evidence of brain inflammation in Michelle. . . .

Thus, the fact that the petitioners failed to demonstrate any evidence of brain inflammation in Michelle adds another reason to reject their theory that her autism was vaccine-caused. . . .

VIII. Petitioners Have Not Demonstrated Either That the MMR Vaccine *Can* Cause Chronic Gastrointestinal Dysfunction, or That an MMR Vaccination *Did* Cause Chronic Gastrointestinal Problems in Michelle

. . . I conclude, however, that the petitioners have *failed* to demonstrate, to the level of "more probable than not," either that the MMR vaccine *can* cause chronic gastrointestinal dysfunction in general, or that an MMR vaccination *did* cause chronic gastrointestinal problems in Michelle. . . .

[Information on the gastrointestinal system and evidence shown in the case has been omitted.]

IX. Petitioners' Evidence Concerning the *Combination* of Regressive Autism Plus Gastrointestinal Dysfunction is Not Persuasive . . .

X. Petitioners Have Not Demonstrated That Michelle's MMR Vaccination Contributed to Her Mental Retardation or Her Seizure Disorder . . .

The problem for petitioners in this regard, of course, is that they have failed to demonstrate that the MMR vaccine contributed to the causation of Michelle's *autism,* for the reasons detailed above. Therefore, their derivative argument, concerning the causation of Michelle's mental retardation and seizure disorder, must fail as well. . . .

[Section XI, in which the petitioners argue that treating physicians did believe that their daughter's autism was caused by vaccines, has been omitted.]

[Section XII, in which the petitioners attempted to tie their daughter's case to other autistic children's cases, has been omitted.]

XIII. Petitioners' Case Fails the *Althen* Test

A. The *Althen* test

In its ruling in *Althen,* the U.S. Court of Appeals for the Federal Circuit discussed the "causation-in-fact" issue in Vaccine Act cases. The court stated as follows:

> Concisely stated, Althen's burden is to show by preponderant evidence that the vaccination brought about her injury by providing: (1) a medical theory causally connecting the vaccination and the injury; (2) a logical sequence of cause and effect showing that the vaccination was the reason for the injury; and (3) a showing of a proximate temporal relationship between vaccination and injury. If Althen satisfies this burden, she is "entitled to recover unless the [government] shows, also by a preponderance of evidence, that the injury was in fact caused by factors unrelated to the vaccine." . . .

XIV. Conclusion

. . . After studying the extensive evidence in this case for many months, I am convinced that the reports and advice given to the Cedillos by Dr. Krigsman and some other physicians, advising the Cedillos that there is a causal connection between Michelle's MMR vaccination and her chronic conditions, have been *very wrong*. Unfortunately, the Cedillos have been misled by physicians who are guilty, in my view, of gross medical misjudgment. Nevertheless, I can understand why the Cedillos found such reports and advice to be believable under the circumstances. I conclude that the Cedillos filed this Program claim in good faith.

. . . However, I must decide this case not on sentiment, but by analyzing the evidence. . . . Accordingly, I conclude that the petitioners in this case are *not* entitled to a Program award on Michelle's behalf.

George L. Hastings, Jr.

Special Master

Source: U.S. Court of Federal Claims. Docket no. 98-916V. "Theresa Cedillo and Michael Cedillo, as Parents and Natural Guardians of Michelle Cedillo, v. Secretary of Health and Human Services." February 12, 2009. www.uscfc.uscourts.gov/sites/default/files/Hastings-Cedillo.pdf.

Snyder v. Secretary of Health and Human Services

February 12, 2009

In the United States Court of Federal Claims

Office of Special Masters

No. 01–162V

Colten Snyder, by and through Kathryn Snyder and Joseph Snyder, his natural guardians and next friends, Petitioners v. Secretary of the Department of Health and Human Services, Respondent.	Omnibus Autism Proceeding; Autism Spectrum Disorder, Pervasive Developmental Disorder, Causation, Measles, MMR, Mercury, Thimerosal, Waiver Applying *Daubert*, Weight of Expert Opinions, Credibility of Witnesses

Filed: February 12, 2009

Christopher W. Wickersham, Sr., Esq., Lloyd Bowers, Esq., and Thomas B. Powers, Esq., for petitioners.

Alexis S. Babcock, Esq., Katherine Esposito, Esq., Voris Johnson, Esq., and Vincent Matanoski, Esq., U.S. Department of Justice, Washington, DC, for respondent.

Decision

Vowell, Special Master:

. . . To be eligible for compensation under the Vaccine Act, a petitioner must either demonstrate a Vaccine Table injury, to which a statutory presumption of causation attaches, or prove by a preponderance of the evidence that a vaccine listed on the Vaccine Table caused or significantly aggravated an injury. The petitioners in this case do not contend that Colten suffered a "Table" injury. Therefore, in order to prevail, they must demonstrate by preponderant evidence: "(1) a medical theory causally connecting the vaccination and the injury; (2) a logical sequence of cause and effect showing that the vaccination was the reason for the injury; and (3) a showing of a proximate temporal relationship between vaccination and injury."

After considering the record as a whole, I hold that petitioners have failed to establish by preponderant evidence that Colten's condition was caused or significantly aggravated by a vaccine or any component thereof. The evidence presented was both voluminous and extraordinarily complex. After careful consideration of all of the evidence, it was abundantly clear that petitioners' theories of causation were speculative and unpersuasive.

Respondent's experts were far more qualified, better supported by the weight of scientific research and authority, and simply more persuasive on nearly every point in contention. Because of pervasive quality control problems at a now-defunct laboratory that tested a key piece of evidence, petitioners could not reliably demonstrate the presence of a persistent measles virus in Colten's central nervous system. Petitioners failed to establish that measles virus can cause autism or that it did so in Colten. They failed to demonstrate that amount of ethyl mercury in TCVs causes immune system suppression or dysregulation. They failed to show that Colten's immune system was dysregulated. Although Colten's condition markedly improved between his diagnosis and the hearing, the experimental treatments he received cannot be logically or scientifically linked to the theories of causation. Given the advice that petitioners received from a treating physician, Colten's parents brought this action in good faith and upon a reasonable basis. However, they have failed to demonstrate vaccine causation of Colten's condition by a preponderance of the evidence. Therefore, I deny their petition for compensation.

Colten's case was heard as part of the largest omnibus proceeding in the history of the Vaccine Act. It was one of three test cases on the first of two theories of causation ["Theory 1"] advanced by petitioners in the Omnibus Autism Proceeding ["OAP"]. Theory 1 is that a combination of the MMR vaccine and TCVs, acting in concert, cause some ASDs. . . .

[Section I, containing information on omnibus proceedings under the Vaccine Act and information on evidence and witnesses has been omitted.]

[Section II, containing information on the causation evidence in the case, has been omitted.]

[Section III, containing the legal standards applied to the case, has been omitted.]

[Section IV, containing information on autism, has been omitted.]

[Section V, detailing the immune system and vaccines, has been omitted.]

[Section VI, outlining the measles theory, has been omitted.]

[Section VII, examining the relationship between autism and vaccines, has been omitted.]

[Section VIII, containing information on Colton's illness, has been omitted.]

SECTION IX. CONCLUSION.

Petitioners have not demonstrated by a preponderance of the evidence that Colten's condition was either caused or significantly aggravated by his vaccinations Thus, they have failed to establish entitlement to compensation and the petition for compensation is therefore DENIED. In the absence of a motion for review filed pursuant to RCFC, Appendix B, the clerk is directed to enter judgment accordingly.

IT IS SO ORDERED.

Denise K. Vowell

Special Master

SOURCE: U.S. Court of Federal Claims. Docket no. 01-162V. "Colten Snyder, By and Through Kathryn Snyder and Joseph Snyder, His Natural Guardians and Next Friends v. Secretary of the Department of Health and Human Services." February 12, 2009. www.uscfc.uscourts.gov/sites/default/files/vaccine_files/Vowell.Snyder.pdf.

Hazlehurst v. Secretary of Health and Human Services

February 12, 2009

In the United States Court of Federal Claims

Office of Special Masters

No. 03–654V

| Rolf and Angela Hazlehurst, parents of William Yates Hazlehurst, Petitioners, *v.* Secretary of the Department of Health and Human Services, Respondent. | } | Omnibus Autism Proceeding; Test Case; Petitioners' First Theory of General Causation; Failure to Prove that the Combination of MMR and Thimerosal-Containing Vaccines Causes Autism |

E-Filed: February 12, 2009

Curtis R. Webb, Twin Falls, ID, for petitioners.

Linda Renzi, United States Department of Justice, Washington, DC, for respondent.

Decision . . .

[The procedural background of the case has been omitted.]

C. The Record in this Case

The Hazlehursts have pursued this vaccine claim on Yates' behalf and have consented to have this case heard as a test case in the OAP. . . . Rather, the task set before the undersigned is to evaluate one particular theory that purports to explain why Yates developed autism. It is extremely important, both for Yates and for all the other families involved in the OAP, that the undersigned analyze this specific theory in great detail. This analysis requires extensive discussion of matters that are clinical and scientific, even abstract. . . .

[The names and backgrounds of the experts and applicable legal standards in the case have been omitted.]

[Section II, describing the legal standards on which the case is based, has been omitted.]

[Section III, containing components of the petitioner's argument, has been omitted.]

[Section IV, containing Yates's medical history, has been omitted.]

V. Conclusion

. . . The undersigned's charge, however, does not permit decision making on the basis of sentiment but rather requires a careful legal analysis of the evidence.

The parties have submitted a wealth of evidence and have presented the testimony of a number of experts, the most persuasive of whom have extensive clinical and research experience in the particular areas of interest in this case, and whose opinions were well supported by reliable and scientifically sound literature. Having carefully and fully considered the evidence, the undersigned concludes that the combination of the thimerosal-containing vaccines and the MMR vaccine are not causal factors in the development of autism and therefore, could not have contributed to the development of Yates' autism. The weight of the presented evidence that is scientifically reliable and methodologically sound does not support petitioners' claim. Petitioners have failed to establish entitlement to compensation under the Vaccine Act. Absent the filing of a timely motion for review, the Clerk of the Court shall enter judgment accordingly.

IT IS SO ORDERED.

Patricia E. Campbell-Smith

Special Master

Source: U.S. Court of Federal Claims. Docket no. 03-654V. "Rolf and Angela Hazlehurst, Parents of William Yates Hazlehurst v. Secretary of the Department of Health and Human Services." February 12, 2009. www.uscfc.uscourts.gov/sites/default/files/vaccine_files/Campbell-Smith_Hazlehurst_Decision.pdf.

Other Historic Documents of Interest

From previous Historic Documents

President Obama's Address Before a Joint Session of Congress and Republican Response

FEBRUARY 24, 2009

As a first-year president who had been in office just over one month, President Barack Obama did not give an official State of the Union address, but rather gave a similar speech in front of a joint session of Congress on February 24, 2009, laying out his plans for the coming years and discussing his views about how the United States should deal with the economy, health care, and foreign policy. A majority of his speech focused on jobs, the housing and credit crisis, the recent American Recovery and Reinvestment Act (ARRA), and the deficit; he made it clear from the beginning that although recovery would not be easy for the United States, it was possible.

Bobby Jindal, Louisiana's governor, was chosen to give the Republican party rebuttal after the speech, and although his message spoke to Republican ideals of overspending by the government, both left- and right-leaning political pundits said his folksy delivery overshadowed what could have been a big moment for a man thought to be a 2012 presidential contender.

THE ECONOMY

Obama's speech before the joint session focused on the economy and how, under his direction, the United States would address the ongoing crisis. Obama made clear that he would need "significant resources" to get the economy back on its feet and people back in jobs and homes. While calling for substantial government investment, Obama also pledged to halve the federal deficit by 2013, the end of his first term in office. This goal of economic recovery had been pervasive in Obama's presidential campaign and during his first month as president. In this speech, the president argued that the economy had deteriorated because of poor decisions made by the federal government and individual citizens. "A surplus became an excuse to transfer wealth to the wealthy instead of an opportunity to invest in our future," he said. He spoke about people who had bought homes they knew they could not afford, and the banks that had given loans they knew people could never repay. "And all the while," the president said, "critical debates and difficult decisions were put off for some other time on some other day."

"The state of our economy is a concern that rises above all others," the president said at the beginning of his speech. "You don't need to hear another list of statistics to know that our economy is in crisis, because you live it every day. It's the worry you wake up with and the source of sleepless nights. It's the job you thought you'd retire from but now have lost; the business you built your dreams upon that's now hanging by a thread; the college acceptance letter your child had to put back in the envelope. The impact of this recession is real, and it is everywhere." However, the president did not spend his entire speech focusing on the negative state of the economy; he also noted what it could be with federal investment and the hard work of Americans. He sounded an optimistic tone during much of his speech, at one point saying, "We will rebuild, we will recover, and the United States of America will emerge stronger than before." There was a lot of work to be done, he reminded listeners, and the turnaround would not be simple. President Obama did not inflate expectations, reminding listeners that "our economy did not fall into decline overnight. Nor did all of our problems begin when the housing market collapsed or the stock market sank," and therefore, it would take awhile to get everything back on track.

President Obama laid out what he called his "blueprint for our future," his federal budget that reflected the reality of the recession. According to the president, the wasteful spending of the past would be stopped, and he had already identified $2 trillion in cuts that could be made over the next decade, without affecting vital services. The president said the first step in a recovery for the United States would be creating and saving jobs for Americans. According to the Obama administration, the ARRA would save or create 3.5 million jobs over two years, most of which would be in the private sector, indicating that the president did not plan to inflate the size of the federal government. He also spoke about how to reverse the credit crisis by starting a new lending fund "that represents the largest effort ever to help provide auto loans, college loans, and small business loans to the consumers and entrepreneurs who keep this economy running." The second part of his credit fix involved the housing market, in dire financial trouble in part because of lenders who had approved mortgages they knew individuals could not repay. His housing plan was meant to help families in danger of foreclosure lower their monthly payments to more manageable levels.

President Obama also spoke to critics of his bailout plan, reiterating his point that he was not trying to rescue Wall Street financiers and executives who earn millions of dollars each year but rather he was trying to save everyday people. "Because when credit is available again," Obama said, "that young family can finally buy a new home. And then some company will hire workers to build it. And then those workers will have money to spend, and if they can get a loan too, maybe they'll finally buy that car, or open their own business. Investors will return to the market, and American families will see their retirement secured once more. Slowly, but surely, confidence will return, and our economy will recover."

President Obama explained that his plan for America would ensure that the nation would never again have to face a recession of this magnitude. But he avoided making lofty promises or overinflating the hopes of Americans looking for an immediate turnaround. To the critics, he said that hope could be found in unlikely places, pointing out an eighth-grade girl from North Carolina who had been invited to the president's speech after writing a letter to legislators asking for help for her school and saying, "We are not quitters."

Foreign Affairs

Economic recovery consumed the bulk of the president's speech, but foreign affairs, and the two ongoing wars, were also included. Unlike his predecessor's last State of the Union speech, President Obama spoke only briefly about the wars in Iraq and Afghanistan, focusing more on how America could restore its image around the world and work with partners abroad to bring about global unity. On the wars, the president said, "We are now carefully reviewing our policies in both wars, and I will soon announce a way forward in Iraq that leaves Iraq to its people and responsibly ends the war." The president vowed that the United States would work to defeat al-Qaida and extremism in Afghanistan and Pakistan, protecting U.S. citizens from terrorism plots. The president also said he wanted to restore "a sense of honesty and accountability" to spending on the war, eliminating supplemental spending practices. "For 7 years, we have been a nation at war," the president said. "No longer will we hide its price."

In his speech President Obama expressed his view that America's foreign policy must include upholding the values that troops in Iraq, Afghanistan, and around the world are fighting for—which, he explained, was why he had ordered the closure of Guantánamo Bay in Cuba. He promised that all terrorists would be brought to justice appropriately, and committed the United States to a policy of never torturing detainees. According to the president, "living our values doesn't make us weaker, it makes us safer and it makes us stronger."

In an effort to combat the international economic crisis and meet the challenges of the twenty-first century, President Obama said the United States would forge new alliances and rekindle old ones. He also indicated that the United States would form a closer bond with nations of the G–20, working to increase demand for American goods and restore international confidence in the economy. "For the world depends on us to have a strong economy, just as our economy depends on the strength of the world's," he said.

The Republicans Respond

Since his election as governor of Louisiana, former Republican congressman Bobby Jindal had been considered an up-and-coming star of the Republican party and a potential candidate in the 2012 presidential election. Jindal's youth, coupled with his Indian heritage, gave the Republican party a combination it rarely had to put front and center on the national stage. Jindal's superstar popularity in his party came to a screeching halt, however, when political analysts began criticizing the eagerness of his rebuttal to Obama's speech. Jindal's simplistic response, and the overwhelmingly negative reaction it received, was unexpected given that just two days earlier, Jindal had given a succinct critique of the ARRA on NBC's *Meet the Press*.

Jindal's speech from the governor's mansion came just days after he had refused to take some of the stimulus money that President Obama had set aside for states and localities in the ARRA. The first state executive to refuse federal recovery funds, Jindal had declared that Louisiana would not accept any money meant to expand unemployment insurance coverage for the state's out-of-work laborers. Jindal said that if the unemployment insurance coverage was expanded at that time, down the road it would lead to higher unemployment insurance taxes. "The federal money in this bill will run out in less than three years for this benefit and our businesses would then be stuck paying the bill," Jindal said. "We must be careful and thoughtful as we examine all the strings attached to the funding in this package. We cannot grow government in an unsustainable way." However, Jindal's criticism of federal government spending programs was called into question given that in 2005 his state had received billions of dollars in aid to help with Hurricane Katrina recovery.

The key point of Jindal's speech was that Obama's plans to fix the economy would continue to increase the federal deficit. "Democratic leaders say their legislation will grow the economy," Jindal said. "What it will do is grow the government, increase our taxes down the line, and saddle future generations with debt." Although the spending programs proposed by the president would have led to more debt, critics argued that the alternatives Jindal proposed would have led to the same problem. Analysts said that Jindal's message did not adequately reflect the gravity of the situation and, given the dire state of the economy, thus seemed too folksy, making him appear "simplistic and almost childish," according to Fox News commentator Juan Williams. Penni Pier, a political communication specialist at Iowa's Wartburg College, said, "Jindal was also trying to be so familiar, he lost credibility. Obama is familiar, but at the same time always a statesman."

Jindal's staff and some Republican commentators, including Rush Limbaugh, tried to counter the backlash. "It's a challenge for anyone to follow Obama," said Jindal's chief of staff Timmy Teepell. "[Obama] is one of the most gifted speakers of our generation." Limbaugh said Jindal was stylistically not as well polished as Obama, but that "[t]he people on our side are making a real mistake if they go after Bobby Jindal. We cannot shun politicians who speak for our beliefs just because we don't like the way he says it."

—Heather Kerrigan

Following is the full text of President Barack Obama's address before a joint session of Congress and the Republican response given by Louisiana governor Bobby Jindal, both on February 24, 2009.

President Obama's Address Before a Joint Session of Congress

February 24, 2009

Madam Speaker, Mr. Vice President, Members of Congress, the First Lady of the United States—she's around here somewhere: I have come here tonight not only to address the distinguished men and women in this great Chamber, but to speak frankly and directly to the men and women who sent us here.

I know that for many Americans watching right now, the state of our economy is a concern that rises above all others, and rightly so. If you haven't been personally affected by this recession, you probably know someone who has: a friend, a neighbor, a member of your family. You don't need to hear another list of statistics to know that our economy is in crisis, because you live it every day. It's the worry you wake up with and the source of sleepless nights. It's the job you thought you'd retire from but now have lost, the business you built your dreams upon that's now hanging by a thread, the college acceptance letter your child had to put back in the envelope. The impact of this recession is real, and it is everywhere.

But while our economy may be weakened and our confidence shaken, though we are living through difficult and uncertain times, tonight I want every American to know this: We will rebuild, we will recover, and the United States of America will emerge stronger than before.

The weight of this crisis will not determine the destiny of this Nation. The answers to our problems don't lie beyond our reach. They exist in our laboratories and our universities, in our fields and our factories, in the imaginations of our entrepreneurs and the pride of the hardest working people on Earth. Those qualities that have made America the greatest force of progress and prosperity in human history, we still possess in ample measure. What is required now is for this country to pull together, confront boldly the challenges we face, and take responsibility for our future once more.

Now, if we're honest with ourselves, we'll admit that for too long, we have not always met these responsibilities as a Government or as a people. I say this not to lay blame or to look backwards, but because it is only by understanding how we arrived at this moment that we'll be able to lift ourselves out of this predicament.

The fact is, our economy did not fall into decline overnight, nor did all of our problems begin when the housing market collapsed or the stock market sank. We have known for decades that our survival depends on finding new sources of energy, yet we import more oil today than ever before. The cost of health care eats up more and more of our savings each year, yet we keep delaying reform. Our children will compete for jobs in a global economy that too many of our schools do not prepare them for. And though all these challenges went unsolved, we still managed to spend more money and pile up more debt, both as individuals and through our Government, than ever before.

In other words, we have lived through an era where too often short-term gains were prized over long-term prosperity, where we failed to look beyond the next payment, the next quarter, or the next election. A surplus became an excuse to transfer wealth to the wealthy instead of an opportunity to invest in our future. Regulations were gutted for the sake of a quick profit at the expense of a healthy market. People bought homes they knew they couldn't afford from banks and lenders who pushed those bad loans anyway. And all the while, critical debates and difficult decisions were put off for some other time, on some other day. Well, that day of reckoning has arrived, and the time to take charge of our future is here.

Now is the time to act boldly and wisely to not only revive this economy, but to build a new foundation for lasting prosperity. Now is the time to jumpstart job creation, restart lending, and invest in areas like energy, health care, and education that will grow our economy, even as we make hard choices to bring our deficit down. That is what my economic agenda is designed to do, and that is what I'd like to talk to you about tonight. It's an agenda that begins with jobs.

As soon as I took office, I asked this Congress to send me a recovery plan by President's Day that would put people back to work and put money in their pockets, not because I believe in bigger Government—I don't—not because I'm not mindful of the massive debt we've inherited—I am. I called for action because the failure to do so would have cost more jobs and caused more hardship. In fact, a failure to act would have worsened our long-term deficit by assuring weak economic growth for years. And that's why I pushed for quick action. And tonight I am grateful that this Congress delivered and pleased to say that the American Recovery and Reinvestment Act is now law.

Over the next 2 years, this plan will save or create 3.5 million jobs. More than 90 percent of these jobs will be in the private sector: jobs rebuilding our roads and bridges, constructing wind turbines and solar panels, laying broadband and expanding mass transit.

Because of this plan, there are teachers who can now keep their jobs and educate our kids, health care professionals can continue caring for our sick. There are 57 police officers who are still on the streets of Minneapolis tonight because this plan prevented the layoffs their department was about to make. Because of this plan, 95 percent of working households in America will receive a tax cut; a tax cut that you will see in your paychecks beginning on April 1st. Because of this plan, families who are struggling to pay tuition costs will receive a $2,500 tax credit for all 4 years of college, and Americans who have lost their jobs in this recession will be able to receive extended unemployment benefits and continued health care coverage to help them weather this storm.

Now, I know there are some in this Chamber and watching at home who are skeptical of whether this plan will work, and I understand that skepticism. Here in Washington, we've all seen how quickly good intentions can turn into broken promises and wasteful spending. And with a plan of this scale comes enormous responsibility to get it right.

And that's why I've asked Vice President Biden to lead a tough, unprecedented oversight effort; because nobody messes with Joe. I—am I right? They don't mess with him. I have told each of my Cabinet, as well as mayors and Governors across the country, that they will be held accountable by me and the American people for every dollar they spend. I've appointed a proven and aggressive Inspector General to ferret out any and all cases of waste and fraud. And we have created a new web site called recovery.gov, so that every American can find out how and where their money is being spent.

So the recovery plan we passed is the first step in getting our economy back on track. But it is just the first step. Because even if we manage this plan flawlessly, there will be no real recovery unless we clean up the credit crisis that has severely weakened our financial system.

I want to speak plainly and candidly about this issue tonight, because every American should know that it directly affects you and your family's well-being. You should also know that the money you've deposited in banks across the country is safe, your insurance is secure, you can rely on the continued operation of our financial system. That's not the source of concern. The concern is that if we do not restart lending in this country, our recovery will be choked off before it even begins.

You see, the flow of credit is the lifeblood of our economy. The ability to get a loan is how you finance the purchase of everything from a home to a car to a college education, how stores stock their shelves, farms buy equipment, and businesses make payroll.

But credit has stopped flowing the way it should. Too many bad loans from the housing crisis have made their way onto the books of too many banks. And with so much debt and so little confidence, these banks are now fearful of lending out any more money to households, to businesses, or even to each other. And when there is no lending, families can't afford to buy homes or cars, so businesses are forced to make layoffs. Our economy suffers even more, and credit dries up even further. That is why this administration is moving swiftly and aggressively to break this destructive cycle, to restore confidence, and restart lending. And we will do so in several ways.

First, we are creating a new lending fund that represents the largest effort ever to help provide auto loans, college loans, and small-business loans to the consumers and entrepreneurs who keep this economy running.

Second, we have launched a housing plan that will help responsible families facing the threat of foreclosure lower their monthly payments and refinance their mortgages. It's a plan that won't help speculators or that neighbor down the street who bought a house he could never hope to afford, but it will help millions of Americans who are struggling with declining home values; Americans who will now be able to take advantage of the lower interest rates that this plan has already helped to bring about. In fact, the average family who refinances today can save nearly $2,000 per year on their mortgage.

Third, we will act with the full force of the Federal Government to ensure that the major banks that Americans depend on have enough confidence and enough money to lend even in more difficult times. And when we learn that a major bank has serious problems, we will hold accountable those responsible, force the necessary adjustments, provide the support to clean up their balance sheets, and assure the continuity of a strong, viable institution that can serve our people and our economy.

Now, I understand that on any given day, Wall Street may be more comforted by an approach that gives bank bailouts with no strings attached and that holds nobody accountable for their reckless decisions. But such an approach won't solve the problem, and our goal is to quicken the day when we restart lending to the American people and American business and end this crisis once and for all.

And I intend to hold these banks fully accountable for the assistance they receive, and this time, they will have to clearly demonstrate how taxpayer dollars result in more lending for the American taxpayer. This time, CEOs won't be able to use taxpayer money to pad their paychecks or buy fancy drapes or disappear on a private jet. Those days are over.

Still, this plan will require significant resources from the Federal Government—and, yes, probably more than we've already set aside. But while the cost of action will be great, I can assure you that the cost of inaction will be far greater, for it could result in an economy that sputters along for not months or years, but perhaps a decade. That would be worse for our deficit, worse for business, worse for you, and worse for the next generation. And I refuse to let that happen.

Now, I understand that when the last administration asked this Congress to provide assistance for struggling banks, Democrats and Republicans alike were infuriated by the mismanagement and the results that followed. So were the American taxpayers; so was I. So I know how unpopular it is to be seen as helping banks right now, especially when everyone is suffering in part from their bad decisions. I promise you, I get it.

But I also know that in a time of crisis, we cannot afford to govern out of anger or yield to the politics of the moment. My job—our job is to solve the problem. Our job is to govern with a sense of responsibility. I will not send—I will not spend a single penny for the purpose of rewarding a single Wall Street executive, but I will do whatever it takes to help the small business that can't pay its workers or the family that has saved and still can't get a mortgage. That's what this is about. It's not about helping banks; it's about helping people—[*applause*].

It's not about helping banks; it's about helping people. Because when credit is available again, that young family can finally buy a new home. And then some company will hire workers to build it. And then those workers will have money to spend. And if they can get a loan too, maybe they'll finally buy that car or open their own business. Investors will return to the market, and American families will see their retirement secured once more. Slowly but surely, confidence will return and our economy will recover.

So I ask this Congress to join me in doing whatever proves necessary, because we cannot consign our Nation to an open-ended recession. And to ensure that a crisis of this magnitude never happens again, I ask Congress to move quickly on legislation that will finally reform our outdated regulatory system. It is time to put in place tough, new, commonsense rules of the road so that our financial market rewards drive and innovation, and punishes shortcuts and abuse.

The recovery plan and the financial stability plan are the immediate steps we're taking to revive our economy in the short term. But the only way to fully restore America's economic strength is to make the long-term investments that will lead to new jobs, new industries, and a renewed ability to compete with the rest of the world. The only way this century will be another American century is if we confront at last the price of our dependence on oil and the high cost of health care, the schools that aren't preparing our children and the mountain of debt they stand to inherit. That is our responsibility.

In the next few days, I will submit a budget to Congress. So often, we've come to view these documents as simply numbers on a page or a laundry list of programs. I see this document differently. I see it as a vision for America, as a blueprint for our future.

My budget does not attempt to solve every problem or address every issue. It reflects the stark reality of what we've inherited, a trillion-dollar deficit, a financial crisis, and a costly recession. Given these realities, everyone in this Chamber, Democrats and Republicans, will have to sacrifice some worthy priorities for which there are no dollars. And that includes me. But that does not mean we can afford to ignore our long-term challenges. I reject the view that says our problems will simply take care of themselves, that says Government has no role in laying the foundation for our common prosperity.

For history tells a different story. History reminds us that at every moment of economic upheaval and transformation, this Nation has responded with bold action and big ideas. In the midst of Civil War, we laid railroad tracks from one coast to another that spurred commerce and industry. From the turmoil of the Industrial Revolution came a system of public high schools that prepared our citizens for a new age. In the wake of war and depression, the GI bill sent a generation to college and created the largest middle class in history. And a twilight struggle for freedom led to a nation of highways, an American on the Moon, and an explosion of technology that still shapes our world. In each case, Government didn't supplant private enterprise; it catalyzed private enterprise. It created the conditions for thousands of entrepreneurs and new businesses to adapt and to thrive.

We are a nation that has seen promise amid peril and claimed opportunity from ordeal. Now we must be that nation again, and that is why, even as it cuts back on programs we don't need, the budget I submit will invest in the three areas that are absolutely critical to our economic future: energy, health care, and education.

It begins with energy. We know the country that harnesses the power of clean, renewable energy will lead the 21st century. And yet, it is China that has launched the largest effort in history to make their economy energy-efficient. We invented solar technology, but we've fallen behind countries like Germany and Japan in producing it. New plug-in hybrids roll off our assembly lines, but they will run on batteries made in Korea. Well, I do not accept a future where the jobs and industries of tomorrow take root beyond our borders, and I know you don't either. It is time for America to lead again.

Thanks to our recovery plan, we will double this Nation's supply of renewable energy in the next 3 years. We've also made the largest investment in basic research funding in American history, an investment that will spur not only new discoveries in energy but breakthroughs in medicine and science and technology.

We will soon lay down thousands of miles of power lines that can carry new energy to cities and towns across this country. And we will put Americans to work making our homes and buildings more efficient so that we can save billions of dollars on our energy bills.

But to truly transform our economy, to protect our security, and save our planet from the ravages of climate change, we need to ultimately make clean, renewable energy the profitable kind of energy. So I ask this Congress to send me legislation that places a market-based cap on carbon pollution and drives the production of more renewable energy in America. That's what we need. And to support that innovation, we will invest $15 billion a year to develop technologies like wind power and solar power, advanced biofuels, clean coal, and more efficient cars and trucks built right here in America.

Speaking of our auto industry, everyone recognizes that years of bad decisionmaking and a global recession have pushed our automakers to the brink. We should not, and will not, protect them from their own bad practices. But we are committed to the goal of a retooled, reimagined auto industry that can compete and win. Millions of jobs depend on it; scores of communities depend on it. And I believe the Nation that invented the automobile cannot walk away from it.

Now, none of this will come without cost, nor will it be easy. But this is America. We don't do what's easy. We do what's necessary to move this country forward.

And for that same reason, we must also address the crushing cost of health care. This is a cost that now causes a bankruptcy in America every 30 seconds. By the end of the year, it could cause 1.5 million Americans to lose their homes. In the last 8 years, premiums have grown four times faster than wages. And in each of these years, 1 million more Americans have lost their health insurance. It is one of the major reasons why small businesses close their doors and corporations ship jobs overseas. And it's one of the largest and fastest growing parts of our budget. Given these facts, we can no longer afford to put health care reform on hold. We can't afford to do it. It's time.

Already, we've done more to advance the cause of health care reform in the last 30 days than we've done in the last decade. When it was days old, this Congress passed a law to provide and protect health insurance for 11 million American children whose parents work full time. Our recovery plan will invest in electronic health records, a new technology that will reduce errors, bring down costs, ensure privacy, and save lives. It will launch a new effort to conquer a disease that has touched the life of nearly every American, including me, by seeking a cure for cancer in our time. And it makes the largest investment ever in preventive care, because that's one of the best ways to keep our people healthy and our costs under control.

This budget builds on these reforms. It includes a historic commitment to comprehensive health care reform, a down payment on the principle that we must have quality, affordable health care for every American. It's a commitment that's paid for in part by efficiencies in our system that are long overdue. And it's a step we must take if we hope to bring down our deficit in the years to come.

Now, there will be many different opinions and ideas about how to achieve reform, and that's why I'm bringing together businesses and workers, doctors and health care providers, Democrats and Republicans to begin work on this issue next week.

I suffer no illusions that this will be an easy process. Once again, it will be hard. But I also know that nearly a century after Teddy Roosevelt first called for reform, the cost of our health care has weighed down our economy and our conscience long enough. So let there be no doubt: Health care reform cannot wait, it must not wait, and it will not wait another year.

The third challenge we must address is the urgent need to expand the promise of education in America. In a global economy where the most valuable skill you can sell is your knowledge, a good education is no longer just a pathway to opportunity, it is a prerequisite. Right now, three-quarters of the fastest growing occupations require more than a high school diploma. And yet, just over half of our citizens have that level of education. We have one of the highest high school dropout rates of any industrialized nation, and half of the students who begin college never finish.

This is a prescription for economic decline, because we know the countries that out-teach us today will out-compete us tomorrow. That is why it will be the goal of this administration to ensure that every child has access to a complete and competitive education, from the day they are born to the day they begin a career. That is a promise we have to make to the children of America.

Already, we've made historic investment in education through the economic recovery plan. We've dramatically expanded early childhood education and will continue to improve its quality, because we know that the most formative learning comes in those first years of life. We've made college affordable for nearly 7 million more students—7 million. And we have provided the resources necessary to prevent painful cuts and teacher layoffs that would set back our children's progress.

But we know that our schools don't just need more resources, they need more reform. And that is why this budget creates new teachers—new incentives for teacher performance, pathways for advancement, and rewards for success. We'll invest in innovative programs that are already helping schools meet high standards and close achievement gaps, and we will expand our commitment to charter schools.

It is our responsibility as lawmakers and as educators to make this system work. But it is the responsibility of every citizen to participate in it. So tonight I ask every American to commit to at least 1 year or more of higher education or career training. This can be community college or a 4-year school, vocational training or an apprenticeship. But whatever the training may be, every American will need to get more than a high school diploma.

And dropping out of high school is no longer an option. It's not just quitting on yourself, it's quitting on your country, and this country needs and values the talents of every American. That's why we will support—we will provide the support necessary for all young Americans to complete college and meet a new goal. By 2020, America will once again have the highest proportion of college graduates in the world. That is a goal we can meet. That's a goal we can meet.

Now, I know that the price of tuition is higher than ever, which is why if you are willing to volunteer in your neighborhood or give back to your community or serve your country, we will make sure that you can afford a higher education. And to encourage a renewed spirit of national service for this and future generations, I ask Congress to send me the bipartisan legislation that bears the name of Senator Orrin Hatch, as well as an American who has never stopped asking what he can do for his country, Senator Edward Kennedy.

These education policies will open the doors of opportunity for our children, but it is up to us to ensure they walk through them. In the end, there is no program or policy that can substitute for a parent, for a mother or father who will attend those parent/teacher conferences or help with homework or turn off the TV, put away the video games, read to their child. I speak to you not just as a President, but as a father, when I say that responsibility for our children's education must begin at home. That is not a Democratic issue or a Republican issue; that's an American issue.

There is, of course, another responsibility we have to our children. And that's the responsibility to ensure that we do not pass on to them a debt they cannot pay. That is critical. [*Applause*] I agree, absolutely. See, I know we can get some consensus in here. [*Laughter*] With the deficit we inherited, the cost of the crisis we face, and the long-term challenges we must meet, it has never been more important to ensure that as our economy recovers, we do what it takes to bring this deficit down. That is critical.

Now, I'm proud that we passed a recovery plan free of earmarks, and I want to pass a budget next year that ensures that each dollar we spend reflects only our most important national priorities.

And yesterday I held a fiscal summit where I pledged to cut the deficit in half by the end of my first term in office. My administration has also begun to go line by line through the Federal budget in order to eliminate wasteful and ineffective programs. As you can imagine, this is a process that will take some time. But we have already identified $2 trillion in savings over the next decade.

In this budget, we will end education programs that don't work and end direct payments to large agribusiness that don't need them. We'll eliminate the no-bid contracts that have wasted billions in Iraq and reform our defense budget so that we're not paying for cold war–era weapons systems we don't use. We will root out the waste and fraud and abuse in our Medicare program that doesn't make our seniors any healthier. We will restore a sense of fairness and balance to our Tax Code by finally ending the tax breaks for corporations that ship our jobs overseas.

In order to save our children from a future of debt, we will also end the tax breaks for the wealthiest 2 percent of Americans. Now, let me be clear—let me be absolutely clear, because I know you'll end up hearing some of the same claims that rolling back these tax breaks means a massive tax increase on the American people: If your family earns less than $250,000 a year, a quarter million dollars a year, you will not see your taxes increased a single dime. I repeat: Not one single dime. In fact—not a dime—in fact, the recovery plan provides a tax cut—that's right, a tax cut—for 95 percent of working families. And by the way, these checks are on the way.

Now, to preserve our long-term fiscal health, we must also address the growing costs in Medicare and Social Security. Comprehensive health care reform is the best way to strengthen Medicare for years to come. And we must also begin a conversation on how to do the same for Social Security, while creating tax-free universal savings accounts for all Americans.

Finally, because we're also suffering from a deficit of trust, I am committed to restoring a sense of honesty and accountability to our budget. That is why this budget looks ahead 10 years and accounts for spending that was left out under the old rules. And for the first time, that includes the full cost of fighting in Iraq and Afghanistan. For 7 years, we have been a nation at war. No longer will we hide its price.

Along with our outstanding national security team, I'm now carefully reviewing our policies in both wars, and I will soon announce a way forward in Iraq that leaves Iraq to its people and responsibly ends this war.

And with our friends and allies, we will forge a new and comprehensive strategy for Afghanistan and Pakistan to defeat Al Qaida and combat extremism, because I will not allow terrorists to plot against the American people from safe havens halfway around the world. We will not allow it.

As we meet here tonight, our men and women in uniform stand watch abroad and more are readying to deploy. To each and every one of them and to the families who bear the quiet burden of their absence, Americans are united in sending one message: We honor your service; we are inspired by your sacrifice; and you have our unyielding support.

To relieve the strain on our forces, my budget increases the number of our soldiers and marines. And to keep our sacred trust with those who serve, we will raise their pay and give our veterans the expanded health care and benefits that they have earned.

To overcome extremism, we must also be vigilant in upholding the values our troops defend, because there is no force in the world more powerful than the example of America. And that is why I have ordered the closing of the detention center at Guantanamo Bay and will seek swift and certain justice for captured terrorists. Because living our values doesn't make us weaker, it makes us safer and it makes us stronger. And that is why I can stand here tonight and say without exception or equivocation that the United States of America does not torture. We can make that commitment here tonight.

In words and deeds, we are showing the world that a new era of engagement has begun. For we know that America cannot meet the threats of this century alone, but the world cannot meet them without America. We cannot shun the negotiating table, nor ignore the foes or forces that could do us harm. We are instead called to move forward with the sense of confidence and candor that serious times demand.

To seek progress towards a secure and lasting peace between Israel and her neighbors, we have appointed an envoy to sustain our effort. To meet the challenges of the 21st century—from terrorism to nuclear proliferation, from pandemic disease to cyber threats to crushing poverty—we will strengthen old alliances, forge new ones, and use all elements of our national power.

And to respond to an economic crisis that is global in scope, we are working with the nations of the G–20 to restore confidence in our financial system, avoid the possibility of escalating protectionism, and spur demand for American goods in markets across the globe. For the world depends on us having a strong economy, just as our economy depends on the strength of the world's.

As we stand at this crossroads of history, the eyes of all people in all nations are once again upon us, watching to see what we do with this moment, waiting for us to lead. Those of us gathered here tonight have been called to govern in extraordinary times. It is a tremendous burden, but also a great privilege, one that has been entrusted to few generations of Americans. For in our hands lies the ability to shape our world for good or for ill.

I know that it's easy to lose sight of this truth, to become cynical and doubtful, consumed with the petty and the trivial. But in my life, I have also learned that hope is found in unlikely places, that inspiration often comes not from those with the most power or celebrity, but from the dreams and aspirations of ordinary Americans who are anything but ordinary.

I think of Leonard Abess, a bank president from Miami who reportedly cashed out of his company, took a $60 million bonus, and gave it out to all 399 people who worked for him, plus another 72 who used to work for him. He didn't tell anyone, but when the local newspaper found out, he simply said, "I knew some of these people since I was 7 years old. It didn't feel right getting the money myself."

I think about Greensburg, Kansas, a town that was completely destroyed by a tornado, but is being rebuilt by its residents as a global example of how clean energy can power an entire community, how it can bring jobs and businesses to a place where piles of bricks and rubble once lay. "The tragedy was terrible," said one of the men who helped them rebuild. "But the folks here know that it also provided an incredible opportunity."

I think about Ty'Sheoma Bethea, the young girl from that school I visited in Dillon, South Carolina, a place where the ceilings leak, the paint peels off the walls, and they have to stop teaching six times a day because the train barrels by their classroom. She had been told that her school is hopeless, but the other day after class she went to the public library and typed up a letter to the people sitting in this Chamber. She even asked her principal for the money to buy a stamp. The letter asks us for help and says: "We are just students trying to become lawyers, doctors, Congressmen like yourself, and one day President, so we can make a change to not just the State of South Carolina but also the world. We are not quitters." That's what she said: "We are not quitters."

These words and these stories tell us something about the spirit of the people who sent us here. They tell us that even in the most trying times, amid the most difficult circumstances, there is a generosity, a resilience, a decency, and a determination that perseveres, a willingness to take responsibility for our future and for posterity. Their resolve must be our inspiration. Their concerns must be our cause. And we must show them and all our people that we are equal to the task before us.

I know—look, I know that we haven't agreed on every issue thus far. [*Laughter*] There are surely times in the future where we will part ways. But I also know that every American who is sitting here tonight loves this country and wants it to succeed. I know that. That must be the starting point for every debate we have in the coming months and where we return after those debates are done. That is the foundation on which the American people expect us to build common ground.

And if we do, if we come together and lift this Nation from the depths of this crisis, if we put our people back to work and restart the engine of our prosperity, if we confront without fear the challenges of our time and summon that enduring spirit of an America that does not quit, then someday years from now our children can tell their children that this was the time when we performed, in the words that are carved into this very Chamber, "something worthy to be remembered."

Thank you. God bless you, and may God bless the United States of America. Thank you.

SOURCE: U.S. Executive Office of the President. "Address Before a Joint Session of the Congress." *Daily Compilation of Presidential Documents* 2009, no. 00105 (February 24, 2009). www.gpo.gov/fdsys/pkg/DCPD-200900105/html/DCPD-200900105.htm.

Louisiana Governor Bobby Jindal
Responds to the President's Address

February 24, 2009

Good evening. I'm Bobby Jindal, Governor of Louisiana.

Tonight, we witnessed a great moment in the history of our Republic. In the very chamber where Congress once voted to abolish slavery, our first African-American

President stepped forward to address the state of our union. With his speech tonight, the President completed a redemptive journey that took our nation from Independence Hall . . . to Gettysburg . . . to the lunch counter . . . and now, finally, the Oval Office.

Regardless of party, all Americans are moved by the President's personal story—the son of an American mother and a Kenyan father, who grew up to become leader of the free world. Like the President's father, my parents came to this country from a distant land. When they arrived in Baton Rouge, my mother was already 4½ months pregnant. I was what folks in the insurance industry now call a "pre-existing condition." To find work, my dad picked up the yellow pages and started calling local businesses. Even after landing a job, he could still not afford to pay for my delivery—so he worked out an installment plan with the doctor. Fortunately for me, he never missed a payment.

As I grew up, my mom and dad taught me the values that attracted them to this country—and they instilled in me an immigrant's wonder at the greatness of America. As a child, I remember going to the grocery store with my dad. Growing up in India, he had seen extreme poverty. And as we walked through the aisles, looking at the endless variety on the shelves, he would tell me: "Bobby, Americans can do anything." I still believe that to this day. Americans can do anything. When we pull together, there is no challenge we cannot overcome.

As the President made clear this evening, we are now in a time of challenge. Many of you listening tonight have lost jobs. Others have seen your college and retirement savings dwindle. Many of you are worried about losing your health care and your homes. And you are looking to your elected leaders in Washington for solutions.

Republicans are ready to work with the new President to provide those solutions. Here in my state of Louisiana, we don't care what party you belong to if you have good ideas to make life better for our people. We need more of that attitude from both Democrats and Republicans in our nation's capital. All of us want our economy to recover and our nation to prosper. So where we agree, Republicans must be the President's strongest partners. And where we disagree, Republicans have a responsibility to be candid and offer better ideas for a path forward.

Today in Washington, some are promising that government will rescue us from the economic storms raging all around us.

Those of us who lived through Hurricane Katrina, we have our doubts.

Let me tell you a story.

During Katrina, I visited Sheriff Harry Lee, a Democrat and a good friend of mine. When I walked into his makeshift office I'd never seen him so angry. He was yelling into the phone: "Well, I'm the Sheriff and if you don't like it you can come and arrest me!" I asked him: "Sheriff, what's got you so mad?" He told me that he had put out a call for volunteers to come with their boats to rescue people who were trapped on their rooftops by the floodwaters. The boats were all lined up ready to go—when some bureaucrat showed up and told them they couldn't go out on the water unless they had proof of insurance and registration. I told him, "Sheriff, that's ridiculous." And before I knew it, he was yelling into the phone: "Congressman Jindal is here, and he says you can come and arrest him too!" Harry just told the boaters to ignore the bureaucrats and start rescuing people.

There is a lesson in this experience: The strength of America is not found in our government. It is found in the compassionate hearts and enterprising spirit of our citizens. We are grateful for the support we have received from across the nation for the ongoing recovery efforts. This spirit got Louisiana through the hurricanes—and this spirit will get our nation through the storms we face today.

To solve our current problems, Washington must lead. But the way to lead is not to raise taxes and put more money and power in hands of Washington politicians. The way to lead is by empowering you—the American people. Because we believe that Americans can do anything.

That is why Republicans put forward plans to create jobs by lowering income tax rates for working families . . . cutting taxes for small businesses . . . strengthening incentives for businesses to invest in new equipment and hire new workers . . . and stabilizing home values by creating a new tax credit for home-buyers. These plans would cost less and create more jobs.

But Democratic leaders in Congress rejected this approach. Instead of trusting us to make wise decisions with our own money, they passed the largest government spending bill in history—with a price tag of more than $1 trillion with interest. While some of the projects in the bill make sense, their legislation is larded with wasteful spending. It includes $300 million to buy new cars for the government, $8 billion for high-speed rail projects, such as a "magnetic levitation" line from Las Vegas to Disneyland, and $140 million for something called "volcano monitoring." Instead of monitoring volcanoes, what Congress should be monitoring is the eruption of spending in Washington, DC.

Democratic leaders say their legislation will grow the economy. What it will do is grow the government, increase our taxes down the line, and saddle future generations with debt. Who among us would ask our children for a loan, so we could spend money we do not have, on things we do not need? That is precisely what the Democrats in Congress just did. It's irresponsible. And it's no way to strengthen our economy, create jobs, or build a prosperous future for our children.

In Louisiana, we took a different approach. Since I became governor, we cut more than 250 earmarks from our state budget. And to create jobs for our citizens, we cut taxes six times—including the largest income tax cut in the history of our state. We passed those tax cuts with bipartisan majorities. Republicans and Democrats put aside their differences, and worked together to make sure our people could keep more of what they earn. If it can be done in Baton Rouge, surely it can be done in Washington, DC.

To strengthen our economy, we need urgent action to keep energy prices down. All of us remember what it felt like to pay $4 at the pump—and unless we act now, those prices will return. To stop that from happening, we need to increase conservation . . . increase energy efficiency . . . increase the use of alternative and renewable fuels . . . increase our use of nuclear power—and increase drilling for oil and gas here at home. We believe that Americans can do anything—and if we unleash the innovative spirit of our citizens, we can achieve energy independence.

To strengthen our economy, we also need to address the crisis in health care. Republicans believe in a simple principle: No American should have to worry about losing their health coverage—period. We stand for universal access to affordable health care coverage. We oppose universal government-run health care. Health care decisions should be made by doctors and patients—not by government bureaucrats. We believe Americans can do anything—and if we put aside partisan politics and work together, we can make our system of private medicine affordable and accessible for every one of our citizens.

To strengthen our economy, we also need to make sure every child in America gets the best possible education. After Katrina, we reinvented the New Orleans school system—opening dozens of new charter schools, and creating a new scholarship program that is giving parents the chance to send their children to private or parochial schools of their choice. We believe that, with the proper education, the children of America can do anything. And it should not take a devastating storm to bring this kind of innovation to education in our country.

To strengthen our economy, we must promote confidence in America by ensuring ours is the most ethical and transparent system in the world. In my home state, there used to be [a] saying: At any given time, half of Louisiana is under water—and the other half is under indictment. No one says that anymore. Last year, we passed some of the strongest ethics laws in the nation—and today, Louisiana has turned her back on the corruption of the past. We need to bring transparency to Washington, DC—so we can rid our Capitol of corruption . . . and ensure we never see the passage of another trillion dollar spending bill that Congress has not even read and the American people haven't even seen.

As we take these steps, we must remember for all our troubles at home, dangerous enemies still seek our destruction. Now is no time to dismantle the defenses that have protected this country for hundreds of years, or make deep cuts in funding for our troops. America's fighting men and women can do anything. And if we give them the resources they need, they will stay on the offensive . . . defeat our enemies . . . and protect us from harm.

In all these areas, Republicans want to work with President Obama. We appreciate his message of hope—but sometimes it seems we look for hope in different places. Democratic leaders in Washington place their hope in the federal government. We place our hope in you—the American people. In the end, it comes down to an honest and fundamental disagreement about the proper role of government. We oppose the National Democrats' view that says—the way to strengthen our country is to increase dependence on government. We believe the way to strengthen our country is to restrain spending in Washington, and empower individuals and small businesses to grow our economy and create jobs.

In recent years, these distinctions in philosophy became less clear—because our party got away from its principles. You elected Republicans to champion limited government, fiscal discipline, and personal responsibility. Instead, Republicans went along with earmarks and big government spending in Washington. Republicans lost your trust—and rightly so.

Tonight, on behalf of our leaders in Congress and my fellow Republican governors, I say: Our party is determined to regain your trust. We will do so by standing up for the principles that we share . . . the principles you elected us to fight for . . . the principles that built this into the greatest, most prosperous country on earth.

A few weeks ago, the President warned that our nation is facing a crisis that he said "we may not be able to reverse." Our troubles are real, to be sure. But don't let anyone tell you that we cannot recover—or that America's best days are behind her. This is the nation that cast off the scourge of slavery . . . overcame the Great Depression . . . prevailed in two World Wars . . . won the struggle for civil rights . . . defeated the Soviet menace . . . and responded with determined courage to the attacks of September 11, 2001. The American spirit has triumphed over almost every form of adversity known to man—and the American spirit will triumph again.

We can have confidence in our future—because, amid today's challenges, we also count many blessings: We have the most innovative citizens . . . the most abundant resources . . . the most resilient economy . . . the most powerful military . . . and the freest political system in the history of the world. My fellow citizens, never forget: We are Americans. And like my dad said years ago, Americans can do anything.

Thank you for listening. God bless you. And God bless America.

SOURCE: Office of the Governor of Louisiana. "Governor Bobby Jindal: 'Americans Can Do Anything.'" February 24, 2009. www.gov.state.la.us/index.cfm?md=newsroom&tmp=detail&catID=3&articleID= 1032.

OTHER HISTORIC DOCUMENTS OF INTEREST

FROM THIS VOLUME

FROM PREVIOUS *HISTORIC DOCUMENTS*

Plane Crash-Lands in the Hudson River

FEBRUARY 24, 2009

On January 15, 2009, U.S. Airways Flight 1549, flying from LaGuardia Airport in New York City to Charlotte, North Carolina, hit a flock of Canadian geese minutes after takeoff, shutting down both of the plane's engines. With no power to get the plane back to LaGuardia, Captain Chesley ("Sully") Sullenberger brought the plane down safely in the Hudson River, in view of the Manhattan skyline. On impact, a hole was ripped in the underside of the plane, causing the back to begin filling up with water. Amazingly, all 155 people on board survived: 150 passengers, three flight attendants, and two pilots. The captain and his crew were hailed as heroes.

FLIGHT 1549

When the pilots brought Flight 1549 down in the frigid Hudson River, it had been airborne for less than six minutes. First Officer Jeffrey Skiles, on his first flight in an Airbus A320 after having passed the certification for that type of plane, was at the controls when a flock of geese flew toward the plane. When the engines lost thrust, Sully took control of the plane and radioed the New York Tracon air traffic control tower—which handles flights after they leave LaGuardia or Teterboro Airports—for assistance. Initially, the air traffic controller asked Sullenberger to bring the plane back to LaGuardia and stopped all inbound and outbound traffic to allow for an emergency landing. When the air traffic controller was told the plane would not be able to make it to LaGuardia, after clearing the George Washington Bridge by just 900 feet, he encouraged the pilot to land at nearby Teterboro Airport in New Jersey. Shortly thereafter, the plane made its last transmission, saying, "We're going to be in the Hudson." The air traffic controller responded, "I'm sorry. Say again?" but there was no reply.

Captain Sullenberger, a certified glider pilot, drew on his years of training and experience to safely "ditch" the plane into the Hudson River. He put the plane into the water near operating boats, knowing the emergency response would be much faster. Landing any plane on water is not an easy task, especially gliding in as the Airbus was forced to do. Flight 1549 was traveling at approximately 150 miles per hour when it crashed in the Hudson River. Luckily, because of the mitigating ground effect, a cushion of air generated by the plane when it flies low to the ground, the plane was not traveling at the speed it would have been otherwise, which could have resulted in a devastating outcome. Police, coast guard, fire crews, and even passenger ferries came quickly to rescue passengers from the plane, many of whom were standing on the plane's wings as it slowly sank into the water. Other passengers swam to shore or nearby boats. The inclusion of many units in the rescue effort, as well as the number of passengers who began walking home, posed a problem for U.S. Airways as it tried to account for all passengers aboard the plane. No passenger on the flight suffered a life-threatening injury, including a baby who was thrown to safety into a life raft, although some passengers were treated for hypothermia and a flight attendant suffered a deep cut in her leg.

Captain Sullenberger was the last person to leave the plane after twice sweeping through the cabin to ensure that no one was left on board. Thirty minutes after the crash, Sullenberger made a call to U.S. Airways headquarters and was nearly hung up on. Sullenberger was told, "Sorry, captain. I can't talk to you now. We have an airplane in the Hudson." Sullenberger promptly responded, "I was flying the airplane."

PRAISE FOR CAPTAIN AND CREW

Praise for the crew and for Captain Sullenberger, who was an air force pilot before joining U.S. Airways in 1980, came quickly from across the country. Passengers called Sullenberger a hero. President George W. Bush commented, "Laura and I are inspired by the skill and heroism of the flight crew as well as the dedication and selflessness of the emergency responders and volunteers who rescued passengers from the icy waters of the Hudson." New York City mayor Michael Bloomberg awarded the crew with the key to the city, and New York's governor, David Paterson, said, "We have had a miracle on 34th Street, I believe now we have a miracle on the Hudson."

The crew was also awarded the Master's Medal of the Guild of Air Pilots and Air Navigators. The organization, upon giving the award, said, "This emergency ditching and evacuation, with the loss of no lives, is a heroic and unique aviation achievement."

Sullenberger became on overnight celebrity after his dramatic landing, appearing on multiple news programs to share his story. Then President-elect Barack Obama invited Sullenberger to attend the presidential inauguration a few days after the crash; Sullenberger was also given the privilege of leading the 2010 Rose Bowl parade. By the end of 2009, books had already been written about the captain and his crew, as well as the tales of passengers on board the flight. Sullenberger took the opportunity to write his own book, *Highest Duty: My Search for What Really Matters,* and he embarked on a cross-country tour to promote it.

BIRD STRIKES AND THE INVESTIGATION

Bird strikes on passenger aircrafts are not uncommon. According to the Federal Aviation Administration (FAA), between 1990 and 2005, 65,000 bird strikes on airplanes were reported. Bird Strike Committee USA, a group that works to gather data on bird strikes in an effort to decrease their frequency, reports that since 1975, five airplanes have had major accidents caused by birds. Given the high likelihood that a bird strike had caused the crash of Flight 1549, the U.S. Department of Agriculture was called in to assist the FAA and National Transportation Safety Board (NTSB) with the investigation into the crash.

After the plane was extracted from the Hudson River on January 18, 2009, the engines were sent to the manufacturer in Ohio, where the NTSB could conduct an in-depth investigation. An initial report released January 16, 2009, suggested that a bird strike had caused the plane crash, which was later confirmed by the cockpit data recorder and flight data recorder. The NTSB also confirmed that debris from Canadian geese had been found in both engines in addition to "dents on both the spinner and inlet lip of the engine cowling." To be doubly certain, material was collected from both engines and sent to the Smithsonian Institution in Washington, D.C., for scientists to identify the type of bird that had struck the plane. In an effort to crackdown on the Canadian goose problem near LaGuardia and New York's other airports, in June and July 2009, the U.S. Department of Agriculture Wildlife Services captured and killed more than 1,000 Canadian geese, and coated eggs with oil to ensure that they not hatch.

SULLY AND HIS CREW TESTIFY BEFORE CONGRESS

Captain Sullenberger and his crew were asked to speak before the U.S. House of Representatives Transportation and Infrastructure Subcommittee on Aviation on February 24, 2009, to give their account of the accident. While Sullenberger began by talking about the flight, he focused a majority of his speech on the financial conditions of the airline industry and pilots, using the opportunity as a forum to tell Congress that without better pay for pilots, the next plane that has to make an emergency landing might not be as lucky as his had been.

In testifying on the crash, air traffic controller Patrick Harten, who had not previously spoken about the flight, said, "People don't survive landings on the Hudson River. . . . I thought it was his own death sentence. . . . I believed at that moment that I was going to be the last person to talk to anyone on that plane alive." Harten said that the worst part about the crash of Flight 1549 was the aftermath. "During the emergency itself, I was hyper-focused. I had no choice but to think and act quickly, and remain calm. But when it was over, it hit me hard. It felt like hours before I learned about the heroic water landing that Captain Sullenberger and his crew had managed. Even after I learned the truth, I could not shake the image of tragedy in my mind. Every time I saw the survivors on the television, I imagined grieving widows."

Sullenberger spoke at length about his pay, which had been cut 40 percent during recent years, and also his pension plan, which had been terminated and replaced by a federal program of the Pension Benefit Guaranty Corporation that Sullenberger said was "worth pennies on the dollar." While the recent financial collapse in the United States had led many airlines to go out of business, Sullenberger said the strained financial status of pilots and flight crews had existed for much longer, since the deregulation of the airline industry in the 1970s.

The current pay rates for flight crews, said Sullenberger, had placed "pilots and their families in untenable financial situations. . . . I do not know a single professional airline pilot who wants his or her children to follow in their footsteps." Sullenberger said that he started his own consulting business and had been working two jobs for many years just to make ends meet, all the while being expected to maintain the safety of hundreds of thousands of passengers on his flights each year. His copilot, Jeffrey Skiles, said that he had been in the same situation. "For the last six years, I have worked seven days a week between my two jobs just to maintain a middle class standard of living."

According to Sullenberger and Skiles, if the airline industry continued to lower the pay for pilots and flight crews, the results could diminish the safety of the flying public, because airlines will be less able to recruit skilled, motivated pilots. According to Skiles, "experienced crews in the cockpit will be a thing of the past." Sullenberger echoed his comments saying, "I am worried that the airline-piloting profession will not be able to continue to attract the best and the brightest. The current experience and skills of our country's professional airline pilots come from investments made years ago when we were able to attract the ambitious, talented people who now frequently seek lucrative professional careers" somewhere else.

—Heather Kerrigan

Following is the text of the speech by Capt. Chesley Sullenberger given before the U.S. House of Representatives Transportation and Infrastructure Subcommittee on Aviation on February 24, 2009.

Captain Sullenberger Testifies Before Congress

DOCUMENT

February 24, 2009

Mr. COSTELLO. And now we will recognize Captain Sullenberger. And let me say that for all of our witnesses on both the first and second panel, that we will be under the 5-minute rule. We would ask that you summarize your testimony. Your entire testimony will be submitted for the record. And of course after your testimony, we will get to questions from Members.

So Captain Sullenberger, you are recognized.

Mr. SULLENBERGER. Thank you, Chairman Costello, Ranking Members Mica and Petri, and other Members of the Committee. It is my great honor to appear before the Aviation Subcommittee today.

I am proud of the fact that I have been involved in aviation for the last 42 years. During that time, I have served our country as a U.S. Air Force pilot, served as an Air Line Pilots Association local Air Safety Committee Chairman, accident investigator, and national technical Committee Member. I have amassed a total flying time of almost 20,000 hours, and flown approximately 1 million passengers in my 29 years as a professional airline pilot.

I have served as a check airman and a Crew Resource Management course developer and facilitator. I am also the founder of Safety Reliability Methods, Inc.

Before I begin, I must first say that my heart goes out to all those affected by the tragic loss of Continental Connection Colgan Air Flight 3407. Words cannot express my sadness and grief at the loss of 50 lives. The families of those no longer with us are in my thoughts and in my heart.

The events of January 15, 2009, have been well documented, and rather than recite them now in great detail, I want only to reiterate to the Subcommittee that the successful outcome was achieved by the actions of many. Lives were saved due to the combination of a very experienced, well-trained crew, First Officer Jeff Skiles, and Flight Attendants Donna Dent, Doreen Welsh, and Sheila Dail, all of whom acted in a remarkable display of teamwork, along with expert air traffic controllers, the orderly cooperation of our cool-headed passengers, and the quick and determined actions of the professional and volunteer first responders in New York City.

The events of January 15th serve as a reminder to us all of the daily devotion to duty of the many thousands of aviation professionals who keep air travel safe, and also as a reminder of what is really at stake. I, like thousands of my professional airline pilots, know that flying a large commercial airline is a tremendous responsibility. We clearly understand that our passengers put their lives in our hands. We know that we must always be prepared; we must always anticipate; we must always be vigilant. Expecting the unexpected and having an effective plan for dealing with it must be in the very makeup of every professional airline pilot.

I am not only proud of my crew, I am proud of my profession. Flying has been my lifelong passion. I count myself fortunate to have spent my life in the profession I love, with colleagues whom I respect and admire.

But while I love my profession, I do not like what has happened to it. I would not be doing my duty if I did not report to you that I am deeply troubled about its future. Americans have been experiencing huge economic difficulties in recent months, but airline employees have been experiencing those challenges and more for 8 years. We have been hit by an economic tsunami.

September 11th, bankruptcies, fluctuating fuel prices, mergers, loss of pensions, and revolving-door management teams who have used airline employees as an ATM have left the people who work for the airlines in the United States with extreme economic difficulties. It is an incredible testament to the collective character, professionalism, and dedication of my colleagues in the industry that they are still able to function at such a high level.

It is my personal experience that my decision to remain in the profession I love has come at a great financial cost to me and to my family. My pay has been cut 40 percent, my pension, like most airline pensions, has been terminated and replaced by a PBGC guarantee worth only pennies on the dollar.

While airline pilots are by no means alone in our financial struggles, I want to acknowledge how difficult it is for everyone right now. It is important to underscore that the terms of our employment have changed dramatically from when I began my career, leading to an untenable financial situation for pilots and their families. When my company offered pilots who had been laid off the chance to return to work, 60 percent refused.

Members, I attempt to speak accurately and plainly, so please do not think I exaggerate when I say I do not know a single professional airline pilot who wants his or her children to follow in their footsteps. I am worried that the airline piloting profession will not be able to continue to attract the best and the brightest.

The current experience and skills of our country's professional airline pilots come from investments made years ago, when we were able to attract the ambitious, talented people who now frequently seek professional careers elsewhere. That past investment was an indispensable element in our commercial aviation infrastructure, vital to safe air travel and our country's economy and security. If we do not sufficiently value the airline piloting profession and future pilots are less experienced and less skilled, it logically follows that we will see negative consequences to the flying public and to our country.

We face remarkable challenges in our industry. In order to ensure economic security and an uncompromising approach to passenger safety, management must work with labor to bargain in good faith, we must find collective solutions that address the huge economic issues we face in recruiting and retaining the experienced and highly-skilled professionals that the industry requires and that passenger safety demands. But further, we must develop and sustain an environment in every airline and aviation organization, a culture that balances the competing needs of accountability and learning.

We must create and maintain the trust that is the absolutely essential element of a successful and sustainable safety reporting system to detect and correct deficiencies before they lead to an accident. We must not let the economic and financial pressures detract from a focus on constantly improving our safety measures and engaging in ongoing and comprehensive training. In aviation, the bottom line is that the single most important piece of safety equipment is an experienced, well-trained pilot.

Despite the bad economic news we have experienced in recent times, despite the many challenges we face as a country, I have faith in America, in our people, in our promise. I briefly touched upon some major problems in my industry today, but I do not believe that they are intractable should we decide to work collectively to solve them.

We all have roles to play in this effort. Despite the economic turbulence hitting our industry, the airline companies must refocus their attention and their resources on the recruitment and retention of highly-experienced and well-trained pilots, and make that a priority that is at least equal to their financial bottom line.

Jeff and I and our fellow pilots will fly our planes and continue to upgrade our education and our skills while we attempt to provide for our families. Patrick and the other talented air traffic controllers will continue to guide us safely through the skies. Our passengers will spend their hard-earned money to pay for their travel. And our flight attendants, mechanics, ground crews, and administrative personnel will deal with the thousands of constant details and demands that keep our planes safely in the air.

You can help us, Mr. Chairman, honorable Members, to work together across party lines and can demand or legislate that labor, management, safety experts, educators, technical experts, and everyday Americans join together to find solutions to these problems.

We all honor our responsibilities in good faith and respect one another. We must keep the American commercial aviation industry safe and affordable for passengers, and financially viable for those who work in the industry day-to-day. And for those talented young men and women considering what to do with their lives, we must restore the narrative of a compelling career path in aviation with sufficient economic resources to once again make this vision a reality.

Thank you for your kind attention and for the opportunity to share my experiences with this Committee.

SOURCE: U.S. House of Representatives Subcommittee on Aviation. Testimony from Captain Chesley Sullenberger. "U.S. Airways Flight 1549 Accident." February 24, 2009. www.gpo.gov/fdsys/pkg/CHRG-111hhrg11147866/pdf/CHRG-111hhrg11147866.pdf.

OTHER HISTORIC DOCUMENTS OF INTEREST

FROM PREVIOUS HISTORIC DOCUMENTS

President Obama Announces Timeline for Ending Iraq War

FEBRUARY 27, 2009

When President Barack Obama stood before 8,000 Marines at Camp Lejeune, North Carolina, on February 27, 2009, explaining his Iraq exit strategy, it had been nearly six years since the United States first entered Iraq. The U.S. death toll in the war stood at 4,425. "By any measure, this has already been a long war," the president said. "Today, I have come to speak to you about how the war in Iraq will end."

Bringing troops out of Iraq was one of the central points in Obama's presidential campaign. He had promised to bring troops home within sixteen months of his inauguration, but the plan he presented at Camp Lejeune would take nineteen months, which had been described by his advisors as a necessary delay of the president's promised time frame because of security concerns on the ground in Iraq.

The Obama withdrawal plan was designed to give the U.S. military more flexibility in moving troops to Afghanistan, a nation where the security situation was increasingly deteriorating, while also freeing up money in the U.S. budget to pay for such options.

OBAMA'S WITHDRAWAL PLAN

Secretary of Defense Robert Gates, chair of the Joint Chiefs of Staff Admiral Mike Mullen, the president, and other senior officials from the Pentagon initially explored three different options for leaving Iraq. The first option was withdrawal in sixteen months, the second was withdrawal in nineteen months, and the third option was withdrawal in twenty-three months. The nineteen-month plan that was chosen featured a steady drawdown of troops, to ensure stability in Iraq during the transition.

At the time of President Obama's announcement, there were 142,000 U.S. troops in Iraq, and under an agreement established by President George W. Bush, troops had already left Iraq's city centers. The plan President Obama proposed at Camp Lejeune would remove between 92,000 to 107,000 troops from Iraq by August 2010. The 50,000 remaining troops were to stay in Iraq until the end of 2011 to continue training Iraqi forces and ensure a smooth transition to a self-governing Iraq without U.S. support. Those remaining troops were to work to transfer power to Iraqi forces and advise them on how best to handle their new situation, including what to do about the growing insurgency in the north, where Kurdish-Arab tensions remained on the rise. Obama's military advisors believed this drawdown plan would satisfy those Americans calling for a quick end to the Iraq war and also satisfy the Iraqis, who still required assistance stabilizing the government and pacifying the insurgency.

"The president has been struck by the fact that there has been a meeting of the minds in a lot of ways among his military advisors about what would be a safe and responsible way to redeploy our troops while protecting our interests in Iraq," one senior administration official told the *Washington Post,* on the condition of anonymity.

According to the top U.S. commander in Iraq, Gen. Raymond Odierno, the remaining troops would be necessary to ensure that the United States leaves behind a stable nation. "We failed the first time in 2003, when things were fairly calm and we didn't have a plan to transition what we had done militarily over to a civilian-led solution to help solve these problems," said General Odierno. "We have another opportunity here in 2010 and 2011 to do this."

President Obama did not indicate during his speech the pace of withdrawals, but he said that he would rely on generals and information coming from Iraq to help him decide the best course. General Odierno expressed his concern that troops needed to be kept in Iraq at least until national elections were held in December 2009. "Between now and May," Odierno said at the time, "I could accelerate the drawdown. If we get through successful elections, and you seat the government peacefully, that provides another level of stability. That will help reduce tensions."

President Obama said during his speech that the United States could no longer stay in Iraq to stabilize the country and needed to trust that the Iraqi people and government are capable of handling everything on their own. While the Bush administration and neoconservatives in Congress had hoped for a fully democratized Iraq that could be a model for the Middle East, the Obama administration seemed ready to accept a less-than-perfect situation in the country. "We cannot rid Iraq of all who oppose America or sympathize with our adversaries. We cannot police Iraq's streets until they are completely safe, nor stay until Iraq's union is perfected. We cannot sustain indefinitely a commitment that has put a strain on our military, and will cost the American people nearly a trillion dollars," the president said.

Some Iraqis had voiced concern that the United States had plans to keep bases in Iraq long term to protect oil interests or influence the decisions of the government. President Obama, in an attempt to alleviate this concern, said, "[T]o the Iraqi people, let me be clear about America's intentions. The United States pursues no claim on your territory or your resources." Some defense analysts, members of the military, and Republicans did not support President Obama's plan for a strict, December 31, 2011, deadline, instead seeing the benefit of a longer-term presence for continued Iraqi troop training. Secretary Gates said he preferred "some very modest-sized presence for training and helping" the Iraqi forces, but thus far, Iraq has not indicated a desire to have U.S. troops remain, in any capacity, past the final troop withdrawal deadline of December 31, 2011.

Many of the troops leaving Iraq will be redeployed to Afghanistan, where insurgency and instability has increased, making Obama's Iraq withdrawal time frame more urgent. In December 2009, the president ordered 30,000 more troops to the region.

BUDGETARY CONSIDERATIONS

The withdrawal from Iraq also meant a slight easing of the budgetary pressure President Obama had been grappling with since taking office. During his campaign, Obama promised to cut the deficit in half by 2013, the end of his first term. Cutting a portion of the billions of dollars budgeted for Iraq and Afghanistan each year would help him meet this goal.

Although President Obama planned to begin a troop withdrawal that could cut U.S. defense expenditures, he asked Congress to approve $83.4 billion to pay for military operations in Iraq and other locations overseas through September 30, 2009. It had been Obama's plan to stop paying for military operations through supplemental funding as his predecessor had done, and instead include operations expenses in the annual budget so that spending on military operations would be clearly defined and transparent at the beginning of each year. Officials in the White House said this one last supplemental request was necessary because the money Bush had budgeted for overseas military operations was set to run out midyear. Secretary Gates said at a press conference, "The alternative to the supplemental is a sudden and precipitous withdrawal of the United States from both places. And I don't know anybody who thinks that's a good idea." White House spokesperson Robert Gibbs said that this would be the last supplemental spending request outside normal budgetary procedures that the president would seek.

REACTION IN CONGRESS

In 2008, the United States and Iraq had worked on a similar withdrawal plan that would have removed most troops from Iraq by August 2010, with some remaining for security and training purposes. After President Obama took office, many Democrats in Congress pressed the administration for a faster withdrawal. The Democratic leadership expressed disapproval of Obama's plan for the length of time that the remaining 50,000 troops would remain in Iraq. Speaker of the House Nancy Pelosi, D-Calif., said, "I don't know what the justification is for . . . the 50,000 troops in Iraq. I would think a third of that, maybe 15,000 or 20,000" would be sufficient. Senate Majority Leader Harry Reid, D-Nev., echoed the Speaker's remarks. "I am happy to listen to the secretary of defense and the president. But when they talk about 50,000, that's a little higher number than I anticipated."

Other Democrats told the president that only a full withdrawal plan, rather than the gradual drawdown he had agreed to, would leave Iraq sovereign and save the United States any further damage to its credibility around the world. "I don't think we need to leave anybody there. They have got to be on their own," said Rep. John Murtha, D-Pa. "[American troops'] presence alone makes them vulnerable." Sen. Carl Levin, D-Mich., the chair of the Senate Armed Services Committee, echoed the leadership in both houses of Congress, calling for a much smaller force to remain in Iraq. "A limited force, following the removal of all combat forces, of a size in the low tens of thousands would be adequate to meet the mission." Most Republicans opposed the president's plan because, they argued, any recent gains in the security and stability of Iraq would be lost with a troop drawdown.

Facing an increasingly unpopular position of support for the war in Iraq, some Republicans, including Sen. John McCain, R-Ariz., Obama's opponent during the presidential election, agreed with the president's plan. "Overall," said Senator McCain, "it is a reasonable plan and one that can work and I support it."

INTERNATIONAL SUPPORT

Turkey stepped forward to help the United States follow through with its withdrawal plans six years after refusing to allow American troops to use Turkish territory to invade Iraq. The Turkish prime minister, Recep Tayyip Erdogan, said, "With regard to the exit of the American soldiers, we are positive on that issue." Erdogan said that if the United States asked for permission, he would consider allowing American troops to exit Iraq across Turkey. One State Department official told CNN, "It's not clear at this point if we'll want to make an extensive use of a Turkish route, but in any case, Turkish remarks that they're willing to help us is a good sign for the future of our relationship." No immediate direct response to the president's decision came from Great Britain, where Prime Minister Gordon Brown was becoming increasingly unpopular; Brown had supported then-candidate Obama's sixteen-month withdrawal timeframe. By July 2009, all British troops had left Iraq under both the prime minister's orders and the expiration of a mandate allowing British troops to remain in the country.

—Heather Kerrigan

Following is the edited text of a speech given by President Barack Obama on February 27, 2009, announcing the United States's strategy for all American troops to leave Iraq by 2011.

 # *President Obama Outlines Iraq Withdrawal Timeline*

February 27, 2009

The President. Thank you very much. Please be seated. To General Hejlik, for the outstanding work that he is doing, thank you so much. Good morning, marines.
  Audience members. Hooah!
  The President. Good morning, Camp Lejeune.
  Audience members. Hooah!

[The president thanks those in attendance]

  The President. Next month will mark the sixth anniversary of the war in Iraq. By any measure, this has already been a long war. For the men and women of America's Armed Forces, and for your families, the war has been one of the most extraordinary chapters of service in the history of our Nation. Many of you have endured tour after tour after tour of duty. You've known the dangers of combat and the lonely distance from loved ones. You have fought against tyranny and disorder. You have bled for your best friends and for unknown Iraqis. And you have borne an enormous burden for your fellow citizens, while extending a precious opportunity to the people of Iraq. Under tough circumstances, the men and women of the United States military have served with honor and succeeded beyond any expectation.

  Today I've come to speak to you about how the war in Iraq will end. To understand where we need to go in Iraq, it's important for the American people to understand where we now stand. Thanks in great measure to your service and your sacrifice, and your family's sacrifices, the situation in Iraq has improved. Violence has been reduced substantially from the horrific sectarian killing of 2006 and 2007. Al Qaida in Iraq has been dealt a serious blow by our troops and Iraq's security forces and through our partnership with Sunni Arabs. The capacity of Iraq's security forces has improved, and Iraq's leaders have taken steps towards political accommodation. The relative peace and strong participation in January's Provincial elections sent a powerful message to the world about how far Iraqis have come in pursuing their aspirations through a peaceful political process.

But let there be no doubt: Iraq is not yet secure, and there will be difficult days ahead. Violence will continue to be a part of life in Iraq. Too many fundamental political questions about Iraq's future remain unresolved. Too many Iraqis are still displaced or destitute. Declining oil revenues will put an added strain on a government that has difficulty delivering basic service. Not all of Iraq's neighbors are contributing to its security. Some are working at times to undermine it. And even as Iraq's Government is on a surer footing, it is not yet a full partner, politically and economically, in the region or with the international community.

In short, today there is a renewed cause for hope in Iraq, but that hope is resting on an emerging foundation. On my first full day in office, I directed my national security team to undertake a comprehensive review of our strategy in Iraq to determine the best way to strengthen that foundation, while strengthening American national security. I have listened to my Secretary of Defense, Robert Gates. I have listened to the Joint Chiefs of Staff, led by Admiral Mullen, as well as the commanders on the ground. We have acted with careful consideration of events on the ground, with respect for the security agreements between the United States and Iraq, and with a critical recognition that the long-term solution in Iraq must be political, not military, because the most important decisions that have to be made about Iraq's future must now be made by Iraqis.

We've also taken into account the simple reality that America can no longer afford to see Iraq in isolation from other priorities. We face the challenge of refocusing on Afghanistan and Pakistan, of relieving the burden of our military and military families, of rebuilding our struggling economy. These are challenges that we must meet and will meet.

Today I can announce that our review is complete, and that the United States will pursue a new strategy to end the war in Iraq through a transition to full Iraqi responsibility. This strategy is grounded in a clear and achievable goal shared by the Iraqi people and the American people: an Iraq that is sovereign, stable, and self-reliant. To achieve that goal, we will work to promote an Iraqi Government that is just, representative, and accountable, and that provides neither support nor safe haven to terrorists. We will help Iraq build new ties of trade and commerce with the world. And we will forge a partnership with the people and Government of Iraq that contributes to the peace and security of the region.

But understand this, we—here's what we will not do: We will not let the pursuit of the perfect stand in the way of achievable goals. We cannot rid Iraq of every single individual who opposes America or sympathizes with our adversaries. We cannot police Iraq's streets indefinitely until they are completely safe, nor can we stay until Iraq's union is perfect. We cannot sustain indefinitely a commitment that has put a strain on our military and will cost the American people nearly a trillion dollars. America's men and women in uniform—so many of you—have fought block by block, Province by Province, year after year, to give the Iraqis this chance to choose a better future. Now we must ask the Iraqi people to seize it.

The first part of this strategy is therefore the responsible removal of our combat brigades from Iraq. As a candidate for President, I made clear my support for a timeline of 16 months to carry out this drawdown, while pledging to consult closely with our military commanders upon taking office to ensure that we preserve the gains we've made and to protect our troops. These consultations are now complete, and I have chosen a timeline that will remove our combat brigades over the next 18 months.

So let me say this as plainly as I can: By August 31, 2010, our combat mission in Iraq will end. As we carry out this drawdown, my highest priority will be the safety and security of our troops and civilians in Iraq. . . . This plan gives our military the forces and flexibility they need to support our Iraqi partners and to succeed.

After we remove our combat brigades, our mission will change from combat to supporting the Iraqi Government and its security forces as they take the absolute lead in securing their country. As I have long said, we will retain a transitional force to carry out three distinct functions: training, equipping, and advising Iraqi security forces as long as they remain nonsectarian; conducting targeted counterterrorism missions; and protecting our ongoing civilian and military efforts within Iraq. Initially, this force will likely be made up of 35,000 to 50,000 U.S. troops.

. . . I intend to remove all U.S. troops from Iraq by the end of 2011. So we will complete this transition to Iraqi responsibility, and we will bring our troops home with the honor that they have earned.

As we remove our combat brigades, we will pursue the second part of our strategy: sustained diplomacy on behalf of a more peaceful and prosperous Iraq. The drawdown of our military should send a clear signal that Iraq's future is now its own responsibility. The long-term success of the Iraqi nation will depend on decisions made by Iraq's leaders and the fortitude of the Iraqi people. Iraq is a sovereign country with legitimate institutions; America cannot and should not take their place. . . .

Going forward, we can make a difference on several fronts. We will work with the United Nations to support national elections, while helping Iraqis improve local government. We can serve as an honest broker in pursuit of fair and durable agreements on issues that have divided Iraq's leaders. And just as we will support Iraq's security forces, we will help Iraq's institutions strengthen their capacity to protect the rule of law, confront corruption, and deliver basic services. . . .

[Obama's description of how the United States can help displaced Iraqis has been omitted.]

Now, before I go any further, I want to take a moment to speak directly to the people of Iraq. . . . In years past, you have persevered through tyranny and terror, through personal insecurity and sectarian violence. And instead of giving in to the forces of disunion, you stepped back from a descent into civil war and showed a proud resilience that deserves our respect. . . .

So to the Iraqi people, let me be clear about America's intentions. The United States pursues no claim on your territory or your resources. We respect your sovereignty and the tremendous sacrifices you have made for your country. We seek a full transition to Iraqi responsibility for the security of your country. And going forward, we can build a lasting relationship founded upon mutual interests and mutual respect as Iraq takes its rightful place in the community of nations.

That leads me to the third part of our strategy, comprehensive American engagement across the region. The future of Iraq is inseparable from the future of the broader Middle East, so we must work with our friends and partners to establish a new framework that advances Iraq's security and the region's. It's time for Iraq to be a full partner in regional dialog and for Iraq's neighbors to establish productive and normalized relations with Iraq. And going forward, the United States will pursue principled and sustained engagement with all of the nations in the region—all the nations in the region, and that, by the way, will include Iran and Syria.

This reflects a fundamental truth: We can no longer deal with regional challenges in isolation. We need a smarter, more sustainable, and comprehensive approach. That is why we are renewing our diplomacy, while relieving the burden on our military. That is why we are refocusing on Al Qaida in Afghanistan and Pakistan, developing a strategy to use all elements of American power to prevent Iran from developing a nuclear weapon, and actively seeking a lasting peace between Israel and the Arab world. . . .

Every nation and every group must know—whether you wish America good or ill—that the end of the war in Iraq will enable a new era of American leadership and engagement in the Middle East. This does not lessen our commitment. We are going to be enhancing that commitment to bring about a better day in that region, and that era has just begun.

Finally, I want to be very clear about my strategy—that my strategy for ending the war in Iraq does not end with military plans or diplomatic agendas; it endures through our commitment to uphold the sacred trust with every man and woman who has served in Iraq. . . .

You and your families have done your duty, now a grateful Nation must do ours. That is why, as reflected in my new budget, I am increasing the number of soldiers and marines, so that we lessen the burden on those who are serving. That is why I've committed to expanding our system of veterans health care to serve more patients and to provide better care in more places. We will continue building new wounded warrior facilities across America and invest in new ways of identifying and treating the signature wounds of this war, Posttraumatic Stress Disorder and traumatic brain injury, as well as other combat injuries.

We also know that service does not end with the person wearing the uniform. In her visits with military families across the country, my wife Michelle has learned firsthand about the unique burden that your families endure every day. I want you to know this: Military families are a top priority for Michelle and me, and they will be a top priority for my administration.

We will raise military pay and continue providing—[*applause*]. . . . We're going to continue providing quality child care, job training for spouses, and expanded counseling and outreach to families that have known the separation and stress of war. We will also heed the lesson of history—that those who fight in battle can form the backbone of our middle class—by implementing a 21st-century GI bill to help our veterans live out their dreams.

As a Nation, we've had our share of debates about the war in Iraq. It has at times divided us as a people. To this very day, there are some Americans who want to stay in Iraq longer and some who want to leave faster. But there should be no disagreement on what the men and women of our military have achieved.

And so I want to be very clear: We sent our troops to Iraq to do away with Saddam Hussein's regime, and you got the job done. We kept our troops in Iraq to help establish a sovereign government, and you got the job done. And we will leave the Iraqi people with a hard-earned opportunity to live a better life. That is your achievement; that is the prospect that you have made possible.

There are many lessons to be learned from what we've experienced. We have learned that America must go to war with clearly defined goals, which is why I've ordered a review of our policy in Afghanistan. We have learned that we must always weigh the costs of action and communicate those costs candidly to the American people, which is why I've put Iraq and Afghanistan into my budget. We have learned that the 21st—in the 21st century, we have to use all elements of American power to achieve our objectives, which is why I'm committed to building our civilian national security capacity so that the burden is not continually pushed onto our military. We have learned that our political leaders must pursue the broad and bipartisan support that our national security policies depend on, which is why I will consult with Congress in carrying out my plans. And we have learned the importance of working closely with friends and allies, which is why we are launching a new era of engagement and diplomacy in the world.

The starting point for our policies must always be the safety and security of the American people. I know that you, the men and women of the finest fighting force in the history of the world, can meet any challenge and defeat any foe. And as long as I am your Commander in Chief, I promise you that I will only send you into harm's way when it is absolutely necessary and provide you with the equipment and support you need to get the job done. That is the most important lesson of all, for the consequences of war are dire, the sacrifices immeasurable. You know because you've seen those sacrifices; you've lived them. And we all honor you for them.

Semper Fidelis—it means always being faithful to the Corps and to country and to the memory of fallen comrades like Corporal Jonathan Yale and Lance Corporal Jordan Haerter. These young men enlisted in a time of war, knowing they would face great danger. They came here, to Camp Lejeune, as they trained for their mission. Last April, they were standing guard in Anbar. In an age when suicide is a weapon, they were suddenly faced with an oncoming truck filled with explosives. These two marines stood their ground; these two marines opened fire; these two marines stopped that truck. When the thousands of pounds of explosives detonated, they had saved 50 fellow marines, they had saved Iraqi police who would have been in the truck's path, but Corporal Yale and Lance Corporal Haerter lost their own lives. Jonathan was 21, and Jordan was 19.

In the town where Jordan Haerter was from, a bridge was dedicated in his name. One marine who traveled to the ceremony said: "We flew here from all over the country to pay tribute to our friend Jordan, who risked his life to save us. We wouldn't be here without him."

America's time in Iraq is filled with stories of men and women like this. Their names are written into the bridges and town squares of this country. They are etched into stone at Arlington and in quiet places of rest across our land. They are spoken in schools and on city blocks. They live on in the memories of those who wear your uniform, in the hearts of those they loved, and in the freedom of the Nation they served.

Each American who has served in Iraq has their own story. Each of you has your own story. And that story is now a part of the history of the United States of America, a Nation that exists only because free men and women have bled for it, from the beaches of Normandy to the deserts of Anbar, from the mountains of Korea to the streets of Kandahar. You teach us that the price of freedom is great. Your sacrifice should challenge all of us—every single American—to ask what we can do to be better citizens.

There will be more danger in the months ahead. We will face new tests and unforeseen trials. But thanks to the sacrifices of those who have served, we have forged hard-earned progress, we are leaving Iraq to its people, and we have begun the work of ending this war.

Thank you. God bless you, God bless the United States of America. Semper Fi. Hooah!

Source: U.S. Executive Office of the President. "Remarks on Military Operations in Iraq at Camp Lejeune, North Carolina." *Daily Compilation of Presidential Documents* 2009, no. 00109 (February 27, 2009). www.gpo.gov/fdsys/pkg/DCPD-200900109/pdf/DCPD-200900109.pdf.

OTHER HISTORIC DOCUMENTS OF INTEREST

FROM THIS VOLUME

- President Obama Announces Troop Increase in Afghanistan, p. 617

FROM PREVIOUS *HISTORIC DOCUMENTS*

- Timetable for Withdrawal of U.S. Troops from Iraq, *2008*, p. 363
- U.S. Intelligence Agencies and General Petraeus on Security in Iraq, *2007*, p. 407
- Iraq Study Group Report on U.S. Policy in Iraq, *2006*, p. 725
- Rep. Murtha and President Bush on U.S. Involvement in Iraq, *2005*, p. 832
- United Nations Security Council on Postwar Iraq, *2003* p. 933

March

CIA Destroyed Ninety-Two Interrogation Tapes

MARCH 2, 2009

It was first disclosed on December 6, 2007, that the Central Intelligence Agency (CIA) had created and later destroyed videotapes of the 2002 interrogation of two detainees being held overseas. On March 2, 2009, a letter sent to Judge Alvin Hellerstein of the U.S. District Court for the Southern District of New York from acting U.S. attorney Lev Dassin disclosed that the total number of destroyed tapes was ninety-two. The letter came as the Justice Department was continuing its criminal investigation into the CIA's destruction of the videotapes.

THE DESTROYED TAPES

The videotapes destroyed by the CIA in 2005 showed the interrogation techniques used on two al-Qaida suspects, Abu Zubaydah and Abd al-Rahim al-Nashiri, that included waterboarding, a technique that simulates the experience of drowning and is considered to be torture in many countries around the world. Only two of the ninety-two destroyed tapes featured Nashiri; the other ninety documented the interrogation and detention of Zubaydah. Both detainees were being held in Thailand, and the tapes remained there at a secret facility until they were destroyed. The only time at which anyone in the United States saw footage from the videotapes was during a one-time electronic transmission of portions of the tapes to the CIA in Langley, Virginia, just outside of Washington, D.C.

The hundreds of hours of videotapes were created initially to protect the CIA interrogators from any fallout after an interrogation—in other words, to show that all interrogation methods used on detainees were in line with what the White House and Justice Department had authorized. According to CIA officials, the CIA also wanted to prove that Zubaydah was receiving medical treatment consistent with gunshot wounds he had received during his capture.

The propriety of destroying the tapes was called into question. At the time, Congress was increasing its scrutiny of CIA interrogation and detention techniques, and the courts were becoming involved. The 9/11 Commission, set up by President George W. Bush, had requested prior to 2005 all information the CIA had related to the detention of terrorism suspects and at the time of its request was not informed of the tapes. "The commission did formally request material of this kind from all relevant agencies," according to Philip Zelikow, executive director of the 9/11 Commission, "and the commission was assured that we had received all the material responsive to our request." Other questions were raised about the timing of the destruction of the tapes as it related to information requested during preparation for the sentencing of Zacarias Moussaoui, the first person to be charged in connection with the September 11, 2001, terrorist attacks. In 2003 and 2005, lawyers for Moussaoui had requested the tapes in an effort to show that the two detainees featured in the tapes did not know him; they believed this would clear Moussaoui of any involvement in the September 11 attacks.

The Case Against the CIA

In addition to congressional inquiries, in September 2004 the American Civil Liberties Union (ACLU) had filed a court order requesting that the CIA retain any evidence of interrogation and detention of suspects being held overseas. The CIA received this court order more than one year before the tapes were destroyed.

There are claims by some in the intelligence community that the Bush White House and Justice Department were contacted regarding destruction of the tapes because the means of interrogation had been, according to the CIA, forced upon them. According to intelligence officers, during a two-year period, even White House lawyer Harriet Miers was asked by the CIA what should be done with the tapes; Miers never gave an order for destruction. It has also been said that CIA lawyer John Rizzo was never comfortable with the decision to destroy the tapes. Then-CIA director Michael Hayden, in an effort to clear the White House and Justice Department of any involvement and further explain the reasoning behind the destruction of the tapes, wrote in a letter to CIA staff that the decision was made "within the CIA."

A select group of legislators, along with the White House and Justice Department, had been told about the existence of the tapes. Rep. Jane Harman, D-Calif., as the senior Democrat on the House Intelligence Committee, was one of only four members of Congress told in 2003 that the tapes existed and later that the CIA intended to destroy them. She said, "I told the CIA that destroying videotapes of interrogations was a bad idea and urged them in writing not to do it." There was, however, no notification sent to key members of Congress that the tapes had in fact been destroyed.

According to the letter from Hayden, who was in charge of the CIA at the time the tapes were destroyed, the reason for destruction was to protect the identities of the CIA interrogators. Hayden said the tapes posed "a serious security risk" and had to be destroyed. "Were they ever to leak," he wrote to CIA staff, "they would permit identification of your CIA colleagues who had served in the program, exposing them and their families to retaliation from al Qaeda and its sympathizers."

In his letter, Hayden also explained that the tapes had first been made to serve as a check on the CIA's interrogation techniques. The tapes, he said, were destroyed only after the organization had determined that they were no longer of value to the CIA or to any legislative inquiries that might arise. Hayden told CIA staff the agency had determined that written notes detailing the interrogations would instead suffice. "The Agency soon determined," Hayden said, "that its documentary reporting was full and exacting, removing any need for tapes. Indeed, videotaping stopped in 2002." Hayden went on to say that there should be no argument over the value of the tapes because everything the CIA did was in accordance with the law and had proved to be valuable to the United States. The tapes, he said, "helped disrupt terrorist operations and saved lives. It was built on a solid foundation of legal review. It has been conducted with careful supervision. If the story of these tapes is told fairly, it will underscore those facts," he wrote.

THE CRIMINAL INVESTIGATION

The letter sent by Dassin on March 2, 2009, came in response to a Freedom of Information Act (FOIA) lawsuit filed by the ACLU in 2008 requesting that the CIA make available all information related to the interrogation of detainees abroad. At the time the FOIA lawsuit was filed, the Justice Department had already begun a formal criminal investigation into the destruction of the CIA videotapes. Attorney General Michael Mukasey upgraded the case to a formal investigation after preliminary evidence showed that the CIA, perhaps acting in cooperation with other government officials, may have committed criminal acts by destroying the tapes. The prosecutor leading the case for the Justice Department, John H. Durham, in cooperation with the Federal Bureau of Investigation (FBI), asked that the ACLU's request be held until he could finish his investigation.

When Durham first began his criminal investigation, the only thing prosecutors knew was that the former head of the CIA's clandestine service, Jose A. Rodriguez Jr., had given the order to destroy the tapes. The investigation sought to figure out whether anyone else had been involved in the physical destruction of the tapes or in ordering the destruction of the tapes. Many of the prosecution's questions centered on the CIA's legal advisors and lawyers who, after reviewing court directives on the matter, had told Rodriquez that it would be a bad decision to destroy the tapes, but not technically against the law.

POSSIBLE CHARGES

By the end of 2009, Durham's case was still ongoing, although he had completed almost all of his interviews with those considered to be major players in the destruction of the tapes, with the exception of Rodriquez.

The findings in the investigation are not expected to bring any charges against any CIA employees, although the ACLU has called on the federal government to hold the CIA in contempt for destroying the videotapes in violation of a court order that required the CIA to make available videotapes or other documented evidence of the interrogation techniques being used abroad. Amrit Singh, a staff lawyer with the ACLU, said, "The sheer number of tapes at issue demonstrates that this destruction was not an accident. There was a deliberate attempt to destroy evidence of what we believe to be illegal conduct." A statement attributable to Singh continued, "Our contempt motion has been pending in court for over a year now—it is time to hold the CIA accountable for its flagrant disregard for the rule of law." In a case such as this, it would be difficult to charge CIA interrogators because the prosecution would need to convince a jury not only of what the CIA operatives knew at the time of the destruction of the tapes but also that their actions were not mistakes but the intentional destruction of evidence. The amount of classified information in this case would also present a major challenge.

Dassin wrote in his letter to Hellerstein regarding the ACLU motion to hold the CIA in contempt, "The CIA intends to produce all of the information requested to the court and to produce as much information as possible on the public record to the plaintiffs." According to CIA spokesperson George Little, the CIA has been cooperating fully with the Justice Department throughout the investigation. "If anyone thinks it's agency policy to impede the enforcement of American law, they simply don't know the facts."

Congress has been carrying on its own investigation into the destruction of the tapes by the CIA, but shortly before Dassin's letter was filed in New York, Sen. Dianne Feinstein, D-Calif., said that the committee she chairs, the Senate Intelligence Committee, would broaden the scope of its investigation to begin looking into the history of the CIA's interrogation program, including when the decision was made to use harsh interrogation techniques, how often the techniques were used, and whether they were effective.

—Heather Kerrigan

Following is the text of a letter sent to Judge Alvin Hellerstein, U.S. District Court, Southern District of New York, from Lev Dassin, acting U.S. attorney, on March 2, 2009, admitting to the destruction of ninety-two tapes, some of which showed harsh interrogation techniques being used on detainees abroad.

DOCUMENT

Letter from Acting U.S. Attorney to Judge Hellerstein Regarding CIA Tapes

March 2, 2009

BY FACSIMILE

Hon. Alvin K. Hellerstein
United States District Court
Southern District of New York
500 Pearl Street, Room 1050
New York, New York 10007–1312

Re: ACLU, et al., v. Department of Defense, et al., No. 04 Civ. 4151 (AKH)

Dear Judge Hellerstein:

The Court's stay of its consideration of Plaintiffs' contempt motion expired on February 28, 2009. John Durham, the Acting United States Attorney for the Eastern District of Virginia who is conducting a criminal investigation into the destruction of certain videotaped interrogations of detainees by the Central Intelligence Agency, did not request a continuation of the stay. Accordingly, it is our expectation that the Court will enter an order requiring the production of the information contemplated in the August 20, 2008 Order Regulating Proceedings; namely:

1. A list identifying and describing each of the destroyed records;

2. A list of any summaries, transcripts, or memoranda regarding the records, and of any reconstruction of the records' contents; and

3. Identification of any witnesses who may have viewed the videotapes or retained custody of the videotapes before their destruction.

With the termination of the stay, the CIA is now gathering information and records responsive to the Court's order. The CIA respectfully requests that it be permitted until Friday, March 6, 2009, to provide the Court with a proposed schedule under which it will respond to each of the three categories of information and records.

In the meantime, the CIA can now identify the number of videotapes that were destroyed, which is information implicated by Point 1 of the August 20, 2008 Order. Ninety-two videotapes were destroyed. This information is included in the CIA Office of Inspector General's Special Review Report, a redacted version of which was previously produced to the Plaintiffs. The CIA will unredact this information from the report and produce it to the Plaintiffs.

Finally, we note that certain of the information contemplated by the August 20, 2008 Order may be classified or statutorily protected from disclosure, such as the names of CIA employees who have reviewed the tapes. The CIA intends to produce all of the information requested to the Court and to produce as much information as possible on the public record to the Plaintiffs.

We thank the Court for considering this submission.

Respectfully,

LEV L. DASSIN
Acting United States Attorney

By:

SEAN H. LANE
PETER M. SKINNER
Assistant United States Attorneys
Telephone: (212) 637–2601
Facsimile: (212) 637–2930

cc: Amrit Singh, Esq. (by facsimile)
Jennifer B. Condon (by facsimile)

Source: American Civil Liberties Union. "Letter to Judge Hellerstein Acknowledging Destroyed CIA Interrogation Tapes." March 2, 2009. www.aclu.org/pdfs/safefree/lettertohellerstein_ciainterroga tiontapes.pdf.

OTHER HISTORIC DOCUMENTS OF INTEREST

FROM THIS VOLUME

FROM PREVIOUS *HISTORIC DOCUMENTS*

President and Army Chief of Guinea-Bissau Assassinated

MARCH 2, 3, AND 21, 2009

On March 2, 2009, Guinea-Bissau's democratically elected president, João Bernadro Vieira, was killed during an apparent clash between two rival groups in the capital of Bissau. Vieira's rival, the head of the military, Gen. Batiste Tagme Na Waie, had been killed only hours earlier. Reports have claimed that Vieira was responsible for the murder of Waie and was killed in retaliation. The murders, which came after legislative elections in November 2008, threw the already troubled nation into turmoil.

GUINEA-BISSAU

Guinea-Bissau, a small African nation, gained independence from Portugal in 1974 and since has been plagued by coups. The nation of more than one and a half million people is one of the world's five poorest countries. Given its weak political and legal structures, South American drug lords have used the nation as a gateway to smuggle drugs into Europe. In the late 1990s, Guinea-Bissau attempted a monetary turnaround by joining the West African Monetary Union and overhauling its tax programs. However, after three years of steady growth in its gross domestic product (GDP), civil war broke out, and GDP quickly decreased by 28 percent. When a sense of order was restored, growth began again, but in 2001, the International Monetary Fund (IMF) ceased its debt-relief assistance for Guinea-Bissau because the nation refused to enforce the reforms the IMF requested. Other international donors began pulling aid from Guinea-Bissau, but a round of legislative elections that resulted in seating democratically elected leaders brought a return of international aid in 2004.

Richard Moncrieff, West Africa project director at the International Crisis Group, a research and advocacy organization, reported, "Guinea-Bissau's institutions remain structurally feeble. Without a real commitment on the part of the ruling elite to end the intrigues and violence that are so damaging to the country's prospects, it will remain unstable and unable to cope with rampant corruption or change its status as a key drugs-transiting country." General Waie and President Vieira each had at times been accused of involvement in the country's lucrative cocaine trade being run by Colombian drug lords.

In addition to the general instability brought on by poverty and the drug trade, underlying ethnic tensions are an issue in Guinea-Bissau. President Vieira was a member of the Papel ethnic group, a minority group in Guinea-Bissau, and he once thought the Balanta, the majority ethnic group, was plotting against him. He became so convinced that Balanta officers were plotting his demise that he condemned some to death and sentenced others to long terms in prison.

BUILD UP TO THE MURDERS

Before becoming president of Guinea-Bissau, Vieira, who was 69 at the time of his death, had been the military commander of guerrilla forces seeking independence for the country from Portugal. Vieira was president for twenty-three years. He was ousted during a coup in 1998 and exiled to Portugal, where he stayed before returning to power in 2005.

Only a few hours before Vieira was murdered, military headquarters had been attacked, and General Waie, one of Vieira's fiercest rivals, had been killed after a bomb went off near his office. Waie, an outspoken critic of Vieira's policies, had been a member of the military government that had overthrown Vieira in the late 1990s, forcing him into exile. Waie remained critical of the president and his party until his death, leading many to allege that Vieira had been responsible for Waie's death. According to Zamora Induta, a military spokesperson, Vieira was "one of the main people responsible for the death of general Tagme [Waie]."

On the morning of Vieira's murder, gunfire was heard near the president's home in Bissau for several hours. Vieira and his wife were asked to immediately leave their house. Vieira refused, but his wife left and remained safe after his murder. The president was killed at approximately 5 A.M. on March 2, 2009.

After the murder, it was unclear what exactly had happened, as conflicting news reports were released. A military spokesperson told the Agence France-Presse (AFP) international news agency, "President Vieira was killed by the army as he tried to flee his house, which was being attacked by a group of soldiers close to the head of the chief of staff, Tagme Na Waie, early this morning." According to the spokesperson, the president had been closely tied to those responsible for the murder of Waie. A statement from the military read on state radio, however, said that there was no connection between the murder of the president and the assassination of Waie and that no retaliation was involved. The statement also said that no coup was under way and placed blame for the president's murder on an unidentified group of soldiers that the military was in the process of locating. Following constitutional order, the statement said, the military would respect the seating of the president of the National People's Assembly, Raimundo Pereira, to succeed Vieira.

Whether the murder of Vieira was in retaliation for the murder of Waie has not yet been determined; neither man was unfamiliar with assassination attempts or coups. During the four months preceding their murders, multiple assassination attempts had been undertaken against both Waie and Vieira. A previous attempt on the life of Vieira had been made in 2008 following the legislative elections, and shortly after, he organized his own 400-member bodyguard unit for his protection. Vieira had an increasingly tense relationship with the military after the disputed parliamentary election results. Following the elections, it seemed that Vieira's bloc had been defeated and that a new regime might be installed. Vieira vehemently opposed this. After the election, the presidential palace was attacked by men with machine guns and rocket-propelled grenades. Vieira eventually conceded defeat and chose as prime minister Carlos Gomes of the African Party for the Independence of Guinea and Cape Verde. In January 2009, Vieira's personal guard was disbanded after being accused of attempting to murder Waie.

Aftermath

Seven days of national mourning and multiple investigations were planned in Guinea-Bissau after the murders. International reaction was strong. The murders of Vieira and Waie were condemned by the United States, United Nations, African Union (AU), European Union, and Portugal. The United Nations strongly condemned the murders and called on the interim government to bring those responsible to justice. The chair of the AU, Jean Ping, said, "I was deeply shocked . . . to hear of the assassination. The AU and myself firmly condemn this criminal act." He continued by calling the murder notable "because it comes at a time when efforts were under way to bolster peace following the November election." According to Mohamed Ibn Chambas, the leader of the Economic Community of West African States (ECOWAS), a regional organization of sixteen countries, the group planned to send a delegation of peacekeepers to the region to assist the interim government, which was seated on March 3, 2009. Chambas said of the murders, "It's not only the assassination of a president or a chief of staff. It's the assassination of democracy." Antonio Mazzitelli, head of the West and Central Africa regional office of the United Nations Office on Drugs and Crime, said the murder was not linked to the drug trade but was "the result of an institutional and personal character crisis rather than anything else." ECOWAS partnered with the United Nations, AU, and nongovernmental organizations to send peacekeepers to Guinea-Bissau to stabilize the government and assist with presidential elections to be held in the summer of 2009.

There was some speculation that the removal of Vieira and Waie, who were not only at odds but also were accused of impeding progress in Guinea-Bissau, could signal a fresh start for the nation. Other observers, however, feared additional political upheaval as the interim government attempted to set up democratic elections under the watch of a strong military. The military in Guinea-Bissau had, since the time of the nation's independence, been involved in the country's politics. According to a statement released after the murders, the military set up "[a] commission of military chiefs" to "manage the crisis," although it was not clear whether they would seek political gain.

In addition, some believed that the president of the assembly, who took on the role of interim president until new elections, would not be powerful enough to enforce Guinea-Bissau's rule of law, leaving the door open for the military to take control of the government. Jan Van Maneen, the honorary consul for the United Kingdom and the Netherlands in Guinea-Bissau, said, "The thing is that we had elections in November, and the new president of the assembly is a very young man with little experience. We are not sure if he is going to respect the constitution." Van Maneen did, however, rule out the possibility that the army might take control of the country, saying, "The rivalry is now over and maybe it [the assassination] is now the beginning of a new solution."

Following the Guinea-Bissau constitution, elections were held during the summer of 2009. Malam Bacai Sanha won and was seated on September 8, 2009. He had previously served as acting president between 1999 and 2000 after Vieira was exiled from the country and had finished runner-up in the 2005 presidential election to Vieira. On taking office, Sanha promised to investigate the murders of Vieira and Waie and also fight drug trafficking, corruption, and other crime.

—Heather Kerrigan

Following is a statement released March 2, 2009, by the chairperson of ECOWAS on the assassinations of the president and army chief in Guinea-Bissau; a March 2, 2009, press release from the African Union calling on the interim government of Guinea-Bissau to work to stabilize the country; a press release from the United Nations Security Council, on March 3, 2009, condemning the murders; and a March 21, 2009, call by ECOWAS for peacekeepers to be sent to Guinea-Bissau.

DOCUMENT

Chairman of ECOWAS on the Assassinations in Guinea-Bissau

March 2, 2009

His Excellency Alhaji Umaru Musa Yar'Adua, Chairman of ECOWAS, has received with deep concern and sadness, news of the assassination of His Excellency, João Bernardo Nino Vieira, President of the Republic of Guinea-Bissau, and General Tagme na Waie, Chief of Defence Staff of the Armed Forces of Guinea-Bissau. The murder of the President and Chief of Defence Staff are condemned in the strongest of terms as reprehensible and acts that undermine democracy, peace and stability in Guinea-Bissau. The fragile political situation in Guinea-Bissau has been further weakened by these events. This is regretted as it comes at a time when the West African region is making a forward march in the development of democratic governance.

President Yar'Adua has emphasized the importance of constitutional succession to the Presidency after the unfortunate events. He called on the Armed Forces and other Security Agencies of Guinea-Bissau to desist from any actions likely to plunge the country further into lawlessness and political instability. All peace loving citizens of Guinea-Bissau are called upon to exercise a high sense of responsibility and moderation in their actions and utterances at this critical and testing period in their national life. The Chairman of ECOWAS will dispatch a foreign ministerial delegation to Bissau comprising Ministers from Nigeria, Burkina Faso, Cape Verde, The Gambia and Senegal, and accompanied by the President of the ECOWAS Commission, on Tuesday, March 3, 2009. The delegation will engage all stakeholders in an effort to restore confidence among the political actors, civil society and security services and return the country to constitutional normalcy.

The Chairman of ECOWAS expresses his deep condolences to the families and loved ones of late President Joao Bernardo Vieira and General Tagme and to the entire people of Guinea-Bissau on their tragic demise. He paid tribute to them as patriots who had fought for the liberation of the country from colonial rule and served in the post-independent period to build the country. He entreated the people of Guinea-Bissau to take their demise, as tragic as it is, as an opportunity for national reconciliation and unity.

SOURCE: Economic Community of West African States. Press release. "ECOWAS Chairman Condemns Killings in Bissau, Urges Security Agencies to Avert Deterioration of Situation." March 2, 2009. http://news.ecowas.int/presseshow.php?nb=020&lang=en&annee=2009.

African Union Press Release on the Assassinations in Guinea-Bissau

March 2, 2009

The Chairperson of the Commission of the African Union, Jean Ping, has learnt with shock of the assassination of the President of Guinea Bissau, João Bernardo "Nino" Vieira, and that of his Army Chief of Staff, General Batista Tagme Na Wai.

The Chairperson condemns in the strongest terms these cowardly and heinous attacks, which have come at a time of renewed efforts by the international community to support peace-building efforts in Guinea Bissau and consolidate progress in the political process in that country in the wake of the legislative elections of November 2008.

The Chairperson calls on all Bissau-Guinean political leaders and stakeholders to rally behind the legitimate authorities of the country, in order to address the current crisis within the framework of the legitimate institutions and the constitution of Guinea Bissau.

The Chairperson reiterates the AU's commitment to the Lomé Declaration and all other AU instruments relating to unconstitutional changes of government, and the total rejection of any attempt at unconstitutional changes of government.

The Chairperson has initiated contact with regional leaders on how best to address the current situation. Consultations are also underway to convene an emergency meeting of the Peace and Security Council (PSC), to review the situation and to take the appropriate steps.

Addis Ababa on 02 March 2009

SOURCE: African Union Press Office. Press release. "Press Statement on the Situation in Guinea Bissau." March 2, 2009. www.africa-union.org/root/UA/Actualites/2009/fev/Communique/Press%20Statement %20on%20Guinea-Bissau%2002-03-2009.pdf.

UN Security Council Condemns the Assassinations of Guinea-Bissau's President and Army Chief

March 3, 2009

Presidential Statement Also Calls for Respect for Democratic Process, Opposes Any Attempt to Change Government Through Unconstitutional Means

Strongly condemning the assassinations of the President of Guinea-Bissau, Joao Bernardo Vieira, and the Chief of Staff of the Armed Forces, Tagme Na Waie, on 1 and 2 March, the

Security Council today called on the Government of Guinea-Bissau to bring to justice those responsible.

In a statement read out by its President, Ibrahim O. A. Dabbashi, the Council also called on the Government, the political leaders, the Armed Forces and the people of Guinea-Bissau to remain calm, exercise restraint, maintain stability and constitutional order, and respect the rule of law and the democratic process.

It also urged all parties to resolve their disputes through political and peaceful means within the framework of its democratic institutions and opposed any attempt to change the Government through unconstitutional means.

It called on the international community to assist in preserving Guinea-Bissau's constitutional order and to continue to support peacebuilding efforts there.

The meeting, which began at 12:08 p.m., ended at 12:13 p.m.

Presidential Statement

The full text of presidential statement S/PRST/2009/2 reads as follows:

"1. The Security Council condemns in the strongest terms the assassinations of the President of Guinea-Bissau, Joao Bernardo Vieira, and the Chief of Staff of the Armed Forces, Tagme Na Waie, on 1 and 2 March 2009. It expresses its deep sympathy and condolences to the families of the victims, and to the people and the Government of Guinea-Bissau.

"2. The Security Council calls on the Government of Guinea-Bissau to bring to justice those responsible for these violent acts. It calls upon the Government, the political leaders, the Armed Forces and the people of Guinea-Bissau to remain calm, exercise restraint, maintain stability and constitutional order and respect the rule of law and the democratic process. It also urges all parties to resolve their disputes through political and peaceful means within the framework of its democratic institutions and opposes any attempt to change the Government through unconstitutional means.

"3. The Security Council welcomes, in this regard, the statements condemning the incidents by the Secretary-General of the United Nations, the African Union, the Economic Community of West African States, the European Union and other members of the international community, and calls on al[l] to assist in preserving the constitutional order in Guinea-Bissau and to continue to support peacebuilding efforts in the country.

"4. The Security Council reaffirms its commitment to support the efforts of the Government and people of Guinea-Bissau to consolidate democratic institutions, peace and stability in that country.

"5. The Security Council shall remain seized of the developments in Guinea-Bissau."

Source: United Nations Security Council. Press release. "Security Council Condemns Assassinations of Guinea-Bissau's President, Army Chief; Calls on Government to Bring Those Responsible to Justice." March 3, 2009. www.un.org/News/Press/docs//2009/sc9605.doc.htm.

ECOWAS Calls for Protection Force in Guinea-Bissau

March 21, 2009

ECOWAS Foreign Ministers on Thursday, 19th March 2009, directed ECOWAS to work with the international community, including the United Nations, towards the deployment of military and police contingents to ensure the protection of republican institutions, VIPs and the electoral process in Guinea Bissau.

At the end of its 26th meeting in Guinea Bissau, Ministers of the Mediation and Security Council also recommended the immediate hosting in Cape Verde of a limited and focused roundtable of financial and technical partners to generate resources for the implementation of the needed security sector reform in Guinea Bissau.

The one-day meeting which was dominated by the situation in Guinea Bissau urged ECOWAS to work with the African Union and the United Nations to facilitate the immediate establishment of an international Commission of Inquiry that will investigate the various events in the country since August 2008 that have the potential to destabilize the country in order to address the problem of impunity and contribute to justice and national reconciliation.

The meeting also considered the issue of drug trafficking through the region and recommended that immediate steps be taken to address the problem through the implementation of the ECOWAS Plan of Action using Cape Verde, Guinea and Guinea Bissau as pilot countries.

In this regard, the ministers urged ECOWAS to facilitate the strengthening of the institutional capacity of the ECOWAS Commission to effectively monitor the situation in collaboration with relevant international agencies, including the UN, INTERPOL and EUROPOL. It further recommended greater cooperation between countries of origin, transit and destination in order to ensure a holistic control of the supply and demand chain.

On the presidential elections to replace former President Joao Bernado Vieira, who was killed on 2nd March 2009, the ministers urged the Interim President to ensure that it was free, fair, transparent and credible in accordance with constitutional provisions. They also called on the Interim President to undertake wide-ranging consultations with all political forces and actors to deepen national consensus on the transition process.

ECOWAS pledged to contribute financially to the election as well as canvas for additional technical and financial support for the election which is constitutionally required to be held two months after the death of the former President.

Moreover, the ministers urged ECOWAS, the AU and the international community to work closely with Guinea Bissau with a view to mobilizing the required resources for the reconstruction of the economy, creating employment opportunities, ensuring fiscal discipline, the efficient management of resources as well as effective revenue generation.

They further stressed the need for the Government of Guinea Bissau to immediately initiate the process of national reconciliation in order to build consensus on the problems that affect the peace, stability and development of the country.

SOURCE: Economic Community of West African States. Press release. "ECOWAS Foreign Ministers Call for Deployment of Protection Force in Guinea Bissau." March 21, 2009. http://news.ecowas.int/presse show.php?nb=029&lang=en&annee=2009.

Arrest Warrant Issued for Sudan's President

MARCH 4, 2009

On March 4, 2009, the International Criminal Court (ICC) in The Hague, The Netherlands, charged Sudan's president, Omar al-Bashir, with war crimes and crimes against humanity and issued a warrant for his arrest. The ICC had never before charged a sitting head of state with war crimes. The charges against Bashir largely stemmed from violence in Darfur, located in western Sudan, where, since 2003, nearly 300,000 people have died, some in combat, others from starvation or after being driven from their homes. The United Nations estimates that nearly 2.5 million citizens of Darfur have fled the fighting.

In 2003 the Sudan Liberation Army and the Justice and Equality Movement attacked government infrastructure in Darfur to retaliate against Sudan's government for oppressing the black Sudanese population while giving favor to Arab Sudanese citizens. The people of Darfur demanded equal access to the economic resources enjoyed by the Arab population. Bashir's government, and his Janjaweed military forces, responded by launching attacks against Darfur, burning cities to the ground and murdering citizens. A peace agreement signed in May 2006 had proved to be ineffective, leading to a rise in violence, and there was some worry that the ICC's decision could completely scuttle the already weak agreement.

THE INTERNATIONAL CRIMINAL COURT'S DECISION

Arrest warrants were issued in 2007 for Humanitarian Affairs Minister Ahmed Haroun and Janjaweed militia leader Ali Abdul Rahman. Two years later a three-judge panel made the decision, in a 2–1 vote, to issue the arrest warrant for Bashir and charge him with war crimes and crimes against humanity, citing such acts as murder, extermination, forcible transfer, torture, rape, pillaging, and directing attacks against civilians. Prosecutors had hoped for a charge of genocide, but the panel decided that there was not enough evidence to support it. Laurence Blairon, spokesperson for the ICC, said, "In this particular case, the pretrial chamber has not been able to find there were reasonable grounds to establish a genocidal intent." To indict someone on charges of genocide, it must be proven that there was a clear intent to destroy all or part of a particular group.

In announcing the indictment, Blairon said that Bashir "is suspected of being criminally responsible . . . for intentionally directing attacks against an important part of the civilian population of Darfur, Sudan; murdering, exterminating, raping, torturing, and forcibly transferring large numbers of civilians, and pillaging their property." The defense in the case argued that the ICC could not directly tie Bashir to the ongoing atrocities in Darfur, but according to an ICC press release, the attacks on Darfur-based rebel groups were "a common plan agreed upon at the highest level of the Government of Sudan by Omar Al-Bashir and other high-ranking Sudanese political and military leaders."

While the ICC's decision is historic, the court has no authority to arrest Bashir in Sudan or any other country. It attempted to pressure Bashir to turn himself in by freezing his assets in Darfur, only to find out that he was hiding everything in accounts under different names. The court is thus forced to rely on the cooperation of other nations to arrest Bashir and bring him to the ICC. Even the United Nations has no authority to make an arrest, but according to Security Council Resolution 1593, Sudan has a legal requirement to arrest Bashir. Although countries that are not a part of the ICC, including Sudan, have the *option* to arrest Bashir and send him to the court, countries that are a part of the ICC are *required* to do so. Amnesty International secretary general Irene Kahn said, "The law is clear. President al Bashir must appear before the ICC to defend himself. If he refuses to do so, the Sudanese authorities must ensure that he is arrested and surrendered immediately to the ICC." Sudan's constitution gives the president immunity from criminal prosecution while serving as head of state. International organizations like the ICC, however, do not recognize such immunity. If Bashir is brought to the ICC, tried, and convicted, he would face life in prison.

Sudan's Reaction to the Warrant

Before the indictment, Sudanese vice president Salva Kiir said, "In the event the court agrees with the chief prosecutor, the [Sudan People's Liberation Movement] will work with its partners in the NCP [National Congress Party] on how to politically and diplomatically handle the decision of the court." He called on the rest of the world to maintain its engagement in Sudan, saying, "The collapse of peace in Sudan shall not only hurt the Sudan itself, but shall also have serious repercussions in the region."

The Sudanese government struck back against the ICC's ruling, calling it a political decision that had no merit and was meant to destabilize the country. The ICC's Blairon, however, said, "The findings of the judges are made on purely legal criteria. This is really important—the court is not a political institution. It speaks the language of the law." The Sudanese government argued that because the chief prosecutor on the case was never allowed into Darfur to investigate anything alleged in the case, the charges were moot.

The Sudanese embassy in Beijing released a statement reasserting its position that it would not give up its president to the ICC. "Sudan is not a member state of the ICC, so it should not be subjected to the ICC's jurisdiction and will not bow to its ruling." The embassy said that the ICC is in violation of international law by trying to force a non-member sovereign state to carry out the wishes of the court.

Mustafa Osman, Sudanese presidential advisor, said, "The court is only one mechanism of neo-colonialist policy used by the West against free and independent countries . . . they do not want Sudan to become stable." Salah Gosh, head of Sudan's intelligence division, called for "the amputation of the hands and the slitting of the throats of any person who dares badmouth al-Bashir or support the International Criminal Court's allegations," which the country sees as a move to collect Sudan's wealth and natural resources.

The Sudanese government compared its decision to not ratify the ICC treaty to that of the United States, another country that is not party to the ICC. "The American government said it was not ready to send any American citizen to the court," said Ghazi Suleiman, a human rights lawyer in Sudan. "So we are just following the steps of our beloved Americans."

After the ICC's ruling, Sudan forced more than ten aid groups, which combined accounted for 60 percent of humanitarian assistance in Darfur, to leave the country, including Oxfam, Doctors Without Borders, and CARE International. These groups help provide medical assistance, food, and clean water to a country that often struggles to provide basic services to its citizens. The humanitarian operation in Darfur is currently the largest effort in the world to provide relief to those suffering from disease, malnutrition, and other problems that result from refugee status. The offices of these organizations based in Sudan were raided, and many of the aid workers who were asked to leave the country said that they were accused of providing information to the ICC for its case against Bashir.

INTERNATIONAL RESPONSE

The issuance of the arrest warrant has some of Sudan's neighbors concerned for the stability of the country and the safety of the region. In opposition to the ICC arrest warrant are the African Union, the Arab League, and the Organization of the Islamic Conference. The African Union and Arab League, fearing the collapse of the fragile peace agreement between Sudan and Darfur, pressured the United Nations to encourage the ICC to wait at least another year to issue its indictment. This time frame, they argued, would allow the peace talks between rebels based in Darfur and officials in Sudan's government to reach a conclusion. African member nations threatened to leave the ICC if an indictment was issued. Of the 108 members of the ICC, thirty are African countries.

Some international analysts thought that it was a bad time for the indictment to be brought against Bashir because Sudan was in a period of particular instability. In Darfur, rebel groups were gaining power and expanding into neighboring countries, causing a new threat of instability that could have jeopardized Darfur's 2009 elections, which were later postponed. The southern part of Sudan, which is considered semiautonomous, had an increasingly tense relationship with Sudan's government in Khartoum. In a statement from its embassy in Berlin, the government of Sudan called the timing of the issuance of the arrest warrant "a huge mistake." The statement continued by explaining that some of the more positive developments in Sudan, including the comprehensive peace agreement, the Abuja peace agreement, and the peace process in Doha, could be threatened by the ICC's decision. "In addition," the embassy statement claimed, "it may send the wrong signal to the rebels who may end up hardening their positions." On the other hand, there were myriad others who maintained that it was time for the international community to come together and bring justice to the people of Darfur. The International Crisis Group's deputy president, Nick Grono, said in response to the ICC's ruling, "The international community should affirm its support for the court and insist that Sudan and other countries cooperate with it as required by the UN Security Council." There was widespread belief that the United Nations would suspend the ICC's decision in an effort to coerce Sudan to peacefully deal with the situation in Darfur and with southern Sudan. The United Nations, however, recognizing the independence of the ICC, let the decision stand.

Bashir Responds

President Bashir, a member of the National Congress Party, continued campaigning to garner support for his government in September 2010 elections, telling the ICC that they could "eat" their decision. The view by the international community was that Bashir would fear traveling outside of Sudan, because any nation, regardless of its membership status in the ICC, could arrest him and turn him over. Bashir, however, has not shown any signs of staying within his own country. After the arrest warrant was issued, Bashir visited Egypt, Ethiopia, Qatar, and Zimbabwe, all without incident.

In March 2009, Bashir took what some interpreted as a victory tour of Darfur, driving through a field while supporters cheered, "Bashir is in our hearts." Sudan had been trying to prove to the world that it does not fear the decision of the ICC and had no plans to carry out an arrest of Bashir. During his trip to Darfur, Bashir told supporters that he does not care if the United Nations votes to reverse the decision of the ICC. "Anyone who supports the court is under my shoe," he told supporters. During a forty-minute speech to the people gathered in Darfur, Bashir blamed the ICC's decision on the United States, asking why the western country is allowed to judge Sudan. "Down, down USA! We won't be ruled by the CIA!" the crowds cheered. Bashir's speech was not only a show of defiance to the ICC but also a rallying cry to the people. "Get ready," Bashir told the crowds, "We are the grandsons of martyrs."

—Heather Kerrigan

Following is the warrant for the arrest of Sudan's president, Omar al-Bashir, issued by the International Criminal Court (ICC) on March 4, 2009, and a press release from the Sudanese embassy in Berlin from March 4, 2009, speaking out against the decision of the ICC to issue an arrest warrant for the leader of a non-ICC signatory.

ICC Decision to Charge Omar al-Bashir with War Crimes and Crimes Against Humanity

March 4, 2009

Situation in Dafur, Sudan

In the case of

The prosecutor v. Omar Hassan Ahmad Al Bashir ("Omar Al Bashir")

Public Document Warrant of Arrest for Omar Hassan Ahmad Al Bashir

PRE-TRIAL CHAMBER I of the International Criminal Court ("the Chamber" and "the Court" respectively);

HAVING EXAMINED the "Prosecution's Application under Article 58" ("the Prosecution Application"), filed by the Prosecution on 14 July 2008 in the record of the situation in Darfur, Sudan ("the Darfur situation") requesting the issuance of a warrant for the arrest of Omar Hassan Ahmad Al Bashir (hereinafter referred to as "Omar Al Bashir") for genocide, crimes against humanity and war crimes;

HAVING EXAMINED the supporting material and other information submitted by the Prosecution;

NOTING the "Decision on the Prosecution's Request for a Warrant of Arrest against Omar Hassan Ahmad Al Bashir" in which the Chamber held that it was satisfied that there are reasonable grounds to believe that Omar Al Bashir is criminally responsible under article 25(3)(a) of the Statute as an indirect perpetrator, or as an indirect co-perpetrator, for war crimes and crimes against humanity and that his arrest appears to be necessary under article 58(1)(b) of the *Rome Statute* ("the Statute");

NOTING articles 19 and 58 of the Statute;

CONSIDERING that, on the basis of the material provided by the Prosecution in support of the Prosecution Application and without prejudice to any subsequent determination that may be made under article 19 of the Statute, the case against Omar Al Bashir falls within the jurisdiction of the Court;

CONSIDERING that, on the basis of the material provided by the Prosecution in support of the Prosecution Application, there is no ostensible cause or self-evident factor to impel the Chamber to exercise its discretion under article 19(1) of the Statute to determine at this stage the admissibility of the case against Omar Al Bashir;

CONSIDERING that there are reasonable grounds to believe that from March 2003 to at least 14 July 2008, a protracted armed conflict not of an international character within the meaning of article 8(2)(f) of the Statute existed in Darfur between the Government of Sudan ("the GoS") and several organised armed groups, in particular the Sudanese Liberation Movement/Army ("the SLM/A") and the Justice and Equality Movement ("the JEM");

CONSIDERING that there are reasonable grounds to believe: (i) that soon after the attack on El Fasher airport in April 2003, the GoS issued a general call for the mobilisation of the Janjaweed Militia in response to the activities of the SLM/A, the JEM and other armed opposition groups in Darfur, and thereafter conducted, through GoS forces, including the Sudanese Armed Forces and their allied Janjaweed Militia, the Sudanese Police Force, the National Intelligence and Security Service ("the NISS") and the Humanitarian Aid Commission ("the HAC"), a counterinsurgency campaign throughout the Darfur region against the said armed opposition groups; and (ii) that the counter-insurgency campaign continued until the date of the filing of the Prosecution Application on 14 July 2008;

CONSIDERING that there are reasonable grounds to believe: (i) that a core component of the GoS counter-insurgency campaign was the unlawful attack on that part of the civilian population of Darfur—belonging largely to the Fur, Masalit and Zaghawa groups—perceived by the GoS as being close to the SLM/A, the JEM and the other armed groups opposing the GoS in the ongoing armed conflict in Darfur; and (ii) that, as part of this core component of the counter-insurgency campaign, GoS forces systematically committed acts of pillaging after the seizure of the towns and villages that were subject to their attacks;

CONSIDERING, therefore, that there are reasonable grounds to believe that from soon after the April 2003 attack in El Fasher airport until 14 July 2008, war crimes within the meaning of articles 8(2)(e)(i) and 8(2)(e)(v) of the Statute were committed by GoS forces, including the Sudanese Armed Forces and their allied Janjaweed Militia, the Sudanese Police Force, the NISS and the HAC, as part of the above-mentioned GoS counter-insurgency campaign;

CONSIDERING, further, that there are reasonable grounds to believe that, insofar as it was a core component of the GoS counter-insurgency campaign, there was a GoS policy to unlawfully attack that part of the civilian population of Darfur—belonging largely to the Fur, Masalit and Zaghawa groups—perceived by the GoS as being close to the SLM/A, the JEM and other armed groups opposing the GoS in the ongoing armed conflict in Darfur;

CONSIDERING that there are reasonable grounds to believe that the unlawful attack on the above-mentioned part of the civilian population of Darfur was (i) widespread, as it affected, at least, hundreds of thousands of individuals and took place across large swathes of the territory of the Darfur region; and (ii) systematic, as the acts of violence involved followed, to a considerable extent, a similar pattern;

CONSIDERING that there are reasonable grounds to believe that, as part of the GoS's unlawful attack on the above-mentioned part of the civilian population of Darfur and with knowledge of such attack, GoS forces subjected, throughout the Darfur region, thousands of civilians, belonging primarily to the Fur, Masalit and Zaghawa groups, to acts of murder and extermination;

CONSIDERING that there are also reasonable grounds to believe that, as part of the GoS's unlawful attack on the above-mentioned part of the civilian population of Darfur and with knowledge of such attack, GoS forces subjected, throughout the Darfur region, (i) hundreds of thousands of civilians, belonging primarily to the Fur, Masalit and Zaghawa groups, to acts of forcible transfer; (ii) thousands of civilian women, belonging primarily to these groups, to acts of rape; and (iii) civilians, belonging primarily to the same groups, to acts of torture;

CONSIDERING therefore that there are reasonable grounds to believe that, from soon after the April 2003 attack on El Fasher airport until 14 July 2008, GoS forces, including the Sudanese Armed Forces and their allied Janjaweed Militia, the Sudanese Police Force, the NISS and the HAC, committed crimes against humanity consisting of murder, extermination, forcible transfer, torture and rape, within the meaning of articles 7(1)(a), (b), (d), (f) and (g) respectively of the Statute, throughout the Darfur region;

CONSIDERING that there are reasonable grounds to believe that Omar Al Bashir has been the *de jure* and *de facto* President of the State of Sudan and Commander-in-Chief of the Sudanese Armed Forces from March 2003 to 14 July 2008, and that, in that position, he played an essential role in coordinating, with other high-ranking Sudanese political and military leaders, the design and implementation of the above-mentioned GoS counter-insurgency campaign;

CONSIDERING, further, that the Chamber finds, in the alternative, that there are reasonable grounds to believe: (i) that the role of Omar Al Bashir went beyond coordinating the design and implementation of the common plan; (ii) that he was in full control of all branches of the "apparatus" of the State of Sudan, including the Sudanese Armed Forces and their allied Janjaweed Militia, the Sudanese Police Force, the NISS and the HAC; and (iii) that he used such control to secure the implementation of the common plan;

CONSIDERING that, for the above reasons, there are reasonable grounds to believe that Omar Al Bashir is criminally responsible as an indirect perpetrator, or as an indirect co-perpetrator, under article 25(3)(a) of the Statute, for:

    i. intentionally directing attacks against a civilian population as such or against individual civilians not taking direct part in hostilities as a war crime, within the meaning of article 8(2)(e)(i) of the Statute;

    ii. pillage as a war crime, within the meaning of article 8(2)(e)(v) of the Statute;

    iii. murder as a crime against humanity, within the meaning of article 7(1)(a) of the Statute;

    iv. extermination as a crime against humanity, within the meaning of article 7(1)(b) of the Statute;

    v. forcible transfer as a crime against humanity, within the meaning of article 7(1)(d) of the Statute;

    vi. torture as a crime against humanity, within the meaning of article 7(1)(f) of the Statute; and

    vii. rape as a crime against humanity, within the meaning of article 7(1)(g) of the Statute;

CONSIDERING that, under article 58(1) of the Statute, the arrest of Omar Al Bashir appears necessary at this stage to ensure (i) that he will appear before the Court; (ii) that he will not obstruct or endanger the ongoing investigation into the crimes for which he is allegedly responsible under the Statute; and (iii) that he will not continue with the commission of the above-mentioned crimes;

    FOR THESE REASONS,

    HEREBY ISSUES:

    A WARRANT OF ARREST for **OMAR AL BASHIR**, a male, who is a national of the State of Sudan, born on 1 January 1944 in Hoshe Bannaga, Shendi Governorate, in the Sudan, member of the Jaáli tribe of Northern Sudan, President of the Republic of the Sudan since his appointment by the RCC-NS on 16 October 1993 and elected as such successively since 1 April 1996 and whose name is also spelt Omar al-Bashir, Omer Hassan Ahmed El Bashire, Omar al-Bashir, Omar al-Beshir, Omar el-Bashir, Omer Albasheer, Omar Elbashir and Omar Hassan Ahmad el-Béshir.

    Done in English, Arabic and French, the English version being authoritative.

    Judge Akua Kuenyehia

    Presiding Judge

    Judge Anita Ušacka

    Judge Sylvia Steiner

    Dated this Wednesday, 4 March 2009

    At The Hague, The Netherlands

SOURCE: The International Criminal Court. Docket no. ICC-02/05-01/09. "Situation in Darfur, Sudan, in the Case of the Prosecutor v. Omar Hassan Ahmad al Bashir ('Omar al Bashir')." March 4, 2009. www.icc-cpi.int/iccdocs/doc/doc639078.pdf.

Sudanese Statement on Arrest Warrant Issued by the ICC

March 4, 2009

Sudan reiterates its well known position to never turn [over] Sudanese citizens for trial abroad. It has not ratified the ICC treaty & consequently the court has no jurisdiction over the country or its citizens. The logic is straightforward and simple: Sudan is not party to the court statute, hence the country owes no treaty obligations to the ICC.

However, the country is keen to end impunity. We emphasize the fact that Sudan, as an independent and sovereign nation, is committed to the principle of prosecuting the perpetrators of Darfur crimes. The country is willing & able to prosecute all offenders. It has a capable, professional and impartial judiciary. We have full confidence in the Sudanese judiciary system's ability to dispense justice. In this case, and according to the complementarity principle, the ICC does not take precedence over domestic courts.

It must be stated on this occasion that the referral of the case against Sudan's president to the ICC, in the first place, was a political exercise par excellence in both substance and style. The Security Council had no right to start with to refer a non-signatory party to the ICC. The Council, in the process of doing this, made [a] mockery of the legal ideal of equality of all before the law. This manifested itself when the Council struck a political deal with the US not to veto resolution 1593 in exchange of exemption of its citizens from any future trial in the ICC. As a result resolution 1593 violated the letter and spirit of the Rome Statute of the ICC. This vintage international power politics in which small countries, like Sudan, are compelled to the will of the powerful reinforces the perception of [a] double standard in matters of global governance. And as a result it severely undermined the court's credibility and legitimacy.

Mr. Ocampo, on his part, made a political rather than a legal or professional case against the president. He cited in his memorandum a considerable amount of hearsay material that has no evidential value and is contrary to the expectation that he should have attempted to verify and corroborate the information. But it was clear that the stockpiling of the allegations to distort the image of Sudan and its president was more important than the legal notion of verification.

Playing politics with the UN processes and norms are not, however, a novel phenomenon in dealing with Sudan. We experienced this throughout the Darfur crisis. The forces, that do not have the interest of Sudan at heart, manipulated the UN process from the beginning of the crisis for nakedly political and geopolitical ends. That was clear in the simplistic characterization of the crisis: instead of being a conflict between local populations over meager resources because of the drought and desertification, it was transformed into a war between "Arabs" and "Africans." It was clear in the insistence that genocide was committed, although the European Union concluded in 2004 that the situation in Darfur was not genocide and so was the conclusion of the UN International Inquiry Commission in 2005. The African Union was of the same opinion. The focus was exclusively on the symptoms of the crisis rather than addressing the root causes of the problem and pushing the peace efforts. The regional dimension which contributes to the complexity of the conflict was always missing from the diagnosis. There was only a deliberate and consistent effort to distort reality and to demonize the country. And the irony of it all is that some of those who are criticizing Sudan in the name of human rights, are busy violating them somewhere else.

We would like also to bring to attention the fact that the timing of the latest move of the ICC was a huge mistake. Some neutral observers have expressed their fears of potential negative ramifications which may threaten a lot of positive developments in Sudan: the Comprehensive Peace Agreement, the Abuja Peace Agreement, the peace process in Doha, the democratic transformation and the elections which [are] scheduled for next September and the cooperation of the government with both AMIS and UNAMAID. In addition it may send the wrong signal to the rebels who may end up hardening their position.

As a country Sudan will do its part to preserve and safeguard these significant developments, but the international community has to do theirs as well. And here we say to the world, small as we are as a country, we want to be a force for good. We will join hands, in this respect, with all nations and people of good will who seek peace and justice.

SOURCE: Embassy of Sudan, in Berlin. Press release. "Sudanese Statement on Arrest Warrant Issued by the ICC." March 4, 2009. www.sudan-embassy.de/pressemitteilungen_11.html#ANCHOR_Text1.

OTHER HISTORIC DOCUMENTS OF INTEREST

FROM PREVIOUS *HISTORIC DOCUMENTS*

- The United Nations and Human Rights Coalition on the Violence in Darfur, *2007*, p. 385
- UN Security Council Resolution on Darfur Crisis in Sudan, *2006*, p. 497
- Secretary of State Powell on Genocide in Western Sudan, *2004*, p. 588

Gov. Bill Richardson Signs Bill to Repeal New Mexico's Death Penalty

MARCH 18, 2009

On March 18, 2009, New Mexico governor Bill Richardson signed into law a repeal of the state's death penalty, replacing it with life in prison without parole. With the governor's signature, New Mexico became the fifteenth state in the United States to abolish the death penalty but only the second state to do so through the legislative process since the U.S. Supreme Court upheld the death penalty in 1976. Other states, including New York, have placed a moratorium on the death penalty, some after declaring the practice in violation of their constitutions.

New Mexico has not often used the death penalty as a means of punishment. Since 1912, twenty-six people have been executed in New Mexico, and no one has been executed since 2001. Only two individuals remained on death row in the state in 2009. After the governor signed the bill, questions remained about whether the new law would lead to legal challenges if someone was sentenced to death before the law took effect on July 1, 2009.

LEGISLATIVE DEBATE

In recent years, the death penalty has engendered increasing debate, some of which has been over the constitutionality of execution methods. In 2008, the U.S. Supreme Court ruled in *Baze v. Rees,* a case brought by two Kentucky death row inmates, that the three-drug combination used for lethal injection is constitutional. In Ohio, the state proposed the use of one drug for lethal injection rather than three, after a botched execution using three drugs. In 2009, the death penalty was a hotly debated topic in state legislatures, and bills to repeal it were introduced in eleven states, including Colorado, Kansas, Maryland, Montana, and New Hampshire. In Colorado, the state planned to use the money it saved by abolishing the death penalty on an investigations unit that would help solve the state's 1,400 unsolved murder cases. In Montana, the state Senate passed a bill to abolish capital punishment, but the House Judiciary Committee voted against it. Maryland narrowed the scope of its use of the death penalty to cases involving conclusive DNA evidence or other biological evidence of guilt, a videotaped confession, or a videotape tying the defendant to the murder. In Connecticut, a legislative attempt to ban capital punishment was vetoed by Gov. Jodi Rell.

The bill to repeal the death penalty in New Mexico was first introduced in the state's legislature in 1999 by Democratic state representative Gail Chasey as a way to

keep victims' families from having to endure lengthy appeals processes. Chasey reintro-
duced the bill during each sixty-day, biannual legislative session, without much success.
In 2005 and 2007, the state House passed her repeal bill only to see it fail in the state
Senate.

In 2009, according to Chasey, the situation in the state was much different,
because of the economy and the election of President Barack Obama. According to
a press release from Chasey, "The time has come to take this step. As long as we
continue to have the death penalty, the risk remains that we will execute innocent
people. A sentence of life in prison without possibility of parole is an effective alternative. New Mexico spends several million dollars a year on death penalty cases, yet only
one person has been executed since 1961. Better that we repeal the death penalty, substitute life without parole and offer the victims' families restitution and support in their
healing process."

The argument from the opposition was that abolishing the death penalty would
excuse the crimes of violent offenders, letting them off with what seemed like a lesser
punishment. Chasey argued, "We are not excusing terribly violent murders, by any means.
. . . We believe society should be protected."

Chasey's bill passed in the state House 40–28, and was sent to the Senate Judiciary
Committee for consideration before bringing it before the full state Senate. A 6–5 vote on
the committee gave the measure the final push it needed to go before the full Senate. Only
one Democrat on the committee joined the four Republicans in opposing it. State senator
Richard Martinez, the lone Democrat, said, "I do believe that the death penalty is a deterrent. . . . In my heart, I think it is."

Debate in the Senate was heated; senators brought the Bible, Navajo beliefs, and
Quakerism into the discussion. On the opposition's side was Sen. Rod Adair, a Republican,
who said that he felt corrections officers were in danger when violent offenders were not
put to death. "There's no incentive for not killing a guard every time you get a chance," he
said. Adair went on to call capital punishment "a just penalty for the most heinous of
crimes in our society." The Democratic argument often rested on the view of the death
penalty shared by many around the world. "We are the last Western society that holds on
to it. . . . It makes us less than we should be," said Democratic state senator Gerald Ortiz
y Piño. The state Senate narrowly passed the measure with a 24-18 vote. All Senate
Republicans voted against abolishing the death penalty, and only three Senate Democrats
voted "no."

A FINANCIAL DECISION

In 2009, a budget deficit in thirty-one states gave a boost to any measure thought to save
money, including the abolition of the death penalty. In New Mexico, supporters thought
that this financial situation created a favorable atmosphere in which to advance their
cause. Governor Richardson, who had supported the death penalty as a member of the
U.S. Congress and opposed abolishing it in past years, said he was keeping an open mind.
It was believed the governor supported abolition of the death penalty partly because of
the cost. According to *State Legislatures* magazine, New Mexico's Supreme Court spends
up to $700,000 on appeals in a typical death penalty case on; only 7 percent of death
penalty cases result in a death sentence, while 68 percent are overturned on appeal, the
highest rate in the United States.

Supporters argued that abolishing the death penalty would save states money in legal fees that would have been spent on cases challenging the death penalty, while opponents said the legal fees would still be paid because of trials brought by inmates contesting life in prison. A report released by the Death Penalty Information Center (DPIC) found that states and localities can save millions of dollars by abolishing the death penalty. In the 1990s, the number of death sentences handed out each year in the United States was approximately 300, and more recently, that number has decreased to 115 per year. The number of executions is falling at a similar rate. According to the DPIC, 2009 was set to end with the lowest number of executions since the death penalty was reinstated in 1976. Richard Dieter, the DPIC's executive director, said, "The death penalty is turning into a very expensive form of life without parole. . . . At a time of budget shortfalls, the death penalty cannot be exempt from reevaluation alongside other wasteful government programs that no longer make sense."

Debate had been ongoing about whether housing and feeding someone sentenced to life in prison is more expensive than executing an inmate, but based on financial data from the states, execution was shown to be far more expensive. For example, California, which has the nation's largest number of people on death row, has carried out eleven executions since 1978, at an average cost of $250 million per person. The state estimates that it costs approximately $137 million per year to maintain the death penalty. However, according to data from the DPIC study, if California moved to a system where life without parole is the harshest sentence handed down, it would cost only $126 million per year to run, saving the state an estimated $11 million each year. In Maryland, the state has spent $186 million since 1978 to keep its death penalty system running and has only executed five inmates during that time. In New Jersey, where the legislature voted to abolish the death penalty, it is estimated that the state had spent more than $250 million between 1983 and 2007 to keep the system running and had not carried out a single execution. The DPIC report estimates that since 1976 $2 billion had been spent nationwide on the death penalty system. These costs, the report claimed, could have been saved if the most severe punishment was life in prison.

The high cost of carrying out a death penalty sentence is multifaceted. One reason is that investigations take more time and money in a death penalty case to reach a conclusion. It can cost up to sixteen times more to litigate a death penalty case than one where the accused is being sentenced to life in prison. After the trial and sentencing, there is often a lengthy appeals process. In total, it is approximated that it costs twenty-one times more to carry out a death sentence than a life sentence. Cutting the cost of capital punishment is not easy and often not an option, because the U.S. Supreme Court has mandated certain trial-and-appeals protections for those convicted and sentenced to death. According to the DPIC, "The choice today is between a very expensive death penalty and one that risks falling below constitutional standards."

RICHARDSON SIGNS THE BILL

Richardson had three days from the time he was given the bill to the time he was required to sign it, and his office received 12,000 phone calls and e-mails from citizens across the state giving their opinion on what the governor should do; more than 75 percent were in favor of repealing the death penalty. Before signing the bill, the governor visited the state penitentiary. He told reporters "I wanted to see for myself the cells. . . . My conclusion is those may be something worse than death."

Richardson called signing Bill 285 the hardest decision he had ever made. "I know we did the right thing, but I'm not totally convinced every argument I made to you is accurate." He stated, however, that he no longer had "confidence in the criminal justice system" in its current form to decide who should live and who should die. He drew on the fact that at the time he signed the bill, 130 death row inmates had been exonerated over the past ten years; four of those exonerations occurred in New Mexico.

Prosecutors made it clear after the governor signed the bill that because the bill did not apply to crimes committed before July 1, 2009, they would still keep the option of the death penalty on the table in all cases where it applied. Others in the state said that pursuing capital punishment after the governor signed the bill would send a contradictory message. According to Viki Elkey, executive director of the New Mexico Coalition to Repeal the Death Penalty, "I find it hard to believe there's support in the state for an execution order after we've passed this bill."

As for the two men remaining on New Mexico's death row, Robert Fry and Timothy Allen, they could still face execution because they were convicted before the new law went into effect. The governor had no plans to commute their sentences.

—Heather Kerrigan

Following are New Mexico governor Bill Richardson's remarks on signing House Bill 285, which repealed the state's death penalty, on March 18, 2009.

Gov. Bill Richardson Signs Repeal of the Death Penalty

March 18, 2009

SANTA FE—Governor Bill Richardson today signed House Bill 285, Repeal of the Death Penalty. The Governor's remarks follow:

Today marks the end of a long, personal journey for me and the issue of the death penalty.

Throughout my adult life, I have been a firm believer in the death penalty as a just punishment—in very rare instances, and only for the most heinous crimes. I still believe that.

But six years ago, when I took office as Governor of the State of New Mexico, I started to challenge my own thinking on the death penalty.

The issue became more real to me because I knew the day would come when one of two things might happen: I would either have to take action on legislation to repeal the death penalty, or more daunting, I might have to sign someone's death warrant.

I'll be honest. The prospect of either decision was extremely troubling. But I was elected by the people of New Mexico to make just this type of decision.

So, like many of the supporters who took the time to meet with me this week, I have believed the death penalty can serve as a deterrent to some who might consider murdering a law enforcement officer, a corrections officer, a witness to a crime or kidnapping and murdering a child. However, people continue to commit terrible crimes even in the face of the death penalty and responsible people on both sides of the debate disagree—strongly—on this issue.

But what we cannot disagree on is the finality of this ultimate punishment. Once a conclusive decision has been made and executed, it cannot be reversed. And it is in consideration of this, that I have made my decision.

I have decided to sign legislation that repeals the death penalty in the state of New Mexico.

Regardless of my personal opinion about the death penalty, I do not have confidence in the criminal justice system as it currently operates to be the final arbiter when it comes to who lives and who dies for their crime. If the State is going to undertake this awesome responsibility, the system to impose this ultimate penalty must be perfect and can never be wrong.

But the reality is the system is not perfect—far from it. The system is inherently defective.

DNA testing has proven that. Innocent people have been put on death row all across the country.

Even with advances in DNA and other forensic evidence technologies, we can't be 100 percent sure that only the truly guilty are convicted of capital crimes. Evidence, including DNA evidence, can be manipulated. Prosecutors can still abuse their powers. We cannot ensure competent defense counsel for all defendants. The sad truth is the wrong person can still be convicted in this day and age, and in cases where that conviction carries with it the ultimate sanction, we must have ultimate confidence—I would say certitude—that the system is without flaw or prejudice. Unfortunately, this is demonstrably not the case.

And it bothers me greatly that minorities are overrepresented in the prison population and on death row.

I have to say that all of the law enforcement officers, and especially the parents and spouses of murder victims, made compelling arguments to keep the death penalty. I respect their opinions and have taken their experiences to heart—which is why I struggled—even today—before making my final decision.

Yes, the death penalty is a tool for law enforcement. But it's not the only tool. For some would-be criminals, the death penalty may be a deterrent. But it's not, and never will be, for many, many others.

While today's focus will be on the repeal of the death penalty, I want to make clear that this bill I'm signing actually makes New Mexico safer. With my signature, we now have the option of sentencing the worst criminals to life in prison without the possibility of parole. They will never get out of prison.

Faced with the reality that our system for imposing the death penalty can never be perfect, my conscience compels me to replace the death penalty with a solution that keeps society safe.

The bill I am signing today, which was courageously carried for so many years by Representative Gail Chasey, replaces the death penalty with true life without the possibility of parole—a sentence that ensures violent criminals are locked away from society forever, yet can be undone if an innocent person is wrongfully convicted. More than 130 death row inmates have been exonerated in the past 10 years in this country, including four New Mexicans—a fact I cannot ignore.

From an international human rights perspective, there is no reason the United States should be behind the rest of the world on this issue. Many of the countries that continue to support and use the death penalty are also the most repressive nations in the world. That's not something to be proud of.

In a society which values individual life and liberty above all else, where justice and not vengeance is the singular guiding principle of our system of criminal law, the potential for wrongful conviction and, God forbid, execution of an innocent person stands as anathema to our very sensibilities as human beings. That is why I'm signing this bill into law.

Source: Office of the Governor of New Mexico. Press release. "Governor Bill Richardson Signs Repeal of the Death Penalty." March 18, 2009. www.governor.state.nm.us/press/2009/march/031809_02.pdf.

OTHER HISTORIC DOCUMENTS OF INTEREST

FROM THIS VOLUME

FROM PREVIOUS *HISTORIC DOCUMENTS*

DOCUMENT IN CONTEXT

Same-Sex Marriage in the States

MARCH 25, JUNE 3 AND 17, DECEMBER 2 AND 3, 2009

Same-sex marriage made headway in the states in 2009, with New Hampshire, Vermont, Maine, Washington, D.C., and New York all seeing legislative action on the issue. Although New Hampshire, Vermont, and Washington, D.C., passed laws to allow same-sex couples to marry within their borders, Maine and New York saw any immediate chance for legalizing same-sex marriage ended by voters and their legislatures. By the end of the year, six states allowed gay couples to marry, and related legal battles were beginning in other states. The uptick in action on the same-sex marriage debate followed on the heels of the California vote in November 2008 that overturned a state Supreme Court decision and banned gay marriage in the state, a decision that at the end of 2009 was mired in a legal battle.

Those in support of legislation legalizing same-sex marriage pointed to the benefit not only to the couples but also to the states that allow the practice. According to Minnesota state senator Scott Dibble, couples that are married are better off both financially and because they receive the benefits of marriage, such as joint credit and the opportunity to have health care insurance through a spouse's employer. Opponents said that allowing same-sex couples to marry would devalue the institution of marriage and be a detriment to society.

According to Gary Gates, a demographer at the University of California, Los Angeles, there is a "noticeable economic benefit" for states to legalize same-sex marriage. This includes an increase in tourism by those living in states without gay marriage laws, which spurs revenue for hotels, banquet facilities, and restaurants, according to Gates, which in turn could lead to an increase in jobs.

Although a state can pass a law legalizing same-sex marriage, under the 1996 Defense of Marriage Act, signed by President Bill Clinton, the federal government will not recognize same-sex marriages and will therefore not extend federal benefits to same-sex couples. President Barack Obama tried to provide greater equality to same-sex couples by signing an executive order in June 2009 that would give some benefits to the same-sex partners of federal employees.

At the signing of the executive order, Obama said, "We've got more work to do to ensure that government treats all its citizens equally, to fight injustice and intolerance in all its forms and to bring about that more perfect union." Obama's executive order gives same-sex partners of federal civil service employees the ability to seek long-term health care under their partner's benefits; the right to use their sick leave to care for a domestic partner; and for those in the Foreign Service, partners of same-sex couples will now be included in evacuation and housing allocations.

Obama's executive order seemed to have little impact on the gay community. Some of the federal employees who would be able to give their partners coverage under the president's memorandum said many of the benefits were already available to both same-sex and heterosexual couples. Others took this opportunity to increase pressure on the president to end the military's "Don't Ask, Don't Tell" policy. Beyond this guarantee of benefits to federal employees, however, decisions on equality for same-sex couples was largely left up to the states.

Since 2003, seven states have legalized same-sex marriage, but in two of those states, the legislation has been overturned—by voters in Maine and in California. Nationwide, pollsters report that the electorate is increasingly in support of gay marriage, but when they perceive the issue is being pushed too quickly, they vote against it. With this knowledge, the states and cities that sought to legalize gay marriage in 2009 had to tread lightly.

VERMONT

In March 2009, Republican governor Jim Douglas vetoed a bill passed by the state legislature that would have allowed same-sex couples to marry in Vermont. The next day, the state Senate, where twenty-six of thirty senators supported the initial same-sex marriage bill, voted to override the governor's veto and sent it to the state House, where 100 of 150 representatives voted for the override. Some of the eleven Democrats who initially voted against the bill in the state House said they would vote for the override in an effort to send the governor a message to discourage him from deciding to override legislation before receiving a copy of the bill, as he had done in this case.

Governor Douglas said that the override was "not unexpected" and called the decision to work on gay marriage legislation a distraction during an economic crisis. "What really disappoints me is that we have spent some time on an issue during which another thousand Vermonters have lost their jobs," said Governor Douglas. "We need to turn our attention to balancing a budget without raising taxes, growing the economy, putting more people to work."

On September 1, 2009, the law went into effect and Vermont became the fourth state in the United States to recognize gay marriage.

MAINE

On May 6, 2009, Democratic governor John Baldacci signed a bill that would allow same-sex couples in Maine to marry. "I did not come to this decision lightly or in haste," Baldacci said. In the past, the governor had supported civil unions for same-sex couples but opposed marriage. In signing the bill, the governor pointed to his responsibility to uphold the state's constitution, which in Article I says "no person shall be deprived of life, liberty or property . . . nor be denied the equal protection of the laws, nor be denied the enjoyment of that person's civil rights or be discriminated against." In a statement, the governor also said that he recognized he would not have the final say on the issue, as he anticipated it would be taken to court or put before voters, but to fulfill his duty as governor, he said he had to sign the legislation.

Although the new law ensured that religious groups did not have to recognize or perform same-sex marriages, opponents, many of whom represented religious organizations, collected 85,000 signatures to bring the bill (Proposition 1) to a vote before the

Maine electorate in November 2009. Collectively, the "No on 1" and "Yes on 1" groups spent $7 million campaigning, with the pro–same-sex marriage lobby ("No on 1") outspending their opponents. When the votes were counted, "Yes on 1" had won by a slim margin, with 52.8 percent of the vote, thereby overturning gay marriage; no same-sex marriages were performed in Maine after the governor signed the bill. With the 2010 election looming, both sides of the debate said they would continue to fight, with opposition groups advocating a constitutional amendment banning gay marriage.

New Hampshire

New Hampshire, a state that had previously legalized same-sex civil unions, took another step in 2009, allowing same-sex couples to marry beginning on January 1, 2010, making it the sixth state to give gay couples this right. Gov. John Lynch, a Democrat, had said that before he would sign the bill it needed to include a measure that would exempt religious organizations from being required to take part in the marriages of gay couples or be required to perform marriage counseling or offer marriage courses to gay couples. "New Hampshire's great tradition has always been to come down on the side of individual liberty and protections," said Lynch. "But following that tradition means we must act to protect both the liberty of same-sex couples and religious liberty." The state House agreed to a Senate compromise bill on May 6, 2009, that included a religious provision and also included a definition of the difference between religious and civil marriage. Opponents of New Hampshire's bill said the language used, while required by Governor Lynch, did not offer enough protection to organizations that do not agree with same-sex marriage.

New York

In December in New York, the state Senate rejected a bill in a 38–24 vote that would have allowed gay couples to marry. Debate was impassioned, with Sen. Diane Savino sharing stories about New York state assembly members who would be able to marry their partners if the bill had passed. "We have nothing to fear from Tom Duane and Louis. We have nothing to fear from Danny O'Donnell and his partner. We have nothing to fear from people who are committed to each other, who want to share their lives and protect one another in the event of sickness, illness, or death. We have nothing to fear from love and commitment."

The bill's defeat shocked some, especially in heavily Democratic New York. Activists on both sides of the issue lobbied the legislature for more than one year. Supporters spent approximately $1 million in legislative races to seat candidates who would support gay marriage. Deputy Republican leader senator Tom Libous blamed the vote on the economy. "I just don't think the majority care too much about [gay marriage] at this time because they're out of work, they want to see the state reduce spending, and they are having a hard time making ends meet. And I don't mean to sound callous, but that's true." Democratic leadership in the state supported the bill, including Gov. David Paterson, but the problem arose on the Senate floor when opponents of the bill remained silent during the debate, giving Democrats false hope that an earlier agreement with Republicans would hold up, and when those from politically vulnerable districts in the upcoming election voted "no." At the time Democrats held thirty-two of sixty-two seats in the New York state Senate. Republicans who supported the measure said the deal they worked out with

Democrats ensured that the limited Democrats would have enough Democratic members to support the bill so that only a limited number of Republicans would have to risk a yes vote. The defeat of the measure almost ensures that it will not come up again, at the earliest, until the new legislature is seated in 2011.

A poll released the day of the vote by the Marist Institute for Public Opinion in Poughkeepsie, New York, showed that 51 percent of registered voters supported same-sex marriage and 42 percent opposed it.

Washington, D.C.

On December 15, 2009, the Washington, D.C., City Council passed a measure that would allow same-sex marriage. The mayor signed the bill, making the District of Columbia the first jurisdiction below the Mason-Dixon line to allow gay couples to marry. Congress was given one month to review the measure because it has constitutional authority to approve or deny any measure passed by the city's government. Opponents of the measure vowed to fight it through Congress by encouraging members to exercise their authority over city regulations, or in the courts. "The city Council's action today is not the final word," said Bishop Harry Jackson, chair of Stand4MarriageDC. In the District bill, churches and other religious organizations would not be required to perform same-sex marriages or provide space for them. The Catholic archdiocese said the church feared being required to provide benefits to same-sex couples.

—Heather Kerrigan

Following is a press release from March 25, 2009, from Vermont governor James Douglas in which he speaks out against same-sex marriage; a statement by New Hampshire governor John Lynch on June 3, 2009, on signing a bill permitting to same-sex marriage; a statement by President Barack Obama on issuing an executive order on June 17, 2009, giving some benefits to same-sex federal employees; and statements by two New York state senators on December 2 and 3, 2009, for and against that state's same-sex marriage legislation.

Vermont Governor James Douglas on Same-Sex Marriage

March 25, 2009

"The urgency of our state's economic and budgetary challenges demands the full focus of every member and every committee of this Legislature. Ensuring that the federal recovery money is spent wisely, that the state budget is balanced and responsible, and that we do all we can to help our employers compete and create jobs is my top priority.

However, I recognize that legislative leaders have different priorities. So long as same-sex marriage consumes the time and energy of legislators, I will urge lawmakers to act quickly so they can turn their full focus to the economic needs of Vermonters as soon as possible.

The question of same sex marriage is an issue that does not break cleanly as Republican or Democrat, rural or urban, religious or atheist. It is an intensely personal decision—a decision informed by all of those things and many more—an amalgam of experience, conviction and faith. These beliefs are deeply held, passionately expressed and, for many legislators, infinitely more complex than the ultimate "yea" or "nay" required to fulfill the duty of their office.

For those on either side of the vote to sternly judge the other's morality and conscience is the only true intolerance in this debate and is a disservice to all Vermonters. I have Republican friends who will vote for this bill and Democratic friends who will vote against—and regardless of their vote, they will still be my friends and have my respect when this issue is resolved.

Vermont's civil union law has extended the same state rights, responsibilities and benefits of marriage to same-sex couples. I believe our civil union law serves Vermont well and I would support congressional action to extend those benefits at the federal level to states that recognize same-sex unions. But like President Obama and other leaders on both sides of the aisle, I believe that marriage should remain between a man and woman.

As you know, it's been a policy of mine not to announce whether or not I will veto a bill before it reaches my desk. But during these extraordinary times, the speculation about my decision has added to the anxiety of the moment and further diverts attention from our most pressing issues—and I cannot allow that to happen.

For those reasons and because I believe that by removing any uncertainty about my position we can move more quickly beyond this debate, I am announcing that I intend to veto this legislation when it reaches my desk.

On such an intensely divisive issue as this, I expect all members will vote as their individual conscience indicates and in the best interest of their districts, and not as the political leadership dictates. That said, I'm sure that legislative leaders would not have advanced this bill if they did not have the votes to override a veto. I will accept the outcome of their vote either way.

In the meantime, I will turn my attention and energy away from this issue and back to the issue that matters most to Vermonters: to growing our economy and creating good jobs.

I respect the passionate opinions of individuals on both sides of this debate and hope that when the Legislature makes their decision, whatever the outcome may be, we can move our state forward, toward a bright future for our children and grandchildren. We still have a great deal of work ahead of us and Vermonters are counting on us to work together to get the job done.

SOURCE: Office of the Governor of Vermont. Press release. "Statement of Governor James H. Douglas Regarding Same-Sex Marriage." March 25, 2009. http://governor.vermont.gov/tools/index.php?topic= GovPressReleases&id=3393&v=Article.

New Hampshire Governor John Lynch Signs Same-Sex Marriage Legislation

June 3, 2009

New Hampshire's great tradition has always been to come down on the side of individual liberties and protections.

That tradition continues today.

Two years ago in this room, I signed civil unions into law. That law gave same-sex couples in New Hampshire the rights and protections of marriage. And while civil unions was recognized as a step forward, many same-sex couples made compelling arguments that a separate system is not an equal system.

They argued that what might appear to be a minor difference in wording to some, lessened the dignity and legitimacy of their families.

At the same time, the word "marriage" has significant and religious connotations to many of our citizens.

They had concerns that this legislation would interfere with the ability of religious groups to freely practice their faiths.

Today, we are standing up for the liberties of same-sex couples by making clear that they will receive the same rights, responsibilities—and respect—under New Hampshire law.

Today, we are also standing up for religious liberties. This legislation makes clear that we understand that certain faiths do not recognize same-sex marriage, and it protects them from having to participate in marriage-related activities that violate their fundamental religious principles.

With the signing of this legislation today, New Hampshire will have taken every action possible to ensure that all families have equal rights to the extent that is possible under state law.

Unfortunately, the federal government does not extend the same rights and protections that New Hampshire provides same-sex families, and that should change.

Here in New Hampshire, this debate has been filled with passion and emotion on both sides.

Two years ago, after an equally passionate debate, the people of New Hampshire embraced civil unions as a natural part of New Hampshire's long tradition of opposing discrimination.

It is my hope, and my belief, that New Hampshire will again come together to embrace tolerance and respect, and to stand against discrimination.

That has [been] how we in New Hampshire have always lived our lives and that is how we will continue as we move forward.

Most families in New Hampshire will awaken tomorrow, go to work and to school, and feel no impact from what we have accomplished today.

But for some, they will awaken tomorrow knowing we have said to them that they are equal, that they have the same rights to live and to love as everyone else.

Today is a day to celebrate in New Hampshire. Today should not be considered a victory for some and a loss for others.

Today is a victory for all the people of New Hampshire, who I believe, in our own independent way, want tolerance for all.

That is truly the New Hampshire way.

SOURCE: Office of the Governor of New Hampshire. "Gov. Lynch Statement Regarding Same-Sex Marriage Legislation Signed into Law Today." June 3, 3009. www.governor.nh.gov/news/2009/060309_marriage.html.

Obama Signs Executive Order Giving Benefits to Some Same-Sex Couples

June 17, 2009

Well, today I'm proud to issue a Presidential memorandum that paves the way for long-overdue progress in our Nation's pursuit of equality. Many of our Government's hard-working and dedicated and patriotic public servants have long been denied basic rights that their colleagues enjoy for one simple reason, the people that they love are of the same sex.

Currently, for example, LGBT Federal employees can't always use sick leave to care for their domestic partners or their partners' children. Their partners aren't covered under long-term care insurance. Partners of American Foreign Service officers abroad aren't treated the same way when it comes to the use of medical facilities or visitation rights in case of an emergency. And these are just some of the wrongs that we intend to right today.

In consultation with Secretary of State Clinton, as well as OPM Director John Berry, my administration has completed a long and thorough review to identify a number of areas where we can extend Federal benefits to the same-sex partners of Foreign Service and executive branch Government employees.

And I'm requesting that Secretary Clinton and Director Berry do so where possible under existing law, and that the heads of all executive departments and agencies conduct reviews to determine where they may do the same.

Hundreds of Fortune 500 companies already offer such benefits, not only because it's the right thing to do, but because they recognize that it helps them compete for and retain the best possible talent, and we need top talent serving their country right now more than ever.

Now, under current law, we cannot provide same-sex couples with the full range of benefits enjoyed by heterosexual married couples. And that's why I'm proud to announce my support for the domestic partners benefits and obligations act; crucial legislation that will guarantee these rights for all Federal employees.

I want to thank Representative Tammy Baldwin, who is behind me somewhere—there she is right there—for her tireless leadership on this bill and in the broader struggle for equality. I want to thank Senators Joe Lieberman—Joe is here—as well as Susan Collins for championing this bill in the Senate, and Representative Barney Frank for his leadership on this and so many other issues. In fact, this is his second trip to the White House today.

It's a day that marks a historic step towards the changes we seek, but I think we all have to acknowledge this is only one step. Among the steps we have not yet taken is to repeal the Defense of Marriage Act. I believe it's discriminatory, I think it interferes with States' rights, and we will work with Congress to overturn it.

We've got more work to do to ensure that Government treats all its citizens equally, to fight injustice and intolerance in all its forms, and to bring about that more perfect union. I'm committed to these efforts, and I pledge to work tirelessly on behalf of these issues in the months and years to come.

Thank you very much everybody, and with that I am going to sign this executive order.

SOURCE: U.S. Executive Office of the President. "Remarks on Signing a Memorandum on Federal Benefits and Non-Discrimination." *Daily Compilation of Presidential Documents* 2009, no. 00475 (June 17, 2009). www.gpo.gov/fdsys/pkg/DCPD-200900475/pdf/DCPD-200900475.pdf.

New York State Senator Diane Savino in Support of Same-Sex Marriage

December 2, 2009

... Tens of thousands of New Yorkers' lives are hanging in the balance in this debate. They are either going to go home today knowing that we made history here in New York State, or they're going to go home incredibly disappointed but certainly unbowed, and the struggle will continue. ...

But this vote is not politics.

It's not about Democratic politics or Republican politics. It's not about who contributed to what campaign. It's not about who tried to make this body one party or another. It has absolutely nothing to do with that. This vote is about an issue of fairness and equality, not political.

It is about the fairness of people who are of the right age, of sound mind, who choose to live together, share everything together, and want to be able to have the protections that government grants those of us who have the privilege of marriage and treat it so cavalierly in our society. That's all this is about. Whether Senator Duane and his partner Louis, who are two of the most committed people I've ever met—I will tell you, I am over the age of 40, and that's all you're going to get from me—but I have never been able to maintain a relationship of the length or the quality that Tom Duane and Louis have. Why should they be denied the right to share their life together?

I don't know Assemblyman O'Donnell's partner, but I know he is as committed to him as Tom is to Louis, and as my friend Matt Titone is to his partner Josh.

These are relationships that I envy, and in fact we all should envy. And all they ask for is to be treated fairly and equally and be able to plan for each other in the event something happens to them . . .

. . . I was on 6th Avenue in Manhattan, I was in my car. . . . I was stopped at a light, I had my window open, and a young man on a pedicab stopped and stuck his head in the window of my car. . . .

And he said to me, "Excuse me. Is there going to be a gay marriage vote in Albany this week?" And I said, "Yes, the Assembly is going to take it up, but the Senate probably won't take it up any time soon. I'm not sure when."

And he said, "Are you going to vote for it?" And I said, "Yes, I am." And he said "Why?" And I said, "Because I believe that people should be able to share their life with whoever they want and the role of government is to administer that contract that they agree to enter into."

And he stopped and he said, "But they're changing the definition of marriage." And I said, "Don't get so excited about this marriage stuff." I said, "Think about this. We just met, you and I, right here at the stoplight. You stuck your head in the window of my car." I said, "Do you know tomorrow we go could go to City Hall, we could apply for a marriage license, and we could get married?" I said, "And nobody there will ask us about the quality of our relationship or whether we've been committed to each other or any of those things. They will issue that marriage license and we can get married."

And he said, "Yes, that's true." I said, "And do you think we're ready for that kind of commitment?"

And he stopped and he said, "I see your point." And that's really what this is about. We in government don't determine the quality or the validity of people's relationships. If we did, we would not issue three-quarters of the marriage licenses we do.

And I know there are many people in the religious community who feel that we're going to force this on them when that in fact is not true. We have never done that.

I'm a Roman Catholic. The Catholic Church has the right to deny me the sacrament of marriage if they determine the person I choose to marry is unfit or our relationship doesn't meet their standards. City Hall does not have that right. That will not change under this bill. . . .

I know many people are concerned about the destruction of the sanctity of marriage as well, and they view this as a threat. But let me ask you something, ladies and gentlemen. What are we really protecting, when you look at the divorce rate in our society? Turn on the television. We have a wedding channel on cable TV devoted to the behavior of people on the way to the altar. They spend billions of dollars, behave in the most appalling way, all in an effort to be princess for a day.

You don't have cable television? Put on network TV. We're giving away husbands on a game show. . . .

That's what we've done to marriage in America, where young women are socialized from the time they're 5 years old to think of being nothing but a bride. They plan every day what they'll wear, how they'll look, their invitations, the whole bit. They don't spend five minutes thinking about what it means to be a wife.

People stand up there before God and man, even in Senator Diaz's church, they swear to love, honor and obey—they don't mean a word of it. And so if there's anything wrong or any threat to the sanctity of marriage in America, it comes from those of us who have the privilege and the right, and we have abused it for decades.

We have nothing to fear from Tom Duane and Louis. We have nothing to fear from Danny O'Donnell and his partner. We have nothing to fear from people who are committed to each other, who want to share their lives and protect one another in the event of sickness, illness, or death. We have nothing to fear from love and commitment.

My only hope, Tom, is that we pass this bill, the Governor signs it, and then we can learn from you and you don't learn from us.

I vote aye.

SOURCE: New York State Senator Diane Savino. *New York State Senate Session Transcripts* (December 2, 2009): 7665–7673.

New York State Senator Carl Kruger Votes No on Same-Sex Marriage

December 3, 2009

Throughout my fifteen years in the Senate I have supported and advocated passionately for legislation that furthers the cause of human rights and fairness for all. Included in this legislation have been measures that have solidified succession rights on apartments, health care proxies, and the right to share property in this state and the legal obligations that go along with it. I was among the earliest supporters of New York State's landmark bias bill that increased criminal penalties against those who single out a victim based on race, gender or sexual orientation.

The community that comprises the 27th District in southern Brooklyn—the community I represent—has made its views on same-sex marriage known to me in no uncertain terms. They have done this through the hundreds of letters that have poured into my office, the thousands of phone calls I have received and the countless people who have stopped me on the street to tell me what they think. The vast majority of people have voiced their opposition to the idea of legalizing same-sex marriage.

Our American government was crafted to function as a representative government. Fifteen years ago, when I voted in support of the death penalty, I was mindful of this fact. We are elected to serve the voters—those who entrusted us with the mission of advocating for their best interests. It is my belief that the overriding sentiment of the district must merit my utmost attention and respect.

Therefore, I voted no to the same-sex marriage bill.

SOURCE: Office of New York State Senator Carl Kruger. Press release. "Same-Sex Legislation Fails in Senate by a Vote of 38–24." December 3, 2009. www.nysenate.gov/press-release/same-sex-legisla tion-fails-senate-vote-38-24.

OTHER HISTORIC DOCUMENTS OF INTEREST

April

The London Summit on Global Economic Recovery

APRIL 2, 2009

In 2009, nations around the world were facing the effects of a serious economic recession—one of the worst in decades—that affected both industrialized and developing countries. Although most analysis indicated that large, industrialized nations were beginning to come out of the recession in 2009, their citizens were still feeling the effects as unemployment continued to rise and social services were strained to their limits. Small- and mid-sized businesses continued to fail throughout 2009, and in an effort to stop further economic damage, many countries introduced stimulus plans to provide an immediate injection of funds.

The policy problems posed by the financial crisis proved just how interconnected the world's economies really are. In an effort to present a united front to combat the economic crisis, international heads of state met throughout 2009 to explore options for a unified solution to the fiscal crisis. During an April 2009 meeting in London, England, the Group of 20 (G-20) pledged $1.1 trillion dollars to the International Monetary Fund (IMF) and other international financial organizations to help shore up the global economy. President Barack Obama called the meeting a "turning point in our pursuit of global economy recovery," but he worked to keep expectations low, reminding world citizens that the pledge was not a guarantee that the recession would end swiftly or that governments could prevent further recessions.

FOUR PHASES OF THE ECONOMIC CRISIS

Across the globe, the financial crisis and attempts at recovery played out in four specific phases: First, nations attempted to stanch the causes of recession and build up financial resources. Second, nations (especially developing markets) dealt with the macroeconomic effects of the recession. Third, nations began to plan to reform the financial sector in an effort to stop a recession of this magnitude from happening again. Fourth, each country dealt with the social impact on its citizens and the political impact for its leaders. Not all nations experienced these phases in the same order; some, like the United States, for example, dealt with the social impact of the recession throughout all of the other three phases.

In the first phase of the economic crisis, addressing the cause of the recession and shoring up resources, countries acted to restore faith in their credit systems. By encouraging consumers to begin spending again and banks to begin lending again, countries hoped to restore a regular flow of credit, necessary not only in strengthening their economies but also keeping them afloat. Some tactics used to accomplish these goals included expanding the availability of money, offering bailout packages to large banks and other vital companies that needed to remain running to keep economies viable, restructuring debt for companies and consumers, and injecting funds into financial sectors as necessary. Without fixing the roots of the problem and helping banks, a nation's economy could remain stagnant or full deeper into recession—as was the case in Japan before a large bailout package was introduced in late 2008.

In the second phase of the economic crisis, many countries were dealing with what was considered the worst macroeconomic downturn (i.e., a downturn that affects all aspects of an economy) since the Great Depression. In addition, developing nations tended to be hardest hit by the macroeconomic effects, as they saw their export numbers drop and the infusion of capital from industrialized nations decline. By the middle of the year, the Organization for Economic Cooperation and Development was predicting that 2009 would be the bottom of the recession for many nations, and was, for the first time in two years, predicting growth for China.

To stem macroeconomic problems caused by the global recession, many countries developed stimulus packages designed to infuse money into government-funded projects and products, such as infrastructure development, health care, and other social services. Some countries used stimulus plans to continue an infusion of funds into banks and other large companies, but for the most part the spending was on government projects. In China, a $586 billion package was rolled out, and packages for individual members of the European Union totaled $396 billion. Around the world, more than $2 trillion in economic stimulus plans were put into place. To ensure that the infusion of funds into these projects was not a short-term boost that would fail to prevent another downturn, many stimulus plans were structured to spread the money out over multiple years.

To address the third phase in this economic crisis, ensuring that another financial collapse of this nature not occur, world leaders worked together in many instances to reform financial markets and increase regulatory control over banks and large companies. The G-20 met three times between late 2008 and the end of 2009 to discuss such reforms. The recommendations they developed included increasing the transparency of the credit markets, reviewing the compensation plans at large corporations, looking to resources available from the IMF, and avoiding quick changes in policy that would damage financial markets in the long run. To meet these goals, at the G-20 meeting in London, leaders formed the Financial Stability Board to work with the IMF to try to predict when economic policies might send the world back into recession.

The fourth phase of the economic crisis, dealing with the social impact on citizens and political impact on leaders, would take time. To truly ameliorate the effects of the economic crisis, social services needed to be expanded (not curtailed, as they had been before the economic downturn) and confidence in the financial markets restored. Such actions will have political implications, as citizens in democratic nations will ultimately determine at the ballot box whether they feel their leaders have done a good enough job combating the crumbling economy. The implications of this final phase are another indication of how linked the global economy is. For example, when the price of oil began to decline, it was reflected in the West by falling gasoline prices. For petroleum-exporting nations, however, a drop in the price per barrel of oil negatively affected the flow of cash into their financial systems that would eventually end up downstream benefitting their citizens. In some countries, such as Pakistan, the decrease in oil prices even had security ramifications. The nation was trying to battle al-Qaida but would be hindered without sufficient funds. In addition, as an increasing number of citizens in Western nations began cutting back on the goods they consumed, exporters such as China, Africa, and Latin America began to feel the pinch.

IMPACT AROUND THE WORLD

The most severely affected countries in the recession were emerging markets, specifically those in central and eastern Europe. The economies of these regions had grown for many years because of the availability of foreign capital that they could borrow. This financial dependence left such nations vulnerable, however, putting their markets in serious danger of collapse once the economic downturn hit because of the decrease in available foreign credit. The IMF responded to the crisis in these markets quickly, guaranteeing an infusion of billions of dollars. Other countries took drastic measures to protect themselves. In October, Brazil, India, Mexico, and Russia reduced their cash reserves by more than $75 billion in an effort to stop their currencies from further devaluation as the U.S. dollar began to rise.

In western Europe, the situation was better, although still precarious. At first, many western European nations saw the collapse of the credit market and economic downturn as a problem exclusively in the United States. However, when revenues began to decline quickly and the economy slipped in Europe as well, leaders there realized they had a true crisis on their hands. Throughout 2009, the European Union worked to restore the financial systems of its member nations and continued in its role as watchdog. Banking and securities committees were given increased power to oversee European markets and make recommendations to stem the outflow of cash. In April, the European Council and European Parliament worked together to increase transparency in credit ratings, and the European Commission took a hard look at executive compensation at the continent's largest corporations. Looking ahead, one of the greater worries for western European nations was how eastern and central Europe would recover from the crisis and whether political instability would arise and threaten western nations.

In Asia, the economic recession compounded problems facing many countries who had been dealing with periods of economic decline during the past decade. An infusion of funds provided by the governments of China and Japan had helped to shore up their respective economies by the second quarter of 2009, and they began to see a slowdown in declining revenues. Economic analysts believe that quick action by large Asian countries put their financial systems on the road to recovery much faster than their Western counterparts. As its economy began to see an upswing, Japan pledged billions of dollars to the IMF to help the financial situation in other countries. China still relies heavily on the revenue stream it receives from exports, which are dependent on consumerism in the rest of the world. China also continues to deal with increasing unemployment, coupled with an increase in migrant workers who came to China looking for work, found none, and remained, drawing on China's resources.

G-20 London Summit

When they met in London, G-20 leaders agreed not only to provide $1.1 trillion dollars to the IMF and other financial organizations to assist with global economic relief, they also reviewed a November 2008 Action Plan on economic recovery and devised new plans to continue economic recovery and to jump-start growth. The plan included ensuring that credit rating agencies were meeting high standards and increasing transparency; increasing scrutiny on banks and other credit-lending institutions; and helping banks develop risk-mitigation strategies. G-20 leaders agreed to meet to share best practices and ensure that their economies worked together to benefit the world—including inviting emerging nations to join the discussion, recognizing the dependency of such nations on members of the G-20.

—Heather Kerrigan

Following are excerpts from the April 2, 2009, plan to combat the international economic crisis agreed to by members of the G-20 when they met in London, England.

Global Plan for Recovery and Reform

April 2, 2009

1.   We, the Leaders of the Group of Twenty, met in London on 2 April 2009.

2.   We face the greatest challenge to the world economy in modern times. . . . A global crisis requires a global solution.

3.   We start from the belief that prosperity is indivisible; that growth, to be sustained, has to be shared; and that our global plan for recovery must have at its heart the needs and jobs of hard-working families, not just in developed countries but in emerging markets and the poorest countries of the world too; and must reflect the interests, not just of today's population, but of future generations too. We believe that the only sure foundation for sustainable globalisation and rising prosperity for all is an open world economy based on market principles, effective regulation, and strong global institutions.

4.   We have today therefore pledged to do whatever is necessary to:

- restore confidence, growth, and jobs;

- repair the financial system to restore lending;

- strengthen financial regulation to rebuild trust;

- fund and reform our international financial institutions to overcome this crisis and prevent future ones;

- promote global trade and investment and reject protectionism, to underpin prosperity; and

- build an inclusive, green, and sustainable recovery.

By acting together to fulfil these pledges we will bring the world economy out of recession and prevent a crisis like this from recurring in the future.

5.   The agreements we have reached today, to treble resources available to the IMF to $750 billion, to support a new SDR [Special Drawing Rights] allocation of $250 billion, to support at least $100 billion of additional lending by the MDBs [multilateral development banks], to ensure $250 billion of support for trade finance, and to use the additional resources from agreed IMF gold sales for concessional finance for the poorest countries, constitute an additional $1.1 trillion programme of support to restore credit, growth and jobs in the world economy. Together with the measures we have each taken nationally, this constitutes a global plan for recovery on an unprecedented scale.

RESTORING GROWTH AND JOBS

6.   We are undertaking an unprecedented and concerted fiscal expansion, which will save or create millions of jobs which would otherwise have been destroyed, and that will, by the end of next year, amount to $5 trillion, raise output by 4 per cent, and accelerate the transition to a green economy. We are committed to deliver the scale of sustained fiscal effort necessary to restore growth.

7. Our central banks have also taken exceptional action. Interest rates have been cut aggressively in most countries, and our central banks have pledged to maintain expansionary policies for as long as needed and to use the full range of monetary policy instruments, including unconventional instruments, consistent with price stability.

8. Our actions to restore growth cannot be effective until we restore domestic lending and international capital flows. We have provided significant and comprehensive support to our banking systems to provide liquidity, recapitalise financial institutions, and address decisively the problem of impaired assets. We are committed to take all necessary actions to restore the normal flow of credit through the financial system and ensure the soundness of systemically important institutions, implementing our policies in line with the agreed G20 framework for restoring lending and repairing the financial sector.

9. Taken together, these actions will constitute the largest fiscal and monetary stimulus and the most comprehensive support programme for the financial sector in modern times. Acting together strengthens the impact and the exceptional policy actions announced so far must be implemented without delay. Today, we have further agreed over $1 trillion of additional resources for the world economy through our international financial institutions and trade finance.

10. Last month the IMF estimated that world growth in real terms would resume and rise to over 2 percent by the end of 2010. We are confident that the actions we have agreed today, and our unshakeable commitment to work together to restore growth and jobs, while preserving long-term fiscal sustainability, will accelerate the return to trend growth. We commit today to taking whatever action is necessary to secure that outcome, and we call on the IMF to assess regularly the actions taken and the global actions required.

11. We are resolved to ensure long-term fiscal sustainability and price stability and will put in place credible exit strategies from the measures that need to be taken now to support the financial sector and restore global demand. We are convinced that

by implementing our agreed policies we will limit the longer-term costs to our economies, thereby reducing the scale of the fiscal consolidation necessary over the longer term.

12. We will conduct all our economic policies cooperatively and responsibly with regard to the impact on other countries and will refrain from competitive devaluation of our currencies and promote a stable and well-functioning international monetary system. We will support, now and in the future, to candid, even-handed, and independent IMF surveillance of our economies and financial sectors, of the impact of our policies on others, and of risks facing the global economy.

STRENGTHENING FINANCIAL SUPERVISION AND REGULATION

13. Major failures in the financial sector and in financial regulation and supervision were fundamental causes of the crisis. Confidence will not be restored until we rebuild trust in our financial system. . . .

14. We each agree to ensure our domestic regulatory systems are strong. But we also agree to establish the much greater consistency and systematic cooperation between countries, and the framework of internationally agreed high standards, that a global financial system requires. Strengthened regulation and supervision must promote propriety, integrity and transparency; guard against risk across the financial system; dampen rather than amplify the financial and economic cycle; reduce reliance on inappropriately risky sources of financing; and discourage excessive risk-taking. Regulators and supervisors must protect consumers and investors, support market discipline, avoid adverse impacts on other countries, reduce the scope for regulatory arbitrage, support competition and dynamism, and keep pace with innovation in the marketplace.

15. To this end we are implementing the Action Plan agreed at our last meeting, as set out in the attached progress report. We have today also issued a Declaration, *Strengthening the Financial System*. In particular we agree:

- to establish a new Financial Stability Board (FSB) with a strengthened mandate, as a successor to the Financial Stability Forum (FSF), including all G20 countries, FSF members, Spain, and the European Commission;

- that the FSB should collaborate with the IMF to provide early warning of macroeconomic and financial risks and the actions needed to address them;

- to reshape our regulatory systems so that our authorities are able to identify and take account of macro-prudential risks;

- to extend regulation and oversight to all systemically important financial institutions, instruments and markets. This will include, for the first time, systemically important hedge funds;

- to endorse and implement the FSF's tough new principles on pay and compensation and to support sustainable compensation schemes and the corporate social responsibility of all firms;

- to take action, once recovery is assured, to improve the quality, quantity, and international consistency of capital in the banking system. In future, regulation must prevent excessive leverage and require buffers of resources to be built up in good times;

- to take action against non-cooperative jurisdictions, including tax havens. We stand ready to deploy sanctions to protect our public finances and financial systems. The era of banking secrecy is over. We note that the OECD [Organization for Economic Cooperation and Development] has today published a list of countries assessed by the Global Forum against the international standard for exchange of tax information;

- to call on the accounting standard setters to work urgently with supervisors and regulators to improve standards on valuation and provisioning and achieve a single set of high-quality global accounting standards; and

- to extend regulatory oversight and registration to Credit Rating Agencies to ensure they meet the international code of good practice, particularly to prevent unacceptable conflicts of interest.

16. We instruct our Finance Ministers to complete the implementation of these decisions in line with the timetable set out in the Action Plan. We have asked the FSB and the IMF to monitor progress, working with the Financial Action Taskforce and other relevant bodies, and to provide a report to the next meeting of our Finance Ministers in Scotland in November.

STRENGTHENING OUR GLOBAL FINANCIAL INSTITUTIONS

17. Emerging markets and developing countries, which have been the engine of recent world growth, are also now facing challenges which are adding to the current downturn in the global economy. It is imperative for global confidence and economic recovery that capital continues to flow to them. This will require a substantial strengthening of the international financial institutions, particularly the IMF. We have therefore agreed today to make available an additional $850 billion of resources through the global financial institutions to support growth in emerging market and developing countries by helping to finance counter-cyclical spending, bank recapitalisation, infrastructure, trade finance, balance of payments support, debt rollover, and social support. To this end:

- we have agreed to increase the resources available to the IMF through immediate financing from members of $250 billion, subsequently incorporated into an expanded and more flexible New Arrangements to Borrow, increased by up to $500 billion, and to consider market borrowing if necessary; and

- we support a substantial increase in lending of at least $100 billion by the Multilateral Development Banks (MDBs), including to low income countries, and ensure that all MDBs have the appropriate capital.

18. It is essential that these resources can be used effectively and flexibly to support growth. We welcome in this respect the progress made by the IMF with its new

Flexible Credit Line (FCL) and its reformed lending and conditionality framework which will enable the IMF to ensure that its facilities address effectively the underlying causes of countries' balance of payments financing needs, particularly the withdrawal of external capital flows to the banking and corporate sectors. We support Mexico's decision to seek an FCL arrangement.

19. We have agreed to support a general SDR allocation which will inject $250 billion into the world economy and increase global liquidity, and urgent ratification of the Fourth Amendment.

20. In order for our financial institutions to help manage the crisis and prevent future crises we must strengthen their longer term relevance, effectiveness and legitimacy. So alongside the significant increase in resources agreed today we are determined to reform and modernise the international financial institutions to ensure they can assist members and shareholders effectively in the new challenges they face. We will reform their mandates, scope and governance to reflect changes in the world economy and the new challenges of globalisation, and that emerging and developing economies, including the poorest, must have greater voice and representation. This must be accompanied by action to increase the credibility and accountability of the institutions through better strategic oversight and decision making. To this end:

- we commit to implementing the package of IMF quota and voice reforms agreed in April 2008 and call on the IMF to complete the next review of quotas by January 2011;

- we agree that, alongside this, consideration should be given to greater involvement of the Fund's Governors in providing strategic direction to the IMF and increasing its accountability;

- we commit to implementing the World Bank reforms agreed in October 2008. We look forward to further recommendations, at the next meetings, on voice and representation reforms on an accelerated timescale, to be agreed by the 2010 Spring Meetings;

- we agree that the heads and senior leadership of the international financial institutions should be appointed through an open, transparent, and merit-based selection process; and

- building on the current reviews of the IMF and World Bank we asked the Chairman, working with the G20 Finance Ministers, to consult widely in an inclusive process and report back to the next meeting with proposals for further reforms to improve the responsiveness and adaptability of the IFIs [international financial institutions].

21. In addition to reforming our international financial institutions for the new challenges of globalisation we agreed on the desirability of a new global consensus on the key values and principles that will promote sustainable economic activity. We support discussion on such a charter for sustainable economic activity with a view to further discussion at our next meeting. We take note of the work started in other fora in this regard and look forward to further discussion of this charter for sustainable economic activity.

Resisting Protectionism and Promoting Global Trade and Investment

22. World trade growth has underpinned rising prosperity for half a century. But it is now falling for the first time in 25 years. Falling demand is exacerbated by growing protectionist pressures and a withdrawal of trade credit. Reinvigorating world trade and investment is essential for restoring global growth. We will not repeat the historic mistakes of protectionism of previous eras. To this end:

- we reaffirm the commitment made in Washington: to refrain from raising new barriers to investment or to trade in goods and services, imposing new export restrictions, or implementing World Trade Organisation (WTO) inconsistent measures to stimulate exports. In addition we will rectify promptly any such measures. We extend this pledge to the end of 2010;

- we will minimise any negative impact on trade and investment of our domestic policy actions including fiscal policy and action in support of the financial sector. We will not retreat into financial protectionism, particularly measures that constrain worldwide capital flows, especially to developing countries;

- we will notify promptly the WTO of any such measures and we call on the WTO, together with other international bodies, within their respective mandates, to monitor and report publicly on our adherence to these undertakings on a quarterly basis;

- we will take, at the same time, whatever steps we can to promote and facilitate trade and investment; and

- we will ensure availability of at least $250 billion over the next two years to support trade finance through our export credit and investment agencies and through the MDBs. We also ask our regulators to make use of available flexibility in capital requirements for trade finance.

23. We remain committed to reaching an ambitious and balanced conclusion to the Doha Development Round, which is urgently needed. This could boost the global economy by at least $150 billion per annum. To achieve this we are committed to building on the progress already made, including with regard to modalities.

24. We will give renewed focus and political attention to this critical issue in the coming period and will use our continuing work and all international meetings that are relevant to drive progress.

Ensuring a Fair and Sustainable Recovery for All

25. We are determined not only to restore growth but to lay the foundation for a fair and sustainable world economy. We recognise that the current crisis has a disproportionate impact on the vulnerable in the poorest countries and recognise our collective responsibility to mitigate the social impact of the crisis to minimise long-lasting damage to global potential. To this end:

- we reaffirm our historic commitment to meeting the Millennium Development Goals and to achieving our respective ODA [official development assistance agencies] pledges, including commitments on Aid for Trade, debt relief, and the Gleneagles commitments, especially to sub-Saharan Africa;

- the actions and decisions we have taken today will provide $50 billion to support social protection, boost trade and safeguard development in low income countries, as part of the significant increase in crisis support for these and other developing countries and emerging markets;

- we are making available resources for social protection for the poorest countries, including through investing in long-term food security and through voluntary bilateral contributions to the World Bank's Vulnerability Framework, including the Infrastructure Crisis Facility, and the Rapid Social Response Fund;

- we have committed, consistent with the new income model, that additional resources from agreed sales of IMF gold will be used, together with surplus income, to provide $6 billion additional concessional and flexible finance for the poorest countries over the next 2 to 3 years. We call on the IMF to come forward with concrete proposals at the Spring Meetings;

- we have agreed to review the flexibility of the Debt Sustainability Framework and call on the IMF and World Bank to report to the IMFC [International Monetary Financial Committee] and Development Committee at the Annual Meetings; and

- we call on the UN, working with other global institutions, to establish an effective mechanism to monitor the impact of the crisis on the poorest and most vulnerable.

26. We recognise the human dimension to the crisis. We commit to support those affected by the crisis by creating employment opportunities and through income support measures. We will build a fair and family-friendly labour market for both women and men. We therefore welcome the reports of the London Jobs Conference and the Rome Social Summit and the key principles they proposed. We will support employment by stimulating growth, investing in education and training, and through active labour market policies, focusing on the most vulnerable. We call upon the ILO [International Labour Organization], working with other relevant organisations, to assess the actions taken and those required for the future.

27. We agreed to make the best possible use of investment funded by fiscal stimulus programmes towards the goal of building a resilient, sustainable, and green recovery. We will make the transition towards clean, innovative, resource efficient, low carbon technologies and infrastructure. We encourage the MDBs to contribute fully to the achievement of this objective. We will identify and work together on further measures to build sustainable economies.

28. We reaffirm our commitment to address the threat of irreversible climate change, based on the principle of common but differentiated responsibilities, and to reach agreement at the UN Climate Change conference in Copenhagen in December 2009.

Delivering Our Commitments

29. We have committed ourselves to work together with urgency and determination to translate these words into action. We agreed to meet again before the end of this year to review progress on our commitments.

Source: The London Summit 2009. "Global Plan for Recovery and Reform." April 2, 2009. www.london summit.gov.uk/resources/en/PDF/final-communique.

OTHER HISTORIC DOCUMENTS OF INTEREST

From this volume

- President Obama Signs the American Recovery and Reinvestment Act of 2009, p. 41
- Economic Outlook in the States, p. 646.

From previous *Historic Documents*

- World Leaders and the IMF on the Global Economic Crisis, *2008*, p. 418
- IMF Director on Asian Financial Crisis, *1998*, p. 832
- World Bank on the Asian Financial Crisis, *1998*, p. 722
- Japanese Prime Minister on Economic Crisis, *1998*, p. 532

Pirates Attack U.S.-Flagged Ship

APRIL 12 AND 30, 2009

On April 8, 2009, an unarmed container ship, the U.S.-flagged MV *Maersk Alabama,* came under attack by pirates off the coast of Somalia. The American crew overtook the pirates, but the ship's captain, Richard Phillips, was taken hostage.

Up to this point, the United States had remained largely uninvolved in the increasing piracy in the waters off of Africa, only recently sending navy ships to assist in the international monitoring of waters off the coast of Somalia. When the *Maersk Alabama* was attacked, however, the United States quickly sprang to action and, under the direction of President Barack Obama, the U.S. Navy rescued the captain in a daring mission and brought back one pirate to the United States for trial.

The attack on the *Maersk Alabama,* the first U.S. commercial ship to be captured during a recent spate of attacks off the Somali coast, raised the question not only of U.S. involvement in the region but also of whether ships should have arms aboard in dangerous waters.

INCREASE IN PIRATE ATTACKS

Pirate attacks off the Horn of Africa had grown significantly during the preceding years. According to the International Maritime Bureau, 111 attacks were recorded in that region in 2008, and by September 2009, the U.S. Department of State reported that 156 attacks had occurred in the first eight months of 2009. The rise in piracy was exacerbated by the lack of a stable government in Somalia, a country long war torn and overrun by corruption.

Fueled by a desire to profit in a place where the most basic necessities are scarce, pirates began undertaking daring missions in small fishing boats to capture large ships, which they then hold for ransom. Many pirates have been killed during these expeditions but the risks have not stopped the growth in piracy, largely because piracy has remained very profitable. In 2008, pirates collected an estimated $30 million in ransoms.

The United Nations has made multiple attempts to stop the rise of piracy, working with nongovernmental organizations and member nations to patrol the waters near Somalia. This, however, has lead to increased violence as pirates broaden the area of attack. According to UN secretary-general Ban Ki-moon, "as a result of the military presence in the region, pirates have employed more daring operational tactics, operating further seawards, toward the Seychelles, and using more sophisticated weaponry."

The growth in piracy threatens Somalia's neighbors with increased violence. Somali citizens and citizens of nearby states that depend on foreign humanitarian aid are put in danger when they are unable to get the basic necessities as ships are sometimes unable or unwilling to make the dangerous passage. Shipping companies are also put in a bind, as the longer, safer shipping route, around the Cape of Good Hope, takes much longer to navigate at a higher cost; it also raises the price of goods to consumers.

Although increased patrolling has been the most prevalent response to the growth of pirate attacks off the Horn of Africa, analysts say that until companies stop paying ransoms demanded by the pirates, it will continue. Disregarding a ransom is, however, often not an option for many shipping companies, because it is far more expensive to buy a new ship and goods and secure a new crew than it is to pay the demanded ransom.

Maersk Alabama Attacked

When the *Maersk Alabama* came under attack on April 8, 2009, it had just finished delivering food aid to Djibouti and was headed toward Kenya. Once crew members spotted the pirates approaching, too late to escape, they decided to disable the ship to prevent the pirates from taking control of it after boarding. Accounts of the incident from the twenty-member crew say that they overtook the pirates within hours of the attack but were unable to rescue their captain, who had been taken hostage. The pirates took the captain from the ship to a lifeboat. From the lifeboat, the pirates began making their ransom demands via a satellite phone.

Many hours into negotiations, which remained at a standstill, the United States sent the U.S.S. *Bainbridge* destroyer to the scene and used aircraft to monitor the lifeboat on which Captain Phillips was being held. When the lifeboat ran out of food, water, and fuel, the pirates accepted assistance from the *Bainbridge* crew, even allowing the navy ship to tow the small lifeboat.

By April 12, negotiations for the release of the hostage between the Federal Bureau of Investigation (FBI) and the U.S. Navy and Somali pirates remained deadlocked, and, determining that the captain's life was in immediate danger, the navy was given permission by President Obama to allow three Navy SEAL snipers to shoot the pirates holding the captain. When a clear shot opened up, each SEAL took one shot, and the nearly week-long standoff quickly came to an end.

Three pirates were killed during the operation and one teenage Somali pirate, Abdiwali Abdiqadir Muse, was taken to the United States, where he pled not guilty to piracy, conspiracy, hostage taking, and weapons charges before the U.S. District Court for the Southern District of New York. After the rescue, Vice Admiral Bill Gortney, commander of the U.S. Naval Forces Central Command, said, "These actions of Capt. Phillips and the civilian mariners of the *Maersk-Alabama* were heroic. They fought back to regain control of their ship, and Captain Phillips selflessly put his life in the hands of these armed criminals in order to protect his crew."

Should Commercial Ships Be Armed?

Like most commercial vessels in international waters, the *Maersk Alabama* was unarmed while sailing in the Indian Ocean. The question of arming commercial vessels has long put mariners at odds with shipping companies and port authorities, and the growth of piracy has reignited the debate. The question comes down in part to whether keeping weapons onboard ships will keep sailors safe or whether it will put them in greater danger if, for example, pirates were to seize the weapons or begin using more deadly techniques against armed mariners. In addition, some ports refuse to allow armed commercial ships to dock.

Captain Phillips testified before Congress that commercial ships operating in dangerous waters *should* be armed. Phillips argued that he and his crew had only knives and fire hoses to combat the Somali pirates, who were carrying automatic weapons and rocket launchers. "It would be my personal preference that a limited number of my crew aboard the vessel have access to effective weaponry," said Captain Phillips during his testimony. Phillips did caution, however, that arming crews will not eradicate piracy; such measures instead would only provide a measure of safety to mariners. "In my opinion, arming the crew cannot and should not be viewed as the best or ultimate solution to the problem. At most, arming the crew should be only one component of a comprehensive plan and approach to combat piracy." Phillips advocated for other solutions as well, such as ships that are stronger structurally to resist pirate attacks.

During the same hearing, Maersk, Inc., chair John P. Clancey offered an opposing opinion: "Arming merchant sailors may result in the acquisition of ever more lethal weapons and tactics by the pirates, a race that merchant sailors cannot win." Clancey also said during his testimony that arming sailors at sea for months could lead to dangerous incidents.

U.S. PIRACY POLICY

Regardless of whether commercial mariners remain unarmed or are given the right to carry weapons, moving forward, the international community will have little choice but to find new ways to combat piracy. At the time of Phillips's release, Somali pirates were holding a total of eighteen ships and nearly 300 non–American crew members hostage. The increase in the number of ships patrolling the waters off the Horn of Africa has pushed pirates farther into international waters, where they capture large vessels and use them as headquarters for their pirating activities.

The United States has particular reason to be wary. After Navy SEALS rescued Captain Phillips, pirates vowed revenge. One group, based in Eyl, Somalia, said, "[T]his matter will lead to retaliation and we will hunt down particularly American citizens traveling in our waters. . . . [N]ext time we get American citizens . . . they [should] expect no mercy from us." A pirate holding a Greek ship hostage told the Associated Press, "Every country will be treated the way it treats us. . . . In the future, America will be the one mourning and crying."

In an attempt to make good on its promise, on April 14, pirates attacked the American-flagged MV *Liberty Sun,* and said "We were not after a ransom. We also assigned a team with special equipment to chase and destroy any ship flying an American flag in retaliation for the brutal killing of our friends." The ship escaped with minimal damage with the assistance of the U.S. Navy.

President Obama promised greater U.S. assistance in combating piracy in international waters in response to the *Maersk Alabama* incident, although he gave no indication of exactly how he planned to carry this out. Obama said that increased prosecution of pirates could lead to a decrease in pirating attacks. Although Navy SEALs were used to bring one pirate in for prosecution in the *Maersk Alabama* case, according to Defense Secretary Robert Gates, there is no "purely military solution" to addressing this situation.

The chair of the Senate Foreign Relations Subcommittee on African Affairs, Sen. Russ Feingold, D-Wis., called on Obama to "personally engage" in Somalia, addressing not just piracy but the root cause of the problem, including government instability.

—Heather Kerrigan

Following is a statement by the commander of the U.S. Naval Forces Central Command, congratulating Capt. Richard Phillips and the Navy SEALs who rescued his ship, and the text of the testimony given by Captain Phillips on April 30, 2009, before the Senate Committee on Foreign Relations.

Statement from Commander Bill Gortney on the Maersk Alabama *Rescue*

DOCUMENT

April 12, 2009

At approximately 7:19 P.M. (12:19 P.M. EDT) April 12 U.S. naval forces rescued Capt. Richard Phillips, the master of Motor Vessel Maersk-Alabama.

"This was an incredible team effort, and I am extremely proud of the tireless efforts of all the men and women who made this rescue possible" said Vice Adm. Bill Gortney, commander, U.S. Naval Forces Central Command.

"The actions of Capt. Phillips and the civilian mariners of *Maersk-Alabama* were heroic. They fought back to regain control of their ship, and Captain Phillips selflessly put his life in the hands of these armed criminals in order to protect his crew."

Following the rescue, Phillips was initially taken aboard the Norfolk, Va., based guided-missile destroyer USS *Bainbridge* (DDG 96). Phillips was subsequently flown to the San Diego based amphibious assault ship USS *Boxer* (LHD 4) where he contacted his family, received a routine medical evaluation and is resting comfortably.

U.S. military forces have one pirate in custody; three were killed in the rescue.

SOURCE: U.S. Navy. "From Commander, U.S. Naval Forces Central Command/5th Fleet Public Affairs." April 12, 2009. www.navy.mil/Search/display.asp?story_id=44268.

DOCUMENT

Statement of Capt. Richard Phillips, Master, Maersk Alabama, *to the Senate Committee on Foreign Relations*

April 30, 2009

Mr. Chairman and Members of the Committee:

I am Captain Richard Phillips. I am a graduate of the Massachusetts Maritime Academy, I have been a member of the International Organization of Masters, Mates & Pilots Union since 1979, and I am a licensed American merchant mariner. I was the captain of the MAERSK ALABAMA when it was attacked by pirates off the coast of Somalia on April 8th. Thankfully, that episode ended with the successful return of the ship, its cargo of US food aid for Africa and, most importantly, my crew. All of us have returned home safely and for that my entire crew and I are deeply appreciative of the actions taken by the Administration, the Department of Defense and, most specifically, the US Navy, the Navy SEALS and the crew aboard the USS *Bainbridge.* All of the US military and government personnel who were involved in this situation are clearly highly trained and motivated professionals and I want to use this opportunity to again say "thank you" to everyone involved in our safe return.

I want to thank the management of Maersk and Waterman Steamship Corp. who handled the situation, the crew and our families with great care and concern.

And equally important, I want to publicly commend all the officers and crew aboard the MAERSK ALABAMA who responded with their typical professionalism in response to this incident. The Licensed Deck Officers who are members of the Masters, Mates & Pilots Union, the Licensed Deck Officer and Licensed Engineers who are members of the Marine Engineers' Beneficial Association, and the unlicensed crew who belong to the Seafarers International Union are dedicated merchant mariners, typical of America's merchant seamen who are well-trained and who are ready and able to respond when necessary to protect the interests of our country.

I am honored to come before this Committee today to discuss my views on making commercial shipping safer, and worldwide sea lanes more secure from the threat of piracy.

I need to make clear at the outset that I am unable to discuss the incident itself because of the ongoing investigation and pending legal action against one of the pirates. But I've had a lot of time to think about the difficult and complex issues of protecting vessel, cargo and crew in crime-ridden waters. So instead of a recount of the MAERSK ALABAMA incident, the focus of my comments will be my beliefs, based on my years of experience at sea, as to what can or should be done to respond to piracy and to protect American vessels and crews.

I should also say at the outset that I realize that my opinions may differ in some ways from other recommendations you have heard before and may hear today from others on the panel. Nevertheless, I do believe that all of us in the maritime industry understand that it is imperative that we work together to address this complex problem, and I believe we are in general agreement on the main principles of keeping crew, cargo and vessel safe.

First, I believe it is the responsibility of our government to protect the United States, including U.S.-flag vessels that are by definition an extension of the United States, their U.S. citizen crews, and our nation's worldwide commercial assets. So, it follows then that the most desirable and appropriate solution to piracy is for the United States government to provide protection, through military escorts and/or military detachments aboard U.S. vessels. That said, I am well aware that some will argue that there is a limit to any government's resources—even America's. In fact, due to the vastness of the area to be covered—and the areas of threat are continually growing larger—our Navy and the coalition of other navies currently positioned in the Gulf of Aden region may simply not have the resources to provide all the protection necessary to prevent and stop the attacks.

So what other things can be done?

In my opinion, the targets—the vessels—can be "hardened" even beyond what's being done today and made even more structurally resistant to pirates. In addition, more can be done in terms of developing specific anti-piracy procedures, tools and training for American crews. I do however want to emphasize that contrary to some reports that I've heard recently, American mariners are highly trained and do receive up-to-date training and upgrading at the private educational training facilities jointly run by the maritime unions and their contracted shipping companies. I believe that discussions are underway now between the industry and government on the details of specific proposals to harden the vessels (the specifics of which should remain secret) and I am confident that we will soon have additional methods for protecting vessel and crew. And while they will be an improvement, there is no way they can be foolproof.

I've also heard the suggestion that all we have to do to counter piracy is "just arm the crews." In my opinion, arming the crew cannot and should not be viewed as the best or ultimate solution to the problem. At most, arming the crew should be only one component of a comprehensive plan and approach to combat piracy. To the extent we go forward in this direction, it would be my personal preference that only the four most senior ranking officers aboard the vessel have access to effective weaponry and that these individuals receive special training on a regular basis. I realize that even this limited approach to arming the crew opens up a very thorny set of issues. I'll let others sort out the legal and liability issues but we all must understand that having weapons on board merchant ships fundamentally changes the model of commercial shipping and we must be very cautious about how it is done. Nevertheless, I do believe that arming the crew, as part of an overall strategy, could provide an effective deterrent under certain circumstances and I believe that a measured capability in this respect should be part of the overall debate about how to defend ourselves against criminals on the sea.

As for armed security details put aboard vessels, I believe, as I indicated earlier, that this idea could certainly be developed into an effective deterrent. My preference would be government protection forces. However, as long as they are adequately trained I would not be opposed to private security on board. Of course, I realize that very clear protocols would have to be established and followed. For example, as a captain, I am responsible for the vessel, cargo and crew at all times. And I am not comfortable giving up command authority to others . . . including the commander of a protection force. In the heat of an attack, there can be only one final decision maker. So command is only one of many issues that would have to be worked out in for security forces to operate effectively.

While there are many new ideas and much discussion going on about how to deal with piracy, I would respectfully ask the Committee to be mindful that the seafarers I've met and worked with over my career are resourceful, hardworking, adventurous, courageous, patriotic and independent. They want whatever help you can offer to make the sea lanes more secure and their work environment safer. But we realize that while preparation is absolutely critical, not every situation can be anticipated. And we accept that as a part of the seafarer's life. So, I will just close with a request for you to please proceed carefully and to please continue to include us in your discussions and debates.

Thank you for this opportunity to speak and I look forward to answering your questions.

Source: U.S. Senate Committee on Foreign Relations. "Statement of Captain Richard Phillips, Master, *Maersk Alabama* to the Senate Committee on Foreign Relations." April 30, 2009. http://foreign.senate .gov/testimony/2009/PhillipsTestimony090430p.pdf.

OTHER HISTORIC DOCUMENTS OF INTEREST

FROM PREVIOUS *HISTORIC DOCUMENTS*

- United Nations and World Leaders on Piracy off the Coast of Somalia, *2008*, p. 625

Mexico and the World Health Organization on the Spread of Swine Flu

APRIL 27 AND JUNE 11, 2009

On June 11, 2009, the World Health Organization (WHO) declared the H1N1 flu virus, nicknamed swine flu, a pandemic—the first pandemic the organization had declared in forty-one years. The long-awaited decision to make this declaration came as countries around the world scrambled to build up vaccine stocks and provide hospitals and health care facilities with the necessary equipment to protect the population against the virus.

"The world is moving into the early days of its first influenza pandemic in the 21st century," said WHO chief Dr. Margaret Chan. "The [swine flu] is now unstoppable." The last declared pandemic, the Hong Kong flu, spread around the world in 1968 and killed approximately one million people. At the time of the 2009 WHO announcement, seventy-four countries had collectively reported nearly 30,000 cases of swine flu, with 144 deaths from the virus.

It was expected that the WHO would declare swine flu a pandemic, but the organization, an arm of the United Nations, did not want to sound the alarm too early. According to the organization, the declaration of a pandemic could have been made earlier if all countries had been properly reporting the count of those with H1N1 or those who had died of H1N1. Accurate counts, however, were not available, as some countries were suspected of underreporting their actual swine flu numbers to prevent panic. Other reports suggested that the WHO had become bogged down in a political battle, with some countries urging the organization not to declare a pandemic, as they suspected it would cause social and economic turmoil within their borders. The WHO would not indicate which nation tipped the scales with regard to the decision to declare a pandemic, but some analysts speculated that countries in the Southern Hemisphere, which was entering its winter season, may have been the deciding factor.

Although some considered the pronouncement of a pandemic too long delayed, Chan said during the declaration, "No previous pandemic has been detected so early or watched so closely, in real-time, right at the very beginning. The world can now reap the benefits of investments, over the last five years, in pandemic preparedness."

SWINE FLU'S ORIGINS

Scientists believe that this strain of swine flu can be traced to the mid-to-late 1980s, but it was not until the late 2000s that the virus began gaining attention. When the H1N1 virus began to spread in early 2009, many fingers pointed to Mexico, particularly to a young boy who had contracted the virus that contained elements of bird, human, and swine flu. Although the early 2009 outbreak may have originated in Mexico, the first incidence of swine flu of recent record had occurred in Wisconsin in 2005 after a teenager participated in a pig slaughter and came into close contact with a chicken, leading to a mutated form of the flu virus. In Sheboygan County, Wisconsin, the local government tried to locate pigs that may have been infected with this illness, but came up largely empty-handed.

In 2006, the American Association of Swine Veterinarians said that the strain of swine flu being seen was not passing from pig to human but rather from human to pig, a theory that may have been confirmed at a county fair in Ohio where pigs had been sickened by the virus, but not humans. In 2008, Iowa State University officials warned hog farmers and facilities that were keeping large numbers of pigs in close quarters that the swine flu virus was becoming increasingly prevalent and was being spread not only by human handlers but also by farm poultry. In late 2008, a Texas resident was sickened by the virus, and it was reported to the Centers for Disease Control and Prevention (CDC); that individual recovered within a few days.

Some health experts believe that had so many people not begun dying from swine flu, it would not have provoked panic, let alone the declaration of a pandemic. The case of Édgar Hernández in Mexico, which many blamed on the American-owned pig farm near his home, was not the only one in Mexico or in the world in early April. In fact, swine flu was rapidly spreading across the Mexican border into the United States. Mexico moved quickly to contain those affected, worked to stop the disease from spreading by shutting down schools and other places where people gather, and increased sanitation efforts. The disease had a faster and more deadly impact in Mexico than in the United States, although investigators were unable to figure out why. In the meantime, the Mexican government worked to calm citizens who lined up at health clinics across the country to have their questions answered and get any medications available. Mexican officials went on national television to order parents to keep their children inside, away from schools and other crowded venues.

At the same time swine flu was beginning to grip North America, in Cairo, Egypt, where a flu strain new to the country was discovered, the government ordered 300,000 pigs to be slaughtered out of fear that they were the cause. It was later found that no confirmed swine flu cases existed at that time in Egypt, but multiple cases of chicken flu did.

THE DANGER OF SWINE FLU

The WHO indicated in its announcement that the declaration of a pandemic did not mean that the virus had become more dangerous, just that it was spreading and showing resilient characteristics. "We also want to make clear that the higher level of the pandemic does not necessarily mean we are going to see a more dangerous virus or see many more people falling severely ill or dying," said Chan. Two characteristics of swine flu that led the WHO to take immediate precautions included the large number of young, healthy people, who are typically resilient to the flu virus, being affected by or dying from swine flu, and the fact that H1N1 was beginning to crowd out other flu strains.

There were indications that swine flu was more virulent than other flu viruses. Typically the "normal" flu virus, which kills approximately 250,000 to 500,000 people worldwide each year, begins to disappear as the weather becomes warmer. In the case of swine flu, the disease was continuing to spread in the Northern Hemisphere just as it entered its summer season and began to take root in the Southern Hemisphere where winter, and therefore typical flu season, was taking hold.

The WHO pointed out that although swine flu could become serious, most cases tended to be mild and did not require any special medical treatment. The fear, however, was that hospitals and health clinics would become crowded with those worried that they had contracted H1N1. In addition, health officials feared that, as with other flu viruses, H1N1 could mutate into a new and more dangerous strain of virus; in this case, the worry was that swine flu could mutate in the Southern Hemisphere and reappear in the Northern Hemisphere in winter.

INTERNATIONAL REACTION

In response to the WHO declaration, countries began pushing for faster production of a large quantity of a swine flu vaccine. According to GlaxoSmithKline PLC, a large pharmaceutical manufacturer, production of a swine flu vaccine could begin in July 2009, but the first vaccines in large enough quantities to be useful would not be available for several months after production began.

Early instructions on how to deal with H1N1 were simple and as common as dealing with the seasonal flu—hand washing and covering one's nose and mouth to sneeze or cough. The WHO did not issue warnings to avoid mass transportation or advocate travel bans, but large countries, in particular those in Asia, began heavily screening passengers entering and leaving to ensure that anyone with an elevated temperature was quarantined until it could be determined whether that person had contracted swine flu. China had one of the quickest and most efficient responses to the outbreak of swine flu, informed largely by recent experience with avian flu. In Hong Kong, the government closed all kindergartens and primary schools for two weeks after twelve students across that country tested positive for swine flu.

Regardless of encouragement by the WHO not to panic over the declaration of a pandemic, some countries were gripped with fear. In Argentina, hospitals were flooded with people worried about the virus, bringing the hospital system nearly to collapse. In fact, fear had been widespread in Argentina even before the announcement. In May, a bus coming from Chile had been stoned by Argentineans who thought someone on the bus had swine flu. Given the level of panic and suspicion of swine flu's originis in Mexico, Argentina canceled all flights to and from Mexico.

In the United States, some panic spread among individual citizens and organizations—many schools shut down over fear that one or two students were sick with swine flu—but the CDC said that it planned no changes in terms of how it was responding to the disease (and did not recommend widespread school closings). Thirteen thousand cases and at least twenty-seven deaths had been recorded in the United States at the time of the WHO declaration. "Our actions in the past month," said Glen Nowak, a CDC spokesperson, "have been as if there was a pandemic in this country." At the time of the actual declaration of the pandemic, the United States had already authorized $1 billion for the development of a swine flu vaccine and had been increasing the availability of seasonal flu vaccines to ensure that the population remained safe. The key goal of the United States with respect to the swine flu, according to CDC director Thomas Frieden, was "to find where [the] virus is spreading and reduce its impact, particularly in those with underlying health conditions and in infants." By the end of 2009, with swine flu vaccines still being slowly produced and distributed, the CDC reported that nearly 50 million Americans had contracted swine flu, with 10,000 reported deaths.

—Heather Kerrigan

Following is an April 27, 2009, press release from the office of Mexican president Filipe Calderón on school closures due to the swine flu outbreak, and a press statement issued on June 11, 2009, by the World Health Organization director-general Margaret Chan, declaring the H1N1 flu virus (swine flu) a global pandemic.

Mexico Cancels School Activities in Response to Swine Flu

April 27, 2009

At approximately 11 A.M. Health Secretary José Ángel Córdova Villalobos gave a press conference to the media during which he reported that to date, the number of persons admitted to hospitals for severe pneumonia in the country is 1,995, of which 776 remain hospitalized, 1,070 have been discharged (53.6%) and 149 have died. Among the latter, research is being carried out to confirm whether the biological agent involved produced severe pneumonia or swine fever.

The Mexican Health Secretary explained that international protocols and recommendations from the World Health Organization (WHO) have been followed and admitted that, "We are at the height of the epidemic," meaning that the number of cases will increase. He therefore stressed five key points:

1. As a "precautionary measure" it has been decided to suspend school activities throughout the country, from tomorrow (April 28) to May 6.

2. An agreement has been reached with CONAGUA to suspend the Cutzamala System Maintenance Program, scheduled for May 1 to 5, to support the health measures implemented in the metropolitan zone.

3. Several permits have been issued by COFEPRIS to facilitate the admission of medicines into the country, for which prescription will be controlled

4. Preventive measures to provide the population with information and advice will continue, such as the following telephone number: 01800–123 10 10.

5. Lastly, all preventive and treatment measures to contain the swine fever outbreak will continue.

SOURCE: Office of the President of Mexico. Press release. "School Activities Throughout Country Suspended: Health Secretariat." April 27, 2009. www.presidencia.gob.mx/en/press/?contenido=44457.

DOCUMENT

WHO *Press Statement Declaring Swine Flu Pandemic*

June 11, 2009

Ladies and gentlemen,

In late April, WHO announced the emergence of a novel influenza A virus.

This particular H1N1 strain has not circulated previously in humans. The virus is entirely new.

The virus is contagious, spreading easily from one person to another, and from one country to another. As of today, nearly 30,000 confirmed cases have been reported in 74 countries.

This is only part of the picture. With few exceptions, countries with large numbers of cases are those with good surveillance and testing procedures in place.

Spread in several countries can no longer be traced to clearly-defined chains of human-to-human transmission. Further spread is considered inevitable.

I have conferred with leading influenza experts, virologists, and public health officials. In line with procedures set out in the International Health Regulations, I have sought guidance and advice from an Emergency Committee established for this purpose.

On the basis of available evidence, and these expert assessments of the evidence, the scientific criteria for an influenza pandemic have been met.

I have therefore decided to raise the level of influenza pandemic alert from phase 5 to phase 6.

The world is now at the start of the 2009 influenza pandemic.

We are in the earliest days of the pandemic. The virus is spreading under a close and careful watch.

No previous pandemic has been detected so early or watched so closely, in real-time, right at the very beginning. The world can now reap the benefits of investments, over the last five years, in pandemic preparedness.

We have a head start. This places us in a strong position. But it also creates a demand for advice and reassurance in the midst of limited data and considerable scientific uncertainty.

Thanks to close monitoring, thorough investigations, and frank reporting from countries, we have some early snapshots depicting spread of the virus and the range of illness it can cause.

We know, too, that this early, patchy picture can change very quickly. The virus writes the rules and this one, like all influenza viruses, can change the rules, without rhyme or reason, at any time.

Globally, we have good reason to believe that this pandemic, at least in its early days, will be of moderate severity. As we know from experience, severity can vary, depending on many factors, from one country to another.

On present evidence, the overwhelming majority of patients experience mild symptoms and make a rapid and full recovery, often in the absence of any form of medical treatment.

Worldwide, the number of deaths is small. Each and every one of these deaths is tragic, and we have to brace ourselves to see more. However, we do not expect to see a sudden and dramatic jump in the number of severe or fatal infections.

We know that the novel H1N1 virus preferentially infects younger people. In nearly all areas with large and sustained outbreaks, the majority of cases have occurred in people under the age of 25 years.

In some of these countries, around 2% of cases have developed severe illness, often with very rapid progression to life-threatening pneumonia.

Most cases of severe and fatal infections have been in adults between the ages of 30 and 50 years.

This pattern is significantly different from that seen during epidemics of seasonal influenza, when most deaths occur in frail elderly people.

Many, though not all, severe cases have occurred in people with underlying chronic conditions. Based on limited, preliminary data, conditions most frequently seen include respiratory diseases, notably asthma, cardiovascular disease, diabetes, autoimmune disorders, and obesity.

At the same time, it is important to note that around one third to half of the severe and fatal infections are occurring in previously healthy young and middle-aged people.

Without question, pregnant women are at increased risk of complications. This heightened risk takes on added importance for a virus, like this one, that preferentially infects younger age groups.

Finally, and perhaps of greatest concern, we do not know how this virus will behave under conditions typically found in the developing world. To date, the vast majority of cases have been detected and investigated in comparatively well-off countries.

Let me underscore two of many reasons for this concern. First, more than 99% of maternal deaths, which are a marker of poor quality care during pregnancy and childbirth, occurs in the developing world.

Second, around 85% of the burden of chronic diseases is concentrated in low- and middle-income countries.

Although the pandemic appears to have moderate severity in comparatively well-off countries, it is prudent to anticipate a bleaker picture as the virus spreads to areas with limited resources, poor health care, and a high prevalence of underlying medical problems.

Ladies and gentlemen,

A characteristic feature of pandemics is their rapid spread to all parts of the world. In the previous century, this spread has typically taken around 6 to 9 months, even during times when most international travel was by ship or rail.

Countries should prepare to see cases, or the further spread of cases, in the near future. Countries where outbreaks appear to have peaked should prepare for a second wave of infection.

Guidance on specific protective and precautionary measures has been sent to ministries of health in all countries. Countries with no or only a few cases should remain vigilant.

Countries with widespread transmission should focus on the appropriate management of patients. The testing and investigation of patients should be limited, as such measures are resource intensive and can very quickly strain capacities.

WHO has been in close dialogue with influenza vaccine manufacturers. I understand that production of vaccines for seasonal influenza will be completed soon, and that full capacity will be available to ensure the largest possible supply of pandemic vaccine in the months to come.

Pending the availability of vaccines, several non-pharmaceutical interventions can confer some protection.

WHO continues to recommend no restrictions on travel and no border closures.

Influenza pandemics, whether moderate or severe, are remarkable events because of the almost universal susceptibility of the world's population to infection.

We are all in this together, and we will all get through this, together.

Thank you.

SOURCE: World Health Organization. "World Now at Start of 2009 Influenza Pandemic." June 11, 2009. www.who.int/mediacentre/news/statements/2009/h1n1_pandemic_phase6_20090611/en/index .html.

OTHER HISTORIC DOCUMENTS OF INTEREST

FROM THIS VOLUME

■ Swine Flu in the United States, p. 467.

FROM PREVIOUS *HISTORIC DOCUMENTS*

■ U.S. Government on Combating an Influenza Pandemic, *2005,* p. 747

■ World Health Organization on Preparing for a Flu Pandemic, *2004,* p. 932

■ Government Accountability on Shortage of Flu Vaccine, *2004,* p. 639

■ Report to Califano on Swine Flu Program, *1978,* p. 669

Congress Passes Credit Card Reform Legislation

APRIL 30 AND MAY 22, 2009

On May 22, 2009, President Obama signed into law legislation reforming the practices of the credit card industry. The new law, known as the Credit CARD (Card Accountability, Responsibility, and Disclosure) Act, places new restrictions on when and how card issuers may charge their customers fees or raise their interest rates. It also requires credit card companies to disclose more financial information to their customers and mail bills three weeks before payment is due, rather than the previously typical two weeks. Both houses of Congress passed the measure with strong bipartisan support. At the signing, President Obama described the act as "some commonsense reforms designed to protect consumers." He added, "Just as we demand credit card users to act responsibly, we demand that credit card companies act responsibly too. And that's not too much to ask." However, banking industry spokespeople and some Republicans warned that the regulations would lead to higher rates and severely reduce the availability of credit, especially to poor individuals.

The debate on the Credit CARD Act came amid the most serious economic distress the nation had seen since the 1930s. As President Obama noted, credit card debt increased 25 percent between 1999 and 2009, ensnaring almost half the U.S. adult population. By the spring of 2009, public opinion had turned sharply against the ongoing bailout of the financial industry. Reports of large compensation packages and bonuses paid to bank executives had provoked voter outrage. On the issue of credit cards, the president positioned himself squarely in the reform camp, pressing Congress to pass legislation and requesting that it reach his desk before his first Memorial Day in office. The Federal Reserve had already approved new rules for the credit card industry in December 2008 that would take effect in July 2010. The Senate legislation, chiefly authored by Sen. Christopher Dodd, D-Conn., went well beyond the specific reforms embraced by the Federal Reserve. The measure passed the Senate Banking Committee by only one vote, but opposition withered once the bill reached the floor. The Senate passed it by a 90–5 vote on May 19, following House approval by 357–70 on April 30. Small-business associations lined up with consumer groups in favor of the reforms.

DEBTS, RATES, AND FEE INCREASES

Credit cards are a comparatively recent financial innovation. The first popular charge cards, such as Diners Club and American Express, appeared in the 1950s. These were originally intended to serve only as a short-term debt vehicle; customers were obligated to pay off their balance each month. The forerunners of Visa and MasterCard emerged in the 1960s, complicating the system by involving networks of cooperating banks and permitting cardholders to carry debt. "Prior to 1990," noted Rep. Ed Perlmutter, D-Colo., "credit cards had more or less standardized rates—around 20 percent—few fees, and they were generally offered to persons with high credit standards. However, since 1990, card issuers have adopted risk-based pricing, and as a result of this new pricing structure, rates have increased and fees have increased dramatically." Banks and card issuers competed for customers by offering low introductory rates, then adjusted those rates based on the customer's credit worthiness. Issuers were free to increase rates at their discretion.

As millions of Americans accrued consumer debt, many paying only the minimum required each month, the industry profited from high rates, penalty fees, and finance charges. One industry analyst reported that the card companies had increased their fee revenues by 43 percent in the five years before 2008. These companies also earned billions of dollars each year from the processing fees charged to merchants each time a customer makes a retail purchase on a credit card.

The severe downturn in the U.S. economy beginning in 2007 and the ongoing mortgage crisis sharply increased the number of credit card delinquencies. Former secretary of labor Robert Reich wrote, "[N]ow that tens of millions of Americans are poorer than they used to be, the credit-card bubble is bursting." Facing losses, the card companies further increased their rate and fee structures and aggressively sought a variety of ways, some obscure, to beef up their bottom line. The industry's tactics led to widespread consumer complaints of abusive practices.

CONTROVERSIAL TACTICS OUTLAWED

The Credit CARD Act contains many specific provisions restricting and regulating the behavior of card issuers that were phased in between August 2009 and February 2010. Although the act does not set a cap on interest rates, it does ban companies from raising those rates arbitrarily. Card companies will only be allowed to raise rates on existing balances if the customer has failed to make the minimum payment for at least sixty days. Even under those conditions, the company will have to reinstate the original rate if the borrower pays on time for six consecutive months. No rate increases will be permitted within the first year of a new borrower's account opening, and any promotional or "teaser" rates must remain effective for a minimum of six months. The act also makes it harder for companies to market or issue cards to people under the age of twenty-one; minors will need a parent or guardian to serve as a cosigner unless they can prove their own source of income.

The legislation targets numerous issuer tactics that had generated vociferous cries of unfairness from consumers. For example, some card accounts include multiple balances at different interest rates, and in recent years card companies have made it standard practice to require the customer to pay off the amount at the lowest rate first. By banning this policy, the Credit CARD Act will help consumers reduce their total debt and pay it off more rapidly. So-called double-cycle billing, in which companies continue to charge interest on portions of a balance that have already been paid, is also outlawed. Some companies had routinely imposed late fees if they received payment late in the day on the due date. The new legislation sets a uniform 5 P.M. standard. Deadlines cannot be set on a Sunday or holiday.

The act imposes several disclosure requirements on card issuers in an attempt to increase transparency in the credit card business and help borrowers understand the terms of their agreements. Credit card statements now must include not only the total balance and the minimum payment due but also the date when the full balance would be paid off if the customer paid no more than each month's minimum and what the total cost would be, including interest. Card companies must post the full terms of card agreements on the Internet. The legislation specifies that certain information formerly relegated to fine print must be printed no smaller than 10-point type. Companies must notify customers forty-five days in advance of any changes to the governing terms and conditions of their agreements and allow customers to close out their account without penalty before the changes, such as higher rates, become effective. Statements must now be mailed twenty-one days ahead of the due date, not the previously accepted fourteen.

WARNINGS OF SHRINKING CREDIT

Republicans opposed to the legislation spoke out against what they perceived as unnecessary federal intervention in the financial market. They also warned that the indirect impact of the reforms would be hazardous to the economy. "If enacted into law, it is not credit card companies that will suffer," said Rep. Pete Sessions, R-Texas, in the House debate. "It will be every single person that has a credit card and for those who even want to have a credit card in the future. Every American will see an increase in their interest rates, and some of the current benefits that encourage responsible lending will most likely disappear." Opponents contended that the act would result in a significant reduction in the overall amount of credit available to American consumers, exacerbating the credit crunch already ongoing and extending the duration of the recession. Critics argued that low-income and poor families could see their access to credit cut off—forcing them into riskier alternatives, like payday lending—and small businesses would have a harder time obtaining the credit they need to grow.

Industry voices also echoed these concerns. According to the head of the American Bankers Association, Edward L. Yingling, "This bill fundamentally changes the entire business model of credit cards by restricting the ability to price credit for risk." The reforms would inevitably raise the costs of offering credit, he argued. Without the ability to offset the risks of supplying credit to those with low credit worthiness and recoup the costs of delinquencies through fees and rate adjustments, there would be a strong likelihood that credit would shrink, perhaps by as much as half of the $5 trillion in currently extended credit. Some industry spokespeople suggested that issuers would find it necessary to restore the annual fees on major credit cards they had dropped decades ago and phase out ancillary benefits, such as cash advances, interest-free balance transfers, and protection for those who surpass their credit limit. Other analysts, such as Peter Dreier and Donald Cohen of the progressive Horizon Institute, dismissed many of these predictions and accused industry advocates of "crying wolf." What seemed clear is that the credit card companies would have to take more care in selecting their customers, having lost some of the flexibility they had to raise rates on existing cardholder balances. The days of the low introductory rate appeared to be numbered. By the fall of 2009, junk mail credit card solicitations had dropped by more than two-thirds.

The first set of Credit CARD Act reforms took effect August 20, 2009, nearly three months after the president signed the bill into law. The delay gave the industry sufficient time to adjust to the new regulatory environment. Some companies, such as Citibank and Capital One, used the intervening period to raise their customers' rates. Many others switched from fixed-interest rates to variable, fluctuating rates. J.P. Morgan Chase doubled minimum payments on some accounts. Of concern was the possibility that companies might find ways to circumvent the new restrictions. A December 2009 report by the Center for Responsible Lending (CRL) alleged that the major issuers were doing just that. The report, titled "Dodging Reform," identified eight ways card companies were gaming the system by imposing "hidden charges" covered by neither the Credit CARD Act nor the new Federal Reserve rules. The CRL recommended the creation of a consumer financial protection agency to monitor the tactics of the credit card industry in an ongoing fashion.

—Roger Smith

Following are remarks from debate in the House of Representatives on April 30, 2009, on the Credit CARD Act by Reps. Ed Perlmutter, D-Colo., and Pete Sessions, R-Texas, and a statement from President Barack Obama on signing the Credit CARD Act on May 22, 2009.

DOCUMENT

Rep. Ed Perlmutter, D-Colo., in Support of the Credit CARD Act

April 30, 2009

Madam Speaker, House Resolution 379 provides for consideration of H.R. 627, the Credit Cardholders' Bill of Rights Act. On a regular basis, constituents of mine from Colorado contact me in disappointment with stories about actions taken by their credit card companies. Hardworking Americans who make payments on time, have good credit, and live within their means see their rates increase without notice and without cause.

In a time when many Americans are struggling to pay their mortgage, when health care costs are increasing and many are out of work, unfair credit card practices threaten many families. Americans deserve a fair shake. They deserve transparency and not smoke and mirrors. They deserve reliability and not chaos within their statements.

The bill brought to us today . . . gives consumers a fair deal. Prior to 1990, credit cards had more or less standardized rates—around 20 percent—few fees, and they were generally offered to persons with high credit standards.

However, since 1990, card issuers have adopted risk-based pricing, and as a result of this new pricing structure, rates have increased and fees have increased dramatically. Today's credit cards feature a wide variety of interest rates that reflect a complex list of factors. The terms of most agreements have become so complicated, consumers don't know what they are getting into when they sign on to a credit card agreement. Most, if not all, agreements allow the issuer to change the interest rate or other terms of agreement at any time for any reason.

For example, there is something called "universal default" in most credit card agreements. Universal default allows the credit card company to change the rate or change the terms of the credit card agreement for something completely unrelated to the credit card. That's got to stop.

There are also practices which allow for credit card companies to apply payments to the lowest rate of interest, not the highest rate of interest, so that amounts continue to grow under the credit card agreements. There are things including double billing cycles so you think that you have paid off a substantial portion of the credit card but, in fact, you continue to get interest charged against the amount you already paid off.

These are excessive practices, and they must be changed.

Under H.R. 627, issuers can only raise interest rates for the reasons provided within the legislation as proposed.

Madam Speaker, the American people have spoken. . . . Americans are tired of opening their monthly credit card bill and noticing that their interest rate has jumped from 8 percent to 15 percent for no reason. H.R. 627 establishes responsible regulation within an industry which has taken advantage of many vulnerable Americans.

Finally, I want to note the careful balance this bill takes. We have had over a half dozen hearings on this bill alone. It's the product of years of meetings and hearings and conversations and input from all interested parties and roughly 60,000 public comments. This bill provides the fairness Americans have asked for from their credit card companies.

I urge my colleagues to vote in favor of the rule and the underlying bill.

With that, I reserve the balance of my time.

SOURCE: Rep. Ed. Perlmutter. "Credit Cardholders' Bill of Rights Act." *Congressional Record* 2009, pt. 155, H5003. www.gpo.gov/fdsys/pkg/CREC-2009-04-30/pdf/CREC-2009-04-30-pt1-PgH5003-2.pdf.

DOCUMENT

Rep. Pete Sessions, R-Texas, in Opposition to the Credit CARD Act

April 30, 2009

Madam Speaker, I rise today in opposition to this rule and to the underlying legislation.

This structured rule does not call for the open and honest debate that has been promised by my Democratic colleagues time after time.

Today's action by my friends on the other side of the aisle is another example of the Federal Government overstepping its boundaries into the private marketplace. And I think it's important for us to note that people who get credit cards get this as an extension of their opportunity and their credit, and they have a responsibility when they sign a contract to live up to that responsibility. It is not a right that is being extended, I believe, today for us to go into the free market and to tinker with on a Federal basis what is a right that is reserved to the States today. We disagree with what is happening today.

Not even 6 months ago, Madam Speaker, the Federal Reserve passed new credit card rules that would protect consumers and provide for more transparency and accountability in the marketplace. These new regulations are set to take effect in July 2010, an agreed-upon date to ensure the necessary time for banks and credit card companies to make crucial and critical adjustments to their business practices without making mistakes and without harming consumers.

Part of what the gentleman from Colorado just described, some of the 60,000 letters of feedback to the industry, took place in that regard. It took place to the Federal Reserve taking information, working with credit card consumer groups to try and alleviate problems or perceived problems in the marketplace. However, with the growing Federal deficit, the current economic crisis, and the growing number of unemployed people, I would simply ask why is Congress passing legislation that already exists? Let's give those statutes and those rules and regulations which are going to be in place time to work.

This legislation allows for the Federal Government to micromanage the way credit card companies and the banking industry does its business. Those hearings have already been held. Decisions have already been made by the Fed. Decisions with credit card companies and consumer groups to understand what changes needed to be made, they've already happened.

If enacted into law, it is not credit card companies that will suffer. It will be every single person that has a credit card and for those who even want to have a credit card in the future. Every American will see an increase in their interest rates, and some of the current benefits that encourage responsible lending will most likely disappear. For example, cash advances, over-the-limit protection, would be just one example.

My friends on the other side of the aisle not only remove any incentive for using credit cards responsibly, but they punish those managing their credit responsibly to subsidize those who are irresponsible. Madam Speaker, the Democrats also want to limit the amount of credit that is available to the middle class and low-income individuals. The very Americans that take the most advantage of credit will be harmed by what we're doing here today.

This legislation prevents credit history from being used to price risk, as an example, meaning that some individuals may not now be able to get a credit card, especially if they are lower-income or they have blemished credit histories or are trying to establish credit for the first time, like college students.

Additionally, the strain of this legislation could have a direct and adverse effect on small businesses which use this credit, especially in times like these where economic and job growth in this country are threatened. For individuals starting in a small business, this legislation means increased interest rates, reduced benefit, and shrinks the availability of credit, potentially limiting their options to even succeed in the marketplace.

Meredith Whitney, a prominent banking analyst, in speaking as a result of this legislation, remarked in *The Wall Street Journal* that she expects a $2.7 trillion decrease in credit by the end of 2010 out of the current $5 trillion credit line available in this country.

Madam Speaker, at a time when we're in economic downturns, the option of credit that is available for people—notwithstanding that they may have to pay a little bit more but will have the flexibility to have that credit—is important.

In the current state of our economy, we urgently would say we need to increase liquidity and lower the cost of credit to stimulate more lending—not raise rates and reduce the availability of credit.

This is not a solution for the ailing economy.

This type of government control of private markets is really what my Democrat colleagues and this new administration have been exploring for quite some time. Whether it is federalizing our banks, federalizing our credit market, federalizing our health care system, federalizing the energy sector, this is what this new administration and my friends in the majority party wish to do.

That said, this administration has taken their power grab a step further, first of all, in this legislation, to write contracts, to hire and fire executives, and to guarantee muffler warranties.

They won't let banks pay back their loans. And now they are plotting a hostile takeover of the financial services industry, converting preferred shares into common equity shares, a drastic shift towards a government strategy of long-term ownership and involvement in some of our banks.

Millions of Americans are outraged at the mismanagement of TARP [Troubled Asset Relief Program] and the reckless use of their tax dollars, and I believe that taxpayers are increasingly uneasy with the Federal Government's growing involvement in financial markets that we see on the floor today.

In an effort to provide more protections to consumers and to taxpayers, I offered an amendment yesterday in the Rules Committee—a Rules Committee of which I have served for 11 years—that was defeated by a party-line vote of 7–3.

Madam Speaker, I would like to insert in the CONGRESSIONAL RECORD a copy of that amendment. . . .

[The text of the amendment, a letter from the House Republican leadership to Treasury Secretary Timothy Geithner, and a letter from Rep. Sessions to Geithner have been omitted.]

As this Democrat majority continues to tax, borrow, and spend Americans' hard-earned tax dollars, we move closer and closer to nationalizing our banking and credit systems that will only deepen our current economic struggle.

The Federal Government is interfering and hindering our progress, not helping it. . . . By not making my amendment in order today, I can say that this Congress has turned its back on what I believe is responsible public policy to say that this Federal Government should not invest in the free enterprise system.

Madam Speaker, it is appropriate to consider new ways to protect credit consumers from unfair and deceptive practices and to ensure that Americans receive useful and complete disclosures about the terms and conditions. But in doing so, we must make sure that we do nothing to make credit cards more expensive for those who use credit responsibly, or to cut off or hinder access to credit for small businesses who count on this credit, but perhaps those with less than perfect credit histories.

While reading *The Wall Street Journal* last week, I came across an op-ed called "Political Credit Cards," discussing this very issue. It states, "Our politicians spend half their time berating banks for offering too much credit on too easy terms and the other half berating banks for handing out too little credit at a high price. The bankers should tell the President that they need to start getting out of the business, and that Washington should quit changing the rules." This speaks to what happened with TARP. It also speaks clearly to health care, welfare, taxes, and this underlying legislation today. Madam Speaker, the American people deserve better from their elected officials.

I would also note that I thought it was interesting that this new Democrat majority, just this week, as we passed what I consider to be an irresponsible $3.5 trillion new budget, the very next vote was on encouraging Americans to understand financial security and integrity. I think Congress could use a little bit of what it hands out to study for itself and to gain the discipline to understand that the free enterprise system works best when we leave it alone.

Madam Speaker, I reserve the balance of my time.

SOURCE: Rep. Pete Sessions. "Credit Cardholders' Bill of Rights Act." *Congressional Record* 2009, pt. 155, H5004–H5006. www.gpo.gov/fdsys/pkg/CREC-2009-04-30/pdf/CREC-2009-04-30-pt1-PgH5003-2.pdf.

President Obama's Remarks on Signing the Credit CARD Act

M A Y   2 2 ,   2 0 0 9

. . . This has been a historic week, a week in which we've cast aside some old divisions and put in place new reforms that will reduce our dependence on foreign oil, prevent fraud against homeowners, and save taxpayers money by preventing wasteful Government contracts, a week that marks significant progress in the difficult work of changing our policies and transforming our politics.

But the real test of change, ultimately, is whether it makes a difference in the lives of the American people. That's what matters to me. That's what matters to my administration. That's what matters to the extraordinary collection of Members of Congress that are standing with me here, but also who are in the audience. And we're here today because of a bill that will make a big difference, the Credit Card Accountability, Responsibility, and Disclosure Act. . . .

We've also seen credit cards become for a minority of customers part of an uneasy, unstable dependence. Some end up in trouble because of reckless spending or wishful thinking. Some get in over their heads by not using their heads. And I want to be clear: We do not excuse or condone folks who've acted irresponsibly. We don't excuse irresponsibility.

But the reason this legislation is so important is because there are many others— many who have written me letters, or grabbed my arm along rope lines, or shared their stories while choking back tears—who have relied on credit cards not because they were avoiding responsibilities, but precisely because they wanted to meet their responsibilities and got trapped.

These are hard-working people whose hours were cut, or the factory closed, who turned to a credit card to get through a rough month, which turned into 2 or 3 or 6 months without a job. These are parents who found, to their surprise, that their health insurance didn't cover a child's expensive procedure and had to pay the hospital bill, families who saw their mortgage payments jump and used the credit card more often to make up the difference.

These are borrowers who discovered that credit card debt is all too easily a one-way street: It's easy to get in, but almost impossible to get out. It's also, by the way, a lot of small-business owners who have helped to finance their dream through credit cards and suddenly, in this economic downturn, find themselves getting hammered.

Part of this is the broader economy, but part of it is the practices of credit card companies. Contracts are drafted not to inform, but to confuse. Mysterious fees appear on statements, payment deadlines shift, terms change, interest rates rise. And suddenly, a credit card becomes less of a lifeline and more of an anchor. . . .

. . . Over the past decade, credit card debt has increased by 25 percent in our country. Nearly half of all Americans carry a balance on their cards. Those who do, carry an average balance of more than $7,000. And as our economic situation worsened—and many defaulted on their debt as a result of a lost job, for example—a vicious cycle ensued. Borrowers couldn't pay their bills, and so lenders raised rates. As rates went up, more borrowers couldn't pay.

Millions of cardholders have seen their interest rates jump in just the past 6 months. One in five Americans carry a balance that has been charged interest rates above 20 percent—one in five.

Now, I also want to emphasize, these are costs that often hit responsible credit card users. . . .

So we're here to put a change to all that. With this bill, we're putting in place some commonsense reforms designed to protect consumers like Janet. I want to be clear about this: Credit card companies provide a valuable service; we don't begrudge them turning a profit. We just want to make sure that they do so while upholding basic standards of fairness, transparency, and accountability. Just as we demand credit card users to act responsibly, we demand that credit card companies act responsibly too. And that's not too much to ask.

And that's why, because of this new law, statements will be required to tell credit card holders how long it will take to pay off a balance and what it will cost in interest if they only make the minimum monthly payments. We also put a stop to retroactive rate hikes that appear on a bill suddenly with no rhyme or reason.

Every card company will have to post its credit card agreements online, and we'll monitor those agreements to see if new protections are needed. Consumers will have more time to understand their statements as well. . . .

Lastly, among many other provisions, there will be no more sudden charges—changes to terms and conditions. We require at least 45 days notice if the credit card company is going to change terms and conditions.

So we're not going to give people a free pass, and we expect consumers to live within their means and pay what they owe. But we also expect financial institutions to act with the same sense of responsibility that the American people aspire to in their own lives. . . .

But I'm heartened by what I'm seeing, by the willingness of old adversaries to seek out new partnerships, by the progress we've made these past months to address many of our toughest challenges. And I'm confident that as a Nation we will learn the lessons of our recent past and that we will elevate again those values at the heart of our success as a people: hard work over the easy buck, responsibility over recklessness, and, yes, moderation over extravagance.

This work has already begun, and now it continues. I thank the Members of Congress for putting their shoulder to the wheel in a bipartisan fashion and getting this piece of legislation done. Congratulations to all of you. . . .

SOURCE: U.S. Executive Office of the President. "Remarks on Signing the Credit Card Accountability, Responsibility, and Disclosure Act of 2009." *Daily Compilation of Presidential Documents* 2009, no. 00395 (May 22, 2009). www.gpo.gov/fdsys/pkg/DCPD-200900395/pdf/DCPD-200900395.pdf.

OTHER HISTORIC DOCUMENTS OF INTEREST

FROM THIS VOLUME

- President Obama Calls for Executive Pay Cap, p. 61

FROM PREVIOUS *HISTORIC DOCUMENTS*

- Passage of the Emergency Economic Stabilization Act of 2008, *2008*, p. 443

May

North Korea Conducts Successful Nuclear Test

MAY 25 AND JUNE 12, 2009

On May 25, 2009, North Korea announced it had successfully conducted an underground nuclear test, its second nuclear missile test in three years. One report initially stated that the size of the blast was comparable to that of atomic bombs dropped on Japan during World War II, but many questioned whether North Korea had officially become a member of the club of nuclear armed-countries. The test brought swift condemnation from government leaders around the world and altered the nature and progression of diplomatic talks.

AN ONGOING STRUGGLE

The missile test dealt a blow to ongoing efforts to persuade President Kim Jong-Il's government to forgo aspirations of becoming a nuclear-armed country in exchange for economic aid and security guarantees. Japan, South Korea, the United States, China, and Russia had been holding talks with North Korea since 2003 in an effort to achieve this goal, but progress had been halting. Talks had been strained since North Korea's first test of a nuclear device in 2006—an act that prompted the United Nations to pass a resolution demanding that Pyongyang (the capital of North Korea) cease activities related to its ballistic missile program and imposing a package of economic sanctions. Some encouraging signs had suggested North Korea was willing to cooperate, such as the country's agreement in 2007 to dismantle its nuclear plants, but that agreement became bogged down in December 2008 because of disputes over how to verify the country's nuclear activities.

Then North Korea launched a long-range rocket on April 5, 2009, claiming the exercise was intended to put a peaceful communications satellite into space. However, the United States, Japan, South Korea, and other countries accused the government of using the launch as a test of its long-range missile technology. The UN Security Council condemned the launch and voted to tighten the sanctions first put in place in 2006, provoking North Korea to declare it would conduct a second nuclear test and launch additional missiles unless the United Nations apologized. Officials also announced the country would abandon the six-party talks, expel international inspectors, and restart its nuclear plants.

ANOTHER PROVOCATION

On May 25, the Korean Central News Agency reported that North Korea had "successfully conducted one more underground nuclear test" as "part of the measures to bolster up its nuclear deterrent for self-defence in every way." The country had given less than one hour's notice through its mission to the United Nations that it would conduct the test. Russian Defense Ministry officials confirmed the test had occurred shortly before 10:00 A.M., approximately 50 miles northwest of the northern city of Kilju. The ministry's early estimates described the size of the explosion as comparable to those of nuclear bombs dropped on Hiroshima and Nagasaki, Japan, during World War II. Further analysis determined that the blast fell far short of these bombs, although it had been nearly twenty times larger than the 2006 nuclear test. The U.S. Geological Survey said it had "registered seismic activity" roughly equivalent to a 4.7 magnitude earthquake. South Korea's Yonhap News Agency reported that North Korea also had fired three short-range ground-to-air missiles with a range of approximately eighty miles, with the intention of keeping U.S. and Japanese surveillance planes away from the nuclear test.

International reactions to the nuclear test were swift and unanimously condemned North Korea's actions. U.S. president Barack Obama declared the tests "a blatant violation of international law" and "a matter of grave concern to all nations." British prime minister Gordon Brown denounced the test as "erroneous, misguided and a danger to the world." Russian and Chinese leaders, who until this point had resisted efforts to harshly punish North Korea for its nuclear activities, denounced the government's actions. China's Ministry of Foreign Affairs said it was "resolutely opposed" to the test and demanded that "North Korea keeps its promise of denuclearization and ceases all actions that could further worsen the situation." The UN Security Council arranged an emergency meeting that same day to discuss how to respond to the test and its "clear violation" of the 2006 resolution. Several diplomats suggested they would push for harsher sanctions, but also noted that the group's "discussions and deliberations will indeed take some time."

Kim Jong-Il's Motivation

Immediately following the test, North Korea experts and other analysts began speculating about Kim Jong-Il's motivation. To some, it seemed clear that he had wanted to provoke the United States in hopes of stimulating direct, high-level negotiations that would result in North Korea's recognition as a nuclear power, new aid and concessions, and a normalization of diplomatic relations. "North Korea has been seeking ways to pressure the United States and South Korea to open up dialogue with them," said Xu Guangyu, a researcher with the China Arms Control and Disarmament Association. "North Korea's strategic objective hasn't changed. The objective is to win the attention of the Obama administration, to push the North Korea issue up the agenda."

The relationship between the two countries was further complicated by North Korea's arrest of two American journalists, Euna Lee and Laura Ling, who had allegedly entered North Korea illegally on March 21, 2009, while working on a story. The women were convicted and sentenced to twelve years of hard labor. Paik Hak-soon of South Korea's Sejong Institute said that North Korea was holding the women as leverage to secure negotiations and that their case provided a "face-saving" way for the United States to send a high-level envoy to Pyongyang. Ling and Lee were later released following a visit to North Korea by former president Bill Clinton.

Although provoking the United States seemed one likely motive for the missile test, other analysts asserted Kim had a different audience in mind. According to Yoon Deokmin of the Institute of Foreign Affairs and National Security in Seoul, "Kim Jong-Il wants to show that he has given his nation mighty nuclear power. This test was absolutely a domestic demonstration." Some thought the missile test was part of a shift toward a more aggressive foreign policy that had begun shortly after Kim had reportedly suffered a stroke, perhaps to assure his government and North Korea's citizens that he was still in control. Others believed the test was his attempt to establish a legacy of technological achievement instead of failure to provide basic needs, such as food and electricity, to impoverished North Koreans.

Still others said the test's greatest significance was its role in the president's selection of a successor. For several months, the international community had been speculating as to which of three sons Kim would choose and when he would make the announcement of succession. South Korean officials believed he had selected his youngest son, Kim Jong-un, an unusual choice for a communist style of government that traditionally had favored the eldest child and in a society that values seniority. Some analysts claimed the missile test was part of the president's strategy to demonstrate his solidarity with the military to win their support and assistance in securing Kim Jong-un as his successor.

New Tension Between North and South Korea

On May 27, two days after the missile test, North Korea announced that it was no longer bound by the 1953 armistice that had brought an end to the Korean War and warned that if any of its ships were stopped by international forces, it would respond "with a powerful military strike." This threat was provoked by South Korea's decision to join the Proliferation Security Initiative (PSI), a collaborative effort among more than ninety countries to stop and inspect suspicious cargo from around the world being transported by land and by sea. The PSI was established by President George W. Bush in 2003 amid increasing suspicion that North Korea was shipping missiles to customers in the Middle East and Southeast Asia. South Korean and Japanese officials believed such a possibility was more troubling than the threat of a direct attack.

North Korea claimed South Korea's decision amounted to a "declaration of war" and moved to intensify naval drills on the two countries' western coastline. On June 2, South Korea deployed a high-speed naval vessel equipped with anti-ship missiles. That same day, U.S. military officials revealed that they had agreed to sell "bunker buster" bombs to South Korea that were capable of destroying underground nuclear facilities. Shortly thereafter, reports surfaced that North Korea was preparing to test launch a long-range intercontinental ballistic missile capable of reaching the United States, as well as several medium-range missiles. The fragile truce that had existed between North Korea and South Korea was effectively shattered.

UN Security Council Resolution 1874

As North Korea continued to make threats, the United States and Japan persisted in their efforts to pass a UN Security Council resolution that would forbid North Korea's government from selling and exporting its weapons and would impose greater economic sanctions. The greatest unknown throughout diplometic negotiations was whether China would support any such resolution. In the past, China had resisted calls to impose harsher financial penalties on North Korea in large part because of their trade relationship. China accounted for 73 percent of North Korea's international trade in 2008, supplying 90 percent of its oil demand, 80 percent of consumer goods, and 45 percent of its food. Chinese officials were also concerned that sanctions might cause North Korea's collapse and spark a refugee crisis on its border.

Yet on June 12, China joined its fellow Security Council members in unanimously condemning North Korea's missile test and passing Resolution 1874. The resolution instituted a mandatory ban on all North Korean arms exports, with the exception of small arms, and called on UN members to inspect all cargo vessels and airplanes suspected of carrying such materials in or out of the country. It also called on states to refrain from providing grants, loans, or public financial support for trade if it was possible that such assistance might contribute to North Korea's nuclear program and similarly required states to deny financial services, such as a freeze on assets, if those assets might contribute to prohibited programs. Explicit exclusions for humanitarian and denuclearization aid as well as legitimate trade and development financing were included.

A Continuing Conversation

North Korea continued to warn of possible conflicts with South Korea throughout the fall and winter of 2009 and rejected calls to abandon its nuclear program. Despite these threats, the Obama administration persisted in its attempts to persuade the country to return to the six-party talks. While officials in Washington and Pyongyang reported that progress had been made following a visit by special U.S. envoy Stephen Bosworth in December, both countries said more discussions were needed before the talks could resume.

—Linda Fecteau

Following is a news release from May 25, 2009, from the Korean Central News Agency of the Democratic People's Republic of Korea announcing North Korea's successful underground nuclear test, and the text of UN Security Council Resolution 1874, released on June 12, 2009, condemning the actions of North Korea and calling for an end to its nuclear tests.

North Korean Announcement of Nuclear Test

May 25, 2009

The Democratic People's Republic of Korea [DPRK] successfully conducted one more underground nuclear test on May 25 as part of the measures to bolster up its nuclear deterrent for self-defence in every way as requested by its scientists and technicians.

The current nuclear test was safely conducted on a new higher level in terms of its explosive power and technology of its control and the results of the test helped satisfactorily settle the scientific and technological problems arising in further increasing the power of nuclear weapons and steadily developing nuclear technology.

The successful nuclear test is greatly inspiring the army and people of the DPRK all out in the 150-day campaign, intensifying the drive for effecting a new revolutionary surge to open the gate to a thriving nation.

The test will contribute to defending the sovereignty of the country and the nation and socialism and ensuring peace and security on the Korean Peninsula and the region around it with the might of Songun.

SOURCE: Korean Central News Agency of the Democratic People's Republic of Korea. "KCNA Report on One More Successful Underground Nuclear Test." May 25, 2009. www.kcna.co.jp.

UN Security Council Resolution Condemning North Korea's Nuclear Test

June 12, 2009

Security Council, Acting Unanimously, Condemns in Strongest Terms Democratic People's Republic of Korea Nuclear Test, Toughens Sanctions

RESOLUTION 1874 (2009) STRENGTHENS ARMS EMBARGO, CALLS FOR INSPECTION OF CARGO, VESSELS IF STATES HAVE "REASONABLE GROUNDS" TO BELIEVE CONTAIN PROHIBITED ITEMS

The Security Council today condemned in the strongest terms the 25 May nuclear test by the Democratic People's Republic of Korea and tightened sanctions against it by blocking funding for nuclear, missile and proliferation activities through targeted sanctions on additional goods, persons and entities, widening the ban on arms imports-exports, and calling on Member States to inspect and destroy all banned cargo to and from that country—on the high seas, at seaports and airports—if they have reasonable grounds to suspect a violation.

Unanimously adopting resolution 1874 (2009) under Chapter VII, the Council sharpened its weapons import-export ban on the Democratic People's Republic of Korea enacted in resolution 1718 (2006)—which included armoured combat vehicles, large calibre artillery systems, attack helicopters, warships and missiles and spare parts—by calling on States to inspect, seize and dispose of the items and by denying fuel or supplies to service the vessels carrying them.

The Council called on all States to cooperate with those inspections, and, if the flag State did not consent to inspection on the high seas, decided that that State should direct the vessel to proceed to an appropriate and convenient port for the required inspection by the local authorities.

Any Member State that undertook an inspection, or seized and disposed of such cargo, was required to promptly submit reports containing the details to the Committee monitoring the sanctions, and to report on any lack of cooperation of a flag State.

It asked the Secretary-General to set up a seven-member expert panel, for an initial one-year period, to assist the Committee in carrying out its mandate and, among other tasks, to gather, examine and analyse information from States, United Nations bodies and other interested parties regarding implementation of resolution 1718 (2006) and today's text, particularly incidents of non-compliance.

Small arms and light weapons were exempted from the inspections, but the Council called on States to exercise vigilance over the direct or indirect supply, sale or transfer to the Democratic People's Republic of those weapons and directed States to notify the "1718" monitoring Committee at least five days prior to selling, supplying or transferring small arms or light weapons to it.

In addition to implementing the asset freeze and travel ban imposed in paragraphs 8(d) and (e) of resolution 1718 (2006), the Council today called on Member States to prevent the provision of financial services or the transfer to, through, or from their territory of any financial or other assets or resources that could contribute to the Democratic People's Republic of Korea's nuclear-related, ballistic missile-related or other weapons of mass destruction-related programmes or activities.

It called on all Member States and international financial and credit institutions not to enter into new commitments for grants, financial assistance or concessional loans to that country, except for humanitarian and developmental purposes directly addressing civilian needs; and on all Member States not to provide public financial support for trade with that country where such support could contribute to the country's nuclear-related or ballistic missile-related or other "WMD"-related programmes or activities. . . .

[Material containing an outline of reporting requirements for all member states related to the new sanctions as well as statements from representatives of UN member states, including China, South Korea, and the United States, have been omitted.]

Background

The Security Council met today to take action on a draft resolution (document S/2009/301), sponsored by France, Japan, Republic of Korea, United Kingdom and the United States, which reads as follows:

"*The Security Council,*

"*Recalling* its previous relevant resolutions, including resolution 825 (1993), resolution 1540 (2004), resolution 1695 (2006), and, in particular, resolution 1718 (2006), as well as the statements of its President of 6 October 2006 (S/PRST/2006/41) and 13 April 2009 (S/PRST/2009/7),

"*Reaffirming* that proliferation of nuclear, chemical and biological weapons, as well as their means of delivery, constitutes a threat to international peace and security,

"*Expressing* the gravest concern at the nuclear test conducted by the Democratic People's Republic of Korea ("the DPRK") on 25 May 2009 (local time) in violation of resolution 1718 (2006), and at the challenge such a test constitutes to the Treaty on Non-Proliferation of Nuclear Weapons ("the NPT") and to international efforts aimed at strengthening the global regime of non-proliferation of nuclear weapons towards the 2010 NPT Review Conference, and the danger it poses to peace and stability in the region and beyond,

"*Stressing* its collective support for the NPT and commitment to strengthen the Treaty in all its aspects, and global efforts towards nuclear non-proliferation and nuclear disarmament, and *recalling* that the DPRK cannot have the status of a nuclear-weapon State in accordance with the NPT in any case,

"*Deploring* the DPRK's announcement of withdrawal from the NPT and its pursuit of nuclear weapons,

"*Underlining* once again the importance that the DPRK respond to other security and humanitarian concerns of the international community,

"*Underlining* also that measures imposed by this resolution are not intended to have adverse humanitarian consequences for the civilian population of the DPRK,

"*Expressing* its gravest concern that the nuclear test and missile activities carried out by the DPRK have further generated increased tension in the region and beyond, and *determining* that there continues to exist a clear threat to international peace and security,

"*Reaffirming* the importance that all Member States uphold the purposes and principles of the Charter of the United Nations,

"*Acting* under Chapter VII of the Charter of the United Nations, and taking measures under its Article 41,

"1. *Condemns* in the strongest terms the nuclear test conducted by the DPRK on 25 May 2009 (local time) in violation and flagrant disregard of its relevant resolutions, in particular resolutions 1695 (2006) and 1718 (2006), and the statement of its President of 13 April 2009 (S/PRST/2009/7);

"2. *Demands* that the DPRK not conduct any further nuclear test or any launch using ballistic missile technology;

"3. *Decides* that the DPRK shall suspend all activities related to its ballistic missile programme and in this context re-establish its pre-existing commitments to a moratorium on missile launches;

"4. *Demands* that the DPRK immediately comply fully with its obligations under relevant Security Council resolutions, in particular resolution 1718 (2006);

"5. *Demands* that the DPRK immediately retract its announcement of withdrawal from the NPT;

"6. *Demands* further that the DPRK return at an early date to the NPT and International Atomic Energy Agency (IAEA) safeguards, bearing in mind the rights and obligations of States Parties to the NPT, and *underlines* the need for all States Parties to the NPT to continue to comply with their Treaty obligations;

"7. *Calls upon* all Member States to implement their obligations pursuant to resolution 1718 (2006), including with respect to designations made by the Committee established pursuant to resolution 1718 (2006) ("the Committee") pursuant to the statement of its President of 13 April 2009 (S/PRST/2009/7);

"8. *Decides* that the DPRK shall abandon all nuclear weapons and existing nuclear programmes in a complete, verifiable and irreversible manner and immediately cease all related activities, shall act strictly in accordance with the obligations applicable to parties under the NPT and the terms and conditions of the IAEA Safeguards Agreement (IAEA INFCIRC/403) and shall provide the IAEA transparency measures extending beyond these requirements, including such access to individuals, documentation, equipment and facilities as may be required and deemed necessary by the IAEA;

"9. *Decides* that the measures in paragraph 8(b) of resolution 1718 (2006) shall also apply to all arms and related materiel, as well as to financial transactions, technical training, advice, services or assistance related to the provision, manufacture, maintenance or use of such arms or materiel;

"10. *Decides* that the measures in paragraph 8(a) of resolution 1718 (2006) shall also apply to all arms and related materiel, as well as to financial transactions, technical training, advice, services or assistance related to the provision, manufacture, maintenance or use of such arms, except for small arms and light weapons and their related materiel, and *calls upon* States to exercise vigilance over the direct or indirect supply, sale or transfer to the DPRK of small arms or light weapons, and further *decides* that States shall notify the Committee at least five days prior to selling, supplying or transferring small arms or light weapons to the DPRK;

"11. *Calls upon* all States to inspect, in accordance with their national authorities and legislation, and consistent with international law, all cargo to and from the DPRK, in their territory, including seaports and airports, if the State concerned has information that provides reasonable grounds to believe the cargo contains items the supply, sale, transfer, or export of which is prohibited by paragraph 8(a), 8(b), or 8(c) of resolution 1718 or by paragraph 9 or 10 of this resolution, for the purpose of ensuring strict implementation of those provisions;

"12. *Calls upon* all Member States to inspect vessels, with the consent of the flag State, on the high seas, if they have information that provides reasonable grounds to believe that the cargo of such vessels contains items the supply, sale, transfer, or export of which is prohibited by paragraph 8(a), 8(b), or 8(c) of resolution 1718 (2006) or by paragraph 9 or 10 of this resolution, for the purpose of ensuring strict implementation of those provisions;

"13. *Calls upon* all States to cooperate with inspections pursuant to paragraphs 11 and 12, and, if the flag State does not consent to inspection on the high seas, *decides* that the flag State shall direct the vessel to proceed to an appropriate and convenient port for the required inspection by the local authorities pursuant to paragraph 11;

"14. *Decides* to authorize all Member States to, and that all Member States shall, seize and dispose of items the supply, sale, transfer, or export of which is prohibited by paragraph 8(a), 8(b), or 8(c) of resolution 1718 or by paragraph 9 or 10 of this resolution that are identified in inspections pursuant to paragraph 11, 12, or 13 in a manner that is not inconsistent with their obligations under applicable Security Council resolutions, including resolution 1540 (2004), as well as any obligations of parties to the NPT, the Convention on the Prohibition of the Development, Production, Stockpiling and Use of Chemical Weapons and on Their Destruction of 29 April 1997, and the Convention on the Prohibition of the Development, Production and Stockpiling of Bacteriological (Biological) and Toxin Weapons and on Their Destruction of 10 April 1972, and *decides* further that all States shall cooperate in such efforts;

"15. *Requires* any Member State, when it undertakes an inspection pursuant to paragraph 11, 12, or 13, or seizes and disposes of cargo pursuant to paragraph 14, to submit promptly reports containing relevant details to the Committee on the inspection, seizure and disposal;

"16. *Requires* any Member State, when it does not receive the cooperation of a flag State pursuant to paragraph 12 or 13 to submit promptly to the Committee a report containing relevant details;

"17. *Decides* that Member States shall prohibit the provision by their nationals or from their territory of bunkering services, such as provision of fuel or supplies, or other servicing of vessels, to DPRK vessels if they have information that provides reasonable grounds to believe they are carrying items the supply, sale, transfer, or export of which is prohibited by paragraph 8(a), 8(b), or 8(c) of resolution 1718 (2006) or by paragraph 9 or 10 of this resolution, unless provision of such services is necessary for humanitarian purposes or until such time as the cargo has been inspected, and seized and disposed of if necessary, and *underlines* that this paragraph is not intended to affect legal economic activities;

"18. *Calls upon* Member States, in addition to implementing their obligations pursuant to paragraphs 8(d) and (e) of resolution 1718 (2006), to prevent the provision of financial services or the transfer to, through, or from their territory, or to or by their nationals or entities organized under their laws (including branches abroad), or persons or financial institutions in their territory, of any financial or other assets or resources that could contribute to the DPRK's nuclear-related, ballistic missile–related, or other weapons of mass destruction–related programmes or activities, including by freezing any financial or other assets or resources on their territories or that hereafter come within their territories, or that are subject to their jurisdiction or that hereafter become subject to their jurisdiction, that are associated with such programmes or activities and applying enhanced monitoring to prevent all such transactions in accordance with their national authorities and legislation;

"19. *Calls upon* all Member States and international financial and credit institutions not to enter into new commitments for grants, financial assistance, or concessional loans to the DPRK, except for humanitarian and developmental purposes directly addressing the needs of the civilian population, or the promotion of denuclearization, and also *calls upon* States to exercise enhanced vigilance with a view to reducing current commitments;

"20. *Calls upon* all Member States not to provide public financial support for trade with the DPRK (including the granting of export credits, guarantees or insurance to their nationals or entities involved in such trade) where such financial support could contribute to the DPRK's nuclear-related or ballistic missile–related or other WMD-related programmes or activities;

"21. *Emphasizes* that all Member States should comply with the provisions of paragraphs 8(a)(iii) and 8(d) of resolution 1718 (2006) without prejudice to the activities of the diplomatic missions in the DPRK pursuant to the Vienna Convention on Diplomatic Relations;

"22. *Calls upon* all Member States to report to the Security Council within forty-five days of the adoption of this resolution and thereafter upon request by the Committee on concrete measures they have taken in order to implement effectively the provisions of paragraph 8 of resolution 1718 (2006), as well as paragraphs 9 and 10 of this resolution, as well as financial measures set out in paragraphs 18, 19 and 20 of this resolution;

"23. *Decides* that the measures set out at paragraphs 8(a), 8(b) and 8(c) of resolution 1718 (2006) shall also apply to the items listed in INFCIRC/254/Rev.9/Part 1a and INFCIRC/254/Rev.7/Part 2a;

"24. *Decides* to adjust the measures imposed by paragraph 8 of resolution 1718 (2006) and this resolution, including through the designation of entities, goods, and individuals, and directs the Committee to undertake its tasks to this effect and to report to the Security Council within 30 days of adoption of this resolution, and further *decides* that, if the Committee has not acted, then the Security Council will complete action to adjust the measures within seven days of receiving that report;

"25. *Decides* that the Committee shall intensify its efforts to promote the full implementation of resolution 1718 (2006), the statement of its President of 13 April 2009 (S/PRST/2009/7) and this resolution, through a work programme covering compliance, investigations, outreach, dialogue, assistance and cooperation, to be submitted to the Council by 15 July 2009, and that it shall also receive and consider reports from Member States pursuant to paragraphs 10, 15, 16 and 22 of this resolution;

"26. *Requests* the Secretary-General to create for an initial period of one year, in consultation with the Committee, a group of up to seven experts ("Panel of Experts"), acting under the direction of the Committee to carry out the following tasks: (a) assist the Committee in carrying out its mandate as specified in resolution 1718 (2006) and the functions specified in paragraph 25 of this resolution; (b) gather, examine and analyse information from States, relevant United Nations bodies and other interested parties regarding the implementation of the measures imposed in resolution 1718 (2006) and in this resolution, in particular incidents of non-compliance; (c) make recommendations on actions the Council, or the Committee or Member States, may consider to improve implementation of the measures imposed in resolution 1718 (2006) and in this resolution; and (d) provide an interim report on its work to the Council no later than 90 days after adoption of this resolution, and a final report to the Council no later than 30 days prior to termination of its mandate with its findings and recommendations;

"27. *Urges* all States, relevant United Nations bodies and other interested parties, to cooperate fully with the Committee and the Panel of Experts, in particular by supplying any information at their disposal on the implementation of the measures imposed by resolution 1718 (2006) and this resolution;

"28. *Calls upon* all Member States to exercise vigilance and prevent specialized teaching or training of DPRK nationals within their territories or by their nationals, of disciplines which could contribute to the DPRK's proliferation sensitive nuclear activities and the development of nuclear weapon delivery systems;

"29. *Calls upon* the DPRK to join the Comprehensive Nuclear-Test-Ban Treaty at the earliest date;

"30. *Supports* peaceful dialogue, *calls upon* the DPRK to return immediately to the Six-Party Talks without precondition, and *urges* all the participants to intensify their efforts on the full and expeditious implementation of the Joint Statement issued on 19 September 2005 and the joint documents of 13 February 2007 and 3 October 2007 . . .

"31. *Expresses* its commitment to a peaceful, diplomatic and political solution to the situation and welcomes efforts by Council members as well as other Member States to facilitate a peaceful and comprehensive solution through dialogue and to refrain from any actions that might aggravate tensions;

"32. *Affirms* that it shall keep the DPRK's actions under continuous review and that it shall be prepared to review the appropriateness of the measures contained in paragraph 8 of resolution 1718 (2006) and relevant paragraphs of this resolution, including the strengthening, modification, suspension or lifting of the measures, as may be needed at that time in light of the DPRK's compliance with relevant provisions of resolution 1718 (2006) and this resolution;

"33. *Underlines* that further decisions will be required, should additional measures be necessary;

"34. *Decides* to remain actively seized of the matter."

The draft resolution (document SC/2009/301) was adopted unanimously by the Security Council, as resolution 1874 (2009). . . .

[Detailed statements from UN members states have been omitted.]

Source: UN Security Council. "Security Council, Acting Unanimously, Condemns in Strongest Terms Democratic People's Republic of North Korea Nuclear Test, Toughens Sanctions." June 12, 2009. www.un.org/News/Press/docs/2009/sc9679.doc.htm.

OTHER HISTORIC DOCUMENTS OF INTEREST

FROM THIS VOLUME

FROM PREVIOUS *HISTORIC DOCUMENTS*

June

DOCUMENT IN CONTEXT

Congress Passes Tobacco Legislation

The Family Smoking Prevention and Tobacco Control Act, signed by President Barack Obama on June 22, 2009, brought sweeping changes to the ways in which tobacco products are marketed and regulated in the United States. The new regulations, which were a blow to many big tobacco companies, gave the Food and Drug Administration (FDA) increased power over the sales and marketing of tobacco products.

At the bill signing, President Obama remarked, "Today, thanks to the work of Democrats and Republicans, health care and consumer advocates, the decades-long effort to protect our children from the harmful effects of tobacco has emerged victorious. Today, change has come to Washington. This law will save American lives and make Americans healthier."

The bill had overwhelming support in both houses of Congress and received major backing from antismoking groups and health organizations, such as the American Cancer Society, as well as Philip Morris, the nation's leading tobacco company.

SUPPORT IN THE HOUSE AND SENATE

Henry Waxman, D-Calif., had introduced the Family Smoking Prevention and Tobacco Control Act in the U.S. House of Representatives. The measure was intended to give new authority to the FDA under the Federal Food, Drug and Cosmetic Act (FD&C Act). When it came up for a vote, the House passed the act 298–112. On May 5, 2009, on behalf of Sen. Edward Kennedy, D-Mass., who was recovering from brain tumor surgery, Majority Leader Harry Reid, D-Nev., introduced the act in the Senate, where it received bipartisan support.

Although the bill received overwhelming backing as it made its way through the House and Senate, a filibuster was attempted by Sen. Richard Burr, R-N.C., who represents a state that is one of the major tobacco producers. A filibuster in the Senate had killed a similar bill in 1998, but before the vote in 2009, Burr recognized that his threatened filibuster would most likely be blocked by a cloture vote. "Clearly the cloture motion will pass," said Burr. His press secretary, David Ward, added "Probably with flying colors." In the end, the bill passed in the Senate 79–17.

A decade earlier, when the filibuster had worked in the Senate, there had been a different attitude toward big tobacco. Regulating these companies used to engender serious debate. However, given the drive of citizens and antismoking groups to pass laws banning smoking in public places, and increased knowledge about the health effects of smoking itself and secondhand smoke, regulation of the tobacco industry was considered an easy win. "There has been a change in attitudes about the need to act to reduce tobacco use and a condemnation of the tobacco industry's continuing behavior," said Matthew Myers, president of the Campaign for Tobacco-Free Kids.

Preventing smoking at an early age was a key topic in the Senate debate. Sen. Frank Lautenberg, D-N.J., stated,

> As we know, since the 1980s, the tobacco industry has continued to engage in one sophisticated marketing campaign after another to get youngsters addicted to nicotine—just get them started and they are yours—even though selling and marketing cigarettes to children is generally against the law. It is our obligation, our responsibility to end the recruitment of kids as the next generation of smokers.

INDUSTRY AND ASSOCIATION RESPONSE

Contrary to what many might have been expected, Philip Morris, the largest cigarette company in the United States, pushed for the legislation in Congress. Smaller tobacco companies, however, were against the bill, and especially against involvement by Philip Morris, seeing this as another way for the large company to dominate the market. With heavier restrictions on marketing, some smaller tobacco companies could be forced out of business because smokers would then rely on big-brand recognition.

In the early to mid-1990s, Philip Morris had opposed legislative efforts on additional regulation of tobacco companies, stating that the powers given to the FDA to regulate tobacco companies and products would have left the agency with no choice but to ban tobacco products from being sold. Beginning in 2001, however, the company pushed to give the FDA more, but not excessive, regulatory power. In a 2001 white paper, Philip Morris asked that the FDA recognize the "unique challenges that cigarettes present" in terms of regulation, as they cannot be considered safe and effective as required of products under the FD&C Act. According to Philip Morris, by increasing tobacco regulation, there would be

> greater consistency in tobacco policy, more predictability for the tobacco industry, and an effective way to address issues that are of concern. . . . These issues include youth smoking; ingredient and [smoke] constituent testing and disclosure; content of health warning on cigarette packages and in advertisements; use of brand descriptors such as "light" and "ultra light"; good manufacturing practices for cigarettes; and standards for defining, and for the responsible marketing of any reduced risk or reduced exposure cigarettes.

The main argument Philip Morris used was that the FDA must recognize that tobacco is not an illegal product and that adults have the right to choose whether to use it. The company was against any regulation that would allow the FDA to ban tobacco products or lower the tar and nicotine content to the point where the product would not be satisfying to adult smokers. The FDA agreed with the Philip Morris argument, seeing the possibility that making tobacco illegal would lead to smuggling and more dangerous products.

Smaller companies, such as R.J. Reynolds and Lorillard, held that although the regulation of products and manufacturers was necessary, too much power invested in the FDA could lead the administration to ban tobacco products altogether. As noted earlier, the smaller companies also argued that changing the marketing structure for tobacco products would mean that consumers would rely more on brand recognition and product placement, an area in which the smaller companies could not compete with Philip Morris. However, Lorillard and R.J. Reynolds—which combined control only 38 percent of the U.S. cigarette market—were not strong enough to affect the legislative decision.

The health care industry also came out in support of the antismoking legislation. The Campaign for Tobacco-Free Kids, one of the largest anti-tobacco lobbies, worked with the American Lung Association, the American Cancer Society, and the American Heart Association to push for increased federal regulation of tobacco products. Their arguments included the following: Tobacco use contributes to more than 400,000 deaths each year, and tobacco-related deaths make up one-third of all cancer deaths. The cost of tobacco use to the public and the health care system is exorbitant, at more than $100 billion annually. One of the major arguments of the Campaign for Tobacco-Free Kids was that cigarette companies had used marketing tools to get a young generation hooked on tobacco products, had misled consumers into believing that some tobacco products are better for one's health than others and not addictive; and, according to these critics, had manipulated tobacco users in ways that prevented them from quitting.

LEGAL LIABILITIES

The FD&C Act had made tobacco regulation a muddy issue. Under this legislation, a manufacturer of food or drug products must be able to prove to the FDA that its product is safe and effective when used properly. Tobacco products, however, are inherently unsafe, and it is therefore impossible for manufacturers to meet FDA standards. In 2000, the U.S. Supreme Court ruled in *FDA v. Brown and Williamson Tobacco Corp.* that the FDA tobacco rule was invalid. The justices wrote in the judgment that if the FDA regulated tobacco products like foods and drugs, it would have no choice but to ban tobacco from the market. This, the Court said, was not what Congress had intended in crafting the FD&C Act. The Family Smoking Prevention and Tobacco Control Act, and other earlier legislative attempts at tobacco regulation, sought to fix what the Supreme Court found to be invalid. Earlier attempts at tobacco regulation had been hampered in both the House and Senate by the clout of representatives from tobacco-producing states and generous campaign contributions from tobacco manufacturers.

The bill signed by President Obama in June 2009 regulates the marketing strategies used by tobacco companies. This calls into question whether the law is in violation of the First Amendment of the Constitution guaranteeing free speech. The Supreme Court has ruled many times on government restriction of commercial speech, in 1980 developing a four-part test to determine whether such commercial speech regulation is constitutional. According to this test, first, the commercial activity must not be false or misleading; second, the government must prove that it is protecting a substantial government interest in restricting commercial speech; third, any restriction must have a direct impact on the government's interest; and fourth, the commercial restriction must not be any more than what is necessary. Tobacco advertising has often been at odds with the government when it comes to commercial free speech. In 2001, Lorillard Tobacco took a case to the Supreme Court in which the justices found that Massachusetts's regulations on outdoor and point-of-sale advertising was unconstitutional, because there was no justifiable reason for the state to use such limiting tactics to reduce the number of children who smoke.

To protect against additional legal battles, the 2009 legislation required that the 1996 tobacco rule, which had previously been overturned by the Supreme Court on the grounds that Congress had not given the FDA regulatory power over tobacco companies, be reenacted. This rule includes regulations on advertising, and among other things, prohibits tobacco manufacturers from distributing promotional items and using outdoor advertising for a tobacco product within 1,000 feet of a school.

PROVISIONS OF THE LAW

The law signed by President Obama in June places multiple restrictions on the tobacco industry. The new law allows the FDA to restrict harmful components in tobacco products. Tobacco companies are required to present a complete product ingredient list to the FDA and submit to mandatory biennial inspections of manufacturing facilities. Marketing techniques are severely limited by this bill: No longer can cigarette companies use the terms "light" or "low tar" on packaging without scientific evidence that such claims are true. In addition, larger health warnings that take up at least 30 percent of the front and back of cigarette packages, in bold type, are required. In addition, if a company wants to produce a new tobacco product, it must first obtain approval from the FDA, unless the product in question is determined to be similar to another product already made by the company or another product already on the market. As noted, tobacco companies can no longer place advertisements near schools or sponsor entertainment or sports events. A fee was levied on tobacco manufacturers to help pay for the additional regulation required of the FDA.

—Heather Kerrigan

Following is a floor statement made on June 2, 2009, by Sen. Richard Burr, R-N.C., in opposition to the Family Smoking Prevention and Tobacco Control Act, a floor statement made on June 3, 2009, by Sen. Frank Lautenberg, D-N.J., in support of tobacco regulation, and a statement by President Barack Obama on June 22, 2009, on signing tobacco regulation into law.

Sen. Richard Burr, R-N.C., on Tobacco Regulation

June 2, 2009

Mr. BURR. Mr. President, as I stated earlier today, I will be back time and time and time again to help my colleagues, one, understand what bill is being considered this week in the Senate but, more importantly, the ramifications of doing the wrong thing.

I think most Americans would agree that we should do everything we can to regulate tobacco products as relates to the youth of our country. . . .

. . . . As a matter of fact, the people now authorizing bills to dump on the FDA the responsibilities for tobacco were very critical of the FDA as it related to their food safety oversight, so it shouldn't shock any of us that I think they are misguided in where they have chosen to focus their efforts toward regulating this industry. . . .

Let me explain. To implement this program, it will cost $787 million a year—$787 million a year. I will propose, along with Senator Hagan, a substitute—that when HHS [Department of Health and Human Services] was asked to tell us how much they needed to absolutely fund that new entity to regulate the tobacco industry they told us they would need $100 million. . . .

Let me say that again, because I don't think everybody realizes what I said. The bill prohibits safer tobacco products and the censoring of potentially lifesaving information about relative risks among tobacco products. But this is being sold as a public health bill. This is being sold as a bill that reduces youth access, youth usage of tobacco products.

Let me tell you what we did in 1998. . . . The tobacco companies, understanding that there was a tremendous health cost that resulted from their products, came up with a settlement with all the States. It was called the Master Settlement Agreement—the MSA—and we will talk about the MSA a lot over the next few days. How much was the MSA? It was a guaranteed award of $280 billion over a period of time, and every year the companies make that payment to the States. These funds were to be used for health care costs and programs associated with tobacco use, mainly cessation programs. The industry was actually paying States to run cessation programs to get people to stop smoking—to stop using tobacco products.

If States spent the MSA money the way the CDC [Centers for Disease Control and Prevention] recommended to them every year, trust me, we wouldn't be here today. We would not be talking about the FDA taking over the jurisdiction of the regulatory responsibilities of tobacco, because had States used the money that was devoted for these cessation programs, the reduction in smoking would have been dramatic.

Let me add that, according to the CDC, smoking rates among Americans decline annually 2 to 4 percent currently—2 to 4 percent a year. The CBO [Congressional Budget Office], when looking at the Kennedy bill, estimated that, when implemented, this legislation would only decrease smoking by 2 percent annually. In other words, doing nothing versus the Kennedy bill, we have a trend line that gets us to a 15.97 percent usage of tobacco products in the year 2016; under the Kennedy bill, as scored by CBO, you would have a usage of cigarettes—of smoking products—of 17 percent in 2016. That is almost a 2-percent difference—a 2-percent additional decline, if we do nothing. And I am not here proposing that we do nothing. I am here proposing we do a new regulation, but we don't do it in a way that necessarily jeopardizes the safety, the gold standard of the Food and Drug Administration. . . .

[A state-by-state analysis of smoking trends has been omitted.]

Read the bill. Actually spend the time to sit down and read the bill. You will find out how we are jeopardizing the future of the American people relative to drug safety . . .

[Quotes from an American Association of Public Health Physicians white paper and statements by other members of Congress have been omitted.]

This bill is going to pass, make no illusions about that. Why? Because Members haven't read it. If they did, there is no way they would vote for it. The truth is, this is going to be popular at home. They will go home and say: I gave the FDA regulation of tobacco products. They will not go home and say: We had an opportunity since 1998 to reduce youth usage of tobacco and our State decided not to even meet the recommendations of the CDC, much less the others. We thought it was more important to build sidewalks or fill budget gaps than to meet these new targets. Now we have the answer to it because giving it to the FDA, no child will ever smoke again. Baloney. If they are under 18 today, they are finding some way to buy tobacco. It is illegal, but it should not surprise us when we look at marijuana usage, where we have a product that is not age limited, it is illegal, and more youth use marijuana than use cigarettes. . . .

[A letter from the American Council on Science and Health has been omitted.]

We are going to see, over the next several days, people come to the floor and say this is about public health, this is about reducing youth usage, this is about addressing the health risks of tobacco. Yet every professional who has written on this issue has said: What we are getting ready to do in the Senate is the worst thing we could do. It is going to make the problem worse. It is going to raise the cost of health care, not lower it. It is going to lock more people into choosing cigarettes versus smokeless products or other nicotine products that might get them off of cigarettes as an addiction.

In addition to not advancing the public health, I firmly believe this bill will further overburden the FDA and doom the FDA at its core mission of safety and efficacy of drugs and devices and biologics and food safety. . . .

If the effort is to get more Americans to make the choice of giving up the habit, then do not create a system that does not allow new products that Sweden and other countries have experienced reduce the amount of usage. Certainly, do not fall prey to the belief that if we pass this legislation we are going to reduce drastically the use of tobacco products. As a matter of fact, as CDC proved, doing nothing reduces the use of tobacco products 2 percent more than if we pass the Kennedy bill. . . . If the effort is to get it right, one would suggest we are doing it wrong. . . .

Our belief that we can just wave a magic wand, give it to a new agency, and that youth numbers are going to go down—well, we might be lucky enough to get them to go down, probably not more than they are naturally going down. I wish we were here debating why the prevalence of marijuana use—an illegal drug—is higher among America's youth than tobacco is. I think the country would be better served if that were the debate we were having on the Senate floor and not a debate about how we jeopardize the safety and efficacy of drugs and devices and cosmetics and food safety in the future.

Mr. President, I yield the floor.

SOURCE: U.S. Senate. "Family Smoking Prevention and Tobacco Control Act." June 2, 2009. *Congressional Record* 2009, 155, pt. S5924–S5926. www.gpo.gov/fdsys/pkg/CREC-2009-06-02/pdf/CREC-2009-06-02-pt1-PgS5922-2.pdf.

Sen. Frank Lautenberg, D-N.J., on Tobacco Regulation

June 3, 2009

Mr. President, basic instinct in humankind directs so much attention to the well-being of our children. . . .

One of the ways we can be effective is to protect our kids against addiction. I use the word deliberately. "Addiction" immediately conjures up a view of drugs—prescription drugs, prohibited drugs. We are not talking about that addiction. I am talking about a serious addiction, an addiction to tobacco—to tobacco—that has such a devastating effect on the people who smoke and often on those who are around the people who smoke. . . .

As a matter of fact, there was a study that was done, and it said even those who never smoked—people who worked in the cabin of the airplane—would show nicotine in their body fluids weeks after they had worked a trip. That is how pervasive this was. But big tobacco fought back. They fought back ferociously. They unleashed their forces. Money flowed to protect their addicted clientele and to keep them there. They brought phony science and high-paid lobbyists to squash this assault on behalf of public health. They had phony experts testify to Congress, up here on television, saying unashamedly that there was no evidence that secondhand smoke was dangerous, even though they knew in the tobacco companies. In the 1930s they learned that nicotine was so addictive and that it would continue to help them earn enormous profits. We fought back, and we succeeded in banning smoking on airplanes. It was a tough fight because of all of the misinformation that the industry spread. That then started a smoke-free revolution, and it did change the world culture on tobacco.

Some years later I authored a law that banned smoking in buildings that provided services to children, any building that had Federal funds. It could have been a library, a clinic, a daycare center; whatever it was, there was no smoking allowed in those buildings, except if it was in a separate room that ventilated directly to the outside. They fought us on that, but the people won. It is as clear to me today as it was then that this industry has not earned the trust to regulate itself. That is a plea they make, but no one believes they mean it.

Ten years ago, I was able to gather unpublished, internal reports by the tobacco industry showing that so-called "light" and "low-tar" cigarettes were a poor disguise of the true harm that these cigarettes brought. The cigarette makers were seducing smokers into thinking that these cigarettes were a healthier choice than those previously generally sold.

Real government oversight was essential to protect the public, especially our young, from this deadly product. As we know, since the 1980s, the tobacco industry has continued to engage in one sophisticated marketing campaign after another to get youngsters addicted to nicotine—just get them started and they are yours—even though selling and marketing cigarettes to children is generally against the law. It is our obligation, our responsibility to end the recruitment of kids as the next generation of smokers. . . .

The legislation we are talking about now that is being debated in this Chamber would finally grant some supervision and give a Federal agency—the Food and Drug Administration—the authority to regulate the tobacco industry. The bill, very simply, would give the FDA jurisdiction over the content and the marketing of tobacco products, and more explicit warning labels would be required. President Obama supports this effort, and it is now our turn and our obligation to safeguard families and children by passing this critical bill.

The legislation would give us more and better information about cigarettes. The fact is that we still don't know a cigarette's exact contents. . . . If this legislation is successful, the FDA would monitor the content of cigarettes and could call for the reduction or removal of the toxic substances.

FDA oversight would also ensure that cigarette makers don't deceive Americans through trick advertising and promotional campaigns. . . .

For years, we have set our sights on getting the FDA to regulate cigarettes. Why? To protect our kids. . . .

For the last 45 years, ever since the Surgeon General's office began issuing warnings about cigarettes, big tobacco has used every tactic imaginable, including sham organizations, influential lobbyists, and powerful lawyers, to avoid public scrutiny. It is time to make big tobacco accountable to the public. It is time to make it accountable so that we can protect our children from the danger that kills more than 400,000 Americans every year.

I, too, was a smoker at one time, until over 30 years ago. Many times I thought about quitting, but the temptation to light up was always there and overcame any decision that could persuade me to stop from lighting up and taking a few drags. . . .

I will close with another hideous reminder about the woman who appeared in front of one of my committees. She had already had an operation on her esophagus, I think, but in her throat, she actually had a hole in her throat. She admitted that despite the fact that she had essentially lost her voice box, she still smoked through the hole in her throat. She said her doctor got angry with her when after this serious surgery she was asking for a cigarette. The hold on people is almost unbreakable. But we can do our part here in the Senate if we pass this bill.

I ask my colleagues to vote yes on this legislation. It is good for your constituents, it is good for your families, it is good for America's financial well-being. We spend over $100 billion a year as a result of premature death and disability from tobacco use.

With that, I yield the floor and note the absence of a quorum.

SOURCE: U.S. Senate. "Family Smoking Prevention and Tobacco Control Act." *Congressional Record* 2009, 155, pt. S6020–S6021. www.gpo.gov/fdsys/pkg/CREC-2009-06-03/pdf/CREC-2009-06-03-pt1-PgS6020-2.pdf.

Remarks by President Obama upon Signing the Tobacco Regulation Bill

DOCUMENT

June 22, 2009

. . . I am thrilled to be here for what is I think an extraordinary accomplishment by this Congress, a bill we're about to sign into law.

I want to acknowledge a few of our special guests. First of all, we've got the crew from the Campaign for Tobacco Free Kids: Eamon, Christopher, Sarah, and Hoai-Nam. We have our FDA Commissioner, Dr. Peggy Hamburg. We have our CDC Director, Tom Frieden. And we have just some extraordinary Members of Congress here on stage—Senator Dodd, Senator Durbin, Senator Enzi, Senator Harkin, Senator Lautenberg, Representative Waxman, Representative Dingell, Representative Christensen, Representative Pallone, and Representative Platts—all of whom did extraordinary work in helping to move this legislation forward. Please give them a big round of applause. I want to thank all of them. . . .

You know, the legislation I'm signing today represents change that's been decades in the making. Since at least the middle of the last century, we've known about the harmful and often deadly effects of tobacco products. More than 400,000 Americans now die of tobacco-related illnesses each year, making it the leading cause of preventable death in the United States. More than 8 million Americans suffer from at least one serious illness caused by smoking, and these health problems cost us all more than $100 billion a year.

What's even worse are the effects on our children. One out of every five children in our country are now current smokers by the time they leave high school. Think about that statistic, one out of every five children in our country are now current smokers by the time they leave high school. Each day, 1,000 young people under the age of 18 become new, regular, daily smokers. And almost 90 percent of all smokers began at or before their 18th birthday.

I know; I was one of these teenagers, and so I know how difficult it can be to break this habit when it's been with you for a long time. And I also know that kids today don't just start smoking for no reason. They're aggressively targeted as customers by the tobacco industry. They're exposed to a constant and insidious barrage of advertising where they live, where they learn, and where they play. Most insidiously, they are offered products with flavorings that mask the taste of tobacco and make it even more tempting.

We've known about this for decades, but despite the best efforts and good progress made by so many leaders and advocates with us today, the tobacco industry and its special interest lobbying have generally won the day up on the Hill. When Henry Waxman first brought tobacco CEOs before Congress in 1994, they famously denied that tobacco was deadly, nicotine was addictive, or that their companies marketed to children. And they spent millions upon millions in lobbying and advertising to fight back every attempt to expose these denials as lies.

Fifteen years later, their campaign has finally failed. Today, thanks to the work of Democrats and Republicans, health care and consumer advocates, the decades-long effort to protect our children from the harmful effects of tobacco has emerged victorious. Today change has come to Washington.

This legislation will not ban all tobacco products, and it will allow adults to make their own choices. But it will also ban tobacco advertising within a thousand feet of schools and playgrounds. It will curb the ability of tobacco companies to market products to our children by using appealing flavors. It will force these companies to more clearly and publicly acknowledge the harmful and deadly effects of the products they sell. And it will allow the scientists at the FDA to take other commonsense steps to reduce the harmful effects of smoking.

This legislation is a victory for bipartisanship, and it was passed overwhelmingly in both Houses of Congress. It's a victory for health care reform, as it will reduce some of the billions we spend on tobacco-related health care costs in this country. It's a law that will reduce the number of American children who pick up a cigarette and become adult smokers. And most importantly, it is a law that will save American lives and make Americans healthier.

We know that even with the passage of this legislation, our work to protect our children and improve the public's health is not complete. Today, tobacco is the leading preventable cause of death not just in America, but also in the world. If current trends continue, 1 billion people will die from tobacco-related illnesses this century. And so the United States will continue to work with the World Health Organization and other nations to fight this epidemic on a global basis.

But no matter how long or how hard this fight may be, what's happening today gives us hope. When I ran for President, I did so because I believed that despite the power of the status quo and the influence of special interests, it was possible for us to bring change to Washington. And the progress we've made these past 5 months has only reinforced my faith in this belief.

Despite the influence of the credit card industry, we passed a law to protect consumers from unfair rate hikes and abusive fees. Despite the influence of banks and lenders, we passed a law to protect homeowners from mortgage fraud. Despite the influence of the defense industry, we passed a law to protect taxpayers from waste and abuse in defense contracting. And today, despite decades of lobbying and advertising by the tobacco industry, we've passed a law to help protect the next generation of Americans from growing up with a deadly habit that so many of our generation have lived with.

When Henry Waxman opened that first hearing back in '94 on tobacco with the industry CEOs, he began by quoting an ancient proverb: "A journey of a thousand miles must begin with a single step." Our journey for change is far from over. But with the package of—passage of the kids tobacco legislation that I'm about to sign, we're taking another big and very important step, a step that will save lives and dollars. So I want to thank not only the Members of Congress who are up on stage, but also all the Members of Congress in the audience and all the health advocates that fought for so long for this to happen. We hope you feel good about the extraordinary service that you've rendered this country. Thank you very much. Let's go sign the bill.

SOURCE: U.S. Executive Office of the President. "Remarks on Signing the Family Smoking Prevention and Tobacco Control Act of 2009." *Daily Compilation of Presidential Documents* 2009, no. 00493 (June 22, 2009). www.gpoaccess.gov/presdocs/2009/DCPD-200900493.pdf.

OTHER HISTORIC DOCUMENTS OF INTEREST

FROM PREVIOUS *HISTORIC DOCUMENTS*

President Obama Speaks at Cairo University

JUNE 4, 2009

On June 4, 2009, President Barack Obama delivered a high-profile speech on U.S. relations with the Muslim world. Speaking at Cairo University in the Egyptian capital, Obama proposed "a new beginning" in these relations, "one based on mutual interest and mutual respect." He conveyed this respect by using the traditional Arabic greeting of *As-salaamu alaykum,* quoting several times from the Quran, and acknowledging Islamic contributions to world civilization as well as American history. The president's speech addressed sensitive policy issues, including the Israeli-Palestinian dispute and the wars in Afghanistan and Iraq. It also dealt with areas where a gulf separates traditional Muslim values and American perspectives, such as democracy and women's rights. Obama's outreach to Muslims was unprecedented for a U.S. leader and clearly intended to reverse the deterioration in the United States' image abroad that had occurred under his predecessor, George W. Bush. Despite Obama's initiative to advance the discourse on Middle East relations, progress toward resolving the region's long-simmering conflicts was slow, with many obstacles in his path. To assist him in improving relations with countries in the Middle East, Obama had named former Senate majority leader George Mitchell to the post of special envoy on January 22, 2009.

Stagnation in the Middle East peace process dates back at least as far as the collapse of the Oslo Accords near the end of Bill Clinton's administration. The September 2001 terrorist attacks on New York and outside Washington, D.C., attributed to al-Qaida, provoked President Bush into declaring a "global war on terror." His administration invaded two predominantly Muslim countries, Afghanistan and Iraq, leading to lengthy occupations, and threatened a third, Iran, declaring it part of an "axis of evil." Terrorist suspects and other prisoners, overwhelmingly Muslim, were tortured by U.S. personnel and detained indefinitely at the Abu Ghraib prison in Iraq, Cuba's Guantánamo Bay, and other secret sites around the world. Bush's policies and rhetoric—he once referred to the campaign against terrorism as a "crusade," invoking that term's historical associations— were deeply alienating to Arab and Muslim populations.

TURNING THE PAGE

As a presidential candidate in 2008, Obama had advocated a new tone in dealing with the Middle East. He had opposed the invasion of Iraq and favored withdrawing American troops from that country. He proposed stronger diplomatic measures to head off the looming crisis over Iran's nuclear ambitions and said the United States should "turn the page" on antiterrorist efforts through public diplomacy. If elected, he promised to deliver a major address from an Islamic capital early in his first year in office.

Between Obama's election in November 2008 and his inauguration two months later, Israel attacked the Gaza Strip, its leaders said in retaliation for rocket attacks launched by Hamas fighters. Benjamin Netanyahu, a Likud party hard-liner on both Iran and the Palestinians, took over as Israeli prime minister in February 2009. Obama's administration formulated a strategy of building a coalition of Arab states to confront Iran. His planned address to the Muslim world would be a key component of his new approach.

Obama's background—an African American with Muslim ancestors in Kenya who spent part of his childhood in Indonesia, home to the world's largest Muslim population—made him uniquely qualified to make such an overture. He told the audience in Cairo, "I have known Islam on three continents before coming to the region where it was first revealed."

"As-Salaamu Alaykum"

According to White House press secretary Robert Gibbs, Obama selected Cairo as the venue for his speech on Islam because "in many ways [it] represents the heart of the Arab world." Egypt is also a key U.S. ally in the Middle East and was the first country in the region to conclude a peace agreement with Israel. Critics wondered how the choice squared with American espousal of democracy, given that Egypt's longtime leader, Hosni Mubarak, has a record of violating civil liberties.

Security was so tight in Cairo at the time of the address that the city was near lockdown as President Obama arrived from Saudi Arabia. The invited guests in Festival Hall had been ushered to their seats nearly three hours before the speech was scheduled to begin. When the American president finally entered, he received an enthusiastic ovation.

Recognizing the tension between his own country and Islamic societies, Obama said, "I am convinced that in order to move forward, we must say openly to each other the things we hold in our hearts and that too often are said only behind closed doors. . . . As the Holy Koran tells us: 'Be conscious of God and speak always the truth.'" Throughout his address, Obama acknowledged dark spots in the historical record, such as colonial and the Cold War interventions, with frankness rarely heard from elected American leaders. He also asserted that "Islam has always been part of America's story," reminding his audience that seven million Muslims now live in the United States. This detail reinforced his overarching message of interdependence and common aspirations.

CONFRONTING THE SOURCES OF TENSION

The bulk of Obama's speech concerned a number of political and cultural issues that he deemed sources of tension between the United States and Islamic societies, beginning with what he called "violent extremism in all of its forms." He defended the U.S. occupation of Afghanistan as a necessary response to the September 11, 2001, terrorist attacks. Obama called the activities of al-Qaida "irreconcilable with the rights of human beings, the progress of nations, and with Islam." In contrast to the Afghanistan war, the president said, "Iraq was a war of choice that provoked strong differences in my country and around the world." Obama repeated his prior pledge to pull all U.S. troops out of Iraq by 2012, the final year of his first term. Recalling the upheaval of September 11, he said, "in some cases, it led us to act contrary to our traditions and our ideals."

Concerning the Israeli-Palestinian conflict, Obama began by declaring that the U.S. alliance with Israel is "unbreakable." He referred to the murder of six million Jews by Nazi Germany and criticized anyone who would deny the historical veracity of the Holocaust. By the same token, he noted, the Palestinian people have been suffering for more than sixty years and continue to "endure the daily humiliations, large and small, that come with occupation." Obama's use of terms such as "occupation" and "Palestine"—highly charged words in the lexicon of Middle East politics—revealed his sensitivity to Arab perspectives. Only a two-state solution, he maintained, will resolve the conflict of "two peoples with legitimate aspirations, each with a painful history that makes compromise elusive." He urged Palestinians to renounce the use of violence and cited the example of the African American civil rights struggle to illustrate the idea that "violence is a dead end." He also insisted that Israel halt the construction of Jewish settlements in the occupied territories. The essence of Obama's public diplomacy effort was crystallized when he said, "[P]rivately, many Muslims recognize that Israel will not go away. Likewise, many Israelis recognize the need for a Palestinian state. It is time for us to act on what everyone knows to be true."

The president then took up another controversial topic, the U.S. dispute with the Islamic Republic of Iran over nuclear weapons. He cleared the air by acknowledging the covert U.S. role in the 1953 coup that overthrew Iran's democratically elected leader, Mohammad Mosaddegh. Despite the "tumultuous history" between the two nations, Obama reiterated his willingness to engage in wide-ranging discussions with Iran's leaders. Yet on the nuclear question, he said, "[W]e have reached a decisive point." Obama did not elaborate on what steps the United States might take to prevent Iran from obtaining the fuel for one or more nuclear weapons, although he has refused to rule out the use of force. He also did not refer to Israel's publicly unacknowledged nuclear arsenal; when meeting with Netanyahu in May, he had agreed to keep mum on this topic, as earlier presidents have. However, he did express his administration's commitment to a future in which all states relinquish this class of weapons, a goal he had articulated in a speech in Prague on April 5 in which he called the worldwide abundance of nuclear weapons "the most dangerous legacy of the Cold War" and outlined steps toward a nuclear-free world. He also said that Iran and any other nation has the right to develop nuclear power, as long as it is done in compliance with the Nuclear Non-Proliferation Treaty, to which Iran is a signatory but Israel is not.

The remainder of the speech focused on democracy, religious freedom, women's rights, and economic development. In each instance, President Obama outlined his conceptions of human rights and American values while making clear that "America does not presume to know what is best for everyone." He emphasized the importance of education and innovation in the twenty-first century, areas that he said had not received sufficient investment in some Muslim societies, including those made prosperous by oil reserves. "No development strategy can be based only upon what comes out of the ground," he quipped, "nor can it be sustained while young people are out of work."

FROM WORDS TO ACTIONS

The president's address unveiled no substantive surprises or new policy initiatives. Apart from the intense publicity that attended the speech, its greatest significance lay in its candor and consistent tone of respect for Muslim traditions and views. There is little evidence that the speech had a major impact on public opinion in the Muslim world, which already held favorable views of the new president but steadfastly negative attitudes toward the United States. Many observers across the political spectrum voiced doubts about whether Obama's oratory would be followed by noticeable changes in U.S. policies toward the region. A spokesperson for Hamas noted the shift in rhetoric between Presidents Obama and Bush but added that Obama's words "did not include a mechanism that can translate his wishes and views into actions." A statement from the Israeli government welcomed Obama's hope for a new beginning while noting the need to protect its national security.

In the longer term, Obama's public diplomacy represented the beginning of a concerted effort to regain the world's respect for American leadership. Obama himself remains a highly popular figure in much of the world. The Norwegian Nobel Committee, in announcing his selection as Nobel Peace Laureate for 2009, declared that "Obama has as president created a new climate in international politics." Nevertheless, his efforts in the Middle East had borne little fruit by year's end. Negotiations between Israel and the Palestinians had slowed to a standstill. Obama's intervention in the peace process, particularly his insistence on a freeze in Israeli settlement construction, which he later dropped, was widely perceived as tactically inept, resulting in a hardening of positions on both sides. His overtures toward Iran led to preliminary diplomatic encounters but no movement toward an agreement that would reduce the threat of nuclear proliferation from Iran's program of uranium enrichment. Resolving these and other pressing political challenges would require sustained engagement and bold actions to back up even the most inspiring words.

—Roger Smith

Following is a transcript of the speech given by U.S. president Barack Obama at Cairo University in Egypt on June 4, 2009.

Obama Speaks on Muslim-American Relations at Cairo University

June 4, 2009

Thank you so much. Good afternoon. I am honored to be in the timeless city of Cairo and to be hosted by two remarkable institutions. . . . And I'm also proud to carry with me the good will of the American people and a greeting of peace from Muslim communities in my country: *As-salaamu alaykum.*

We meet at a time of great tension between the United States and Muslims around the world, tension rooted in historical forces that go beyond any current policy debate. The relationship between Islam and the West includes centuries of coexistence and cooperation, but also conflict and religious wars. More recently, tension has been fed by colonialism that denied rights and opportunities to many Muslims and a cold war in which Muslim-majority countries were too often treated as proxies without regard to their own aspirations. Moreover, the sweeping change brought by modernity and globalization led many Muslims to view the West as hostile to the traditions of Islam.

Violent extremists have exploited these tensions in a small, but potent minority of Muslims. The attacks of September 11, 2001, and the continued efforts of these extremists to engage in violence against civilians has led some in my country to view Islam as inevitably hostile not only to America and Western countries, but also to human rights. All this has bred more fear and more mistrust.

So long as our relationship is defined by our differences, we will empower those who sow hatred rather than peace, those who promote conflict rather than the cooperation that can help all of our people achieve justice and prosperity. And this cycle of suspicion and discord must end.

I've come here to Cairo to seek a new beginning between the United States and Muslims around the world, one based on mutual interest and mutual respect and one based upon the truth that America and Islam are not exclusive and need not be in competition. Instead, they overlap and share common principles, principles of justice and progress, tolerance and the dignity of all human beings.

I do so recognizing that change cannot happen overnight. . . . But I am convinced that in order to move forward, we must say openly to each other the things we hold in our hearts and that too often are said only behind closed doors. There must be a sustained effort to listen to each other, to learn from each other, to respect one another, and to seek common ground. As the Holy Koran tells us: "Be conscious of God and speak always the truth." That is what I will try to do today, to speak the truth as best I can, humbled by the task before us and firm in my belief that the interests we share as human beings are far more powerful than the forces that drive us apart.

Now part of this conviction is rooted in my own experience. I'm a Christian, but my father came from a Kenyan family that includes generations of Muslims. As a boy, I spent several years in Indonesia and heard the call of the *azaan* at the break of dawn and at the fall of dusk. As a young man, I worked in Chicago communities where many found dignity and peace in their Muslim faith. As a student of history, I also know civilization's debt to Islam.

It was Islam, at places like Al-Azhar, that carried the light of learning through so many centuries, paving the way for Europe's renaissance and enlightenment. It was innovation in Muslim communities that developed the order of algebra, our magnetic compass and tools of navigation, our mastery of pens and printing, our understanding of how disease spreads and how it can be healed. Islamic culture has given us majestic arches and soaring spires, timeless poetry and cherished music, elegant calligraphy and places of peaceful contemplation. And throughout history, Islam has demonstrated through words and deeds the possibilities of religious tolerance and racial equality.

I also know that Islam has always been a part of America's story. The first nation to recognize my country was Morocco. In signing the Treaty of Tripoli in 1796, our second President, John Adams, wrote: "The United States has in itself no character of enmity against the laws, religion, or tranquillity of Muslims." And since our founding, American Muslims have enriched the United States. They have fought in our wars; they have served in our government; they have stood for civil rights; they have started businesses; they have taught at our universities; they've excelled in our sports arenas; they've won Nobel Prizes, built our tallest building, and lit the Olympic Torch. And when the first Muslim American was recently elected to Congress, he took the oath to defend our Constitution using the same Holy Koran that one of our Founding Fathers, Thomas Jefferson, kept in his personal library.

So, I have known Islam on three continents before coming to the region where it was first revealed. That experience guides my conviction that partnership between America and Islam must be based on what Islam is, not what it isn't. And I consider it part of my responsibility as President of the United States to fight against negative stereotypes of Islam wherever they appear.

But that same principle must apply to Muslim perceptions of America. Just as Muslims do not fit a crude stereotype, America is not the crude stereotype of a self-interested empire. . . .

Now, much has been made of the fact that an African American with the name Barack Hussein Obama could be elected President. But my personal story is not so unique. The dream of opportunity for all people has not come true for everyone in America, but its promise exists for all who come to our shores, and that includes nearly 7 million American Muslims in our country today, who, by the way, enjoy incomes and educational levels that are higher than the American average.

Moreover, freedom in America is indivisible from the freedom to practice one's religion. That is why there is a mosque in every State in our Union and over 1,200 mosques within our borders. That's why the United States Government has gone to court to protect the right of women and girls to wear the *hijab* and to punish those who would deny it.

So let there be no doubt, Islam is a part of America. . . .

Of course, recognizing our common humanity is only the beginning of our task. Words alone cannot meet the needs of our people. These needs will be met only if we act boldly in the years ahead and if we understand that the challenges we face are shared and our failure to meet them will hurt us all. . . .

And this is a difficult responsibility to embrace, for human history has often been a record of nations and tribes and, yes, religions subjugating one another in pursuit of their own interests. Yet in this new age, such attitudes are self-defeating. Given our interdependence, any world order that elevates one nation or group of people over another will inevitably fail. . . . Our problems must be dealt with through partnership; our progress must be shared.

Now, that does not mean we should ignore sources of tension. Indeed, it suggests the opposite. We must face these tensions squarely. And so in that spirit, let me speak as clearly and as plainly as I can about some specific issues that I believe we must finally confront together.

The first issue that we have to confront is violent extremism in all of its forms. In Ankara, I made clear that America is not, and never will be, at war with Islam. We will, however, relentlessly confront violent extremists who pose a grave threat to our security, because we reject the same thing that people of all faiths reject: the killing of innocent men, women, and children. And it is my first duty as President to protect the American people.

The situation in Afghanistan demonstrates America's goals and our need to work together. Over 7 years ago, the United States pursued Al Qaida and the Taliban with broad international support. We did not go by choice; we went because of necessity. I'm aware that there's still some who would question or even justify the events of 9/11. But let us be clear: Al Qaida killed nearly 3,000 people on that day. The victims were innocent men, women, and children from America and many other nations who had done nothing to harm anybody. And yet, Al Qaida chose to ruthlessly murder these people, claimed credit for the attack, and even now states their determination to kill on a massive scale. They have affiliates in many countries and are trying to expand their reach. These are not opinions to be debated; these are facts to be dealt with.

Make no mistake, we do not want to keep our troops in Afghanistan. . . . We would gladly bring every single one of our troops home, if we could be confident that there were not violent extremists in Afghanistan and now Pakistan determined to kill as many Americans as they possibly can. But that is not yet the case.

And that's why we're partnering with a coalition of 46 countries. And despite the costs involved, America's commitment will not weaken. Indeed, none of us should tolerate these extremists. They have killed in many countries. They have killed people of different faiths, but more than any other, they have killed Muslims. Their actions are irreconcilable with the rights of human beings, the progress of nations, and with Islam. The Holy Koran teaches that "whoever kills an innocent" is as—"it is as if he has killed all mankind." And the Holy Koran also says, "whoever saves a person, it is as if he has saved all mankind." The enduring faith of over a billion people is so much bigger than the narrow hatred of a few. Islam is not part of the problem in combating violent extremism, it is an important part of promoting peace.

Now, we also know that military power alone is not going to solve the problems in Afghanistan and Pakistan. That's why we plan to invest $1.5 billion each year over the next 5 years to partner with Pakistanis to build schools and hospitals, roads and businesses, and hundreds of millions to help those who've been displaced. That's why we are providing more than $2.8 billion to help Afghans develop their economy and deliver services that people depend on.

Let me also address the issue of Iraq. Unlike Afghanistan, Iraq was a war of choice that provoked strong differences in my country and around the world. Although I believe that the Iraqi people are ultimately better off without the tyranny of Saddam Hussein, I also believe that events in Iraq have reminded America of the need to use diplomacy and build international consensus to resolve our problems whenever possible. . . .

Today, America has a dual responsibility to help Iraq forge a better future and to leave Iraq to Iraqis. And I have made it clear to the Iraqi people that we pursue no bases and no claim on their territory or resources. Iraq's sovereignty is its own. And that's why I ordered the removal of our combat brigades by next August. . . .

And finally, just as America can never tolerate violence by extremists, we must never alter or forget our principles. Nine-eleven was an enormous trauma to our country. The fear and anger that it provoked was understandable, but in some cases, it led us to act contrary to our traditions and our ideals. We are taking concrete actions to change course. I have unequivocally prohibited the use of torture by the United States, and I have ordered the prison at Guantanamo Bay closed by early next year.

So America will defend itself, respectful of the sovereignty of nations and the rule of law, and we will do so in partnership with Muslim communities, which are also threatened. The sooner the extremists are isolated and unwelcome in Muslim communities, the sooner we will all be safer.

The second major source of tension that we need to discuss is the situation between Israelis, Palestinians, and the Arab world. America's strong bonds with Israel are well known. This bond is unbreakable. It is based upon cultural and historical ties and the recognition that the aspiration for a Jewish homeland is rooted in a tragic history that cannot be denied.

Around the world, the Jewish people were persecuted for centuries, and anti-Semitism in Europe culminated in an unprecedented Holocaust. Tomorrow I will visit Buchenwald, which was part of a network of camps where Jews were enslaved, tortured, shot, and gassed to death by the Third Reich. Six million Jews were killed, more than the entire Jewish population of Israel today. Denying that fact is baseless, it is ignorant, and it is hateful. Threatening Israel with destruction or repeating vile stereotypes about Jews is deeply wrong and only serves to evoke in the minds of Israelis this most painful of memories while preventing the peace that the people of this region deserve.

On the other hand, it is also undeniable that the Palestinian people, Muslims and Christians, have suffered in pursuit of a homeland. . . .

For decades then, there has been a stalemate: two peoples with legitimate aspirations, each with a painful history that makes compromise elusive. It's easy to point fingers . . . But if we see this conflict only from one side or the other, then we will be blind to the truth. The only resolution is for the aspirations of both sides to be met through two states, where Israelis and Palestinians each live in peace and security.

That is in Israel's interest, Palestine's interest, America's interest, and the world's interest. And that is why I intend to personally pursue this outcome with all the patience and dedication that the task requires. The obligations that the parties have agreed to under the road map are clear. For peace to come, it is time for them, and all of us, to live up to our responsibilities.

Palestinians must abandon violence. . . . For centuries, black people in America suffered the lash of the whip as slaves and the humiliation of segregation. But it was not violence that won full and equal rights. It was a peaceful and determined insistence upon the ideals at the center of America's founding. . . .

Now is the time for Palestinians to focus on what they can build. . . . Hamas must put an end to violence, recognize past agreements, recognize Israel's right to exist.

At the same time, Israelis must acknowledge that just as Israel's right to exist cannot be denied, neither can Palestine's. The United States does not accept the legitimacy of continued Israeli settlements. This construction violates previous agreements and undermines efforts to achieve peace. It is time for these settlements to stop.

And Israel must also live up to its obligation to ensure that Palestinians can live and work and develop their society. Just as it devastates Palestinian families, the continuing humanitarian crisis in Gaza does not serve Israel's security, neither does the continuing lack of opportunity in the West Bank. Progress in the daily lives of the Palestinian people must be a critical part of a road to peace, and Israel must take concrete steps to enable such progress.

And finally, the Arab States must recognize that the Arab Peace Initiative was an important beginning, but not the end of their responsibilities. The Arab-Israeli conflict should no longer be used to distract the people of Arab nations from other problems. Instead, it must be a cause for action to help the Palestinian people develop the institutions that will sustain their state, to recognize Israel's legitimacy, and to choose progress over a self-defeating focus on the past.

America will align our policies with those who pursue peace, and we will say in public what we say in private to Israelis and Palestinians and Arabs. We cannot impose peace. But privately, many Muslims recognize that Israel will not go away. Likewise, many Israelis recognize the need for a Palestinian state. It is time for us to act on what everyone knows to be true. . . .

The third source of tension is our shared interest in the rights and responsibilities of nations on nuclear weapons. This issue has been a source of tension between the United States and the Islamic Republic of Iran. . . .

I recognize it will be hard to overcome decades of mistrust. . . . There will be many issues to discuss between our two countries, and we are willing to move forward without preconditions on the basis of mutual respect. But it is clear to all concerned that when it comes to nuclear weapons, we have reached a decisive point. This is not simply about America's interests. It's about preventing a nuclear arms race in the Middle East that could lead this region and the world down a hugely dangerous path.

I understand those who protest that some countries have weapons that others do not. No single nation should pick and choose which nation holds nuclear weapons. And that's why I strongly reaffirmed America's commitment to seek a world in which no nations hold nuclear weapons. And any nation, including Iran, should have the right to access peaceful nuclear power, if it complies with its responsibilities under the Nuclear Non-Proliferation Treaty. . . .

The fourth issue that I will address is democracy. I know there has been controversy about the promotion of democracy in recent years, and much of this controversy is connected to the war in Iraq. So let me be clear: No system of government can or should be imposed by one nation by [*sic*] any other.

That does not lessen my commitment, however, to governments that reflect the will of the people. Each nation gives life to this principle in its own way, grounded in the traditions of its own people. America does not presume to know what is best for everyone . . . But I do have an unyielding belief that all people yearn for certain things: the ability to speak your mind and have a say in how you are governed, confidence in the rule of law and the equal administration of justice, government that is transparent and doesn't steal from the people, the freedom to live as you choose. These are not just American ideas, they are human rights. And that is why we will support them everywhere.

Now, there is no straight line to realize this promise, but this much is clear: Governments that protect these rights are ultimately more stable, successful, and secure. Suppressing ideas never succeeds in making them go away. America respects the right of all peaceful and law-abiding voices to be heard around the world, even if we disagree with them. And we will welcome all elected, peaceful governments, provided they govern with respect for all their people. . . .

The fifth issue that we must address together is religious freedom. Islam has a proud tradition of tolerance. . . . That is the spirit we need today. People in every country should be free to choose and live their faith based upon the persuasion of the mind and the heart and the soul. This tolerance is essential for religion to thrive, but it's being challenged in many different ways.

Among some Muslims, there's a disturbing tendency to measure one's own faith by the rejection of somebody else's faith. . . .

Likewise, it is important for Western countries to avoid impeding Muslim citizens from practicing religion as they see fit, for instance, by dictating what clothes a Muslim woman should wear. We can't disguise hostility towards any religion behind the pretence of liberalism.

In fact, faith should bring us together. And that's why we're forging service projects in America to bring together Christians, Muslims, and Jews. That's why we welcome efforts like Saudi Arabian King Abdallah's interfaith dialog and Turkey's leadership in the Alliance of Civilizations. . . .

The sixth issue that I want to address is women's rights. I know . . . and you can tell from this audience, that there is a healthy debate about this issue. I reject the view of some in the West that a woman who chooses to cover her hair is somehow less equal, but I do believe that a woman who is denied an education is denied equality. . . .

Now, let me be clear: Issues of women's equality are by no means simply an issue for Islam. In Turkey, Pakistan, Bangladesh, Indonesia, we've seen Muslim-majority countries elect a woman to lead. Meanwhile, the struggle for women's equality continues in many aspects of American life and in countries around the world.

I am convinced that our daughters can contribute just as much to society as our sons. . . . And that is why the United States will partner with any Muslim-majority country to support expanded literacy for girls and to help young women pursue employment through microfinancing that helps people live their dreams.

Finally, I want to discuss economic development and opportunity. I know that for many, the face of globalization is contradictory. The Internet and television can bring knowledge and information, but also offensive sexuality and mindless violence into the home. Trade can bring new wealth and opportunities, but also huge disruptions and change in communities. . . .

But I also know that human progress cannot be denied. There need not be contradictions between development and tradition. . . .

And this is important, because no development strategy can be based only upon what comes out of the ground, nor can it be sustained while young people are out of work. Many Gulf States have enjoyed great wealth as a consequence of oil, and some are beginning to focus it on broader development. But all of us must recognize that education and innovation will be the currency of the 21st century, and in too many Muslim communities there remains underinvestment in these areas. . . .

On education, we will expand exchange programs and increase scholarships like the one that brought my father to America. . . .

On economic development, we will create a new corps of business volunteers to partner with counterparts in Muslim-majority countries. . . .

On science and technology, we will launch a new fund to support technological development in Muslim-majority countries and to help transfer ideas to mark—to the marketplace so they can create more jobs. We'll open centers of scientific excellence in Africa, the Middle East, and Southeast Asia and appoint new science envoys to collaborate on programs that develop new sources of energy, create green jobs, digitize records, clean water, grow new crops. . . .

All these things must be done in partnership. Americans are ready to join with citizens and governments, community organizations, religious leaders, and businesses in Muslim communities around the world to help our people pursue a better life.

And the issues that I have described will not be easy to address, but we have a responsibility to join together on behalf of the world that we seek, a world where extremists no longer threaten our people and American troops have come home, a world where Israelis and Palestinians are each secure in a state of their own and nuclear energy is used for peaceful purposes, a world where governments serve their citizens and the rights of all God's children are respected. Those are mutual interests. That is the world we seek, but we can only achieve it together.

I know there are many, Muslim and non-Muslim, who question whether we can forge this new beginning.... There's so much fear, so much mistrust that has built up over the years. But if we choose to be bound by the past, we will never move forward. And I want to particularly say this to young people of every faith in every country: You, more than anyone, have the ability to reimagine the world, to remake this world.

All of us share this world for but a brief moment in time. The question is whether we spend that time focused on what pushes us apart, or whether we commit ourselves to an effort, a sustained effort to find common ground, to focus on the future we seek for our children, and to respect the dignity of all human beings.

It's easier to start wars than to end them. It's easier to blame others than to look inward. It's easier to see what is different about someone than to find the things we share. But we should choose the right path, not just the easy path....

The Holy Koran tells us: "O mankind! We have created you male and a female, and we have made you into nations and tribes so that you may know one another." The Talmud tells us: "The whole of the Torah is for the purpose of promoting peace." The Holy Bible tells us: "Blessed are the peacemakers, for they shall be called sons of God." The people of the world can live together in peace. We know that is God's vision, now that must be our work here on Earth.

Thank you, and may God's peace be upon you. Thank you very much. Thank you.

SOURCE: U.S. Executive Office of the President. "Remarks in Cairo, Egypt." *Daily Compilation of Presidential Documents* 2009, no. 00436 (June 4, 2009). www.gpoaccess.gov/presdocs/2009/DCPD-200900436.pdf.

OTHER HISTORIC DOCUMENTS OF INTEREST

FROM PREVIOUS *HISTORIC DOCUMENTS*

U.S. Supreme Court on Campaign Contributions to Judges

JUNE 8, 2009

On June 8, 2009, the U.S. Supreme Court, for the first time addressed the question of judicial recusal in the increasingly big-money context of state judicial elections. Justice Anthony M. Kennedy, writing for the 5-4 majority in *Caperton v. A.T. Massey Coal Company,* held that the Due Process Clause of the Fourteenth Amendment was violated when a West Virginia supreme court justice refused to disqualify himself from the appeal of a $50 million verdict against a company whose CEO had spent extraordinary sums to get the judge elected; the CEO knew his appeal would be heard by that justice's court. The finding was not based on any actual proof of bias on the part of the judge but because the "probability of actual bias on the part of the judge ... [was] too high to be constitutionally tolerable."

ELECTIONS FOR STATE COURT JUDGES

The *Caperton* case arose in a context of increasing concern over the potentially corrupting role of big money in state judicial elections. Unlike federal judges, who are appointed by the president and confirmed by the Senate and serve lifetime terms, some judges in thirty-eight states are elected. Thirteen of these states, including West Virginia, select some of their judges through highly partisan contests. Elections have become increasingly expensive as candidates come to rely on thirty-second television spots, realizing that the candidate with the most ad exposure usually wins. As a consequence, the funds being raised for judicial campaigns have been skyrocketing. According to the judicial reform organization Justice at Stake, from 1999 to 2008, state supreme court candidates nationally raised more than $200.4 million, more than double the $84.4 raised from 1989 to 1998. Much of this money comes from groups with an interest in the outcome of litigation. Many of the organizations that filed *amici* briefs in *Caperton* argued that big money undermines the fundamental requirement that judges be neutral and impartial, creating the impression that justice is for sale. According to Justice at Stake, there is already the perception that this is happening: Polls show that more than three out of four Americans believe campaign cash affects courtroom decisions.

WHAT HAPPENED IN WEST VIRGINIA

In 2002, a jury in West Virginia found that Massey Coal, the fourth largest coal-producing company in the country, intentionally destroyed Hugh Caperton's mining business, through fraud and interference with contracts, and ordered Massey to pay $50 million in compensatory and punitive damages. Before the appeal could be heard by the state supreme court, West Virginia held judicial elections. Massey Coal's chair, chief executive and president Don Blankenship, supported a relatively unknown attorney, Brent Benjamin, to replace a sitting state supreme court justice. Blankenship contributed the statutory maximum of $1,000 directly to Benjamin's campaign, another $2.5 million to fund a 527 organization that opposed the incumbent, and $500,000 to create his own ads supporting Benjamin. In total, he spent $1 million more on getting his candidate elected than the campaigns of both candidates combined. His $3 million in contributions were more than the total amount spent by all other Benjamin supporters and three times the amount spent by Benjamin's own committee.

Benjamin won the election with 53.3 percent of the vote. After joining the West Virginia Supreme Court of Appeals, Justice Benjamin denied Caperton's motion that he recuse himself based on the conflict caused by Blankenship's involvement with his campaign. He then joined the majority to cast the deciding vote to overturn the $50 million judgment against Blankenship's company, on the grounds that Harman Mining, under the direction of Caperton, should not have been allowed to file a case in West Virginia after previously being awarded $6 million from Massey in damages in Virginia.

Caperton filed for a rehearing and, between them, the parties moved to disqualify three of the five justices who had decided the appeal. After the first appeal, photographs turned up of then-Chief Justice Elliot "Spike" Maynard, one of the other judges who voted with the majority, on vacation in the French Riviera with Blankenship while the case was pending. Justice Maynard agreed to disqualify himself from the rehearing. On the other side, Justice Larry Starcher agreed to recuse himself as well based on his very public criticism of Blankenship's role in the 2004 elections. According to Justice Starcher, "Blankenship's bestowal of his personal wealth, political tactics, and 'friendship' have created a cancer in the affairs of this Court." Caperton once again moved to have Justice Benjamin recuse himself from hearing the case and, once more Justice Benjamin, by then chief justice of the state supreme court, denied the motion. On rehearing, a divided court again ruled 3-2 to overturn the jury verdict against Massey Coal.

THE U.S. SUPREME COURT REVERSES THE WEST VIRGINIA SUPREME COURT

Caperton's appeal to the U.S. Supreme Court raised the question of "whether Justice Benjamin's failure to recuse himself from participation in his principal financial supporter's case violated the Due Process Clause of the Fourteenth Amendment." Due process, the Court emphasized, requires a "fair trial in a fair tribunal." In the past, the Supreme Court had only rarely reviewed disputes over when a judge should be disqualified, with only a few that did not involve a judge with a "direct, personal, substantial, pecuniary interest" in the outcome. The *Caperton* case was the first such case to arise in the context of judicial elections. Writing for a Court divided 5-4, Justice Kennedy found that at a point clearly crossed in this case, a judge hearing a case involving a major campaign donor will violate due process.

The main issue was one that had split the lower courts: whether due process requires recusal only on proof of "actual" bias or also for the "appearance" of bias on the part of the judge. Justice Benjamin urged that there was no basis for recusal because Caperton provided no "objective evidence" of bias, only "subjective belief" of bias. Adopting "a standard merely of 'appearances,'" he argued "seems little more than an invitation to subject West Virginia's justice system to the vagaries of the day—a framework in which predictability and stability yield to supposition, innuendo, half-truths, and partisan manipulations." The Supreme Court, however, rejected a standard that relies exclusively on a judge's own inquiry into his or her actual bias, an inquiry that cannot be reviewed. Instead, Justice Kennedy preferred objective standards that do not require proof of actual bias. The test Kennedy adopted in this case requires an objective inquiry into whether a substantial campaign donation, under all the circumstances, poses such a risk of actual bias or prejudgment that it is constitutionally impermissible.

Not every campaign contribution, the Court emphasized, creates a probability of bias, but the opinion repeatedly described this as an exceptional case—"extraordinary" and "extreme." In this instance, the disproportionate size of the campaign contributions in comparison to the total amount spent in the election and the temporal relationship between the campaign and the pending appeal, taken together, created a "serious, objective risk of actual bias that required Justice Benjamin's recusal."

The dissent, written by Chief Justice John G. Roberts Jr., argued that the majority's standard, "probability of bias," is unmanageable because it does not give clear, workable, guidance for future cases. By way of illustration, Roberts's dissent included forty numbered questions that he said he feared are just some of the many that future courts would have to determine. Among them, how much money is too much money? What about contributions from trade associations? What if the case involves social or ideological issues rather than financial ones? Roberts predicted that the majority opinion would result in a flood of groundless recusal motions that would undermine confidence in the judiciary. "It is an old cliché," he wrote, "but sometimes the cure is worse than the disease." Justice Antonin Scalia, in a separate dissent, derided the opinion for doing more harm than good as the Court "continues its quixotic quest to right all wrongs and repair all imperfections through the Constitution. Alas the quest cannot succeed—which is why some wrongs and imperfections have been called nonjusticiable."

Justice Kennedy disagreed that this case would lead to a flood of recusal motions given the extreme nature of its facts. He also highlighted judicial reforms that have been implemented by the states that provide for even stricter standards. For instance, almost every state, including West Virginia, has adopted the American Bar Association's objective standard: "A judge shall avoid impropriety and the appearance of impropriety." The test for the appearance of impropriety is "whether the conduct would create in reasonable minds a perception that the judge's ability to carry out judicial responsibilities with integrity, impartiality and competence is impaired." These more rigorous tests would, he argued, resolve most disputes without resort to the Constitution.

IMPACT OF THE *CAPERTON* DECISION

Many establishment legal groups, including the American Bar Association and former state supreme court justices as well as judicial reform organizations had joined this case to urge the Court to rule that the Constitution requires elected judges to disqualify themselves from cases involving substantial contributors to their campaigns. These groups applauded the decision. For example, hailing the decision as a "major victory for the rule of law," James Sample of the Brennan Center for Justice stated that "the Supreme Court has reaffirmed the fundamental principle that money should not influence the courts, and that justice should not be for sale."

In the majority opinion, Justice Kennedy made clear that due process set a floor for judicial disqualifications, but that states are free to adopt more rigorous requirements. Since *Caperton,* many states have accepted that challenge. For instance, Michigan, West Virginia, Ohio, Texas, California, and Washington have all taken steps to implement specific policies and establish clear guidelines to govern judicial disqualifications. These efforts have run into much resistance.

On a more personal level, the impact of this landmark case on its litigants was short-lived. The Supreme Court sent the case back to the West Virginia Supreme Court for rehearing without Justice Benjamin. There, on November 12, 2009, the court, for the third time, overturned the 2002 jury verdict that had awarded Caperton $50 million from coal giant Massey, this time by a vote of 4-1. Massey general counsel Shane Harvey stated, "We are pleased that this decision today brings this lengthy legal proceeding to an appropriate close."

—Melissa Feinberg

Following is the June 8, 2009, opinion of the U.S. Supreme Court in Caperton v. A.T. Massey Coal Company, *in which the Court decided 5-4 that a judge ruling on a case of his or her major campaign donor is in violation of due process, and an excerpt from Chief Justice John G. Roberts Jr.'s dissenting opinion.*

Caperton v. A.T. Massey Coal Company

June 8, 2009

No. 08-22

| Hugh M. Caperton, et al., Petitioners *v.* A.T. Massey Coal Company, Inc. et al. | } | On writ of certiorari to the Supreme Court of Appeals of West Virginia |

[June 8, 2009]

JUSTICE KENNEDY delivered the opinion of the Court.

In this case the Supreme Court of Appeals of West Virginia reversed a trial court judgment, which had entered a jury verdict of $50 million. Five justices heard the case, and the vote to reverse was 3 to 2. The question presented is whether the Due Process Clause of the Fourteenth Amendment was violated when one of the justices in the majority denied a recusal motion. The basis for the motion was that the justice had received campaign contributions in an extraordinary amount from, and through the efforts of, the board chairman and principal officer of the corporation found liable for the damages.

Under our precedents there are objective standards that require recusal when "the probability of actual bias on the part of the judge or decisionmaker is too high to be constitutionally tolerable." Applying those precedents, we find that, in all the circumstances of this case, due process requires recusal.

I

[Discussion of the facts in this case has been omitted.]

II

It is axiomatic that "[a] fair trial in a fair tribunal is a basic requirement of due process." As the Court has recognized, however, "most matters relating to judicial disqualification [do] not rise to a constitutional level." The early and leading case on the subject is *Tumey* v. *Ohio,* 273 U.S. 510 (1927). There, the Court stated that "matters of kinship, personal bias, state policy, remoteness of interest, would seem generally to be matters merely of legislative discretion."

The *Tumey* Court concluded that the Due Process Clause incorporated the common-law rule that a judge must recuse himself when he has "a direct, personal, substantial, pecuniary interest" in a case. This rule reflects the maxim that "[n]o man is allowed to be a judge in his own cause; because his interest would certainly bias his judgment, and, not improbably, corrupt his integrity." [citation omitted] Personal bias or prejudice "alone would not be sufficient basis for imposing a constitutional requirement under the Due Process Clause."

As new problems have emerged that were not discussed at common law, however, the Court has identified additional instances which, as an objective matter, require recusal. These are circumstances "in which experience teaches that the probability of actual bias on the part of the judge or decisionmaker is too high to be constitutionally tolerable." To place the present case in proper context, two instances where the Court has required recusal merit further discussion. . . .

[A detailed description of precedents has been omitted.]

III

Based on the principles described in these cases we turn to the issue before us. This problem arises in the context of judicial elections, a framework not presented in the precedents we have reviewed and discussed.

Caperton contends that Blankenship's pivotal role in getting Justice Benjamin elected created a constitutionally intolerable probability of actual bias. Though not a bribe or criminal influence, Justice Benjamin would nevertheless feel a debt of gratitude to Blankenship for his extraordinary efforts to get him elected. That temptation, Caperton claims, is as strong and inherent in human nature as was the conflict the Court confronted in *Tumey* and *Monroeville* when a mayor-judge (or the city) benefited financially from a defendant's conviction, as well as the conflict identified in *Murchison* and *Mayberry* when a judge was the object of a defendant's contempt.

Justice Benjamin was careful to address the recusal motions and explain his reasons why, on his view of the controlling standard, disqualification was not in order. In four separate opinions issued during the course of the appeal, he explained why no actual bias had been established. He found no basis for recusal because Caperton failed to provide "objective evidence" or "objective information," but merely "subjective belief" of bias. Nor could anyone "point to any actual conduct or activity on [his] part which could be termed 'improper.'" In other words, based on the facts presented by Caperton, Justice Benjamin conducted a probing search into his actual motives and inclinations; and he found none to be improper. We do not question his subjective findings of impartiality and propriety. Nor do we determine whether there was actual bias.

Following accepted principles of our legal tradition respecting the proper performance of judicial functions, judges often inquire into their subjective motives and purposes in the ordinary course of deciding a case. This does not mean the inquiry is a simple one. "The work of deciding cases goes on every day in hundreds of courts throughout the land. Any judge, one might suppose, would find it easy to describe the process which he had followed a thousand times and more. Nothing could be farther from the truth."

The judge inquires into reasons that seem to be leading to a particular result. Precedent and *stare decisis* and the text and purpose of the law and the Constitution; logic and scholarship and experience and common sense; and fairness and disinterest and neutrality are among the factors at work. To bring coherence to the process, and to seek respect for the resulting judgment, judges often explain the reasons for their conclusions and rulings. There are instances when the introspection that often attends this process may reveal that what the judge had assumed to be a proper, controlling factor is not the real one at work. If the judge discovers that some personal bias or improper consideration seems to be the actuating cause of the decision or to be an influence so difficult to dispel that there is a real possibility of undermining neutrality, the judge may think it necessary to consider withdrawing from the case.

The difficulties of inquiring into actual bias, and the fact that the inquiry is often a private one, simply underscore the need for objective rules. Otherwise there may be no adequate protection against a judge who simply misreads or misapprehends the real motives at work in deciding the case. The judge's own inquiry into actual bias, then, is not one that the law can easily superintend or review, though actual bias, if disclosed, no doubt would be grounds for appropriate relief. In lieu of exclusive reliance on that personal inquiry, or on appellate review of the judge's determination respecting actual bias, the Due Process Clause has been implemented by objective standards that do not require proof of actual bias. In defining these standards the Court has asked whether, "under a realistic appraisal of psychological tendencies and human weakness," the interest "poses such a risk of actual bias or prejudgment that the practice must be forbidden if the guarantee of due process is to be adequately implemented."

We turn to the influence at issue in this case. Not every campaign contribution by a litigant or attorney creates a probability of bias that requires a judge's recusal, but this is an exceptional case. We conclude that there is a serious risk of actual bias—based on objective and reasonable perceptions—when a person with a personal stake in a particular case had a significant and disproportionate influence in placing the judge on the case by raising funds or directing the judge's election campaign when the case was pending or imminent. The inquiry centers on the contribution's relative size in comparison to the total amount of money contributed to the campaign, the total amount spent in the election, and the apparent effect such contribution had on the outcome of the election.

Applying this principle, we conclude that Blankenship's campaign efforts had a significant and disproportionate influence in placing Justice Benjamin on the case. Blankenship contributed some $3 million to unseat the incumbent and replace him with Benjamin. His contributions eclipsed the total amount spent by all other Benjamin supporters and exceeded by 300% the amount spent by Benjamin's campaign committee. Caperton claims Blankenship spent $1 million more than the total amount spent by the campaign committees of both candidates combined.

Massey responds that Blankenship's support, while significant, did not cause Benjamin's victory. In the end the people of West Virginia elected him, and they did so based on many reasons other than Blankenship's efforts. Massey points out that every major state newspaper, but one, endorsed Benjamin. It also contends that then-Justice McGraw cost himself the election by giving a speech during the campaign, a speech the opposition seized upon for its own advantage.

Justice Benjamin raised similar arguments. He asserted that "the outcome of the 2004 election was due primarily to [his own] campaign's message," as well as McGraw's "devastat[ing]" speech in which he "made a number of controversial claims which became a matter of statewide discussion in the media, on the internet, and elsewhere."

Whether Blankenship's campaign contributions were a necessary and sufficient cause of Benjamin's victory is not the proper inquiry. Much like determining whether a judge is actually biased, proving what ultimately drives the electorate to choose a particular candidate is a difficult endeavor, not likely to lend itself to a certain conclusion. This is particularly true where, as here, there is no procedure for judicial factfinding and the sole trier of fact is the one accused of bias. Due process requires an objective inquiry into whether the contributor's influence on the election under all the circumstances "would offer a possible temptation to the average . . . judge to . . . lead him not to hold the balance nice, clear and true." In an election decided by fewer than 50,000 votes (382,036 to 334,301), Blankenship's campaign contributions—in comparison to the total amount contributed to the campaign, as well as the total amount spent in the election—had a significant and disproportionate influence on the electoral outcome. And the risk that Blankenship's influence engendered actual bias is sufficiently substantial that it "must be forbidden if the guarantee of due process is to be adequately implemented."

The temporal relationship between the campaign contributions, the justice's election, and the pendency of the case is also critical. It was reasonably foreseeable, when the campaign contributions were made, that the pending case would be before the newly elected justice. The $50 million adverse jury verdict had been entered before the election, and the Supreme Court of Appeals was the next step once the state trial court dealt with post-trial motions. So it became at once apparent that, absent recusal, Justice Benjamin would review a judgment that cost his biggest donor's company $50 million. Although there is no allegation of a *quid pro quo* agreement, the fact remains that Blankenship's extraordinary contributions were made at a time when he had a vested stake in the outcome. Just as no man is allowed to be a judge in his own cause, similar fears of bias can arise when—without the consent of the other parties—a man chooses the judge in his own cause. And applying this principle to the judicial election process, there was here a serious, objective risk of actual bias that required Justice Benjamin's recusal.

Justice Benjamin did undertake an extensive search for actual bias. But, as we have indicated, that is just one step in the judicial process; objective standards may also require recusal whether or not actual bias exists or can be proved. Due process "may sometimes bar trial by judges who have no actual bias and who would do their very best to weigh the scales of justice equally between contending parties." The failure to consider objective standards requiring recusal is not consistent with the imperatives of due process. We find that Blankenship's significant and disproportionate influence—coupled with the temporal relationship between the election and the pending case—"would offer a possible temptation to the average . . . judge to . . . lead him not to hold the balance nice, clear and true." On these extreme facts the probability of actual bias rises to an unconstitutional level.

IV

Our decision today addresses an extraordinary situation where the Constitution requires recusal. Massey and its *amici* predict that various adverse consequences will follow from recognizing a constitutional violation here—ranging from a flood of recusal motions to unnecessary interference with judicial elections. We disagree. The facts now before us are extreme by any measure. The parties point to no other instance involving judicial campaign contributions that presents a potential for bias comparable to the circumstances in this case. . . .

[Discussion of the ABA Model Code and West Virginia Code of Judicial conduct has been omitted.]

"The Due Process Clause demarks only the outer boundaries of judicial disqualifications. Congress and the states, of course, remain free to impose more rigorous standards for judicial disqualification than those we find mandated here today." Because the codes of judicial conduct provide more protection than due process requires, most disputes over disqualification will be resolved without resort to the Constitution. Application of the constitutional standard implicated in this case will thus be confined to rare instances.

* * *

The judgment of the Supreme Court of Appeals of West Virginia is reversed, and the case is remanded for further proceedings not inconsistent with this opinion.
It is so ordered.

CHIEF JUSTICE ROBERTS, with whom JUSTICE SCALIA, JUSTICE THOMAS, and JUSTICE ALITO join, dissenting.
I, of course, share the majority's sincere concerns about the need to maintain a fair, independent, and impartial judiciary—and one that appears to be such. But I fear that the Court's decision will undermine rather than promote these values.
Until today, we have recognized exactly two situations in which the Federal Due Process Clause requires disqualification of a judge: when the judge has a financial interest in the outcome of the case, and when the judge is trying a defendant for certain criminal contempts. Vaguer notions of bias or the appearance of bias were never a basis for disqualification, either at common law or under our constitutional precedents. Those issues were instead addressed by legislation or court rules.

Today, however, the Court enlists the Due Process Clause to overturn a judge's failure to recuse because of a "probability of bias." Unlike the established grounds for disqualification, a "probability of bias" cannot be defined in any limited way. The Court's new "rule" provides no guidance to judges and litigants about when recusal will be constitutionally required. This will inevitably lead to an increase in allegations that judges are biased, however groundless those charges may be. The end result will do far more to erode public confidence in judicial impartiality than an isolated failure to recuse in a particular case. . . .

II

In departing from this clear line between when recusal is constitutionally required and when it is not, the majority repeatedly emphasizes the need for an "objective" standard. The majority's analysis is "objective" in that it does not inquire into Justice Benjamin's motives or decisionmaking process. But the standard the majority articulates—"probability of bias"—fails to provide clear, workable guidance for future cases. At the most basic level, it is unclear whether the new probability of bias standard is somehow limited to financial support in judicial elections, or applies to judicial recusal questions more generally.

But there are other fundamental questions as well. With little help from the majority, courts will now have to determine:

1. How much money is too much money? What level of contribution or expenditure gives rise to a "probability of bias"?

2. How do we determine whether a given expenditure is "disproportionate"? Disproportionate *to what?*

3. Are independent, non-coordinated expenditures treated the same as direct contributions to a candidate's campaign? What about contributions to independent outside groups supporting a candidate?

4. Does it matter whether the litigant has contributed to other candidates or made large expenditures in connection with other elections? . . .

[Questions 5–40 have been omitted.]

These are only a few uncertainties that quickly come to mind. Judges and litigants will surely encounter others when they are forced to, or wish to, apply the majority's decision in different circumstances. Today's opinion requires state and federal judges simultaneously to act as political scientists (why did candidate X win the election?), economists (was the financial support disproportionate?), and psychologists (is there likely to be a debt of gratitude?).

The Court's inability to formulate a "judicially discernible and manageable standard" strongly counsels against the recognition of a novel constitutional right. The need to consider these and countless other questions helps explain why the common law and this Court's constitutional jurisprudence have never required disqualification on such vague grounds as "probability" or "appearance" of bias. . . .

[Section III, an argument against considering this case as "extreme," has been omitted.]

* * *

It is an old cliché, but sometimes the cure is worse than the disease. I am sure there are cases where a "probability of bias" should lead the prudent judge to step aside, but the judge fails to do so. Maybe this is one of them. But I believe that opening the door to recusal claims under the Due Process Clause, for an amorphous "probability of bias," will itself bring our judicial system into undeserved disrepute, and diminish the confidence of the American people in the fairness and integrity of their courts. I hope I am wrong.

I respectfully dissent.

SOURCE: U.S. Supreme Court. *Caperton v. A.T. Massey Coal Co.,* 556 U.S. ___ (2009). www.supreme courtus.gov/opinions/08pdf/08-22.pdf.

OTHER HISTORIC DOCUMENTS OF INTEREST

FROM THIS VOLUME

- U.S. Supreme Court on DNA Testing for Prisoners, p. 254
- U.S. Supreme Court on the Voting Rights Act, p. 263
- U.S. Supreme Court on Strip Searches of Students, p. 272
- U.S. Supreme Court on Civil Rights Act in Hiring Practices, p. 292

FROM PREVIOUS *HISTORIC DOCUMENTS*

- Supreme Court on Federal Campaign Finance Law, *2003,* p. 1155
- Supreme Court on Federal Election Campaign Financing, *1976,* p. 71

New York State to Pay Women for Egg Donations for Stem Cell Research

JUNE 11, 2009

In a first for states, New York decided on June 11, 2009, that stem cell research groups based in the state could pay women to donate their eggs for research and made it possible for the state to allocate funds for such compensation. The decision touched on a long-running ethical debate over stem cell research conducted on embryos (because donated eggs are then fertilized for the purposes of research). Some groups consider embryos, or fertilized eggs, to be humans with rights, whereas others see the embryos used in stem cell research as a necessary component for modern medical advancement. The decision by the Empire State Stem Cell Board, the group charged with overseeing and awarding stem cell research grants in the state, raises new bioethics questions that have yet to be answered. Spokespersons for the board noted that it had wanted to legalize compensating women for their eggs as a way to advance science. "We want to enhance the potential of stem cell research," said David Hohn, the vice chairman of the ethics and financial committees of the board. "If we are going to encourage stem cell research as a solution for a variety of diseases, we should remove barriers to the greatest extent possible. We decided to break some new territory."

The board debated for more than a year before it recommended that women be paid for their egg donations. In their decision, which was released quietly in the hopes of avoiding public backlash, the board members said that they had "agreed that it is ethical and appropriate for women donating oocytes for research purposes to be compensated in the same manner as women who donate oocytes for reproductive purposes and for such payments to be reimbursable as an allowable expense" under state grants backed by tax-payer dollars.

Stem cell research had been gaining traction in the states, with an increasing number setting aside funding for adult or embryonic stem cell research. Adult stem cell research causes less controversy as a person is able to voluntarily donate their cells, but such cells have less potential because adult stem cells typically cannot be reprogrammed to form many different types of cells, as can embryonic stem cells. In 2002 California became the first state to pass a law to encourage the use of embryonic stem cells for research. Following the success of this law, which brought many stem cell researchers to the state, in 2004 voters established the California Institute for Regenerative Medicine and amended the state constitution to support embryonic stem cell research through various measures, including a bond sale to raise $3 billion for projects through 2014. New Jersey became the second state to pass a law to encourage embryonic stem cell research and the first to commit state funds to it. Connecticut, Illinois, Maryland, Massachusetts, and Ohio have also since set up research programs and set aside funds for embryonic stem cell programs.

New York State's Decision

Stem cells are the root from which all cells in the human body are formed, and research currently being conducted on them has the potential to unlock new treatments for some of the most serious diseases facing humans today, including cancer, Parkinson's, Alzheimer's, and paralysis. Before this decision, researchers in New York and the other forty-nine states had to rely on leftover embryos that were being used for in vitro fertilization or skin cells that had been reprogrammed. Little success in developing useful stem cells had come from these methods.

The U.S. Congress banned the use of federal tax dollars for stem cell research in 1995 because it involved the destruction of human embryos, but in March 2009, President Barack Obama made it clear that his administration intended to help scientists advance research by removing the restrictions on the use of human embryos in federally funded stem cell research. They, however, have not yet been lifted.

New York state had been progressive in the area of stem cell research as one of only twelve states to finance projects; in 2007 it pledged $600 million to help fund an eleven-year stem cell research project that is overseen by the Empire State Stem Cell Board. The board's June 2009 decision will allow research groups to pay up to $10,000 to each woman who agrees to donate her eggs. The compensation, according to the board, is for time, out-of-pocket expenses, and the burden of egg donation.

Although the eggs that research organizations in the state can now purchase will provide many of the same research tools as leftover in vitro embryos, the harvested eggs open up greater possibilities. A Harvard stem cell researcher, Dr. George Daley, said that he believed the decision was a step in the right direction for science. "I think it's a gold step for New York State, and it will mean a tremendous advantage for New York," he said. Daley added that he has used eggs that had been discarded from in vitro fertilization attempts, but had not been successful in creating stem cells because the eggs were of a lower quality because of their age and time outside of the body.

Some stem cell research institutes in New York remained unable to pay women for their egg donations after the board's decision because their internal guidelines prohibit it. These institutions, including Rockefeller University and Cornell University, risk falling behind other groups that are able and willing to pay women for their donations.

Support and Opposition

The debate over stem cells has been ongoing since researchers realized the potential medical benefits of the cells. Much of the debate about the use of stem cells has rested on when life begins. As noted earlier, to use eggs for stem cell research, researchers must first fertilize the eggs, thus creating an embryo. This is where the ethical questions come into play. By fertilizing the egg, some argue that life has begun and that life is later wrongfully ended when the stem cell research has been completed and the embryo is destroyed. On the other side of the argument are those who believe this research is necessary for medical advancement; they note that the embryos typically used for this form of research would have been thrown away regardless, as they were left over from other procedures. These supporters believe that without placing the embryo inside a woman for development, there is no moral dilemma in its subsequent destruction. Opponents say that even leftover embryos can be adopted and used for in vitro fertilization. Such procedures produce what are sometimes referred to as snowflake children, so named because they were born from embryos that had been frozen. President George W. Bush appeared with many snowflake children while speaking against embryonic stem cell research.

Scientists are attempting to produce cells designed for individual patients. This technique is known as somatic cell nuclear transfer, and it relies on human eggs. To complete the cells for each patient, scientists must replace the genetic material in an egg with genes from the particular patient being treated and then encourage the egg to develop into an embryo. In so doing, scientists hope that this will produce cells that will not be rejected by the patient's immune system, as some stem cells are. However, because of the rarity of eggs donated for research, scientists have not yet been able to build stem cells that can be used in this fashion.

Because eggs have often been difficult to obtain for use in somatic cell nuclear transfer and other research, supporters of New York's decision say that paying women to donate their eggs to science is a necessary incentive, the rationale being that women are paid if they donate their eggs to be used in a fertility treatment, and thus donations for the purpose of research should be no different. Many researchers argue that women are unlikely to donate eggs without compensation, because they must undergo weeks of hardship, including hormone injections and a painful procedure to actually retrieve the eggs from the body. This procedure can sometimes lead to complications for the donor. Dr. Robert Klitzman, a member of the Empire State Stem Cell Board's ethics committee, said, "What we're doing is making it in some ways more reasonable for women who are interested in donating for research to do so." He added, "And at the same time, the goal is to move the science ahead, but we don't want to just move science ahead regardless of people's rights." In an effort to soothe the concerns of those who believe women are being exploited, the stem cell board decided that payments of more than $5,000 would be scrutinized.

Scrutiny of payments did little to calm critics, however. "You don't have to be a rocket scientist to understand that this is going to create a kind of undue inducement, a scenario in which a person can feel unduly compelled to take advantage of a situation," said Rev. Thomas Berg, the director of a Roman Catholic research group. Opponents said that offering payment for donating eggs to research is simply exploiting women who need the money and reducing the human body to a commodity. Other opponents expressed concern that in an economic downturn, a program like this would exploit women who are in disadvantaged economic situations.

The National Academy of Sciences (NAS), while recognizing how difficult it is to encourage women to donate their eggs without compensation, came down on the side of the opposition. The NAS already had guidelines in place prohibiting researchers from paying for women's eggs.

Some researchers thought the payments unwarranted. Jonathan Moreno, a professor of bioethics at the University of Pennsylvania, questioned whether research institutions have done a good enough job encouraging women to donate without compensation. "I wonder if all the expertise that could be brought to bear on this problem of getting unreimbursed donation have been explored." However, there is documented evidence that even a large campaign to donate eggs for free will not necessarily produce the desired result. A Harvard University researcher spent $100,000 over two years to encourage women to donate their eggs for free and found only a single donor.

Supporters of the board's decision have rejected the argument that women are being exploited and point to the fact that it would be wrong to think that women cannot make their own decision about whether to donate. "Women are perfectly capable in our society in deciding to get plastic surgery, Botox, donate a kidney," said Susan Solomon, the CEO of the New York Stem Cell Foundation. "I find it patronizing beyond belief. We compensate people in clinical trials for time and burden all the time," and she argued that scientists should be able to do the same for research purposes.

In a rebuttal to Solomon's argument that payment for egg donations for research is essentially like paying women to donate eggs for fertilization treatments, Moreno said, "People recognize that eggs can make a baby. That's a very concrete good for society. But you can't be sure any biological material you collect for research will be part of a medical breakthrough. That's the goal, but you can't be sure."

—Heather Kerrigan

Following is a statement by the Empire State Stem Cell Board on June 11, 2009, announcing its decision to pay women who donate their eggs for stem cell research.

Empire State Stem Cell Board on Its Decision to Pay for Egg Donations

June 11, 2009

On June 11, 2009, the Empire State Stem Cell Board (the "Board") voted to allow funding of research on stem cell lines derived using eggs (called "oocytes") donated solely for research purposes where the donor was, or will be, compensated for the expense, time, burden and discomfort associated with the donation process—within specified limits—as is currently permitted when women donate oocytes for reproductive purposes in New York State. The Board's decision followed extensive deliberation that included consideration of the great potential of stem cell research, national and international ethical standards, and mechanisms to safeguard the rights and welfare of oocyte donors. The Board agreed that it is ethical and appropriate for women donating oocytes for research purposes to be compensated in the same manner as women who donate oocytes for reproductive purposes and for such payments to be reimbursable as an allowable expense under NYSTEM [New York State Stem Cell Science] contracts.

This measure affects *only* donations of oocytes specifically and solely to stem cell research. NYSTEM does not permit payment for donation to stem cell research of oocytes or embryos that are in excess of clinical need from *in vitro* fertilization processes.

The Board offers the following brief statement on its oocyte donor payment decision:

Sources of recently-harvested oocytes are necessary for certain stem cell research pursuing medical advances to alleviate pain and suffering by people afflicted with debilitating and life-threatening diseases. Experiences in other jurisdictions indicate that lack of reasonable compensation to women who donate their oocytes to stem cell research has created a significant impediment to such donation, limiting the progress of stem cell research. Accordingly, over the past year, the ESSCB [Empire State Stem Cell Board] has intensively examined and discussed the issue of whether it is ethically appropriate to provide women who donate their oocytes to stem cell research with any form of reimbursement, in recognition of the considerable financial and physical burdens associated with the donation process.

When women donate their oocytes for reproductive purposes (*i.e.*, for *in vitro* fertilization), New York State permits reasonable reimbursements for out-of-pocket expenses, time, burden and discomfort associated with the donation, in amounts consistent with the guidelines developed by the American Society for Reproductive Medicine (ASRM). Such reimbursements are widely accepted as ethical, so long as they are not made contingent upon the quality or number of oocytes retrieved, the amount does not act as an undue inducement to donate, and the short- and long-term risks and benefits of donation are fully disclosed to the donor.

There is no principled reason to distinguish between donation of oocytes for reproductive purposes and research purposes when determining the ethicality of reimbursement. The risks associated with donating oocytes to stem cell research are no greater than those associated with reproductive donations. Moreover, donating oocytes to stem cell research arguably confers a greater benefit to society than does oocyte donation for private reproductive use.

Similarly, there is no ethical basis for promulgating different payment policies for women who donate oocytes to stem cell research and for participants in other types of human subjects research. National and international consensus bodies, as well as ethics scholars, generally have found it acceptable to provide reasonable compensation to subjects who participate in human subjects research to remunerate for the time and discomfort associated with participation in such research. To treat differently women who donate oocytes to stem cell research would be unjust, and would demean the significant contribution that oocyte donors make to society by participating in stem cell research.

The Board acknowledges that excessively high payments to oocyte donors could act as an undue influence to donate, or cause a woman to discount the risks associated with donation. However, the Board believes that reasonable reimbursement coupled with other safeguards protects against this possibility, and that a policy prohibiting reasonable payments because they may interfere with a woman's ability to weigh the risks and benefits of donation is unnecessarily paternalistic. In addition to the safeguards specified in NYSTEM's new donor payment contract provisions (*e.g.*, rigorous review by an institutional oversight committee, prohibition against payment of valuable consideration, and adherence to ASRM's guidelines), the Board has previously instituted by contract a number of important safeguards, including requiring full disclosure of all physical and psychological risks associated with oocyte donation, directing that informed consent be obtained through a dynamic process focused on the donor's comprehension of the information provided, and mandating availability of psychological counseling prior to donation.

We are confident that procedures implemented by institutional oversight commit-tees (IRBs [Institutional Review Boards] and ESCROs [Embryonic Stem Cell Research

Oversight Committees]), as mandated by law and by NYSTEM contract requirements, will protect against potential exploitation of donors and will ensure equitable access to opportunities.

On these bases, the Ethics Committee recommended, and the Funding Committee adopted, a measure to allow NYSTEM-funded research to proceed on cell lines created from oocytes donated solely to research, where the oocyte donor was provided with reimbursement for: (1) out-of-pocket expenses, which may include the costs associated with travel, housing, child care, and medical care, incurred as a result of the donation process; and (2) the time, burden and inconvenience associated with oocyte donation, in an amount consistent with New York State standards applicable to donations of oocytes for reproductive purposes and not to exceed the range permitted by ASRM. The measure requires that all payments be reviewed rigorously by an institutional oversight body to ensure that the amount would not constitute an undue inducement to donate, and that no consideration of any kind may be given for the number or quality of the oocytes themselves.

With respect to the source of funds for these payments, the Board believes that since it is ethical to provide NYSTEM funds for research on cell lines derived from an oocyte from which the donor was paid in accordance with the strict standards of the NYSTEM contract, it is also ethical to permit NYSTEM funds to be used for the payment of the donor. Therefore, the measure also includes a provision allowing use of NYSTEM funds for oocyte donor payment where that payment complies with all of the NYSTEM contract requirements.

SOURCE: Empire State Stem Cell Board. "Statement of the Empire State Stem Cell Board on Compensation of Oocyte Donors." June 11, 2009. http://stemcell.ny.gov/docs/ESSCB_Statement_on_Compensation_of_Oocyte_Donors.pdf.

OTHER HISTORIC DOCUMENTS OF INTEREST

FROM PREVIOUS HISTORIC DOCUMENTS

Conflict over Iranian Presidential Elections

JUNE 14, 15, AND 19, 2009

In June 2009, Iranians headed to the polls for the country's tenth presidential election. The resulting reelection of President Mahmoud Ahmadinejad and accompanying allegations of election fraud fueled unprecedented public protests. The massive demonstrations and signs of dissent within the country's traditionally conservative clergy generated international speculation that the Iranian regime was beginning to fray.

THE CAMPAIGN

President Ahmadinejad first took office in 2005, when he won in a runoff against Ali Akbar Hashemi Rafsanjani. Following his election, Ahmadinejad earned praise for his promise to share Iran's oil wealth more equally among all citizens. Over the course of his first four years in office, Iran generated approximately $280 billion in oil income, some of which Ahmadinejad distributed in cash handouts to facilitate loans to lower-income families, provide housing subsidies, and raise wages and pensions for government employees. Yet some criticized him for his hostile stance toward Western countries, particularly the United States, and his stated desire to build and acquire nuclear weapons, which made Iran a pariah among the international community.

The 2009 election pitted the president against reformist candidates Mir Hossein Mousavi and Mehdi Karroubi and conservative candidate Mohsen Rezai. Ahmadinejad's greatest challenge came from Mousavi, a former prime minister who supported plans to introduce more freedom and democracy. Mousavi enjoyed the backing of Ahmadinejad's former opponent, Rafsanjani, as well as former president Mohammad Khatami, who had dropped out of the 2009 campaign and supported Mousavi.

The *Daily Telegraph* described the campaign as "unusually open by Iranian standards but also highly acrimonious." Ahmadinejad argued that under his leadership, unemployment and unequal distribution of wealth were on the decline. He also claimed the rate of inflation had decreased to 15 percent, while official numbers placed it closer to 25 percent. Such claims prompted Mousavi to declare, "We're dealing with someone who looks you in the eyes and says white is black. . . . He has turned the country into a place full of lies and hypocrisy." Ahmadinejad in turn accused his rivals of using "Hitler-style" smear tactics against him, threatening them with jail time for insulting the president.

Thousands of supporters of both parties turned out for political rallies in the weeks preceding the election, and government officials predicted record voter turnout. Some speculated that the excitement could only benefit Mousavi. "A lot of people who have never voted are planning to vote," said Nasser Hadian, a professor at the University of Tehran. "This is a referendum on Ahmadinejad. It's more a movement against the President than anything else." Opinion polls were generally unreliable, however, with some indicating a comfortable lead for Ahmadinejad but others pointing to a clear win for Mousavi.

THE RESULTS

On Friday, June 12, Iranians headed to the polls to cast their votes. Turnout exceeded 80 percent, and election officials extended the polling deadline several times to accommodate voters. By 11:00 P.M., Mousavi was confident enough in the results to hold a press conference and declare, "I am the absolute winner of the election by a very large margin."

Yet one hour later, the Interior Ministry's election commission announced that initial results showed Ahmadinejad had won reelection. The next day, the ministry confirmed that with 80 percent of the ballots counted, Ahmadinejad had received 63.8 percent of the vote, compared to 32.7 percent of the vote for Mousavi. Rezai and Karroubi finished a distant third and fourth, respectively.

ALLEGATIONS OF FRAUD

While Ahmadinejad asserted that the results gave him a clear mandate to govern, members of the opposition immediately claimed there was significant evidence of election fraud. They pointed to reports that opposition election observers had been barred from entering some voting stations and that text messaging and pro-Mousavi Web sites had been blocked during the last few hours of voting. A number of polling locations in northwestern and southern Iran had run out of ballots, and the number of Iranians voting in some locations did not correspond to the number of eligible voters in those areas.

Opposition officials also questioned the unusually fast announcement of the results, claiming it would not be possible to count so many paper ballots by hand in such a short period of time. Others pointed to seemingly odd vote totals as evidence of election fraud. The president received a consistent percentage of the vote across the entire country, yet these numbers typically vary by region. He also won in Tabriz, Mousavi's hometown, despite Mousavi's popularity among the residents there. In addition, official figures gave Karroubi less than 1 percent of the vote, a total far less than expected and drastically divergent from the pattern of support for minor candidates in past elections.

OUTRAGE IN THE STREETS

On June 13, thousands of opposition supporters took to the streets to protest Ahmadinejad's reelection, burning buses and tires, chanting "Death to the Dictator" and carrying signs reading "Where is my vote?" Such demonstrations against the government were unprecedented in a country known for its tight-fisted control of criticism. The police immediately cracked down on the protestors, beating them with batons and using tear gas to disperse the crowds. Approximately 1,000 Iranians were arrested, including nearly 100 prominent opposition members.

The following day, the president spoke to thousands of his supporters at a rally in Tehran and refuted the opposition's allegations of widespread voting fraud. He compared the protestors to disappointed soccer fans after a losing match and dismissed them as "dust." On June 15, hundreds of thousands of Iranians marched in silence through central Tehran in another demonstration of dissent. Later that evening, seven protestors were killed when a crowd attempted to set fire to the headquarters of the volunteer Basij militia. Shortly thereafter, the supreme leader, Ayatollah Ali Khamenei, called for a formal review of the election results, and the Guardian Council announced it would be willing to conduct a partial recount of the votes. Members of the opposition rejected the offer and demanded a new election.

The government also sought to control media coverage by revoking the press credentials of those temporarily in Iran to cover the election and requiring journalists stationed in the country to receive explicit government permission before reporting beyond their offices. Protestors were able to use social networking sites, such as Facebook and Twitter, as well as YouTube, to distribute videos, photographs, and other material, providing updates on the demonstrations and subsequent government crackdown. Perhaps the most striking example of citizen journalism was an amateur video of a young woman named Neda Agha-Soltan bleeding to death on a Tehran street after being shot in the chest by security forces.

As demonstrations continued, prosecutors warned protestors they could face execution for "waging war on God." Four members of the Iranian soccer team received a lifetime ban after wearing bright green ribbons, the signature color of Mousavi supporters, during a game with South Korea. Hundreds more opposition supporters were jailed and beaten, leading the United Nations High Commissioner for Human Rights, Navi Pillay, to express her concern about the excessive use of force and violence. "What are the grounds for the arrests? Have proper warrants been issued in accordance with Iranian law? Why have some of those who have been arrested been denied access to lawyers and members of their families? And why is the whereabouts of others unknown?" she asked.

Hope for Compromise Dies

On June 19, Khamenei shattered any remaining hope of compromise between the government and reformists when he delivered a lengthy, hard-line sermon declaring the election results valid and warning opposition leaders they "would be responsible for bloodshed and chaos" if they continued to protest. Police officers and militiamen were sent into the streets to quiet protestors and detain hundreds of independent and opposition journalists. Ten days later, the Guardian Council officially certified the election results.

The government also established a special court system for trying protestors and in early July began broadcasting their "confessions," in which detainees admitted participating in a Western-backed plot to topple the government. Reports circulated that many of the detainees were being beaten, and their confessions had been coerced. "Many of the detainees, especially the higher-ranking leaders of the opposition, are coming under a great deal of pressure to make false confessions which we fear may be used in show trials in the future," said Tom Porteous, London director of Human Rights Watch.

A Divided Clergy

Signs of dissent also appeared among Iran's clergy. The Association of Combatant Clergy issued a statement claiming the vote had been rigged and calling for the results to be annulled, and the Association of Researchers and Teachers of Qum released a statement declaring the new government to be illegitimate. Grand Ayatollah Hoseyn Ali Montazeri, one of Shia Islam's most respected theologians, issued a fatwa condemning Ahmadinejad's government, claiming the president's actions were "mainly against the interests of the country" and urging fellow clerics to act to bring about reform. Some clerics expressed their shock that the government was using such violent and oppressive tactics in the name of Islam, while others questioned the impartiality of the Guardian Council given that several members had campaigned for Ahmadinejad.

CONTINUED UNREST

Although for the most part the government succeeded in subduing public protests through the remainder of the year, resistance to Ahmadinejad's government remained. Tempers flared again in late December, when opposition supporters publicly mourned the death of Grand Ayatollah Montazeri. After several days, the mourners staged a major antigovernment protest during the festival of Ashura, one of the holiest holidays for Shia Muslims. In what became the most violent protest since the election, police killed eight protestors, including Mousavi's nephew.

Such demonstrations and disagreements among the clergy have led some in the international community to speculate that the Iranian regime has begun to self-destruct, and that it is only a matter of time before the people act to install a more open and democratic government.

—Linda Fecteau

Following is a press release on Iranian president Mahmoud Ahmadinejad's reelection on June 14, 2009, a press release from Ahmadinejad on June 15, 2009, in response to those who challenged his reelection, and a news release from the United Nations on June 19, 2009, expressing concern about the Iranian presidential elections and subsequent violence.

DOCUMENT

President Ahmadinejad Addresses Iran *after His Reelection*

June 14, 2009

On a nationwide TV speech, re-elected President Mahmoud Ahmadinejad said Saturday evening he would do his best to strengthen position of Iran in the world.

At the beginning, the president felicitated the nation on the august occasion of birthday of Prophet Mohammad's daughter Fatemah (as) as well as birthday anniversary of the late Imam Khomeini.

He said election is an important work which indicates nation's desires and intentions and makes people ready to move towards their own high ideals and progress.

Calling election as a big test, the president said, "Although we had already had good elections, but this was exceptional, because the world is forming a new politico-economic framework."

"While financial, political and propaganda possibilities had been equipped both abroad and inside the country against the Iranian nation and a number of international networks with complicated methods had imposed pressure and organized a psychological war, the nation with almost 40 million participants in election created an honorable record in the world," the president said.

"A big nation has big capacities and will have big achievements. A new era has started in the history of Iran and a constructive future full of honor is in front."

President Ahmadinejad appreciated all people, clegymen [*sic*], media persons and all those who voted for him or others and participated in creation of such a great epic.

He also praised supreme leader for his guidlines [*sic*] and said that the level of hope in the Iranian nation is in the highest degree; hope for solving problems and removing obstacles in the way of country's progress.

Ahmadinejad said people voted for programs and they show their desires, so we have to provide them with their desires.

"People want problems concerning youth, occupation, and housing be solved. They are seeking justice, ending discrimination, protection of public wealth and are against special privileges for special people."

"People want progress and honor for their country in all fields and they desire their country take its deserving position in the world.

Although I respect political parties, the government belongs to the whole people and I don't believe in different groups with different names."

"People want me to choose efficient and committed colleagues who understand people's sufferings and problems," the newly re-elected president said.

"One of my big commitments before people is campaign against mischief and improving affairs."

At the end, President Ahmadinejad invited everybody to cooperate with him to build our dear country.

SOURCE: Office of the President of the Islamic Republic of Iran. "Re elected President Speaks to Nation on TV." June 14, 2009. www.president.ir/en/?ArtID=16895.

President Ahmadinejad Responds to Protests

DOCUMENT

June 15, 2009

President Ahmadinejad in a meeting with the press in Tehran on sunday [*sic*] night said; The Iranian nation is true manifestation of peoples' right to decide their own destiny.

He said that the fact that over 84 percent of the eligible voters took part in the presidential election no [*sic*] [F]riday dealt a severe blow to the foundations of the "oppressive system now ruling the world."

[S]tressing that Iranian [*sic*] want sustainable peace and security based on respect and justice, he said that Iran has often demonstrated that it wants dialogue on an equal and fair basis and never allows others to make decision on its behalf.

He went onto [*sic*] add "The fact that some protest and question the election results is not important; rather it is natural because they would win but they did not. So it is understandable that they will be upset and respond or write letters. . . ."

Responding to a question from a western reporter that his huge election victory is open to question, he said,: They (Westerners) have been behaving like this for almost 30 years. What would they do if they stop behaving like this!? On what documents do they make such claimes [*sic*]. They only say that the result was contrary to their expectations . . . they should correct their expectation. Some western media, like their government, say some thing, keep on repeating it and then end up believing it."

On the same highly sensitive issue he said "The answer our people gave them is quite clear: 40-million-strong voter-turnout with about 25 million having voted for me. This means 40 million Iranian are against the interference of the western media in their domestic affair."

MILITARY THREAT

In responde [*sic*] to a japenes [*sic*] reporter who asked him about the possibility of military action by the US and Israel against Iran, Ahmadinejad said; no power in the world is capable of threatening Iran or even think about attacking Iran.

He underscored the peace-loving and logical nature of the Iranians and said Iran IS capable of defending itself in the face of threats and intimidations. The press conference was held two days after his landslide reelection with an overwhelming 24 million votes.

[O]ver 200 reporters attended the press conference.

US TALKS

Ahmadinejad said he is ready to holds debates with Barak [*sic*] Obama.

Iran is monitoring the attitudes of different countries toward the presidential election in Iran and was assessing their positions, he said.

He noted that Iran's nuclear case now belongs to the past and cooperation and interaction among nations cannot achieved but through a global alliance for disarmament.

SOURCE: Office of the President of the Islamic Republic of Iran. "Ahmadinejad Public Opinion Not Affected by Movement." June 15, 2009. www.president.ir/en/?ArtID=16923.

 *United Nations Expresses Concern over Violence after Iranian Elections*

June 19, 2009

The top United Nations human rights official today expressed concern over reports of the use of excessive force and violence, as well as rising numbers of potentially extralegal arrests, in Iran following last week's contested presidential polls.

According to media reports, hundreds of thousands of people have taken to the streets, and Mir Hossein Mousavi has said he believes the vote was fixed in favour of President Mahmoud Ahmadinejad, while the incumbent said the vote was fair.

"The legal basis of the arrests that have been taking place, especially those of human rights defenders and political activists, is not clear," said High Commissioner for Human Rights Navi Pillay.

"What are the grounds for the arrests? Have proper warrants been issued in accordance with Iranian law? Why have some of those who have been arrested been denied access to lawyers and members of their families? And why is the whereabouts of others unknown?" she asked, urging the Government to guarantee that due process is followed to prevent fanning "the feelings of injustice."

Stressing that the freedoms of expression and assembly are fundamental human rights, Ms. Pillay hailed the largely peaceful and dignified massive demonstrations in the capital, Tehran.

She voiced concern over reported violence by members of the Basij militia, which could be in violation of international and Iranian national law.

"It is the responsibility of the government to ensure that militia members and regular law enforcement agencies do not resort to illegal acts of violence," the High Commissioner said. "If they are perceived to be acting outside the law, it could provoke a serious deterioration in the security situation, which would be a great tragedy and is in nobody's interests."

Also expressing their concern over the situation in post-election Iran today were five UN independent human rights experts who stressed that excessive police force, arbitrary arrests and killings in the wake of the recent elections thwart the freedom of expression and assembly.

Violent clashes with security forces have resulted in the death, injury and arrest of several people, the experts said in a press release. Further, they noted reports that students and others who may have contested the election results have been attacked.

"We are gravely concerned that the recent arrests and the use of excessive police force against opposition supporters may be a direct attempt to stifle freedom of assembly and expression in the country," said Frank La Rue, Special Rapporteur on freedom of opinion and expression.

He pointed to reports of online news services and social networking Internet sites have been blocked after election results were announced.

"Human rights defenders are often the first target in situations as this one, but each State has a prime responsibility and duty to protect them against any violence, threats, retaliation, de facto or de jure adverse discrimination, pressure or any other arbitrary action," stressed Margaret Sekaggya, Special Rapporteur on the situation of human rights defenders.

For her part, Manuela Carmena Castrillo, the Chairperson-Rapporteur of the Working Group on Arbitrary Detention, underscored that it is the Government's "obligation to take all necessary measures to guarantee the right of everyone not to be deprived arbitrarily of their liberty and to have fair proceedings before an independent and impartial tribunal."

On the reported killings in Iran, Philip Alston, Special Rapporteur on extrajudicial, summary or arbitrary executions, emphasized that "law enforcement officials should apply non-violent means before resorting to the use of force and firearms," while

Mannfred Nowak, the Special Rapporteur on torture and other cruel, inhuman or degrading treatment or punishment, highlighted that "excessive violence may constitute ill treatment which contravenes international human rights law."

Earlier this week, Secretary-General Ban Ki-moon said today he is keeping an eye on the post-election situation in Iran.

"At the same time, I have also taken note of the instruction by the religious leaders that there should be an investigation into this issue," Mr. Ban told reporters in New York.

"In any country, when there is an election, the genuine will of the people should be reflected and respected in a most transparent and fair and objective manner," he added.

SOURCE: UN News Centre. "Iran: UN Rights Chief Concerned over Arrests, Excessive Force Following Polls." June 19, 2009. www.un.org/apps/news/story.asp?NewsID=31196&Cr=iran&Cr1.

OTHER HISTORIC DOCUMENTS OF INTEREST

FROM PREVIOUS *HISTORIC DOCUMENTS*

U.S. Supreme Court on DNA Testing for Prisoners

JUNE 18, 2009

In June 2009, the Supreme Court again addressed the question of whether the federal judiciary should be involved in making rules that could overturn state laws and decisions. In *District Attorney's Office for the Third Judicial District v. Osborne*, in which a prisoner came to the Supreme Court seeking access to the DNA collected at the crime scene that had been used to convict him of murder, the Court ruled 5-4 against imposing rules that could overturn state decisions. In this specific case, that meant the petitioner would have to abide by state law in the jurisdiction in which he was convicted to gain access to DNA evidence against him.

OSBORNE'S CRIME

The petitioner in this case, William Osborne, had been convicted of a crime in 1993 in which two men raped and assaulted a prostitute in Alaska. The men buried the woman in the snow, leaving her for dead. A passing motorist found her alive. Forensic evidence found at the crime scene included a blue condom, which one of the men was alleged to have worn. Dexter Jackson was picked up for questioning a week after the assault and told police that another man, Osborne, had been with him when the crime occurred and that Osborne had taken part in it. When brought in for questioning, the victim identified Jackson and Osborne as the men who had raped and assaulted her although she had earlier given a description of someone who was heavier and older than Osborne appeared; she also said the man had no facial hair, while Osborne had a mustache.

In an attempt to link Osborne to the crime, Alaskan detectives tested the sperm found in the blue condom using the DQ Alpha DNA test, which can identify genes on a specific spot on the DNA chromosome. The DQ Alpha type that was detected in this case could be found among one in every six or seven African Americans, including Osborne. Although another, more advanced DNA test was available, Osborne's attorney did not request the sample be run using it.

At his 1994 trial, Osborne was convicted of kidnapping and rape. He was later sentenced to twenty-six years in prison. While serving his sentence, Osborne appealed to the Alaska Court of Appeals, claiming that he had a right to have the DNA in the case retested using a new and better testing method that had not been available at the time his case was tried. The court denied Osborne's request to access the DNA because better DNA testing *had* been available at the time of his trial. During the state appeals process, Osborne took the case to the federal level, filing a civil rights suit and claiming that the state of Alaska had violated his due process rights by not allowing him to use the DNA evidence at the crime scene to prove his innocence. In his federal suit, Osborne asked that the court force Alaska to provide him the DNA found at the crime scene so that additional tests could be run using new technology, which could winnow the match to only one in one billion people.

The federal district court that received Osborne's case dismissed it, saying that he could not ask for access to DNA evidence through a civil rights suit. The district court also said that he could not receive access to evidence at a due process trial because it could invalidate the conviction that was handed down from the state court. Thus, the district court said, he would have to file a much lengthier and difficult habeas case and exhaust all state court avenues before bringing his case before a federal court.

OSBORNE'S ARGUMENT

Much of Osborne's argument in this case and the cases he brought to trial in lower courts rested on the precedent in *Heck v. Humphrey* (1994), in which the defendant had brought a civil rights suit on the basis of malicious prosecution. Heck claimed that he had been improperly convicted. The Supreme Court, however, said that Heck would have to go through all necessary state courts before bringing his case before the federal court, as a decision in federal court could overturn his state-ordered conviction. To bring the case to trial, the judges said, Heck would have to file a habeas motion.

When Osborne appealed his case to the federal Ninth Circuit Court of Appeals, the court ruled to reverse the decision of the federal district court, stating that access to DNA to conduct another test would not necessarily overturn the conviction he had already received in the state court. In fact, the Ninth Circuit said, it could prove his guilt, or even prove to be inconclusive, in which case his conviction would still stand. In a separate decision, the court also said that the Fourteenth Amendment, and its Due Process Clause, gave Osborne the right to access the DNA evidence that had been used to convict him.

Alaska's attorney general called on the Supreme Court in a petition for *certiorari* to overturn the two decisions of the Ninth Circuit court. According to the petition, *Heck* would disallow Osborne access to DNA evidence because he could use it as a means to overturn his conviction. It also noted that the Supreme Court had never heard a case using the actual, or freestanding, innocence argument, in which the accused need only raise a reasonable doubt that he or she was not the person who committed the crime. Attorneys acting for Osborne responded to the attorney general's petition with evidence that most states already had laws in place that in some instances allow offenders to access the DNA evidence against them after they have been convicted.

The Supreme Court agreed to hear the arguments, and said, in granting *certiorari*, that it would also look at whether a civil rights suit, rather than a habeas case, could be used to access DNA evidence after a conviction.

In its decision, the Supreme Court justices took into account the forty-four states that have laws that give some prisoners access to DNA evidence. Alaska contended that by upholding the decision of the Ninth Circuit and agreeing with the forty-four other states, the Supreme Court would be stopping Alaska from determining how to give prisoners access to new technologies that could be used in conjunction with DNA to prove their innocence. Osborne's attorneys contended that because Alaska is one of only six states that does not allow at least some access to DNA evidence postconviction, the standards being applied to Osborne are unconstitutional. Osborne also argued that his right to prove his innocence did not end when he was convicted. Furthermore, because Osborne wanted to pay for the DNA testing himself, the state would incur no expense, and therefore denial of access to the DNA evidence was unfounded. The state argued that as in *Brady v. Maryland,* a case in which the prosecution withheld evidence from the defendant, a person must only be allowed access to the evidence against them before a trial. No requirements existed for allowing access to evidence after a conviction.

The other issue at trial was whether a freestanding innocence claim should or could nullify Osborne's claim. According to Osborne, even if he had access to the DNA evidence, there was no way to prove that he would use the DNA to file a case to reverse his conviction; he could simply apply for a pardon or clemency or do nothing at all. On the other hand, the state argued that there would be no way to overlook freestanding innocence in this case.

Court Upholds States Rights

In its 5-4 decision, the Court found that there was nothing in the Constitution that limited a person convicted of a crime from the constitutional right to access DNA evidence for further tests but that it should be left to each individual state to decide how to regulate access to evidence after a trial. Chief Justice John G. Roberts Jr., writing for the majority, stated, "We are reluctant to enlist the Federal Judiciary in creating a new constitutional code of rules for handling DNA."

In leaving the decision regarding DNA access up to the states, the Court simply ruled that there was no legal requirement to give access to that evidence and that the states will make the ultimate decision of who should have access to DNA evidence. This means that different people will be subjected to different laws and specifications based on the location in which they are convicted. What the Court majority did not want to do in its decision was create a federal standard for accessing DNA evidence that would invalidate what the states allowed. The Court did, however, hold that if an individual wants to access DNA evidence after being convicted of a crime, he or she must file a habeas case and pursue the matter in all state-level courts before suing in federal court.

The overarching question raised by this case is whether new constitutional rights should be created by Supreme Court interpretation. Chief Justice Roberts indicated in his opinion that it was not the place of the Court to create new constitutional rights. He wrote that the biggest issue presented in this case was "whether the Federal Judiciary must leap ahead—revising (or even discarding) the [current system of criminal justice] by creating a new constitutional right and taking over responsibility for refining it." He did not call for an end to the Court's ability to create new rights, but did call for caution.

Justice Samuel A. Alito Jr., writing a separate, concurring opinion, said that he had two additional reasons for rejecting Osborne's claim that he had a right to access DNA evidence in his case. First, Alito stated, Osborne should have pursued his claim through a habeas case rather than a civil rights suit. Second, Osborne had access to additional DNA tests during his trial but decided not to ask for them, making his case moot.

In his dissenting opinion, Justice John Paul Stevens, joined by Justices Ruth Bader Ginsburg and Stephen G. Breyer, wrote that rights go "far deeper" than what the Constitution itself has laid out. First, Stevens wrote, the Due Process Clause gave Osborne a right to postconviction DNA testing. Stevens relied heavily on the states that currently allow access to postconviction DNA testing in his dissent. "The fact that nearly all the States have now recognized some post-conviction right to DNA evidence makes it more, not less, appropriate to recognize a limited federal right to such evidence in cases where litigants are unfairly barred from obtaining relief in state court." The three dissenters also wrote that giving different access rights to convicted persons and individuals pretrial brought up the question of "fundamental fairness" that must be reconsidered.

In his dissent, Justice David H. Souter wrote, "Changes in societal understanding of the fundamental reasonableness of government actions work out in much the same way that individuals reconsider issues of fundamental belief. We can change our own inherited views just so fast, and a person is not labeled a stick-in-the-mud for refusing to endorse a new moral claim without having some time to work through it intellectually and emotionally." Souter warned that caution and care should be used in making determinations in these types of cases moving forward.

—Heather Kerrigan

Following is the text of District Attorney's Office v. Osborne, *the U.S. Supreme Court decision in which it ruled 5-4 on June 18, 2009, that it is not the place of the federal judiciary to overturn state laws when deciding who has access to evidence after a trial and conviction have occurred.*

District Attorney's Office v. Osborne

June 18, 2009

No. 08–6

District Attorney's Office for
the Third Judicial District,
et al., petitioners

v.

William G. Osborne

On writ of certiorari to
the United States Court
of Appeals for the
Ninth Circuit

[June 18, 2009]

CHIEF JUSTICE ROBERTS delivered the opinion of the Court.

DNA testing has an unparalleled ability both to exonerate the wrongly convicted and to identify the guilty. It has the potential to significantly improve both the criminal justice system and police investigative practices. The Federal Government and the States have recognized this, and have developed special approaches to ensure that this evidentiary tool can be effectively incorporated into established criminal procedure—usually but not always through legislation.

Against this prompt and considered response, the respondent, William Osborne, proposes a different approach: the recognition of a freestanding and far-reaching constitutional right of access to this new type of evidence. The nature of what he seeks is confirmed by his decision to file this lawsuit in federal court under 42 U.S.C. §1983, not within the state criminal justice system. This approach would take the development of rules and procedures in this area out of the hands of legislatures and state courts shaping policy in a focused manner and turn it over to federal courts applying the broad parameters of the Due Process Clause. There is no reason to constitutionalize the issue in this way. Because the decision below would do just that, we reverse. . . .

[Section I, containing background on the case, has been omitted.]

II

Modern DNA testing can provide powerful new evidence unlike anything known before. Since its first use in criminal investigations in the mid-1980s, there have been several major advances in DNA technology, culminating in STR technology. It is now often possible to determine whether a biological tissue matches a suspect with near certainty. While of course many criminal trials proceed without any forensic and scientific testing at all, there is no technology comparable to DNA testing for matching tissues when such evidence is at issue. DNA testing has exonerated wrongly convicted people, and has confirmed the convictions of many others.

At the same time, DNA testing alone does not always resolve a case. Where there is enough other incriminating evidence and an explanation for the DNA result, science alone cannot prove a prisoner innocent. The availability of technologies not available at trial cannot mean that every criminal conviction, or even every criminal conviction involving biological evidence, is suddenly in doubt. The dilemma is how to harness DNA's power to prove innocence without unnecessarily overthrowing the established system of criminal justice.

That task belongs primarily to the legislature. "[T]he States are currently engaged in serious, thoughtful examinations," *Washington* v. *Glucksberg,* 521 U.S. 702, 719 (1997), of how to ensure the fair and effective use of this testing within the existing criminal justice framework. Forty-six States have already enacted statutes dealing specifically with access to DNA evidence. . . .

Alaska is one of a handful of States yet to enact legislation specifically addressing the issue of evidence requested for DNA testing. But that does not mean that such evidence is unavailable for those seeking to prove their innocence. Instead, Alaska courts are addressing how to apply existing laws for discovery and post conviction relief to this novel technology.

First, access to evidence is available under Alaska law for those who seek to subject it to newly available DNA testing that will prove them to be actually innocent. Under the State's general post conviction relief statute, a prisoner may challenge his conviction when "there exists evidence of material facts, not previously presented and heard by the court, that requires vacation of the conviction or sentence in the interest of justice." Such a claim is exempt from otherwise applicable time limits if "newly discovered evidence," pursued with due diligence, "establishes by clear and convincing evidence that the applicant is innocent." §12.72.020(b)(2). . . .

[Further discussion of Alaskan law has been omitted.]

III

The parties dispute whether Osborne has invoked the proper federal statute in bringing his claim. He sued under the federal civil rights statute, 42 U.S.C. §1983, which gives a cause of action to those who challenge a State's "deprivation of any rights . . . secured by the Constitution." The State insists that Osborne's claim must be brought under 28 U.S.C. §2254, which allows a prisoner to seek "a writ of habeas corpus . . . on the ground that he is in custody in violation of the Constitution."

While Osborne's claim falls within the literal terms of §1983, we have also recognized that §1983 must be read in harmony with the habeas statute. "Stripped to its essence," the State says, "Osborne's §1983 action is nothing more than a request for evidence to support a hypothetical claim that he is actually innocent. . . . [T]his hypothetical claim sounds at the core of habeas corpus."

Osborne responds that his claim does not sound in habeas at all. Although invalidating his conviction is of course his ultimate goal, giving him the evidence he seeks "would not necessarily imply the invalidity of [his] confinement." If he prevails, he would receive only *access* to the DNA, and even if DNA testing exonerates him, his conviction is not automatically invalidated. He must bring an entirely separate suit or a petition for clemency to invalidate his conviction. If he were proved innocent, the State might also release him on its own initiative, avoiding any need to pursue habeas at all.

Osborne also invokes our recent decision in *Wilkinson v. Dotson*, 544 U.S. 74 (2005). There, we held that prisoners who sought new hearings for parole eligibility and suitability need not proceed in habeas. We acknowledged that the two plaintiffs "hope[d]" their suits would "help bring about earlier release," *id.*, at 78, but concluded that the §1983 suit would not accomplish that without further proceedings. "Because neither prisoner's claim would necessarily spell speedier release, neither l[ay] at the core of habeas corpus." Every Court of Appeals to consider the question since *Dotson* has decided that because access to DNA evidence similarly does not "necessarily spell speedier release," *ibid.*, it can be sought under §1983. See 423 F. 3d, at 1055-1056; *Savory v. Lyons*, 469 F. 3d 667, 672 (CA7 2006); *McKithen v. Brown*, 481 F. 3d 89, 103, and n. 15 (CA2 2007). On the other hand, the State argues that *Dotson* is distinguishable because the challenged procedures in that case did not affect the ultimate "exercise of discretion by the parole board." It also maintains that *Dotson* does not set forth "the *exclusive* test for whether a prisoner may proceed under §1983."

While we granted certiorari on this question, our resolution of Osborne's claims does not require us to resolve this difficult issue. Accordingly, we will assume without deciding that the Court of Appeals was correct that *Heck* does not bar Osborne's §1983 claim. Even under this assumption, it was wrong to find a due process violation.

IV

A

"No State shall . . . deprive any person of life, liberty, or property, without due process of law." This Clause imposes procedural limitations on a State's power to take away protected entitlements. Osborne argues that access to the State's evidence is a "process" needed to vindicate his right to prove himself innocent and get out of jail. Process is not an end in itself, so a necessary premise of this argument is that he has an entitlement (what our precedents call a "liberty interest") to prove his innocence even after a fair trial has proved otherwise. We must first examine this asserted liberty interest to determine what process (if any) is due. . . .

[The state of Alaska's argument and the argument of Osborne have been omitted.]

The Court of Appeals went too far, however, in concluding that the Due Process Clause requires that certain familiar pre conviction trial rights be extended to protect Osborne's post conviction liberty interest. After identifying Osborne's possible liberty interests, the court concluded that the State had an obligation to comply with the principles of *Brady* v. *Maryland,* 373 U.S. 83. In that case, we held that due process requires a prosecutor to disclose material exculpatory evidence to the defendant before trial. The Court of Appeals acknowledged that nothing in our precedents suggested that this disclosure obligation continued after the defendant was convicted and the case was closed, 521 F. 3d, at 1128, but it relied on prior Ninth Circuit precedent applying "*Brady* as a post-conviction right," *id.,* at 1128-1129 (citing *Thomas* v. *Goldsmith,* 979 F. 2d 746, 749-750 (1992)). Osborne does not claim that *Brady* controls this case, Brief for Respondent 39–40, and with good reason.

A criminal defendant proved guilty after a fair trial does not have the same liberty interests as a free man. At trial, the defendant is presumed innocent and may demand that the government prove its case beyond reasonable doubt. But "[o]nce a defendant has been afforded a fair trial and convicted of the offense for which he was charged, the presumption of innocence disappears." "Given a valid conviction, the criminal defendant has been constitutionally deprived of his liberty."

The State accordingly has more flexibility in deciding what procedures are needed in the context of post conviction relief. "[W]hen a State chooses to offer help to those seeking relief from convictions," due process does not "dictat[e] the exact form such assistance must assume." Osborne's right to due process is not parallel to a trial right, but rather must be analyzed in light of the fact that he has already been found guilty at a fair trial, and has only a limited interest in post conviction relief. *Brady* is the wrong framework.

Instead, the question is whether consideration of Osborne's claim within the framework of the State's procedures for post conviction relief "offends some principle of justice so rooted in the traditions and conscience of our people as to be ranked as fundamental," or "transgresses any recognized principle of fundamental fairness in operation." Federal courts may upset a State's post conviction relief procedures only if they are fundamentally inadequate to vindicate the substantive rights provided.

We see nothing inadequate about the procedures Alaska has provided to vindicate its state right to post conviction relief in general, and nothing inadequate about how those procedures apply to those who seek access to DNA evidence. . . .

Establishing a freestanding right to access DNA evidence for testing would force us to act as policymakers, and our substantive-due-process rulemaking authority would not only have to cover the right of access but a myriad of other issues. We would soon have to decide if there is a constitutional obligation to preserve forensic evidence that might later be tested. If so, for how long? Would it be different for different types of evidence? Would the State also have some obligation to gather such evidence in the first place? How much, and when? No doubt there would be a miscellany of other minor directives. . . . .

DNA evidence will undoubtedly lead to changes in the criminal justice system. It has done so already. The question is whether further change will primarily be made by legislative revision and judicial interpretation of the existing system, or whether the

Federal Judiciary must leap ahead—revising (or even discarding) the system by creating a new constitutional right and taking over responsibility for refining it.

Federal courts should not presume that state criminal procedures will be inadequate to deal with technological change. The criminal justice system has historically accommodated new types of evidence, and is a time-tested means of carrying out society's interest in convicting the guilty while respecting individual rights. That system, like any human endeavor, cannot be perfect. DNA evidence shows that it has not been. But there is no basis for Osborne's approach of assuming that because DNA has shown that these procedures are not flawless, DNA evidence must be treated as categorically outside the process, rather than within it. That is precisely what his §1983 suit seeks to do, and that is the contention we reject.

The judgment of the Court of Appeals is reversed, and the case is remanded for further proceedings consistent with this opinion.

It is so ordered.

JUSTICE ALITO, with whom JUSTICE KENNEDY joins, and with whom JUSTICE THOMAS joins as to Part II, concurring.

Respondent was convicted for a brutal sexual assault. At trial, the defense declined to have DNA testing done on a semen sample found at the scene of the crime. Defense counsel explained that this decision was made based on fear that the testing would provide further evidence of respondent's guilt. After conviction, in an unsuccessful attempt to obtain parole, respondent confessed in detail to the crime. Now, respondent claims that he has a federal constitutional right to test the sample and that he can go directly to federal court to obtain this relief without giving the Alaska courts a full opportunity to consider his claim.

I agree with the Court's resolution of respondent's constitutional claim. In my view, that claim also fails for two independent reasons beyond those given by the majority. First, a state prisoner asserting a federal constitutional right to perform such testing must file a petition for a writ of habeas corpus, not an action under 42 U.S.C. §1983, as respondent did here, and thus must exhaust state remedies, see 28 U.S.C. §2254(b)(1)(A). Second, even though respondent did not exhaust his state remedies, his claim may be rejected on the merits, see §2254(b)(2), because a defendant who declines the opportunity to perform DNA testing at trial for tactical reasons has no constitutional right to perform such testing after conviction. . . .

[Further dissent has been omitted.]

JUSTICE STEVENS, with whom JUSTICE GINSBURG and JUSTICE BREYER join, and with whom JUSTICE SOUTER joins as to Part I, dissenting.

The State of Alaska possesses physical evidence that, if tested, will conclusively establish whether respondent William Osborne committed rape and attempted murder. If he did, justice has been served by his conviction and sentence. If not, Osborne has needlessly spent decades behind bars while the true culprit has not been brought to justice. The DNA test Osborne seeks is a simple one, its cost modest, and its results uniquely precise. Yet for reasons the State has been unable or unwilling to articulate, it refuses to allow Osborne to test the evidence at his own expense and to thereby ascertain the truth once and for all.

On two equally problematic grounds, the Court today blesses the State's arbitrary denial of the evidence Osborne seeks. First, while acknowledging that Osborne may have a due process right to access the evidence under Alaska's post conviction procedures, the Court concludes that Osborne has not yet availed himself of all possible avenues for relief in state court. As both a legal and factual matter, that conclusion is highly suspect. More troubling still, based on a fundamental mischaracterization of the right to liberty that Osborne seeks to vindicate, the Court refuses to acknowledge "in the circumstances of this case" any right to access the evidence that is grounded in the Due Process Clause itself. Because I am convinced that Osborne has a constitutional right of access to the evidence he wishes to test and that, on the facts of this case, he has made a sufficient showing of entitlement to that evidence, I would affirm the decision of the Court of Appeals. . . .

[The remainder of Justice Stevens's dissent has been omitted.]

JUSTICE SOUTER, dissenting.

I respectfully dissent on the ground that Alaska has failed to provide the effective procedure required by the Fourteenth Amendment for vindicating the liberty interest in demonstrating innocence that the state law recognizes. I therefore join Part I of JUSTICE STEVENS's dissenting opinion.

I would not decide Osborne's broad claim that the Fourteenth Amendment's guarantee of due process requires our recognition at this time of a substantive right of access to biological evidence for DNA analysis and comparison. I would reserve judgment on the issue simply because there is no need to reach it; at a general level Alaska does not deny a right to post conviction testing to prove innocence, and in any event, Osborne's claim can be resolved by resort to the procedural due process requirement of an effective way to vindicate a liberty interest already recognized in state law, see *Evitts* v. *Lucey*, 469 U.S. 387, 393 (1985). My choice to decide this case on that procedural ground should not, therefore, be taken either as expressing skepticism that a new substantive right to test should be cognizable in some circumstances, or as implying agreement with the Court that it would necessarily be premature for the Judicial Branch to decide whether such a general right should be recognized.

There is no denying that the Court is correct when it notes that a claim of right to DNA testing, post-trial at that, is a novel one, but that only reflects the relative novelty of testing DNA, and in any event is not a sufficient reason alone to reject the right asserted, see *Reno* v. *Flores*, 507 U.S. 292, 318-319 (1993) (O'Connor, J., concurring). . . .

[The remainder of Justice Souter's argument has been omitted.]

SOURCE: U.S. Supreme Court. *District Attorney v. Osborne,* 557 U.S. ___ (2009). www.supremecourtus.gov/opinions/08pdf/08-6.pdf.

OTHER HISTORIC DOCUMENTS OF INTEREST

FROM THIS VOLUME

U.S. Supreme Court on the Voting Rights Act

JUNE 22, 2009

After the Supreme Court heard oral arguments on April 29, 2009, in the case of *Northwest Austin Municipal Utility District Number One v. Holder,* a majority of the justices appeared poised to strike down the core oversight provision of the 1965 Voting Rights Act, widely touted as one of the country's most effective civil rights laws. Instead of the extremely divisive opinion that had been widely predicted, however, on June 22, 2009, a virtually unanimous court sidestepped the constitutional issues entirely to decide the case on narrow statutory grounds. Although civil rights groups were relieved, there was not much in the opinion to give them long-term comfort. Chief Justice John G. Roberts Jr., writing for the majority, questioned whether the forty-five-year-old Voting Rights Act would pass a constitutional test. "In part due to the success of that legislation," Roberts wrote, "we are now a very different Nation. Whether conditions continue to justify such legislation is a difficult constitutional question we do not answer today."

THE VOTING RIGHTS ACT AND THE AUSTIN UTILITY DISTRICT

The Fifteenth Amendment, passed in 1870, guarantees that the "right of citizens of the United States to vote shall not be denied or abridged by the United States or any State on account of race, color, or previous condition of servitude." It also gives Congress the authority to enforce the amendment legislatively. For a hundred years, the Fifteenth Amendment was an unfulfilled promise. African Americans who attempted to vote were often met with coordinated intimidation and violence at the polls. Jim Crow laws passed by the states were designed to deny them the right to vote by requiring literacy tests, poll taxes, "good character" tests, and grandfather clauses. Enforcement statutes passed in the 1950s and early 1960s required time-consuming and expensive individual lawsuits by the Justice Department to challenge each discriminatory law. By the time one law was over-turned, the states had created another in its place. Justice Clarence Thomas wrote in his dissent in *Northwest Austin Municipal Utility v. Holder* that "the massive scale of disenfranchisement efforts made case-by-case enforcement of the Fifteenth Amendment impossible, if not Sisyphean."

By 1965, Congress had become convinced that more sweeping powers were needed to make the promise of a right to vote into a reality and responded with the Voting Rights Act. Section 2 of the act is permanent and applies nationwide; it forbids any "standard, practice, or procedure" that "results in a denial or abridgment of the right of any citizen of the United States to vote on account of race or color." This provision was not in play in this case. What was at issue were the oversight powers of section 5 that apply only to states found to have a sustained history of racial bias in voting and were originally intended to last for five years. Currently the requirements apply to nine southern states in their entireties and parts of seven other states, including California and North Carolina. Under this law, all covered states and jurisdictions must approach the Justice Department or the District of Columbia federal court to get preclearance for any proposed changes in the way they hold elections. This provision was extended in 1970 for five years, in 1975 for seven years, and in 1982 for twenty-five years. In 1982, Congress added a "bailout" provision allowing local jurisdictions to seek exemption from the preclearance requirements if they could demonstrate that they had not actually been engaging in discrimination and had worked to end it. The most recent reauthorization of section 5 came in 2006 when it was overwhelmingly renewed for another twenty-five years by a Republican-controlled Congress (unanimously in the Senate and by a vote of 390–33 in the House) and signed into law by President George W. Bush.

Ten days after the latest extension became law, Northwest Austin Municipal Utility District No. 1, in Austin, Texas, challenged it in district court. This Austin utility district had been created in 1987 to provide waste collection and other public works services for a small, affluent suburb of about 3,500 residents, and it had no history of disenfranchising voters on the basis of race. The preclearance requirements of the Voting Rights Act applied to it only because it is a local jurisdiction in Texas. Elections in the utility district had been held in private homes or garages, and the board wanted to change the polling location to a school. To do this they had to seek federal clearance.

Rather than seek federal approval, the utility district filed suit seeking to be exempted from the preclearance obligation under the "bailout" provisions of the Voting Rights Act that allow "political subdivisions" that have met certain rigorous standards to seek release from section 5 from a three-judge district court in Washington, D.C. The suit argued that it should be able to bail out from the requirements, or in the alternative, that the requirements of section 5 were unconstitutional. The district court denied both claims, finding that a subdivision such as the utility district that did not register its own voters was not eligible under the act for bailout, and that section 5 was constitutional. The utility district appealed to the Supreme Court.

The case attracted much attention. In his opinion, Chief Justice Roberts described the briefs filed on the constitutional question by dozens of interested parties as "ardent." Hostile questioning from the justices at oral arguments convinced many voting rights experts that the Court was poised to overturn the historic law. Justice Anthony M. Kennedy, often a swing vote, repeatedly asked how Congress could justify subjecting some states but not others to the preclearance requirements, how "Congress has made the finding that the sovereignty and dignity of Georgia is less than the sovereign dignity of Ohio, and that of Alabama less than that of Michigan?" Chief Justice Roberts compared the voting rights rule to an "elephant whistle" to illustrate that it may have outlasted its usefulness. "'I have this whistle to keep away the elephants.' You know well, that's silly. 'Well, there are no elephants, so it must work.'"

The Court's Unexpectedly Narrow Ruling

Chief Justice Roberts, in an 8-1 opinion, with only Justice Clarence Thomas dissenting in part, relied on the principle of constitutional avoidance to skirt the central constitutional issue in this case. Under this principle, the Court avoids deciding a constitutional question if there is some other ground available to resolve the case. Here, the Court chose to expand a limiting statutory definition of "political subdivision" to reach the conclusion that "the Voting Rights Act permits all political subdivisions, including the district in this case, to seek relief from its preclearance requirements." With the Austin utility district able to bailout from the Voting Rights Act, there was no need for the Court to resolve whether the Voting Rights Act could survive constitutional scrutiny.

However, before reaching this narrow conclusion, the Roberts opinion hints openly that the preclearance requirements of the Voting Rights Act may no longer be constitutional. The requirement that states must first get federal approval for all changes to election laws—regardless of how innocuous—represents a significant intrusion into areas of state and local responsibility, posing significant burdens on states, with substantial "federalism costs," he wrote, that "have caused Members of this Court to express serious misgivings about" its constitutionality. According to Roberts, there is also a federalism cost to treating states differently, despite fundamental principles of equal sovereignty. Such a departure from these principles requires proof, he writes, that the disparate coverage, based on data that is now more than thirty-five years old, accounts for current political conditions. Roberts acknowledges the dramatic civil rights gains that are "no doubt due in significant part to the Voting Rights Act itself, and stand as a monument to its success," but adds that this past success cannot, in his view, be sufficient justification to retain the preclearance requirements. The current burdens being imposed by the act, he wrote, "must be justified by current needs." Whether they are still justified was a question that the opinion described as "difficult" and left for another day.

Writing separately, Justice Thomas noted that he would reach the constitutional question and hold that section 5 of the Voting Rights Act exceeds Congress's power to enforce the Fifteenth Amendment. To Thomas, the preclearance requirements of the act are an extraordinary exercise of congressional power that could only be justified by extreme circumstances. Justice Thomas concluded that such circumstances no longer exist: "[N]ow—more than 40 years later—the violence, intimidation, and subterfuge that led Congress to pass Section 5 and this Court to uphold it no longer remains. An acknowledgment of Section 5's unconstitutionality represents a fulfillment of the Fifteenth Amendment's promise and full enfranchisement and honors the success achieved by the VRA [Voting Rights Act]."

Impact of the Decision

Although the Austin decision avoided the constitutionality of the Voting Rights Act, it is not a question that has gone away, and more conservative challenges are likely. How far they will go depends in part on why the Court chose to rule narrowly on this case. Some theorize that Chief Justice Roberts was unable to secure Justice Kennedy's vote to overrule the statute and chose to rule narrowly rather than issue a divided opinion. Laughlin McDonald, director of the American Civil Liberties Union Voting Rights Project, expressed satisfaction that the Court, presented with the opportunity to declare section 5 unconstitutional, "declined that invitation." Moreover, he predicted that by liberalizing the bailout provisions of the act, the Court had made it "more difficult for jurisdictions covered by Section 5 to complain that there is no escape from its preclearance requirements." If more jurisdictions with no record of discrimination successfully seek an escape from federal scrutiny, there may be less dissatisfaction with section 5, but bailout has been available to 12,000 jurisdictions since 1982, and to date, it has only been granted to seventeen jurisdictions.

The timing of this issue is important as the 2010 Census will bring about a new round of political redistricting. With section 5 of the Voting Rights Act still in place, all jurisdictions that it covers must obtain preapproval from the Justice Department before redrawing district boundaries.

—Melissa Feinberg

Following is the June 22, 2009, U.S. Supreme Court opinion in Northwest Austin Municipal Utility District Number One v. Holder, *in which the Court decided 8-1 that all jurisdictions are eligible to seek relief from preclearance requirements to changing their election laws.*

Northwest Austin Municipal v. Holder

June 22, 2009

No. 08–322

Northwest Austin
Municipal Utility District
Number One, Appellant
v.
Eric H. Holder, Jr., Attorney
General, et al.

}

On appeal from
the United States
District Court for the
District of Columbia

[June 22, 2009]

CHIEF JUSTICE ROBERTS delivered the opinion of the Court.

The plaintiff in this case is a small utility district raising a big question—the constitutionality of §5 of the Voting Rights Act. The district has an elected board, and is required by §5 to seek preclearance from federal authorities in Washington, D. C., before it can change anything about those elections. This is required even though there has never been any evidence of racial discrimination in voting in the district.

The district filed suit seeking relief from these preclearance obligations under the "bailout" provision of the Voting Rights Act. That provision allows the release of a "political subdivision" from the preclearance requirements if certain rigorous conditions are met. The court below denied relief, concluding that bailout was unavailable to a political subdivision like the utility district that did not register its own voters. The district appealed, arguing that the Act imposes no such limitation on bailout, and that if it does, the preclearance requirements are unconstitutional.

That constitutional question has attracted ardent briefs from dozens of interested parties, but the importance of the question does not justify our rushing to decide it. Quite the contrary: Our usual practice is to avoid the unnecessary resolution of constitutional questions. We agree that the district is eligible under the Act to seek bailout. We therefore reverse, and do not reach the constitutionality of §5. . . .

[Section I, containing information on the Fifteenth Amendment and its relation to this case, has been omitted.]

II

The historic accomplishments of the Voting Rights Act are undeniable. When it was first passed, unconstitutional discrimination was rampant and the "registration of voting-age whites ran roughly 50 percentage points or more ahead" of black registration in many covered States. Today, the registration gap between white and black voters is in single digits in the covered States; in some of those States, blacks now register and vote at higher rates than whites. Similar dramatic improvements have occurred for other racial minorities. "[M]any of the first generation barriers to minority voter registration and voter turnout that were in place prior to the [Voting Rights Act] have been eliminated."

At the same time, §5, "which authorizes federal intrusion into sensitive areas of state and local policymaking, imposes substantial 'federalism costs.'" These federalism costs have caused Members of this Court to express serious misgivings about the constitutionality of §5.

Section 5 goes beyond the prohibition of the Fifteenth Amendment by suspending *all* changes to state election law—however innocuous—until they have been precleared by federal authorities in Washington, D.C. The preclearance requirement applies broadly, *NAACP* v. *Hampton County Election Comm'n*, 470 U.S. 166, 175-176 (1985), and in particular to every political subdivision in a covered State, no matter how small, *United States* v. *Sheffield Bd. of Comm'rs*, 435 U.S. 110, 117-118 (1978).

Some of the conditions that we relied upon in upholding this statutory scheme in *Katzenbach* and *City of Rome* have unquestionably improved. Things have changed in the South. Voter turnout and registration rates now approach parity. Blatantly discriminatory evasions of federal decrees are rare. And minority candidates hold office at unprecedented levels.

These improvements are no doubt due in significant part to the Voting Rights Act itself, and stand as a monument to its success. Past success alone, however, is not adequate justification to retain the preclearance requirements. It may be that these improvements are insufficient and that conditions continue to warrant preclearance under the Act. But the Act imposes current burdens and must be justified by current needs.

The Act also differentiates between the States, despite our historic tradition that all the States enjoy "equal sovereignty." Distinctions can be justified in some cases. "The doctrine of the equality of States . . . does not bar . . . remedies for *local* evils which have subsequently appeared." But a departure from the fundamental principle of equal sovereignty requires a showing that a statute's disparate geographic coverage is sufficiently related to the problem that it targets.

These federalism concerns are underscored by the argument that the preclearance requirements in one State would be unconstitutional in another. . . . Yet considerations of race that would doom a redistricting plan under the Fourteenth Amendment or §2 seem to be what save it under §5. Additional constitutional concerns are raised in saying that this tension between §§2 and 5 must persist in covered jurisdictions and not elsewhere.

The evil that §5 is meant to address may no longer be concentrated in the jurisdictions singled out for preclearance. The statute's coverage formula is based on data that is now more than 35 years old, and there is considerable evidence that it fails to account for current political conditions. For example, the racial gap in voter registration and turnout is lower in the States originally covered by §5 than it is nationwide. Congress heard warnings from supporters of extending §5 that the evidence in the record did not address "systematic differences between the covered and the non-covered areas of the United States[,] . . . and, in fact, the evidence that is in the record suggests that there is more similarity than difference."

The parties do not agree on the standard to apply in deciding whether, in light of the foregoing concerns, Congress exceeded its Fifteenth Amendment enforcement power in extending the preclearance requirements. The district argues that "'[t]here must be a congruence and proportionality between the injury to be prevented or remedied and the means adopted to that end,'" Brief for Appellant 31, quoting *City of Boerne* v. *Flores,* 521 U.S. 507, 520 (1997); the Federal Government asserts that it is enough that the legislation be a "'rational means to effectuate the constitutional prohibition,'" Brief for Federal Appellee 6, quoting *Katzenbach, supra,* at 324. That question has been extensively briefed in this case, but we need not resolve it. The Act's preclearance requirements and its coverage formula raise serious constitutional questions under either test.

In assessing those questions, we are keenly mindful of our institutional role. We fully appreciate that judging the constitutionality of an Act of Congress is "the grave stand most delicate duty that this Court is called on to perform." The Fifteenth Amendment empowers "Congress," not the Court, to determine in the first instance what legislation is needed to enforce it. Congress amassed a sizable record in support of its decision to extend the preclearance requirements, a record the District Court determined "document[ed] contemporary racial discrimination in covered states." The District Court also found that the record "demonstrat[ed] that section 5 prevents discriminatory voting changes" by "quietly but effectively deterring discriminatory changes."

We will not shrink from our duty "as the bulwar[k] of a limited constitution against legislative encroachments," The Federalist No. 78, p. 526 (J. Cooke ed. 1961) (A. Hamilton), but "[i]t is a well-established principle governing the prudent exercise of this Court's jurisdiction that normally the Court will not decide a constitutional question if there is some other ground upon which to dispose of the case," *Escambia County* v. *McMillan,* 466 U.S. 48, 51 (1984) (*per curiam*). Here, the district also raises a statutory claim that it is eligible to bail out under §§4 and 5.

JUSTICE THOMAS argues that the principle of constitutional avoidance has no pertinence here. He contends that even if we resolve the district's statutory argument in its favor, we would still have to reach the constitutional question, because the district's statutory argument would not afford it all the relief it seeks.

We disagree. The district expressly describes its constitutional challenge to §5 as being "in the alternative" to its statutory argument. The district's counsel confirmed this at oral argument. We therefore turn to the district's statutory argument.

III

Section 4(b) of the Voting Rights Act authorizes a bailout suit by a "State or political subdivision." There is no dispute that the district is a political subdivision of the State of Texas in the ordinary sense of the term. The district was created under Texas law with "powers of government" relating to local utilities and natural resources.

The Act, however, also provides a narrower statutory definition in §14(c)(2): "'[P]olitical subdivision' shall mean any county or parish, except that where registration for voting is not conducted under the supervision of a county or parish, the term shall include any other subdivision of a State which conducts registration for voting." The District Court concluded that this definition applied to the bailout provision in §4(a), and that the district did not qualify, since it is not a county or parish and does not conduct its own voter registration.

"Statutory definitions control the meaning of statutory words, of course, in the usual case. But this is an unusual case." Were the scope of §4(a) considered in isolation from the rest of the statute and our prior cases, the District Court's approach might well be correct. But here specific precedent, the structure of the Voting Rights Act, and underlying constitutional concerns compel a broader reading of the bailout provision. . . .

[Discussion of statutory interpretation has been omitted.]

The Government's contrary interpretation has helped to render the bailout provision all but a nullity. Since 1982, only 17 jurisdictions—out of the more than 12,000 covered political subdivisions—have successfully bailed out of the Act. It is unlikely that Congress intended the provision to have such limited effect.

We therefore hold that all political subdivisions—not only those described in §14(c)(2)—are eligible to file a bailout suit.

* * *

More than 40 years ago, this Court concluded that "exceptional conditions" prevailing in certain parts of the country justified extraordinary legislation otherwise unfamiliar to our federal system. In part due to the success of that legislation, we are now a very different Nation. Whether conditions continue to justify such legislation is a difficult constitutional question we do not answer today. We conclude instead that the Voting Rights Act permits all political subdivisions, including the district in this case, to seek relief from its preclearance requirements.

The judgment of the District Court is reversed, and the case is remanded for further proceedings consistent with this opinion.

It is so ordered.

JUSTICE THOMAS, concurring in the judgment in part and dissenting in part. . . .

II

The Court quite properly alerts Congress that §5 tests the outer boundaries of its Fifteenth Amendment enforcement authority and may not be constitutional. And, although I respect the Court's careful approach to this weighty issue, I nevertheless believe it is necessary to definitively resolve that important question. For the reasons set forth below, I conclude that the lack of current evidence of intentional discrimination with respect to voting renders §5 unconstitutional. The provision can no longer be justified as an appropriate mechanism for enforcement of the Fifteenth Amendment. . . .

Indeed, §5's preclearance requirement is "one of the most extraordinary remedial provisions in an Act noted for its broad remedies. Even the Department of Justice has described it as a 'substantial departure . . . from ordinary concepts of our federal system'; its encroachment on state sovereignty is significant and undeniable." This "encroachment is especially troubling because it destroys local control of the means of self-government, one of the central values of our polity." More than 40 years after its enactment, this intrusion has become increasingly difficult to justify.

Third, to accommodate the tension between the constitutional imperatives of the Fifteenth and Tenth Amendments—a balance between allowing the Federal Government to patrol state voting practices for discrimination and preserving the States' significant interest in self-determination—the constitutionality of §5 has always depended on the proven existence of intentional discrimination so extensive that elimination of it through case-by-case enforcement would be impossible. . . .

C

The extensive pattern of discrimination that led the Court to previously uphold §5 as enforcing the Fifteenth Amendment no longer exists. Covered jurisdictions are not now engaged in a systematic campaign to deny black citizens access to the ballot through intimidation and violence. And the days of "grandfather clauses, property qualifications, 'good character' tests, and the requirement that registrants 'understand' or 'interpret' certain matter," *Katzenbach*, 383 U.S., at 311, are gone. There is thus currently no concerted effort in these jurisdictions to engage in the "unremitting and ingenious defiance of the Constitution," *id.*, at 309, that served as the constitutional basis for upholding the "uncommon exercise of congressional power" embodied in §5, *id.*, at 334. . . .

* * *

In 1870, the Fifteenth Amendment was ratified in order to guarantee that no citizen would be denied the right to vote based on race, color, or previous condition of servitude. Congress passed §5 of the VRA in 1965 because that promise had remained unfulfilled for far too long. But now—more than 40 years later—the violence, intimidation, and subterfuge that led Congress to pass §5 and this Court to uphold it no longer remains. An acknowledgment of §5's unconstitutionality represents a fulfillment of the Fifteenth Amendment's promise of full enfranchisement and honors the success achieved by the VRA.

SOURCE: U.S. Supreme Court of the United States. *Northwest Austin Municipal Utility District Number One v. Holder,* 557 U.S. ___ (2009). www.supremecourtus.gov/opinions/08pdf/08-322.pdf.

OTHER HISTORIC DOCUMENTS OF INTEREST

U.S. Supreme Court on Strip Searches of Students

JUNE 25, 2009

On June 25, 2009, when the U.S. Supreme Court ruled in the case of *Safford Unified School District v. Redding,* it was not the first time the Court had addressed the issue of students' rights while on school property. Four decades ago, the Court ruled that when children are on public school property, they retain constitutional rights. In addition, more than two decades ago, the Court ruled that although public school students do not have full access to the constitutional right to privacy while under the supervision of adults on school property, they still have some privacy protections. On the other hand, the Court has also ruled that because public school students are minors, if school officials can prove that what a student does is in some way detrimental to other students, rights to privacy and free speech can be curtailed.

In the case of *Safford v. Redding,* the Court looked at drug use in public schools. In the past, the Court had ruled that schools can impose mandatory drug testing on students who want to participate in school activities. In addition, searches of school children have been deemed proper as long as a school official has a reasonable belief that the student is carrying drugs; "probable cause" is not required for such searches. In this particular case, the Supreme Court took up the issue of whether strip searches are warranted when school officials suspect a student of carrying substances banned by school policy, in this case prescription-strength ibuprofen.

ARE STRIP SEARCHES LEGAL?

The case of *Safford v. Redding* originated in October 2003, when school officials in Safford, Arizona, acting on a tip they received from an eighth-grade student, strip-searched Savana Redding on the suspicion that she was carrying prescription-strength ibuprofen on school property for nonmedical purposes and distributing it to other students. The vice principal first searched Redding's backpack, and finding no prescription medications, sent Redding to the school nurse, where two female staff members forced the student to remove her clothing and expose her breasts and pelvic area. No prescription medications were found during the search.

In response to the search, Redding's mother sued the school in district court, where it was determined that the tip given to school officials by another student gave the vice principal just cause for strip-searching Redding. The strip search was ruled as not "excessively intrusive" in the case, a decision that a Ninth Circuit Court panel agreed with on appeal. However, when the full Ninth Circuit heard the case, the ruling was reversed. The action by the full Ninth Circuit court was based on the fact that a strip search is more intrusive than a simple bag search, or pocket search, and therefore probable cause, which the school did not have, was needed to conduct the strip search.

Not satisfied with the results of the appeal, the school district asked the Supreme Court to hear the case, citing the rise in the number of students who abuse prescription medications and over-the-counter drugs as a reason why such strip searches were necessary. The school district's petition asked the Court to review the Fourth Amendment as it relates to searching school children suspected of distributing drugs to other students at school and whether school officials should be given legal immunity when conducting such searches. The district rested most of its case on the social problem of drug abuse by young children. In its petition to the Supreme Court, the school district wrote, "Students have begun to experiment with drugs at a progressively earlier age. . . . [S]treet drugs used to be the primary concern. . . . Teens are now abusing prescription drugs far more than any illicit drug except marijuana." The school district also argued that the Ninth Circuit had been unreasonable in its judgment that schools need probable cause, rather than a reasonable suspicion, to justify a strip search, a situation, they maintained, that can prove confusing for school officials at all levels. In fact, the school district pointed out, this was exactly the idea that the Supreme Court overturned in its first school search case, *New Jersey v. T.L.O.*, in which the Court ruled that the principal who had searched a teenage girl's bag after she was caught smoking on school grounds had had reason to do so, therefore setting the reasonableness standard for searches of students, rather than a probable-cause standard.

In response, attorneys for Redding argued that to make their case for the search, the school had acted on "unreliable information" and that the search had traumatized Redding. They added that although another student had reported that Redding had distributed medication on school property, there was no hard evidence to prove that she was in fact involved in such activity.

SUPPORT FOR REDDING AND THE SCHOOL DISTRICT

School associations, including the American Association of School Administrators and National School Boards Association, became involved in the debate, urging the Supreme Court to take the case to provide more complete instructions to school districts on how they should properly deal with property and strip searches or what conditions they must meet to conduct such searches. These associations accused the Ninth Circuit of looking lightly upon the drug problem that is a part of many schools.

The Justice Department sent the court an *amicus* brief that stated that a new constitutional standard should be developed, specifically one that looks at strip searches as illegal under most circumstances. The new rule proposed by the Justice Department held, "Strip searches are impermissible in the public schools unless the officials reasonably suspect not only that the student possesses contraband but also that it is hidden in a place that such a search will reveal." Using this argument, the search of Redding would be ruled unconstitutional. The Justice Department also argued, however, that because the constitutionality of the strip search was not clear during the time the search was conducted, school officials should receive qualified immunity.

THE COURT'S DECISION

When hearing oral arguments, justices appeared disturbed by the idea that school officials should be able to subject students to exposing their private parts to school officials with whom they have daily contact. However, the question raised by both the school district and the justices was whether school officials should allow embarrassing strip searches or if they should take the risk that a student might be injured or killed while under school supervision. Justice David H. Souter said during oral arguments, "My thought process is I would rather have the kid embarrassed by a strip search, if we can't find anything short of that, than to have some other kids dead because the stuff is distributed at lunchtime and things go awry."

However, Souter, writing for the 8-1 majority, said that in this case, Redding's Fourth Amendment rights had been violated by the strip search. The majority also agreed with the Justice Department, deciding that school officials would receive qualified immunity because the question of constitutionality had not been determined at the time of the search.

The Court disagreed with the school district that the case of *New Jersey v. T.L.O.* could be used to justify its position. According to the *T.L.O.* opinion, the search must not be "excessively intrusive in light of the age and sex of the student and the nature of the infraction," of which the school district in *Redding* was in violation. "The content of the suspicion failed to match the degree of intrusion" and school officials were not able to provide evidence that the intrusiveness of their search was justified for "nondangerous school contraband." There was no reason, according to the Court, to believe that Redding was carrying drugs in her underwear or that the drugs she was suspected of possessing posed a serious danger. As for the *T.L.O.* argument,

> The . . . concern to limit a school search to reasonable scope required the support of reasonable suspicion of danger or of resort to underwear for hiding evidence of wrongdoing before a search can reasonably make the quantum leap from outer clothes and backpacks to exposure of intimate parts. The meaning of such a search, and the degradation its subject may reasonably feel, place a search that intrusive in a category of its own demanding its own specific suspicions.

Justice Clarence Thomas wrote an opinion in which he agreed in part with the majority and dissented in part. He wrote that there was no violation of Fourth Amendment rights. Justice Thomas said that although the Court agreed that the school could demonstrate "reasonable suspicion that Redding was in possession of drugs in violation of these policies," he believed that this "justified a search extending to any area where small pills could be concealed." Thomas wrote in his opinion that the decision of the majority could have a detrimental effect. "Redding would not have been the first person to conceal pills in her undergarments. Nor will she be the last after today's decision, which announces the safest place to secrete contraband in school."

Justices Ruth Bader Ginsburg and John Paul Stevens wrote separate opinions that agreed with the majority on the Fourth Amendment argument but disagreed with qualified immunity being given to school officials. Stevens called this "a case in which clearly established law meets clearly outrageous conduct." Ginsburg wrote that she found qualified immunity to be an inappropriate decision because, "In contrast to *T.L.O.*, where a teacher discovered a student smoking in the lavatory, and where the search was confined to the student's purse, the search of Redding involved her body and rested on the bare accusation of another student whose reliability the Assistant Principal had no reason to trust. The Court's opinion in *T.L.O.* plainly stated the controlling Fourth Amendment law: A search ordered by a school official, even if 'justified at its inception,' crosses the constitutional boundary if it becomes 'excessively intrusive in light of the age and sex of the student and nature of the infraction.'" In this case, Ginsburg said, the vice principal could not reasonably believe that the search he conducted was permitted by law, especially given Redding's age and gender.

—Heather Kerrigan

Following is the text of the U.S. Supreme Court's 5-4 decision of June 25, 2009, in Safford Unified School District v. Redding, *in which the Court ruled strip searches of public school students unconstitutional.*

Safford Unified School District v. Redding

June 25, 2009

No. 08–479

Safford Unified School District #1, et al., petitioners *v.* April Redding	}	On writ of certiorari to the United States Court of Appeals for the Ninth Circuit

[June 25, 2009]

JUSTICE SOUTER delivered the opinion of the Court.

The issue here is whether a 13-year-old student's Fourth Amendment right was violated when she was subjected to a search of her bra and underpants by school officials acting on reasonable suspicion that she had brought forbidden prescription and over-the-counter drugs to school. Because there were no reasons to suspect the drugs presented a danger or were concealed in her underwear, we hold that the search did violate the Constitution, but because there is reason to question the clarity with which the right was established, the official who ordered the unconstitutional search is entitled to qualified immunity from liability.

I

[Background on the case has been omitted.]

II

The Fourth Amendment "right of the people to be secure in their persons . . . against unreasonable searches and seizures" generally requires a law enforcement officer to have probable cause for conducting a search. "Probable cause exists where 'the facts and circumstances within [an officer's] knowledge and of which [he] had reasonably trustworthy information [are] sufficient in themselves to warrant a man of reasonable caution in the belief that' an offense has been or is being committed," *Brinegar* v. *United States*, 338 U.S. 160, 175-176 (1949) (quoting *Carroll* v. *United States*, 267 U.S. 132, 162 (1925)), and that evidence bearing on that offense will be found in the place to be searched.

In *T.L.O.*, we recognized that the school setting "requires some modification of the level of suspicion of illicit activity needed to justify a search," 469 U.S., at 340 and held that for searches by school officials "a careful balancing of governmental and private interests suggests that the public interest is best served by a Fourth Amendment standard of reasonableness that stops short of probable cause," *id.*, at 341. We have thus applied a standard of reasonable suspicion to determine the legality of a school administrator's search of a student, *id.*, at 342, 345, and have held that a school search "will be permissible in its scope when the measures adopted are reasonably related to the objectives of the search and not excessively intrusive in light of the age and sex of the student and the nature of the infraction," . . .

[Examples of reasonable suspicion cases have been omitted.]

III . . .

[Additional background on the case has been omitted.]

B

. . . The indignity of the search does not, of course, outlaw it, but it does implicate the rule of reasonableness as stated in *T.L.O.*, that "the search as actually conducted [be] reasonably related in scope to the circumstances which justified the interference in the first place." The scope will be permissible, that is, when it is "not excessively intrusive in light of the age and sex of the student and the nature of the infraction."

Here, the content of the suspicion failed to match the degree of intrusion. . . .

Nor could Wilson have suspected that Savana was hiding common painkillers in her underwear. . . .

In sum, what was missing from the suspected facts that pointed to Savana was any indication of danger to the students from the power of the drugs or their quantity, and any reason to suppose that Savana was carrying pills in her underwear. We think that the combination of these deficiencies was fatal to finding the search reasonable.

In so holding, we mean to cast no ill reflection on the assistant principal, for the record raises no doubt that his motive throughout was to eliminate drugs from his school and protect students from what Jordan Romero has gone through. . . .

We do mean, though, to make it clear that the *T.L.O.* concern to limit a school search to reasonable scope requires the support of reasonable suspicion of danger or of resort to underwear for hiding evidence of wrongdoing before a search can reasonably make the quantum leap from outer clothes and backpacks to exposure of intimate parts.

The meaning of such a search, and the degradation its subject may reasonably feel, place a search that intrusive in a category of its own demanding its own specific suspicions.

IV

A school official searching a student is "entitled to qualified immunity where clearly established law does not show that the search violated the Fourth Amendment." To be established clearly, however, there is no need that "the very action in question [have] previously been held unlawful." . . .

We think these differences of opinion from our own are substantial enough to require immunity for the school officials in this case. We would not suggest that entitlement to qualified immunity is the guaranteed product of disuniform views of the law in the other federal, or state, courts, and the fact that a single judge, or even a group of judges, disagrees about the contours of a right does not automatically render the law unclear if we have been clear. . . . We conclude that qualified immunity is warranted.

V

The strip search of Savana Redding was unreasonable and a violation of the Fourth Amendment, but petitioners Wilson, Romero, and Schwallier are nevertheless protected from liability through qualified immunity. Our conclusions here do not resolve, however, the question of the liability of petitioner Safford Unified School District #1 under *Monell* v. *New York City Dept. of Social Servs.,* 436 U.S. 658, 694 (1978), a claim the Ninth Circuit did not address. The judgment of the Ninth Circuit is therefore affirmed in part and reversed in part, and this case is remanded for consideration of the *Monell* claim.

It is so ordered.

JUSTICE STEVENS, with whom JUSTICE GINSBURG joins, concurring in part and dissenting in part.

In *New Jersey* v. *T.L.O.,* 469 U.S. 325 (1985), the Court established a two-step inquiry for determining the reasonableness of a school official's decision to search a student. First, the Court explained, the search must be "'justified at its inception'" by the presence of "reasonable grounds for suspecting that the search will turn up evidence that the student has violated or is violating either the law or the rules of the school." Second, the search must be "permissible in its scope," which is achieved "when the measures adopted are reasonably related to the objectives of the search and *not excessively intrusive in light of the age and sex of the student and the nature of the infraction.*"

Nothing the Court decides today alters this basic framework. . . .

The Court reaches a contrary conclusion about qualified immunity based on the fact that various Courts of Appeals have adopted seemingly divergent views about *T.L.O.*'s application to strip searches. . . .

The Court of Appeals properly rejected the school official's qualified immunity defense, and I would affirm that court's judgment in its entirety.

JUSTICE GINSBURG, concurring in part and dissenting in part.

I agree with the Court that Assistant Principal Wilson's subjection of 13-year-old Savana Redding to a humiliating strip down search violated the Fourth Amendment. But

I also agree with JUSTICE STEVENS, *ante,* at 1–2, that our opinion in *New Jersey* v. *T.L.O,* 469 U.S. 325 (1985), "clearly established" the law governing this case. . . .

[A discussion on the differences between the Redding and T.L.O. cases has been omitted.]

JUSTICE THOMAS, concurring in the judgment in part and dissenting in part.

I agree with the Court that the judgment against the school officials with respect to qualified immunity should be reversed. Unlike the majority, however, I would hold that the search of Savana Redding did not violate the Fourth Amendment. The majority imposes a vague and amorphous standard on school administrators. It also grants judges sweeping authority to second-guess the measures that these officials take to maintain discipline in their schools and ensure the health and safety of the students in their charge. This deep intrusion into the administration of public schools exemplifies why the Court should return to the common-law doctrine of *in loco parentis* under which "the judiciary was reluctant to interfere in the routine business of school administration, allowing schools and teachers to set and enforce rules and to maintain order." . . .

I

"Although the underlying command of the Fourth Amendment is always that searches and seizures be reasonable, what is reasonable depends on the context within which a search takes place." Thus, although public school students retain Fourth Amendment rights under this Court's precedent, those rights "are different . . . than elsewhere; the 'reasonableness' inquiry cannot disregard the schools' custodial and tutelary responsibility for children." . . .

A

A "search of a student by a teacher or other school official will be 'justified at its inception' when there are reasonable grounds for suspecting that the search will turn up evidence that the student has violated or is violating either the law or the rules of the school." . . .

[Discussion of why the search was justifiable has been omitted.]

B

The remaining question is whether the search was reasonable in scope. Under *T.L.O.,* "a search will be permissible in its scope when the measures adopted are reasonably related to the objectives of the search and not excessively intrusive in light of the age and sex of the student and the nature of the infraction." The majority concludes that the school officials' search of Redding's underwear was not "'reasonably related in scope to the circumstances which justified the interference in the first place,'" . . . notwithstanding the officials' reasonable suspicion that Redding "was involved in pill distribution." . . .

1

The majority finds that "subjective and reasonable societal expectations of personal privacy support . . . treat[ing]" this type of search, which it labels a "strip search," as "categorically distinct, requiring distinct elements of justification on the part of school authorities for going beyond a search of clothing and belongings." Thus, in the majority's view, although the school officials had reasonable suspicion to believe that Redding had the pills on her person, see *ante*, at 7, they needed some greater level of particularized suspicion to conduct this "strip search." There is no support for this contortion of the Fourth Amendment.

The Court has generally held that the reasonableness of a search's scope depends only on whether it is limited to the area that is capable of concealing the object of the search . . .

[Further discussion of the scope of the strip search has been omitted.]

2

The majority compounds its error by reading the "nature of the infraction" aspect of the *T.L.O.* test as a license to limit searches based on a judge's assessment of a particular school policy. According to the majority, the scope of the search was impermissible because the school official "must have been aware of the nature and limited threat of the specific drugs he was searching for" and because he "had no reason to suspect that large amounts of the drugs were being passed around, or that individual students were receiving great numbers of pills." *Ante*, at 9-10. Thus, in order to locate a rationale for finding a Fourth Amendment violation in this case, the majority retreats from its observation that the school's firm no-drug policy "makes sense, and there is no basis to claim that the search was unreasonable owing to some defect or coming of the rule it was aimed at enforcing."

Even accepting the majority's assurances that it is not attacking the rule's reasonableness, it certainly is attacking the rule's importance. This approach directly conflicts with *T.L.O.* in which the Court was "unwilling to adopt a standard under which the legality of a search is dependent upon a judge's evaluation of the relative importance of school rules." Indeed, the Court in *T.L.O.* expressly rejected the proposition that the majority seemingly endorses—that "some rules regarding student conduct are by nature too 'trivial' to justify a search based upon reasonable suspicion."

The majority's decision in this regard also departs from another basic principle of the Fourth Amendment: that law enforcement officials can enforce with the same vigor all rules and regulations irrespective of the perceived importance of any of those rules. . . .

[Discussion of who is best suited to make decisions on school policies has been omitted.]

3

Even if this Court were authorized to second-guess the importance of school rules, the Court's assessment of the importance of this district's policy is flawed. It is a crime to possess or use prescription-strength Ibuprofen without a prescription. . . .

[Further information on use of prescription drugs without a prescription has been omitted.]

School administrators can reasonably conclude that this high rate of drug abuse is being fueled, at least in part, by the increasing presence of prescription drugs on school campuses. In a 2008 survey, "44 percent of teens sa[id] drugs are used, kept or sold on the grounds of their schools." The risks posed by the abuse of these drugs are every bit as serious as the dangers of using a typical street drug.

Teenagers are nevertheless apt to "believe the myth that these drugs provide a medically safe high." . . .

Admittedly, the Ibuprofen and Naproxen at issue in this case are not the prescription painkillers at the forefront of the prescription-drug-abuse problem. . . .

If a student with a previously unknown intolerance to Ibuprofen or Naproxen were to take either drug and become ill, the public outrage would likely be directed toward the school for failing to take steps to prevent the unmonitored use of the drug. . . .

* * *

In determining whether the search's scope was reasonable under the Fourth Amendment, it is therefore irrelevant whether officials suspected Redding of possessing prescription-strength Ibuprofen, nonprescription-strength Naproxen, or some harder street drug. Safford prohibited its possession on school property. Reasonable suspicion that Redding was in possession of drugs in violation of these policies, therefore, justified a search extending to any area where small pills could be concealed. The search did not violate the Fourth Amendment.

II

By declaring the search unreasonable in this case, the majority has "'surrender[ed] control of the American public school system to public school students'" by invalidating school policies that treat all drugs equally and by second-guessing swift disciplinary decisions made by school officials. . . .

. . . So empowered, schoolteachers and administrators had almost complete discretion to establish and enforce the rules they believed were necessary to maintain control over their classrooms. The perils of judicial policymaking inherent in applying Fourth Amendment protections to public schools counsel in favor of a return to the understanding that existed in this Nation's first public schools, which gave teachers discretion to craft the rules needed to carry out the disciplinary responsibilities delegated to them by parents.

If the common-law view that parents delegate to teachers their authority to discipline and maintain order were to be applied in this case, the search of Redding would stand. There can be no doubt that a parent would have had the authority to conduct the search at issue in this case. . . .

Restoring the common-law doctrine of *in loco parentis* would not, however, leave public schools entirely free to impose any rule they choose. "If parents do not like the rules imposed by those schools, they can seek redress in school boards or legislatures; they can send their children to private schools or home school them; or they can simply move." Indeed, parents and local government officials have proved themselves quite capable of challenging overly harsh school rules or the enforcement of sensible rules in insensible ways. . . .

[Examples of schools changing policies have been omitted.]

These local efforts to change controversial school policies through democratic processes have proven successful in many cases. . . .

In the end, the task of implementing and amending public school policies is beyond this Court's function. . . .

III

"[T]he nationwide drug epidemic makes the war against drugs a pressing concern in every school." And yet the Court has limited the authority of school officials to conduct searches for the drugs that the officials believe pose a serious safety risk to their students. By doing so, the majority has confirmed that a return to the doctrine of *in loco parentis* is required to keep the judiciary from essentially seizing control of public schools. Only then will teachers again be able to "'govern the[ir] pupils, quicken the slothful, spur the indolent, restrain the impetuous, and control the stubborn'" by making "'rules, giv[ing] commands, and punish[ing] disobedience'" without interference from judges. By deciding that it is better equipped to decide what behavior should be permitted in schools, the Court has undercut student safety and undermined the authority of school administrators and local officials. Even more troubling, it has done so in a case in which the underlying response by school administrators was reasonable and justified. I cannot join this regrettable decision. I, therefore, respectfully dissent from the Court's determination that this search violated the Fourth Amendment.

SOURCE: U.S. Supreme Court. *Safford Unified School District v. Redding,* 557 U.S. ___ (2009). www.supreme courtus.gov/opinions/08pdf/08-479.pdf.

OTHER HISTORIC DOCUMENTS OF INTEREST

FROM THIS VOLUME

FROM PREVIOUS *HISTORIC DOCUMENTS*

Political Crisis in Honduras

JUNE 29 AND JULY 25, 2009

On June 28, 2009, the democratically elected president of Honduras, Manuel Zelaya, was ousted from power in a military-backed coup d'état. In the months before his removal from office, Zelaya had become embroiled in a conflict between the government and its opponents, namely the military and the judiciary. The tensions stemmed from Zelaya's proposal to hold a "popular consultation," a nonbinding referendum, on constitutional reform. The referendum, which was due to take place on June 28, would have asked Hondurans to decide if a question asking whether a constitutional assembly should be convened could be added to the ballot at the next general election in November 2009. The purpose of convening a constitutional assembly would have been to reform the country's constitution, which does not allow a president to seek a second term in office. Opponents saw Zelaya's moves as a thinly veiled attempt to rewrite the constitution, paving the way for his (potential) reelection.

HONDURAS'S MILITARY COUP

The president's attempt to hold a referendum had been spurred by the Honduran supreme court, which had ruled that a so-called popular consultation was illegal. The Honduran Congress subsequently backed the supreme court's decision. Despite this, Zelaya remained committed to holding the referendum and demanded the military's support. (The Honduran military is tasked with distributing ballots and maintaining security during elections.) However, the commander of Honduras's military forces, General Romeo Vásquez, refused and was subsequently fired by Zelaya. On June 26, the supreme court ruled that the firing of Vásquez was invalid and reinstated him. Furthermore, the supreme court issued a warrant for Zelaya's arrest, charging him with abuse of power and treason, among other offenses.

Some of the details of the military coup that followed two days later are not entirely clear. Zelaya maintains that he was "kidnapped" by military personnel and flown to Costa Rica on Honduran military aircraft. However, his opponents assert that they had a resignation letter from the ousted president, a claim that Zelaya steadfastly denies. Immediately after the coup, Zelaya was replaced in office by the head of the legislature, Roberto Micheletti, who under Honduran law was next in the line of succession. Despite hailing from the same party, the ruling Partido Liberal (PL), Micheletti was a known political rival of the deposed president. Micheletti denies that the ousting of Zelaya was a coup, instead arguing that the president was relieved of office by a judicial order after conspiring to hold a referendum that was ruled unconstitutional by the supreme court.

The coup received widespread condemnation from governments around the world. The Organization of American States, a regional body tasked with monitoring countries' adherence to democratic principles in the region, subsequently suspended Honduras's membership, while all countries in the region refused to recognize the interim administration and recalled their ambassadors. Meanwhile, the political crisis triggered financial problems for the country, which is heavily reliant on international aid. Both the World Bank and the Inter-American Development Bank suspended their financing to Honduras in the aftermath of the coup, while on September 8 the International Monetary Fund (IMF) decided to withhold funds until a decision was made as to whether it would recognize the interim administration. In addition, the Honduras-based Banco Centroamericano de Integración Económica (Central American Bank for Economic Integration) halted its disbursement of funds, leading to the suspension of numerous development projects in the country.

ATTEMPTS AT NEGOTIATIONS

Zelaya attempted to return to Honduras on July 5, but the interim government blocked the runways at the airport in the capital, Tegucigalpa, preventing the former president's plane from landing. Micheletti warned Zelaya that he would be arrested if he was successful in entering the country. In the days that followed, the president of Costa Rica, Oscar Arias, attempted to broker a deal between Zelaya and Micheletti and his supporters. However, the interim president remained steadfast in his opposition to Zelaya's return to office, even if presidential powers were curtailed. Zelaya was similarly stubborn in his demand that he be reinstated as president, and the negotiations quickly collapsed.

A subsequent round of negotiations, held in Costa Rica on July 18 and 19, was also unsuccessful. An agreement put forth by Arias proposed that Zelaya return to his former position until his term in office ended on January 27, 2010. The so-called Acuerdo de San José also recommended that a national reconciliation government preside over the country until a new president took office in late January. The reconciliation government would include members of both of the country's main political parties, the PL and the opposition Partido Nacional (PN). The proposition also included a provision for a general amnesty for political crimes to prevent a witch hunt for individuals involved in planning and executing the coup. Zelaya accepted the terms of the agreement, but Micheletti and his interim government again refused to budge on the issue of the former president's return to office. As the two sides were unable to come to an agreement on this key issue, negotiations were once again shelved. Zelaya's government called on the United States for assistance in late July, asking President Barack Obama to help restore constitutional rule to the nation. "We believe that the measures that we are asking the U.S. administration to take will exercise direct pressure on the perpetrators of the coup without causing any sort of negative impact on the people of Honduras," said Enrique Reina, Zelaya's ambassador designee to the United States. Despite the political crisis, plans remained in place to hold the general election in late November 2009; campaigning began in early September. Many observers argued that a free and fair election was the only way to end the country's international isolation, although it was feared that the results of the election would not be recognized internationally. The main opposition PN fared well in the polls in the run-up to the election, reflecting in large part the public's belief that the ruling PL was responsible for the political crisis. The presidential candidate for the PN, Porfirio "Pepe" Lobo Sosa, insisted that he stood for "new politics" and was committed to leading a united national government. Meanwhile, the PL's presidential candidate, Elvin Santos, struggled to gain voter support. Supporters of the PL had divided their support between rival factions within the party, leaving Santos hard-pressed to make gains in the polls.

Zelaya Returns to Honduras

On September 21, Zelaya unexpectedly returned to Honduras and sought refuge in the Brazilian embassy. Zelaya then called for his supporters to demonstrate in the streets. The interim administration reacted by sending riot police to disperse demonstrators, imposing a curfew and shutting down the country's airports. In addition, police surrounded the Brazilian embassy and cut off the building's supply of electricity and water as well as its telephone lines. The Brazilian government called the Honduran administration's moves a breach of international law and a violation of its territory.

Entangling Brazil in the political controversy forced the U.S. government, which had previously been hesitant to intervene, into action. On October 28, high-level diplomats, including the U.S. assistant secretary of state for Western Hemisphere affairs, Thomas Shannon, and the National Security Council's representative for the Western Hemisphere, Dan Restrepo, arrived in Honduras to help negotiate an agreement. The deal envisaged Zelaya's return to office; the creation of a national unity government; a truth commission to investigate the events surrounding the coup; and an agreement by all Honduran political parties to honor the outcome of the November election. If these conditions were met, international aid inflows would resume and various international sanctions would be lifted. Micheletti's interim government stipulated that the agreement would only be valid if both the legislature and the supreme court agreed to the terms.

Both Zelaya and Micheletti agreed to the terms, the former undoubtedly assuming that Congress and the supreme court would allow him to return to office prior to the November 29 election and finish out his term. However, in late October, Congress delayed the vote on the reinstatement of Zelaya until December 2—after the general election scheduled for November 29. Moreover, the Micheletti administration did not include any of Zelaya's political allies in the national unity government. As a result, with just weeks until the election, the former president pulled out of the accord and called on his supporters to boycott the polls.

As was widely expected, Lobo was victorious in the November election. In the days following, Congress voted overwhelmingly not to restore Zelaya to power for the remainder of his term. This left the former president with little choice but to determine an appropriate exit strategy from Honduras. In due course, Zelaya requested that the interim administration allow him safe passage to Mexico. However, owing to a disagreement over Zelaya's status—he wanted to travel as a "distinguished guest" of Mexico, but the interim administration insisted that instead he be labeled a political refugee—his request was denied by the Honduran authorities. The former president was expected to leave the country by the time Lobo took office, although it was unclear how this would be accomplished. Zelaya feared arrest if he left the Brazilian embassy, and was therefore unlikely to do so without first being granted amnesty. A bill before the Honduran Congress could give him just that. The legislation would offer amnesty to any individual involved in the events surrounding the coup.

—Hilary Ewing

Following is a release from the UN General Assembly on June 29, 2009, express-
ing outrage about the coup d'état in Honduras, and a statement released by the
Honduran embassy in Washington, D.C., on July 25, 2009, calling on President
Barack Obama to help restore constitutional rule in Honduras.

UN General Assembly Responds to Coup d'État in Honduras

June 29, 2009

With a heavy heart and a sense of outrage, General Assembly President Miguel d'Escoto Brockmann today urged the world community to consider ways to effect the peaceful restoration of Honduran President Jose Manuel Zelaya, as he convened a meeting of the Assembly to consider the situation following that leader's ouster by a military-led coup d'état Sunday.

"This is a throwback to another era that we hoped was now a distant nightmare," Mr. d'Escoto said, stressing that Central America's record as the world's most coup-filled region had no place in the twenty-first century.

Describing those bloody, oppressive years as "lost years" in the region's development, he said it was appropriate and crucial for the world community, as the "G-192," to underscore the coup's illegality and stand as one in their condemnation. To that end, he had invited President Zelaya, who was exiled to Costa Rica, to personally update the General Assembly on the situation in Honduras. That offer had been accepted and an address scheduled for 11 A.M. tomorrow.

Turning to the reasons cited by the military for its actions, he stressed that President Zelaya's call for an amendment to extend the limits of a presidential term was not illegitimate. Indeed, other countries in the region had done so through various plebiscites. President Zelaya's removal ran counter to the democratic trends in the region and he remained "the only legitimate and constitutional head of the Honduran Government."

Saying he represented Jose Manuel Zelaya, the "true President of Honduras," the Permanent Representative of Honduras to the United Nations emphasized that his Government's mandate to govern had been gained in fully transparent elections. A non-binding referendum on constitutional issues, that was to have taken placed on Sunday, was an insufficient motive for violating the constitutional order of the country. The President had, in fact, aimed to strengthen the country's constitution and democracy.

He hoped the Assembly would, as many other countries and regional groups already had, universally condemn the coup d'état by forces that opposed the will [of] the people.

It should also avoid recognizing any illegitimate Government that might be proclaimed through the coup. A resolution on this matter would be tabled as soon as possible.

During the meeting, which was convened amidst the ongoing Conference on the World Financial and Economic Crisis and Its Impact on Development, over two dozen speakers took the floor to condemn President Zelaya's ouster. Among them, the representative of Venezuela, who spoke on behalf of the Bolivarian Alliance for the Americas, demanded the immediate return of the rule of law and restoration of the President's functions. He called on the Honduran armed forces to immediately return to their headquarters and avoid any incident that might lead to bloodshed.

Calling the weekend's events in Honduras an "anachronism," Guatemala's representative stressed the progress the region as a whole, and Honduras in particular, had made on the road to peace and democracy. The laws and Constitution of Honduras contained mechanisms for resolving differences between the State's different powers within an institutional framework and, to that end, the use of force by the Honduran armed forces to resolve such differences was to be condemned.

Joining the 20 other speakers from the Americas in rejecting the coup, the United States delegate said her country had also joined its colleagues in the Organization of American States yesterday in condemning the coup. United States President Barack Obama had also called on all actors to resolve any dispute peacefully through dialogue and free of any outside influence. Her country would continue to work through the Organization of American States to help the Honduran people.

Nicaragua's representative urged the people of Honduras to arm themselves with courage and let the "putschists" know that their time had passed. All of America, both North and South, rejected their coup, and no more banana republics where oligarchs could continue to exploit the people with impunity existed. Although they claimed to be acting in support of democracy, they acted with bare-faced illogic that went against the region's recent democratic history.

She particularly condemned the abduction of Patricia Rodas, the Foreign Minister of Honduras, as well as the kidnapping of the ambassadors of Cuba, Venezuela and Nicaragua. That flagrant violation of international law was an act of aggression against each respective country that would not go unpunished.

Also speaking were the representatives of Mexico (on behalf of the Rio Group), Czech Republic (on behalf of the European Union), Chile (on behalf of the Union of South American Nations), Cuba (on behalf of the Non-Aligned Movement), Jamaica (on behalf of the Caribbean Community), Dominican Republic, Bahrain (on behalf of the Arab Group), Brazil, Ecuador, Algeria, Bolivia, Argentina, Colombia, Saint Vincent and the Grenadines, El Salvador, Spain, Costa Rica, Panama, Belize, Peru, Uruguay and Cape Verde.

The General Assembly will reconvene to take action on the reports of its Fifth Committee (Administrative and Budgetary) at 10 A.M. on Tuesday, 30 June, after which it will hear an address by the President of Honduras and act on a related resolution.

BACKGROUND

The General Assembly this morning reopened to consider agenda item 20 entitled "The situation in Central America: progress in forming a region of peace, freedom, democracy and development" in response to the situation in Honduras.

Statements

Assembly President Miguel d'Escoto Brockmann said he called the meeting with a heavy heart and, indeed, a sense of outrage, so that the world community might consider ways for the peaceful restoration of Honduran President Jose Manuel Zelaya, who was ousted in a coup d'état Sunday.

"This is a throwback to another era that we hoped was now a distant nightmare," he said, stressing that Central America's record as the world's most coup-filled region had no place in the twenty-first century. As a Nicaraguan, he expressed shame that the coup d'état had taken place during his term at the head of the General Assembly.

Briefly outlining the history of the region's coups in the 1970s and 1980s, he said they had been bloody, oppressive years that represented lost years in the region's development. Against the recent trends of democracy in the region, armed men had forced President Zelaya into exile in Costa Rica on Sunday morning. The region had responded with outrage, demanding the Government's immediate restoration. Regional groups, as well as leaders around the world, had also done so. It was appropriate and crucial for the world community, in the "G-192," to underscore the illegality of this crime, standing as one in their condemnation.

President Zelaya's call for an amendment to extend the limits of a presidential term was not, he stressed, illegitimate. Indeed, other countries in the region had done so through various plebiscites. Moreover, the peoples of the world should be allowed to choose their Governments. Underlining his total and unconditional solidarity with President Zelaya and calling him "the only legitimate and constitutional Head of the Honduran Government," he said he had already sent a letter to President Zelaya inviting him to come and update the General Assembly on the situation in Honduras.

JORGE ARTURO REINA IDIAQUEZ (*Honduras*) said he came before the Assembly at a tragic moment, but he was sure it would be a transitory one and the country would emerge strengthened. He represented the true President of Honduras, Manuel Zelaya. It was a pity that the coup d'état had come on the scene at this time. But, once again forces that were opposed to democracy and the will of the people had a lease on life. It was not pleasant to denounce a violation of a Government. The Government had a mandate to govern that was gained in fully transparent elections.

Civilization as we know it today would not exist without democracy. His country had lost its democratic system of government. A coup against the legitimate President, President Zelaya, had sent him, in the middle of the night, into a neighbouring country, and his human rights had been violated. A non-binding referendum on constitutional issues, that was to have taken placed [*sic*] on Sunday, was not enough motive to have very conservative forces violate the constitutional order of the country, he said. There was not enough violent motive to violate the country's Constitution and laws. The President had aimed to strengthen the Constitution and democracy of the country.

Honduras hoped that the Assembly would, as many other countries and regional groups already had, universally condemn the coup d'état in Honduras. He hoped that the President would be restored and that human rights would be upheld and no other Government would be recognized that would be born through this coup. He was very thankful to many countries, especially Costa Rica, for their support. He called for the saving of the life of the President and his family and upholding the rights of all

Hondurans; the return of the President; and that any illegitimate Government that tried to take the place of the present Government not be accepted.

JORGE VALERO (*Venezuela*), speaking on behalf of the Bolivarian Alliance for the Americas, rejected and condemned the coup d'état against President Jose Manuel Zeyala, the constitutional President of Honduras, launched by the armed forces in connivance with reactionary forces. He demanded the immediate return of the rule of law and restoration of the President's functions. His delegation did not—and would not—recognize any Government that was not the democratically elected Government of President Zeyala, and he urged that the international community not recognize any other Government in Honduras. He called on the Honduran armed forces to immediately return to their headquarters and avoid any incident that might lead to bloodshed. He denounced the kidnapping of the Honduran Foreign Minister and other prominent Honduran figures, and demanded full respect for the dignity of President Zelaya's family and all members of the Honduran Government. He expressed solidarity with civic demonstrations by Hondurans, who called for the return of President Zeyala, and unconditional solidarity with President Zeyala.

Speaking next in his national capacity, he expressed Venezuela's support to the Government of President Zelaya and demanded that the coup d'état-instated Government step down. That Government should not be recognized and he demanded President Zeyala's immediate return. He congratulated the General Assembly President for calling the meeting today and supporting a process of change. In the Americas, the "time of the peoples" was dawning; a new world was emerging and it was breaking the mould of corrupt political groups that oppressed people—neo-liberal dictatorships that denied human rights. New, plural forms of democracy were being built—participatory democracies. That process would not come to a halt over the coup d'état in Honduras. Countries must help stop this attempt to turn a regressive tide in history.

Describing past events of torture and murder in the region, he said hope was coming to life again and Honduras would decide the future. That was why Honduras could not be allowed to fall into the hands of oligarchs that had no country to call their own. Coups d'état would not end democratic progress taking place on the continent. A spark of peace had been ignited—it was a message in the name of the Earth that said no to death and yes to hope. Humankind would free itself and no army or tyrant would be able to overcome that. President Zeyala had been deposed because he wanted to consult the people and pave the way for open participation—oligarchies feared that, which was why they were conspiring in various countries in the hemisphere. Venezuela did not and would not accept any President other than President Zelaya. Democracy had taken deep root in Honduras and would emerge strengthened after this process. He expressed Venezuela's firm solidarity with Hondurans. In closing, he called for an international front against fascism.

CLAUDE HELLER (*Mexico*), speaking on behalf of the Rio Group, said the coup had breached the democratic order of Honduras. The Rio Group rejected the use of the armed forces and the arbitrary detention of the head of the Government. This breach was unacceptable and inadmissible and was a practice that the countries of the region had categorically rejected. The Rio Group reiterated its adherence to the rule of law, which it believed should transcend any political difference. The immediate order of the Honduran Government should be returned immediately and the constitutional President restored, as should all constitutional powers.

He went on to say that the Organization of American States (OAS) had also agreed on a statement condemning the coup and had called for President Zelaya's immediate return. No Government issuing from this breach would be recognized. The Organization's permanent council had also condemned all acts of violence, including the arbitrary detention of members of the Honduran Government's Cabinet. He had been tasked with submitting this statement to the General Assembly of the United Nations.

MARTIN PALOUŠ (*Czech Republic*), speaking on behalf of the European Union, said he strongly condemned the coup that violated the constitutional order of Honduras. He urged the immediate release of the President and called on all to refrain from violence. He said that all activities should be carried out in accordance with the rule of law. The European Union called for the restoration of the political situation in the country, and called for fair and transparent elections in 2009.

HERALDO MUÑOZ (*Chile*), speaking on behalf of the Union of South American Nations (UNASUR), vehemently rejected the attempted coup d'état in Honduras, giving his fullest support to President Zeyala. His delegation did not recognize any situation that breached the rule of law or jeopardized stability. He objected to the President's kidnapping and expressed his delegation's determination not to recognize any Government other than that of democratically elected President Zeyala. He called for the restoration of democracy and the President, saying that internal conflicts should be solved only in the framework of democratic institutions and the rule of law.

Speaking in his national capacity, he said Chile's declaration, made yesterday, emphatically condemned the coup d'état in Honduras, which flouted the provisions of the Organization of American States. His Government called for the restoration of democracy and immediate reinstatement of the legitimately elected President, Jose Manuel Zeyala.

In his as [*sic*] role as chairman of the Coordinating Bureau of the Non-Aligned Movement (NAM), ABELARDO MORENO (*Cuba*) said the Bureau's 118 members strongly condemned the coup d'état carried out against the constitutional President of Honduras, a sister nation that was a member of the Non-Aligned Movement. The Bureau rejected the breach of the democratic constitutional order that had taken place in Honduras and called upon the international community to strongly condemn the coup. It called for the reinstatement of the rule of law in that country and the immediate and unconditional reinstatement of the legitimate representative of the Honduran people, President Zelaya.

Speaking on behalf of the Cuban people and Government, he called for the immediate reinstatement of the rule of law in Honduras. The coup had prevented an important democratic referendum from taking place in Honduras on Sunday. He said the Foreign Minister, Patricia Rodas, and the Ambassadors of Cuba, Nicaragua, and Venezuela were kidnapped and beaten by the pro-coup military. Other members of the Honduran constitutional Government and their relatives were facing persecution. Cuba called upon all States and members of the international community to condemn the coup and demand the reinstatement of the rule of law in that country and the immediate and unconditional return and full reinstatement of the only legitimate representative of the Honduran people, President Manuel Zelaya.

MARIA RUBIALES DE CHAMORRO (*Nicaragua*), joining her voice to statements made on behalf of the Rio Group, Bolivarian Alliance for the Americas and the Non-Aligned Movement, said that today, Central America had committed itself to never again allowing such aggression as a coup d'état to take place in its region. The President had been humiliated by a group of armed mercenaries in the payment of the oligarchy. Nicaragua vigorously condemned the coup and would spare no effort in ensuring that the President was restored to his position. She called on the people of Honduras to arm themselves with courage and let the "putschists" know that their time had passed. All of America, both North and South, rejected their coup.

Calling for respect for the rule of law and the immediate return of the only constitutional leader of Honduras, she stressed that the people of Honduras should further be aware that last night the Bolivarian Alliance for the Americas had met in Managua, where it unequivocally condemned the coup. There were no more banana republics where oligarchs could continue to exploit the people with impunity. While these people said they acted in support of democracy, they acted with bare-faced illogic that went against the region's recent history. All Cabinet members should be released, as should all citizens. She condemned the abduction of the Foreign Minister of Honduras as well as the kidnapping of the ambassadors of Cuba, Venezuela and Nicaragua. This flagrant violation of international law was an act of aggression against each respective country that would not go unpunished. Above all, the main breach was against the Honduran democracy. Nothing would quell the desire of the Honduran people for the liberty of which they were currently deprived. . . .

[Statements by other UN delegates have been omitted.]

SOURCE: UN General Assembly. Press release. "General Assembly President Expresses Outrage at Coup D'etat in Honduras, Says Crucial for World Community to 'Stand as One' in Condemnation." June 29, 2009. www.un.org/News/Press/docs/2009/ga10840.doc.htm.

Honduran President Zelaya Calls on United States to Help Restore Rule in Honduras

July 25, 2009

With the aim of restoring constitutional order and ending the repression and violation of human rights taking place in Honduras, president Manuel Zelaya has asked president Barack Obama to take a series of concrete measures directed at the main perpetrators of the military coup of June 28, 2009. In a letter sent to the U.S. head of state, via the State Department, the constitutional president of Honduras has requested that the U.S. administration prohibit the bank transactions and cancel the U.S. visas of those "directly responsible for my abduction and the interruption of constitutional order in my country."

President Zelaya has sent to President Obama the list of the individuals who these specific measures should be directed towards. This list includes the following individuals:

- Division General Romeo Vásquez Velázquez, head of the Joint Chiefs of Staff of the Armed Forces of Honduras

- Brigadier General Miguel Angel Garcia Padget, commanding general of the Army

- Rear Admiral Juan Pablo Rodriguez, commanding general of the Navy

- Brigadier General Luis Javier Prince Suazo, commanding general of the Air Force

- Roberto Micheletti, President of the National Congress

- Luis Alberto Rubí, Attorney General of Honduras

- Rosa America Miranda, Public Prosecutor of Honduras

These individuals, who played a key role in planning and executing the June 28th coup, have thus far disregarded the international community's calls for the immediate and unconditional return of President Zelaya to his constitutional post. Furthermore, while President Zelaya agreed to Costa Rican President Oscar Arias' framework agreement that would have allowed for the rapid restitution of democracy in Honduras, the coup regime, headed by Roberto Micheletti, has systematically rejected to compromise in any way.

Given the continued deterioration of the human rights situation in Honduras, with for instance a growing number of extrajudicial killings of leaders of the popular movements opposed to the coup, the constitutional government of Honduras considers it urgent for the U.S. and other countries to step up their efforts to pressure the coup regime.

"We believe that the measures that we are asking the U.S. administration to take will exercise direct pressure on the perpetrators of the coup without causing any sort of negative impact on the people of Honduras," said Enrique Reina, the Communications Minister of Honduras' constitutional government, and President Zelaya's new ambassador designee to the U.S.

SOURCE: Embassy of Honduras, Washington, D.C. Press release. "Honduran President Manuel Zelaya Asks President Barack Obama to Take Further Measures to Help Restore Constitutional Rule in Honduras." July 25, 2009. http://hondurasemb.org.

OTHER HISTORIC DOCUMENTS OF INTEREST

FROM PREVIOUS *HISTORIC DOCUMENTS*

U.S. Supreme Court on Civil Rights Act in Hiring Practices

JUNE 29, 2009

In New Haven, Connecticut, during the fall of 2003, the city offered a promotion exam for firefighters to fill vacant captain and lieutenant positions. More than one hundred firefighters took the test, but all of the scores—and the test itself—were thrown out because none of the twenty-seven African American firefighters who had taken the exam passed, meaning none qualified for a promotion.

In response, seventeen white firefighters and one Hispanic firefighter sued the city on the grounds of reverse discrimination. New Haven argued that it was trying to follow the federal law that looks suspiciously on exams and job qualifications that give a disadvantage to majorities.

The Supreme Court ruled 5-4 in *Ricci v. DeStefano* that white firefighters had been discriminated against by New Haven by not being allowed the chance at a promotion after qualifying based on the test. The Court considered the city to be in violation of Title VII of the Civil Rights Act, which seeks to prevent African Americans from unfairly losing out on employment opportunities to white candidates. When the law was originally passed, Congress was attempting to stop discriminatory hiring practices that had been prevalent for decades, especially in police forces and firefighting.

A REVERSED RULING

The federal judge who first heard the case ruled in favor of New Haven, saying, "The decision to disregard the test results affected all applicants equally." In her forty-eight-page opinion, U.S. district court judge Janet Bond Arterton said that taking the test never guaranteed a promotion; it only offered the possibility of one.

The firefighters in the lawsuit alleged that the department gave in to pressure from city government to increase diversity among the leadership at the fire department. There was no indication, they said, that any part of the test caused the eight African Americans vying for captain and the nineteen vying for lieutenant to fail.

Before the U.S. district court, New Haven officials said that they threw the test out because no black applicant would be eligible for a promotion, therefore affecting black applicants disproportionately. In response, Arterton said the city was correct in using this method to be sensitive to the issue of race. "New Haven did not race-norm the scores. . . . [T]hey simply decided to start over. While the evidence shows that race was taken into account in the decision not to certify the test results, the result was race neutral: all the test results were discarded," said Arterton.

Judge Arterton argued that although some might look at New Haven as simply a city trying to escape criticism and lawsuits from minority applicants, the actual motive of the city, to increase diversity in the highest ranks of the fire department, were legal. There was no reason for the city to have to explain why the test did not reflect positively on white, Hispanic, and African American candidates alike. It only mattered, in Judge Arterton's opinion, that based on federal guidelines, discrimination would have to be assumed because the African American applicants would have been promoted at a rate of less than 80 percent of the white applicants. In the case of this exam, the African American applicants passed the test at half the rate of the white applicants. New Haven would not have been able to promote low-testing applicants to increase racial equality because the city's charter requires a "rule of three" in which the positions must be offered to the top three exam scorers when they become available.

More than one and a half years later, the district court's decision was appealed and the case went to the Second U.S. Circuit Court of Appeals, which reached the same conclusion as Judge Arterton. The panel's one-paragraph decision complemented Arterton's decision and said, "We are not unsympathetic to the plaintiffs' expression of frustration." The panel commented specifically on Ricci and his struggle with dyslexia in preparing for the exam. Ricci came in sixth on the test. The city, however, acted appropriately, according to the panel. Supreme Court associate justice Sonia Sotomayor was at the time a member of the three-judge panel that released this opinion, which became a point of contention during her confirmation hearings, as conservatives tried to argue that Sotomayor would reflexively be on the side of minorities in cases before the Court.

The debate among the judges was particularly contentious, with six of the thirteen on the full Second Circuit voting to re-hear the case. The dissent was twelve pages long and scolded the majority for not releasing a full opinion on the case. "This court has failed to grapple with the questions of exceptional importance raised in this appeal," said Judge José Cabranes. The minority said the case deserved the review of the U.S. Supreme Court.

THE FIREFIGHTER'S ARGUMENT

The argument brought by petitioners in the case was one of reverse discrimination. Because a race-based decision was made by the city of New Haven, the white firefighters argued, there was an increased level of scrutiny that must be placed on their ultimate decision. According to the firefighters, when the city threw out the test, it benefited the minority applicants and put white applicants at a disadvantage simply because of their race. The petitioners argued that an attempt to avoid an unfair advantage to one race or another did not represent a compelling government interest, as required in this case. Claiming a compelling interest, petitioners said, would mean a government surrender "to organized racial lobbies." Their evidence, they said, was that the city had no way to prove that the test in itself disadvantaged minority applicants. Therefore, the petitioners said, if the city claimed it was trying to comply with Title VII of the Civil Rights Act, it was using the act itself as a means for discrimination, not to avoid discrimination. If the city felt strongly that minority applicants were disadvantaged, the petitioners argued, the city should have offered tutorials or study aids for future exams.

The keystone of the argument brought by the white firefighters was that the city was in direct violation of Title VII. According to petitioners, section 2000e-2(j) prohibits any employer from "granting preferences to prevent racial imbalances." If the city wanted to prove that it was in fact complying with Title VII, petitioners said, they would have to prove that the test did in fact show a "strong basis in evidence" that minority candidates were put at a disadvantage. Because no proof was uncovered during discovery motions for the case, the decision made by the city was inappropriate and prohibited by Title VII, according to the white firefighters.

In their merits brief, respondents argued that if the Supreme Court accepted the argument given by petitioners that Title VII was violated, down the road Title VII could prove to be a shield used by those who benefit from an unfair advantage in a promotion or hiring exam. Next, respondents answered the question of when test results could be rejected. They indicated that as long as an employer had a "good faith" belief that the test was disadvantaging one group or another, it could be thrown out. If employers were required to come up with solid evidence that a test was unfair, many would be unable to comply with Title VII, respondents argued. Respondents said that New Haven could prove that it had a prima facie case, one in which facts or evidence presented are sufficient for a decision, based on the fact that it could be subject to liability if it had certified the test results. In the end, the city argued, no race benefited. All exam scores were thrown out, regardless of race.

CIVIL RIGHTS VIOLATION

Chief Justice John G. Roberts Jr. had heard civil rights cases in the past and had most often greeted them with apparent hostility, noting the "sordid business" of categorizing everyone on the basis of race. Roberts wrote in a 2007 opinion by the court that public schools would not be allowed to take race into account as a determining factor when attempting to maintain a policy of school integration. "The way to stop discrimination on the basis of race is to stop discriminating on the basis of race," Roberts wrote. Although the Court had looked into race in education in 2007, it had not taken up race in hiring and promotions in decades.

In its 5-4 decision, the Supreme Court ruled in favor of the petitioners, stating that the federal civil rights of the seventeen white firefighters and one Hispanic firefighter who brought the case had been violated. According to the Court, when the city of New Haven decided to throw out the test results, it violated Title VII of the Civil Rights Act by not giving a promotion to any of the firefighters who had qualified. The Court did say, however, that an employer could decide, after giving a promotion exam, to not hand out any promotions to those who took the exam, as long as it was not based on race.

In its decision, the Court said that the New Haven test had been valid, that the city had not proved that it could have used a different test to avoid the supposed discrimination, that the city had no way to prove that it actually feared being sued by minority groups if it certified the test results, and that minority firefighters had no legal right to a complaint in this case on the basis of discrimination because the city was attempting to follow Title VII by giving promotions to those firefighters who scored best on the exam, regardless of race.

Justice Antonin Scalia, while concurring with the Court's decision, wrote a separate opinion in which he called *Ricci v. DeStefano* a postponement of the inevitable: At some point, Scalia said, the Court will have to decide whether "the disparate-impact provisions of Title VII of the Civil Rights Act of 1964" are "consistent with the Constitution's guarantee of equal protection." Justice Scalia also joined the concurring, but separate, opinion of Justices Samuel A. Alito Jr. and Clarence Thomas, who wrote that given the reasoning the dissenters used to justify their decision, they should have reached the same conclusion as the majority of the Court. According to Alito, the dissent "provides an incomplete description of the events that led to New Haven's decision to reject the results of the exam."

Dissenting from the majority decision were Justices Ruth Bader Ginsburg, John Paul Stevens, David H. Souter, and Stephen G. Breyer. Ginsburg argued that the majority had overlooked the purpose of Title VII of the Civil Rights Act of 1964, which was enacted to end discrimination against minorities and has taken decades to come to fruition. According to Ginsburg, because of the struggle for minority firefighters to achieve equality in cities such as New Haven, and because the test results proved unequal among different races, the white firefighters who scored highest on the test had no "vested right to promotion." In addition, the dissenters argued that because no firefighter had received a promotion after the test, regardless of race, there was no reason for the white firefighters to allege reverse discrimination.

The Court's decision left many questions unanswered, including how an employer should deal with test results that seem to favor one race over another. There is also uncertainty in New Haven. Since the test was given in 2003, no promotions have been handed out within the fire department, and there is no indication that moving forward any of the firefighters who scored high enough on the 2003 exams will be promoted, or if a list of those scores even exists anymore. Good faith that a test disadvantaged one racial group or another would no longer be permitted, according to the Supreme Court's decision. However, the Court failed to lay out what or how an employer would have to prove discrimination.

—Heather Kerrigan

Following are excerpts from the U.S. Supreme Court's opinion in Ricci v. DeStefano *on June 29, 2009, in which the Court found that the city of New Haven, Connecticut, had violated the Civil Rights Act by throwing out a promotion exam that white firefighters had passed but African American firefighters had not.*

Ricci v. DeStefano

June 29, 2009

Nos. 07–1428 and 08–328

Frank Ricci, et al.,
petitioners 07–1428

v.

John DeStefano et al.

Frank Ricci, et al.,
petitioners 08–0328

v.

John DeStefano et al.

On writs of certiorari
to the United States
Court of Appeals for
the Second Circuit

[June 29, 2009]

JUSTICE KENNEDY delivered the opinion of the Court.

In the fire department of New Haven, Connecticut—as in emergency-service agencies throughout the Nation—firefighters prize their promotion to and within the officer ranks. An agency's officers command respect within the department and in the whole community; and, of course, added responsibilities command increased salary and benefits. Aware of the intense competition for promotions, New Haven, like many cities, relies on objective examinations to identify the best qualified candidates.

In 2003, 118 New Haven firefighters took examinations to qualify for promotion to the rank of lieutenant or captain. Promotion examinations in New Haven (or City) were infrequent, so the stakes were high. The results would determine which firefighters would be considered for promotions during the next two years, and the order in which they would be considered. Many firefighters studied for months, at considerable personal and financial cost.

When the examination results showed that white candidates had outperformed minority candidates, the mayor and other local politicians opened a public debate that turned rancorous. Some firefighters argued the tests should be discarded because the results showed the tests to be discriminatory. They threatened a discrimination lawsuit if the City made promotions based on the tests. Other firefighters said the exams were neutral and fair. And they, in turn, threatened a discrimination lawsuit if the City, relying on the statistical racial disparity, ignored the test results and denied promotions to the candidates who had performed well. In the end the City took the side of those who protested the test results. It threw out the examinations.

Certain white and Hispanic firefighters who likely would have been promoted based on their good test performance sued the City and some of its officials. Theirs is the suit now before us. The suit alleges that, by discarding the test results, the City and the named officials discriminated against the plaintiffs based on their race, in violation of both Title VII of the Civil Rights Act of 1964, 78 Stat. 253, as amended, 42 U.S.C. §2000e *et seq.*, and the Equal Protection Clause of the Fourteenth Amendment. The City and the officials defended their actions, arguing that if they had certified the results, they could have faced liability under Title VII for adopting a practice that had a disparate impact on the minority firefighters. The District Court granted summary judgment for the defendants, and the Court of Appeals affirmed.

We conclude that race-based action like the City's in this case is impermissible under Title VII unless the employer can demonstrate a strong basis in evidence that, had it not taken the action, it would have been liable under the disparate-impact statute. The respondents, we further determine, cannot meet that threshold standard. As a result, the City's action in discarding the tests was a violation of Title VII. In light of our ruling under the statutes, we need not reach the question whether respondents' actions may have violated the Equal Protection Clause. . . .

[Most of Section I, containing background on the case, has been omitted.]

After full briefing and argument by the parties, the Court of Appeals affirmed in a one-paragraph, unpublished summary order; it later withdrew that order, issuing in its place a nearly identical, one-paragraph *per curiam* opinion adopting the District Court's reasoning. 530 F. 3d 87 (CA2 2008). Three days later, the Court of Appeals voted 7 to 6 to deny rehearing en banc, over written dissents by Chief Judge Jacobs and Judge Cabranes.

This action presents two provisions of Title VII to be interpreted and reconciled, with few, if any, precedents in the courts of appeals discussing the issue. Depending on the resolution of the statutory claim, a fundamental constitutional question could also arise. We found it prudent and appropriate to grant certiorari.

We now reverse.

II . . .

A

Title VII of the Civil Rights Act of 1964, 42 U.S.C. §2000e *et seq.*, as amended, prohibits employment discrimination on the basis of race, color, religion, sex, or national origin. Title VII prohibits both intentional discrimination (known as "disparate treatment") as well as, in some cases, practices that are not intended to discriminate but in fact have a disproportionately adverse effect on minorities (known as "disparate impact"). . . .

[Further discussion on the history and meaning of the Civil Rights Act has been omitted.]

B

Petitioners allege that when the CSB [Civil Service Board] refused to certify the captain and lieutenant exam results based on the race of the successful candidates, it discriminated against them in violation of Title VII's disparate-treatment provision. The City counters that its decision was permissible because the tests "appear[ed] to violate Title VII's disparate impact provisions."

Our analysis begins with this premise: The City's actions would violate the disparate-treatment prohibition of Title VII absent some valid defense. All the evidence demonstrates that the City chose not to certify the examination results because of the statistical disparity based on race—*i.e.*, how minority candidates had performed when compared to white candidates. As the District Court put it, the City rejected the test results because "too many whites and not enough minorities would be promoted were the lists to be certified." Without some other justification, this express, race-based decision making violates Title VII's command that employers cannot take adverse employment actions because of an individual's race.

The District Court did not adhere to this principle, however. It held that respondents' "motivation to avoid making promotions based on a test with a racially disparate impact . . . does not, as a matter of law, constitute discriminatory intent." And the Government makes a similar argument in this Court. It contends that the "structure of Title VII belies any claim that an employer's intent to comply with Title VII's disparate-impact provisions constitutes prohibited discrimination on the basis of race." But both of those statements turn upon the City's objective—avoiding disparate-impact liability—while ignoring the City's conduct in the name of reaching that objective. Whatever the City's ultimate aim—however well intentioned or benevolent it might have seemed—the City made its employment decision because of race. The City rejected the test results solely because the higher scoring candidates were white. The question is not whether that conduct was discriminatory but whether the City had a lawful justification for its race-based action.

We consider, therefore, whether the purpose to avoid disparate-impact liability excuses what otherwise would be prohibited disparate-treatment discrimination. Courts often confront cases in which statutes and principles point in different directions. Our task is to provide guidance to employers and courts for situations when these two prohibitions could be in conflict absent a rule to reconcile them. In providing this guidance our decision must be consistent with the important purpose of Title VII—that the workplace be an environment free of discrimination, where race is not a barrier to opportunity. . . .

[The petitioners' and respondents' arguments and past cases of the Court have been omitted.]

If an employer cannot rescore a test based on the candidates' race, §2000e–2(l), then it follows *a fortiori* that it may not take the greater step of discarding the test altogether to achieve a more desirable racial distribution of promotion-eligible candidates—absent a strong basis in evidence that the test was deficient and that discarding the results is necessary to avoid violating the disparate-impact provision. Restricting an employer's ability to discard test results (and thereby discriminate against qualified candidates on the basis of their race) also is in keeping with Title VII's express protection of bona fide promotional examinations.

For the foregoing reasons, we adopt the strong-basis-in evidence standard as a matter of statutory construction to resolve any conflict between the disparate-treatment and disparate-impact provisions of Title VII.

Our statutory holding does not address the constitutionality of the measures taken here in purported compliance with Title VII. We also do not hold that meeting the strong-basis-in-evidence standard would satisfy the Equal Protection Clause in a future case. As we explain below, because respondents have not met their burden under Title VII, we need not decide whether a legitimate fear of disparate impact is ever sufficient to justify discriminatory treatment under the Constitution.

Nor do we question an employer's affirmative efforts to ensure that all groups have a fair opportunity to apply for promotions and to participate in the process by which promotions will be made. But once that process has been established and employers have made clear their selection criteria, they may not then invalidate the test results, thus upsetting an employee's legitimate expectation not to be judged on the basis of race. Doing so, absent a strong basis in evidence of an impermissible disparate impact, amounts to the sort of racial preference that Congress has disclaimed, §2000e–2(j), and is antithetical to the notion of a workplace where individuals are guaranteed equal opportunity regardless of race. . . .

C

The City argues that, even under the strong-basis-in evidence standard, its decision to discard the examination results was permissible under Title VII. That is incorrect. Even if respondents were motivated as a subjective matter by a desire to avoid committing disparate-impact discrimination, the record makes clear there is no support for the conclusion that respondents had an objective, strong basis in evidence to find the tests inadequate, with some consequent disparate-impact liability in violation of Title VII.

On this basis, we conclude that petitioners have met their obligation to demonstrate that there is "no genuine issue as to any material fact" and that they are "entitled to judgment as a matter of law." . . .

The racial adverse impact here was significant, and petitioners do not dispute that the City was faced with a prima facie case of disparate-impact liability. . . .

1

There is no genuine dispute that the examinations were job-related and consistent with business necessity. The City's assertions to the contrary are "blatantly contradicted by the record." . . .

[Further arguments presented by the City and firefighters have been omitted.]

3

On the record before us, there is no genuine dispute that the City lacked a strong basis in evidence to believe it would face disparate-impact liability if it certified the examination results.

In other words, there is no evidence—let alone the required strong basis in evidence—that the tests were flawed because they were not job-related or because other, equally valid and less discriminatory tests were available to the City. Fear of litigation alone cannot justify an employer's reliance on race to the detriment of individuals who passed the examinations and qualified for promotions. The City's discarding the test results was impermissible under Title VII, and summary judgment is appropriate for petitioners on their disparate-treatment claim. . . .

Our holding today clarifies how Title VII applies to resolve competing expectations under the disparate-treatment and disparate-impact provisions. If, after it certifies the test results, the City faces a disparate-impact suit, then in light of our holding today it should be clear that the City would avoid disparate-impact liability based on the strong basis in evidence that, had it not certified the results, it would have been subject to disparate-treatment liability.

Petitioners are entitled to summary judgment on their Title VII claim, and we therefore need not decide the underlying constitutional question. The judgment of the Court of Appeals is reversed, and the cases are remanded for further proceedings consistent with this opinion.

It is so ordered.

JUSTICE SCALIA, concurring.

I join the Court's opinion in full, but write separately to observe that its resolution of this dispute merely postpones the evil day on which the Court will have to confront the question: Whether, or to what extent, are the disparate-impact provisions of Title VII of the Civil Rights Act of 1964 consistent with the Constitution's guarantee of equal protection? The question is not an easy one.

The difficulty is this: Whether or not Title VII's disparate-treatment provisions forbid "remedial" race-based actions when a disparate-impact violation would *not* otherwise result—the question resolved by the Court today—it is clear that Title VII not only permits but affirmatively *requires* such actions when a disparate-impact violation *would* otherwise result. But if the Federal Government is prohibited from discriminating on the basis of race, *Bolling* v. *Sharpe,* 347 U. S. 497, 500 (1954), then surely it is also prohibited from enacting laws mandating that third parties—*e.g.,* employers, whether private, State, or municipal—discriminate on the basis of race. As the facts of these cases illustrate, Title VII's disparate impact provisions place a racial thumb on the scales, often requiring employers to evaluate the racial outcomes of their policies, and to make decisions based on (because of) those racial outcomes. That type of racial decisionmaking is, as the Court explains, discriminatory.

To be sure, the disparate-impact laws do not mandate imposition of quotas, but it is not clear why that should provide a safe harbor. . . .

The Court's resolution of these cases makes it unnecessary to resolve these matters today. But the war between disparate impact and equal protection will be waged sooner or later, and it behooves us to begin thinking about how—and on what terms—to make peace between them.

JUSTICE ALITO, with whom JUSTICE SCALIA and JUSTICE THOMAS join, concurring.

I join the Court's opinion in full. I write separately only because the dissent, while claiming that "[t]he Court's recitation of the facts leaves out important parts of the story," *post,* at 2 (opinion of GINSBURG, J.), provides an incomplete description of the events that led to New Haven's decision to reject the results of its exam. The dissent's omissions are important because, when all of the evidence in the record is taken into account, it is clear that, even if the legal analysis in Parts II and III–A of the dissent were accepted, affirmance of the decision below is untenable.

I . . .

The question on which the opinion of the Court and the dissenting opinion disagree concerns the objective component of the determination that must be made when an employer justifies an employment decision, like the one made in this litigation, on the ground that a contrary decision would have created a risk of disparate-impact liability. The Court holds—and I entirely agree—that concern about disparate-impact liability is a legitimate reason for a decision of the type involved here only if there was a "substantial basis in evidence to find the tests inadequate." The Court ably demonstrates that in this litigation no reasonable jury could find that the city of New Haven (City) possessed such evidence and therefore summary judgment for petitioners is required. Because the Court correctly holds that respondents cannot satisfy this objective component, the Court has no need to discuss the question of the respondents' actual intent. As the Court puts it, "[e]ven if respondents were motivated as a subjective matter by a desire to avoid committing disparate-impact discrimination, the record makes clear there is no support for the conclusion that respondents had an objective, substantial basis in evidence to find the tests inadequate."

The dissent advocates a different objective component of the governing standard. According to the dissent, the objective component should be whether the evidence provided "good cause" for the decision, *post,* at 19, and the dissent argues—incorrectly, in my view—that no reasonable juror could fail to find that such evidence was present here. But even if the dissent were correct on this point, I assume that the dissent would not countenance summary judgment for respondents if respondents' professed concern about disparate-impact litigation was simply a pretext. Therefore, the decision below, which sustained the entry of summary judgment for respondents, cannot be affirmed unless no reasonable jury could find that the City's asserted reason for scrapping its test—concern about disparate-impact liability—was a pretext and that the City's real reason was illegitimate, namely, the desire to placate a politically important racial constituency. . . .

[Further discussion of the dissent has been omitted.]

JUSTICE GINSBURG, with whom JUSTICE STEVENS, JUSTICE SOUTER, and JUSTICE BREYER join, dissenting.

In assessing claims of race discrimination, "[c]ontext matters." In 1972, Congress extended Title VII of the Civil Rights Act of 1964 to cover public employment. At that time, municipal fire departments across the country, including New Haven's, pervasively discriminated against minorities. The extension of Title VII to cover jobs in firefighting effected no overnight change. It took decades of persistent effort, advanced by Title VII litigation, to open firefighting posts to members of racial minorities.

The white firefighters who scored high on New Haven's promotional exams understandably attract this Court's sympathy. But they had no vested right to promotion. Nor have other persons received promotions in preference to them. . . .

I

A

The Court's recitation of the facts leaves out important parts of the story. Firefighting is a profession in which the legacy of racial discrimination casts an especially long shadow. . . .

[Further dissent from Justice Ginsburg has been omitted.]

SOURCE: U.S. Supreme Court. *Ricci v. DeStefano,* 557 U.S. _____ (2009). www.supremecourtus.gov/opinions/08pdf/07-1428.pdf.

OTHER HISTORIC DOCUMENTS OF INTEREST

FROM THIS VOLUME

- U.S. Supreme Court on Campaign Contributions to Judges, p. 230
- U.S. Supreme Court on DNA Testing for Prisoners, p. 254
- U.S. Supreme Court on the Voting Rights Act, p. 263
- U.S. Supreme Court on Strip Searches of Students, p. 272

FROM PREVIOUS *HISTORIC DOCUMENTS*

- Court on Seniority/Affirmative Action, *1984*, p. 365
- Court on Job-Related Affirmative Action Programs, *1979*, p. 493
- Supreme Court Decision on Reverse Discrimination, *1976*, p. 405

July

Delhi Court Overturns Ban on Homosexuality

JULY 2, 2009

In a 105-page decision by the Delhi High Court, the colonial-era ban criminalizing homosexuality was overturned, ushering in a new period for gay men and lesbians in India. According to the judges of the High Court, "The inclusiveness that Indian society traditionally displayed, literally in every aspect of life, is manifest in recognizing a role in society for everyone." The decision represents the first time India has directly addressed the rights of its homosexual citizens. More than eighty countries around the world currently make it illegal for homosexual couples to have consensual sex, a trend that the UN Joint Program on HIV/AIDS (UNAIDS) says leads to such problems as a lack of knowledge about protection against HIV/AIDS and other sexually transmitted diseases. In India, approximately 2.5 million people have contracted HIV.

Although the decision applies only to India's capital, New Delhi, international analysts and Indian lawyers agree that the decision will force the Indian government to challenge the ruling in the nation's Supreme Court or change the Delhi law to apply to the whole country. The transition will not be easy, however, because Indian society is reserved and frowns on displays of affection.

Great Britain had instituted a ban on homosexuality in many of its colonies (including India) and at home. In England and Wales, the ban was overturned in 1967, but in the former colonies, including Singapore, Zimbabwe, and Malaysia, strict laws are still in place banning homosexual relationships.

INDIA'S BAN

Section 377 of India's penal code, instituted in 1861 by British colonial rulers, banned "carnal intercourse against the order of nature with any man, woman, or animal," considering it an "unnatural offense." While this law does not specifically mention homosexuality, it has always been interpreted as such. The law had long been viewed in the nation as archaic, but few attempts were made to overturn it. Although not many people have been prosecuted under the law in modern times, it has been used as a form of blackmail and harassment against members of the gay and lesbian community. The law makes homosexual sex punishable by up to ten years in prison. Indian officials have maintained that reversing the ban on homosexuality would demoralize Indian society, leading to an increase in delinquent behavior and more health problems. Indian government officials, in a statement to the High Court, said, "Every citizen has the right to lead a decent and moral life in society and the right would be violated if such behavior is legalized in the country."

Although the government and religious leaders have taken a strong line against homosexuality, the general public's opinion has been mixed. India reveres men known as "hijras" or eunuchs, who are mostly homosexual men who dress as women and have been castrated. These hijras are often asked to bless weddings or births. In India's Rajpipla royal family, Manvendra Singh Gohil, the scion of the family who was once shunned for his homosexuality, is now set to become the first openly homosexual maharajah in Indian history. Gohil was initially shunned by his community as well; after revealing his homosexuality in 2005, the people of his village burned his picture. By 2009, the Indian people had backed off of their calls for him to be stripped of his title.

The law persisted and Indian society has largely remained hostile toward the idea of homosexuality and toward homosexuals. In many cases, to avoid embarrassment to themselves and their families, homosexual Indian men and women marry heterosexuals and have children. Although they maintain a heterosexual relationship, many have secret homosexual relationships as well.

Although petitions to change the law sent to the Indian government have fervently been rejected, there had been some indication in recent years, as discontent from gay rights advocates grew, that the government might consider overturning the ban. Although Delhi's High Court can rule against the ban, the law can only be amended by India's national parliament. Such a decision by the High Court, however, can stop imprisonment and unlawful treatment of homosexuals in Delhi.

In this heavily religious society, gay rights have increasingly gained traction in recent years, as more Bollywood films include gay themes, and young people frequently attend gay pride parades held in India's most populous cities. Acceptance in pop culture has not truly affected India's homosexual population, however, as gay men and lesbians still face attacks and are often forced from homes and shunned by families.

THE COURT'S DECISION

The lawsuit against Section 377 that led to the Delhi High Court decision was brought eight years earlier by the Naz Foundation, an AIDS awareness group in India. The Naz Foundation, and other gay rights groups, had been campaigning for nearly a decade to encourage the High Court to overturn the ban on homosexuality. AIDS awareness groups around the world joined in the fight, in an attempt to increase education about safe sex and protect India's population, which has one of the world's largest number of people living with AIDS. Many advocates of overturning the ban against homosexuality saw it as a barrier to educating India's citizens; the government has at times used Section 377 to stop HIV/AIDS education groups from spreading health information around the country. In its ruling, the court said that the government's argument that banning homosexuality stops the spread of HIV/AIDS was "completely unfounded" and "based on incorrect and wrong notions."

With its decision, the High Court sought to stop discrimination against India's gay population. "Those perceived by the majority as 'deviants' or 'different' are not on that score excluded or ostracized," the court's opinion read. Chief Justice A. P. Shah and Justice S. Muralidhar, who wrote the opinion, said that Section 377 of the penal code was in violation of India's constitution. "Consensual sex amongst adults is legal," the justices said, "which includes even gay sex and sex among the same sexes." The opinion noted that Article 14 guarantees equal protection for all Indians; Article 15 bans discrimination; and Article 21 protects life and personal liberty. All are violated by the ban on homosexuality. "It cannot be forgotten that discrimination is antithesis of equality and that it is the recognition of equality which will foster dignity of every individual," the justices wrote.

It is now up to India's parliament to decide whether it will pass a law that will reverse the court's decision or alter the penal code in line with the court's ruling. Until that time, the decision by the High Court will be the precedent only within Delhi's city limits.

DEBATE CONTINUES

As noted, the High Court's decision only applies to the capital area: Debate about the decision continues in New Delhi and in other areas of the country. Many who wanted to preserve India's history and culture called the decision wrong. Maulana Abdul Khaliq Madrasi, a vice chancellor of Dar ul-Uloom, India's major university for Islamic education, said the decision would increase the prevalence of Western norms in India's society and "corrupt Indian boys and girls." Others, including Murli Manohar Joshi, a leader of the Hindu nationalist Bharatiya Janata party, the main opposition group to the court's decision, said that the court should not be given authority to rule on cases such as this.

Those who supported the court's decision saw it as the first step on a long path toward educating India's society about homosexuals and toward increasing awareness about safe sex. The stigma attached to homosexuals in rural parts of India is greater than in urban areas, which have been increasingly accepting of gay culture. In some rural areas, groups try to "cure" men and women of homosexuality by forcing them to have sex with members of the opposite sex. The Delhi High Court decision "is a first major step" toward challenging such stigmas, said Anjali Gopalan, the executive director and founder of the Naz Foundation, but, she continued "there are many more battles."

Other supporters celebrated the freedom that homosexual Indians in New Delhi will now have, at least within the city limits. "I'm so proud of India," said Sumith Baudh, a member of Voices Against 377, a coalition of groups advocating for gay rights in India. "We know this will translate for the lives of many Indians into creating more tolerance, fighting harassment, isolation and depression they have long suffered."

Opponents, including many Muslim, Hindu, and Christian leaders, quickly denounced the court's ruling. The Catholic Bishops Conference of India, in a statement read by Babu Joseph, the group's spokesperson, said, "[W]hile respecting the judgment of the court, we still hold that homosexuality is not an acceptable behaviour in society." Supporters countering the church's argument noted that Hindu scripture makes reference to homosexuality as a natural part of human existence.

Those who supported the court's decision saw it as a message to the rest of the world, including nations that are still holding on to laws created by earlier rulers. "Most of the world's sodomy laws are relics of colonialism," said Scott Long, who directs the Lesbian, Gay, Bisexual and Transgender Rights Program at Human Rights Watch. "As the world's largest democracy, India has shown the way for other countries to rid themselves of these repressive burdens."

—Heather Kerrigan

Following is the text of the Delhi High Court's decision in Naz Foundation v. The Government of Delhi, *issued on July 2, 2009, lifting the ban on homosexuality within New Delhi's city limits.*

New Delhi Court Ruling on Ban on Homosexuality

July 2, 2009

In the High Court of Delhi at New Delhi

WP(C) N0.7455/2001

Date of decision: 2nd July, 2009

Naz Foundation. . . . Petitioner
versus
Government of NCT of Delhi and Others. . . . Respondents

AJIT PRAKASH SHAH, CHIEF JUSTICE:

1. This writ petition has been preferred by Naz Foundation, a Non Governmental Organisation (NGO) as a Public Interest Litigation to challenge the constitutional validity of Section 377 of the Indian Penal Code, 1860 (IPC), which criminally penalizes what is described as "unnatural offences," to the extent the said provision criminalises consensual sexual acts between adults in private. The challenge is founded on the plea that Section 377 IPC, on account of it covering sexual acts between consenting adults in private infringes the fundamental rights guaranteed under Articles 14, 15, 19 & 21 of the Constitution of India. Limiting their plea, the petitioners submit that Section 377 IPC should apply only to non-consensual penile non-vaginal sex and penile non-vaginal sex involving minors. The Union of India is impleaded as respondent No.5 through Ministry of Home Affairs and Ministry of Health & Family Welfare. Respondent No.4 is the National Aids Control Organisation (hereinafter referred to as "NACO"), a body formed under the aegis of Ministry of Health & Family Welfare, Government of India. NACO is charged with formulating and implementing policies for the prevention of HIV/AIDS in India. Respondent No.3 is the Delhi State Aids Control Society. Respondent No.2 is the Commissioner of Police, Delhi. Respondents No.6 to 8 are individuals and NGOs, who were permitted to intervene on their request. The writ petition was dismissed by this Court in 2004 on the ground that there is no cause of action in favour of the petitioner and that such a petition cannot be entertained to examine the academic challenge to the constitutionality of the legislation. The Supreme Court vide order dated 03.02.2006 in Civil Appeal No.952/2006 set aside the said order of this Court observing that the matter does require consideration and is not of a

nature which could have been dismissed on the aforesaid ground. The matter was remitted to this Court for fresh decision. . . .

[The history of the litigation and proceedings has been omitted.]

THE CLASSIFICATION BEARS NO RATIONAL NEXUS TO THE OBJECTIVE SOUGHT TO BE ACHIEVED

91. The petitioner's case is that public morality is not the province of criminal law and Section 377 IPC does not have any legitimate purpose. Section 377 IPC makes no distinction between acts engaged in the public sphere and acts engaged in the private sphere. It also makes no distinction between the consensual and non-consensual acts between adults. Consensual sex between adults in private does not cause any harm to anybody. Thus it is evident that the disparate grouping in Section 377 IPC does not take into account relevant factors such as consent, age and the nature of the act or the absence of harm caused to anybody. Public animus and disgust towards a particular social group or vulnerable minority is not a valid ground for classification under Article 14. Section 377 IPC targets the homosexual community as a class and is motivated by an animus towards this vulnerable class of people.

92. According to Union of India, the stated object of Section 377 IPC is to protect women and children, prevent the spread of HIV/AIDS and enforce societal morality against homosexuality. It is clear that Section 377 IPC, whatever its present pragmatic application, was not enacted keeping in mind instances of child sexual abuse or to fill the lacuna in a rape law. It was based on a conception of sexual morality specific to Victorian era drawing on notions of carnality and sinfulness. In any way, the legislative object of protecting women and children has no bearing in regard to consensual sexual acts between adults in private. The second legislative purpose elucidated is that Section 377 IPC serves the cause of public health by criminalising the homosexual behaviour. As already held, this purported legislative purpose is in complete contrast to the averments in NACO's affidavit. NACO has specifically stated that enforcement of Section 377 IPC adversely contributes to pushing the infliction underground, make risky sexual practices go unnoticed and unaddressed. Section 377 IPC thus hampers HIV/AIDS prevention efforts. Lastly, as held earlier, it is not within the constitutional competence of the State to invade the privacy of citizens lives or regulate conduct to which the citizen alone is concerned solely on the basis of public morals. The criminalisation of private sexual relations between consenting adults absent any evidence of serious harm deems the provision's objective both arbitrary and unreasonable. The state interest "must be legitimate and relevant" for the legislation to be non-arbitrary and must be proportionate towards achieving the state interest. If the objective is irrational, unjust and unfair, necessarily classification will have to be held as unreasonable. The nature of the provision of Section 377 IPC and its purpose is to criminalise private conduct of consenting adults which causes no harm to anyone else. It has no other purpose than to criminalise conduct which fails to conform with the moral or religious views of a section of society. The discrimination severely affects the rights and interests of homosexuals and deeply impairs their dignity.

93. We may also refer to Declaration of Principles of Equality issued by the Equal Rights Trust in April, 2008, which can be described as current international understanding of Principles on Equality. This declaration was agreed upon by a

group of experts at a conference entitled "Principles on Equality and the Development of Legal Standard on Equality" held on 3–5 April, 2008 in London. Participants of different backgrounds, including academics, legal practitioners, human rights activists from all regions of the world took part in the Conference. The Declaration of Principles on Equality reflects a moral and professional consensus among human rights and equality experts. The declaration defines the terms "equality" and "equal treatment" as follows:

> "THE RIGHT TO EQUALITY
>
> The right to equality is the right of all human beings to be equal in dignity, to be treated with respect and consideration and to participate on an equal basis with others in any area of economic, social, political, cultural or civil life. All human beings are equal before the law and have the right to equal protection and benefit of the law.
>
> EQUAL TREATMENT
>
> Equal treatment, as an aspect of equality, is not equivalent to identical treatment. To realise full and effective equality, it is necessary to treat people differently according to their different circumstances, to assert their equal worth and to enhance their capabilities to participate in society as equals."

Part-II of the Declaration lays down the right to non-discrimination. The right to non-discrimination is stated to be a free-standing fundamental right, subsumed in the right to equality. Discrimination is defined as follows:

> "Discrimination must be prohibited where it is on grounds of race, colour, ethnicity, descent, sex, pregnancy, maternity, civil, family or carer [*sic*] status, language, religion or belief, political or other opinion, birth, national or social origin, nationality, economic status, association with a national minority, *sexual orientation, gender identity*, age, disability, health status, genetic or other predisposition toward illness or a combination of any of these grounds, or on the basis of characteristics associated with any of these grounds. (*emphasis supplied*)
>
> Discrimination based on any other ground must be prohibited where such discrimination (i) causes or perpetuates systemic disadvantage; (ii) undermines human dignity; or (iii) adversely affects the equal enjoyment of a person's rights and freedoms in a serious manner that is comparable to discrimination on the prohibited grounds stated above.
>
> Discrimination must also be prohibited when it is on the ground of the association of a person with other persons to whom a prohibited ground applied or the perception, whether accurate or otherwise, of a person as having a characteristic associated with a prohibited ground.
>
> Discrimination may be direct or indirect.
>
> Direct discrimination occurs when for a reason related to one or more prohibited grounds a person or group of persons is treated less favourably than another person or another group of persons is, has been, or would be treated in a comparable situation; or when for a reason related to one or more prohibited grounds a person or group of persons is subjected to a detriment. Direct discrimination may be permitted only very exceptionally, when it can be justified against strictly defined criteria.

> *Indirect discrimination occurs when a provision, criterion or practice would put persons having a status or a characteristic associated with one or more prohibited grounds at a particular disadvantage compared with other persons, unless that provision, criterion or practice is objectively justified by a legitimate aim, and the means of achieving that aim are appropriate and necessary.*
>
> *Harassment constitutes discrimination when unwanted conduct related to any prohibited ground takes place with the purpose or effect of violating the dignity of a person or of creating an intimidating, hostile, degrading, humiliating or offensive environment. (emphasis supplied)"*

[Declaration of Principles on Equality 2008—The Equal Rights Trust]

Section 377 IPC Targets Homosexuals as a Class

94. Section 377 IPC is facially neutral and it apparently targets not identities but acts, but in its operation it does end up unfairly targeting a particular community. The fact is that these sexual acts which are criminalised are associated more closely with one class of persons, namely, the homosexuals as a class. Section 377 IPC has the effect of viewing all gay men as criminals. When everything associated with homosexuality is treated as bent, queer, repugnant, the whole gay and lesbian community is marked with deviance and perversity. They are subject to extensive prejudice because [of] what they are or what they are perceived to be, not because of what they do. The result is that a significant group of the population is, because of its sexual nonconformity, persecuted, marginalised and turned in on itself. . . .

[Previous cases dealing with gay rights around the world have been omitted.]

98. The inevitable conclusion is that the discrimination caused to MSM [men who have sex with men] and gay community is unfair and unreasonable and, therefore, in breach of Article 14 of the Constitution of India.

Infringement of Article 15—Whether "Sexual Orientation" Is a Ground Analogous to "Sex"

99. Article 15 is an instance and particular application of the right of equality which is generally stated in Article 14. Article 14 is genus while Article 15 along with Article 16 are species although all of them occupy [the] same field and the doctrine of "equality" embodied in these Articles has many facets. Article 15 prohibits discrimination on several enumerated grounds, which include "sex." The argument of the petitioner is that "sex" in Article 15(1) must be read expansively to include a prohibition of discrimination on the ground of sexual orientation as the prohibited ground of sex discrimination cannot be read as applying to gender *simpliciter*. The purpose underlying the fundamental right against sex discrimination is to prevent behaviour that treats people differently for reason of not being in conformity with generalization concerning "normal" or "natural" gender roles. Discrimination on the basis of sexual orientation is itself grounded in stereotypical judgments and generalization about the conduct of either sex. This is stated to be the legal position in International Law and comparative jurisprudence. Reliance was placed on judgments of Human Rights Committee and also on the judgments of Canadian and South African courts.

100. International Covenant on Civil and Political Rights (ICCPR) recognises the right to equality and states that, "the law shall prohibit any discrimination on any ground

such as race, colour, sex, language, religion, political or other opinion, national or social region, property, birth or other status." In *Toonen v. Australia* (supra), the Human Rights Committee, while holding that certain provisions of the Tasmanian Criminal Code which criminalise various forms of sexual conduct between men violated the ICCPR, observed that the reference to "sex" in Article 2, paragraphs 1 and 26 (of the ICCPR) is to be taken as including "sexual orientation." . . .

104. We hold that sexual orientation is a ground analogous to sex and that discrimination on the basis of sexual orientation is not permitted by Article 15. Further, Article 15(2) incorporates the notion of horizontal application of rights. In other words, it even prohibits discrimination of one citizen by another in matters of access to public spaces. In our view, discrimination on the ground of sexual orientation is impermissible even on the horizontal application of the right enshrined under Article 15. . . .

[Previous cases and constitutional powers of the court have been omitted.]

DOCTRINE OF SEVERABILITY

127. The prayer of the petitioner is to declare Section 377 IPC as unconstitutional to the extent the said provision affects private sexual acts between consenting adults in private. The relief has been sought in this manner to ensure the continuance of applicability of Section 377 IPC to cases involving non-consensual sex. Our attention was drawn to a passage from Constitutional Law of India. . . .

CONCLUSION

129. The notion of equality in the Indian Constitution flows from the "Objective Resolution" moved by Pandit Jawaharlal Nehru on December 13, 1946. Nehru, in his speech, moving this Resolution wished that the House should consider the Resolution not in a spirit of narrow legal wording, but rather look at the spirit behind that Resolution. He said, "Words are magic things often enough, but even the magic of words sometimes cannot convey the magic of the human spirit and of a Nation's passion . . . . [*sic*] (The Resolution) seeks very feebly to tell the world of what we have thought or dreamt of so long, and what we now hope to achieve in the near future."

130. If there is one constitutional tenet that can be said to be underlying theme of the Indian Constitution, it is that of "inclusiveness." This Court believes that Indian Constitution reflects this value deeply ingrained in Indian society, nurtured over several generations. The inclusiveness that Indian society traditionally displayed, literally in every aspect of life, is manifest in recognising a role in society for everyone. Those perceived by the majority as "deviants" or "different" are not on that score excluded or ostracised.

131. Where society can display inclusiveness and understanding, such persons can be assured of a life of dignity and nondiscrimination. This was the "spirit behind the Resolution" of which Nehru spoke so passionately. In our view, Indian Constitutional law does not permit the statutory criminal law to be held captive by the popular misconceptions of who the LGBTs are. It cannot be forgotten that discrimination is antithesis of equality and that it is the recognition of equality which will foster the dignity of every individual.

132. We declare that Section 377 IPC, insofar it criminalises consensual sexual acts of adults in private, is violative of Articles 21, 14 and 15 of the Constitution. The provisions of Section 377 IPC will continue to govern non-consensual penile non-vaginal sex and penile non-vaginal sex involving minors. By "adult" we mean everyone who is 18 years of age and above. A person below 18 would be presumed not to be able to consent to a sexual act. This clarification will hold till, of course, Parliament chooses to amend the law to effectuate the recommendation of the Law Commission of India in its 172nd Report which we believe removes a great deal of confusion. Secondly, we clarify that our judgment will not result in the re-opening of criminal cases involving Section 377 IPC that have already attained finality.

We allow the writ petition in the above terms.

CHIEF JUSTICE

S. MURALIDHAR, J

JULY 2, 2009

Source: Delhi High Court. Judgment Information System. *Naz Foundation (India) Trust v. Government of NCT of Delhi and Others*. WP(C) No. 7455/2001. July 2, 2009. http://lobis.nic.in/dhc.

OTHER HISTORIC DOCUMENTS OF INTEREST

FROM THIS VOLUME

■ Same-Sex Marriage in the States, p. 143

Congress Briefed on Secret CIA Program

JULY 8, 2009

In early July, it became public knowledge that Central Intelligence Agency (CIA) director Leon Panetta had briefed Congress in June 2009 on a secret CIA program to assassinate top al-Qaida leaders that had been authorized by the George W. Bush administration. According to Panetta's briefing, former vice president Dick Cheney had told the CIA to conceal details of the program from Congress and the public. The *New York Times,* which first broke the story, reported that President Bush had given permission to the CIA in 2001 to capture or kill top-level al-Qaida members.

The CIA program was first revealed to Panetta on June 23, 2009, as tensions between the agency and Congress escalated over activities, both secret and public, carried out after the September 11, 2001, terrorist attacks. According to Democrats on the House Intelligence Committee, current CIA director Panetta knew that the agency had not received the proper authorization from Congress to carry out such a program at a time when the CIA was under the direction of George Tenet. According to members of the committee, however, when Panetta became aware of the program after taking his position in early 2009, he was encouraged by CIA officials to bring the matter to the attention of Congress, which could give him authorization to carry out the previous administration's plans. The secret and still unnamed program was ended by Panetta in late June 2009. According to one former CIA employee, "Because this program never went fully operational and hadn't been briefed as Panetta thought it should have been, his decision to kill it was neither difficult nor controversial." Full details of the program have not yet been released. Silvestre Reyes, D-Texas, chair of the House Intelligence Committee, said, "This was a very highly classified program that had been in place since right after the attacks of 9/11 and involved a worldwide effort. It's a very serious program."

There has always been debate in Congress about whether it should be more involved in security and intelligence matters, but the Bush administration drew harsher criticism of its secret programs than previous administrations because of the tactics used in pursuing al-Qaida members.

LONG-RUNNING DEBATE

The revelation of the secret CIA program was just another piece in a long-running debate between the legislative and executive branches about oversight and whether the CIA must fully disclose its programs to Congress. Although members of the House Intelligence Committee had pushed for greater oversight, administrations have resisted, wanting to keep certain things within the executive branch. President Barack Obama has made it clear that he will veto any bill that attempts to radically change the National Security Act, including a significant increase in the number of CIA briefings before Congress.

Tensions had been high when the CIA assassination program came to light, just as debates were raging over the appropriateness of waterboarding and other interrogation methods the CIA had been using and that the CIA had destroyed tapes detailing the interrogation of two al-Qaida suspects detained in Thailand.

According to U.S. law, it is the duty of the president to keep congressional intelligence committees "fully and currently informed of the intelligence activities of the United States, including any significant anticipated intelligence activity." However, since the National Security Act of 1947 was amended in 1949, the information from the president is now required "to the extent consistent with due regard for the protection from unauthorized disclosure of classified information relating to sensitive intelligence sources and methods or other exceptionally sensitive matters." This stipulation in effect has left the sharing of information up to the discretion of the president. An argument often used against fully briefing Congress on CIA operations is that with any covert operation, the National Security Act says that the information disseminated on the program can be limited to the Gang of Eight, which consists of Democratic and Republican leaders in the House and Senate and their intelligence committees.

Although Democrats have largely been on the side of increased disclosure of CIA programs, Republicans have been ok with leaving it up to the executive branch and the CIA to decide whether lawmakers should be involved. Some Democrats who want increased disclosure, however, have said that this particular program was probably not as important as many thought originally. On the other hand, the bits and pieces of information revealed by former CIA officials indicate that this *was* an operation that should have been brought to the attention of Congress immediately.

SECRET CIA PROGRAM

When the story came to light in July, Sen. Dianne Feinstein, D-Calif., chair of the Senate Intelligence Committee, said that the day after Panetta had learned of the program he told members of Congress in a forty-five-minute briefing that Cheney had ordered the CIA to keep the operation secret from the public as well as from Congress. The program and Cheney's effort to keep Congress out of the loop became public knowledge on July 8, when a letter, written on June 26 by seven House Democrats to Panetta, was released, citing his remark that the CIA had "concealed significant actions from all Members of Congress, and misled Members for a number of years from 2001 to this week."

Bush had authorized the CIA to investigate whether a program of this nature would be viable through a legal pronouncement known as a finding. The CIA, according to former officials, began planning operations to capture or kill senior al-Qaida members and may have begun training some of its members to carry out this operation. The entire program, however, was stopped by Panetta in 2009 before it became operational.

According to a former senior intelligence official and Republicans on the intelligence committee, the program had not advanced to a stage where Congress needed to be involved in the process. The senior official claimed that Congress had long known that

President Bush had issued the finding directing the CIA to look into such a program and that it was not necessarily a complete program but rather "many ideas suggested over the course of years."

As tensions ran high after the September 11, 2001, terrorist attacks, and as the United States prepared troops to enter Afghanistan, military officials sent cables among themselves, according to those who have seen them, that authorized killing senior al-Qaida officials on site. President Bush had not authorized these memos or directives, but did eventually give permission to military leaders to kill al-Qaida leaders if it was determined that capturing them would prove too dangerous for the Americans or civilians involved. According to Rep. Peter Hoekstra, R-Mich., the ranking Republican on the House Intelligence Committee, Congress most likely would have approved such a CIA program in the days after September 11 amid fear that al-Qaida could attack the United States again at any time.

Spokespersons for the CIA said that although years went into planning and deciding what methods would be most logical to carry out these assassinations, no plans were ever put into action because agreed upon methods could not be reached. There were many difficult questions and details to decide, including how to stage the paramilitary members, whether to inform allies of the plans, and whether the assassinations could be sanctioned under the rules of war. The Bush administration held off giving the CIA the official go-ahead on the program, because officials hoped that the assassinations could be carried out with drones or other airstrikes, which would be more in line with typical military activities during a time of war.

How much the CIA spent on the program has been a subject of debate. According to some reports, the costs of training and investigation into how the operations would be carried out may have been as high as $50 million. According to Hoekstra, the spending was closer to $1 million. "The idea for this kind of program was tossed around in fits and starts," he said.

The CIA and members of the Bush administration have refused to comment on the program or any of its details, and it remains classified. Democratic members of Congress have called for an investigation into why the CIA withheld information about the program.

Although some former CIA operatives have said that there was no reason to inform Congress of its plans because the program was never fully operational, others have said that Panetta's move to quickly end the program indicated that it may have been higher on the CIA's priority list than originally noted.

POSSIBLE INVESTIGATION

Beyond the 2001 finding issued by President Bush, members of the CIA had continued to be briefed on a potential undertaking of this kind by the agency. According to senior CIA officials, two to three more briefings occurred, with the last one taking place in early 2008. At this point, the CIA made the determination that Congress should be briefed on the program in an effort to limit the scope and objectives. However, no congressional briefing occurred.

Former CIA officials have characterized the program in various ways, from an idea being casually tossed around to an expectation that the agency was preparing for an all-out attack on al-Qaida leaders. One former official told the *Wall Street Journal*, "It was straight out of the movies. It was like: Let's kill them all." This same official, however, said that President Bush and Vice President Cheney did not support such an all-out program and that any discussions moving in this direction were quickly stopped within the CIA. Democrats in Congress, however, said they planned to carry out investigations into the program, regardless of how far it had progressed. According to Senate majority whip Dick Durbin, D-Ill., "To have a massive program that is concealed from the leaders in Congress is not only inappropriate—it could be illegal."

Republicans have expressed concern at a Democratic investigation, saying that it could set the country back to the 1970s, when Frank Church's Committee looked into whether the Mafia had been hired to kill Fidel Castro. "We're heading back into this Frank Church atmosphere in this Senate and in this Congress, where, basically, where people use the CIA as a whipping boy," said Sen. Judd Gregg, R-N.H.

—Heather Kerrigan

Following is a press release from Silvestre Reyes, R-Texas, chair of the House Intelligence Committee on July 8, 2009, regarding the secret program run by the CIA about which CIA director Leon Panetta testified before Congress, and a letter from seven representatives sent on June 26, 2009, but released on July 8, 2009, questioning whether the CIA had misled Congress.

DOCUMENT

Rep. Silvestre Reyes, R-Texas, on CIA Director Leon Panetta's Testimony Before Congress

July 8, 2009

I appreciate Director Panetta's recent efforts to bring issues to the Committee's attention that, for some reason, had not been previously conveyed, and to make certain that the Committee is fully and currently briefed on all intelligence activities. I understand his direction to be that the Agency does not and will not lie to Congress, and he has set a high standard for truth in reporting to Congress.

I believe that CIA has, in the vast majority of matters, told the truth. But in rare instances, certain officers have not adhered to the high standards held, as a rule, by the CIA with respect to truthfulness in reporting. Both Director Panetta and I are determined to make sure this does not happen again.

The men and women of the CIA are honest, hard-working patriots, and they do not deserve the distraction to their mission that this current issue has caused.

SOURCE: Rep. Silvestre Reyes. Press release. "Reyes Statement on Recent Correspondence regarding the CIA." July 8, 2009. http://intelligence.house.gov/Media/PDFS/ReyesRelease070809.pdf.

Release of a Letter to the CIA from Seven Members of Congress on Misleading Information

July 8, 2009

June 26, 2009

The Honorable Leon E. Panetta, Director
Central Intelligence Agency
Washington, DC 20505

Dear Director Panetta:

You recall, no doubt, that on May 15, 2009, you stated the following in a letter to CIA employees:

"Let me be clear: It is not our policy or practice to mislead Congress. That is against our laws and values."

Recently you testified that you have determined that top CIA officials have concealed significant actions from all Members of Congress, and misled Members for a number of years from 2001 to this week. This is similar to other deceptions of which we are aware from other recent periods.

In light of your testimony, we ask that you publically correct your statement of May 15, 2009.

Sincerely,

Anna G. Eshoo
Rush D. Holt
Alcee L. Hastings
John F. Tierney
Mike Thompson
Janice D. Schakowsky
Adam Smith

Source: Rep. Anna Eshoo. Press release. "Rep. Eshoo Releases Letter to CIA Dir. Panetta." July 8, 2009. http://eshoo.house.gov/images/2009.06.26.panetta.pdf.

OTHER HISTORIC DOCUMENTS OF INTEREST

FROM THIS VOLUME

FROM PREVIOUS *HISTORIC DOCUMENTS*

Sonia Sotomayor Confirmed as First Hispanic Supreme Court Justice

JULY 13 AND AUGUST 5, 2009

On August 6, 2009, Sonia Sotomayor, who had served previously for seventeen years as a judge at the federal level, was confirmed by the U.S. Senate in a 68–31 vote to become the nation's first Hispanic Supreme Court associate justice, replacing retiring associate justice David H. Souter. Although her confirmation hearings went smoothly, with many assuming she would be confirmed from the beginning, questions about her votes on civil rights issues and how she would vote based on her ethnicity and background arose during the hearings.

In casting their votes, Senate Republicans had to decide whether they should risk voting against Sotomayor and further alienating Hispanic voters; the party had lost Hispanic support in the 2008 presidential election. The final Senate vote was not along party lines, with nine Republicans joining Democrats to confirm Sotomayor. Political analysts noted that it was interesting that no Republican who voted for Sotomayor was up for reelection in 2010.

SOTOMAYOR'S JUDICIAL RECORD

Sotomayor's record as a judge on the Second U.S. Circuit Court of Appeals, during which she authored more than 150 opinions, was closely focused on during her confirmation process, especially decisions made on abortion rights, civil rights, and the Second Amendment.

Although she had never handled a case dealing directly with the abortion rights of U.S. citizens, Sotomayor did write the decision in *Center for Reproductive Law and Policy v. Bush,* which involved the so-called Mexico City policy of the United States denying funds to any nation that planned to use the money for performing or counseling about abortions. An abortion rights group, Center for Reproductive Law and Policy, had brought the case, saying that its First Amendment, due process, and equal protection rights had been violated. Sotomayor wrote that the First Amendment and due process were not violated—the latter because the group claimed harm on a foreign entity rather than themselves. She also wrote that although equal protection could legitimately be claimed in this case, it failed because the government, when spending public funds, "is free to favor the anti-abortion position over the pro-choice position."

Sotomayor also tried multiple civil rights cases during her time as a judge, ruling on race, sex, age, and disability discrimination. In most cases, Sotomayor sided with the plaintiff. In what is considered her most strongly worded opinion, Sotomayor wrote the dissent in *Gant v. Wallingford Board of Education*, a case in which the parents of a student who had been transferred from first grade to kindergarten because of academic problems claimed that the school had disregarded racial discrimination against him. Although Sotomayor agreed with the court's majority that there was no harassment based on race, she disagreed with their ruling that demoting the student was not racially charged. According to Sotomayor, white students in the plaintiff's class who were struggling academically were given additional assistance, while the plaintiff, the only African American student in his class, was sent back to kindergarten without additional assistance from teachers.

The most high profile civil rights case Sotomayor participated in during her time as a federal judge was *Ricci v. DeStefano*, in which a group of white firefighters accused the city of New Haven, Connecticut, of racial discrimination. According to the firefighters, the city had offered a promotions test, and when no African American firefighter passed, the city threw the test out and did not grant promotions, believing the test had a racial bias. Sotomayor, as a member of a Second Circuit panel, sided with the city. The circuit court refused to hear the case, which reached the U.S. Supreme Court in 2009. The Court voted 5–4 that New Haven's decision to throw out all test results was a violation of Title VII of the Civil Rights Act.

The right to bear arms also came up during Sotomayor's time on the Second Circuit. In the case of *Maloney v. Cuomo*, a New York attorney claimed that a state law that prohibited people from carrying a chuka stick, used in martial arts practice, violated Second Amendment rights. Sotomayor's court rejected the claim, saying that the Second Amendment is a federal standard that does not apply to the states.

Supreme Court Nomination and Confirmation

After her nomination by President Barack Obama on May 26 to replace Justice Souter, supporters of Sotomayor said that during her seventeen years at the federal court level, she had been popular with both Republicans and Democrats. Before her nomination, Sotomayor had served as a judge on the Second Circuit after having been nominated by former president Bill Clinton, and before that had been named a district judge by President George H.W. Bush in 1992. Although Democrats thought her confirmation would be smooth given that they held the majority of seats in the Senate, it did not go without strong Republican opposition.

President Obama called Sotomayor shortly before her confirmation hearings began. According to a statement from the White House, the president "complimented the judge for making courtesy calls to 89 senators in which she discussed her adherence to the rule of law throughout her 17 years on the federal bench." In addition, "The president expressed his confidence that Judge Sotomayor would be confirmed to serve as a justice on the Supreme Court for many years to come," the statement said.

Sen. Mitch McConnell, R-Ky., was an outspoken critic of Sotomayor's confirmation, saying that he would oppose the nomination because her "record of written statements suggest an alarming lack of respect for the notion of equal justice, and, therefore, in my view, an insufficient willingness to abide by the judicial oath." McConnell called the notion of equal justice "particularly important" when deciding whether to confirm a Supreme Court nominee because "there would be no higher court to deter or prevent her from injecting into the law the various disconcerting principles that recur throughout her public statements." Other Republicans joined McConnell, complaining that the Republican leadership had not done enough to try and stall Sotomayor's confirmation. However, Sotomayor's performance in her confirmation hearings impressed Democrats and Republicans alike. Sen. Olympia Snowe, R-Maine, said she was "impressed with Judge Sotomayor's comportment and obvious mastery of the law during this weeks' nomination hearings." Other Republicans disagreed with some of Sotomayor's constitutional interpretations, including her assessment that the Second Amendment, which concerns the right to bear arms, is not a fundamental right.

McConnell's remarks came at the same time some of his Republican colleagues said that they would vote to confirm Sotomayor. Regardless of McConnell's disapproval of Sotomayor, the Democratic majority in Congress and the Republicans who said they would cross the aisle in her support, would eliminate any chance of a filibuster and ensure a smooth confirmation. Sen. Mel Martinez, R-Fla., a Cuban American, said that Sotomayor's rise through the judicial ranks indicated "that the American dream continues to be attainable."

During her first day of questioning before the Senate Judiciary Committee, Democrats worked to portray Sotomayor as a role model. They said she would bring balance to the Court, attempting to counter Republican charges that Sotomayor would become a liberal activist on the Court.

Sotomayor defended herself against Republican questioning, saying, "The task of a judge is not to make law. It is to apply law. And it is clear, I believe, that my record in two courts reflects my rigorous commitment to interpreting the Constitution according to its terms, interpreting statutes according to their terms and Congress's intent, and hewing faithfully to precedents established by the Supreme Court and by my circuit court."

During her confirmation hearing, Sotomayor spoke about her background, being raised in a housing project in the Bronx by her mother after her father had passed away, learning English at a young age, and being drawn to a career in law after watching the "Perry Mason" show on television. Sotomayor's determination earned her an undergraduate degree from Princeton University and a law degree from Yale. Sotomayor had said in speech that because of her experiences, she hoped that as a "wise Latina woman" she would be able to reach better conclusions than those who had not had as many diverse experiences. This quote first appeared in documents sent to Congress ahead of her confirmation hearings. Republicans set out to challenge Sotomayor not only on her "wise Latina" remark but also on her comments that her race and past life experiences could give her a better view of cases at hand.

"I will not vote for, and no senator should vote for, anyone who will not render justice impartially," said Sen. Jeff Sessions, R-Ala. "Call it empathy, call it prejudice or call it sympathy, but whatever it is, it's not the law," he continued. Sotomayor responded by saying, "My personal and professional experiences help me to listen and understand, with the law always commanding the result in every case." Republicans, however, were cognizant that with an extensive judicial resume that spanned three different presidential nominations, she most likely would be confirmed.

Conservative radio personality Rush Limbaugh and Republican former House majority leader Newt Gingrich called the "wise Latina" remark racist, but most Republicans at her confirmation hearings, although questioning the remark, were less bombastic. Sen. Susan Collins, R-Maine, told reporters that Sotomayor said she had used the phrase in the past but would not use it again in the future.

Sotomayor was given the opportunity to explain her "wise Latina" remark during her congressional hearings. She explained that when she used the phrase during a 2001 speech, she was trying "to inspire young Hispanics, Latino students, and lawyers to believe that their life experiences added value to the process." However, she apologized, saying that her comment was regrettable and a "rhetorical flourish that fell flat." Sotomayor further noted that she does not believe that a Latina woman would necessarily always make better decisions than a white male.

During the debate and vote, Democrats focused on Sotomayor's record as an impartial judge with an uplifting background. Republicans continued to call her a liberal activist judge who would make determinations in an effort to enforce laws in a liberal manner. Chair of the Senate Judiciary Committee, Sen. Patrick Leahy, D-Vt., called Sotomayor's nomination historic. "It is distinctively American to continually refine our union, moving us closer to our ideals. Our union is not yet perfected, but with this confirmation, we will be making progress." He continued, "Years from now, we will remember this time, when we crossed paths with the quintessentially American journey of Sonia Sotomayor, and when our nation took another step forward through this historic confirmation process."

In the end, Sotomayor was confirmed by a 68–31 vote in the Senate with nine Republicans voting for her confirmation, and only one senator, Ted Kennedy, D-Mass., missing the vote, while recovering from brain surgery. "This is a wonderful day for Judge Sotomayor and her family, but I also think it's a wonderful day for America," said President Obama.

Latino Reaction

Latinos around the country celebrated Sotomayor's confirmation. It was a big step for Latinos, who make up 15 percent of the population yet only account for 3 percent of U.S. judges.

After senators in the Sotomayor confirmation hearings raised questions about her "wise Latina woman" remarks, as noted earlier, Latinos used the phrase as a rallying cry. A popular artist, Lalo Alcaraz, said that Sotomayor's confirmation would mean a lot for his daughter, who by seeing a Latino woman on the nation's high court could grow up knowing that she could achieve any of her dreams.

—Heather Kerrigan

Following is Judge Sonia Sotomayor's opening statement before the Senate Judiciary Committee on July 13, 2009; a floor statement from August 5, 2009, by Sen. Jeff Sessions, R-Ala., on Sotomayor's nomination to the Supreme Court; and a floor statement by Sen. Patrick Leahy, D-Vt., on August 5, 2009, on Sotomayor's nomination to the Supreme Court.

Judge Sonia Sotomayor's Opening Statement Before the Senate Judiciary Committee

July 13, 2009

Thank you, Mr. Chairman. I also want to thank Senators Schumer and Gillibrand for that kind introduction. In recent weeks, I have had the privilege and pleasure of meeting eighty-nine gracious Senators, including all the members of this Committee. I thank you for the time you have spent with me. Our meetings have given me an illuminating tour of the fifty states and invaluable insights into the American people.

There are countless family members, friends, mentors, colleagues, and clerks who have done so much over the years to make this day possible. I am deeply appreciative for their love and support. I want to make one special note of thanks to my mom. I am here today because of her aspirations and sacrifices for both my brother Juan and me. Mom, I love that we are sharing this together. I am very grateful to the President and humbled to be here today as a nominee to the United States Supreme Court.

The progression of my life has been uniquely American. My parents left Puerto Rico during World War II. I grew up in modest circumstances in a Bronx housing project. My father, a factory worker with a third grade education, passed away when I was nine years old.

On her own, my mother raised my brother and me. She taught us that the key to success in America is a good education. And she set the example, studying alongside my brother and me at our kitchen table so that she could become a registered nurse. We worked hard. I poured myself into my studies at Cardinal Spellman High School, earning scholarships to Princeton University and then Yale Law School, while my brother went to medical school. Our achievements are due to the values that we learned as children, and they have continued to guide my life's endeavors. I try to pass on this legacy by serving as a mentor and friend to my many godchildren and students of all backgrounds.

Over the past three decades, I have seen our judicial system from a number of different perspectives—as a big-city prosecutor, a corporate litigator, a trial judge and an appellate judge. My first job after law school was as an assistant District Attorney in New York. There, I saw children exploited and abused. I felt the suffering of victims' families torn apart by a loved one's needless death. And I learned the tough job law enforcement has protecting the public safety. In my next legal job, I focused on commercial, instead of criminal, matters. I litigated issues on behalf of national and international businesses and advised them on matters ranging from contracts to trademarks.

My career as an advocate ended—and my career as a judge began—when I was appointed by President George H.W. Bush to the United States District Court for the Southern District of New York. As a trial judge, I decided over four hundred and fifty cases, and presided over dozens of trials, with perhaps my best known case involving the Major League Baseball strike in 1995.

After six extraordinary years on the district court, I was appointed by President William Jefferson Clinton to the United States Court of Appeals for the Second Circuit. On that Court, I have enjoyed the benefit of sharing ideas and perspectives with wonderful colleagues as we have worked together to resolve the issues before us. I have now served as an appellate judge for over a decade, deciding a wide range of Constitutional, statutory, and other legal questions.

Throughout my seventeen years on the bench, I have witnessed the human consequences of my decisions. Those decisions have been made not to serve the interests of any one litigant, but always to serve the larger interest of impartial justice.

In the past month, many Senators have asked me about my judicial philosophy. It is simple: fidelity to the law. The task of a judge is not to make the law—it is to apply the law. And it is clear, I believe, that my record in two courts reflects my rigorous commitment to interpreting the Constitution according to its terms; interpreting statutes according to their terms and Congress's intent; and hewing faithfully to precedents established by the Supreme Court and my Circuit Court. In each case I have heard, I have applied the law to the facts at hand.

The process of judging is enhanced when the arguments and concerns of the parties to the litigation are understood and acknowledged. That is why I generally structure my opinions by setting out what the law requires and then by explaining why a contrary position, sympathetic or not, is accepted or rejected. That is how I seek to strengthen both the rule of law and faith in the impartiality of our justice system. My personal and professional experiences help me listen and understand, with the law always commanding the result in every case.

Since President Obama announced my nomination in May, I have received letters from people all over this country. Many tell a unique story of hope in spite of struggles. Each letter has deeply touched me. Each reflects a belief in the dream that led my parents to come to New York all those years ago. It is our Constitution that makes that Dream possible, and I now seek the honor of upholding the Constitution as a Justice on the Supreme Court.

I look forward in the next few days to answering your questions, to having the American people learn more about me, and to being part of a process that reflects the greatness of our Constitution and of our nation. Thank you

SOURCE: Sonia Sotomayor. "Testimony of Judge Sonia Sotomayor." July 13, 2009. http://judiciary.senate .gov/hearings/testimony.cfm?id=3959&wit_id=8102.

Sen. Jeff Sessions, R-Ala., Floor Statement on Sotomayor

August 5, 2009

Mr. SESSIONS. Mr. President, we had a number of Members discuss the second amendment issue that was dealt with by Judge Sotomayor in two different cases. It is an important question and I think her nomination raises very serious concerns about it. I would like to try as fairly as I can to analyze the circumstances in her dealing with these issues and why I think it is a problem that Senators rightly have objections to.

The second amendment is in the Constitution. It is the second of the first 10 amendments. It is part of the Bill of Rights. If you remember, the people were not so happy with the Constitution. They wanted to have a guarantee of individual rights that they as American citizens would possess no matter what the Federal Government or anyone else wanted to do about it. So they passed the right not to establish a religion, free speech, free press, the right to jury trial and other matters of that kind in the first 10 amendments, as adopted.

The second amendment was one of those, of course. It says:

A well regulated militia being essential to the security of a free State, the right of the people to keep and bear arms shall not be infringed.

The right of the people to keep and bear arms shall not be infringed.

Over the years, laws have been passed that caused difficulties and that began to overreach with respect to the second amendment right. . . .

I think most scholars have believed for some time that it is, in fact, an individual right, that the first clause regarding the well-regulated militia did not undermine the final declaratory clause which said:

The right of the people to keep and bear arms shall not be infringed.

But no Supreme Court case had ruled on that squarely until last year when the Supreme Court took up the Heller case, which was in the Federal city we are in today, DC. The Supreme Court in the Heller case said it was an individual right and it prohibited the city of Washington, DC, from effectively barring any citizen in the District from having a gun.

It was an exceedingly broad ban on guns. But I would note something that ought to be remembered: It was a 5-to-4 decision—four members of the Supreme Court did not agree. Some people do not agree.

One of our Democratic colleagues yesterday said of the result in Heller, that it was "a newly minted and narrowly enacted constitutional right."

That is cause for concern. The Constitution, I don't think, is newly minted. I don't think the Court created a right. I think the Court simply declared a right that was plainly in the Constitution. So this is part of our concern.

I would suggest that it is a fragile right, however, based on the way some of the courts have been ruling and based on how Judge Sotomayor ruled.

Somebody had raised the point several times that it is somehow not right that the National Rifle Association here, at the end, after the hearings, declared that they think that Judge Sotomayor should not be confirmed. Certainly they were reluctant to be engaged in this debate.

But for the reasons I would note—and Senator Murkowski and others have noted—I don't think they had much choice, because it is a critical thing we are dealing with here, the next appointment to the U.S. Supreme Court.

In a year after the Heller case was decided that the right to keep and bear arms is a personal or individual right and it cannot be abridged by the Federal Government, the case came before her as to whether the second amendment applied to States and cities.

What if other cities were to declare that you couldn't have a gun in the city, or a State were to declare you couldn't have a firearm, or if a State were to place massive restrictions on the use of personal weapons? She took that case, the first major case after Heller to deal with this issue. Anyone who is familiar with the appellate courts in America, as this judge would be, would know this was a big, big, big case, a case of great importance coming on the heels of the widely discussed Heller decision. In it, she rendered an exceedingly short opinion. In it, she found it was "settled law" that the second amendment does not apply to individual Americans in States or cities. The city or State could completely bar them from having any kind of gun. . . .

My first point is this: I don't believe it would be appropriate to say it is settled law that the second amendment does not apply to the States after the Heller case. That troubled me that she said that.

Judge Sotomayor made a decision in the Maloney case, the first major case after Heller. It was only eight paragraphs in a case that everyone knew was of great importance. And only one paragraph dealt with the question of whether the second amendment would apply to the States.

Those who have supported Judge Sotomayor have correctly noted that the seventh circuit heard the same kind of case some months later and they agreed with the Maloney case and Judge Sotomayor. They spent, however, a number of pages on it. They spent 2½ pages on the question of whether it was incorporated against the States. But they concluded that even with the footnote in the Heller case, they concluded that the more clear authority was still this old case that is out there in the 1800s. They did not say, however, that it was settled law.

The ninth circuit took up the very same case just a few months after Judge Sotomayor's Maloney decision. In a 19-page opinion that discussed in great depth the important constitutional issues, the panel said, when you read the Heller decision, when you consider the footnote of the Supreme Court's opinion where they said they didn't explicitly decide whether it applied to the States, they found differently. They found the second amendment does apply to the States and cities, and the States and cities must comply with it, and they can't ban all guns. They found not only that it was not settled law. To the contrary, they found that the footnote in the Supreme Court opinion "explicitly left open this question." And because they found the question was left open by the Supreme Court, they felt they were authorized to consider the constitutional laws and questions that are important and render a decision that they thought was the right constitutional decision. That is why they went forward in that fashion.

At the hearing, the judge was asked a number of questions about this. I didn't find those questions answered very persuasive [*sic*], frankly. In some instances, I found them confusing. There was no retreat that I heard from this untenable position. . . .

In the course of her decision she also found a critical question, that the second amendment is not a fundamental question. The judge was just wrong on that in a big, big case. It is the kind of thing you shouldn't make a mistake on. In the majority's footnote on this issue, the Court expressly reserved the question of whether the second amendment applies to the States. . . .

So they explicitly said that they didn't [*sic*] were addressing this issue. But it is pretty clear that the doctrine that allows the Bill of Rights, the first 10 amendments, to apply to the States [*sic*]. That doctrine has developed dramatically in the 20th century, over the last 100 years. Virtually every one of the 10 amendments has been incorporated against the States. But the Second Amendment has not yet been applied to the States. To me, that is an odd thing in light of the doctrine of the incorporating of the first 10 amendments as protections for individual Americans against both the Federal Government and State and local governments. That doctrine has developed great strength and power over the last 100 years. Few people would want to go back. I think most people would be awfully surprised to learn that the second amendment would not be one of those applied to the States. It certainly, in my opinion, is not settled law.

This case was dealt with in a most cursory manner. It dealt with a matter of huge national importance. It is the kind of case that legal scholars watch closely. It was an exceedingly short opinion, a few paragraphs. It showed little respect for the seriousness of the issue.

It didn't discuss it in any depth. It incorrectly stated it was settled law that the second amendment would not apply to the States. These are the problems we have with it.

Judge Sotomayor now seeks to be on the Supreme Court. And with regard to the 5-to-4 decision in Heller and to the question of whether she should recuse herself, as asked by Senator Kyl, she indicated that if her case came up, she would recuse herself. It could come before the Supreme Court. It is that important. But if one of the other cases raising exactly the same issue came up, she refused to say she would recuse herself. Of course, if her case comes up, it is a matter of ethics that she would have to recuse herself. I thought that since having already clearly decided precisely the same issue the Supreme Court would have to deal with, she ought to have indicated to us that since she expressed her opinion on it, she wouldn't sit on the case. But that did not happen.

I will share likewise another concern we have about the firefighters case and how that was handled in such a short manner. The firefighters contended that they had studied hard. They had passed a promotion exam. They were on the road to being promoted. The city, because of political complaints about the fact that certain groups did not pass the test in a way that raised concerns, decided they would give up and not have the test and wipe out the test and not follow through with the test. The firefighters felt they had done everything possible, and they challenged that. Indeed, later the Supreme Court held that no evidence was ever presented that the test was not a fair and good test. Indeed, they had taken great care to get good people to help write the test in a way that would be neutral and fair to all groups of people and would not have any kind of unfair advantage.

When that case came before the judge, I was very disappointed that she and her panel treated it as a summary order. A summary order is reserved for cases that present no real legal question. Summary orders are not even circulated among the other judges in the circuit. Here, it was a summary order that did not even adopt the opinion of the lower courts that had ruled in this fashion. It just summarily dismissed the firefighters' claim and rendered judgment in favor of the city which had altered the plan for promotion. It was basically done because of their race.

The equal protection clause of the Constitution says that all American citizens are entitled to equal protection of the laws, regardless of race. That is what their complaint was, one of the complaints. I would note that this was not even an opinion. It was basically a line or two summarily dismissing this.

Then one of the other judges on the court apparently found out this opinion had been rendered in a case that struck him, apparently, as a matter of real importance, a case that ought not to be disposed of by a summary order, that the firefighters were at least entitled to an opinion. And by the way, they never got a trial. Basically it was dismissed prior to trial on motions. So after great debate within the circuit, a little bit of a dust-up within the circuit, by a 7-to-6 margin, Judge Sotomayor casting the decisive seventh vote, they decided not to rehear the case and any precedent that may exist in the circuit. But at that point, I guess as part of the process of confrontation that arose there, the panel issued an opinion that adopted the lower court opinion, a procuring opinion. They didn't write their own opinion but basically adopted the lower court's opinion. . . .

SOURCE: Sen. Jeff Sessions. "Nomination of Sonia Sotomayor to Be an Associate Justice of the Supreme Court of the United States." August 5, 2009. *Congressional Record* 2009, 155, pt. S88542–S8843. www.gpo .gov/fdsys/pkg/CREC-2009-08-05/pdf/CREC-2009-08-05-pt1-PgS8822-2.pdf.

Sen. Patrick Leahy, D-Vt., Floor Statement on Sotomayor

August 5, 2009

Mr. LEAHY. Mr. President, many independent studies that have closely examined Judge Sotomayor's record have concluded that hers is a record of applying the law, not bias. For example, the American Bar Association's Standing Committee on the Federal Judiciary unanimously found Judge Sotomayor to be "well qualified"—its highest rating—after conducting a thorough evaluation that included an examination of her integrity and freedom from bias. The Chair of the Standing Committee testified, "the committee unanimously found an absence of any bias in the nominee's extensive work," and described Judge Sotomayor's opinions as "show[ing] an adherence to precedent and an absence of attempts to set policy based on the judge's personal views."

Numerous other studies from groups such as the Congressional Research Service, the New York City Bar Association, the Transactional Records Access Clearinghouse, the National Association of Women Lawyers, and the nonpartisan Brennan Center for Justice, have reached similar conclusions. These studies were entered into the record during Judge Sotomayor's confirmation hearings. Nothing in these studies or in her 17 year record on the bench raises a concern that Judge Sotomayor would substitute feelings for the command of the law.

Judge Sotomayor's critics attack her by pretending that President Obama does not respect the Constitution and the rule of law. . . .

They attack her by misconstruing what empathy means. Empathy is understanding and awareness. . . .

When she was designated by the President, Judge Sotomayor said: "The wealth of experiences, personal and professional, have helped me appreciate the variety of perspectives that present themselves in every case that I hear. It has helped me to understand, respect, and respond to the concerns and arguments of all litigants who appear before me, as well as to the views of my colleagues on the bench. I strive never to forget the real-world consequences of my decisions on individuals, businesses, and government."

It took a Supreme Court that understood the real world to see that the seeming fair-sounding doctrine of "separate but equal" was a straightjacket of inequality. We do not need more conservative activists second guessing Congress and who through judicial extremism override congressional judgments intended to protect Americans' voting rights, privacy rights and access to health care and education.

In her widely misconstrued speech at the University of California at Berkeley, Judge Sotomayor said: "[J]udges must transcend their personal sympathies and prejudices and aspire to achieve a greater degree of fairness and integrity based on the reason of law." That parallels what Chief Justice Roberts said at his confirmation hearing when he testified about "the ideal in the American justice system" and judges "doing their best to interpret the law, to interpret the Constitution, according to the rule of law" and not substituting their own personal agenda.

Those who spent days asking Judge Sotomayor to explain what she meant in a partial quotation from that speech about the decisions reached by a "wise Latina woman with the richness of her experiences" miss that she begins that statement with the words,

"I would hope." They miss that her statement is aspirational. She would "hope" that she and the other Hispanic women judges would be "wise" in their decisionmaking and that their experiences would help inform them and help provide that wisdom. Judge Sotomayor's critics have ignored her modesty in not claiming to be perfect, but rather in aspiring to the greatest wisdom and fairness she can achieve.

These critics also miss that Judge Sotomayor was pointing out a path to greater fairness and fidelity to law by acknowledging that despite the aspiration she shares with other judges, there are imperfections of human judging. By acknowledging rather than ignoring that while all judges seek to set aside their personal views, they do not always succeed, and we can be on guard against those views influencing judicial outcomes. . . .

We have a long and important tradition in the law of seeking justice and fairness and equity. Judge Sotomayor spoke about the meaning of the word "justice" a decade ago and said: "Almost every person in our society is moved by that one word. It is a word embodied with a spirit that rings in the hearts of people. It is an elegant and beautiful word that moves people to believe that the law is something special." . . .

We need judges who appreciate when and how to use their equitable powers. Judges who follow the law are empowered to enjoin illegal behavior, as the Supreme Court did in its historic series of orders enjoining the States and others from segregating schools on the basis of race. This does not mean that our courts have the power to remedy every problem in America. They do not . . . In that regard, I believe that the experience and wisdom Judge Sotomayor has gained from an extraordinary life will benefit all Americans.

Mr. President, I yield the floor and suggest the absence of a quorum.

Source: Sen. Patrick Leahy. "Nomination of Sonia Sotomayor to Be an Associate Justice of the Supreme Court of the United States." *Congressional Record* 2009, 155, pt. S8850–S8851. www.gpo.gov/fdsys/pkg/CREC-2009-08-05/pdf/CREC-2009-08-05-pt1-PgS8822-2.pdf.

OTHER HISTORIC DOCUMENTS OF INTEREST

FROM THIS VOLUME

■ U.S. Supreme Court on Civil Rights Act in Hiring Practices, p. 292

FROM PREVIOUS *HISTORIC DOCUMENTS*

■ U.S. Supreme Court on Personal Right to Possess Firearms, *2008,* p. 264
■ First Woman Appointed to Supreme Court, *1981,* p. 575

Centers for Disease Control and Prevention Reports Rise in Pregnancy and STD Rates During Bush Administration

JULY 17, 2009

During his eight years in office, President George W. Bush was a stalwart supporter of abstinence-only sex education, both in the United States and abroad, in an effort to reduce teenage pregnancies and sexually transmitted diseases (STDs). His administration's policies included decreasing or eliminating funding for safe-sex programs and increasing funding for abstinence education. According to a July 17, 2009, report from the Centers for Disease Control and Prevention (CDC) examining 10- to 24-year-olds, the Bush-era policies proved largely ineffective, especially in poor and minority areas. In fact, after 2006, after more than a decade of decline, teenage pregnancy and syphilis rates rose sharply in half the U.S. states, according to the report.

From 1987 to 1991, the birthrate for teenage girls rose steadily, which was followed by a decade of significant decrease. In 1991, the teenage birth rate hit a high of 62.1 per 1,000 teenagers aged 15 to 19, and fell to a record low of 45.9 per 1,000 in 2001. Between 2000 and 2001, the birthrate for those aged 15 to 17 fell by 8 percent; and although all states saw a decline in their teenage birth rates between 1991 and 2000, ten states saw record declines of greater than 20 percent.

"It is disheartening that after years of improvement with respect to teen pregnancy and sexually transmitted diseases, we now see signs that progress is stalling and many of these trends are going in the wrong direction," said Janet Collins, a CDC director.

DEPARTMENT OF HEALTH AND HUMAN SERVICES ABSTINENCE-ONLY EDUCATION

Beginning in 1991, the United States began to see a significant decrease in the number of girls aged 15 to 19 who reported being pregnant or having contracted an STD. This trend continued through 2006, when the rates showed a sharp uptick. During this time, the Bush administration and the U.S. Department of Health and Human Services (HHS) were working to increase funding and the availability of abstinence-only education programs to teenagers, specifically those in underserved communities, while decreasing the money available to states for safe-sex programs.

President Bush made it a goal to increase abstinence-only funding to $135 million per year by the time he left office in January 2009. To help achieve his goal, the president used the welfare reform law of 1996, which had created the Abstinence Education Program. Through this program, the federal government provided grants to organizations that taught abstinence-only sex education. From 1998 through 2002, this law provided $50 million per fiscal year to promote abstinence until marriage. In addition to the Abstinence Education Program, the HHS also administered grants that supported both public and private entities teaching abstinence education. The first grant through this program was provided in 2001.

Although each state was encouraged to apply for grants through these two programs and various others working to decrease teenage pregnancy and STD rates through abstinence, some states, such as California, did not choose to do so, citing restrictions placed on the grants by the federal government. "We're walking a tightrope: one side wants us to apply for the money, and the other says 'Don't you dare,'" said Catherine Camacho, then–deputy director of family health in California's Department of Health Services. "We firmly believe that abstinence is the foundation on which every teen pregnancy prevention program should be built," she continued. "But if you look at the studies, the data is going to tell you that it isn't necessarily realistic."

The stipulations on how states could use the money from the federal government gave many public health experts reason to believe that the policies would not be very popular with a majority of the population. If accepting the money, states were required to teach that sex before marriage "is likely to have harmful psychological and physical effects" and that abstinence is the only foolproof way to prevent pregnancy and STDs. While there is general agreement with the latter, according to some studies, parents also wanted their children to be told about the use of contraception to protect themselves. The programs funded by the federal government, however, discussed contraception only to explain what happens when it fails. According to a study conducted in 2000 by the Kaiser Family Foundation, a nonprofit organization focusing on health care, of 4,000 educators, parents, and others, 85 percent wanted children to learn about different forms of contraception, as well as how to talk to a partner about the use of contraception.

CENTERS FOR DISEASE CONTROL AND PREVENTION REPORT

The CDC was not the first organization to find that abstinence-only education programs are not the most effective with teenagers. In November 2007, at the time President Bush was calling for more funding for abstinence-only sex education, the National Campaign to Prevent Teen and Unplanned Pregnancy released a report indicating that sex-ed programs that encompass abstinence as well as information on contraception were the most effective at preventing teenage pregnancy and STDs. Even before this report was released, the Guttmacher Institute had reported that "a nine-year $8 m evaluation of federally funded abstinence-only-until-marriage programs found that these programs have no beneficial impact on young people's sexual behavior." Democratic members of Congress, led by Rep. Henry Waxman, D-Calif., had also pointed to reports indicating the failure of abstinence-only programs. A report requested by Waxman in 2004 had found that 80 percent of abstinence-only programs teach "false, misleading, or distorted information about reproductive health," which nearly ensured, the report said, that pregnancy and STD rates would rise.

According to CDC researcher Lorrie Gavin, "You see overall patterns through the '90s and early 2000s of general improvements in the sexual and reproductive health of our young people." Younger teens, and specifically African Americans, who have historically had the highest teenage birth rate, saw a decrease from 59.3 percent of teens reporting sexual activity in 1991 to 46 percent reporting such activity in 2007. Those reporting that they had engaged in sexual conduct reported having used a condom. This decrease in sexual activity led to a decrease in the rate of teenage births and abortions, especially among African American teenagers.

In 2006, this trend slowed, and later reversed. Birth rates among young people were up two years in a row. In 2006, the rate was up 3 percent, and in 2007 it increased another 1 percent. The greatest increase was among African American teenagers, at 5 percent in 2006; white and Hispanic teenagers saw flattened rates. In addition, the occurrence of STDs showed a significant rise, with one million teenagers reporting an infection to health care providers in the past 10 years. Researchers at the CDC said that although the trend in greater numbers of STDs is alarming, the increase in STD rates also reflects better testing and reporting. Still, the number of teenage girls reporting having contracted syphilis rose by nearly half and the number of teenage boys diagnosed with AIDS almost doubled during the past ten years.

THE DEBATE

The CDC report sparked increased debate among those supporting abstinence-only sex education and those supporting comprehensive sex education programs. The abstinence-only camp argued that the report indicates only that a greater effort needed to be made to get teenagers information about postponing sex until marriage. Kristi Hamrick, a spokesperson for American Values, a nonprofit organization that works to encourage traditional marriage and families, said that the difficulty for groups such as hers is an American culture that has become obsessed with sex. "It is ridiculous to say that a program we nominally invest in has failed when it fails to overcome the most sexualized culture in world history. Education that emphasizes abstinence as the best option for teens makes up a minuscule part of overall sex education in the United States," she said. She compared sex education to other choices that teenagers make, saying that when it comes to food, drugs, or alcohol, we tell teenagers which choice is best for them to make, but don't do the same for sex. "We don't take vodka to drivers education because children will drink and drive," she said.

Groups that support comprehensive sex education programs for teenagers have used the CDC report as evidence that abstinence-only education has failed. Planned Parenthood, one of the nation's largest supporters of comprehensive sex education, called the report "alarming" and a confirmation that teenagers need "medically accurate, age-appropriate, comprehensive sex education."

The CDC says it is still too early to tell whether this upswing in pregnancy and STD rates represents a true reversal of the decade-long trend toward safer sexual activity or a temporary variation.

MINORITIES DISPROPORTIONATELY AFFECTED

The CDC and other health organizations have long known that poor and minority women are more likely to be affected by STDs and teenage pregnancy than others. A report conducted in 2006 found that "[w]omen living in poverty are now almost four times more likely to become pregnant unintentionally than women of greater means." Although the

2009 CDC report left out an investigation specifically based on poverty, the report does indicate that when race and geography are taken into account, there is a greater chance that poor and minority teenage girls will be affected by higher pregnancy and STD rates.

Geographically, southern states "tend to have the highest rate of negative sexual and reproductive health outcomes, including early pregnancy and STDs," according to the report. In these states, there is a greater reliance on religion and abstinence-only education.

AIDS and pregnancy rates among girls aged 15–19 are highest in Hispanic and non–Hispanic black communities, while chlamydia, gonorrhea, and syphilis most greatly affect non–Hispanic black men and women between the ages of 10 and 24.

GLOBAL ABSTINENCE-ONLY EDUCATION

During his presidency, Bush banned U.S. government funding to any nongovernmental organization that provided abortion services and counseling around the world. In his President's Emergency Plan for AIDS Relief (PEPFAR) program, Bush allocated funding so that one-third went to abstinence-only education. However, when the money was actually distributed, two-thirds delegated to preventing the spread of HIV went to abstinence-only education.

—Heather Kerrigan

Following is an excerpt of the report released by the Centers for Disease Control and Prevention on July 17, 2009, detailing the rise in pregnancy and STD rates among teenagers between 2002 and 2007.

CDC Reports Rise in Teen Pregnancy and STD Rates

July 17, 2009

Sexual and Reproductive Health of Persons Aged 10–24 Years—United States, 2002–2007

[Table and note references have been omitted.]

SUMMARY

This report presents data for 2002–2007 concerning the sexual and reproductive health of persons aged 10–24 years in the United States. Data were compiled from the National Vital Statistics System and multiple surveys and surveillance systems that monitor sexual and reproductive health outcomes into a single reference report that makes this information more easily accessible to policy makers, researchers, and program providers who are working to improve the reproductive health of young persons in the United States. The report addresses three primary topics: 1) current levels of risk behavior and health outcomes; 2) disparities by sex, age, race/ethnicity, and geographic residence; and 3) trends over time.

The data presented in this report indicate that many young persons in the United States engage in sexual risk behavior and experience negative reproductive health outcomes. In 2004, approximately 745,000 pregnancies occurred among U.S. females aged <20 years. In 2006, approximately 22,000 adolescents and young adults aged 10–24 years in 33 states were living with human immunodeficiency virus/acquired immune deficiency syndrome (HIV/AIDS), and approximately 1 million adolescents and young adults aged 10–24 years were reported to have chlamydia, gonorrhea, or syphilis. One-quarter of females aged 15–19 years and 45% of those aged 20–24 years had evidence of infection with human papillomavirus during 2003–2004, and approximately 105,000 females aged 10–24 years visited a hospital emergency department (ED) for a nonfatal sexual assault injury during 2004–2006. Although risks tend to increase with age, persons in the youngest age group (youths aged 10–14 years) also are affected. For example, among persons aged 10–14 years, 16,000 females became pregnant in 2004, nearly 18,000 males and females were reported to have sexually transmitted diseases (STDs) in 2006, and 27,500 females visited a hospital ED because of a nonfatal sexual assault injury during 2004–2006.

Noticeable disparities exist in the sexual and reproductive health of young persons in the United States. For example, pregnancy rates for female Hispanic and non–Hispanic black adolescents aged 15–19 years are much higher (132.8 and 128.0 per 1,000 population) than their non–Hispanic white peers (45.2 per 1,000 population). Non–Hispanic black young persons are more likely to be affected by AIDS: for example, black female adolescents aged 15–19 years were more likely to be living with AIDS (49.6 per 100,000 population) than Hispanic (12.2 per 100,000 population), American Indian/Alaska Native (2.6 per 100,000 population), non–Hispanic white (2.5 per 100,000 population) and Asian/Pacific Islander (1.3 per 100,000 population) adolescents. In 2006, among young persons aged 10–24 years, rates for chlamydia, gonorrhea, and syphilis were highest among non–Hispanic blacks for all age groups. The southern states tend to have the highest rates of negative sexual and reproductive health outcomes, including early pregnancy and STDs.

Although the majority of negative outcomes have been declining for the past decade, the most recent data suggest that progress might be slowing, and certain negative sexual health outcomes are increasing. For example, birth rates among adolescents aged 15–19 years decreased annually during 1991–2005 but increased during 2005–2007, from 40.5 live births per 1,000 females in 2005 to 42.5 in 2007 (preliminary data). The annual rate of AIDS diagnoses reported among males aged 15–19 years has nearly doubled in the past 10 years, from 1.3 cases per 100,000 population in 1997 to 2.5 cases in 2006. Similarly, after decreasing for >20 years, gonorrhea infection rates among adolescents and young adults have leveled off or had modest fluctuations (e.g., rates among males aged 15–19 years ranged from 285.7 cases per 100,000 population in 2002 to 250.2 cases per 100,000 population in 2004 and then increased to 275.4 cases per 100,000 population in 2006), and rates for syphilis have been increasing (e.g., rates among females aged 15–19 years increased from 1.5 cases per 100,000 population in 2004 to 2.2 cases per 100,000 population in 2006) after a significant decrease during 1997–2005.

BACKGROUND

Early, unprotected sex among young persons can have negative consequences. Pregnancy and sexually transmitted diseases (STDs), including human immunodeficiency virus/ acquired immune deficiency syndrome (HIV/AIDS), result in high social, economic, and health costs for affected persons, their children, and society.

CDC operates multiple nationally representative surveys and surveillance systems that track patterns of sexual risk behavior and reproductive health outcomes in the U.S. population. In addition, CDC's National Vital Statistics System (NVSS) provides information from vital records in the United States. These surveys, surveillance, and vital records systems collect information that includes age at initiation of sexual intercourse, frequency of sexual intercourse, number of sexual partners, contraceptive use and use of prevention services, pregnancies, births, abortions, cases of HIV/AIDS and other STDs, and reports of sexual violence.

Each source of information reports data separately and in different formats, which can make interpreting the data difficult. This report combines available data from multiple sources for the first time into a single report concerning the sexual and reproductive health of persons in the United States aged 10–24 years. The report addresses three main questions:

- How many young persons currently engage in sexual risk behaviors and experience related health outcomes?

- What are the greatest disparities in terms of age, sex, race/ethnicity, and geographic location?

- How do recent data compare with previously reported data, i.e., what are the historical trends?

This report includes the most recent data that were available when the report was produced. The findings can be used to guide the work of policy makers, researchers, and program providers. . . .

[A description of the research methods used in the study has been omitted.]

RESULTS

Current Levels of Sexual Risk Behavior and Health Outcomes

Sexual Behaviors

NSFG [National Survey of Family Growth] data for 2002 were used to present the percentage of adolescents and young adults who engaged in a range of sexual risk behaviors. Among female adolescents aged 15–17 years, 30.0% reported ever having had sex, compared with 70.6% of those aged 18–19 years. Among adolescent males aged 15–17 years, 31.6% reported ever having had sex, compared with 64.7% of those aged 18–19 years. Among females aged 18–24 years, 9.6% who had sex by age 20 years reported having had nonvoluntary first intercourse. Having ever been forced to have intercourse was reported by 14.3% of females aged 18–19 years and 19.1% of females aged 20–24 years. Among teenagers aged 15–19 years, 13.1% of females and 14.8% of males reported having had sex at age <15 years. The majority (58.7%) of females aged 15–19 years reported that their first sex partners were 1–3 years older than they were, and 22.4% reported that their first partners were >4 years older than they were. Approximately three in 10 female and male adolescents aged 15–19 years reported having had two or more sexual partners.

Among never-married adolescents aged 15–19 years who were sexually active, 75.2% of females and 82.3% of males reported using a method of contraception at first intercourse. Condom use at first intercourse was reported by 67.5% of females and 70.7% of males. Adolescents also were likely to have used contraception at their most recent intercourse (83.2% of never-married females and 90.7% of never-married males). Never-married females aged 20–24 years were somewhat more likely than adolescent females to have used contraception at last sex (87.3%); never-married males aged 20–24 years were somewhat less likely than adolescent males to have done so (84.8%).

A substantial majority of adolescents aged 15–19 years (85.5% of females and 82.6% of males) reported having received formal instruction before reaching age 18 years on how to say no to sex, and 69.9% of adolescent females and 66.2% of adolescent males reported receiving instruction on methods of birth control. Among adolescents aged 18–19 years, 49.8% of females and 35.1% of males had talked with a parent before reaching age 18 years about methods of birth control. Approximately three fourths of adolescents aged 15–17 years (74.6% of females and 71.5% of males) reported having talked to their parents about at least one of five sex education topics included in the survey.

Use of reproductive and medical services varied by age. For example, 37.6% of females aged 15–17 years and 80.5% of females aged 20–24 years had received at least one family planning or medical service during the preceding 12 months. Among males aged 15–19 years, 72.3% received at least one health or family planning service during the preceding 12 months, but that percentage decreased to 51.9% among young adult males aged 20–24 years.

Pregnancies among adolescents are very likely to be unintended (unwanted or mistimed) at conception. Among females aged 15–17 years, 88.0% of births during the preceding 5 years were the result of unintended pregnancies.

Pregnancy, Births, Birth Characteristics, and Abortions

In 2004, an estimated 2.4 million pregnancies occurred among U.S. females aged <25 years, with 30% of those pregnancies occurring among adolescent females aged 15–19 years and <1% among females aged aged [sic] <15 years. The total number of pregnancies reported for U.S. females aged <25 years for 2004 included 1.5 million live births, 613,000 induced abortions, and 341,000 fetal losses (e.g., stillbirths and miscarriages; data not presented in table). Among adolescents aged 15–19 years, 57% of pregnancies ended in a live birth, 27% ended in induced abortion, and 16% were fetal losses.

In 2006, a total of 435,436 births occurred to adolescent mothers aged 15–19 years, with almost one third occurring among adolescents aged 15–17 years (preliminary data indicate that this number increased to 445,045 in 2007). Initiation of prenatal care in the first trimester typically increases with age. In 2006, according to data for 32 states, the District of Columbia, and New York City, less than half of pregnant youths aged 10–14 years initiated prenatal care in the first trimester. This proportion increased to 64.9% for those aged 15–17 years and 72.3% of those 18–19 years. A total of 92% of births among females aged 15–17 years and 81% among those aged 18–19 years were to unmarried mothers (data not presented in table). Mothers aged <15 years were more likely than adolescent females aged 15–19 years or young women aged 20–24 years to receive late or no prenatal care, to have a preterm or very preterm infant, and to have a low or very low birthweight infant. Smoking during pregnancy also typically increases with age through age 18–19 years. In 2006, on the basis of data for 33 states, the District of Columbia, and New York City, adolescents aged 15–17 years were three times more likely to smoke during pregnancy as youths aged 10–14 years (10.3 compared with. 3.3%).

In 2004, an estimated 199,000 abortions were reported for female adolescents aged 15–19 years, with more than one third occurring among adolescents aged 15–17 years and nearly two thirds among those aged 18–19 years. Among young women aged 20–24 years, the estimated number of abortions was approximately twice that for adolescents aged 15–19 years. The abortion rates in 2004 varied substantially by age, with the rate for women aged 20–24 years (39.9 per 1,000 population) double the rate for adolescents aged 15–19 years (19.8 per 1,000).

HIV/AIDS

In 2006, a total of 2,194 persons (668 females and 1,526 males) in the United States aged 10–24 years received a diagnosis of AIDS, and a cumulative total of 9,530 persons (3,914 females and 5,616 males) were living with AIDS. The majority of persons aged 10–24 years who received an AIDS diagnosis in 2006 were young adults aged 20–24 years (71% of females and 80% of males), and 72% of total diagnoses were received by males (1,526 of 2,194 total diagnoses). However, among persons aged 10–14 years, the majority of AIDS diagnoses (61%) were received by females.

The number of young persons living with HIV/AIDS in the 38 areas with stable (i.e., confidential name-based) HIV reporting also is presented. In 2006, a total of 5,396 young persons (1,540 females and 3,856 males) received a diagnosis of HIV/AIDS, and a cumulative total of 21,890 young persons were living with HIV/AIDS in these 38 areas (9,024 females and 12,866 males). As with AIDS diagnoses, the majority of HIV/AIDS diagnoses occurred among young adults aged 20–24 years (1,049 [68%] of 1,540 females and 2,922 [76%] of 3,856 males) and were male (3,856 [71%] of 5,396 total diagnoses). Among youths aged 10–14 years, more diagnoses were received by females than by males (44 [70%] and 19 [30%], respectively).

Sexually Transmitted Diseases

Adolescents and young adults aged 15–24 years have high rates for the most common STDs. Persons in this age group have been estimated to acquire nearly half of all incident STDs although they represent only 25% of the sexually active population. Reasons for the increased rates include biologic susceptibility, risky sexual behavior, and limited access to health care.

Cases of chlamydia, gonorrhea, and syphilis diagnosed in the United States are reported to CDC via NNDSS [Nationally Notifiable Disease Surveillance System]. Of these three STDs, for which federally funded control programs exist, chlamydia is the most frequently reported among all age groups of young persons. In 2006, among youths aged 10–14 years, 12,364 cases of chlamydia were reported in females and 1,238 in males; among adolescents aged 15–17 years, 130,569 cases were reported in females and 23,665 in males; among adolescents aged 18–19 years, 162,823 cases were reported in females and 35,155 in males; and among young adults aged 20–24 years, 284,763 cases were reported in females and 93,035 in males. Chlamydia screening is not recommended for males, so the consistently higher reported rates of chlamydia among females probably reflects compliance with recommendations for chlamydia screening for all sexually active females aged <26 years and thus underestimates the disease burden among males. Population-based NHANES [National Health and Nutrition Examination Survey] data demonstrate that prevalence of chlamydia among adolescents aged 14–19 years is somewhat greater among females (4.6%; 95% confidence interval [CI] = 3.7–5.8) than among males (2.3% [CI = 1.5–3.5]). However, the trend is the opposite among young adults aged 20–29 years, for whom chlamydia prevalence is greater among males (3.2%; CI = 2.4–4.3) than among females (1.9%; CI = 1.0–3.4).

Gonorrhea was the second most commonly reported STD in 2006. Among youths aged 10–14 years, 3,574 cases were reported in females and 675 cases in males; among younger adolescents aged 15–17 years, 30,703 cases were reported in females and 11,242 in males; among older adolescents aged 18–19 years, 35,701 cases were reported in females and 18,877 in males; among young adults aged 20–24 years, 61,665 cases were reported in females and 49,304 in males.

Of the three STDs for which federally funded control programs exist, primary and secondary syphilis is the least frequently reported STD. In 2006, among youths aged 10–14 years, 11 cases were reported in females and two in males; among younger adolescents aged 15–17 years, 96 cases were reported in females and 94 in males; among older adolescents aged 18–19 years, 137 cases were reported in females and 238 in males; and among young adults aged 20–24 years, 299 cases were reported in females and 1,083 in males.

NHANES data for 2003–2004 indicate that the prevalence of HPV DNA was 24.5% (CI = 19.6–30.5) among females aged 14–19 years and 44.8% (CI = 36.3–55.3) among females aged 20–24 years. The overall prevalence of HPV DNA among females aged 14–24 years was 33.8%, representing approximately 7.5 million females with HPV infection in the United States. NHANES data for 1999–2004 indicated that prevalence of HSV-2 among persons aged 14–19 years was 2.3% (CI = 1.7–3.2) among females and 0.9% (CI = 0.5–1.5) among males.

Sexual Violence

During 2004–2006, an estimated 105,187 females and 6,526 males aged 10–24 years received medical care in U.S. EDs as a result of nonfatal injuries sustained from a sexual assault (data not presented). The rate was significantly higher (t = 5.75; p < 0.001) among females aged 10–24 years than among males (114.8 and 6.8 ED visits per 100,000 population, respectively). Among females, rates were 90.0 per 100,000 females aged 10–14 years, 152.6 per 100,000 females aged 15–17 years, 163.7 per 100,000 females aged 18–19 years, and 97.1 per 100,000 females aged 20–24 years. Nonfatal injury rates sustained from sexual assaults were significantly higher among females aged 15–17 years (t = 2.0; p < 0.05) and 18–19 years (t = 2.44; p < 0.05) than among females aged 20–24 years. Other differences between age groups for females were not statistically significant. Among males aged 10–14 years, the rate for nonfatal sexual assault–related injury was 11.1 ED visits per 100,000 population. Estimates for other age groups of males (ages 15–17, 18–19, and 20–24 years) are not reported because of the limited sample size.

Disparities in Race/Ethnicity, Mode of Transmission for HIV/AIDS, and Geographic Residence

Sexual Behavior

Sexual risk behavior varied among non–Hispanic black, Hispanic, and non–Hispanic white females and males. Among female adolescents aged 15–19 years, 40.4% of Hispanic females reported ever having had sex, compared with 46.4% of non–Hispanic white females and 57.0% of non–Hispanic black females. Having first sex at age <15 years was reported by 22.9% of non–Hispanic black adolescent females aged 15–19 years, compared with 11.6% of non–Hispanic white females in the same age group. This estimate does not meet the NSFG standard of reliability for Hispanic females. . . . Among adolescent females aged 15–19 years, Hispanics were more likely (35.2%) than non–Hispanic whites (19.6%) and non–Hispanic blacks (19.0%) to report having had sex for the first time with a partner who was substantially older (>4 years). Among adolescent females aged 15–19 years, 40.8% of Hispanics reported using no method of contraception at last intercourse, compared with 25.2% of non–Hispanic blacks and 10.3% of non–Hispanic whites.

The majority (56.5%) of non–Hispanic black females aged 15–19 years reported having used at least one family planning or medical service during the preceding 12 months, compared with 41.2% of Hispanic females and 49.4% of non–Hispanic white females. Among adolescent males aged 15–19 years, 29.6% of non–Hispanic blacks reported having had four or more lifetime partners, compared with 25.4% of Hispanic males and 12.1% of non–Hispanic white males. Reported use of condoms at first and most recent intercourse was higher among non–Hispanic black males aged 15–19 years (85.3% and 86.1%, respectively) than non–Hispanic white males (68.6% and 69.2%, respectively) and Hispanic males (66.5% and 59.9%, respectively) in the same age group. Non–Hispanic blacks males aged 15–19 years were also more likely to report always using condoms during the previous 4 weeks than their non–Hispanic white and Hispanic counterparts (86.8% compared with 68.0% and 53.1%, respectively).

Among adolescents and young adults who reported being sexually active, non–Hispanic black females aged 20–24 years were more likely to have ever been tested for HIV, STDs, or both (62.4%, compared with 47.9% of Hispanic females and 45.4% of non–Hispanic white females). Among males aged 20–24 years, use of condoms at most recent intercourse also was higher among non–Hispanic black males (62.3%) than non–Hispanic white males and Hispanic males (46.5% and 47.3%, respectively).

Data from multiple studies for selected measures of pregnancies, births, birth characteristics, induced abortions, cases of HIV/AIDS, STDs, and sexual violence among persons aged 10–24 years are reported.

Pregnancy, Births, Birth Characteristics, and Abortions

Pregnancy rates varied by race and ethnicity. In 2004, the highest pregnancy rates for adolescents aged 15–19 years were reported among Hispanic and non–Hispanic black adolescents (132.8 and 128.0, respectively), compared with 45.2 among non–Hispanic white adolescents. Among young women aged 20–24 years, rates per 1,000 population were 259.0 among non–Hispanic black women and 244.8 among Hispanic women, compared with 122.8 among non–Hispanic white women.

Birth rates also varied by race and ethnicity. Among females aged 10–24 years, birth rates were lowest among APIs [Asian and Pacific Islanders] and non–Hispanic whites in every age group and highest among non–Hispanic blacks and Hispanics. The majority of births to adolescent mothers are nonmarital; in 2006, the proportion of births among unmarried adolescents aged 15–19 years ranged from 77.3% among APIs to 96.9% among non–Hispanic blacks.

The risk for having a low and very low birthweight baby was highest among mothers in the youngest age group (age 10–14 years) and decreased linearly with age. Non-Hispanic black mothers aged 15–19 years were more likely to have a low or very low birthweight infant than mothers in all other racial and ethnic populations. Similarly, the proportion of preterm and very preterm births was higher among non–Hispanic black mothers than among other groups .

HIV/AIDS

Rates for AIDS and HIV/AIDS diagnoses and for living with AIDS and HIV/AIDS have been tabulated by age group, sex, and race/ethnicity. In 2006, non–Hispanic blacks experienced the highest rates of AIDS and HIV/AIDS diagnoses and the highest rate for living with AIDS and HIV/AIDS across all age groups. Rates among non–Hispanic blacks were three to five times higher than those among Hispanics, the population that had the second highest rates. For example, 141.7 per 100,000 non–Hispanic black males aged 15–19 years were living with HIV/AIDS compared with 39.8 per 100,000 Hispanic males that same age. Further, 129.5 per 100,000 non–Hispanic black females aged 15–19 years were living with HIV/AIDS compared with 40.2 per 100,000 Hispanic females aged 15–19 years. AI/ANs [American Indians/Alaska Natives] and non–Hispanic whites experienced the next highest rates, whereas API experienced the lowest rates of HIV/AIDS. For example, among males aged 15–19 years, the rates were 6.7 per 100,000 population for non–Hispanic whites, 7.3 per 100,000 population for AI/AN, and 4.7 per 100,000 population among APIs.

The frequency of HIV/AIDS diagnoses in 2006 by age, transmission category, sex and race/ethnicity has been calculated. Among females of all ages and racial/ethnic populations, the primary transmission category was heterosexual contact, followed by injection-drug use (IDU). Among males of all age groups and racial/ethnic populations, the primary transmission category was men who have sex with men (MSM). For non–Hispanic black males and for Hispanic males, the second most important transmission category was heterosexual contact; for non–Hispanic white males, it was IDU.

The frequency of persons aged 10–24 years who were living with HIV/AIDS in 2006 has been calculated by transmission category, age group, and sex. The primary transmission category for persons aged 10–17 years was perinatal (92.5% among males aged 10–14 years and 90.1% among females aged 10–14 years). Among persons aged 20–24 years, the primary transmission category was MSM for males (74.9%) and heterosexual sex for females (78.7%). The frequency of persons aged 10–24 years who were living with AIDS in 2006 also has been calculated by transmission category, age group, and sex. The patterns were similar to those for persons living with HIV/AIDS (i.e., the primary transmission category for youths and adolescents was perinatal transmission). Among males aged 20–24 years, the primary transmission category was MSM; among females, it was heterosexual.

Sexually Transmitted Diseases

Substantial disparities in STD rates exist among racial and ethnic populations. In 2006, rates for chlamydia, gonorrhea, and syphilis were highest among non–Hispanic blacks for all age groups. Among adolescents aged 15–19 years, the highest rates of chlamydia occurred among non–Hispanic black females (8,858.1 cases per 100,000 population), compared with non–Hispanic black males (2,195.4 cases per 100,000 population) and non–Hispanic white females (1,374.9 cases per 100,000 population). A similar pattern among adolescents aged 15–19 years was recorded for gonorrhea, with the highest rates occurring among non–Hispanic black females (2,829.6 cases per 100,000 population), compared with non–Hispanic black males (1,467.6 cases per 100,000 population) and non–Hispanic white females (208.3 cases per 100,000 population). The pattern varied slightly for syphilis, with non–Hispanic black males aged 20–24 years experiencing the highest rates (41.0 cases per 100,000 population), compared with non–Hispanic black females (14.8 cases per 100,000 population) and non–Hispanic white males (3.7 cases per 100,000 population) of the same age.

AI/AN and Hispanic young persons also experienced high rates of sexually transmitted diseases. For example, among females aged 20–24 years, rates for chlamydia were 5,008.5 cases per 100,000 population among AI/AN females and 3,301.5 cases per 100,000 population among Hispanic females, and gonorrhea rates were 634.8 cases per 100,000 population among AI/AN females and 326.7 cases per 100,000 population among Hispanic females. Among males aged 20–24 years, syphilis rates were 6.3 cases per 100,000 population among AI/AN males and 9.2 cases per 100,000 population among Hispanic males. Chlamydia, gonorrhea, and syphilis rates also are provided for youths aged 10–14 years, but the rates are substantially lower compared with older age groups. In this age group, the highest rates occurred among non–Hispanic black females: 462.2 cases per 100,000 population for chlamydia, 168.6 cases per 100,000 population for gonorrhea, and 0.6 cases per 100,000 population for syphilis.

Sexual Violence

During 2004–2006, among adolescents and young adults aged 10–24 years, an estimated 45,485 non–Hispanic white females, 24,121 black females (i.e., inclusive of Hispanic black and non–Hispanic black), and 10,733 Hispanic females (i.e., excluding Hispanic black) were treated in EDs of U.S. hospitals as a result of nonfatal injuries sustained from a sexual assault. Among males aged 10–24 years, an estimated 2,361 non–Hispanic white, 1,663 black (including black Hispanic and non–Hispanic black), and 907 Hispanic (i.e., excluding Hispanic black) male adolescents and young adults were treated in EDs as a result of nonfatal injuries sustained from sexual assaults. Because of the low numbers and the high frequency of missing data concerning race/ethnicity, all estimates for males by age and race/ethnicity are unstable and not reported. For both females and males, 21% of the sexual assault injury cases are missing data on race/ethnicity, so rates by race/ethnicity were not calculated, and caution should be used when interpreting counts by race/ethnicity.

Geographic Distribution of Births, HIV/AIDS, and STD Cases

Birth rates for adolescents varied considerably by state. Birth rates for adolescents were lower among states in the North and Northeast and higher among states in the South and Southwest. These geographic patterns largely reflect the composition (e.g., race/ethnicity and socioeconomic factors such as educational attainment) of each state's population. The number and rates of young persons living with HIV/AIDS in each of the 38 areas (i.e., 33 states and five U.S. territories) that had stable (i.e., confidential name-based) HIV reporting in 2006 has been calculated, as has the number and rates of young persons living with AIDS in each of the 50 states, the District of Columbia, and U.S. territories in 2006. The highest rates of young persons living with AIDS were clustered in the eastern and southern regions of the United States. National rates have been calculated for chlamydia, gonorrhea, and syphilis (primary and secondary) by age group and region. Across all regions, overall rates for chlamydia and gonorrhea were higher among persons aged 18–19 years than among those aged 10–14, 15–17, and 20–24 years. Among persons aged 15–24 years, rates for syphilis increased with age group in all regions. Rates were higher for chlamydia, gonorrhea, and syphilis in the South for all age groups, compared with other regions and with the U.S. total. However, variation in racial composition account for much of the difference by region. . . .

[Additional examination of trends over time has been omitted.]

CONCLUSION

The data presented in this report indicate that the sexual and reproductive health of America's young persons remains an important public health concern: a substantial number of youths are affected, disparities exist, and earlier progress appears to be slowing and perhaps reversing. These patterns exist for a range of health outcomes (i.e., sexual risk behavior, pregnancy and births, STDs, HIV/AIDS, and sexual violence), highlighting the magnitude of the threat to young persons' sexual and reproductive health.

These findings underscore the importance of sustaining efforts to promote adolescent reproductive health. Effective screening, treatment, and referral services exist, and a growing number of evidence-based sexuality education, parent–child communication, and youth development programs are available to promote adolescent sexual and reproductive health. A key challenge is to ensure that these services are delivered so all youths can benefit. Continued support also is needed to monitor trends in sexual risk behavior and to promote research on new ways to help young persons achieve reproductive health.

The data presented in this report are subject to several limitations.

First, self-reported data are subject to social desirability and response bias. Second, cases of disease often remain undetected and are unreported. Third, estimating pregnancy rates is challenging because of the difficulty in measuring the number of abortions and fetal losses. Finally, the data summarized in this report describe risk behaviors and negative reproductive health outcomes among young persons, but the data do not explain the causes of sexual risk behavior nor what interventions are most effective. Research is needed that identifies both the key determinants of sexual risk behavior and those interventions that are effective in reducing risk behavior.

Despite these limitations, understanding temporal trends and which subpopulations are at greatest risk is a critical first step that guides other public health action. Practitioners can use the information provided in this report when making decisions about how to allocate resources and identify those subpopulations that are in greatest need. Researchers can use the information provided in this report to guide future study on youths at highest risk to better understand the causes of sexual risk behavior and ways to reduce it. Finally, policy makers can use the information provided in this report to justify expanded funding of effective programs, new research on innovative intervention strategies, and continued monitoring of sexual risk behavior and reproductive health outcomes. . . .

[The acknowledgements and the references have been omitted.]

SOURCE: Centers for Disease Control and Prevention. "Sexual and Reproductive Health of Persons Aged 10–24 Years—United States, 2002–2007." *Morbidity and Mortality Weekly Report*, 58, No. SS-6 (July 17, 2009). www.cdc.gov/mmwr/PDF/ss/ss5806.pdf.

OTHER HISTORIC DOCUMENTS OF INTEREST

FROM THIS VOLUME

- HIV Vaccine Study Shows Promising Results in Thailand, p. 458

FROM PREVIOUS *HISTORIC DOCUMENTS*

- Surgeon General on Promoting Sexual Health, *2001*, p. 456
- Federal Report on Teen Pregnancy, *1998*, p. 260

New Jersey and New York Government Officials Arrested in Corruption Probe

JULY 23, 2009

On July 23, 2009, a major raid involving 300 law enforcement agents in New York and New Jersey led to the arrests of forty-four people, including three New Jersey mayors, a city council president, and two state legislators accused of involvement in a ten-year-long corruption, bribery, and money-laundering ring. The federal investigation, which began in 1999, was related to two earlier cases and made use of a Federal Bureau of Investigation (FBI) informant who wore a wire and videotaped his negotiations with public officials, rabbis, and others involved in the crime ring.

According to the acting U.S. attorney in New Jersey, Ralph Marra Jr., "for these defendants, corruption was a way of life. They existed in an ethics-free zone, and they exploited giant loopholes in the state's contribution rules."

New Jersey has a long history of corruption in government, with Newark seemingly the epicenter of such crime. Three ex-mayors of Newark had been convicted of crimes, although there was no link between their convictions and the crimes at hand. "New Jersey's corruption problem is one of the worst, if not the worst, in the nation. It has become ingrained in New Jersey's political culture," said Ed Kahrer, special agent in charge of the FBI's white collar crime and public corruption program in New Jersey.

MONEY LAUNDERING

Officials had begun their investigation in mid-2006 by looking into money laundering in New York and New Jersey. Investigators believed the accused were funneling tens of millions of dollars through nonprofit and charitable organizations run by rabbis. The investigation source evolved from charges of bank fraud against a Syrian Jew named Solomon Dwek who, when charged, became an informant for the FBI. He then approached members of the ring, pretending to be a real estate developer looking to give kickbacks to politicians who would help him with favorable building and development contracts. Dwek had been arrested in May 2006 after passing a bad $25 million check at a bank in New Jersey. Using Dwek in their investigation, FBI and local authorities funneled nearly $3 million through the ring between June 2007 and July 2009.

Dwek enticed rabbis and other members of his Syrian Jewish community in New York and New Jersey into money laundering. In luring the accused into different schemes, he told them that he was bankrupt and was trying to keep his assets secret from the government while he faced bank fraud charges. Dwek would write a check to charities run by those involved in the ring, the target would take a fee from it, and give the rest of the money back to Dwek in cash. The cash that exchanged hands during the investigation came mostly through a man in Israel who told investigators after his arrest that he had received the money from another man in Switzerland.

The U.S. attorney also charged a Brooklyn, New York, resident involved in the ring with trafficking human organs, including kidneys, which he bought for $10,000 each and sold for up to $160,000.

PUBLIC CORRUPTION

In 2007, investigators shifted their focus from money laundering to corruption at some of the highest levels of New York and New Jersey government. Although the investigations were conducted separately, in many instances, the same people were involved. One indication of political corruption came when Moshe Altman, a Hudson County, New York, developer introduced Dwek to a Jersey City building official and a city official named Maher Khalil in an effort to help Dwek obtain favorable building permits. Soon after, Dwek paid these officials to receive favorable zoning changes and building inspections. In one case, a future Hoboken mayor, Peter Cammarano, agreed to expedite building contracts through Hoboken's city council in exchange for $10,000—$5,000 immediately and $5,000 after being elected mayor. As mayor, Cammarano, who ran a campaign based on reforming government, pled not guilty to corruption charges.

Prosecutors believed that Cammarano was willing to accept the bribes because the amount was small enough that it might stay under the radar. According to the complaint from the prosecutor, Cammarano told Dwek that he was not concerned about losing the election. "Right now," he told Dwek, "the Italians, the Hispanics, the seniors are locked down. Nothing could change that now. I could be . . . indicted, and I'm still going to win 85 to 95 percent of those populations."

Other officials arrested on public corruption charges included Mayor Dennis Elwell of Secaucus, New Jersey; L. Harvey Smith, a New Jersey state assembly member representing Jersey City; Jersey City deputy mayor Leona Beldini; Ridgefield mayor Anthony Suarez; and assembly member Daniel Van Pelt, representing Ocean City. In addition to his position in the New Jersey assembly, Van Pelt was also mayor of Ocean Township, New Jersey. Van Pelt was accused of accepting $10,000 from Dwek, who wanted a building permit in Ocean County, New Jersey. Smith had once run for mayor of Jersey City on the platform of eliminating corruption from government, telling the *New York Times,* "I don't take cash. I don't let people give me things." Smith was charged with accepting $15,000 in bribes. Jersey City, Mayor Jerramiah Healy called Deputy Mayor Beldini's arrest and charge "a little shocking." Beldini was charged with conspiracy to commit extortion after accepting $20,000 in illegal campaign contributions. Elwell was charged with accepting $10,000 in bribes. Overall, according to Marra, more than $650,000 in bribes were paid to those charged in the criminal complaint.

The fallout extended beyond local government officials. Joseph Doria, New Jersey's community affairs commissioner, was asked by Gov. Jon Corzine to step down from his position; he had not been charged, but his name was floated as someone potentially involved in the corruption ring, and his home and offices were searched. Doria, a former speaker of New Jersey's assembly and mayor of Bayonne, New Jersey, resigned hours after the search took place.

In total, forty-four public officials, rabbis, and others were arrested and charged. Twenty-nine faced corruption charges and fifteen faced charges of money laundering. The special agent in charge of Newark's FBI office, Weysan Dun, said, "The list of names and titles of those arrested today sounds like a roster for a community leaders meeting. Sadly," he said, "these prominent individuals were not in a meeting room but were in the FBI booking room this morning."

The rabbis involved in the ring were arrested for money laundering, kidney trafficking, bank and bankruptcy fraud, and selling fake Gucci and Prada brand bags. They had set up charities at their synagogues to funnel the money through them. "These complaints paint a disgraceful picture of religious leaders heading money-laundering crews, acting as crime bosses. They used purported charities . . . as vehicles for laundering millions of dollars in illicit funds," said Marra.

The rabbis and public officials, who appeared in ankle shackles and handcuffs before a judge on July 23, had bail set between $25,000 and $3 million. The three New Jersey mayors were bonded at $100,000 and were required to give up passports and limit any travel to New Jersey and New York. Some of those accused of money laundering were thought to be flight risks and were held on higher bonds.

EFFECT ON THE GUBERNATORIAL RACE

New Jersey governor Corzine, a Democrat against at the time facing a difficult reelection battle against a Republican and an independent candidate, said, "[A]ny corruption is unacceptable—anywhere, anytime, by anybody. The scale of corruption we're seeing as this unfolds is simply outrageous and cannot be tolerated." Corzine explained that he was "sickened" by the charges brought that day in July. "Whenever an elected or appointed official violates the public trust, it's crossed the bright line of right and wrong. New Jersey citizens have long been outraged by the repeated and deep vein of political corruption in our state and justifiably so. . . . But the scope of corruption that has been unmasked today is simply beyond any pale. It is outrageous, and there are no worthier words that fit but 'outrageous.'"

His Republican opponent, Christopher Christie, a former U.S. attorney, seized on the sting to insinuate that Corzine's administration was corrupt, pointing to the resignation of Doria, and argued that Corzine had yet to clean up and reform government in New Jersey, calling the arrests a "really tragic day" for New Jersey. He said that he had worked "extraordinarily hard" to stop the pervasive corruption in New Jersey during his time as a prosecutor, but, he added, "unfortunately today is another example that there is much work still to be done."

The corruption scandal, coupled with Corzine's other missteps as governor, cost him the election in November 2009. Christie suceeded him as governor.

—Heather Kerrigan

Following is the text of a press release from the U.S. Attorney's Office, District of New Jersey, on July 23, 2009, announcing the results of its investigation into money laundering and corruption against public officials and rabbis in New York and New Jersey.

DOCUMENT

U.S. Attorney's Office Press Release on Money Laundering and Corruption Probe

July 23, 2009

The mayors of Hoboken, Secaucus and Ridgefield, the Jersey City deputy mayor and council president, two state assemblymen, numerous other public officials and political figures and five rabbis from New York and New Jersey were among 44 individuals charged today in a two-track federal investigation of public corruption and a high-volume, international money laundering conspiracy, Acting U.S. Attorney Ralph J. Marra, Jr., announced.

Among those charged in criminal Complaints are:

- Peter Cammarano III, the newly elected mayor of Hoboken and an attorney, charged with accepting $25,000 in cash bribes, including $10,000 last Thursday, from an undercover cooperating witness.

- L. Harvey Smith, a New Jersey Assemblyman and recent mayoral candidate in Jersey City, charged along with an aide of taking $15,000 in bribes to help get approvals from high-level state agency officials for building projects.

- Daniel Van Pelt, a New Jersey Assemblyman, charged with accepting a $10,000 bribe.

- Dennis Elwell, mayor of Secaucus, charged with taking a $10,000 cash bribe.

- Anthony Suarez, mayor of Ridgefield and an attorney, charged with agreeing to accept a $10,000 corrupt cash payment for his legal defense fund.

- Louis Manzo, the recent unsuccessful challenger in the Jersey City mayoral election and former state Assemblyman, and his brother and political advisor Ronald Manzo, both with taking $27,500 in corrupt cash payments for use in Louis Manzo's campaign.

- Leona Beldini, the Jersey City deputy mayor and a campaign treasurer, charged with taking $20,000 in conduit campaign contributions and other self-dealing in her official capacity.

- Eliahu Ben Haim, of Long Branch, N.J., the principal rabbi of a synagogue in Deal, N.J., charged with money laundering of proceeds derived from criminal activity.

- Saul Kassin, of Brooklyn, N.Y., the chief rabbi of a synagogue in Brooklyn, New York, charged with money laundering of proceeds derived from criminal activity.

- Edmund Nahum, of Deal, N.J., the principal rabbi of a synagogue in Deal, charged with money laundering of proceeds derived from criminal activity.

- Mordchai Fish, of Brooklyn, N.Y., a rabbi at a synagogue in Brooklyn, charged with money laundering of proceeds derived from criminal activity. His brother, also a rabbi, was charged as well.

Most of the defendants were arrested early this morning by a large contingent of federal agents, led by Special Agents of the FBI Newark Division and IRS Criminal Investigation Division. Court-authorized search warrants were also being executed approximately 20 locations in New Jersey and New York, to recover, among other things, large sums of cash and other evidence of criminal conduct. Additionally, 28 seizure warrants were being executed against bank accounts in the names of the money laundering defendants and entities they control.

One criminal Complaint charges a Brooklyn man, Levy Izhak Rosenbaum, with conspiring to broker the sale of a human kidney for a transplant, at a cost of $160,000 to the transplant recipient. According to the Complaint, Rosenbaum said he had been brokering the sale of kidneys for 10 years. . . .

[Court appearance information has been omitted.]

The cooperating witness told targets of the money laundering investigation that he was involved in illegal businesses and bank frauds. He also openly discussed with targets that he was in bankruptcy and was attempting to conceal cash and assets, and told them he wanted to launder criminal proceeds in increments ranging from tens of thousands of dollars to $150,000 or more at a time, often at the rate of several transactions per week. According to the criminal Complaints, the money laundering operations run by the rabbis laundered a total of approximately $3 million for the cooperating witness alone between about June 2007 and July 2009.

The investigation veered onto its public corruption track in July 2007 in Hudson County, where the cooperating witness represented himself to be a developer and owner of a tile business who wanted to build high rises and other projects and get public contracts in Hudson County schools. Through an intermediary, the cooperating witness was introduced to a Jersey City building inspector who, in return for $40,000 in bribes, promised to smooth the way for approvals of the cooperating witness's building projects, according to the criminal Complaints.

From there, introductions and referrals spread amongst a web of public officials, council and mayoral candidates, their operatives and associates—mostly in Hudson County, and primarily in Jersey City—who took bribes. In return, they pledged their official assistance in getting the cooperating witness's projects prioritized and approved or to steer contracts to him.

In part, the bribe-taking was connected to fund raising efforts in heavily contested mayoral and city council campaigns in Jersey City and Hoboken, and the bribes were often parceled out to straw donors, who then wrote checks in their names or businesses to the campaigns in amounts that complied with legal limits on individual donations—so-called conduit or conversion donations. Other bribe recipients took cash for direct personal use and benefit; others kept some of the cash and used the rest for political campaigns, according to the criminal Complaints.

The investigation produced hundreds of hours of video and audio recordings documenting much of the money laundering and bribe-taking.

"This investigation has once again identified a corrupt network of public officials who were all too willing to take cash in exchange for promised official action," said Marra. "It seemed that everyone wanted a piece of the action. The corruption was widespread and pervasive."

"In both parts of this investigation," Marra said, "respected figures in positions of public and private trust engaged in conduct behind closed doors that belied the faces of honesty, integrity and rectitude they displayed daily to their respective constituencies."

"The list of names and titles of those arrested today sounds like a roster for a community leaders meeting," said Weysan Dun, Special Agent In Charge of the FBI in Newark. "Sadly, these prominent individuals were not in a meeting room but were in the FBI booking room this morning. We hope that our actions today will be the clarion call that prompts significant change in the way business and politics are conducted in the State of New Jersey. Those who engage in this culture of corruption should know the cross hairs of justice will continue to be focused on them."

"Traditional money laundering used to be confined to narcotics traffickers and organized crime," said Julio La Rosa, Acting Special Agent in Charge of the IRS Criminal Investigation Division (CID). "Based on the allegations contained in today's complaints, money laundering has no boundaries and impacts every segment of our society."

The investigation is the third phase of the FBI, IRS-CID and U.S. Attorney's Office "Bid Rig" investigations that began first in Monmouth and Ocean counties in New Jersey. The initial investigation became public in 2002 with the guilty plea of Ocean Township mayor Terrence Weldon, who admitted extorting cash from developers to influence approval of projects. The second Bid Rig phase resulted in the arrests in February 2005 of 11 sitting and former mayors and other elected officials in Monmouth County. Those public officials took bribes from someone they believed was a contractor and money launderer seeking municipal work but who was, in fact, an undercover cooperating witness.

The Money Laundering Investigation

The money laundering conspiracy involved high-ranking religious figures and their associates in Brooklyn, N.Y., and Deal, N.J. Among them was Eliahu Ben Haim, of Long Branch, N.J., the principal rabbi of Congregation Ohel Yaacob in Deal, N.J. Typically, according to the criminal Complaints, Haim received bank checks in amounts ranging from tens of thousands of dollars up to $160,000 at a time made payable to a charitable, tax exempt organization associated with Haim and his synagogue. To complete the money laundering cycle, Haim would return the amount of the check in cash to the cooperating witness, less a cut for Haim, typically 10 percent.

Haim's source of cash for funding the money laundering was, according to the Complaints, an Israeli in Israel who, Haim said, he had worked with for years. For a fee, that source would make cash available through other individuals charged today who ran cash houses in Brooklyn. Hundreds of thousands of dollars were regularly available from the cash houses for Haim to return to his money laundering clients, including the government's cooperating witness.

Similar circles of money launderers in Brooklyn and Deal, N.J., operated separately but occasionally co-mingled activities and participants. In most cases, the rings were led by rabbis who used charitable, non-profit entities connected to their synagogues to "wash" money that they understood came from criminal activity like bank fraud, counterfeit goods and other illegal sources, according to the criminal Complaints. . . .

One of the other money laundering operations was allegedly led by Saul Kassin, a leading Brooklyn rabbi, and another by Edmund Nahum, the leader of a synagogue in Deal. In one secretly recorded conversation, Nahum tells the cooperating witness that he should launder his money through a number of rabbis. "The more it's spread the better," Nahum said, according to his criminal Complaint. . . .

Also arrested today was Levi Deutsch, an Israeli living in Israel who, according to the Complaints, was a high-level source of cash from overseas for funding the bank checks that passed through charitable entities. Deutsch, who traveled frequently between Israel and New York, explained to the cooperating witness that the source of his cash was the "diamond business (and) other, other things," according to the Complaints. He further explained that he was associated with a Swiss banker who charged "two, three points" per $1 million laundered through him. (Deutsch is a different person than the Israeli working with Haim.)

Finally, another alleged money launderer was Moshe "Michael" Altman, a Hudson County real estate developer who, according to the criminal Complaints, "washed" more than $600,000 in dirty checks to cash for the cooperating witness through charitable, non-profit entities. Altman is also the intermediary who introduced the cooperating witness to Jersey City building inspector John Guarini, who allegedly took $20,000 from the cooperating witness in July 2007, and $40,000 in total over time. That initial bribe is what gave rise to the public corruption portion of the investigation.

THE PUBLIC CORRUPTION INVESTIGATION

Guarini introduced the cooperating witness to Maher A. Khalil, deputy director of the Jersey City Department of Health and Human Services and a former member of the Jersey City Zoning Board of Adjustment. Khalil—who accepted $30,000 in cash payments from the cooperating witness—made key referrals that set in motion a kind of "corruption networking" amongst the defendants charged today, as well as others, Marra said. The investigation is continuing.

Introductions usually took place at diners and restaurants in Jersey City, Bayonne, Weehawken, Hoboken, Staten Island, Toms River, Atlantic City and elsewhere. Envelopes stuffed with cash were often passed from the cooperating witness to recipients or their intermediaries in parking lots after such meetings, according to the criminal Complaints. Khalil pledged to the cooperating witness to make introductions only to "players" who would "do the right thing" by approving the cooperating witness's development plans in exchange for payments, according to his criminal Complaint. All along the way, each of the individuals charged allegedly took cash bribes up to $20,000 at a time—often numerous times—either taking the money outright or scheming to direct conduit payments through others to political campaigns in Jersey City or Hoboken. In each instance, the defendants acknowledged that, in exchange for the cash or cash campaign contributions, they would vote for and/or use their official influence to expedite and get approvals for the cooperating witness's projects.

Following are the individuals charged in the public corruption investigation, with the exception of Khalil and Guarini above, and summaries of their alleged conduct from the criminal Complaints (All defendants are presumed innocent unless proven guilty beyond a reasonable doubt):

- Leona Beldini, deputy mayor of Jersey City and a realtor. Beldini planned to become broker [sic] for his purported 750-unit condominium project on Garfield Avenue, where units would sell for $500,000 each. Beldini, who was treasurer of a Jersey City official's reelection campaign (that official is identified only as Jersey City Official 4 in the Complaints), also accepted $20,000 in campaign donations, which she said would be divided between "donors" who would return the money to the campaign in increments of $2,600, the maximum individual donation allowed under law.

- Jack M. Shaw, a Hudson County political consultant. As described in the Complaint, he took $10,000 from the cooperating witness for himself and proposed that the cooperating witness pay $10,000 in campaign contributions for the re-election campaign of Jersey City Official 4.

- Edward Cheatam, the affirmative action officer for Hudson County, a commissioner with the Jersey City Housing Authority and, until May, vice president of the Jersey City Board of Education. Cheatam took $15,000 in cash bribes. (Khalil had introduced Cheatam to the cooperating witness; Cheatam then introduced Beldini and Shaw to the cooperating witness, all of whom then went on to extend introductions of the cooperating witness to many others.)

- Mariano Vega, Jr., the Jersey City council president. He met several times with the cooperating witness and ultimately accepted three $10,000 payments, two of which Vega instructed an intermediary to have broken down and converted into individual contributions for his re-election campaign and the third which he received after his election victory.

- Louis Manzo, a defeated candidate for Jersey City mayor, and his brother and political advisor, Ronald. Together, they accepted $27,500 in three cash payments intended for Louis Manzo's campaign. The cooperating witness was told that giving money to Louis Manzo was "insurance" to secure his influence for the cooperating witness in the event the incumbent for mayor lost.

- Lavern Webb-Washington, an unsuccessful candidate for the Jersey City council and a self-described housing activist. She accepted $15,000 in three cash installments of $5,000 for her political campaign.

- Lori Serrano, an unsuccessful candidate for the Jersey City council and former chair of the Jersey City Housing Authority. Serrano accepted $10,000 in two cash payments of $5,000 for her political campaign.

- James P. King, an unsuccessful candidate for Jersey City Council, former head of the Jersey City Parking Authority, former chairman of the Jersey City Incinerator Authority and a former Hudson County undersheriff. He accepted two payments of $5,000 each for his political campaign.

- Michael J. Manzo (no relation to the other Manzos), an unsuccessful candidate for Jersey City Council, and a Jersey City arson investigator. He agreed to accept a $5,000 cash payment from the cooperating witness for his campaign.

- Joseph Castagna, a health officer with the Jersey City Department of Health and Human Services, and a close associate of Michael Manzo. Castagna took the $5,000 payment from the cooperating witness to pass to Michael Manzo.

- Dennis Jaslow, an investigator for the Hudson County Board of Elections and formerly a state corrections officer. Jaslow accepted $2,500, but complained that he wanted $5,000.

- Joseph Cardwell, a political consultant and a commissioner of the Jersey City Municipal Utilities Authority. He accepted two payments of $10,000 in cash to assist the cooperating witness with local government officials in Jersey City and other municipalities, and another $10,000, most of which was used for the purchase of fundraising event tickets.

- Guy Catrillo, a Jersey City planning aide and member of the mayor's "Action Bureau," and an unsuccessful candidate for the city council. Catrillo took $10,000 in campaign cash and another $5,000.

- L. Harvey Smith, state Assemblyman, a Jersey City mayoral candidate and former three term councilman in Jersey City and a Hudson County under-sheriff. Smith took two cash payments, one for $5,000, the other for $10,000, in exchange for approaching high-level contacts with the state Department of Transportation and Department of Environmental Protection to clear the way for approvals of the cooperating witness's project on Garfield Avenue in Jersey City and another project off Route 440 in Bayonne. Smith's aide, Richard Greene, is charged in the same criminal Complaint, and is accused of taking the $5,000 payment from the cooperating witness and passing it to Smith.

- Peter Cammarano III, previously a Hoboken councilman and now mayor, and a lawyer specializing in election law. While a candidate for mayor, then-councilman Cammarano and his close associate, Michael Schaffer, a commissioner on the North Hudson Utilities Authority, took three payments of $5,000 each with the promise that, in return, Cammarano would sponsor zoning changes and push through building plans for high-rise development in Hoboken by the cooperating witness. After the conclusion of their first meeting at a Hoboken diner, the cooperating witness stated, "Make sure you get my stuff expedited." To which Cammarano replied: "I promise you . . . you're gonna be treated like a friend." Moments later, in the parking lot, Schaffer took the first $5,000 in cash. On July 16, Cammarano and Schaffer met the cooperating witness again at a Hoboken diner and accepted another $10,000, which Cammarano said was needed to pay campaign debts, bringing the total in bribes accepted by Cammarano and Schaffer to $25,000.

- Dennis Elwell, mayor of Secaucus, and Ronald Manzo (Manzo is charged in this Complaint in addition to the one with his brother Louis). Elwell received a $10,000 cash bribe—through Manzo as the middleman—to assist the cooperating witness with plans to build a hotel in Secaucus. Manzo took $5,000 from the cooperating witness as a reward for bringing Elwell to him.

- Anthony Suarez, mayor of Ridgefield Borough and an attorney, and co-defendant Vincent Tabbachino, owner of a tax preparation business in Guttenberg. Suarez accepted $10,000 from the cooperating witness through Tabbachino as a middleman, for Suarez's promised assistance in getting approvals to develop properties in Ridgefield. Tabbachino said he kept the cash and, in turn, would write checks totaling $10,000 (one check for $2,500 was cashed) to a legal defense fund for Suarez related to an allegation made by a political opponent of Suarez.

Tabbachino also laundered $100,000 in cash from the cooperating witness's purported knock-off handbag business.

- Daniel M. Van Pelt, state Assemblyman and administrator for Lumberton Township. Van Pelt accepted $10,000 from the cooperating witness for his influence as a state Assemblyman to help in getting the necessary permits for a purported project the cooperating witness was planning in Waretown, Ocean Township. Van Pelt particularly offered his influence in obtaining the necessary permits from the state Department of Environmental Protection.

- Jeffrey Williamson, a Lakewood housing inspector, who was also a state Assembly candidate in 2007. He accepted a total of more than $16,000 in bribes in regular payments of $1,000 between about May 2007 and the last one on July 10, to provide lenient inspections on rental and other properties owned by the cooperating witness in Lakewood. Williamson also allowed the cooperating witness to illegally use a residence in Lakewood as a commercial office. Charles "Shaul" Amon aided in the Lakewood payoff scheme by introducing Williamson to the cooperating witness.

- Charles "Shaul" Amon, previously worked for the cooperating witness managing properties in Lakewood. Amon aided in the Lakewood payoff scheme by introducing Williamson to the cooperating witness. Amon described how he had previously made payoffs to Williamson to go light on housing inspections.

The Money Laundering Defendants

Following are the individuals charged in the money laundering investigation and summaries of their alleged conduct as described in the criminal Complaints (All defendants are presumed innocent unless proven guilty beyond a reasonable doubt):

- Saul Kassin, the chief rabbi of Sharee Zion in Brooklyn, who laundered more than $200,000 with the cooperating witness between June 2007 and December 2008 by accepting "dirty" bank checks from the cooperating witness and exchanging them for clean checks from Kassin's charitable organization, after taking a fee of 10 percent for each transaction.

- Edmund Nahum, principal rabbi at Deal Synagogue in Deal, N.J., who laundered money both acting alone and with Kassin. Nahum laundered $185,000 between June 2007 and December 2008 by accepting dirty checks from the cooperating witness and exchanging them for clean checks from his own and Kassin's charitable organizations, after taking a fee of 10 percent for each transaction. . . .

- Eli Ben Haim, principal rabbi of Congregation Ohel Yaacob in Deal, N.J., laundered $1.5 million with the cooperating witness between June 2007 and February 2009 by accepting dirty checks from the cooperating witness and exchanging them for cash, after taking a fee of approximately 10 percent for each transaction. His source for the cash was an Israeli who, for a fee of 1.5 percent, supplied the cash through intermediary cash houses. . . .

[Names of Cash House Operators for Haim transactions have been omitted.]

[Prosecutorial information has been omitted.]

SOURCE: U.S. Attorney's Office, District of New Jersey. Press release. "Two-Track Investigation of Political Corruption and International Money Laundering Rings Net 44 Individuals." July 23, 2009. www.justice .gov/usao/nj/press/press/files/pdffiles/bidrig0723.rel.pdf.

OTHER HISTORIC DOCUMENTS OF INTEREST

FROM THIS VOLUME

U.S. Department of Transportation's Cash for Clunkers Program

JULY 27 AND SEPTEMBER 25, 2009

On July 27, 2009, the U.S. Department of Transportation (DOT) announced a new program to help revive the struggling U.S. auto industry. The Car Allowance Rebate System (CARS), known as Cash for Clunkers, allowed consumers to trade in older model vehicles with low gas mileage for new vehicles with better gas mileage in return for up to $4,500 in credit toward the purchase. Not only was the Obama administration looking to increase car sales to help automakers, many of whom were being subsidized by loans from the federal government, it also wanted to help reduce dependence on foreign oil and the amount of greenhouse gases entering the atmosphere. "With this program, we are giving the auto industry a shot in the arm and struggling consumers can get rid of their gas-guzzlers and buy a more reliable, fuel-efficient vehicle," said DOT secretary Ray LaHood. "This is good news for our economy, the environment and consumers' pocketbooks."

Upon approving the program, lawmakers expected their $1 billion allocation for credits to last from July 1, 2009, through November 1, 2009. Because of the overwhelming success of the program, however, the $1 billion was exhausted during the first week, prompting lawmakers to extend the program with another $2 billion in Troubled Asset Relief Program (TARP) funds.

SPECIFICATIONS OF THE PROGRAM

On June 24, President Barack Obama had signed the Consumer Assistance to Recycle and Save Act of 2009 into law, which created the Cash for Clunkers program. Under the legislation developed by Congress, the National Highway Traffic Safety Administration (NHTSA) was given thirty days to define how the program would be run and publish details for the public.

According to the NHTSA, which oversaw the program, those who wanted to participate had to trade in a car that was at most twenty-five years old, got eighteen or fewer miles per gallon, was in working order and properly registered, and was insured during the previous year. Anyone trading in an old vehicle for a new one could receive up to $4,500. If the new vehicle got four more miles per gallon or better than the vehicle traded in, the buyer received a $3,500 voucher toward purchasing the new vehicle. Any vehicle getting ten miles or more per gallon over the traded-in vehicle would get $4,500 in credit toward the purchase. To attract buyers, some car manufacturers added additional bonuses to those of the program.

The popular program caused a number of problems for auto dealers, who had to complete a certification process with the NHTSA. On the first day the credit was available, buyers flooded car dealers, and when employees began entering data for the certification process, the NHTSA computer system crashed. The backlog of reimbursements due to car dealers led DOT to triple the number of employees it had hired to work on the program. Some dealers decided not to participate because it cost them too much time and money to wait on the government to reimburse them. General Motors, in an effort to ensure that all its dealers participated in the program, said on August 20 that it would advance money to dealers to cover the credits until the government reimbursed them.

After the first week of the program, the $1 billion allocation from Congress had been exhausted, and the Obama administration announced that it was working with Congress to keep the program running. "It has succeeded well beyond our expectations and all expectations," said Obama. "We're doing everything possible to continue this program." The House of Representatives easily passed a $2 billion extension for the program, although some Republicans tried to hold up the vote while portraying this as another Democratic spending program that would increase the nation's budget deficit. "Cash for Clunkers is another example of the government picking winners and losers and enshrines us as a bailout nation," said Rep. Jeb Hensarling, R-Texas. Passage of the extension in the Senate was not as swift, as Republican lawmakers called for senators to take time to think about what the extension could mean. Sen. Mitch McConnell, R-Ky., said, "We were told this program would last for several months. As it turned out, it ran out of money in a week, prompting the House to rush $2 billion extension before anybody even had time to figure out what happened to the first billion."

INDUSTRY RESPONSE

Programs similar to Cash for Clunkers have been used around the world including in European and Asian countries, to jump start auto sales. In Germany, auto sales during a similar program rose between 25 and 40 percent, France saw an increase of 8 percent, and China saw an increase of 15 percent. This was not the first program of its kind in the United States. In 1992, President George H.W. Bush had developed a similar type of program as part of his environmental policy.

According to Edmunds.com, an automotive Web site to educate consumers, a total of 690,000 cars were sold during the program's run. Of those sales, 125,000 would not have happened if it were not for the rebate program. According to the site, this means that the government spent $24,000 to sell each of the 125,000 vehicles. However, economists applauded the program, because it added 1.7 percent to the gross domestic product (GDP) in the third quarter of 2009. The growth was aided by a 10.6 percent jump in auto sales, which boosted retail sales 2.7 percent. In addition to a growth in GDP, several auto plants that had been closed when auto manufacturers began cutting back were reopened to increase production and restock inventories, leading to job creation.

The chief executive of Edmunds.com, Jeremy Anwyl, said the Cash for Clunkers program would not help the auto industry out of the slump it was in, nor would it help companies receiving bailout dollars pay the money back to the government. "The scale is all wrong," Anwyl said. According to his estimates, auto sales would have to increase by three million or more vehicles, not a number in the hundreds of thousands expected to be sold during the life of the program. A *Washington Post* editorial echoed these concerns. "Those paltry results will merely represent the shifting of future demand for cars to the present; they will also come at the expense of sales of other goods that people might have chosen to buy this summer or fall," according to the *Post*.

The negative assessment by Edmunds.com drew anger from some quarters. "It is unfortunate that Edmunds.com has had nothing but negative things to say about a wildly successful program that sold nearly 250,000 cars in its first four days alone," said Bill Adams, a spokesperson for DOT. "There can be no doubt that CARS drummed up more business for car dealers at a time when they needed help the most," he continued. George Pipas, a sales analyst with Ford Motor Company, agreed. "The whole purpose of the program was to provide some kind of catalyst to kick-start the economy, and by all accounts the extra production that was added this year was a boost to the economy," he said.

J.D. Power and Associates forecasted that because of the Cash for Clunkers program, August retail car sales would exceed one million. "Improved consumer confidence and credit availability during the past six months have combined with the CARS program to lift industry sales out of their slumping year-to-date levels, which have been down approximately 35 percent year-over-year," said Gary Dilts, senior vice president of global automotive operations at J.D. Power and Associates.

ENVIRONMENTAL QUESTIONS

Many environmentalists were against the Cash for Clunkers program, even though it replaced less fuel efficient vehicles with more fuel efficient ones, thus reducing the amount of greenhouse gases entering the atmosphere. Environmental lobbies said that although the program promoted better fuel mileage, vehicles that were still drivable were being taken off the roads and thrown away, not recycled or driven until they were no longer useful. Sen. Dianne Feinstein, D-Calif., submitted an alternate bill to Congress, and dubbed the Cash for Clunkers program "Handouts for Hummer," saying that the program undermined fuel efficiency by allowing families to purchase trucks and SUVs that despite getting better fuel mileage than the "clunkers" required a greater amount of fuel than other automotive alternatives. Feinstein noted that there was no program for used cars that were cheaper and more fuel efficient, an argument given by economists who feared that families buying new cars under the program would have to forgo other purchases later in the year, such as holiday gifts, thus reducing retail sales for businesses other than automotives.

Given the number of vehicles traded in during the program, fuel economy was improved overall by 60 percent, according to statistics from Hyundai Motor America. "[W]hen the federal government and the private sector team up to take bold action, the American public reaps the rewards," said LaHood. "Working together, we have delivered on our promise to improve the environment, create jobs and get this struggling economy back on its feet, not to mention the millions of dollars the CARS program generated in local and state sales tax revenue to help cash-strapped states," he said.

—Heather Kerrigan

Following is a press release of July 27, 2009, from the Department of Transportation announcing the start of the Cash for Clunkers program, and a department press release of September 25, 2009, on the end of Cash for Clunkers payouts.

Department of Transportation
Announces Cash for Clunkers Program

July 27, 2009

U.S. Transportation Secretary Ray LaHood today kicked off a buyer incentive program designed to help consumers purchase new fuel efficient vehicles and boost the economy at the same time. The Car Allowance Rebate System (CARS), commonly referred to as Cash for Clunkers, is a new federal program that gives buyers up to $4,500 towards a new, more environmentally-friendly vehicle when they trade-in their old gas guzzling cars or trucks.

"With this program, we are giving the auto industry a shot in the arm and struggling consumers can get rid of their gas-guzzlers and buy a more reliable, fuel-efficient vehicle," Secretary LaHood said. "This is good news for our economy, the environment and consumers' pocketbooks."

The National Highway Traffic Safety Administration (NHTSA) also released the final eligibility requirements to participate in the program. Under the CARS program, consumers receive a $3,500 or $4,500 discount from a car dealer when they trade in their old vehicle and purchase or lease a new, qualifying vehicle. In order to be eligible for the program, the trade-in passenger vehicle must: be manufactured less than 25 years before the date it is traded in; have a combined city/highway fuel economy of 18 miles per gallon or less; be in drivable condition; and be continuously insured and registered to the same owner for the full year before the trade-in. Transactions must be made between now and November 1, 2009 or until the money runs out.

The vehicle that is traded in will be scrapped. NHTSA estimates the program could take approximately 250,000 vehicles that are not fuel efficient off the road.

In the coming, days, NHTSA will launch an all-out effort to raise public awareness about this program. On Monday, July 27, NHTSA will hold a Webinar with dealers from across the country to explain the program and make sure the process is as user-friendly as possible. Dealers and interested participants are encouraged to visit the official website www.cars.gov for more information. In addition, NHTSA has established a toll-free hotline that consumers can call to get information on the program 866-CAR-7891. In early August, NHTSA will launch a national television and Internet advertising campaign to further educate the public about CARS. Consumers are reminded that they do not need to register for the program in order to participate.

# # #

Car Allowance Rebate System (CARS) Fact Sheet

About CARS:

The Car Allowance Rebate System (CARS) is a $1 billion government program that helps consumers buy or lease a more environmentally-friendly vehicle from a participating dealer when they trade in a less fuel-efficient car or truck. The program is designed to energize the economy, boost auto sales and put safer, cleaner and more fuel-efficient vehicles on the nation's roadways.

Legislative History:

On June 24, the President signed into law the Consumer Assistance to Recycle and Save Act of 2009. The Act established a temporary program under the National Highway Traffic Safety Administration (NHTSA) called the Car Allowance Rebate System (CARS), referred to commonly as Cash for Clunkers.

Under the legislation, NHTSA had 30 days from the time the President signed the bill to fine-tune administrative aspects of the Car Allowance Rebate System (CARS) including dealer registration, vehicle eligibility requirements, payment transfers and anti-fraud and abuse protections. The agency met the statutory requirement and issued the implementation rule on July 24. The program ends on November 1, 2009.

Eligibility:

To be eligible for a trade-in rebate, cars and light trucks must be at least a 1984 model-year vehicle or newer. The vehicle must be drivable, insured and licensed for at least a year, and get 18 miles per gallon or less combined highway/city rating. Both domestic and imported vehicles are eligible for the program. The credit cannot be applied toward the purchase or lease of used vehicles. Requirements for work trucks are slightly different.

How It Works:

Consumers bring their vehicles, title, proof of registration and proof of insurance to the dealership. The rebate amount, at the time of purchase, will depend on the improved mileage of the new vehicle.

- For passenger cars, consumers will receive a $3500 rebate if the new vehicle gets at least 4 mpg higher than the trade-in. To receive $4500, the new vehicle needs to get at least 10 mpg higher than the trade-in.

- For light trucks, the $3500 rebate would require at least 2 mpg higher than the trade-in. To receive the $4500 rebate, the new vehicle must be at least 4 mpg higher than the trade-in.

The dealers are later reimbursed by NHTSA through an electronic funds transfer. The vehicles traded in under the CARS program will be scrapped. Dealers are required under law to use a NHTSA approved salvage facility for vehicle disposal. Vehicles are required to be shredded or crushed within 6 months. The entity crushing or shredding the vehicles can sell some parts of the vehicle prior to crushing or shredding it, but these parts cannot include the engine or the drive train (unless the drive train, the transmission, drive shaft, or rear end are sold as separate parts).

NHTSA estimates that the program could remove approximately 250,000 fuel-inefficient vehicles from U.S. roads. . . .

Frequently Asked Questions:

What Is the Car Allowance Rebate System?
The Car Allowance Rebate System is a new program from the government that will help you pay for a new, more fuel efficient car or truck from a participating dealer when you trade in a less fuel efficient car or truck.

Do I need to get a voucher or sign up for this program?
No. You do not need a voucher and you are not required to sign up or enroll in this program. Participating new car dealers will apply a credit, reducing the price you pay at the time of your purchase or lease, provided the vehicle you buy or lease and the vehicle you trade in meet the program requirements. The dealer will then obtain reimbursement from the government.

How do I know if a dealer is participating in the program?
The law requires dealers to be registered to participate in the program. We will be moving as quickly as possible to register interested dealers as soon as the registration process begins in the near future. As dealers are registered, we will list them on this website. Meanwhile, you may wish to contact dealers in your area to ask whether they plan to participate in the program. The CARS Act requires that dealers be licensed by their respective state for the sale of new automobiles in order for them to participate in the program.

How do I know if my car or truck is an eligible trade-in vehicle?
There are several requirements (but you also have to meet certain conditions for the car or truck you wish to buy). Your dealer can help you determine whether you have an eligible trade in vehicle.

Your trade-in vehicle must: have been manufactured less than 25 years before the date you trade it in; have a "new" combined city/highway fuel economy of 18 miles per gallon or less; be in drivable condition and be continuously insured and registered to the same owner for the full year preceding the trade-in. The trade-in vehicle must have been manufactured not earlier than 25 years before the date of trade in and, in the case of a category 3 vehicle, must also have been manufactured not later than model year 2001. Note that work trucks (i.e., very large pickup trucks and cargo vans) have different requirements.

What will I need to bring to the dealer in order to participate in the program?
You should bring documentation establishing the identity of the person who currently owns the vehicle, preferably the title of the vehicle, and documentary proof that the vehicle "has been continuously insured consistent with the applicable State law and registered to the same owner for a period of not less than 1 year immediately prior

to the trade-in." The final rule will specify what types of documentation would be acceptable. . . .

SOURCE: U.S. Department of Transportation. Office of Public Affairs. Press release. "Transportation Secretary Ray LaHood Kicks-Off CARS Program, Encourages Consumers to Buy More Fuel Efficient Cars and Trucks." July 27, 2009. www.cars.gov/files/official-information/July27PR.pdf.

Department of Transportation Declares Cash for Clunkers Payouts Nearly Complete

September 25, 2009

With final dealer payments being processed under the enormously successful CARS program, U.S. Transportation Secretary Ray LaHood announced today that the agency has crossed the finish line for paying back eligible and complete dealer submissions.

"This is the final curtain call for a program that took the entire nation by storm and succeeded beyond expectations," said Secretary LaHood. "There can be no doubt that this program drummed up more business, for more people, in more places, at a time when our economy needed help the most."

With the $3 billion provided by Congress to run the CARS program, consumers turned in gas guzzlers and bought nearly 700,000 more fuel efficient vehicles in fewer than 30 days. In August alone, retail sales rose by 2.7 percent, due in large part to a notable 10.6 percent boost in sales by auto dealers.

Ford and General Motors recently announced production increases for both the third and fourth quarters as a result of the demand generated by the program. Honda also said it will be increasing production at its U.S. plants in East Liberty and Marysville, Ohio and in Lincoln, Alabama.

In addition, the program provides good news for the environment, a 60 percent improvement in fuel economy between the trade-in and new cars purchased.

"When the federal government and the private sector team up to take bold action, the American public reaps the rewards," said Secretary LaHood. "Working together, we have delivered on our promise to improve the environment, create jobs and get this struggling economy back on its feet, not to mention the millions of dollars the CARS program generated in local and state sales tax revenue to help cash-strapped states."

To date, 98 percent of CARS program rebates totaling $2,799,077,000 have been approved for payment under the program. All applications for rebates have been reviewed at least once, and all eligible and complete applications have been approved for payment. The agency will continue to work directly with dealers to help them correct and complete the remaining two percent of submitted applications.

The government reached this milestone in payment of valid submissions just 90 days after the law creating this program was enacted, 60 days after issuing its rule setting the requirements for the program and 30 days after closing the program due to exhaustion of funds.

[A chart listing the requested reimbursements per state has been omitted.]

Source: U.S. Department of Transportation. Office of Public Affairs. Press release. "Cash for Clunkers Payout Nearly Complete." September 25, 2009. www.cars.gov/files/official-information/September25PR .pdf.

OTHER HISTORIC DOCUMENTS OF INTEREST

FROM THIS VOLUME

- President Obama Signs the American Recovery and Reinvestment Act of 2009, p. 41
- The Department of Transportation and the Environmental Protection Agency Release New Fuel Economy Standards, p. 442

FROM PREVIOUS *HISTORIC DOCUMENTS*

- California Sues the EPA over Emissions Standards, *2008,* p. 3
- President Bush on Gasoline Prices and Oil Dependence, *2006,* p. 140
- EPA Report on Global Warming, *2002,* p. 298

U.S.-Russian Relations in the Obama Administration

JULY 28 AND SEPTEMBER 17, 2009

After assuming office in January 2009, U.S. president Barack Obama sought to "reset" relations with Russia. The relationship between the two countries had been strained in recent years, owing in part to U.S. plans to build antimissile facilities in the Czech Republic and Poland; the planned enlargement of the North Atlantic Treaty Organization (NATO) into eastern Europe; Russia's war with Georgia in August 2008; and U.S. recognition of Kosovo as a sovereign state in early 2008. By the end of 2008, relations between the United States and Russia had deteriorated to their lowest point since the end of the Cold War. President Obama acknowledged the poor state of bilateral relations in April 2009, stating that "over the last several years, the relationship between our two countries has been allowed to drift."

At a meeting between U.S. secretary of state Hillary Rodham Clinton and Russia's foreign minister, Sergei Lavrov, on March 6, 2009, both parties agreed to reset their relations and to begin negotiations on a new nuclear arms control agreement by the end of the year. The Strategic Arms Reduction Treaty (START I), which went into effect in 1994, limited both Russia and the United States to possessing 6,000 warheads and 1,600 bombs and missiles. Both countries have a strong interest in furthering disarmament. For its part, the United States was eager to avoid major expenditures on nuclear arms to achieve parity (or near parity) with Russia. Meanwhile, Russia was likely equally keen to avoid another expensive arms race with the United States. But perhaps more important, the decision to begin negotiations on another arms control agreement signaled to Russia that the United States was ready to discuss its planned missile defense system in eastern Europe.

On April 2, 2009, President Obama and his Russian counterpart, President Dmitri Medvedev, met in London for the first time, after which they announced that significant negotiations on a new arms control agreement would be undertaken to "move beyond Cold War mentalities." The two leaders also acknowledged areas of ongoing disagreement, most notably the breakaway regions of Abkhazia and South Ossetia in Georgia. President Obama indicated that the United States would not recognize the independence of the regions, over which Russia and Georgia fought a brief war in mid-2008.

U.S.-RUSSIAN SUMMIT

It was not only nuclear policy that led the United States to reengage with Russia. The Obama administration was interested also in diffusing tensions so that the two states could cooperate in areas of special interest to the United States. In particular, the United States was eager to work together on issues relating to Iran's nuclear program, as well as the NATO-led war in Afghanistan. President Obama has asked President Medvedev for assistance in urging Iran to abandon its pursuit of a nuclear weapons program. Russia has opposed UN sanctions against Iran in response to the latter's controversial nuclear program, which is unsurprising given that Russia has strong economic ties to Iran. Indeed, Russia is Iran's number one supplier of nuclear materials and technology, as well as arms.

A number of political developments added to existing tensions between the two states in the days leading up to a summit held in Moscow, July 6–7, 2009. The Russian government had officially recognized the reelection of the Iranian president, Mahmoud Ahmadinejad, and had performed major military exercises in the Caucasus. The latter raised concerns that another war with Georgia could be in the cards, particularly as Russia had also expelled monitors from the United Nations and the Organization for Security and Cooperation in Europe (OSCE) from Georgia. Furthermore, the Russian government had unexpectedly dropped its bid for accession to the World Trade Organization (WTO), stating that instead of gaining membership as a state it would seek to join the international organization as a customs bloc with Kazakhstan and Belarus. WTO rules do not allow states to join as a customs bloc.

The summit, which President Obama and President Medvedev attended, was a qualified success. The centerpiece of the summit was the signing of a framework agreement on cutting each country's stockpile of nuclear weapons. The two sides officially agreed to undertake negotiations on the successor to START I that will seek to cut the number of nuclear-armed missiles and bombs to 500–1,100 and the number of nuclear warheads to a maximum of 1,650 by 2017. A number of other important agreements were also signed by the two leaders, including one establishing a high-level bilateral commission tasked with increasing ties on a range of topics, including economic issues. The commission will be headed by President Obama and his Russian counterpart, and Clinton and Lavrov also will be heavily involved. In addition, Russia agreed to allow the U.S. military to use its airspace when transporting troops and supplies to Afghanistan. Doing so helps Russia to secure its southern border with Afghanistan while also saving the U.S. military time and money. This was a tangible outcome and an obvious step forward in relations between the two countries. Moreover, a new framework for cooperation between Russian and U.S. military forces was signed.

However, outside of the areas in which both countries have a strong mutual interest, namely Afghanistan and nuclear nonproliferation, little progress was made. Undoubtedly the most contentious issue was the U.S. plan to build a missile defense system in the Czech Republic and Poland that Russia vehemently opposed. The proposed system was intended to protect U.S. allies in Europe against a potential Iranian missile launch. Russia loathed the idea of U.S. missiles situated in countries that at one time were within the Soviet Union's sphere of influence, as well as the fact that the defense system would have been capable of monitoring activities in a significant area of Russian airspace. Moreover, the Russian government viewed the missile defense system as antagonistic and as a way for the United States to try to curb Russian military power. During the summit, Obama stated that it would be reasonable to discuss defensive as well as offensive weapons during negotiations for the successor to START I. This implied a U.S. willingness to negotiate on plans for the missile defense program. However, President Obama also inferred that there would have to be a trade-off, likely in the form of Russian help in stopping Iran from further developing its nuclear program.

RESETTING RELATIONS WITH RUSSIA

In mid-September 2009, the Obama administration moved to reset relations with Russia by ending the planned missile defense system in the Czech Republic and Poland, indicating that the threat of Iranian weapons was not aimed at the United States. To better combat the threat of Iran's ballistic missiles, the United States would place a "distributed sensor network" in northern and southern Europe, as well as on ships in nearby waters. Announcing the end of the program, Obama said, "To put it simply, our new missile defense architecture in Europe will provide stronger, smarter, and swifter defenses of American forces and America's allies. It is more comprehensive than the previous program, it deploys capabilities that are proven and cost effective, and it sustains and builds upon our commitment to protect the U.S. homeland against long-range ballistic missile threats, and it ensures and enhances the protection of all our NATO allies."

A week after announcing that the old, proposed missile defense system would be canceled, President Obama and President Medvedev met again on the sidelines of the UN General Assembly. The two leaders spoke at length about Iran's nuclear program; President Medvedev promised, in a shift in Russian policy toward Iran, that Russia would encourage Iran to make "a right decision" and that "in some cases sanctions are inevitable."

Russia has fiercely opposed the enlargement of NATO on the grounds that it would constitute a military threat. The potential future membership of Ukraine and Georgia, both of which are former Soviet states, has proved to be a particular irritant in relations between the United States and Russia. The issue of NATO enlargement will continue to be a topic of intense discussion at meetings of the NATO-Russia Council.

START I expired on December 5, 2009, and negotiators from the United States and Russia were unable to conclude a new agreement by the end-of-2009 deadline. Russia is determined to ensure that the number of missiles and delivery vehicles in the two country's arsenals be equal. The principle of symmetry is also important to Russia. START I required that the United States and Russia exchange flight data from missile tests, but this provision had a greater impact on Russia because its weapons development program has been more active than that of the United States since START I went into force. Russian officials are concerned that the valuable data the United States has received about the latter's weapons could be used to develop a missile defense system that would be highly effective against Russian warheads.

The Obama administration was eager to conclude a successor agreement by the end of April 2010, ahead of the next review conference on the Nuclear Non-Proliferation Treaty. The outcome of the conference is considered to be important to strengthening the global nuclear nonproliferation movement.

—Hilary Ewing

Following is the text of a statement by Philip Gordon, assistant secretary of state for European and Eurasian affairs, given on July 28, 2009, before the House Foreign Relations Committee on the relationship between the United States and Russia, and a statement by President Barack Obama on September 17, 2009, announcing the end of the Bush-era missile defense system in Europe.

Philip Gordon's Statement Before the House Foreign Relations Committee

July 28, 2009

Chairman Wexler, Congressman Gallegly, members of the Committee, thank you for the opportunity to speak to you today about the Administration's achievements in Moscow as a result of the summit meeting of President Obama and President Medvedev July 6–8. I would like to submit my full testimony for the record, and would like to take this opportunity to make a few brief remarks.

Let me begin by putting the results of the summit into a somewhat wider context. The Obama Administration entered office seeking to put an end to the dangerous drift in our bilateral relations with Russia. Last December, then President-elect Obama called for a "reset" in our relations with Russia. He argued that the United States and Russia have mutual interests in a number of areas—including nuclear nonproliferation, terrorism, and Afghanistan for example—and argued that it should be possible to cooperate practically in these areas even as we disagreed on other issues. The results of the Moscow Summit demonstrate that the President's instincts were correct.

In the six months since President Obama took office, the United States and Russia worked hard to achieve such a fresh start. Not only have our leaders made progress in improving the tone of our relations and helping to build goodwill between our two countries, but as the Moscow Summit demonstrates, we have succeeded in translating the rhetoric about potential collaboration into identifiable, concrete actions that are fundamental to the security and the prosperity of both our countries.

This significant progress in our relations with Russia, moreover, did not in any way come at the expense of our principles or partnerships with friends and allies. There are still many areas where the United States and Russia disagree and will continue to disagree. Nevertheless, in Moscow we demonstrated in real terms our shared desire to build a relationship based on respect, cooperation, and common interests.

First and foremost, the United States and Russia took important steps to increase nuclear security and prevent the spread of nuclear weapons, beginning with the reduction of our own nuclear arsenals. The two Presidents signed a Joint Understanding for a follow-on agreement to START that commits both parties to a legally binding treaty that will reduce our nuclear warheads and delivery systems by at least one third of our current treaty limitations. They also agreed to participate in a joint threat assessment of the ballistic missile challenges of the 21st century, including those posed by Iran and North Korea. Wasting no time in launching this effort, an interagency team of experts is heading out to Moscow this week to begin discussions.

Second, we made concrete commitments to deepen security cooperation, including by working together to defeat violent extremists and to counter transnational threats, including those of piracy and narcotics trafficking. At the summit, Chairman of the Joint Chiefs of Staff Admiral Mullen and Russian Chief of the General Staff General Makarov agreed to work plan for resuming military-to-military cooperation in areas such as counter-terrorism, search and rescue, and counterpiracy.

Another very tangible result of the summit was Russia's agreement to allow the United States to transport its military personnel and equipment across Russia in support of the NATO-led International Security Assistance Force as well as our Coalition Forces in Afghanistan. This agreement will add flexibility and further diversify our crucial supply routes, resulting in a potential savings of up to $133 million in fuel, maintenance, and other transportation costs. The significance of this contribution to our efforts to bring about peace and stability to Afghanistan, which is also of strategic benefit to Russia as well, should not be understated. It is an excellent example of how the two countries can cooperate in the pursuit of common interests, without any quid pro quos.

We also agreed to strengthen cooperation in non-strategic areas. For example, the United States and Russia took steps to build cooperation in public health, which could include strengthening work between U.S. and Russian scientific research institutions on HIV/AIDS and tuberculosis and prevention and treatment of cardiovascular disease. And we agreed to restore the work of the Joint Commission on Prisoners of War and Missing in Action.

Finally, President Obama and President Medvedev recognized the need for a more structured foundation for advancing our cooperation in key areas across our respective inter-agencies. The Bilateral Presidential Commission—to be chaired by the two presidents and led by Secretary Clinton and Foreign Minister Lavrov—will provide a mechanism for sustaining and expanding on the progress we achieved in Moscow, while also proving a for a [sic] in which we can work together effectively to narrow our differences.

Notwithstanding all of these positive developments, we have no illusions that our reset of relations will be easy, or that we will not continue to have differences with Russia. Nonetheless, we are confident that the United States and Russia can still work together where our interests coincide while at the same time seeking to narrow our differences in an open and mutually respectful way, be it on issues of human rights or Russia's unlawful recognition of Georgia's separatist regions. In this regard, the President was unequivocal in his message that the "reset" in our bilateral relationship will not come at the expense of our friends and allies. More than in words, but in actions, we have demonstrated our commitment to the territorial integrity and independence of Russia's neighbors, including Ukraine and Georgia. President Obama made very clear in Moscow that we will continue to support their sovereignty and their right to choose their own security alliances, a message reinforced by the Vice President's trip to those two countries just last week. The President also stressed, both privately and publicly, America's enduring support for democracy, human rights and the rule of law.

To conclude, at the Moscow Summit the United States and Russia took significant steps forward in translating the "reset" in relations into concrete achievements to benefit both our nations and our global partners. Without abandoning our principles or our friends and allies, we demonstrated that the United States and Russia can work effectively together on a broad range of issues where our interests coincide.

Mr. Chairman, Congressman Gallegly, members of the Committee, I am grateful for the opportunity to speak before you today, and I welcome the opportunity to respond to your questions.

SOURCE: U.S. Department of State. Bureau of European and Eurasian Affairs. "Statement Before the House Foreign Relations Committee." July 28, 2009. www.state.gov/p/eur/rls/rm/2009/126537.htm.

President Obama Announces End of Bush-era Missile Defense Program in Europe

September 17, 2009

Good morning. As Commander in Chief, I'm committed to doing everything in my power to advance our national security, and that includes strengthening our defenses against any and all threats to our people, our troops, and our friends and allies around the world.

And one of those threats is the danger posed by ballistic missiles. As I said during the campaign, President Bush was right that Iran's ballistic missile program poses a significant threat. And that's why I'm committed to deploying strong missile defense systems which are adaptable to the threats of the 21st century.

The best way to responsibly advance our security and the security of our allies is to deploy a missile defense system that best responds to the threats that we face and that utilizes technology that is both proven and cost effective.

In keeping with that commitment and a congressionally mandated review, I ordered a comprehensive assessment of our missile defense program in Europe. And after an extensive process, I have approved the unanimous recommendations of my Secretary of Defense and my Joint Chiefs of Staff to strengthen America's defenses against ballistic missile attack.

This new approach will provide capabilities sooner, build on proven systems, and offer greater defenses against the threat of missile attack than the 2007 European missile defense program.

This decision was guided by two principal factors. First, we have updated our intelligence assessment of Iran's missile programs, which emphasizes the threat posed by Iran's short- and medium-range missiles, which are capable of reaching Europe. There's no substitute for Iran complying with its international obligations regarding its nuclear program, and we, along with our allies and partners, will continue to pursue strong diplomacy to ensure that Iran lives up to these international obligations. But this new ballistic missile defense program will best address the threat posed by Iran's ongoing ballistic missile defense program.

Second, we have made specific and proven advances in our missile defense technology, particularly with regard to land- and sea-based interceptors and the sensors that support them. Our new approach will therefore deploy technologies that are proven and cost effective and that counter the current threat, and do so sooner than the previous program. Because our approach will be phased and adaptive, we will retain the flexibility to adjust and enhance our defenses as the threat and technology continue to evolve.

To put it simply, our new missile defense architecture in Europe will provide stronger, smarter, and swifter defenses of American forces and America's allies. It is more comprehensive than the previous program, it deploys capabilities that are proven and cost effective, and it sustains and builds upon our commitment to protect the U.S. homeland against long-range ballistic missile threats, and it ensures and enhances the protection of all our NATO allies.

Now, this approach is also consistent with NATO missile—NATO's missile defense efforts and provides opportunities for enhanced international collaboration going forward. We will continue to work cooperatively with our close friends and allies, the Czech Republic and Poland, who had agreed to host elements of the previous program. I've spoken to the Prime Ministers of both the Czech Republic and Poland about this decision and reaffirmed our deep and close ties. Together, we are committed to a broad range of cooperative efforts to strengthen our collective defense, and we are bound by the solemn commitment of NATO's Article 5 that an attack on one is an attack on all.

We've also repeatedly made clear to Russia that its concerns about our previous missile defense programs were entirely unfounded. Our clear and consistent focus has been the threat posed by Iran's ballistic missile program, and that continues to be our focus and the basis of the program that we're announcing today.

In confronting that threat, we welcome Russians' cooperation to bring its missile defense capabilities into a broader defense of our common strategic interests, even as we continue to—we continue our shared efforts to end Iran's illicit nuclear program.

Now, going forward, my administration will continue to consult closely with Congress and with our allies as we deploy this system, and we will rigorously evaluate both the threat posed by ballistic missiles and the technology that we are developing to counter it. I'm confident that with the steps we've taken today, we have strengthened America's national security and enhanced our capacity to confront 21st century threats.

Thank you very much, everybody.

SOURCE: U.S. Executive Office of the President. "Remarks on Missile Defense Systems in Europe." *Daily Compilation of Presidential Documents* 2009, no. 00720 (September 17, 2009). www.gpo.gov/fdsys/pkg/DCPD-200900720/pdf/DCPD-200900720.pdf.

OTHER HISTORIC DOCUMENTS OF INTEREST

FROM PREVIOUS *HISTORIC DOCUMENTS*

- Kosovo Declares Independence from Serbia, *2008*, p. 70
- Medvedev on His Inauguration as President of Russia, *2008*, p. 169
- Georgian, Russian and U.S. Officials on the Conflict in South Ossetia, *2008*, p. 346
- Russian President Putin on World Affairs and Russian Politics, *2007*, p. 62
- President Bush on Plans for a Missile Defense System, *2007*, p. 1026
- Energy Commission Report on Russian Nuclear Weapons, *2001*, p. 17
- NATO Members and Russia on a "New Relationship," *2001*, p. 892
- Yeltsin's Summit with Bush, Address to Congress, *1992*, p. 519

August

American Journalists Freed in North Korea

AUGUST 5, 2009

Two American journalists reporting on the plight of North Korean refugees in China were arrested on March 17, 2009, at the border between the two nations and were accused by North Korean authorities of illegally entering the country to commit "hostile acts."

The two women, Laura Ling and Euna Lee, were held for more than four months. They were tried and sentenced to hard labor in North Korea's judicial system. On August 5, 2009, former president Bill Clinton undertook a successful mission to North Korea to free the two journalists and escort them back to the United States.

Clinton's twenty-hour trip in August raised questions about whether it would lead North Korea to think that the United States was prepared for bilateral talks on North Korea's nuclear program. The State Department denied that Clinton had spent any time discussing the North Korean nuclear issue, maintaining that the former president was simply there on a humanitarian mission to negotiate the release of Lee and Ling. North Korean media sources put a different spin on the talks, reporting that Clinton had come at the request of North Korean leader Kim Jong Il to discuss the journalists and the nation's nuclear weapons program.

DETENTION OF LEE AND LING

Lee and Ling worked for Current TV, a media venture based in San Francisco, California, and founded by former vice president Al Gore. At the time of their capture, the women were at the China–North Korea border to report on the condition of refugees who had escaped North Korea to live in China.

Ling, Lee, their families, and Current TV consistently denied that the two had ventured into North Korea, an act that would have been illegal for Americans, who are not allowed to enter the country without permission. South Korea became involved, claiming that the North Korean guards who had captured Ling and Lee had crossed into China to seize them.

In June, the journalists were quickly tried and convicted for illegally crossing the North Korean border. They were sentenced to twelve years of "reform through labor." This sentence dashed the hopes of their families, who feared that they might never see the two women again given North Korea's record of having one of the world's most brutal penal systems. The two women were fed meals of rice that, according to Ling, sometimes contained rocks, and they were rarely allowed to communicate with each other.

North Korean officials claimed that Ling and Lee had admitted during their trial that they had entered North Korea illegally and that the two had accepted their sentences. The state-run Korean Central News Agency (KCNA) reported that the women had said that they had entered North Korea to collect evidence for a smear campaign about human rights violations.

UNITED STATES WORKS FOR RELEASE

The families of Lee and Ling pleaded publicly with North Korean authorities to release the two women, fearing for their emotional well-being and physical safety. Ling's family told the media that she suffered from ulcers, and Lee's family pleaded for the return of their daughter so that she could care for her child. Lee and Ling were able to write to their families during their captivity, expressing their fear of being held in a North Korean prison indefinitely. "While I am trying to remain hopeful," wrote Ling in one letter, "each day becomes harder and harder to bear. I am so lonely and scared."

The United States relied heavily on the Swedish ambassador, Mats Foyer, in North Korea throughout the detention of the two journalists, using him to send messages to North Korea to ensure that mail and medicine reached the two women. It was during phone calls facilitated by Sweden's embassy that Ling and Lee were able to relay messages to their families that were then sent on to the State Department, including the revelation that North Korea would consider releasing the two journalists if former president Clinton was sent as an envoy.

Ling and Lee were held in North Korea for 140 days before Clinton arrived to secure their release. The North Koreans had made two demands of the United States—to meet with a top diplomat and to receive an apology. When former president Clinton arrived in North Korea, he met with North Korea's leader, Kim Jong Il, for one hour and fifteen minutes. Reports from U.S. news agencies and North Korea's KCNA differed concerning what happened during the meeting. KCNA reported that former president Clinton had apologized for the actions of the two journalists, while Secretary of State Hillary Rodham Clinton and the Obama administration were quick to deny through the U.S. media that an apology had been offered. In the end, both nations got what they wanted—Kim received a visit from a well-regarded U.S. leader and the United States succeeded in freeing the two journalists.

Ling and Lee arrived back in the United States in August. Questions were immediately raised about why Bill Clinton, rather than his wife, the secretary of state, had gone to North Korea. After their release, President Barack Obama expressed satisfaction with Clinton's trip, saying that he was "very pleased with the outcome." His administration was mum, however, on how involved Obama had been in the planning stages of the release of the journalists. Former vice president Gore said, "President Obama and countless members of his administration have been deeply involved in this humanitarian effort. They have really put their hearts in this."

Secretary Clinton was naturally quite involved in the release. Deputy State Department spokesperson Robert Wood said that it had been President Obama's idea to send Bill Clinton on the "private humanitarian mission" to secure the women's release. One reason for not sending the secretary of state may have been North Korea's July 2009 reference to her as a "funny lady" whom they did not consider intelligent. The North Korean Foreign Ministry said she sometimes "looks like a primary-school girl and sometimes a pensioner going shopping." Secretary Clinton said after the journalists's release, "We have successfully completed a humanitarian mission, it was a private mission, but now we have to go back to the ongoing efforts to enlist the North Koreans in discussions the world wants to see them participate in."

More details came to light after Lee and Ling arrived home, including the fact that the rescue trip had been in the works for months, and contrary to what many expected, Lee and Ling had been kept in a guesthouse in Pyongyang rather than a prison. They were surprised to have former president Clinton actually come to their aid. "We feared that at any moment we could be sent to a hard labor camp, and then suddenly we were told that we were going to a meeting. When we walked through the doors, we saw standing before us President Bill Clinton," said Ling. "We were shocked," she continued, "but we knew instantly in our hearts that the nightmare of our lives was finally coming to an end."

It was believed that North Korea had detained Ling and Lee to use them as leverage to set up direct talks with the United States on a number of issues, perhaps including its nuclear program. The United States has refused to engage North Korea on the nuclear issue unless it was in six-party talks that also included South Korea, Japan, China, and Russia. President Clinton has maintained that he only discussed Ling and Lee during his meetings with North Korean diplomats.

INTERPRETATIONS

There were differing ideas about what Clinton's trip might mean. Clinton was only the second U.S. president to visit the country; former president Jimmy Carter had visited the communist nation in 1994 during the Clinton administration. Some suspected that although Clinton had been asked to avoid the issue, the former president may have given Kim his views on North Korea's nuclear tests. North Korea could potentially use this as leverage to secure bilateral talks on nuclearization with the United States. The trip received extensive attention on state-run media, which had implied that the United States was to begin direct talks. John Bolton, former U.S. ambassador to the United Nations, called the visit to North Korea "a classic case of rewarding bad behavior."

North Korea's news agency trumpeted the arrival of Clinton in a bold headline, "Bill Clinton Arrives Here," followed by boxes featuring links to "Nuclear Talks; Trial of American Journalists," indicating that the government wanted to leave the impression that Clinton had arrived for nuclear negotiations.

In the United States, officials maintained that Clinton's was simply a humanitarian mission and that it would have no effect on the multilateral six-party talks regarding North Korea's nuclear program. The negotiations for Ling and Lee's release and visit of a high-level U.S. official may have sparked the detention of three Americans who had entered Iran while hiking near the Iran-Iraq border. The State Department tried to calm fears that Iran had detained the Americans simply to secure a U.S. diplomat for negotiations, saying that each case would be handled based on its own merits.

—Heather Kerrigan

Following is the text of remarks on August 5, 2009, by U.S. secretary of state Hillary Rodham Clinton on the release of U.S. journalists Laura Ling and Euna Lee from North Korea, and a report from the Korean Central News Agency issued on August 5, 2009, on the visit of former president Bill Clinton.

Secretary of State Hillary Rodham Clinton on the Release of American Journalists from North Korea

August 5, 2009

We have been working hard on the release of the two journalists. We have always considered that a totally separate issue from our efforts to reengage the North Koreans and have them return to the Six-Party Talks and work toward a commitment for the full, verifiable denuclearization of the Korean Peninsula. I was very pleased to get the news that my husband's plane had taken off from Pyongyang with the two young women on board. They are on their way to California where they will be reunited with their families. I had a very brief conversation with my husband, we did not go into the details of some of the questions that you are asking, there will be time to talk about that later. This was mostly just to communicate directly how relieved and pleased he was and we are with the successful completion of this mission. As I said in a long set of remarks in Thailand about two weeks ago, the future of our relationships with the North Koreans are really up to them. They have a choice; they can continue to follow a path that is filled with provocative actions which further isolates them from the international community, which resulted in the imposition of sanctions by the Security Council and the full cooperation of the international community, including and led by China, for the implementation of those sanctions under the resolution. Or they can decide to renew their discussions with the partners in the Six-Party Talks. We have always said there would be a chance to discuss bilateral matters with the North Koreans within that regional context and that is still the offer today.

SOURCE: U.S. Department of State. "Release of Two Journalists from North Korea." August 5, 2009. www.state.gov/secretary/rm/2009a/08/126880.htm.

North Korean News Report on Visit of Former President Bill Clinton

August 5, 2009

Former U.S. President Bill Clinton and his party visited the Democratic People's Republic of Korea from August 4 to 5.

Kim Jong Il, general secretary of the Workers' Party of Korea and chairman of the National Defence Commission of the DPRK, met with Bill Clinton and his party.

During their stay Clinton and his party paid a courtesy call on Kim Yong Nam, president of the Presidium of the Supreme People's Assembly.

Clinton expressed words of sincere apology to Kim Jong Il for the hostile acts committed by the two American journalists against the DPRK after illegally intruding into it. Clinton courteously conveyed to Kim Jong Il an earnest request of the U.S. government to leniently pardon them and send them back home from a humanitarian point of view.

The meetings had candid and in-depth discussions on the pending issues between the DPRK and the U.S. in a sincere atmosphere and reached a consensus of views on seeking a negotiated settlement of them.

Kim Jong Il issued an order of the Chairman of the DPRK National Defence Commission on granting a special pardon to the two American journalists who had been sentenced to hard labor in accordance with Article 103 of the Socialist Constitution and releasing them.

Clinton courteously conveyed a verbal message of U.S. President Barack Obama expressing profound thanks for this and reflecting views on ways of improving the relations between the two countries.

The measure taken to release the American journalists is a manifestation of the DPRK's humanitarian and peaceloving policy.

The DPRK visit of Clinton and his party will contribute to deepening the understanding between the DPRK and the U.S. and building the bilateral confidence.

SOURCE: Korean Central News Agency. "Report on Bill Clinton's Visit to DPRK Made Public." August 5, 2009. www.kcna.co.jp/item/2009/200908/news05/20090805-01ee.html.

OTHER HISTORIC DOCUMENTS OF INTEREST

FROM THIS VOLUME

- North Korea Conducts Successful Nuclear Test, p. 195

FROM PREVIOUS *HISTORIC DOCUMENTS*

- North Korea Removed from U.S. List of State Sponsors of Terrorism, *2008*, p. 489
- UN Security Council on Nuclear Tests by North Korea, *2006*, p. 606
- Joint Statement on Six-Party Talks on North Korean Nuclear Programs, *2005*, p. 604

Sen. Edward Kennedy Dies

After a highly public struggle with brain cancer, Sen. Edward M. Kennedy, D-Mass., succumbed to his illness on August 25, 2009, at his family home in Hyannis Port, Massachusetts, at the age of 77. Often called the "Lion of the Senate," Kennedy left behind an extensive legacy of legislative triumphs and public service. As many wondered who would fill the prominent Democrat's Senate seat, Kennedy was remembered across the nation as a person of great achievement, despite well-publicized personal failings.

President Barack Obama said during his eulogy, "Ted Kennedy has gone home now, guided by his faith and by the light of those that he has loved and lost. At last he is with them once more, leaving those of us who grieve his passing with the memories he gave, the good that he did, the dream he kept alive, and a single, enduring image, the image of a man on a boat, white mane tousled, smiling broadly as he sails into the wind, ready for whatever storms may come, carrying on toward some new and wondrous place just beyond the horizon."

BORN INTO A FAMILY DYNASTY

Edward "Ted" Moore Kennedy was born the youngest of nine children on February 22, 1932, to Joseph and Rose Fitzgerald Kennedy. As a successful businessman and U.S. ambassador to Great Britain, father Joe Kennedy had high expectations for all of his sons. He felt they should serve in public office and hoped that at least one of them would become president of the United States. Ted's eldest brother, Joseph Jr., served as a pilot during World War II and was killed in a bombing mission in 1944. His two other brothers, John and Robert, each served in the Senate before rising to the offices of president and attorney general, respectively.

Ted would soon follow his brothers' path into public service. He first became involved in politics while attending law school at the University of Virginia, helping to manage John's reelection campaign to the U.S. Senate in 1958. The following year, Ted went to the West to work on John's successful presidential campaign. The Kennedy family decided Ted should fill his brother's vacant Senate seat, but at twenty-eight years of age, he did not meet the Senate's minimum age requirement. With the new president's help, the family persuaded Massachusetts governor Foster Furcolo to appoint a family loyalist to fill the seat until November 1962, when Ted would be of age. In the intervening years, Ted prepared himself by participating in a Senate fact-finding mission to Africa and touring Latin America, Israel, and West Germany. On March 14, 1962, he announced his candidacy for the U.S. Senate and went on to win 54 percent of the vote in the special election, defeating Republican George Cabot Lodge, son of another New England political dynasty.

Less than one year later, President Kennedy was assassinated in Dallas, Texas. The tragedy had a profound impact on Ted personally and professionally. When he returned to the Senate, he committed himself to passing several of John's legislative priorities, including the historic Civil Rights Act of 1964 and immigration reform. Ted kicked off a campaign for his first full Senate term in 1964, but was dealt a major setback early in the campaign. Flying back to Massachusetts from Washington, D.C., his plane crashed into an apple orchard, critically injuring the senator. After a six-month period of recuperation, Ted went on to face Republican Howard Whitmore in the election. Whitmore had declined to campaign against Kennedy, saying, "My opponent is flat on his back, and, from a gentleman's standpoint, I can't campaign against that." Kennedy won handily, with approximately 74 percent of the vote.

A Flawed Man

Beginning in his youth, Kennedy had a reputation for irresponsible behavior. As an undergraduate at Harvard University in 1951, he had arranged for a classmate to take a Spanish test for him. A proctor recognized the substitution and both Ted and his peer were expelled but also told they could be readmitted to Harvard if they showed evidence of "constructive and responsible citizenship." Ted completed his Harvard degree, after serving briefly in the Army. The cheating incident would be used against him in future campaigns.

The most infamous moment of Kennedy's life came on July 18, 1969. That evening, Kennedy had hosted a small reunion party on Chappaquiddick Island in Massachusetts for six women who had worked on his brother Robert's 1968 presidential campaign. Late in the evening, Kennedy left the party with Mary Jo Kopechne. Along the way, Kennedy's car skidded off a narrow bridge and landed upside down in the water. Kennedy managed to escape the vehicle, but Kopechne drowned. For unknown reasons, Kennedy did not report the accident to police until ten hours later. He pled guilty to leaving the scene of an accident and received a two-month suspended sentence.

The incident further fueled rumors of Kennedy's womanizing and suspected infidelities to his first wife, Joan. The pair separated in 1978 and divorced in 1982, ending what had long been a troubled marriage.

Presidential Aspirations

After Robert Kennedy was assassinated during his bid in the 1968 presidential campaign, many speculated that Ted would pursue the presidency. When Jimmy Carter took the White House in 1976, Kennedy made no effort to conceal his ideological disagreements with the new president. He found Carter to be conservative and thought some of his programs were too "timid." On November 7, 1979, Senator Kennedy declared his candidacy for president in an unusual challenge—to an incumbent of his own party. Indeed, Democratic party officials were reluctant to abandon Carter, and Kennedy's actions at Chappaquiddick remained in the minds of many. Facing such obstacles, Kennedy won only 10 of the 35 presidential primaries. He would withdraw from the race and formally endorse Carter at the Democratic National Convention in New York, delivering what would become his most famous speech.

"For me, a few hours ago, this campaign came to an end," he said. "For all those whose cares have been our concern, the work goes on, the cause endures, the hope still lives, and the dream shall never die."

BUILDING A LEGISLATIVE RECORD

Kennedy would not run for president again, telling Massachusetts voters in 1985 that "the pursuit of the presidency is not my life. Public service is." At the time of his death, Kennedy boasted one of the longest congressional careers in history, having won nine elections, serving in the Senate for forty-seven years. He was regarded as a bastion of liberalism—a symbol of strength for the left, and a valuable political target for the right. Yet Kennedy was also known for his bipartisanship, working with such conservative stalwarts as Sens. Robert Dole, R-Kan., Orrin Hatch, R-Utah, and Alan Simpson, R-Wyo., on several initiatives. "He is famous among his colleagues in the Senate for his warmth, good humor and his simply astonishing will and ability to get things done," said Sen. Mitch McConnell, R-Ky.

Kennedy's legislative record spanned many issues, including allowing eighteen-year-olds the right to vote and the landmark Voting Rights Act of 1965. He consistently worked to raise the minimum wage and was a driving force behind the Freedom of Information Act, the Occupational Safety and Health Act, and the Americans with Disabilities Act. In 1988 Kennedy worked with Senator Hatch to pass the first major piece of AIDS legislation in the United States, securing approval for a $1 billion spending measure for treatment, education, and research.

Kennedy also led the Senate's antiwar faction when President George W. Bush sought congressional authorization for the use of military force in Iraq. He provided one of twenty-three votes in opposition to the president's proposal, saying it was the "best vote" he ever cast. Yet Kennedy also worked with President Bush on the No Child Left Behind Act, legislation that mandated testing in schools to measure student progress. Kennedy was a lead author of the bill, but would later criticize Bush for his failure to adequately fund the program. The senator also worked to pass the Edward M. Kennedy Serve America Act of 2009, expanding support for national community-service programs.

Kennedy was widely known for his four-decade crusade to implement universal health insurance, an issue he described as "the cause of my life." As he worked to attain this goal, Kennedy secured federal support for neighborhood health clinics, helped conceptualize the Consolidated Omnibus Budget Reconciliation Act (COBRA) (for portable insurance), and helped create the Family and Medical Leave Act, along with laws providing Medicare prescriptions. As the chair of the Senate Health, Education, Labor, and Pensions Committee, Kennedy also played a major role in shaping President Barack Obama's proposed health care reform and worked tirelessly to generate Senate support for the package until his death.

FATAL DIAGNOSIS

On May 20, 2008, Kennedy was diagnosed with a malignant brain tumor, after he had suffered a seizure at his family home in Hyannis Port. He underwent surgery to remove the tumor in June, as well as radiation and chemotherapy treatments. Doctors warned that although surgery had improved his prognosis, most patients in Kennedy's situation did not survive longer than one year. Kennedy was not deterred from his legislative responsibilities, returning to the Senate floor to cast several votes a little more than a month after his surgery. He also made time to announce he was endorsing then-Senator Barack Obama, D-Ill., for president in the 2008 election, and made a moving surprise speech at the Democratic National Convention.

Kennedy's condition continued to worsen. He collapsed at Obama's Inauguration Day luncheon after suffering another seizure and left Washington in spring 2009. He missed the Presidential Medal of Freedom award ceremony in August, although President Obama had named him as one of the recipients, and he was unable to attend the funeral of his sister Eunice Kennedy Shriver, who passed away a few weeks before he did.

A Nation Mourns

Kennedy succumbed to his illness on August 25, surrounded by his family. "We've lost the irreplaceable center of our family and joyous light in our lives, but the inspiration of his faith, optimism, and perseverance will live in our hearts forever," said a statement released by the Kennedy family. "He always believed that our best days were still ahead, but it's hard to imagine any of them without him."

An outpouring of grief and accolades from Capitol Hill greeted the news of his death. Sen. Chris Dodd, D-Conn., said, "I will always remember Teddy as the ultimate example for all of us who seek to serve, a hero for those Americans in the shadow of life who so desperately needed one." Senator Hatch declared Kennedy's influence "cannot be overstated" and that "many will come after, but Ted Kennedy's name will always be remembered as someone who lived and breathed the United States Senate and the work completed within its chamber."

Kennedy laid in repose at the John F. Kennedy Presidential Library and Museum in Boston before a funeral on August 29 at Our Lady of Perpetual Help Basilica, where President Obama eulogized the senator as "the greatest legislator of our time." Later that afternoon, Kennedy was buried at Arlington National Cemetery beside his assassinated brothers.

—Linda Fecteau

Following is the text of the eulogy delivered by President Barack Obama at the funeral of Sen. Edward Kennedy, D-Mass., on August 29, 2009, in Boston, Massachusetts.

Eulogy Given by President Barack Obama at the Funeral of Sen. Edward Kennedy

August 29, 2009

Your Eminence, Vicki, Kara, Edward, Patrick, Curran, Caroline, members of the Kennedy family, distinguished guests, and fellow citizens: Today we say goodbye to the youngest child of Rose and Joseph Kennedy. The world will long remember their son Edward as the heir to a weighty legacy, a champion for those who had none, the soul of the Democratic Party, and the lion of the United States Senate, a man who graces nearly 1,000 laws and who penned more than 300 laws himself.

But those of us who loved him and ache with his passing know Ted Kennedy by the other titles he held: father; brother; husband; grandfather; Uncle Teddy, or as he was often known to his younger nieces and nephews, "the Grand Fromage" or "the Big Cheese." I, like so many others in the city where he worked for nearly half a century, knew him as a colleague, a mentor, and above all, as a friend.

Ted Kennedy was the baby of the family who became its patriarch, the restless dreamer who became its rock. He was the sunny, joyful child who bore the brunt of his brothers' teasing, but learned quickly how to brush it off. When they tossed him off a boat because he didn't know what a jib was, 6-year-old Teddy got back in and learned to sail. When a photographer asked the newly elected Bobby to step back at a press conference because he was casting a shadow on his younger brother, Teddy quipped, "It'll be the same in Washington."

That spirit of resilience and good humor would see Teddy through more pain and tragedy than most of us will ever know. He lost two siblings by the age of 16. He saw two more taken violently from a country that loved them. He said goodbye to his beloved sister, Eunice, in the final days of his life. He narrowly survived a plane crash, watched two children struggle with cancer, buried three nephews, and experienced personal failings and setbacks in the most public way possible.

It's a string of events that would have broken a lesser man. And it would have been easy for Ted to let himself become bitter and hardened, to surrender to self-pity and regret, to retreat from public life and live out his years in peaceful quiet. No one would have blamed him for that.

But that was not Ted Kennedy. As he told us: "[I]ndividual faults and frailties are no excuse to give in and no exemption from the common obligation to give of ourselves." Indeed, Ted was the "Happy Warrior" that the poet Wordsworth spoke of when he wrote: "As tempted more; more able to endure, / As more exposed to suffering and distress; / Thence, also, more alive to tenderness."

Through his own suffering, Ted Kennedy became more alive to the plight and the suffering of others: the sick child who could not see a doctor; the young soldier denied her rights because of what she looks like or who she loves or where she comes from. The landmark laws that he championed—the Civil Rights Act, the Americans With Disabilities Act, immigration reform, children's health insurance, the Family and Medical Leave Act—all have a running thread: That's Kennedy's life work was not to champion the causes of those with wealth or power or special connections; it was to give a voice to those who were not heard, to add a rung to the ladder of opportunity, to make real the dream of our founding. He was given the gift of time that his brothers were not, and he used that gift to touch as many lives and right as many wrongs as the years would allow.

We can still hear his voice bellowing through the Senate Chamber, face reddened, fists pounding the podium, a veritable force of nature, in support of health care or workers' rights or civil rights. And yet, as has been noted, while his causes became deeply personal, his disagreements never did. While he was seen by his fiercest critics as a partisan lightning rod, that's not the prism through which Ted Kennedy saw the world, nor was it the prism through which his colleagues saw Ted Kennedy. He was a product of an age when the joy and nobility of politics prevented differences of party and platform and philosophy from becoming barriers to cooperation and mutual respect, a time when adversaries still saw each other as patriots.

And that's how Ted Kennedy became the greatest legislator of our time. He did it by hewing to principle, yes, but also by seeking compromise and common cause, not through deal-making and horse-trading alone, but through friendship and kindness and humor. There was the time he courted Orrin Hatch for support of the Children's Health Insurance Program by having his chief of staff serenade the Senator with a song Orrin had written himself, the time he delivered shamrock cookies on a china plate to sweeten up a crusty Republican colleague, the famous story of how he won the support of a Texas committee chairman on an immigration bill. Teddy walked into a meeting with a plain manila envelope and showed only the chairman that it was filled with the Texan's favorite cigars. When the negotiations were going well, he would inch the envelope closer to the chairman [*Laughter*]. When they weren't, he'd pull it back [*Laughter*]. Before long, the deal was done [*Laughter*].

It was only a few years ago, on St. Patrick's Day, when Teddy buttonholed me on the floor of the Senate for my support of a certain piece of legislation that was coming up for a vote. I gave him my pledge, but I expressed skepticism that it would pass. But when the roll call was over, the bill garnered the votes that it needed and then some. I looked at Teddy with astonishment and asked how had he done it. He just patted me on the back and said, "Luck of the Irish." [*Laughter*]

Of course, luck had little to do with Ted Kennedy's legislative success; he knew that. A few years ago, his father-in-law told him that he and Daniel Webster just might be the two greatest Senators of all time. Without missing a beat, Teddy replied, "What did Webster do?" [*Laughter*]

But though it is Teddy's historic body of achievements that we will remember, it is his giving heart that we will miss. It was the friend and the colleague who was always the first to pick up the phone and say, "I'm sorry for your loss," or, "I hope you feel better," or, "What can I do to help?" It was the boss so adored by his staff that over 500, spanning five decades, showed up for his 75th birthday party. It was the man who sent birthday wishes and thank-you notes and even his own paintings to so many who never imagined that a U.S. Senator of such stature would take the time to think about somebody like them. I have one of those paintings in my private study off the Oval Office, a Cape Cod seascape that was a gift to a freshman legislator who had just arrived in Washington and happened to admire it when Ted Kennedy welcomed him into his office. That, by the way, is my second gift from Teddy and Vicki after our dog Bo. And it seems like everyone has one of those stories, the ones that often start with "You wouldn't believe who called me today."

Ted Kennedy was the father who looked not only after his own three children but John's and Bobby's as well. He took them camping and taught them to sail. He laughed and danced with them at birthdays and weddings, cried and mourned with them through hardship and tragedy, and passed on that same sense of service and selflessness that his parents had instilled in him. Shortly after Ted walked Caroline down the aisle and gave her away at the altar, he received a note from Jackie that read: "On you the carefree youngest brother fell a burden a hero would have begged to have been spared. We are all going to make it because you were always there with your love."

Not only did the Kennedy family make it because of Ted's love, he made it because of theirs, especially because the love and the life he found in Vicki. After so much loss and so much sorrow, it could not have been easy for Ted to risk his heart again. And that he did is a testament to how deeply he loved this remarkable woman from Louisiana. And she didn't just love him back. As Ted would often acknowledge, Vicki saved him. She gave him strength and purpose, joy and friendship, and stood by him always, especially in those last, hardest days.

We cannot know for certain how long we have here. We cannot foresee the trials or misfortunes that will test us along the way. We cannot know what God's plan is for us. What we can do is to live out our lives as best we can with purpose and with love and with joy. We can use each day to show those who are closest to us how much we care about them and treat others with the kindness and respect that we wish for ourselves. We can learn from our mistakes and grow from our failures. And we can strive at all costs to make a better world so that someday, if we are blessed with the chance to look back on our time here, we know that we spent it well, that we made a difference, that our fleeting presence had a lasting impact on the lives of others.

This is how Ted Kennedy lived. This is his legacy. He once said, as has already been mentioned, of his brother Bobby that he need not be idealized or enlarged in death [beyond] what he was in life, and I imagine he would say the same about himself. The greatest expectations were placed upon Ted Kennedy's shoulders because of who he was, but he surpassed them all because of who he became. We do not weep for him today because of the prestige attached to his name or his office. We weep because we loved this kind and tender hero who persevered through pain and tragedy, not for the sake of ambition or vanity, not for wealth or power, but only for the people and the country that he loved.

In the days after September 11th, Teddy made it a point to personally call each one of the 177 families of this State who lost a loved one in the attack. But he didn't stop there. He kept calling and checking up on them. He fought through redtape to get them assistance and grief counseling. He invited them sailing, played with their children, and would write each family a letter whenever the anniversary of that terrible day came along. To one widow, he wrote the following: "As you know so well, the passage of time never really heals the tragic memory of such a great loss, but we carry on, because we have to, because our loved ones would want us to, and because there is still light to guide us in the world from the love they gave us." We carry on.

Ted Kennedy has gone home now, guided by his faith and by the light of those that he has loved and lost. At last he is with them once more, leaving those of us who grieve his passing with the memories he gave, the good that he did, the dream he kept alive, and a single, enduring image, the image of a man on a boat, white mane tousled, smiling broadly as he sails into the wind, ready for whatever storms may come, carrying on toward some new and wondrous place just beyond the horizon. May God bless Ted Kennedy, and may he rest in eternal peace.

SOURCE: U.S. Executive Office of the President. "Eulogy at the Funeral Service for Senator Edward M. Kennedy in Boston, Massachusetts." *Daily Compilation of Presidential Documents* 2009, no. 00669 (August 29, 2009). www.gpo.gov/fdsys/pkg/DCPD-200900669/pdf/DCPD-200900669.pdf.

OTHER HISTORIC DOCUMENTS OF INTEREST

FROM THIS VOLUME

- Roland Burris and Al Franken Seated During Dynamic Year in U.S. Senate, p. 13

FROM PREVIOUS HISTORIC DOCUMENTS

- President Bush Signs Mental Health Parity Law, *2008*, p. 474
- Sen. Edward M. Kennedy's Eulogy for John F. Kennedy Jr., *1999*, p. 422
- Senator Kennedy's Apology for Faults in His Private Life, *1991*, p. 713
- Kennedy Convention Speech, *1980*, p. 701
- Kennedy's Rejection of 1976 Presidential Race, *1974*, p. 853

September

Court Finds New York Discriminated Against Mentally Ill

SEPTEMBER 8, 2009

A federal district court ruled on September 8, 2009, that the state of New York had discriminated against New York City's mentally ill residents when moving them from psychiatric hospitals into adult homes. According to Judge Nicholas Garaufis in his ruling in *Disability Advocates, Inc., v. David A. Paterson et al.*, the 4,300 mentally ill residents who were not considered a danger to themselves or others faced dire conditions that were no better than the psychiatric hospitals of a generation ago when they were moved from traditional psychiatric hospitals to group homes. The state's actions isolated residents and failed to provide them with the chance to learn and use skills needed to function in society. Such an overly restrictive environment violates the Americans with Disabilities Act (ADA). According to Title II of the ADA, disabled citizens cannot be segregated into institutions. This means that care facilities must provide the least restrictive environment possible in proportion to the mental illnesss, with the appropriate level of access to activities and programs outside the group home, to mentally ill individuals. In this case, group homes were providing residents little access to visitors, jobs, and activities outside of the group home itself, leading to the claim of discrimination.

GROUP HOMES IN NEW YORK CITY

The group home system in New York state developed in the 1960s and 1970s, when the state implemented deinstitutionalization in an effort to move some mentally ill patients from state-run psychiatric hospitals into adult homes. At that time, the state set up for-profit group homes that would be much easier to maintain than traditional psychiatric hospitals. The state used federal money allocated for disability programs to set up and run the homes.

Disability Advocates was not the first instance in which advocacy groups questioned the conditions of the group homes. In 2002 the *New York Times* published a story about state inspection reports on these adult homes. According to the article, some group homes housed too many mentally ill patients, while other group homes forced residents to have unnecessary medical procedures to bring in more money from Medicare and Medicaid. Some group homes failed to keep proper files on their residents, and instead created fake files when state inspectors came to the facilities.

Disability Advocates, a nonprofit legal services group, brought their case against the state of New York in 2003, hoping the court system would require the state to stop steering mentally ill residents of New York City into group homes. According to the executive director of Disability Advocates, Cliff Zucker, "even if you made [group homes] spick-and-span, there's something wrong with having people live with 200 to 300 people under one roof." He continued, "You can't cook your own food. You can't do your own laundry. A certain type of dependence is mandatory. Pretty soon you start to wonder whether you can do it anymore." In this case, spokespersons for Disability Advocates argued that residents of group homes could be moved into supported housing, where residents live on their own in apartments and are visited by health care workers to receive necessary services. A program such as this, according to these advocates, would cost the state no more than housing mentally ill individuals in group homes.

TRIAL AGAINST NEW YORK

The trial generated by Disability Advocates' complaint lasted for five weeks, in May and June 2009. Testimony was heard from state mental health officials, mental health experts, and those who advocated for better living conditions for the state's mentally ill residents. State mental health officials testifying in the trial said group homes are good places for the mentally ill to live, because the group homes are close to community amenities and allow residents to come and go at will. Judge Garaufis, however, found that the adult homes "are even more restrictive or 'institutional' than psychiatric hospitals." In addition, the judge said that the homes cut down on work or social interaction with the outside world. "Living in a place where the phone is answered 'Brooklyn Adult Care Center' diminishes work options and social contacts, and being subject to visiting hours diminishes opportunities to cultivate social or family relationships."

According to Judge Garaufis's decision, although New York state had earlier cracked down on group homes and forced them to maintain a better environment for residents and to keep better records, that fact had no bearing on this case, because the original claim was that there had been no reason for many of the residents to be housed in group homes when they were capable of living on their own.

Zucker's organization applauded the court's decision, although there are still questions about what comes next, even after the state submits a remedial plan. "This is an extraordinarily important decision that is going to improve the lives of 4,300 people who are now being warehoused in institutions unnecessarily," said Zucker.

Although the judge did not specifically demand that the state stop sending mentally ill individuals to group homes, he required it to develop the remedial plan by late October 2009. In his ruling, Judge Garaufis wrote that the group homes in New York City were no more than centers that segregated residents from their communities, giving them little access to the care and programs that would help them develop necessary skills. The state, said Garaufis, "denied thousands of individuals with mental illness in New York City the opportunity to receive services in the most integrated setting appropriate to their needs." Further, he wrote, "To the extent that mental health programs or case management aim to teach independent living skills, like cooking, budgeting and grocery shopping, residents have little or no opportunity to practice these skills in their present living situation."

The 210-page opinion described the living conditions of these adult homes, in which residents were herded into lines for meals and medicines and participated in group activities such as bingo, a situation that Garaufis described as little more than being a psychological prisoner. The group homes never took residents into the community, to a park, or to concerts; residents rarely left the facility for any reason, even though they were free to come and go so long as they signed in and out and arrived back by curfew.

The decision all but forced the state to find apartments or other living quarters in supported housing—which is supposed to be a more independent living situation in which specialty care nurses visit as the patient requires—for all 4,300 group home residents where they would be able to live less regulated, more independent lives. According to Garaufis, it would even cost the state less to house these residents in supported housing. His estimates indicate that supported housing costs a little more than $40,000 per year per resident, whereas it costs the state more than $47,000 per resident living in a group adult home. In addition, the cost to Medicaid for those in adult homes is nearly double what it would cost Medicaid to assist someone in supported housing. Spokespersons for New York disagreed with this finding during the case, but the judge said in his decision that the state had failed to take into account millions of dollars for non–care-related expenses, such as air conditioning.

The U.S. Supreme Court had ruled on a similar case in 1999, on which Garaufis based some of his findings in the New York state case. In *Olmstead v. L.C.*, the Court ruled that segregating disabled residents into institutions is considered discrimination under Title II of the ADA. Title II of the ADA rests on an "integration mandate" that holds that "[a] public entity shall administer services, programs, and activities in the most integrated setting appropriate to the needs of qualified individuals with disabilities." Garaufis stated in his finding that because the group homes in question did little to integrate their residents into the community, or help them excel at basic skills, such as grocery shopping, the state in this instance was in violation of the ADA.

Families Left Without Answers

The decision has put the families of those in adult group homes in a difficult situation. Those mentally ill individuals who are channeled into adult homes rather than psychiatric facilities are not considered to be a danger to themselves or the community. By state definition, they are legal adults who are able to care for themselves. Advocates who support nonpsychiatric settings for mentally ill individuals argue that if done properly, group homes can give necessary care while allowing residents to maintain their freedom. But this has done little to calm concerns of families who do not know whether to invite mentally ill family members to live in their private homes or to put them into another form of group care. Families interviewed by the *New York Times* told the newspaper about experiences of bringing unhappy mentally ill residents out of group homes. One woman, Florence Weil, took her daughter out of an adult home because the daughter had called it a prison. One day when Weil left the house briefly, her daughter took twenty-five or thirty heart pills and drank furniture polish, which led to organ failure ten days later. Because of this, Weil is trying to discourage other families from simply removing their loved ones from the adult care system; instead, she advocates evaluating what type of treatment they truly need. "Many of the people in the adult homes are well enough to live in a freer environment, to be part of the world," said Weil. "In my daughter's case, she was just so sick."

Zucker understands the concerns of families now left with questions after Judge Garaufis's decision. "It's not surprising that family members have anxiety. But what the judge is talking about is not abandoning people in apartments, but helping them have the supports they need."

New York state has approximately 12,000 residents statewide who live in adult homes, 13,000 in supported housing, and more than 4,000 in psychiatric hospitals. Because Judge Garaufis's ruling in this case only applies to New York City, it leaves the door open for future action regarding the other state residents living in adult homes.

—Heather Kerrigan

Following is an excerpted version of the 210-page decision released on September 8, 2009, in Disability Advocates, Inc. v. David A. Paterson et al., *in which New York was found to be in violation of the Americans with Disabilities Act for the way in which it placed mentally ill residents in group homes.*

U.S. District Court on Rights of Mentally Ill New York City Residents

September 8, 2009

United States District Court
Eastern District of New York
Disability Advocates, Inc., Plaintiff,
-against-

David A. Paterson, in his official capacity as Governor of the State of New York, Richard F. Daines, in his official capacity as Commissioner of the New York State Department of Health, Michael F. Hogan, in his official capacity as Commissioner of the New York State Office of Mental Health, the New York State Department of Health, and the New York State Office of Mental Health, Defendants

Case: 03-CV-3209 (NGG)

MEMORANDUM & ORDER SETTING FORTH FINDINGS OF FACT AND CONCLUSIONS OF LAW

NICHOLAS G. GARAUFIS, United States District Judge.

The Supreme Court held in *Olmstead v. L.C.*, 527 U.S. 581 (1999), that "[u]njustified isolation . . . is properly regarded as discrimination based on disability," observing that "institutional placement of persons who can handle and benefit from community settings perpetuates unwarranted assumptions that persons so isolated are incapable of or unworthy of participating in community life." The "integration mandate" of Title II of the American with Disabilities Act, 42 U.S.C. § 12101 et seq., and Section 504 of the Rehabilitation Act, 29 U.S.C. § 791 et seq., as expressed in federal regulations and *Olmstead*, requires that when a state provides services to individuals with disabilities, it must do so "in the most integrated setting appropriate to their needs." The "most integrated setting," according to the federal regulations, is "a setting that enables individuals with disabilities to interact with non-disabled persons to the fullest extent possible."

Plaintiff Disability Advocates, Inc. ("DAI"), a protection and advocacy organization authorized by statute to bring suit on behalf of individuals with disabilities, brings this action on behalf of individuals with mental illness residing in, or at risk of entry into, "adult homes" in New York City with more than 120 beds and in which twenty-five residents or 25% of the resident population (whichever is fewer) have a mental illness. Adult homes are for-profit residential adult care facilities licensed by the State of New York (the "State").

Following a five-week bench trial, DAI has proven by a preponderance of the evidence that its constituents, approximately 4,300 individuals with mental illness, are not receiving services in the most integrated setting appropriate to their needs. The adult homes at issue are institutions that segregate residents from the community and impede residents' interactions with people who do not have disabilities. DAI has proven that virtually all of its constituents are qualified to receive services in "supported housing," a far more integrated setting in which individuals with mental illness live in apartments scattered throughout the community and receive flexible support services as needed. DAI has also proven that its constituents are not opposed to receiving services in more integrated settings. Therefore, DAI has established a violation of the integration mandate of the ADA and the Rehabilitation Act. . . .

[Background on the case and information on the Americans with Disabilities Act has been omitted.]

III. Plaintiff's Claims Under the ADA and Rehabilitation Act

As set forth below, DAI has proven by a preponderance of the evidence that Defendants have discriminated against DAI's constituents by reason of their disability. DAI has established that the adult homes at issue are not the most integrated setting appropriate to the needs of DAI's constituents: the adult homes do not "enable interactions with nondisabled persons to the fullest extent possible," especially compared to supported housing, a far more integrated setting. DAI has established that virtually all its constituents are qualified to move to supported housing and are not opposed to receiving services in more integrated settings. . . .

[Additional findings in the case, including why Disability Advocates has legal standing to sue under the ADA, have been omitted.]

b. Adult Homes Are Institutions That Segregate Individuals with Mental Illness from the Community

i. Adult Homes Are Institutions

The overwhelming evidence in the record compels the court to find, as a factual matter, that Adult Homes are institutions:

> as a consequence of poor access to community housing, inadequate levels of mental health housing, and clinical programs that do not support people in getting/keeping housing successfully, many people with mental illness are poorly housed or institutionalized. *Thus, many people with mental illness are "stuck" in . . . institutional settings (nursing homes, adult homes, state psychiatric centers).*

The court uses the term "institution" as defined by Elizabeth Jones, one of DAI's experts, who explained that: "[An] [i]nstitution, in my mind, and in my experience, and in the literature, is a segregated setting for a large number of people that through its restrictive practices and its controls on individualization and independence limits a person's ability to interact with other people who do not have a similar disability."

As set forth more fully below, the evidence demonstrates that Adult Homes have the characteristics Ms. Jones described. Witnesses for both sides testified that Adult Homes share many salient features of State psychiatric hospitals. First, Adult Homes house a large number of people with psychiatric disabilities in a congregate setting. As Defendants' expert Alan Kaufman observed, "significant numbers of residents suffer from serious mental illness. . . . The number of beds in many of the larger Adult Homes, as well as their physical layout, furnishings, and decorations, also give an appearance similar to that in an institutional setting." Second, life in the Adult Homes is highly regimented. Adult Homes, like other types of institutions, "are designed to manage and control large numbers of people . . . by eliminating choice and personal autonomy, establishing inflexible routines for the convenience of staff, restricting access, implementing measures which maximize efficiency, and penalizing residents who break the rules." In particular, there are inflexible schedules for meals, taking medication, receiving public benefits, and other daily activities. Residents are assigned roommates and are required to sit at a specific seat at a specific table in the cafeteria; they must seek permission to change these assignments. Most Adult Home residents line up to receive their medications at scheduled times. Long lines also form for receiving personal needs allowances, the portion of residents' Supplemental Security Income allocated for the residents' personal use. Witnesses observed that Adult Homes had the look and feel of "back wards" of [*sic*] State hospitals and were "reminiscent of a state psychiatric hospital and its culture." . . .

ii. Much of Residents' Daily Lives Takes Place Inside the Adult Homes

Much of Adult Home residents' daily lives takes place inside the Adult Homes. As Ms. Jones observed, "[t]here is a large number of people who seem to stay in the homes and don't really go out a whole lot at all." Residents spend most of their days in activities organized for them by the Adult Homes and/or mental health providers associated with the Adult Homes. Adult Homes are required to provide a program of activities in the facility as well as in the community, and DOH has cited Adult Homes for failing to provide a sufficient program of activities. Activities provided by Adult Homes include games, puzzles, and other child-appropriate leisure activities. For example, activities provided on-site at Riverdale Manor through the case management program include computer games suitable "for a three- or four-year-old," and a calendar of recreational activities at Surfside Manor lists activities such as beads, nail painting, and bingo. A former Adult Home resident testified that the activities "had you coloring, like a little kid; you play Bingo, like a little kid; you play domino, like a little kid; and you play cards, like a little kid." When asked at trial about the Adult Home's activities, an Adult Home resident answered, "[t]hey really don't have too much of anything. It's like just maybe playing cards, cribbage, puzzles, stuff like that; but they really don't have anything much to do." Adult Homes also arrange for religious services and musical performances inside the facilities. . . .

[Information on adult home activities, access to outside locations, and non–mentally ill residents has been omitted.]

vii. Adult Homes Discourage Residents from Engaging in Activities of Daily Living and Foster "Learned Helplessness"

The Adult Homes foster what witnesses for both sides have referred to as "learned help-lessness": when individuals are "treated as if they're completely helpless, the helplessness becomes a learned phenomenon." This is consistent with Defendant OMH Commissioner Hogan's testimony to the Legislature that in institutions in general, "the skills of community living are eroded by the routines of institutional life." The Adult Homes discourage—and some outright prohibit—residents from cooking, cleaning, doing their own laundry, and administering their own medication. The Adult Homes also generally manage residents' personal needs allowances, distributing cash to residents on specified dates and times. The result is that Adult Home residents lose skills that they had prior to living in the Adult Home—such as medication management—because they are forbidden from practicing those skills in the Adult Home. As one former Adult Home resident testified, "[W]hen you go to an adult home, number one, you're treated like a little kid. And if you stay there long enough, you're going to act like a little kid and you ain't going to want to leave because you being taken care of. . . . [I]t's like an institution to me." Similarly, another former resident testified, "the adult home fosters complete dependency upon them to do everything for you, discourages independence." . . . Plaintiff's expert Dennis Jones—who had been the Commissioner of Department of Mental Health in two states and a transitional receiver for the District of Columbia's public mental health system—testified that Adult Homes are a "residency based model which means the goal there is not really to promote independence, it's to promote dependence and sustain dependency."

That the Adult Homes are a setting that fosters learned helplessness, however, does not mean that the individuals who live in the Adult Homes are helpless, or that they cannot and do not manage their activities of daily living. . . .

3. Conclusions of Law

. . . The court's factual finding that the Adult Homes are institutions is compelling evidence supporting the conclusion that such a setting does not enable interactions with nondisabled people to the fullest extent possible. Adult Homes are institutions that house well over 100 people, all of whom have disabilities and most of whom have mental illness. Adult Homes are designed to manage and control large numbers of people and do so by establishing inflexible routines, restricting access, and limiting personal choice and autonomy. Residents line up to receive meals, medication, and money at inflexibly scheduled times during the day. They are assigned seats in the cafeteria, roommates, and treatment providers. They have next to no privacy or autonomy in their own daily lives, and they are discouraged, and most often prohibited, from managing their own activities of daily living, such as cooking, taking medication, cleaning, and budgeting.

These institutional qualities of the Adult Homes are relevant to the issue of integration because they influence the extent to which residents can interact with individuals who do not have disabilities. The large population of the Adult Homes is relevant because many people with mental illness living together in one setting with few or no nondisabled persons contributes to the segregation of Adult Home residents from the community. . . .

Regardless of whether the Adult Homes at issue are "institutions" per se or merely a setting with "institutional characteristics," as Defendants contend, the overwhelming evidence demonstrates that the institutional characteristics of Adult Homes impede residents' ability to develop relationships with nondisabled persons. Thus, the Adult Homes do not enable interactions with nondisabled persons "to the fullest extent possible." . . .

[Rejection of arguments from the defense and testimony from each expert in the trial have been omitted.]

h. There Are No Material Differences Between Adult Home Residents and Supported Housing Residents

Adult Home residents do not have more severe disabilities than individuals already served by Defendants in supported housing. As noted above, DAI's constituents have one or more major mental illnesses, such as schizophrenia, bipolar disorder, and/or depression. There is generally little distinction between the psychiatric characteristics of Adult Home residents and supported housing residents.

People with mental illness are often placed in Adult Homes not for clinical reasons, but because the Adult Home is the only housing available when they are discharged from the psychiatric hospital. . . .

Nor are Adult Homes designed to provide individuals with mental illness with the intensive levels of care and supervision that Defendants claim Adult Home residents require. To the contrary, because supervision in Adult Homes is minimal, individuals in Adult Homes must be able to live with some degree of independence. . . .

[Further rejection of arguments from the defense has been omitted.]

3. Conclusions of Law

a. Virtually All of DAI's Constituents Meet the Essential Eligibility Requirements of Supported Housing

Part of the inquiry as to whether supported housing is "appropriate to the needs" of DAI's constituents is whether DAI's constituents are qualified to be served in supported housing. In *Olmstead,* the Supreme Court held that states have an obligation to provide services and programs in community-based settings only if the individual with disabilities "meets the 'essential eligibility requirements' for habilitation in a community-based program," referring to the "most integrated setting appropriate" language in the regulations. . . .

Applying the law to the facts, the court concludes that DAI has proven that virtually all of its constituents meet the essential eligibility requirements of supported housing. For virtually all of DAI's constituents, nothing about their disabilities necessitates living in the Adult Homes as opposed to supported housing, nor would they require services that are not already provided to people living in supported housing. The evidence at trial demonstrates that Defendants expect New York's supported housing programs to serve individuals with serious mental illness who have a wide range of support needs—including individuals transitioning directly from psychiatric hospitals and inpatient psychiatric centers, whom OMH terms "high need." The evidence at trial further demonstrates that the supports that would be needed by Adult Home residents to live independently are well within the capabilities of New York's supported housing providers to accommodate. Indeed, many of DAI's constituents would need only minimal supports.

Voluminous evidence supports the court's conclusion. After extensive investigations that included interviews with hundreds of residents and review of hundreds of mental health records, DAI's experts credibly and persuasively concluded that virtually all Adult Home residents could be served in supported housing. OMH's own former Senior Deputy Commissioner agrees with the conclusions of these experts that virtually all Adult Home residents could be appropriately served in supported housing. . . .

[Desires of adult home residents, as gathered by polling and interviewing, have been omitted. The fundamental alteration defense has also been omitted.]

2. The Requested Relief Would Not Increase Costs to the State

The parties do not dispute that moving Adult Home residents to supported housing would require the development of additional supported housing beds. The evidence demonstrates that serving DAI's constituents in supported housing rather than Adult Homes would not increase costs to the State. . . .

i. Defendants' Own Analysis Demonstrates That Medicaid Costs in Supported Housing Are Significantly Lower Than Medicaid Costs in Adult Homes

At DAI's request, the State undertook a comparison of the Medicaid costs for residents of Adult Homes and residents of supported housing for the fiscal year 2004–2005 ("State Analysis"). In that analysis, the overall annual Medicaid costs for an individual residing in an Adult Home were, on average, roughly $15,000 higher than the average Medicaid costs for an individual with mental illness in supported housing . . . the total average Medicaid expenditures, including the State and federal shares, were $31,530 per Medicaid-eligible individual in the Adult Homes at issue, and $16,467 per Medicaid-eligible individual with mental illness in supported housing. . . .

[Additional cost analysis has been omitted.]

VI. Remedy

. . . Plaintiff's proposed relief would require Defendants to provide a plan conforming to ten guidelines. These proposed guidelines include a four-year transition period, by the end of which Defendants would achieve the following goals: (1) all current Adult Home residents who desire placement in supported housing have been afforded such a placement if qualified; (2) all future Adult Home residents—including individuals admitted to the Adult Homes both during and after the four-year transition period—who desire placement in supported housing are afforded such a placement if qualified; and (3) no individual who is qualified for supported housing will be offered placement in an Adult Home at public expense unless, after being fully informed, he or she declines the opportunity to receive services in supported housing. . . .

VII. Conclusion

DAI has proven that Defendants have discriminated against DAI's constituents in violation of the integration mandate of the Americans with Disabilities Act and the

Rehabilitation Act. In carrying out their administration of New York's mental health service system, Defendants have denied thousands of individuals with mental illness in New York City the opportunity to receive services in the most integrated setting appropriate to their needs. DAI has proven that the large, impacted Adult Homes at issue are not the most integrated setting appropriate to the needs of DAI's constituents, especially compared to supported housing, in which individuals with mental illness live in apartments and receive flexible support services as needed. DAI has also proven that virtually all of DAI's constituents are qualified to receive services in supported housing and are unopposed to receiving services in a more integrated setting. Defendants have failed to prove that the relief DAI seeks would constitute a "fundamental alteration" of the State's mental health service system. Accordingly, DAI is entitled to declaratory and injunctive relief. Following additional briefing from the parties, the court will issue a separate Order and Judgment once it determines the appropriate injunctive remedy.

SO ORDERED.

Dated: Brooklyn, New York

September 8, 2009

Nicholas G. Garaufis

United States District Judge

SOURCE: U.S. District Court for the Eastern District of New York. Decisions of Interest. 1:03-cv-03209-NGG-MDG Disability Advocates, Inc., v. Pataki et al. September 8, 2009. www.nyed.uscourts.gov/pub/rulings/cv/2009/03cv3209mo090809.pdf. Governor George Pataki had been the lead defendant when the suit was filed; when the trial began, David A. Paterson had assumed the office of governor.

OTHER HISTORIC DOCUMENTS OF INTEREST

FROM PREVIOUS HISTORIC DOCUMENTS

President Obama Speaks to Congress on Health Care Reform

SEPTEMBER 9, 2009

In the first year of Barack Obama's presidency, no domestic issue received more attention in Washington than health care. As a candidate, Obama had declared his determination to reform the nation's system of health care and health insurance. Once in office, he charged Congress with negotiating the details of the reform bill and pass it by the end of 2009. The complex legislative process, involving five congressional committees, Republican resistance, and industry lobbyists, stoked public frustration. Opposition to the emerging plan intensified during the August congressional recess. When the legislators returned, President Obama attempted to recapture the momentum for reform in a speech to a joint session of Congress on September 9. He clarified his goals and priorities for reform and admonished the legislators saying, "[T]he time for bickering is over."

URGENT PROBLEM, ELUSIVE SOLUTION

In 2009 there was broad agreement that the American system of delivering health care was deeply flawed. Compared to other industrialized democracies, the United States spend far more per patient, with notably worse health outcomes. In 2000, the World Health Organization ranked the United States as thirty-seventh among the world's most effective health care systems, putting it between Costa Rica and Slovenia. The number of uninsured Americans had steadily risen over a decade, with more than 46 million lacking basic coverage in 2008. Millions more were underinsured. The rising cost of health services, prescription drugs, and insurance premiums far outstripped inflation, leading to bankruptcies and home foreclosures even when families were covered. Health insurance companies came under a barrage of criticism for denying coverage to people with "preexisting conditions" and for abusive practices, such as "rescission," or revoking customers' policies once they fall ill.

Despite the clear need for a remedy, the goal of achieving comprehensive health care reform had eluded political leaders, particularly Democrats, for decades, since Medicare and Medicaid were created under President Lyndon Johnson in 1965. The State Children's Health Insurance Program (SCHIP) came into being in 1997, during Bill Clinton's administration, after the major health care overhaul spearheaded by then-first lady Hillary Rodham Clinton was defeated. The program, later known as CHIP, was created by the federal government to provide funds to states to provide health insurance for children whose parents earned a modest income that was nevertheless too much to qualify for

Medicaid assistance. The health care, insurance, and pharmaceutical industries represent some of the nation's most powerful lobbies and have traditionally opposed legislation that threatened their business interests. "I am not the first President to take up this cause," President Obama told Congress in his September 2009 speech, "but I am determined to be the last."

Health care reform had been a central issue of Obama's 2008 campaign for the presidency. He discussed reform proposals in great detail over dozens of debates with his Democratic rival, Sen. Hillary Rodham Clinton. Both candidates advocated universal health care with subsidies for low-income individuals not offered coverage through their employer. Both favored creating a public insurance option to compete with private industry, but opposed universalizing coverage through a government-run single-payer system such as Canada's. Although Senator Clinton's proposal included a mandate requiring individuals to carry health insurance, Obama opposed the idea of mandates in favor of making voluntary insurance more affordable for working families. As the Democratic nominee, Obama pledged to pass a reform plan in his first year in office that would cut the average family's health care costs by thousands of dollars per year.

Obama, however, was forced first to contend with the financial crisis that sent the nation into the worst economic downturn since the Great Depression. Nevertheless, Obama maintained that containing the rise in health costs was integral to the nation's economic well-being and that reform could not wait. On February 4, 2009, the president signed a bill reinstating the SCHIP program, which President George W. Bush had vetoed. Obama's economic stimulus package, passed later in February, included $87 billion to help states maintain their Medicaid programs.

FIVE COMMITTEES, ONE ANOINTED

Although the president made clear that health care reform was one of his highest priorities for 2009, he decided to take a back seat while Congress began shaping the complex details of the legislation. The bill was assigned to three committees in the House and two in the Senate. A comfortable Democratic majority in the House made it likely that a bill would reach the floor and pass, but matters were different in the Senate. Because of Senate rules regarding filibusters, sixty votes would be necessary to move any significant legislation through the chamber. The defection of Republican Pennsylvania senator Arlen Specter to the Democrats on April 28, and the seating of Minnesota's Al Franken on July 7 after a lengthy electoral dispute with his Republican opponent, Norm Coleman, brought the Democratic caucus to the magic number sixty. Thus hopes for the health care bill rested on either attracting some Republican support or maintaining unanimity among the Democrats.

The congressional committee most likely to craft a bipartisan bill was the Senate Finance Committee, chaired by conservative Democrat Max Baucus of Montana. Long after the other committees had completed their work, Baucus was still negotiating, privately with two other centrist Democrats and three Republicans. Insiders increasingly suggested—to the consternation of single-payer supporters and more liberal Democrats— that whatever language this "gang of six" came up with was likely to make it into the final bill. Industry lobbyists concentrated their attentions on the Finance Committee. In the previous year, Baucus had received $1.5 million in campaign contributions from the health care industry, more than any other legislator.

One of the key lessons the Obama administration took from the failure of the 1993 Clinton reform effort was the importance of enlisting support from the powerful health and drug lobbies. Behind the scenes, the administration began a series of meetings with the Pharmaceutical Research and Manufacturers of America (PhRMA). The head of PhRMA at the time was Billy Tauzin, a former congressional leader who had been instrumental in shaping the Medicare prescription drug bill that became law in 2003. Obama had campaigned against the influence of lobbyists, even targeting Tauzin specifically in a television ad during the primaries. Nevertheless, in early 2009 Tauzin and other pharmaceutical industry executives were invited to dozens of meetings with White House and congressional leaders.

Together they hammered out a secret deal. PhRMA would support the bill and pay for advertising to promote it; in exchange, the administration agreed that the reform bill would not force the drug industry to cut its costs by more than $80 billion. The legislation would also prohibit Medicare and Medicaid from negotiating lower drug prices or importing cheaper drugs from foreign countries, measures that could potentially lower health costs and pharmaceutical company profits. These compromises would be inserted into the Senate Finance Committee's markup of the bill. In August, Tauzin leaked the specifics of this agreement to the press, after the House Energy and Commerce Committee had approved a bill with more stringent cost-cutting provisions. The White House was forced into an embarrassing acknowledgment of the backroom deal.

An Industry-Friendly Package

With 3,000 registered lobbyists representing the health sector in Washington—many of them former members of Congress and legislative aides—there was no denying the influence of the industry throughout the legislative process and the likelihood that other bargains were being made outside the public eye. The insurance trade group America's Health Insurance Plans (AHIP), like PhRMA, was generally supportive of the reform effort but adamantly opposed to the creation of a government-run "public option," initially one of the most popular planks of the legislation with the Obama administration. The U.S. Chamber of Commerce, which spent more than $50 million in lobbying in 2009, lined up against the bill. The American Association of Retired Persons (AARP), the well-funded lobby group for seniors, supported reform. The highly vocal constituency advocating for a single-payer (or "Medicare for all") plan was conspicuously left out of congressional deliberations.

In addition to lobbying, industry interest groups spent lavishly on campaign contributions to lawmakers as well as advertising and public relations. One former insurance executive, Wendell Potter, blew the whistle on the industry's efforts to rid themselves of unhealthy policyholders as well as allegedly deceptive public relations tactics. Potter testified before Congress that insurance companies aimed "to shape reform in a way that benefits Wall Street far more than average Americans."

As the legislative process unfolded, it became clear that the bill would indeed boost industry profits if enacted, at least in the short run. All versions of the bill centered on a mandate for individuals to purchase insurance, which would guarantee tens of millions of new paying customers in the market. Although candidate Obama had opposed the mandate, President Obama appeared to bow to its inevitability. "Unless everybody does their part," he said in his speech to Congress, "many of the insurance reforms we seek, especially requiring insurance companies to cover preexisting conditions, just can't be achieved." Obama also steadily backed away from his earlier support of the public option, denying that it had ever been a central component of his reform package and refusing to fight for its inclusion in the final Senate bill. Some liberal Democrats, assessing a bill with an individual mandate but without a public insurance option, began to question whether the reform would truly improve on the status quo.

"YOU LIE!"

At the same time, attacks on the "Obamacare" proposal from the right grew in ferocity. Republicans prepared to filibuster the legislation, especially the public option. In town hall meetings during the summer recess, anxious constituents gave legislators an earful, voicing concerns about a major expansion of government involvement in health care and its potential impact on the deficit. Former Republican vice presidential candidate Sarah Palin worried aloud that the reform would create "death panels" to ration end-of-life care—an erroneous claim, but one that nevertheless resounded for weeks through the media.

In this acrimonious environment, the president sought to refocus the debate with his September 9 address to Congress. Placing health care in the context of the nation's economic distress, Obama invoked the burden that rising health costs are placing on taxpayers and employers: "Put simply, our health care problem is our deficit problem. Nothing else even comes close." The reform plan, the president said, would not add a dime to the nation's present or future deficits. He defended his program against the bogus "death panel" charge and against the claim that his plan would insure illegal immigrants. The latter assertion prompted a spontaneous cry of "You lie!" from Rep. Joe Wilson, R-S.C.; Republican leaders later expressed regret for this breach of decorum. Republicans applauded when Obama expressed support for reforming medical malpractice law, a longstanding GOP objective.

Although seeking bipartisan support, against the odds, and expressing openness to any serious ideas, the president also gave notice to his opponents: "I will not waste time with those who have made the calculation that it's better politics to kill this plan than to improve it." Reminding his audience that Social Security and Medicare had also faced stiff opposition in their day, he concluded, "I still believe we can act even when it's hard."

Hours before the president spoke, Senator Baucus announced that the Senate Finance Committee would soon bring the health care measure to a vote, with or without Republican supporter. One Republican, Olympia Snowe of Maine, voted in favor when the markup passed the committee, 14–9, on October 13. The full Senate allowed the reform bill to come to a vote and passed it on December 24, following House approval on November 7. Significant differences between the two bills remained, such as over the public option, which had been excluded from the Senate bill. Additional difficult compromises would be necessary as the legislation entered its reconciliation phase.

—Roger Smith

Following is the text of the speech given by President Obama to a joint session of Congress on the subject of health care on September 9, 2009.

President Obama Speaks to Joint Session of Congress on Health Care

September 9, 2009

. . . When I spoke here last winter, this Nation was facing the worst economic crisis since the Great Depression. We were losing an average of 700,000 jobs per month, credit was frozen, and our financial system was on the verge of collapse.

Now, as any American who is still looking for work or a way to pay their bills will tell you, we are by no means out of the woods. A full and vibrant recovery is still many months away. And I will not let up until those Americans who seek jobs can find them, until those businesses that seek capital and credit can thrive, until all responsible homeowners can stay in their homes. That is our ultimate goal. But thanks to the bold and decisive action we've taken since January, I can stand here with confidence and say that we have pulled this economy back from the brink.

I want to thank the Members of this body for your efforts and your support in these last several months, and especially those who've taken the difficult votes that have put us on a path to recovery. I also want to thank the American people for their patience and resolve during this trying time for our Nation. But we did not come here just to clean up crises. We came here to build a future. So tonight, I return to speak to all of you about an issue that is central to that future, and that is the issue of health care.

I am not the first President to take up this cause, but I am determined to be the last. . . .

Our collective failure to meet this challenge, year after year, decade after decade, has led us to the breaking point. Everyone understands the extraordinary hardships that are placed on the uninsured who live every day just one accident or illness away from bankruptcy. These are not primarily people on welfare; these are middle class Americans. Some can't get insurance on the job. Others are self-employed and can't afford it since buying insurance on your own costs you three times as much as the coverage you get from your employer. Many other Americans who are willing and able to pay are still denied insurance due to previous illnesses or conditions that insurance companies decide are too risky or too expensive to cover.

We are the only democracy—the only advanced democracy on Earth—the only wealthy nation that allows such hardship for millions of its people. There are now more than 30 million American citizens who cannot get coverage. In just a 2-year period, one in every three Americans goes without health care coverage at some point. And every day, 14,000 Americans lose their coverage. In other words, it can happen to anyone.

But the problem that plagues the health care system is not just a problem for the uninsured. Those who do have insurance have never had less security and stability than they do today. More and more Americans worry that if you move, lose your job, or change your job, you'll lose your health insurance too. More and more Americans pay their premiums only to discover that their insurance company has dropped their coverage when they get sick or won't pay the full cost of care. It happens every day. . . .

Then there's the problem of rising cost. We spend one and a half times more per person on health care than any other country, but we aren't any healthier for it. This is one of the reasons that insurance premiums have gone up three times faster than wages. It's why so many employers, especially small businesses, are forcing their employers— employees to pay more for insurance or are dropping their coverage entirely. It's why so many aspiring entrepreneurs cannot afford to open a business in the first place and why American businesses that compete internationally, like our automakers, are at a huge disadvantage. And it's why those of us with health insurance are also paying a hidden and growing tax for those without it, about $1,000 per year that pays for somebody else's emergency room and charitable care.

Finally, our health care system is placing an unsustainable burden on taxpayers. . . .

. . . We know we must reform this system. The question is how. Now, there are those on the left who believe that the only way to fix the system is through a single-payer system like Canada's, where we would severely restrict the private insurance market and have the Government provide coverage for everybody. On the right, there are those who argue that we should end employer-based systems and leave individuals to buy health insurance on their own.

. . . I have to say that there are arguments to be made for both these approaches. But either one would represent a radical shift that would disrupt the health care most people currently have. Since health care represents one-sixth of our economy, I believe it makes more sense to build on what works and fix what doesn't, rather than try to build an entirely new system from scratch. . . .

But what we've also seen in these last months is the same partisan spectacle that only hardens the disdain many Americans have towards their own government. Instead of honest debate, we've seen scare tactics. Some have dug into unyielding ideological camps that offer no hope of compromise. Too many have used this as an opportunity to score short-term political points, even if it robs the country of our opportunity to solve a long-term challenge. And out of this blizzard of charges and countercharges, confusion has reigned.

Well, the time for bickering is over. The time for games has passed. Now is the season for action. Now is when we must bring the best ideas of both parties together and show the American people that we can still do what we were sent here to do. Now is the time to deliver on health care.

The plan I'm announcing tonight would meet three basic goals: It will provide more security and stability to those who have health insurance; it will provide insurance for those who don't; and it will slow the growth of health care costs for our families, our businesses, and our Government. It's a plan that asks everyone to take responsibility for meeting this challenge, not just government, not just insurance companies, but everybody, including employers and individuals. And it's a plan that incorporates ideas from Senators and Congressmen, from Democrats and Republicans, and yes, from some of my opponents in both the primary and general election.

Here are the details that every American needs to know about this plan. First, if you are among the hundreds of millions of Americans who already have health insurance through your job or Medicare or Medicaid or the VA, nothing in this plan will require you or your employer to change the coverage or the doctor you have. Let me repeat this: Nothing in our plan requires you to change what you have.

What this plan will do is make the insurance you have work better for you. Under this plan, it will be against the law for insurance companies to deny you coverage because of a preexisting condition. . . . We will place a limit on how much you can be charged for out-of-pocket expenses, because in the United States of America, no one should go broke because they get sick. And insurance companies will be required to cover, with no extra charge, routine checkups and preventive care, like mammograms and colonoscopies, because there's no reason we shouldn't be catching diseases like breast cancer and colon cancer before they get worse. That makes sense, it saves money, and it saves lives.

Now, that's what Americans who have health insurance can expect from this plan, more security and more stability. Now, if you're one of the tens of millions of Americans who don't currently have health insurance, the second part of this plan will finally offer you quality, affordable choices. If you lose your job or you change your job, you'll be able to get coverage. If you strike out on your own and start a small business, you'll be able to get coverage. We'll do this by creating a new insurance exchange, a marketplace where individuals and small businesses will be able to shop for health insurance at competitive prices. Insurance companies will have an incentive to participate in this exchange because it lets them compete for millions of new customers. As one big group, these customers will have greater leverage to bargain with the insurance companies for better prices and quality coverage. This is how large companies and Government employees get affordable insurance, it's how everyone in this Congress gets affordable insurance, and it's time to give every American the same opportunity that we give ourselves.

Now, for those individuals and small businesses who still can't afford the lower priced insurance available in the exchange, we'll provide tax credits, the size of which will be based on your need. . . .

Now, even if we provide these affordable options, there may be those, especially the young and the healthy, who still want to take the risk and go without coverage. There may still be companies that refuse to do right by their workers by giving them coverage. The problem is, such irresponsible behavior costs all the rest of us money. . . . And unless everybody does their part, many of the insurance reforms we seek, especially requiring insurance companies to cover preexisting conditions, just can't be achieved.

And that's why under my plan, individuals will be required to carry basic health insurance, just as most States require you to carry auto insurance. Likewise, businesses will be required to either offer their workers health care or chip in to help cover the cost of their workers. There will be a hardship waiver for those individuals who still can't afford coverage, and 95 percent of all small businesses, because of their size and narrow profit margin, would be exempt from these requirements. But we can't have large businesses and individuals who can afford coverage game the system by avoiding responsibility to themselves or their employees. Improving our health care system only works if everybody does their part. . . .

Some of people's concerns have grown out of bogus claims spread by those whose only agenda is to kill reform at any cost. The best example is the claim made not just by radio and cable talk show hosts, but by prominent politicians, that we plan to set up panels of bureaucrats with the power to kill off senior citizens. Now, such a charge would be laughable if it weren't so cynical and irresponsible. It is a lie, plain and simple.

Now, there are also those who claim that our reform efforts would insure illegal immigrants. This too is false. . . .

[*Representative Joe Wilson*] You lie!

[*The President*] It's not true. And one more misunderstanding I want to clear up, under our plan, no Federal dollars will be used to fund abortions, and Federal conscience laws will remain in place.

Now, my health care proposal has also been attacked by some who oppose reform as a Government takeover of the entire health care system. As proof, critics point to a provision in our plan that allows the uninsured and small businesses to choose a publicly sponsored insurance option, administered by the Government just like Medicaid or Medicare.

So let me set the record straight here. My guiding principle is, and always has been, that consumers do better when there is choice and competition. . . .

Now, I have no interest in putting insurance companies out of business. They provide a legitimate service and employ a lot of our friends and neighbors. I just want to hold them accountable. And the insurance reforms that I've already mentioned would do just that. But an additional step we can take to keep insurance companies honest is by making a not-for-profit public option available in the insurance exchange. Now, let me be clear. Let me be clear. It would only be an option for those who don't have insurance. No one would be forced to choose it, and it would not impact those of you who already have insurance. In fact, based on Congressional Budget Office estimates, we believe that less than 5 percent of Americans would sign up.

Despite all this, the insurance companies and their allies don't like this idea. . . .

Now, it's worth noting that a strong majority of Americans still favor a public insurance option of the sort I've proposed tonight. But its impact shouldn't be exaggerated by the left or the right or the media. It is only one part of my plan and shouldn't be used as a handy excuse for the usual Washington ideological battles. To my progressive friends, I would remind you that for decades, the driving idea behind reform has been to end insurance company abuses and make coverage available for those without it. The public option is only a means to that end, and we should remain open to other ideas that accomplish our ultimate goal. And to my Republican friends, I say that rather than making wild claims about a Government takeover of health care, we should work together to address any legitimate concerns you may have. . . .

Finally, let me discuss an issue that is a great concern to me, to Members of this Chamber, and to the public, and that's how we pay for this plan. And here's what you need to know. First, I will not sign a plan that adds one dime to our deficits, either now or in the future. . . .

Second, we've estimated that most of this plan can be paid for by finding savings within the existing health care system. . . .

Reducing the waste and inefficiency in Medicare and Medicaid will pay for most of this plan. Now, much of the rest would be paid for with revenues from the very same drug and insurance companies that stand to benefit from tens of millions of new customers. And this reform will charge insurance companies a fee for their most expensive policies, which will encourage them to provide greater value for the money, an idea which has the support of Democratic and Republican experts. And according to these same experts, this modest change could help hold down the costs of health care for all of us in the long run.

Now, finally, many in this Chamber, particularly on the Republican side of the aisle, have long insisted that reforming our medical malpractice laws can help bring down the cost of health care. Now—[applause]—there you go. There you go. Now, I don't believe malpractice reform is a silver bullet, but I've talked to enough doctors to know that defensive medicine may be contributing to unnecessary costs. So I'm proposing that we move forward on a range of ideas about how to put patient safety first and let doctors focus on practicing medicine. . . .

Now, add it all up, and the plan I'm proposing will cost around $900 billion over 10 years, less than we have spent on the Iraq and Afghanistan wars and less than the tax cuts for the wealthiest few Americans that Congress passed at the beginning of the previous administration. Now, most of these costs will be paid for with money already being spent, but spent badly, in the existing health care system. The plan will not add to our deficit. The middle class will realize greater security, not higher taxes. And if we are able to slow the growth of health care costs by just one-tenth of 1 percent each year—one-tenth of 1 percent—it will actually reduce the deficit by $4 trillion over the long term. . . .

That is why we cannot fail, because there are too many Americans counting on us to succeed, the ones who suffer silently and the ones who share their stories with us at town halls, in e-mails, and in letters. I received one of those letters a few days ago. It was from our beloved friend and colleague Ted Kennedy. He had written it back in May, shortly after he was told that his illness was terminal. He asked that it be delivered upon his death.

In it he spoke about what a happy time his last months were, thanks to the love and support of family and friends, his wife Vicki, his amazing children, who are all here tonight. And he expressed confidence that this would be the year that health care reform, "that great unfinished business of our society," he called it, would finally pass. He repeated the truth that health care is decisive for our future prosperity, but he also reminded me that "it concerns more than material things." "What we face," he wrote, "is above all a moral issue; at stake are not just the details of policy, but fundamental principles of social justice and the character of our country." . . .

That large-heartedness, that concern and regard for the plight of others, is not a partisan feeling; it's not a Republican or a Democratic feeling. It too is part of the American character, our ability to stand in other people's shoes, a recognition that we are all in this together, and when fortune turns against one of us, others are there to lend a helping hand, a belief that in this country, hard work and responsibility should be rewarded by some measure of security and fair play, and an acknowledgment that sometimes government has to step in to help deliver on that promise.

This has always been the history of our progress. In 1935, when over half of our seniors could not support themselves and millions had seen their savings wiped away, there were those who argued that Social Security would lead to socialism, but the men and women of Congress stood fast, and we are all the better for it. In 1965, when some argued that Medicare represented a Government takeover of health care, Members of Congress, Democrats and Republicans, did not back down. They joined together so that all of us could enter our golden years with some basic peace of mind.

You see, our predecessors understood that government could not, and should not, solve every problem. They understood that there are instances when the gains in security from government action are not worth the added constraints on our freedom. But they also understood that the danger of too much government is matched by the perils of too little, that without the leavening hand of wise policy, markets can crash, monopolies can stifle competition, the vulnerable can be exploited. And they knew that when any government measure, no matter how carefully crafted or beneficial, is subject to scorn; when any efforts to help people in need are attacked as un-American, when facts and reason are thrown overboard and only timidity passes for wisdom, and we can no longer even engage in a civil conversation with each other over the things that truly matter, that at that point we don't merely lose our capacity to solve big challenges, we lose something essential about ourselves.

That was true then; it remains true today. I understand how difficult this health care debate has been. I know that many in this country are deeply skeptical that government is looking out for them. I understand that the politically safe move would be to kick the can further down the road, to defer reform one more year or one more election or one more term.

But that is not what the moment calls for. That's not what we came here to do. We did not come to fear the future. We came here to shape it. I still believe we can act even when it's hard. I still believe. I still believe that we can act when it's hard. I still believe we can replace acrimony with civility and gridlock with progress. I still believe we can do great things and that here and now we will meet history's test, because that's who we are. That is our calling. That is our character.

Thank you, God bless you, and may God bless the United States of America.

SOURCE: U.S. Executive Office of the President. "Address Before the Joint Session of the Congress on Health Care Reform." *Daily Compilation of Presidential Documents* 2009, no. 00693 (September 9, 2009). www.gpo.gov/fdsys/pkg/DCPD-200900693/pdf/DCPD-200900693.pdf.

OTHER HISTORIC DOCUMENTS OF INTEREST

FROM THIS VOLUME

FROM PREVIOUS *HISTORIC DOCUMENTS*

Iran Calls for Diplomatic Talks

SEPTEMBER 9, 2009

The long-running issue on the international stage over Iran's nuclear program renewed on September 9, 2009, when Iran submitted a proposal for discussions not on its own nuclear program but on other nations' nuclear programs and revisions to the UN Charter. After President Barack Obama had earlier indicated that he would entertain unconditional discussions with Iran, the United States, while skeptical that any discussion with Iran would lead to disarmament, said it welcomed Iran's proposal to engage in multiparty discussions. Other nations, such as the United Kingdom, simply called for tougher sanctions imposed on Iran by the United Nations rather than further discussions, while China said that any additional sanctions would not be well received. These nations characterized more discussions as useless, as Iran had already indicated that it would not discontinue its nuclear program, instead telling the International Atomic Energy Agency (IAEA) that it was building a second uranium enrichment plant.

Representatives of Iran, the United Kingdom, China, Germany, France, Russia, and the United States in Geneva on October 1, 2009, met to discuss Iran's need for a nuclear program. During the meetings, a proposal to send Iran enriched uranium for the purpose of fuel production was presented, and although it initially seemed that Iran would accept the proposal, it later balked, announcing that it would not allow another country to enrich uranium for its use. By the end of 2009, talks between Iran and the six nations had broken down.

IRAN'S NUCLEAR PROGRAM

Iran has always claimed that the nuclear program it has been developing on and off since the 1950s is for the purpose of creating energy and fuel, not for building nuclear weapons. However, because it has run the program in near secrecy, the international community, led by Western nations, has called for the country to answer extensive questions on its program and allow weapons inspectors into all its nuclear facilities to verify this claim. Iran has refused. When the IAEA conducted inspections of Iran's nuclear program, officials in Tehran destroyed evidence and lied to the agency about aspects of it. While Iran has worked with the IAEA, it has still been criticized by the organization for false reports and not allowing timely access to information. Iran said it must conduct its program in secret because Western nations would otherwise try to deny it the capability to produce nuclear fuel and conduct additional research on possible technologies. Although officials are skeptical about this claim, a 1997 Central Intelligence Agency (CIA) report agreed with it. The IAEA in recent reports, however, has said that it is unclear whether Iran is producing nuclear weapons. In 2007, the group reported that Iran had "halted its nuclear weapons program" in 2003, but continued that the nation was "keeping open the option to develop nuclear weapons."

The IAEA reported that it took Iran until September 2009 to reveal that it was constructing a new nuclear facility in Qom. In late September, the IAEA called on Iran to provide the organization with "further information with respect to the name and location of the pilot enrichment facility, the current status of its construction and plans for the introduction of nuclear material into the facility." The letter also requested that inspectors from the organization be allowed to enter the facility. Iran granted the IAEA full access to its facility near Qom between October 25 and 28. After its inspection, the IAEA reported that it still had questions on the "purpose and chronology" of the facility and asked for more information. The remaining questions led the IAEA to say that "Iran's late declaration of the new facility reduces confidence in the absence of other nuclear facilities under construction in Iran which have not been declared to the Agency."

International observers have questioned why Iran has a nuclear program for the purpose of producing energy when it has some of the world's largest oil and gas reserves. Many nations that use nuclear energy purchase nuclear fuel from other nations rather than producing it themselves. Russia has agreed to sell Iran nuclear fuel, but until September 2009, Iran had turned down the offer, focusing instead on ramping up its own program. Iran has called international suppliers unreliable, and thus chooses to produce its own fuel.

In response to Iran's nuclear program, the United Nations has placed multiple sanctions on Iran. The United States has a history of sanctions against Iran, first doing so in response to the hostage situation in 1979; a trade embargo followed later in 1995, in response to Iran's supposed support of terrorism and desire to develop nuclear weapons. The UN Security Council imposed restrictions in 2006, 2007, and 2008 in response to the country's nuclear program. Sanctions included stopping all member nations from sending Iran materials that could be used for uranium enrichment purposes, preventing contact with and travel of Iranians thought to be connected to the nation's Revolutionary Guard, and the importing and selling of arms. The sanctions have done little to dissuade Iran from continuing to enrich uranium, building additional enrichment plants, conducting centrifuge research, and building a heavy-water reactor.

SEPTEMBER 9 PROPOSAL

On September 9, 2009, Iran submitted to representatives of the European Union and other permanent members of the UN Security Council a five-page proposal titled Cooperation for Peace, Justice and Progress, which called for discussions on multiple international issues, including nuclear disarmament. The proposal, however, did not say anything about Iran's nuclear program. The missing piece of the proposal did not come as a surprise to international observers, after Iranian president Mahmoud Ahmadinejad said he was "finished" discussing the nuclear program because he saw no reason to negotiate on "the Iranian nation's obvious rights."

President Obama had said previously that he was willing to talk with Iran about its nuclear program, and the September 9 proposal was largely seen as a response to him. The United States disregarded many of Iran's remarks in the proposal, stating that they were the same as past promises; however, spokespersons for the United States did indicate that the administration wanted to work with Iran in an effort to stop uranium enrichment programs in Iran and halt additional research on centrifuges and heavy-water reactors. The proposal could possibly provide an opening to discuss these issues with Iran. Other suspicions about the timing of Iran's proposal involved the work of international agencies, including the CIA, that were attempting to uncover additional information about Iran's program. Iran's proposal noted that the nation was planning to enrich uranium up to 5 percent, which would only be enough for power production, not weapons production, but that "[F]urther complementary information will be provided in an appropriate and due time."

REACTION IN THE WEST

In late September, the Group of 20 met in Pittsburgh, Pennsylvania, and, speaking with President Obama and French president Nicolas Sarkozy, British prime minister Gordon Brown said that investigations into Iran's nuclear facilities and capabilities had produced information that would "shock and anger the whole international community, and it will harden our resolve" in calling for change in Iran. This announcement came after the United States had been meeting with Iranian officials for a week trying to come to an agreement about how to move forward. According to officials with knowledge of the event, it was revealed at the meeting that Iran's nuclear facilities were not yet operational but would be able to produce one bomb per year beginning in 2010.

President Obama has been criticized for being willing to work diplomatically and unconditionally with Iran on its nuclear facilities, something his predecessor strongly opposed. But Obama sternly called on the Iranian government to work with the international community and be welcomed by it if Iran was willing to cooperate. Obama said, "[T]he Iranian government must now demonstrate through deeds its peaceful intentions or be held accountable to international standards and international law."

Russia, a member of the UN Security Council and a nation closely tied economically and diplomatically to Iran, has encouraged the West to work with Iran rather than imposing additional sanctions. According to Russian foreign minister Sergei Lavrov, the proposal sent by Iran indicated that Iran was ready for negotiations. "Based on a brief review of the Iranian papers, my impression is there is something there to use," Lavrov said. "The most important thing is Iran is ready for a comprehensive discussion of the situation, what positive role it can play in Iraq, Afghanistan and the region." Russia has the ability to veto sanctions imposed by the United Nations, and in some remarks has indicated that it might do so if Western nations are unwilling or unable to diplomatically work with Iran. "Iran is a partner that has never harmed Russia in any way," said Lavrov. Russia also indicated that Iran had made little progress, contrary to Western media reports, in building nuclear weapons. Russia has most recently been caught up in the Iran controversy when it was accused of sending an air-defense system to Iran. Israel claimed that it detected the system being delivered by cargo ship. Russia denied any involvement.

GENEVA MEETINGS

In advance of the October 1 P5+1 meetings in Geneva (ambassadors of the five permanent Security Council members plus Germany are often referred to as P5+1), international leaders called for increased action on Iran. Up to this point, nations had mainly worked through the United Nations to place sanctions on the country, with individual countries promising to open up trade if it would release additional information on its nuclear program. Israeli prime minister Benjamin Netanyahu called for "crippling sanctions" against Iran.

During the October 1 Geneva meetings, officials from Iran stressed the importance of continuing discussion on its September proposal. Although talks at the meeting did not get far, Iran mostly approved the proposal that came out of this meeting calling for it to receive enriched fuel for a research reactor originally supplied by the United States that produces isotopes for medical purposes and is closely monitored by the IAEA. The United States and Russia wrote the official proposal, which the IAEA presented to Iran. Iran indicated that if it was not provided fuel for the reactor, it would produce its own. Based on the proposal, Russia would receive 1,200 kilograms of enriched uranium hexafluoride from Iran. Russia would then further enrich it and pass it to France, at which point the material would be added to fuel assemblies. After France transferred the material back to Russia, Russia would send it back to Iran. On October 19, 2009, France, Russia, the United States, the IAEA, and Iran began negotiating over the proposal. Although Iran had agreed to much of the proposal, it still wanted some modifications to the agreement. In mid-November, Iran's foreign minister stated that the nation would not provide its uranium to any foreign country for further enrichment, indicating that it was growing cold to the deal. By the end of 2009, the group had yet to get official approval of the plan from Iran.

Officials involved in the P5+1 proposal expressed disappointment because Iran seemingly had been willing to negotiate in September, but then failed to work with the group on an agreement or even set up additional meetings to discuss the proposal. After the breakdown of talks, the P5+1 said that it was likely that the United Nations would impose additional sanctions.

—Heather Kerrigan

Following is the text of Iran's Cooperation for Peace, Justice and Progress proposal submitted on September 9, 2009, to representatives of European Union nations and other permanent members of the UN Security Council and passed by the Swiss government to the United States.

Cooperation for Peace, Justice and Progress

September 9, 2009

In the Name of the Almighty

Cooperation for Peace, Justice and Progress

Package of Proposals by the Islamic Republic of Iran for Comprehensive and Constructive Negotiations

There is no doubt that our world is at the threshold of entering a new era. The difficult era characterized by domination of empires, predominance of military powers, dominance of organized and interrelated media networks and competitions on the basis of offensive capability and the power from conventional and non-conventional weapons is coming to an end. A new era characterized by cultural approach and rational thinking, and respect for the true godly essence of humankind is flourishing and blossoming. Many of the predicaments facing our world today, such as the unprecedented economic crisis, cultural and identity crisis, political and security dilemmas, and the mushrooming of terrorism, organized crimes and the illicit drugs are the products of the fading era of domination of ungodly ways of thinking prevailing in the global relations and the ominous legacy for present and future generations of humanity.

Resolution of these problems and creating a world filled with spirituality, friendship, prosperity, wellness and security requires reorganization and creating an opportunity for broad and collective participation in the management of the world. The existing mechanisms are not capable to meet the present needs of humankind and their ineffectiveness has been clearly proven in the realms of economy, politics, culture and security. These mechanisms and structures are the direct product of relations based on brute power and domination, while our world today needs mechanisms that come from divine and godly thinking and an approach based on human values and compassion. The new mechanisms should pave the way for the advancement, full blossoming of the talents and potentials of all nations and establishment of lasting world peace and security.

The Iranian nation is prepared to enter into dialogue and negotiation in order to lay the ground for lasting peace and regionally inspired and generated stability for the region and beyond and for the continued progress and prosperity of the nations of the region and the world. Our desire to enter into this dialogue and cooperative relationships proceeds from our inherent national, regional and international capacity and strength, our principled and historical commitment in applying this capacity to foster peace, tranquility, progress and well-being for nations in our region and beyond. We stand ready to enter into this dialogue on the basis of godly and human principles and values, including the recognition of the rights of nations, respect for sovereignty and principles of democracy and the right of people to have free elections, as well as refraining from imposing pressure or threats and moving forward on the solid foundation of justice and law.

The Islamic Republic of Iran believes that within the framework of principles of justice, democracy and multilateralism, a wide range of security, political, economic and cultural issues at regional and global levels could be included in these negotiations with a view of fostering constructive cooperation for advancement of nations and promotion of peace and stability in the region and the world.

As it was clearly stated last year in our proposed package, the Islamic Republic or Iran believes that drawing lessons from the past mistakes and not insisting on futile and pointless paths that have proven to be of no avail is the prerequisite for the success in the upcoming negotiations. Accordingly, the commitment of all parties involved to, firstly, composition of new structure of international interactions that is free from past errors, and secondly expression of good intent by all parties both in words and deeds in demonstrating commitment to justice and law can lead to a new phase in negotiations for a long-term cooperation with a view to consolidating lasting peace and security in the region and the world.

Political, security, economic and international issues are the primary subjects that have raised shared concerns in the region and the world for governments and nations. The Islamic Republic of Iran firmly believes that proceeding from principles and fundamentals stated above and in light of the present state of affairs in our world we all need to show compassion and concern for the destiny of humanity and to turn these shared concerns into collective commitments for the purpose of paving the way for effective regional and international cooperation.

The Islamic Republic of Iran voices its readiness to embark on comprehensive, all-encompassing and constructive negotiations, aiming at acquiring a clear framework for cooperative relationships by ensuring the adherence of all parties to collective commitments, a future free from injustice that promises welfare and progress free from double standards for all nations of the region and the world.

Proceeding from regional and international priorities, the axes of the negotiations for peace and prosperity can be included in three main areas: political-security issues, international issues and economic issues.

1. POLITICAL-SECURITY ISSUES

1.1 Protecting human dignity, respect for their culture and their rights.

1.2 Consolidating stability and fostering just peace, promotion of democracy and enhancement of prosperity of nations in regions that suffer from instability, militarism, violence and terrorism on the basis of:

First: Respect for the rights of nations and national interests of sovereign states.

Second: Consolidating the national sovereignty of countries in the framework of democratic practices.

Third: Refraining from violence and militarism.

Fourth: Tackling the root causes of terrorism.

Some parts of the world, especially in the Middle East, the Balkans, parts of Africa, South America and East Asia, need to be accorded priority. Joint efforts and interactions to help the people of Palestine to draw a comprehensive, democratic and equitable plan in order to help the people of Palestine to achieve all-embracing peace, lasting security and to secure their fundamental rights could be good examples of those cooperative relations.

1.3 Combating common security threats by dealing effectively and firmly with the main causes of security threats including terrorism, illicit drugs, illegal migrations, organized crimes and piracy.

2. International Issues

2.1 Reform of the United Nations and the Security Council and raising their effectiveness on the basis of principles of democracy and justice

2.2 Elevating the weight and position of environmental issues in the international relations and fostering collective participation in the management of environmental issues.

2.3 Equitable definition and codification of the rights to space and sharing of all possessors of space technologies in the management and fair use of space.

2.4 Definition and codification of the rights relating to new and advanced technologies.

2.5 Promoting a rule-based and equitable oversight function of the IAEA and creating the required mechanisms for use of clean nuclear energy in agriculture, industry, and medicine and power generation.

2.6 Promoting the universality of NPT mobilizing global resolve and putting into action real and fundamental programmes toward complete disarmament and preventing development and proliferation of nuclear, chemical and microbial weapons.

2.7 Enhancement of ethical and human considerations and their full observance in international mechanisms, ties and practices.

3. Economic Issues

3.1 Energy and its security in production, supply, transport and consumption.

3.2 Trade and investment.

3.3 Capacity-building for promotion of public welfare, global poverty alleviations reducing social gaps and bridging the gap between the South and the North.

3.4 Finding the root causes of global economic and financial crisis and preventing the occurrence of other manifestations of crisis in the world economy and designing new and just mechanisms.

3.5 Combating underground economy, economic corruption, financial frauds and organized crime activities that are detrimental to economic security.

Source: Islamic Republic of Iran."Cooperation for Peace Justice and Progress." September 9, 2009. http://s3.documentcloud.org/documents/503/iran-nuclear-program-proposal.pdf

OTHER HISTORIC DOCUMENTS OF INTEREST

FBI Report on Crime in the United States

SEPTEMBER 14, 2009

The Federal Bureau of Investigation (FBI) released an annual statistical report, *Crime in the United States, 2008,* on September 14, 2009; the document lays out the number of crimes committed in the United States from January 1 through December 31, 2008. The report shows that the volume of violent crime declined for the second year in a row, by 0.7 percent in 2007 and 1.9 percent in 2008. The number of property crimes also decreased in 2008, by 0.8 percent, making 2008 the sixth straight year in a row in which the volume of property crime had fallen. The volume of the four types of violent crime—murder and nonnegligent manslaughter, aggravated assault, robbery, and forcible rape, a category that includes assaults, attempt to commit rape, and forcing a female to have sex against her will, but does not include nonforcible rape (i.e., statutory)—all declined from 2007 to 2008. Murder and nonnegligent manslaughter decreased by 3.9 percent; aggravated assault decreased by 2.5 percent; robbery decreased by 0.7 percent; and forcible rape dropped by 1.6 percent.

In 2009 geography and density in population played a roll in crime rate increases and decreases. In some large cities, there were increases in the number of violent crimes. Cities with a population of fewer than 10,000 saw the rate of murder and nonnegligent manslaughter grow by 5.5 percent and forcible rape rise by 1.4 percent, according to the FBI's preliminary June 2009 report. The Northeast saw an increase in the number of murders, up 1.4 percent over 2007, and also experienced an increase in property crime, up 2.5 percent. The Midwest and West saw a decrease across the violent crime and property crime categories, and the South experienced 0.6 percent growth in property crime from 2007 to 2008. In rural areas, forcible rape decreased by 7.3 percent, but in urban areas, the volume of forcible rape increased by 0.6 percent, according to preliminary statistics.

The FBI notes that the crimes included in the annual report are only those that were reported to law enforcement. Therefore, the organization cautions against using its report to determine the safest places to live in the United States or to rank cities against one another. According to the FBI, "[T]hese rough rankings provide no insight into the numerous variables that mold crime in a particular town, city, county, state or region." As such, the FBI says, using the statistics to make comparisons can "lead to simplistic and/or incomplete analyses that often create misleading perceptions adversely affecting communities and their residents." The U.S. Department of Justice conducts the National Crime Victimization Survey, which estimates unreported crimes. When the two studies are looked at together, they give the most accurate representation of the actual crime rate in the United States. The version of the National Crime Victimization Survey released on September 2, 2009, showed no change in violent crime between 2007 and 2008, and only a slight decrease in property crime. In addition, if multiple crimes are committed during one incident, only the most serious offense is reported in the FBI report; this practice obviously has an effect on the overall numbers associated with certain crimes.

CRIME RATES

The FBI does not indicate reasons for the rise and fall of crime rates. According to FBI spokesperson Bill Carter, "We leave that up to the academics and the criminologists and the sociologists." However, Carter did speculate that one reason for a drop in the number of homicides over recent years could be attributed to better medical care, which means more assault victims are able to recover, rather than die.

The rate of property crime, including burglary, larceny-theft, motor vehicle theft, and arson, fell 1.6 percent from 2007 to 2008, to a rate of 3,212.5 crimes committed per 100,000 people. The property crime rate in 2008 was 8.6 percent lower than in 2004 and 14.2 percent lower than in 1999. The FBI estimates that $17.2 billion in losses were caused by property crime, of which larceny-theft accounted for 67.5 percent, burglary 22.7, and motor vehicle theft 9.8 percent.

Nationwide, 62,807 arsons were reported in 2008, of which 43.4 percent involved structures, including houses, storage units, and office buildings; 28.9 percent involved mobile property; and 27.7 percent involved another form of property, such as crops and fences. Per person, the average dollar amount lost per arson was estimated at $16,015. Arsons decreased 3.6 percent from 2007 to 2008.

In each violent crime category—murder and nonnegligent manslaughter, forcible rape, robbery, and aggravated assault—the number of offenses declined from 2007 to 2008. The violent crime rate in 2008 was 454.5 offenses per 100,000 people, a decrease of 2.7 percent since 2007. The 2008 estimate of violent crime showed an increase over the 2004 level, by 1.6 percent, but was 3.1 percent below the level of violent crime in 1999. Aggravated assaults made up the greatest portion of all violent crimes, at 60.4 percent, while robbery accounted for 32 percent, murder accounted for 1.2 percent, and forcible rape made up 6.4 percent. The FBI data also gives a breakdown of murderers and their victims. According to the report, 23.3 percent of murder victims were killed by a family member, a total of 54.7 percent of victims were killed by someone they knew, and only 22 percent of murder victims were killed by strangers. Of all homicides committed in the United States in 2008, 9,484 involved firearms.

In 2008, 14,005,615 arrests were reported by the FBI for all offenses, excluding traffic violations. Of those, nearly 595,000 were for violent crime, while more than 1.6 million were for property crime. The largest number of arrests, at more than 1.7 million, were for drug abuse. From 2007 to 2008, the number of violent crime arrests declined 0.6 percent; arrests for property crime increased 5.6 percent; arrests of juveniles decreased 2.8 percent; and arrests of adults decreased 1.3 percent.

The falling crime rate reported across the nation did not mean all cities, counties, and states saw a decrease. In Providence, Rhode Island, for example, the number of violent crimes in 2008 was up 19.5 percent over those committed in 2007. Property crimes also increased after years of flat or decreasing crime rates there. Providence police chief Dean Esserman said the level of violent crime was "of great concern" to the department, which was responding by refocusing energies and resources on combating violent crime in the region. "We also remain committed to the concept of neighborhood policing, and working together with community partners," said Esserman.

Prison Trends

As violent crime and property crime fell in 2008, those who support the idea of decreasing the use of prison sentences for nonviolent offenders saw these statistics as encouraging to their cause. According to the Justice Policy Institute, a think tank that promotes placing limits on incarcerations, the FBI report, coupled with a decreasing rate of incarceration, could indicate "that decreasing the number of people incarcerated can be part of an effective public safety strategy." According to Tracy Velazquez, the group's executive director, the FBI report "shows that we can preserve public safety while expanding the use of community supervision and improving the systems that help people be successful, including treatment, housing and job services."

The Justice Policy Institute analysis of the FBI's statistics showed that as violent crime fell 1.9 percent, the growth rate in the number of prisoners slowed from 1.6 percent in 2006–2007 to 1.0 percent in 2007–2008. These statistics, gathered from the Bureau of Justice Statistics, an arm of the Department of Justice, indicate that the prison population in the United States grew only slightly in 2008, and twenty states saw a decrease in their total number of inmates.

The trend away from prison and jail time has been multifaceted. For some localities, there is not enough money in the public safety and corrections budgets to be able to house and feed a growing number of prison or jail inmates. Other areas have moved away from prison and jail time, favoring instead community intervention and rehabilitation. Ram Cnann, a professor at the University of Pennsylvania, said prisons "simply cost too much. If you can prevent opening a new prison, you can save lots of money." Cnann continued, saying that decreasing budgets are forcing states to take a hard look at all costs, including corrections. "It's not ideological, it's pragmatic," he said. "This is the first time that we have alliances on the right and left on this issue, and it's the money that has forced the issue."

Race in Crime

The FBI report in 2009 indicated that African American and white males were nearly as likely to be victims of a homicide in 2008, a shocking number when compared to data from the U.S. Census Bureau, which indicates that 80 percent of Americans are white and 13 percent are African American. This makes an African American male six times more likely to be the victim of a homicide. Among African Americans and whites, men between the ages of 17 and 30 were the most likely to be homicide victims or killers.

According to the report, approximately 17,000 homicides were committed in 2008, and of those, 6,782 had African American victims and 6,838 had white victims. As has long been the case, men are more likely to be homicide victims than women. Parity between white and African American males was shown in statistics of those arrested for homicide. Out of more than 16,000 people arrested for homicide, 5,943 were African American and 5,334 were white.

In addition to producing an annual report on crime, each year the FBI also releases a report on the number of hate crimes in the United States. The 2009 report, based on data from 2008, found hate crimes to be at their highest levels since 2001. "Hate violence in America is a serious national problem that shows little sign of slowing," according to Robert G. Sugarman, national chair of the Anti-Defamation League, an organization that works to combat anti-Semitism, racism, and bigotry. Sugarman called for "a coordinated campaign to prevent, deter, and respond effectively to criminal violence motivated by bigotry and prejudice."

The FBI hate crimes report stated that 7,783 bias-motivated crimes occurred in 2008. Broken down by subgroup, lesbians, gay men, Jews, and African Americans saw the highest number of crimes committed against them since 2001. There is some indication that the increasing rate of hate crimes can be attributed to better reporting systems rather than an increase in incidences.

To work toward combating hate crime targeting members of the gay and lesbian community, President Barack Obama signed a law on October 28, 2009, making it a federal crime to assault anyone based on their sexual orientation. According to Obama, statistics show that 12,000 hate crimes aimed at gay men and lesbians were reported during the past decade. Obama called the legislation, hailed as the first major federal gay rights bill ever signed, a step in the right direction to "help protect our citizens from violence based on what they look like, who they love, how they pray."

—Heather Kerrigan

Following are excerpts from the Federal Bureau of Investigation annual report Crime in the United States, 2008, *released on September 14, 2009.*

FBI Statistics on Crime in the United States

September 14, 2009

Violent Crime

Definition

In the FBI's Uniform Crime Reporting (UCR) Program, violent crime is composed of four offenses: murder and nonnegligent manslaughter, forcible rape, robbery, and aggravated assault. Violent crimes are defined in the UCR Program as those offenses which involve force or threat of force. . . .

Overview

- An estimated 1,382,012 violent crimes occurred nationwide in 2008, showing a decrease of 1.9 percent from the 2007 estimate.

- The 2008 estimated violent crime total was 1.6 percent above the 2004 level but 3.1 percent below the 1999 level.

- There were an estimated 454.5 violent crimes per 100,000 inhabitants in 2008.

- Aggravated assaults accounted for 60.4 percent of violent crimes, the highest number of violent crimes reported to law enforcement. Robbery comprised 32.0 percent of violent crimes, forcible rape accounted for 6.4 percent, and murder accounted for 1.2 percent of estimated violent crimes in 2008.

- In 2008, offenders used firearms in 66.9 percent of the Nation's murders, 43.5 percent of robberies, and 21.4 percent of aggravated assaults. . . .

MURDER

Definition

The FBI's Uniform Crime Reporting (UCR) Program defines murder and nonnegligent manslaughter as the willful (nonnegligent) killing of one human being by another.

The classification of this offense is based solely on police investigation as opposed to the determination of a court, medical examiner, coroner, jury, or other judicial body. The UCR Program does not include the following situations in this offense classification: deaths caused by negligence, suicide, or accident; justifiable homicides; and attempts to murder or assaults to murder, which are scored as aggravated assaults. . . .

Overview

- An estimated 16,272 persons were murdered nationwide in 2008. This number was a 3.9 percent decrease from the 2007 estimate, a 0.8 percent increase from the 2004 figure, and a 4.8 percent increase from the 1999 estimate.

- There were an estimated 5.4 murders per 100,000 inhabitants in 2008, a 4.7 percent decrease from the estimated 2007 rate.

- 89.4 percent of the murders that occurred in the United States in 2008 were within Metropolitan Statistical Areas, 6.3 percent were in nonmetropolitan counties, and the remainder (4.3 percent) occurred in cities outside metropolitan areas. . . .

FORCIBLE RAPE

Definition

Forcible rape, as defined in the FBI's Uniform Crime Reporting (UCR) Program, is the carnal knowledge of a female forcibly and against her will. Attempts or assaults to commit rape by force or threat of force are also included; however, statutory rape (without force) and other sex offenses are excluded. . . .

Overview

- In 2008, the estimated number of forcible rapes (89,000)—the lowest figure in the last 20 years—decreased 1.6 percent from the 2007 estimate. The estimated volume of rapes in 2008 was 6.4 percent lower than in 2004 and was 0.5 percent below the 1999 level. . . .

- The rate of forcible rapes in 2008 was estimated at 57.7 offenses per 100,000 female inhabitants, a 2.4 percent decrease when compared with the 2007 estimated rate of 59.2.

- Rapes by force comprised 92.5 percent of reported rape offenses, and attempts or assaults to commit rape accounted for 7.5 percent of reported rapes. . . .

ROBBERY

Definition

The FBI's Uniform Crime Reporting (UCR) Program defines robbery as the taking or attempting to take anything of value from the care, custody, or control of a person or persons by force or threat of force or violence and/or by putting the victim in fear. . . .

Overview

- In 2008, the estimated robbery total (441,855) decreased 0.7 percent from the 2007 estimate. However, the 5-year robbery trend (2004 data compared with 2008 data) showed an increase of 10.1 percent.

- The 2008 estimated robbery rate (145.3 per 100,000 inhabitants) showed a decrease of 1.5 percent when compared with the 2007 rate. . . .

- Losses estimated at $581 million were attributed to robberies in 2008.

- The average dollar loss per robbery offense was $1,315. The highest average dollar loss was for banks, which lost $4,854 per offense. . . .

- Firearms were used in 43.5 percent of robberies in 2008. Strong-arm robberies accounted for 40.2 percent of the total. . . .

AGGRAVATED ASSAULT

Definition

The FBI's Uniform Crime Reporting (UCR) Program defines aggravated assault as an unlawful attack by one person upon another for the purpose of inflicting severe or aggravated bodily injury. The UCR Program further specifies that this type of assault is usually accompanied by the use of a weapon or by other means likely to produce death or great bodily harm. Attempted aggravated assault that involves the display of—or threat to use—a gun, knife, or other weapon is included in this crime category because serious personal injury would likely result if the assault were completed. When aggravated assault and larceny-theft occur together, the offense falls under the category of robbery. . . .

Overview

- In 2008, there were an estimated 834,885 aggravated assaults in the Nation.

- According to 2- and 10-year trend data, the estimated number of aggravated assaults in 2008 declined 2.5 percent and 8.4 percent, respectively, when compared with the estimates for 2007 and 1999.

- The estimated rate of aggravated assaults was 274.6 offenses per 100,000 inhabitants in 2008.

- A comparison of 10-year trend data for 2008 and 1999 showed that the rate of aggravated assaults in 2008 dropped 17.9 percent. . . .

- Of the aggravated assault offenses for which law enforcement agencies provided expanded data in 2008, 33.5 percent were committed with blunt objects or other dangerous weapons; 26.2 percent involved personal weapons such as hands, fists, and feet; 21.4 percent were committed with firearms; and 18.9 percent involved knives or other cutting instruments. . . .

PROPERTY CRIME

Definition

In the FBI's Uniform Crime Reporting (UCR) Program, property crime includes the offenses of burglary, larceny-theft, motor vehicle theft, and arson. The object of the theft-type offenses is the taking of money or property, but there is no force or threat of force against the victims. The property crime category includes arson because the offense involves the destruction of property; however, arson victims may be subjected to force. Because of limited participation and varying collection procedures by local law enforcement agencies, only limited data are available for arson. Arson statistics are included in trend, clearance, and arrest tables throughout Crime in the United States, but they are not included in any estimated volume data. The arson section in this report provides more information on that offense. . . .

Overview

- There were an estimated 9,767,915 property crime offenses in the Nation in 2008.

- The 2-year trend showed property crime decreased 0.8 percent in 2008 compared with 2007 estimates. The 5-year trend, comparing 2008 with 2004, showed a 5.3 percent drop in property crime.

- In 2008, the rate of property crimes was estimated at 3,212.5 offenses per 100,000 inhabitants, a 1.6 percent decrease when compared with the rate in

2007. The 2008 property crime rate was 8.6 percent lower than the 2004 rate and 14.2 percent under the 1999 rate. . . .

- Larceny-theft accounted for 67.5 percent of all property crimes in 2008. Burglary accounted for 22.7 percent and motor vehicle theft for 9.8 percent. . . .

- An estimated 17.2 billion dollars in losses resulted from property crimes in 2008. . . .

BURGLARY

Definition

The FBI's Uniform Crime Reporting (UCR) Program defines burglary as the unlawful entry of a structure to commit a felony or theft. To classify an offense as a burglary, the use of force to gain entry need not have occurred. The UCR Program has three subclassifications for burglary: forcible entry, unlawful entry where no force is used, and attempted forcible entry. The UCR definition of "structure" includes apartment, barn, house trailer or houseboat when used as a permanent dwelling, office, railroad car (but not automobile), stable, and vessel (i.e., ship). . . .

Overview

- In 2008, there were an estimated 2,222,196 burglaries—an increase of 2.0 percent when compared with 2007 data.

- There was an increase of 3.6 percent in the number of burglaries in 2008 when compared with the 2004 estimate and an increase of 5.8 percent when compared with the 1999 estimate. . . .

- Burglary accounted for 22.7 percent of the estimated number of property crimes committed in 2008. . . .

- Of all burglaries, 61.2 percent involved forcible entry, 32.3 percent were unlawful entries (without force), and the remainder (6.4 percent) were forcible entry attempts. . . .

- Victims of burglary offenses suffered an estimated $4.6 billion in lost property in 2008; overall, the average dollar loss per burglary offense was $2,079. . . .

- Burglaries of residential properties accounted for 70.3 percent of all burglary offenses. . . .

LARCENY-THEFT

Definition

The FBI's Uniform Crime Reporting (UCR) Program defines larceny-theft as the unlawful taking, carrying, leading, or riding away of property from the possession or constructive possession of another. Examples are thefts of bicycles, motor vehicle parts and accessories, shoplifting, pocket-picking, or the stealing of any property or article that is not taken by force and violence or by fraud. Attempted larcenies are included. Embezzlement, confidence games, forgery, check fraud, etc., are excluded.

Overview

- There were an estimated 6.6 million (6,588,873) larceny-thefts nationwide in 2008.

- There was a 0.3 percent increase in the estimated number of larceny-thefts in 2008 compared with the 2007 estimate. The 2008 figure showed a 5.3 percent decline compared with the 1999 estimate.

- The estimated rate of larceny-thefts in 2008 was 2,167.0 per 100,000 inhabitants.

- The rate of larceny-thefts declined 0.5 percent from 2007 to 2008, and the rate declined 15.0 percent from 1999 to 2008. . . .

- Larceny-thefts accounted for an estimated 67.5 percent of property crimes in 2008. . . .

- The average value of property taken during larceny-thefts was $925 per offense. When the average value was applied to the estimated number of larceny-thefts, the loss to victims nationally was nearly $6.1 billion. . . .

- Thefts of motor vehicle parts, accessories, and contents made up the largest portion of reported larcenies—35.8 percent. . . .

Motor Vehicle Theft

Definition

In the FBI's Uniform Crime Reporting (UCR) Program, motor vehicle theft is defined as the theft or attempted theft of a motor vehicle. In the UCR Program, a motor vehicle is a self-propelled vehicle that runs on land surfaces and not on rails. Examples of motor vehicles include sport utility vehicles, automobiles, trucks, buses, motorcycles, motor scooters, all-terrain vehicles, and snowmobiles. Motor vehicle theft does not include farm equipment, bulldozers, airplanes, construction equipment, or water craft such as motor-boats, sailboats, houseboats, or jet skis. The taking of a motor vehicle for temporary use by persons having lawful access is excluded from this definition.

Overview

- There were an estimated 956,846 thefts of motor vehicles nationwide in 2008.

- In terms of a nationwide rate, there were 314.7 motor vehicle thefts per 100,000 inhabitants.

- The estimated number of motor vehicle thefts declined 12.7 percent when compared with data from 2007, 22.7 percent when compared with 2004 figures, and 16.9 percent when compared with 1999 figures. . . .

- Nationwide, more than $6.4 billion was lost to motor vehicle thefts in 2008. The average dollar loss per stolen vehicle was $6,751. . . .

- More than 72 percent (72.4) of all motor vehicles reported stolen in 2008 were automobiles. . . .

ARSON

Definition

The FBI's Uniform Crime Reporting (UCR) Program defines arson as any willful or malicious burning or attempting to burn, with or without intent to defraud, a dwelling house, public building, motor vehicle or aircraft, personal property of another, etc.

Data Collection

Only the fires that investigation determined to have been willfully set—not fires labeled as suspicious or of unknown origin—are included in this arson data collection. . . .

Overview

- Nationally, 62,807 arson offenses were reported by 14,011 law enforcement agencies that provided 1–12 months of arson data in 2008. Of those agencies, 13,980 provided expanded offense data concerning 56,972 arsons.

- Arsons involving structures (residential, storage, public, etc.) accounted for 43.4 percent of the total number of arson offenses; arsons involving mobile property accounted for 28.9 percent; and other types of property (such as crops, timber, fences, etc.) accounted for 27.7 percent of reported arsons.

- The average dollar loss per arson offense was $16,015.

- Arsons of industrial/manufacturing structures resulted in the highest average dollar losses (an average of $212,388 per offense).

- In 2008, arson offenses decreased 3.6 percent when compared with the 2007 number. . . .

- Nationwide, the rate of arson was 24.1 offenses for every 100,000 inhabitants. . . .

OFFENSES CLEARED

Within the FBI's Uniform Crime Reporting (UCR) Program, law enforcement agencies can clear, or "close," offenses in one of two ways: by arrest or by exceptional means. Although agencies may administratively close a case, it does not necessarily mean that the agency can clear the offense for UCR purposes. To clear an offense within the Program's guidelines, the reporting agency must adhere to certain criteria, which are outlined in the following text. . . .

Clearances Involving Only Persons Under 18 Years of Age

When an offender under the age of 18 is cited to appear in juvenile court or before other juvenile authorities, the UCR Program considers the incident for which the juvenile is being held responsible to be cleared by arrest, even though a physical arrest may not have occurred. When clearances involve both juvenile and adult offenders, those incidents are classified as clearances for crimes committed by adults. Because the clearance percentages for crimes committed by juveniles include only those clearances in which no adults were involved, the figures in this publication should not be used to present a definitive picture of juvenile involvement in crime.

Overview

- In 2008, 45.1 percent of violent crimes and 17.4 percent of property crimes nationwide were cleared by arrest or exceptional means.

- Of the violent crimes of murder and nonnegligent manslaughter, forcible rape, robbery, and aggravated assault, murder had the highest percentage—63.6 percent—of offenses cleared.

- Of the property crimes of burglary, larceny-theft, and motor vehicle theft, larceny-theft was the offense most often cleared with 19.9 percent cleared by arrest or exceptional means.

- Nationwide in 2008, 38.2 percent of arson offenses cleared by arrest or exceptional means involved juveniles (persons under age 18), the highest percentage of all offense clearances involving only juveniles. . . .

Arrests

Definition

The FBI's Uniform Crime Reporting (UCR) Program counts one arrest for each separate instance in which a person is arrested, cited, or summoned for an offense. The UCR Program collects arrest data on 29 offenses, as described in Offense Definitions. Because a person may be arrested multiple times during a year, the UCR arrest figures do not reflect the number of individuals who have been arrested. Rather, the arrest data show the number of times that persons are arrested, as reported by law enforcement agencies to the UCR Program.

Data Collection—Juveniles

The UCR Program considers a juvenile to be an individual under 18 years of age regardless of state definition. The program does not collect data regarding police contact with a juvenile who has not committed an offense, nor does it collect data on situations in which police take a juvenile into custody for his or her protection, e.g., neglect cases.

Overview

- The FBI estimated that 14,005,615 arrests occurred in 2008 for all offenses (except traffic violations). Of these arrests, 594,911 were for violent crimes and 1,687,345 were for property crimes.

- The most frequent arrests made in 2008 were for drug abuse violations (estimated at 1,702,537 arrests). These arrests comprised 12.2 percent of the total number of all arrests.

- The rate of arrests was estimated at 4,637.7 arrests per 100,000 inhabitants in 2008. The arrest rate for violent crime was 198.2 per 100,000 inhabitants, and the arrest rate for property crime was 565.2 per 100,000 inhabitants.

- Violent crime arrests in 2008 declined 0.6 percent when compared with 2007 arrest data.

- Arrests for property crime increased 5.6 percent in 2008 when compared with the 2007 arrests.

- Arrests of juveniles decreased 2.8 percent in 2008 when compared with the 2007 number; arrests of adults declined 1.3 percent.

- Arrests of males accounted for the following: 75.5 percent of all persons arrested; 81.7 percent of persons arrested for violent crime; and 65.2 percent of persons arrested for property crime.

- In 2008, 69.2 percent of all persons arrested were white; 28.3 percent were black; and the remaining 2.4 percent were of other races. . . .

Hate Crimes

Incidents and Offenses

The Uniform Crime Reporting (UCR) Program collects data about both single-bias and multiple-bias hate crime incidents. For each offense type reported, law enforcement must indicate at least one bias motivation. A single-bias incident is defined as an incident in which one or more offense types are motivated by the same bias. A multiple-bias incident is defined as an incident in which more than one offense type occurs and at least two offense types are motivated by different biases.

- In 2008, 13,690 law enforcement agencies submitted hate crime data to the UCR Program. Of these agencies, 2,145 reported 7,783 hate crime incidents involving 9,168 offenses.

- Of the 7,783 reported incidents, 7,780 were single-bias and involved 9,160 offenses, 9,683 victims, and 6,921 offenders.

- The 3 multiple—bias incidents reported in 2008 involved 8 offenses, 8 victims, and 6 offenders. . . .

Single-bias Incidents

Of the 7,780 single-bias incidents reported in 2008:

- 51.3 percent were racially motivated.

- 19.5 percent were motivated by religious bias.

- 16.7 percent stemmed from sexual-orientation bias.

- 11.5 percent resulted from ethnicity/national origin bias.

- 1.0 percent were motivated by disability bias. . . .

Offenses by Bias Motivation within Incidents

There were 9,160 single-bias hate crime offenses reported in the above incidents. Of these:

- 51.4 percent stemmed from racial bias.

- 17.7 percent were motivated by sexual-orientation bias.

- 17.5 percent resulted from religious bias.

- 12.5 percent were motivated by ethnicity/national origin bias.

- 0.9 percent resulted from biases against disabilities. . . .

SOURCE: Federal Bureau of Investigation. "Crime in the United States 2008." September 14, 2009. www.fbi.gov/ucr/cius2008/index.html.

OTHER HISTORIC DOCUMENTS OF INTEREST

FROM THIS VOLUME

- Hate Crimes Bill Becomes Law, p. 502

FROM PREVIOUS *HISTORIC DOCUMENTS*

Federal Reserve Board Chair Announces End of Recession

SEPTEMBER 15, 2009

What was widely considered the worst economic recession since the Great Depression of the 1930s officially ended on September 15, 2009, according to Federal Reserve chair Ben Bernanke. Bernanke spoke on the one-year anniversary of the collapse of financial giant Lehman Brothers, which had been blamed for causing economic panic around the world. Although Bernanke told listeners that it was "very likely" the United States was seeing the end of this recession, he cautioned that it would still take time for the unemployment numbers to drop and individual Americans to begin seeing their personal economic situation improve. "Even though from a technical perspective the recession is very likely over at this point, it's still going to feel like a very weak economy for some time as many people will still find that their job security and their employment status is not what they wish it was. That's a challenge for us and all policy makers going forward," Bernanke said in response to a question after his September 15 speech.

The Federal Reserve, or Fed, worked to improve the economy by cutting key interest rates to near-zero levels. The Fed also bought mortgage-related securities and long-term debt from the Treasury to encourage economic growth. Bernanke had previously spoken positively about the economy in August 2009, when he said that there were indications that the market might have begun an upswing.

ECONOMIC INDICATORS

In economic terms, two quarters of negative growth indicates a recession. The United States, until September 2009, had seen four quarters of negative growth, meaning that the economy was shrinking. When the shrinking stopped in the third quarter of 2009, economists could say, at least from the perspective of economic growth, that the recession had ended.

According to Bernanke, he and other economists were forecasting only moderate growth for the fourth quarter of 2009 and into 2010, because it would take time for jobs to come back and for consumers to regain confidence, two vital indicators needed to fix the credit market. Without more money exchanging hands, recovery would continue to be slow. "The general view of forecasters is that growth in 2010 will be moderate, less than you might expect given the depth of the recession," Bernanke said.

In his September 2009 remarks, Bernanke reminded listeners that despite growth for the first time in four quarters, recovery might not be as quick or as strong as the country would like. However, he said, it could be faster than expected. "There are risks on both sides of that forecast," said Bernanke. "But if we do in fact see moderate growth, but not growth much more than the underlying potential growth rate, then unfortunately, unemployment will be slow to come down." At the time of Bernanke's speech, unemployment was at 9.7 percent, a twenty-six-year high.

Economists said that there had been some bright spots involving growth in the retail sector of the economy, specifically the Cash for Clunkers program, in which Americans were encouraged to trade in old cars and get a rebate toward a more fuel efficient model. From July to August 2009, automobile and automobile parts sales jumped 10.6 percent. Some hints of consumer confidence were also seen as discretionary spending on nonessential items and dining out rose 0.3 percent from July to August 2009. This was the largest increase seen in the nonessential items category over the previous six months. However, retail sales were still more than 5 percent lower than in 2008, and retailers were projecting further decreases. According to Rosalind Wells, chief economist of the National Retail Federation, "[S]hoppers were a bit more comfortable digging into their wallets [in August], and retailers are hopeful that we've turned a corner. It is encouraging to see some momentum building as retailers anticipate the all-important holiday season." Unfortunately, after the holiday season, retailers reported spending that was lower than in 2008. Some economists and retail experts had expected this, as families used programs, such as Cash for Clunkers, to make purchases they may otherwise have held off on, which meant they would have to cut back on other purchases, such as holiday gifts.

Although the stock market surged on Bernanke's announcement, and the Department of Commerce reported that the Cash for Clunkers program had brought car sales their largest monthly increase since January 2006, politicians were cautious, realizing that an economic indication of the end of a recession does not translate into much for families losing their homes and jobs.

POLITICAL IMPACT

People in Washington, D.C., had a different view of the end of the recession. Many members of Congress were facing reelection in 2010 and had to contend with constituents who were seeing little improvement in their own economic situation. According to political analysts, when politicians focus on economic indicators that do not necessarily translate well in citizens' lives, they put themselves in a politically dangerous situation. Voters often punish lawmakers at the ballot box for not improving a situation that by all economic indications has begun improving. This was a problem for President George H.W. Bush during his reelection campaign in 1992. In 1991 the United States experienced two quarters of economic decline, but it stopped before the end of the year. Bush's economic advisers told him that the economy was recovering, and he told voters, but they were unwilling to believe—or reelect—him because their personal economic situation had not improved.

In addition, with the increasing number of stimulus programs, projects, and money flowing from the federal government, there was the lingering question about when these programs should end. Secretary of the Treasury Timothy Geithner cautioned officials that ending any program too early could throw the economy quickly back into recession. Bernanke agreed. In fact, both appeared to heed the message of historians who pointed out that when federal programs ended early in the 1930s during the Great Depression, it led to greater problems later in the decade. On the other hand, there were economists who said that if the federal government waited too long to begin scaling back these spending programs, it could lead to inflation, which also would hurt the already damaged economy.

As these programs begin to wind down and if the Fed continues to keep interest rates low, there is some expectation that the cost of borrowing could go up, not only for the government but also for individuals. This would drive the already sky-high deficit higher and slow the return of consumer confidence.

Given the large federal government deficit, Republicans attacked Democrats on Capitol Hill for increasing spending through stimulus and other programs and criticized the president for continuously touting a spending program that they said had yet to produce the results promised. During his speech, however, Bernanke defended the programs, calling them necessary to the recovery the economy was seeing. "Without these speedy and forceful actions," said Bernanke, "last October's panic would likely have continued to intensify, more major financial firms would have failed, and the entire global financial system would have been at serious risk." He added that there is no way to know whether the economy would have recovered without the federal government's intervention. But, he added, "what we know about the effects of financial crises suggests that the resulting global downturn could have been extraordinarily deep and protracted."

Although President Barack Obama inherited an already declining economy when he took office in 2009, he was held responsible by U.S. citizens for fixing it quickly. Despite starting his administration with the highest approval rating since John F. Kennedy, Obama's approval numbers dropped from an all-time high of 69 percent immediately after his inauguration to the mid-50s, which could reflect poorly on his party in Congress in the 2010 midterm elections. Any referendum on the president's party at the ballot box, or backpedaling by members of Congress to appease voters, could hurt the president's chances at securing health care reform and success on other programs he has pushed for, including those focusing on energy and the environment.

President Obama's economic team has worked to portray the president as being a man of the people who understands the economic plight of the country. Geithner, during a congressional hearing, called unemployment levels "unacceptably high." Rather than focusing on the minimal economic growth, he said, "For every person out of work, for every family facing foreclosure, for every small business facing a credit crunch, the recession remains alive and acute."

Before Bernanke's announcement, the Obama administration had been pushing for an overhaul of financial regulation in the United State, releasing an eighty-nine-page proposal that included direction to assist consumers in the event of another crisis, strengthen the international economy, and impose additional regulations on financial markets and financial firms. Bernanke, when asked about the program after his announcement, said, "I feel quite confident that a comprehensive reform will be forthcoming. This has just been too big a calamity and too serious a problem, and clearly regulatory problems were part of it." Bernanke indicated that he supported the creation of a resolution authority, one idea circulating in Congress, that would work with financial firms on the verge of collapse that are large enough to have an impact on the economy as a whole. This power would rest not with the Fed but with the Federal Deposit Insurance Corporation, which currently oversees bad banks, those that hold on to toxic assets.

—Heather Kerrigan

Following is a speech given by Federal Reserve chair Ben Bernanke on September 15, 2009, on the economic situation in the United States.

Federal Reserve Chair Bernanke on the U.S. Economy

September 15, 2009

[All footnotes have been omitted.]

By the standards of recent decades, the economic environment at the time of this symposium one year ago was quite challenging. A year after the onset of the current crisis in August 2007, financial markets remained stressed, the economy was slowing, and inflation—-driven by a global commodity boom—had risen significantly. What we could not fully appreciate when we last gathered here was that the economic and policy environment was about to become vastly more difficult. In the weeks that followed, several systemically critical financial institutions would either fail or come close to failure, activity in some key financial markets would virtually cease, and the global economy would enter a deep recession. My remarks this morning will focus on the extraordinary financial and economic events of the past year, as well as on the policy responses both in the United States and abroad.

One very clear lesson of the past year—no surprise, of course, to any student of economic history, but worth noting nonetheless—is that a full-blown financial crisis can exact an enormous toll in both human and economic terms. A second lesson—once again, familiar to economic historians—is that financial disruptions do not respect borders. The crisis has been global, with no major country having been immune.

History is full of examples in which the policy responses to financial crises have been slow and inadequate, often resulting ultimately in greater economic damage and increased fiscal costs. In this episode, by contrast, policymakers in the United States and around the globe responded with speed and force to arrest a rapidly deteriorating and dangerous situation. Looking forward, we must urgently address structural weaknesses in the financial system, in particular in the regulatory framework, to ensure that the enormous costs of the past two years will not be borne again.

SEPTEMBER–OCTOBER 2008: THE CRISIS INTENSIFIES

When we met last year, financial markets and the economy were continuing to suffer the effects of the ongoing crisis. We know now that the National Bureau of Economic Research has determined December 2007 as the beginning of the recession. The U.S. unemployment rate had risen to 5–3/4 percent by July, about 1 percentage point above its level at the beginning of the crisis, and household spending was weakening. Ongoing declines in residential construction and house prices and rising mortgage defaults and foreclosures continued to weigh on the U.S. economy, and forecasts of prospective credit losses at financial institutions both here and abroad continued to increase. Indeed, one of the nation's largest thrift institutions, IndyMac, had recently collapsed under the weight of distressed mortgages, and investors continued to harbor doubts about the condition of the government-sponsored enterprises (GSEs) Fannie Mae and Freddie Mac, despite the approval by the Congress of open-ended support for the two firms.

Notwithstanding these significant concerns, however, there was little to suggest that market participants saw the financial situation as about to take a sharp turn for the worse.

For example, although indicators of default risk such as interest rate spreads and quotes on credit default swaps remained well above historical norms, most such measures had declined from earlier peaks, in some cases by substantial amounts. And in early September, when the target for the federal funds rate was 2 percent, investors appeared to see little chance that the federal funds rate would be below 1–3/4 percent six months later. That is, as of this time last year, market participants evidently believed it improbable that significant additional monetary policy stimulus would be needed in the United States.

Nevertheless, shortly after our last convocation, the financial crisis intensified dramatically. Despite the steps that had been taken to support Fannie Mae and Freddie Mac, their condition continued to worsen. In early September, the companies' regulator placed both into conservatorship, and the Treasury used its recently enacted authority to provide the firms with massive financial support.

Shortly thereafter, several additional large U.S. financial firms also came under heavy pressure from creditors, counterparties, and customers. The Federal Reserve has consistently maintained the view that the disorderly failure of one or more systemically important institutions in the context of a broader financial crisis could have extremely adverse consequences for both the financial system and the economy. We have therefore spared no effort, within our legal authorities and in appropriate cooperation with other agencies, to avert such a failure. The case of the investment bank Lehman Brothers proved exceptionally difficult, however. Concerted government attempts to find a buyer for the company or to develop an industry solution proved unavailing, and the company's available collateral fell well short of the amount needed to secure a Federal Reserve loan of sufficient size to meet its funding needs. As the Federal Reserve cannot make an unsecured loan, and as the government as a whole lacked appropriate resolution authority or the ability to inject capital, the firm's failure was, unfortunately, unavoidable. The Federal Reserve and the Treasury were compelled to focus instead on mitigating the fallout from the failure, for example, by taking measures to stabilize the triparty repurchase (repo) market.

In contrast, in the case of the insurance company American International Group (AIG), the Federal Reserve judged that the company's financial and business assets were adequate to secure an $85 billion line of credit, enough to avert its imminent failure. Because AIG was counterparty to many of the world's largest financial firms, a significant borrower in the commercial paper market and other public debt markets, and a provider of insurance products to tens of millions of customers, its abrupt collapse likely would have intensified the crisis substantially further, at a time when the U.S. authorities had not yet obtained the necessary fiscal resources to deal with a massive systemic event.

The failure of Lehman Brothers and the near-failure of AIG were dramatic but hardly isolated events. Many prominent firms struggled to survive as confidence plummeted. The investment bank Merrill Lynch, under pressure in the wake of Lehman's failure, agreed to be acquired by Bank of America; the major thrift institution Washington Mutual was resolved by the Federal Deposit Insurance Corporation (FDIC) in an assisted transaction; and the large commercial bank Wachovia, after experiencing severe liquidity outflows, agreed to be sold. The two largest remaining free-standing investment banks, Morgan Stanley and Goldman Sachs, were stabilized when the Federal Reserve approved, on an emergency basis, their applications to become bank holding companies.

Nor were the extraordinary pressures on financial firms during September and early October confined to the United States: For example, on September 18, the U.K. mortgage lender HBOS, with assets of more than $1 trillion, was forced to merge with Lloyds TSB.

On September 29, the governments of Belgium, Luxembourg, and the Netherlands effectively nationalized Fortis, a banking and insurance firm that had assets of around $1 trillion. The same day, German authorities provided assistance to Hypo Real Estate, a large commercial real estate lender, and the British government nationalized another mortgage lender, Bradford and Bingley. On the next day, September 30, the governments of Belgium, France, and Luxembourg injected capital into Dexia, a bank with assets of more than $700 billion, and the Irish government guaranteed the deposits and most other liabilities of six large Irish financial institutions. Soon thereafter, the Icelandic government, lacking the resources to rescue the three largest banks in that country, put them into receivership and requested assistance from the International Monetary Fund (IMF) and from other Nordic governments. In mid-October, the Swiss authorities announced a rescue package for UBS, one of the world's largest banks, that consisted of a capital injection and a purchase of assets. The growing pressures were not limited to banks with significant exposure to U.S. or U.K real estate or to securitized assets. For example, unsubstantiated rumors circulated in late September that some large Swedish banks were having trouble rolling over wholesale deposits, and on October 13 the Swedish government announced measures to guarantee bank debt and to inject capital into banks.

The rapidly worsening crisis soon spread beyond financial institutions into the money and capital markets more generally. As a result of losses on Lehman's commercial paper, a prominent money market mutual fund announced on September 16 that it had "broken the buck"—that is, its net asset value had fallen below $1 per share. Over the subsequent several weeks, investors withdrew more than $400 billion from so-called prime money funds. Conditions in short-term funding markets, including the interbank market and the commercial paper market, deteriorated sharply. Equity prices fell precipitously, and credit risk spreads jumped. The crisis also began to affect countries that had thus far escaped its worst effects. Notably, financial markets in emerging market economies were whipsawed as a flight from risk led capital inflows to those countries to swing abruptly to outflows.

The Policy Response

Authorities in the United States and around the globe moved quickly to respond to this new phase of the crisis, although the details differed according to the character of financial systems. The financial system of the United States gives a much greater role to financial markets and to nonbank financial institutions than is the case in most other nations, which rely primarily on banks. Thus, in the United States, a wider variety of policy measures was needed than in some other nations.

In the United States, the Federal Reserve established new liquidity facilities with the goal of restoring basic functioning in various critical markets. Notably, on September 19, the Fed announced the creation of a facility aimed at stabilizing money market mutual funds, and the Treasury unveiled a temporary insurance program for those funds. On October 7, the Fed announced the creation of a backstop commercial paper facility, which stood ready to lend against highly rated commercial paper for a term of three months. Together, these steps helped stem the massive outflows from the money market mutual funds and stabilize the commercial paper market.

During this period, foreign commercial banks were a source of heavy demand for U.S. dollar funding, thereby putting additional strain on global bank funding markets, including U.S. markets, and further squeezing credit availability in the United States. To address this problem, the Federal Reserve expanded the temporary swap lines that had been established earlier with the European Central Bank (ECB) and the Swiss National Bank, and established new temporary swap lines with seven other central banks in September and five more in late October, including four in emerging market economies. In further coordinated action, on October 8, the Federal Reserve and five other major central banks simultaneously cut their policy rates by 50 basis points.

The failure of Lehman Brothers demonstrated that liquidity provision by the Federal Reserve would not be sufficient to stop the crisis; substantial fiscal resources were necessary. On October 3, on the recommendation of the Administration and with the strong support of the Federal Reserve, the Congress approved the creation of the Troubled Asset Relief Program, or TARP, with a maximum authorization of $700 billion to support the stabilization of the U.S. financial system.

Markets remained highly volatile and pressure on financial institutions intense through the first weeks of October. On October 10, in what would prove to be a watershed in the global policy response, the Group of Seven (G-7) finance ministers and central bank governors, meeting in Washington, committed in a joint statement to work together to stabilize the global financial system. In particular, they agreed to prevent the failure of systemically important financial institutions; to ensure that financial institutions had adequate access to funding and capital, including public capital if necessary; and to put in place deposit insurance and other guarantees to restore the confidence of depositors. In the following days, many countries around the world announced comprehensive rescue plans for their banking systems that built on the G-7 principles. To stabilize funding, during October more than 20 countries expanded their deposit insurance programs, and many also guaranteed nondeposit liabilities of banks. In addition, amid mounting concerns about the solvency of the global banking system, by the end of October more than a dozen countries had announced plans to inject public capital into banks, and several announced plans to purchase or guarantee bank assets. The comprehensive U.S. response, announced on October 14, included capital injections into both large and small banks by the Treasury; a program which allowed banks and bank holding companies, for a fee, to issue FDIC-guaranteed senior debt; the extension of deposit insurance to all noninterest-bearing transactions deposits, of any size; and the Federal Reserve's continued commitment to provide liquidity as necessary to stabilize key financial institutions and markets.

This strong and unprecedented international policy response proved broadly effective. Critically, it averted the imminent collapse of the global financial system, an outcome that seemed all too possible to the finance ministers and central bankers that gathered in Washington on October 10. However, although the intensity of the crisis moderated and the risk of systemic collapse declined in the wake of the policy response, financial conditions remained highly stressed. For example, although short-term funding spreads in global markets began to turn down in October, they remained elevated into this year. And, although generalized pressures on financial institutions subsided some-what, government actions to prevent the disorderly failures of individual, systemically significant institutions continued to be necessary. In the United States, support packages were announced for Citigroup in November and Bank of America in January. Broadly similar support packages were also announced for some large European institutions, including firms in the United Kingdom and the Netherlands.

Although concerted policy actions avoided much worse outcomes, the financial shocks of September and October nevertheless severely damaged the global economy—starkly illustrating the potential effects of financial stress on real economic activity. In the fourth quarter of 2008 and the first quarter of this year, global economic activity recorded its weakest performance in decades. In the United States, real GDP plummeted at nearly a 6 percent average annual pace over those two quarters—an even sharper decline than had occurred in the 1981–82 recession. Economic activity contracted even more precipitously in many foreign economies, with real GDP dropping at double-digit annual rates in some cases. The crisis affected economic activity not only by pushing down asset prices and tightening credit conditions, but also by shattering household and business confidence around the world.

In response to these developments, the Federal Reserve expended the remaining ammunition in the traditional arsenal of monetary policy, bringing the federal funds rate down, in steps, to a target range of 0 to 25 basis points by mid-December of last year. It also took several measures to further supplement its traditional arsenal. In particular, on November 25, the Fed announced that it would purchase up to $100 billion of debt issued by the housing-related GSEs and up to $500 billion of agency-guaranteed mortgage-backed securities, programs that were expanded substantially and augmented by a program of purchases of Treasury securities in March. The goal of these purchases was to provide additional support to private credit markets, particularly the mortgage market. Also on November 25, the Fed announced the creation of the Term Asset-Backed Securities Loan Facility (TALF). This facility aims to improve the availability and affordability of credit for households and small businesses and to help facilitate the financing and refinancing of commercial real estate properties. The TALF has shown early success in reducing risk spreads and stimulating new securitization activity for assets included in the program.

Foreign central banks also cut policy rates to very low levels and implemented unconventional monetary measures. For example, the Bank of Japan began purchasing commercial paper in December and corporate bonds in January. In March, the Bank of England announced that it would purchase government securities, commercial paper, and corporate bonds, and the Swiss National Bank announced that it would purchase corporate bonds and foreign currency. For its part, the ECB injected more than €400 billion of one-year funds in a single auction in late June. In July, the ECB began purchasing covered bonds, which are bonds that are issued by financial institutions and guaranteed by specific asset pools. Actions by central banks augmented large fiscal stimulus packages in the United States, China, and a number of other countries.

On February 10, Treasury Secretary Geithner and the heads of the federal banking agencies unveiled the outlines of a new strategy for ensuring that banking institutions could continue to provide credit to households and businesses during the financial crisis. A central component of that strategy was the exercise that came to be known as the bank stress test. Under this initiative, the banking regulatory agencies undertook a forward-looking, simultaneous evaluation of the capital positions of 19 of the largest bank holding companies in the United States, with the Treasury committing to provide public capital as needed. The goal of this supervisory assessment was to ensure that the equity capital held by these firms was sufficient—in both quantity and quality—to allow those institutions to withstand a worse-than-expected macroeconomic environment over the subsequent two years and yet remain healthy and capable of lending to creditworthy borrowers. This exercise, unprecedented in scale and scope, was led by the Federal Reserve in cooperation with the Office of the Comptroller of the Currency and the FDIC. Importantly, the agencies' report made public considerable information on the projected losses and revenues of the 19 firms, allowing private analysts to judge for themselves the credibility of the exercise. Financial market participants responded favorably to the announcement of the results, and many of the tested banks were subsequently able to tap public capital markets.

Overall, the policy actions implemented in recent months have helped stabilize a number of key financial markets, both in the United States and abroad. Short-term funding markets are functioning more normally, corporate bond issuance has been strong, and activity in some previously moribund securitization markets has picked up. Stock prices have partially recovered, and U.S. mortgage rates have declined markedly since last fall. Critically, fears of financial collapse have receded substantially. After contracting sharply over the past year, economic activity appears to be leveling out, both in the United States and abroad, and the prospects for a return to growth in the near term appear good. Notwithstanding this noteworthy progress, critical challenges remain: Strains persist in many financial markets across the globe, financial institutions face significant additional losses, and many businesses and households continue to experience considerable difficulty gaining access to credit. Because of these and other factors, the economic recovery is likely to be relatively slow at first, with unemployment declining only gradually from high levels.

INTERPRETING THE CRISIS: ELEMENTS OF A CLASSIC PANIC

How should we interpret the extraordinary events of the past year, particularly the sharp intensification of the financial crisis in September and October? Certainly, fundamentals played a critical role in triggering those events. As I noted earlier, the economy was already in recession, and it had weakened further over the summer. The continuing dramatic decline in house prices and rising rates of foreclosure raised serious concerns about the values of mortgage-related assets, and thus about large potential losses at financial institutions. More broadly, investors remained distrustful of virtually all forms of private credit, especially structured credit products and other complex or opaque instruments.

At the same time, however, the events of September and October also exhibited some features of a classic panic, of the type described by Bagehot [a British businessman who wrote extensively about financial crisis] and many others. A panic is a generalized run by providers of short-term funding to a set of financial institutions, possibly resulting in the failure of one or more of those institutions. The historically most familiar type of panic, which involves runs on banks by retail depositors, has been made largely obsolete by deposit insurance or guarantees and the associated government supervision of banks. But a panic is possible in any situation in which longer-term, illiquid assets are financed by short-term, liquid liabilities, and in which suppliers of short-term funding either lose confidence in the borrower or become worried that other short-term lenders may lose confidence. Although, in a certain sense, a panic may be collectively irrational, it may be entirely rational at the individual level, as each market participant has a strong incentive to be among the first to the exit.

Panics arose in multiple contexts last year. For example, many financial institutions, notably including the independent investment banks, financed a portion of their assets through short-term repo agreements. In repo agreements, the asset being financed serves as collateral for the loan, and the maximum amount of the loan is the current assessed value of the collateral less a haircut. In a crisis, haircuts typically rise as short-term lenders attempt to protect themselves from possible declines in asset prices. But this individually rational behavior can set off a run-like dynamic: As high haircuts make financing portfolios more difficult, some borrowers may have no option but to sell assets into illiquid markets. These forced sales drive down asset prices, increase volatility, and weaken the financial positions of all holders of similar assets, which in turn increases the risks borne by repo lenders and thus the haircuts they demand. This unstable dynamic was apparent around the time of the near-failure of Bear Stearns in March 2008, and haircuts rose particularly sharply during the worsening of the crisis in mid-September. As we saw last fall, when a vicious funding spiral of this sort is at work, falling asset prices and the collapse of lender confidence may create financial contagion, even between firms without significant counterparty relationships. In such an environment, the line between insolvency and illiquidity may be quite blurry.

Panic-like phenomena occurred in other contexts as well. Structured investment vehicles and other asset-backed programs that relied heavily on the commercial paper market began to have difficulty rolling over their short-term funding very early in the crisis, forcing them to look to bank sponsors for liquidity or to sell assets. Following the Lehman collapse, panic gripped the money market mutual funds and the commercial paper market, as I have discussed. More generally, during the crisis runs of uninsured creditors have created severe funding problems for a number of financial firms. In some cases, runs by creditors were augmented by other types of "runs"—for example, by prime brokerage customers of investment banks concerned about the funds they held in margin accounts. Overall, the role played by panic helps to explain the remarkably sharp and sudden intensification of the financial crisis last fall, its rapid global spread, and the fact that the abrupt deterioration in financial conditions was largely unforecasted by standard market indicators.

The view that the financial crisis had elements of a classic panic, particularly during its most intense phases, has helped to motivate a number of the Federal Reserve's policy actions. Bagehot instructed central banks—the only institutions that have the power to increase the aggregate liquidity in the system—to respond to panics by lending freely against sound collateral. Following that advice, from the beginning of the crisis the Fed (like other central banks) has provided large amounts of short-term liquidity to financial institutions. As I have discussed, it also provided backstop liquidity support for money market mutual funds and the commercial paper market and added significant liquidity to the system through purchases of longer-term securities. To be sure, the provision of liquidity alone can by no means solve the problems of credit risk and credit losses; but it can reduce liquidity premiums, help restore the confidence of investors, and thus promote stability. It is noteworthy that the use of Fed liquidity facilities has declined sharply since the beginning of the year—a clear market signal that liquidity pressures are easing and market conditions are normalizing.

What does this perspective on the crisis imply for future policies and regulatory reforms? We have seen during the past two years that the complex interrelationships among credit, market, and funding risks of key players in financial markets can have far-reaching implications, particularly during a general crisis of confidence. In particular, the experience has underscored that liquidity risk management is as essential as capital adequacy and credit and market risk management, particularly during times of intense financial stress. Both the Basel Committee on Banking Supervision and the U.S. bank regulatory agencies have recently issued guidelines for strengthening liquidity risk management at financial institutions. Among other objectives, liquidity guidelines must take into account the risks that inadequate liquidity planning by major financial firms pose for the broader financial system, and they must ensure that these firms do not become excessively reliant on liquidity support from the central bank.

But liquidity risk management at the level of the firm, no matter how carefully done, can never fully protect against systemic events. In a sufficiently severe panic, funding problems will almost certainly arise and are likely to spread in unexpected ways. Only central banks are well positioned to offset the ensuing sharp decline in liquidity and credit provision by the private sector. They must be prepared to do so.

The role of liquidity in systemic events provides yet another reason why, in the future, a more systemwide or macroprudential approach to regulation is needed. The hallmark of a macroprudential approach is its emphasis on the interdependencies among firms and markets that have the potential to undermine the stability of the financial system, including the linkages that arise through short-term funding markets and other counterparty relationships, such as over-the-counter derivatives contracts. A comprehensive regulatory approach must examine those interdependencies as well as the financial conditions of individual firms in isolation.

Conclusion

Since we last met here, the world has been through the most severe financial crisis since the Great Depression. The crisis in turn sparked a deep global recession, from which we are only now beginning to emerge.

As severe as the economic impact has been, however, the outcome could have been decidedly worse. Unlike in the 1930s, when policy was largely passive and political divisions made international economic and financial cooperation difficult, during the past year monetary, fiscal, and financial policies around the world have been aggressive and complementary. Without these speedy and forceful actions, last October's panic would likely have continued to intensify, more major financial firms would have failed, and the entire global financial system would have been at serious risk. We cannot know for sure what the economic effects of these events would have been, but what we know about the effects of financial crises suggests that the resulting global downturn could have been extraordinarily deep and protracted.

Although we have avoided the worst, difficult challenges still lie ahead. We must work together to build on the gains already made to secure a sustained economic recovery, as well as to build a new financial regulatory framework that will reflect the lessons of this crisis and prevent a recurrence of the events of the past two years. I hope and expect that, when we meet here a year from now, we will be able to claim substantial progress toward both those objectives.

Source: Board of Governors of the Federal Reserve System. Testimony and speeches. "Reflections on a Year of Crisis." September 15, 2009. www.federalreserve.gov/newsevents/speech/bernanke20090821a.htm.

OTHER HISTORIC DOCUMENTS OF INTEREST

FROM THIS VOLUME

FROM PREVIOUS *HISTORIC DOCUMENTS*

The Department of Transportation and the Environmental Protection Agency Release New Fuel Economy Standards

SEPTEMBER 15, 2009

During the 2008 presidential campaign, Barack Obama promised that if elected he would work to lessen the effects of global climate change. On September 15, 2009, four months after announcing his intention to have the Environmental Protection Agency (EPA) and the Department of Transportation (DOT) draft new fuel economy standards in an effort to curb global warming attributed to the greenhouse effect, President Obama stood at a General Motors plant in Ohio to tell the crowd that he was moving forward on this agenda.

"We are launching—for the first time in history—a new national standard aimed at both increasing gas mileage and decreasing greenhouse gas pollution for all new cars and trucks sold in America. This action will give our auto companies some long-overdue clarity, stability and predictability. In the past, an agreement like this would have been impossible—but this time was different," he said.

The EPA and National Highway Traffic Safety Administration (NHTSA) on September 15, 2009, released a new set of fuel economy standards, the first in thirty years, that would help reduce greenhouse gas emissions, save consumers money at the pump, and decrease dependence on oil.

Climate change is one of the most pressing environmental issues today. Greenhouse gases, more than 28 percent of which are emitted by vehicles, trap heat within Earth's atmosphere, causing the temperature to rise. Although no one knows the precise effects global warming might precipitate, such changes could include heat waves, severe drought, wildfires, flooding, increasingly violent hurricanes feeding off warmer seas, and a significant rise in sea levels. All of these changes can damage ecosystems, animals, and crops.

Sixty percent of U.S. greenhouse gas emissions from vehicles are produced by light-duty vehicles—in other words, those weighing less than 8,500 pounds. These vehicles are regulated by the new standards, but heavy-duty vehicles, including semitrucks and buses, are not.

Regulating the fuel efficiency of light-duty vehicles also helps decrease the U.S. dependence on oil, a goal of the United States since the 1970s, when oil prices rose sharply. In 2008, another oil crisis hit the United States, sending prices to more than $100 per barrel, which translated into gasoline prices at the pump of $4 and more per gallon, igniting a greater sense of urgency to reduce oil use. The light-duty vehicles being regulated by these standards account for 40 percent of all U.S. oil use.

Obama's Promise

In May 2009, President Obama, in a Rose Garden ceremony that included executives from ten major automakers, announced plans for new national fuel economy standards. The president's proposal came in part in response to the 2007 Supreme Court decision in *Massachusetts v. EPA,* in which the Court held that the EPA has the right to regulate greenhouse gas emissions because they are considered air pollutants for the purposes of the Clean Air Act, signed into law in 1970. President Obama called the decision to move forward with new fuel economy standards "an historic agreement to help America break its dependence on oil, reduce harmful pollution and begin the transition to a clean energy economy."

This initiative by President Obama is the first use of federal standards to reduce greenhouse gas emissions since passage of the Clean Air Act. The new standards, which would affect model years 2012 through 2016, include a requirement for automakers to gradually work toward an average gas mileage of 35.5 miles per gallon for cars and 30 miles per gallon for trucks by 2016. At the time of the president's announcement, fuel economy for all vehicles was set at an average of 25 miles per gallon.

Although many automakers had fought previous attempts to increase fuel efficiency, they joined President Obama in May and applauded his decision, recognizing that although it would cost billions to get light-duty fleet vehicles up to the new standards, it would mean that a national program would be in place, rather than a more unwieldy fifty-state patchwork. In part, auto manufacturers were motivated to participation by California's suit against the EPA in 2007 and 2008 in which the state sought the right to regulate the fuel economy standard of cars sold in California in an effort to control greenhouse gas emissions. Spokespersons on behalf of California argued that the Clean Air Act gave states the right to control emissions in whatever way they saw fit. Automakers, however, said that allowing California to have its own standards would translate into huge costs for them, because automakers in effect would be forced to make different cars for different states. After California's lawsuit, and victory in June 2009, thirteen other states and the District of Columbia lined up to adopt California standards as well. The U.S. Chamber of Commerce and the National Automobile Dealers Association filed a lawsuit with the U.S Circuit Court of Appeals in Washington, D.C., requesting that the court review the EPA's decision to allow California to regulate its own fuel economy standards; it was expected that this would be the first of many lawsuits challenging individual state emissions regulations, as well as the federal government's new standards.

President Obama's push for nationwide fuel economy standards that would protect automakers from a patchwork of standards while also reducing greenhouse gases was not the first of his climate change initiatives. He had been pressing Congress to pass a bill to limit all U.S. greenhouse gas emissions. Nations that had ratified the Kyoto protocol, the international agreement on climate change (signed by many industrialized nations but not the United States), had moved to cut theirs. By September, however, House majority leader Harry Reid informed the president and the nation that given the pressing issues on health care, Congress would not take up climate change until 2010.

Nevertheless, President Obama has worked to push the United States toward becoming a major player in combating climate change. The effort at increasing fuel efficiency and reducing emissions represented a step to which the administration could point before heading into UN-sponsored climate negotiations with 180 other nations in Copenhagen in December 2009. Before the Copenhagen summit, the administration hoped to have in place cap and trade legislation as well as the new emissions standards.

THE ENVIRONMENTAL PROTECTION AGENCY/ NATIONAL HIGHWAY TRAFFIC SAFETY ADMINISTRATION FUEL ECONOMY DECISION

The EPA and NHTSA's new standards were a second-phase response to the Supreme Court's 2007 decision in *Massachusetts v. EPA,* in which the Court held that it was the responsibility of the EPA to determine whether new vehicle emissions cause greenhouse gases that contribute to air pollution and whether those greenhouse gases are detrimental to human health. The first response from the EPA came in April 2009, when the agency proposed to find research that could support the negative health effects caused by greenhouse gas emissions as well as determining whether four gases—carbon dioxide, methane, nitrous oxide, and hydrofluorocarbons—emitted by new engines contributed to the level of greenhouse gases in the atmosphere. On December 7, 2009, the EPA released its findings in response to *Massachusetts v. EPA,* stating that greenhouses gases "threaten public health and welfare of current and future generations" and that motor vehicles contribute to this health-threatening pollution. At a press conference announcing the new fuel economy standards, Secretary of Transportation Ray LaHood said the new rules "would bring about a new era in automotive history." The standards put together by the EPA in cooperation with DOT would not go into effect until model year 2012, or October 2011, when the new model year begins. At this time, automakers would have to have begun increasing fuel mileage, with a goal of 35.5 miles per gallon for all light-duty vehicles by 2016. The light-duty vehicles covered by these new standards include passenger cars, light-duty trucks, and medium-duty passenger vehicles. In 2007 Congress had proposed similar standards, but with a goal of increasing fuel mileage by 2020. The EPA program would also limit the amount of carbon dioxide each light-duty vehicle could omit to 250 grams per mile per vehicle by 2016, compared to an average of 424 in model year 2008.

GOALS OF THE NEW PROGRAM

One goal of the new rules was to ensure that although car manufacturers would be required to institute new standards, American drivers would still be able fo afford a full line of vehicles. The expectation is that each car produced with advanced systems and additional equipment to make them more fuel efficient between model years 2012 and 2016 will cost approximately $1,000 more than previous model years. However, because these cars will be more fuel efficient, any consumer paying cash for their car would be able to cover the additional $1,000 within three years in savings on gas, assuming prices remain steady. More consumers pay for cars through credit, however, so with a typical five-year loan, the fuel savings to the consumer would outweigh the cost of a loan payment by $130 to $160 per year. This means that over the lifetime of a model year 2012–2016 vehicle, consumers would save approximately $3,000 in fuel—again, assuming steady gas prices.

"American drivers will keep more money in their pockets, put less pollution into the air, and help reduce a dependence on oil that sends billions of dollars out of our economy every year," said EPA administrator Lisa Jackson. "By bringing together a broad coalition of stakeholders—including an unprecedented partnership with American automakers—we have crafted a path forward that is win-win for our health, our environment, and our economy. Through that partnership, we've taken the historic step of proposing the nation's first ever greenhouse gas emissions standards for vehicles, and moved substantially closer to an efficient, clean energy future."

The new fuel economy and carbon dioxide emissions standards were expected to have a significant impact on the environment. According to White House reports, the plan will prevent 950 million metric tons of greenhouse gas emissions from entering the atmosphere. During the total lifetime of any vehicle purchased with new standards between 2012 and 2016, 1.8 billion barrels of oil will be saved, most of which comes from foreign sources. Carbon dioxide emissions will be reduced by 21 percent by 2030. Although there will be a cost of approximately $60 billion to manufacturers and the U.S. government to implement these new standards, the expected benefits could be greater than $250 billion.

Studies conducted by the EPA and the NHTSA indicate that there are many ways for auto manufacturers to comply with the new standards, including improving engines, transmissions, tires, air conditioners, and reducing the weight of each vehicle. In addition to these improvements, the EPA will give car manufacturers credit for producing more hybrid and electric vehicles. In earning credits by producing these vehicles, and also looking at total carbon dioxide emissions across an entire fleet, automakers will be able to trade credits from one vehicle type to another to meet the new requirements. Credits will be tradable among companies as well, but all credits will be phased out after model year 2015.

On hearing the announcement of new fuel economy standards, the National Auto Dealers Association said that although it supports a national fuel economy standard that would protect auto manufacturers from producing different cars for different states, the new rules could prove confusing. The Union of Concerned Scientists responded by calling on the government to carefully monitor the work of auto manufacturers to ensure that they were not trying to play the system. The Alliance of Automobile Manufacturers backed the new standards. "This is really the road map for automakers to follow," said Charlie Territo, a spokesperson for the group. On the opposite side automakers saw the move as a decrease in the uncertainty currently in the auto market when states are allowed to regulate their own emissions with a waiver under the Clean Air Act. President Obama agreed, saying that the new regulations would "give auto companies some long-overdue clarity, stability and predictability." The new standards are set to take effect in 2011; the EPA and the NHTSA were in the meantime to finalize the rules of the program, by March 31, 2010. Before the new rules go into effect, the EPA is required to review and finalize its findings that greenhouse gas emissions pose a danger to human health.

—Heather Kerrigan

Following is a press release from Secretary of Transportation Ray LaHood and EPA administrator Lisa Jackson on September 15, 2009, announcing new nationwide fuel economy standards.

Department of Transportation and Environmental Protection Agency Leaders Propose New National Fuel Economy Standards

September 15, 2009

U.S. Department of Transportation (DOT) Secretary Ray LaHood and U.S. Environmental Protection Agency (EPA) Administrator Lisa P. Jackson today jointly proposed a rule establishing an historic national program that would improve vehicle fuel economy and reduce greenhouse gases. Their proposal builds upon core principles President Obama announced with automakers, the United Auto Workers, leaders in the environmental community, governors and state officials in May, and would provide coordinated national vehicle fuel efficiency and emissions standards. The proposed program would also conserve billions of barrels of oil, save consumers money at the pump, increase fuel economy, and reduce millions of tons of greenhouse gas emissions.

"American drivers will keep more money in their pockets, put less pollution into the air, and help reduce a dependence on oil that sends billions of dollars out of our economy every year," said EPA Administrator Lisa P. Jackson. "By bringing together a broad coalition of stakeholders—including an unprecedented partnership with American automakers—we have crafted a path forward that is win-win for our health, our environment, and our economy. Through that partnership, we've taken the historic step of proposing the nation's first ever greenhouse gas emissions standards for vehicles, and moved substantially closer to an efficient, clean energy future."

"The increases in fuel economy and the reductions in greenhouse gases we are proposing today would bring about a new era in automotive history," Transportation Secretary Ray LaHood said. "These proposed standards would help consumers save money at the gas pump, help the environment, and decrease our dependence on oil—all while ensuring that consumers still have a full range of vehicle choices."

Under the proposed program, which covers model years 2012 through 2016, automobile manufacturers would be able to build a single, light-duty national fleet that satisfies all federal requirements as well as the standards of California and other states. The proposed program includes miles per gallon requirements under NHTSA's Corporate Average Fuel Economy Standards (CAFE) program and the first-ever national emissions standards under EPA's greenhouse gas program. The collaboration of federal agencies for this proposal also allows for clearer rules for all automakers, instead of three standards (DOT, EPA, and a state standard).

Specifically, the program would:

Increase fuel economy by approximately five percent every year

Reduce greenhouse gas emissions by nearly 950 million metric tons

Save the average car buyer more than $3,000 in fuel costs

Conserve 1.8 billion barrels of oil

Increase Fuel Economy and Reduce Carbon Dioxide Emissions:

The proposed national program would require model year 2016 vehicles to meet an estimated combined average emission level of 250 grams of carbon dioxide per mile. Under the proposed program, the overall light-duty vehicle fleet would reach 35.5 miles per gallon (mpg) in model year 2016, if all reductions were made through fuel economy improvements. If this occurs, Congress' fuel economy goal of 35.0 mpg by 2020 will be met four years ahead of schedule. This would surpass the CAFE law passed by Congress in 2007, which required an average fuel economy of 35 mpg in 2020.

Reduce Greenhouse Gases:

Climate change poses a significant long-term threat to America's environment. The vehicles subject to the proposed rules announced today are responsible for almost 60 percent of all U.S. transportation-related greenhouse gas emissions. These will be the nation's first ever national greenhouse gas standards. The proposed standards would require model year 2016 vehicles to meet an estimated combined average emission level of 250 grams of carbon dioxide per mile under EPA's greenhouse gas program. The combined EPA and NHTSA standards would reduce carbon dioxide emissions from the light-duty vehicle fleet by about 21 percent in 2030 over the level that would occur in the absence of any new greenhouse gas or fuel economy standards. The greenhouse gas emission reductions this program would bring about are equivalent to the emissions of 42 million cars.

Save Consumers Money:

NHTSA and EPA estimate that U.S. consumers who purchase their vehicle outright would save enough in lower fuel costs over the first three years to offset the increases in vehicle costs. Consumers would save more than $3,000 due to fuel savings over the lifetime of a model year 2016 vehicle.

Conserve Oil and Increase Energy Security:

The light-duty vehicles subject to this proposed National Program account for about 40 percent of all U.S. oil consumption. The program will provide important energy security benefits by conserving 1.8 billion barrels of oil, which is twice the amount of oil (crude oil and products) imported in 2008 from the Persian Gulf countries, according to the Department of Energy's Energy Information Administration Office. These standards also provide important energy security benefits as light-duty vehicles account for about 60 percent of transportation oil use.

Within the Auto Industry's Reach:

EPA and NHTSA have worked closely to develop this coordinated joint proposal and have met with many stakeholders including automakers to insure the standards proposed today are both aggressive and achievable given the current financial state of the auto industry.

NHTSA and EPA expect automobile manufacturers would meet these proposed standards by improving engine efficiency, transmissions and tires, as well as increasing the use of start-stop technology and improvements in air conditioning systems. EPA and NHTSA also anticipate that these standards would promote the more widespread use of advanced fuel-saving technologies like hybrid vehicles and clean diesel engines. . . .

SOURCE: Environmental Protection Agency. Press release. "DOT Secretary Ray LaHood and EPA Administrator Lisa P. Jackson Propose National Program to Improve Fuel Economy and Reduce Greenhouse Gases/New Interagency Program to Address Climate Change and Energy Security." September 15, 2009. http://yosemite.epa.gov/opa/admpress.nsf/6427a6b7538955c585257359003f0230/522d0a809f6b7f9c8525763200562534!OpenDocument.

OTHER HISTORIC DOCUMENTS OF INTEREST

FROM THIS VOLUME

- U.S. Department of Transportation's Cash for Clunkers Program, p. 356

FROM PREVIOUS HISTORIC DOCUMENTS

- California Sues the EPA over Emissions Standards, *2008*, p. 3
- President Bush on Gasoline Prices and Oil Dependence, *2006*, p. 140
- EPA Report on Global Warming, *2002*, p. 298

Democratic Party Wins Landmark Election in Japan

SEPTEMBER 16, 2009

On August 30, 2009, Japanese citizens dealt what many considered a final blow to a party that had held power mostly unchallenged since the 1950s. When Japanese voters went to the polls, they voted to end the reign of the Liberal Democratic party, which had won all but one election since the end of World War II, and install, in a landslide victory, the Democratic party, which promised to stop the economic decline that began the 1990s. The Democratic party won 308 of 480 seats in Japan's lower house, a 175 percent increase over the number of seats previously held by the party. The Democrats had gained control of the upper house in July 2007 amid growing discontent with the Liberal Democratic party. "This has been a revolutionary election," said Democratic party leader Yukio Hatoyama. "The people have shown the courage to take politics into their own hands." The election was considered less an endorsement of the Democratic party and more a referendum on the Liberal Democrats, who had held power for sixty-two of the previous sixty-three years. Some analysts in Japan said the defeat could be the end of the Liberal Democratic party in Japan.

Hatoyama's party campaigned to realign Japan with Asia, rather than continuing in what it considered a U.S.-dominated relationship. This raised the question of what would happen to the 50,000-strong U.S. military force on the island nation. The question of what to do with the air base located on Okinawa has long been a point of contention in U.S.-Japan relations, as many residents want the American forces gone, and the Japanese government has long advocated, although not forcefully, relocating the base.

After the election, Prime Minister Taro Aso, who had held his post since September 2008, announced his resignation, saying that he would accept full responsibility for the defeat of the Liberal Democratic party. Elections in Japan's Diet, or parliament, for a new prime minister were held September 16, 2009, and Hatoyama was chosen to lead the new government.

GROWING DISCONTENT WITH THE LIBERAL DEMOCRATS

In Japan, citizens had long expressed discontent with the Liberal Democratic party. However, the party had such a strong hold on the Diet that no other party had been able to make headway in an election, even though the Liberal Democrats had done little to stop Japan from slipping into economic stagnation and lacked a coherent approach to fixing Japan's most pressing problems and moving the country forward. In addition, over the previous three years, the Japanese had been extremely discontent with their leaders, with two prime ministers stepping down after less than a year on the job because of low approval ratings. From the start of his tenure as prime minister in September 2008, Aso was seen as out of touch with ordinary Japanese citizens, who were experiencing one of the worst economic climates since the 1970s oil crisis. Aso's political missteps and public gaffes had members of his own party criticizing his policies, including a proposal of $130 payments to each person in Japan that was largely considered no more than an attempt to buy popularity. Aso was also criticized for speaking publicly about drinking at expensive hotel bars while citizens struggled to make ends meet.

Five months into Aso's rule, his finance minister resigned after being videotaped in what many thought was a drunken stupor at a global economic summit news conference. The finance minister said he had taken too much cold medication. Following this incident, Liberal Democrats, recognizing that Aso was leading the least popular government in recent history, began calling for Aso's resignation, which he staunchly rejected. Masazumi Gotoda, a Liberal Democratic lawmaker, said, "The prime minister no longer has the ability, trust or integrity to manage the current political crisis." Aso's poll numbers fell to single digits, and the popularity of his party slipped to just under 27 percent. Some lawmakers continued to back Aso and the Liberal Democratic party, saying that it had faced unpopularity in the past and would simply redefine itself to remain in power. However, party leaders showed little or no ability to figure out a new way to govern.

Promises of the Democratic Party

The possibility of electing a new party to lead Japan brought 70 percent of eligible voters to the polls, the highest turnout in almost twenty years. Voters indicated that their participation was not about support for one party or the other, but displeasure with the way the country was being run. One voter, Akiki Tanaka, said, "If we keep going like we've been, nothing will get better. We need a new government."

The biggest challenge for the new government will be to maintain unity among its members, made up mostly of former Socialists and former Liberal Democrats. The only other non–Liberal Democratic government to lead postwar Japan took power in 1993 and lasted for eleven months before the party fell apart and new elections were held, putting Liberal Democrats back in power. Given the broad coalition of the Democratic party, there is an expectation that few radical changes will be made, at least in the near term, while the party forms a complete government and governing platform that ensures nearly total agreement among party members. This means that although the Democrats campaigned on changing the relationship between the United States and Japan, this promise may be put on hold while the new government attempts to shore up the economy. Japan has experienced growing unemployment, as well as increasing numbers of migrants drawing on the country's social services. The gap has widened between Japan's most affluent and least fortunate citizens.

In addition to the economy, the new government has promised to focus on fixing the social issues plaguing the nation, including its low birthrate. The Democrats have proposed giving families $270 per month per child to encourage families to grow. The aging population of Japan has been a serious drain on social service funding, something voters want to see changed but do not necessarily expect that this government can fix. Critics of the Liberal

Democrats had complained about the party's perceived focus on aiding corporations rather than citizens, something the Democrats have promised to change. Hatoyama's party promised to increase the availability of welfare funds, especially because nearly one-third of Japanese citizens are now pensioners. The growing number of pensioners will increase the drain on the economy with less tax revenue coming in. The crumbling economy means that Japan could fall to the third largest economy (behind the United States and China) by the end of 2010.

JAPANESE EXPECTATIONS FOR NEW AND CHANGED ALLIANCES

The relationship between the United States and Japan is expected to change as a result of the election of the Democratic party, which opposed the U.S.-led invasion of Iraq and the Liberal Democratic party's decision to use Japanese naval ships to refuel U.S. and allied ships being used to fight in Iraq. There is some expectation that the newly empowered Democrats will decide to end this agreement. There is also concern that the U.S. Marine Corps's Futenma airfield, on Okinawa, might be closed or downsized, which could lead to a relocation or eviction of military forces.

The White House released a statement from President Barack Obama at the time of the Democratic party's victory, saying the administration was "confident that the strong U.S.–Japan alliance and the close partnership between our two countries will continue to flourish." The statement continued, "President Obama looks forward to working closely with the new Japanese prime minister on a broad range of global, regional and bilateral issues."

Analysts in the United States, although agreeing that the U.S. and Japanese governments will continue to work together on not only domestic issues but ones of global importance, including the economy, say that the nations may hit some bumps, because the Democratic party in Japan has made it clear that it will assert its power and not immediately agree with or follow the lead of the United States. According to Daniel Sneider, a Stanford University researcher, "This is what happens when you have a government in Japan that must be responsive to public opinion." He continued that the new government "will end the habits from decades of a relationship in which Japan didn't challenge the United States." However, Democrats in Japan have sought to dismiss rumors that they are only playing to their base with such rhetoric while also letting the United States know that Japan still values its relationship with it. "It's complete nonsense that a non–Liberal Democratic government will hurt U.S.-Japan relations," said Democratic lawmaker Tetsuro Fukuyama. "But there are many things left unchanged from the last 50 years that need to be re-examined."

Because Japanese public opinion concerning the relationship between the United States and Japan has been low in recent years, the new government has planned to focus more on improving relations with other Asian nations and becoming more involved on the continent. Under the Liberal Democratic party, Japan isolated itself from Asia, aligning itself more with Western nations, a policy the Democrats want to reverse.

—Heather Kerrigan

Following is the text of a speech by newly elected Japanese prime minister Yukio Hatoyama delivered on September 16, 2009.

Speech by Newly Elected Japanese Prime Minister Hatoyama

September 16, 2009

Earlier, at the moment when I was elected Prime Minister by both the House of Representatives and the House of Councillors, I was deeply moved, trembling at the thought that Japanese history was in the making. At the same time I felt a great sense of responsibility at the privilege of serving at the forefront in transforming this country into one of popular sovereignty in the true sense of the word.

The Democratic Party of Japan (DPJ) will be playing a central role, in a coalition with the Social Democratic Party and People's New Party. The DPJ must work, whatever may stand in the way, to meet the expectations of the Japanese public. This is the strong sense of mission that I now have.

The DPJ and its allied parties emerged triumphantly from the major struggle that this election was. Needless to say, however, this victory was not the triumph of the DPJ. It is the result of the public casting votes for the DPJ and its partners with a sense of expectation. History has not yet been made in the true sense. Whether it will be depends on our work from now on.

During this election, we often heard all around the country numerous expressions of anger, dissatisfaction and sorrow from the public. How did Japan turn out like this, why did my hometown become like this—these thoughts we must keep firmly in mind. And we must assume the heavy mantle of squarely meeting those concerns.

That is to say, the victors in this election were you, the entire Japanese nation, and in order to make this triumph of yours ring true, we will persevere throughout in forging politics for you the people. And in order to do so, we will in turn present to you now politics that sheds its dependence on the bureaucracy, so to speak, and put it into practice. Within various structures, we intend to engage in politics in which politicians shed their dependency on bureaucrats, with politicians maintaining the initiative while still using the brilliant minds of civil servants.

Beyond that, it is obvious. It is politicians who connect with your minds, those of the people. In that spirit, we will take to heart the various thoughts among the Japanese people, about changing politics, and why they want us to change politics. I intend to keep these thoughts firmly in mind as we depart, prepared as best possible, on a major voyage.

To make this possible, I ask the public not to be content just in having cast their ballots but urge them to voice their views on various matters to the government. I should like you to participate in this administration. I should think it can be said that the degree to which the thoughts of the public can be solidly encapsulated into public policy depends upon the participation we have from the general public.

It was in such a context that we wrote up our Manifesto. Whether the issue be "child allowances" or others, such as to somehow rectify the pensions system, which is now in tatters, we must first and foremost eliminate waste, amidst concerns over how to pay for them. This has also been the thought behind creating the Government Revitalisation Unit.

In addition, I intend to launch a National Policy Unit [*Kokka Senryaku-shitsu*]. My idea is to meet the expectations of the public by having the Unit outline major roles to be played by the state as well as the guiding principles.

I suspect that we will fail at times in a series of trial and error. I should very much like to ask people to be tolerant in this regard. After all, in a sense we are encountering the unknown, that is, taking a plunge into a world in which we have no experience. In order to forge a nation of political leadership, popular sovereignty, and local sovereignty in the truest sense, we will have to conduct various kinds of trial experiments. Therefore, I would be most grateful if the public could patiently foster this new government.

These were the thoughts we had when we resolved to form a coalition government. At all events we will introduce a new kind of politics that meets public expectations. That is the sole thought on which we established a coalition government. As we launch this government with everyone savouring that thought, I hope most sincerely for the guidance and support of the public, alongside their patience.

[Q&As]

QUESTION: What do you see as the most important policy issues for your administration in the near term? Also, with regard to the child allowance that you mentioned just now and the like, the question of fiscal resources is still being pointed out. How will you address this situation? At the same time, there are concerns regarding adverse effects on the economy as a result of cancellations in budget execution. How will you reconcile these two aspects [of budget re-allocation]? Please answer these two questions.

PRIME MINISTER YUKIO HATOYAMA: First of all, on the policy issues I attach importance to, these are quite evident. They are those in the Manifesto, which I earlier mentioned briefly. Since this is a coalition government, we will in this government be firmly implementing the contents on which we have reached agreement within the coalition. As for the DPJ, the party hopes before all else to initiate a child allowance, as well as abolish the provisional tax rates [which raise the petrol and automobile weight taxes]: policies and measures that stimulate people's domestic finances. As you just said, we want to carry out very quickly policies which would make the public feel that their financial condition has improve [*sic*] a little, and that they can place hope in this government.

That leads us to the issue of fiscal resources. We will immediately put into operation the Government Revitalisation Unit, which will, in addition to doing other work, thoroughly separate out the various operations conducted by the government. I should like all government ministries and agencies to do their utmost to eliminate governmental waste. I believe we have more or less worked out how to secure the necessary resources; as for the first fiscal year, we are certain that we can secure the necessary amount, which is somewhat over seven trillion yen.

I believe we need completely to overhaul the package of economic countermeasures and the supplementary budget [that was being implemented by the previous government]. Therefore, I expect that there will be areas where I will ask for a halt in budget execution. That said, as far as the regions where budget execution is going ahead, we would like this in principle to continue, provided that the budget item in question is deemed to be helping the revitalisation of that region. On the other hand, those budget items which do not meet this requirement, those whose implementation has not begun, will need to be reviewed radically. That is where I stand on this issue.

What we would like to say, as I just mentioned, is that we will give careful consideration to such cases where work has already begun and there would be serious consequences should this be halted. At the same time, we will be reviewing those budget items that are wasteful or whose money could be better spent, thereby setting out more effective steps forward.

QUESTION: Prime Minister Hatoyama, you reiterated your strong determination to make politics that sheds its dependence on the bureaucracy a reality. Strong resistance to this is to be expected among bureaucrats. Please explain in concrete terms how you intend to bring about politics that sheds its dependence on the bureaucracy, including the positioning of the National Policy Unit [*Kokka Senryaku-kyoku*].

PRIME MINISTER YUKIO HATOYAMA: First of all, we intend to have decisions on policy made in the various government ministries by Minister, State Secretary and Parliamentary Vice Minister, i.e. the incumbents of the so-called "three politically-appointed top posts." It goes without saying that we do not have any reason to reprimand excellent bureaucrats who work hard for the Japanese people.

However, to deal with [government activity which does not quite benefit the people], we will be creating a system in which essentially politicians play the main role in the decision-taking concerning the operations of government ministries. As I believe I've mentioned, we will set up Cabinet committees [on each important policy matter]. Particularly in the case of projects that fall within the remit of several government ministries, we will have these committees do most of the decision-taking, with the [full] Cabinet meeting to take the final decisions on these matters. As we have abolished [permanent] vice ministers' meeting [which used to be held the day before each Cabinet meeting], I do not foresee this process being distorted due to resistance from bureaucrats.

Obviously, leadership will be assumed by politicians at the National Policy Unit [*Kokka Senryaku-kyoku*] and Government Revitalisation Unit. In particular, the National Policy Unit [*Kokka Senryaku-shitsu*] will debate in particular the overall framework of the budget, and I have entrusted Minister [Naoto] Kan with those duties. Let me state here my great expectations on Minister Kan's tremendously capable leadership. Likewise, I hope Minister [Yoshito] Sengoku will fully exert his leadership at the Government Revitalisation Unit, with those at the level of State Secretaries at various ministries also assuming suitable roles within the Unit. I hope those concerned shall exert political leadership to ensure that wasteful projects are thoroughly eliminated, starting with work in order thoroughly to separate out the various operations conducted by the government. I intend to carry out politics that sheds its dependence on bureaucrats by making full use of this range of approaches.

QUESTION: Prime Minister Hatoyama, with regard to [the fiscal resources required] next year [to implement] the Manifesto, you stated that you have more or less worked out how to secure the necessary 7.1 trillion yen (*sic*). But, presumably the formulation of the budget for next fiscal year will be a pressing issue. My first question is, will you be reviewing the budget "ceiling" from a zero-based budgeting approach? Also, will you formulate this budget by the end of the calendar year? And would you aim to enact the budget by the end of the present fiscal year [March 2010]? What are your current ideas concerning the schedule of such matters?

PRIME MINISTER YUKIO HATOYAMA: My fundamental stance is to have discussions conducted urgently and in depth with the Finance Minister as well as

Minister Kan of the National Policy Unit [*Kokka Senryaku-shitsu*] playing the central roles. What I would venture to say is that the methodology employed thus far will be reconsidered from a zero-based budgeting approach. I intend to have the "ceiling" method fundamentally rethought. Although we are starting somewhat late, my intended schedule at this point to is to formulate the budget [for fiscal 2010] by the end of this calendar year.

QUESTION: You will be visiting the United States for the United Nations General Assembly, and I presume you will also take part in a Japan-US summit meeting. In concrete terms, what sort of policies will you be pursuing in order to deepen Japan-US relations? The coalition agreement states that it is now a turning point so far as the revision of the Status of Forces Agreement is concerned. I would like to know in concrete terms whether or not you plan to put this matter on the table [at the forthcoming summit meeting with the US].

PRIME MINISTER YUKIO HATOYAMA: While I am still hopeful that a date and time for a Japan-US summit meeting [next week] will be set, we are not yet in a situation to know what that date and time would be.

Speaking to you on a hypothetical basis then, I would say that the first step that needs to be taken is to build a relationship of trust with President Obama. In that sense I would suggest that the most important thing in this [meeting with the President Obama during my] visit [next week] to the US is enhancing that sense of trust through a frank mutual exchange of views.

As for issues such as what is known as the Status of Forces Agreement, I am currently of the opinion that, obviously, our fundamental stance will not change. It is also true that the coalition agreement states that we will make efforts towards a revision of this Agreement.

Nevertheless, the main thrust of this [summit] meeting will be to foster a relationship of trust. I believe it important to spend a certain amount of time on a comprehensive review of the range of issues in the Japan-US relationship, including that of security-related issues. And it would be important to advance discussions during the time that we set aside. I should like you to understand that we consider the creation of a relationship of trust to be the key [at next week's summit meeting]. At the risk of repeating myself here, in order to do that, I believe that we need to create a rapport which enables us to speak to each other without reservation.

Japan has until now has tended to be somewhat passive within the Japan-US relationship. I should like to foster a relationship in which Japan plays a proactive role and can discuss its views frankly with the US. I will work to achieve a conclusion [on the matters you raised] within such a relationship.

QUESTION: I would like to ask about the government's stance on the abduction issue.

There are two ministers in your Cabinet, Minister Kan and Minister [Keiko] Chiba, who signed a petition for the release of former death row inmate Shin Kwang-soo, a criminal responsible for the abduction of Megumi Yokota by North Korea. It seems to me that there is a risk of sending the wrong message to the North Koreans as we are about to press them for the resolution of the abduction issue. What are your thoughts on that?

In addition, do you intend to ask these two ministers to express remorse or apology to the families of the abduction victims?

These are my questions.

PRIME MINISTER YUKIO HATOYAMA: I believe that the events of the past you cite are true. However, what is of paramount importance in dealing with North Korea is that we move forward pragmatically in seeking to resolve the abduction issue. For that reason, as well as others, in my Cabinet I have appointed Hiroshi Nakai, Minister of State and National Public Safety Chairman to be the Minister in charge of the abduction issue as well.

I place great value on the fact that he has been extremely assertive in taking action on the abduction issue thus far and I myself intend to spare no effort so that we see good progress on the abduction issue. I have no intention at present to question the two ministers regarding matters of the past.

QUESTION: I have two questions, one being a point of confirmation related to the formulation of the budget as mentioned earlier, and the other a question with regard to the new Cabinet. Insofar as the formulation of the budget will be an urgent issue in the near future, will the command centre for its formulation be the National Policy Unit [*Kokka Senryaku-kyoku*], or will the Ministry of Finance assume that role?

My second question is, when you were Secretary-General of the DPJ, you said with regard to the Nishimatsu Construction Co. illegal donations incident that the investigation was "politically-motivated." Now, having assumed governmental power, do you still maintain that position? And, if you maintain this view on the investigation, did you take any particular points into account when selecting your Justice Minister?

PRIME MINISTER YUKIO HATOYAMA: First, on formulation of the budget, I will have the National Policy Unit [*Kokka Senryaku-shitsu*] discuss the fundamental structure of the budget. That is to say I will have the National Policy Unit [*Kokka Senryaku-shitsu*] design the framework, as opposed to drafting the details. It was with that in mind that I created the National Policy Unit [*Kokka Senryaku-shitsu*].

Fleshing out the specific details from a well-designed framework is a role that will be centred on the Finance Minister and the Ministry of Finance. As both will be involved in how much waste can be eliminated, together with the Government Revitalisation Unit, the three should advance their discussions cohesively and divide their respective roles as appropriate.

Next, I did indeed once use the words "politically-motivated investigation" with regard to the Nishimatsu incident, but I did not use them twice. That is to say that I have been refraining from using them again, regretting having used those words on one occasion. I hope you understand that that is my position.

QUESTION: With regard to the East Asian community that you advocate, when and in what form do you intend to make it more widely known to the international community during the upcoming diplomatic calendar?

In addition, your views on a common Asian currency for this community seem to be interpreted in the United States as an intention to move away from the US or away from the US dollar. How would you respond to such concerns?

PRIME MINISTER YUKIO HATOYAMA: As you know, the spirit of fraternity in one sense serves as a starting line. In the case of the EU this has extended as far as a common currency, the euro. I feel that to envisage a regional community in Asia, particularly in East Asia in the medium to long term is the correct path to take, even though in a sense there are major differences in our countries' systems.

This idea certainly is not intended to exclude the US dollar or the United States. Quite the contrary, as a step beyond this initiative I believe we should envisage an

Asia-Pacific community, and I do not think that this could readily be achieved without the United States. I should like to elaborate on this vision as early as possible, and leaving aside the degree of detail that can be discussed, I am planning to speak about this idea in some form or another in my forthcoming address at the United Nations. So I am thinking about raising the idea in a preliminary manner, but I haven't thought this through yet.

QUESTION: I would like to ask you about the issue of political donations you received from individuals.

You have consistently maintained that you have sufficiently fulfilled your responsibility to explain this issue of donations from individuals. However, it is I think inevitable that you will be subjected to very pointed questions from the opposition parties in the extraordinary session of the Diet and elsewhere. What do you have to say on the effect that this issue will have on your handling of the government, and on whether you intend to offer any further explanation in the future?

PRIME MINISTER YUKIO HATOYAMA: I have apologised to the Japanese people for the extensive consternation I have cause [sic] because of this matter, and have made my best efforts to rectify and remedy [the report on receipts and disbursements of political funds].

I accept that indeed I have struggled to gain the understanding of the public on this matter. Thus I should like to make further efforts to explain it more fully. I intend make efforts to convey my thoughts to the Japanese people as honestly and accurately as possible, taking into account developments surrounding the matter, so that they will be able to improve their understanding of it.

SOURCE: Office of the Prime Minister of Japan and His Cabinet. "Press Conference by Prime Minister Yukio Hatoyama." September 16, 2009. www.kantei.go.jp/foreign/hatoyama/statement/200909/16 kaiken_e.html.

OTHER HISTORIC DOCUMENTS OF INTEREST

FROM THIS VOLUME

FROM PREVIOUS *HISTORIC DOCUMENTS*

HIV Vaccine Study Shows Promising Results in Thailand

SEPTEMBER 29, 2009

On September 24, 2009, researchers in Thailand announced that a vaccine combination that they had tested could be used to prevent the spread of human immunodeficiency virus (HIV), the disease that develops into acquired immune deficiency syndrome (AIDS). AIDS kills approximately two million people worldwide each year.

This was the first study conducted in which scientists have seen positive results; participants were administered two separate HIV vaccines. "For the first time, an investigational HIV vaccine has demonstrated some ability to prevent HIV infection among vaccinated individuals. Additional research is needed to better understand how this vaccine regimen reduced the risk of HIV infection, but certainly this is an encouraging advance for the HIV vaccine field," said National Institute of Allergy and Infectious Diseases (NIAID) director Anthony Fauci.

The two vaccines used by medical researchers in this study have in the past proven to be ineffective when used separately, and scientists do not yet know why, when used in combination, they can help stop the spread of HIV. This development could lead to a reduction in the number of people suffering worldwide from HIV and AIDS. However, questions remain from this first study, including whether the vaccine combination, which was used against strains of HIV that circulate in Thailand, would be viable in the rest of the world and whether a 30 percent success rate, as was seen in this study, is enough to constitute a successful vaccine.

EARLIER VACCINE TRIALS

The six-year, $105 million study in Thailand was the third major study conducted in search of an HIV vaccine since the virus was identified as the cause of AIDS in 1983. Attempts have been made in the past to produce a vaccine, a combination of vaccines, or a secondary method for the prevention of HIV, but none have proven successful. These failures had led some scientists to question whether a vaccine for HIV would ever be possible.

In 2007, two international studies were conducted using a vaccine produced by the pharmaceutical company Merck. Going into each study, expectations of a positive outcome were high; however, in each case, the trial was stopped before completion because of complications with the vaccine. Later studies showed that the vaccine actually *increased* each participant's risk of developing HIV rather than decreasing it.

Unrelated studies conducted in Africa have shown a 60 percent success rate in reducing the risk of HIV infection through male circumcision.

THAILAND'S STUDY

The vaccine study conducted in Thailand, the largest HIV study in vaccine history, began in 2003. The study was supported by the Walter Reed Army Institute of Research and NIAID, and it was conducted by the Thai Ministry of Public Health. The U.S. Army chose Thailand as the best place to site this study because it has been tracking and studying the virus strains there since the 1990s. Based on this early research, scientists were able to identify the strains of HIV prevalent in Thailand and compile a full genetic description of it, which vaccine makers could use.

After identifying the strains of HIV, the World Health Organization (WHO) and Joint United Nations Programme on HIV/AIDS (UNAIDS) began compiling additional data and support for the study. Although UNAIDS and the WHO began preliminary research in 1991, the study did not get under way fully until 2003, when participants were invited to receive the vaccine.

A total of 16,402 men and women participated. Each person in the study was between the ages of 18 and 30 and at differing levels of risk of contracting HIV. Participants were administered the vaccine and counseled on other methods of protecting themselves from contracting the virus, such as practicing safe sex.

To halt multiplication of the HIV virus, researchers gave participants a two-drug combination. In this study, the goal was to halt the B and E strains, which are most common in Thailand. The two drugs administered were ALVAC, distributed by Sanofi Pasteur SA, a division of Sanofi-Aventis, a French drug company; and AIDSVAX, made by the nonprofit organization Global Solutions. The ALVAC vaccine includes a bird virus, canarypox, which helps the vaccine locate the HIV genes but cannot itself cause an infection in humans. AIDSVAX, produced synthetically, is a replica of a protein found on the surface of the HIV vaccine. Neither AIDSVAX nor ALVAC can cause HIV.

Half of the participants in the study were given a placebo and the other half were given a "prime-boost" vaccine combination—six shots over a six-month period in which the first four prime, or prepare, the body to fight HIV and the final two doses help strengthen the immune system's response to the disease.

At the end of the study, 51 of the 8,197 participants who received the prime-boost vaccine had contracted HIV, whereas 74 of the 8,198 who received the placebo had tested positive for HIV. Two placebo participants died during the study.

These results show a 31 percent lower rate of HIV infection for those who received the vaccine; however, in most vaccine trials, only results that block infection at a rate of 50 percent or greater are considered successful enough to produce the vaccine for mass use.

Medical experts recognized that although the study produced some positive results, much more work remains. "This is a world first which proves that vaccine development is possible," said Supachi Rerks-Ngarm, the Thai health official who oversaw the study. "But this is not to the level where we can license or manufacture the vaccine yet."

In addition to protecting participants from contracting the disease, another goal of the study had been to reduce the levels of HIV in the bloodstream when those who had received the vaccine contracted the virus. Scientists in Thailand were unable to meet this goal. The vaccine combination did not reduce the damage caused by the virus. A vaccine typically considered successful would result in a lower "viral load," an indicator for measuring the amount of HIV in the bloodstream, in the vaccine group compared to the placebo group, an indicator physicians use when identifying HIV in the bloodstream.

Because scientists were unable to determine why the vaccine combination was to an extent successful or why RV144, as the vaccine combination is known, does not decrease the viral load in a patient's bloodstream, medical experts said it indicates a lack of complete understanding of what success means in terms of combating HIV/AIDS. "We don't know whether our current measures of the human immune response are even relevant to the protection that we see in this trial. [That is] a humbling reminder of how little we know, and how much work remains to be done in our search for an optimal HIV vaccine," said Fauci.

After the initial findings of Thailand's study were released, a second analysis of the data was completed. This second evaluation excluded any participants who had not completed the full vaccine course. With a reduced population in the pool, the new analysis revealed only 26 percent protection from HIV in participants who received the vaccine. This, some scientists said, meant the Thai study was not statistically significant, leading to questions about whether the results were simply a matter of chance.

MORE STUDIES TO BE CONDUCTED

Although the production of a vaccine combination that prevented contracting HIV in some study participants left scientists with renewed hope of one day developing an effective vaccine, it also raised many questions, particularly regarding the validity of the results given the small sample population. In this study, 125 participants contracted HIV, while in previous studies, the number was ten times as much.

As noted, scientists are not yet sure why this combination of vaccines produced positive results but did not affect the viral load in the vaccine group. Jonathan Weber, an HIV expert at Imperial College in London, said that the study indicates that antibody production had a hand in the outcome. However, scientists have long known that antibodies can prevent infection but cannot change the disease once it has been contracted.

Of greater concern is that scientists could not figure out why this particular combination of vaccines had an effect, a concern that was first voiced before the study began. "We have no idea why this series of vaccinations worked," said Col. Nelson Michael, director of the U.S. Military HIV Research Program. Additional studies will have to be conducted to back up the Thai study and figure out, through isolation, which parts of each vaccine prevented the virus from being contracted. The U.S. Army is planning to take the data from this study and work in conjunction with medical researchers and institutions to find ways to use it in future research.

Scientists do not know whether the vaccine has any long-lasting effects or if booster shots will be necessary. Some results in the Thai study suggest that one vaccination may not provide life-long protection against HIV. There is also no indication whether the vaccine would protect gay men or intravenous drug users from contracting the disease. Most study participants were heterosexual nondrug users.

There is also no indication that the vaccine combination used in this study would have a positive effect in the United States or the rest of the world. HIV strains B and E are the most common in Thailand, but are not jointly most prevalent in most other countries. "Given its modest level of efficacy, this prime boost regimen is likely unsuitable in its current form for public health purposes. . . . Based on the available published data, it is likely that different vaccines may be required for different regions in the world," said Col. Jerome Kim, HIV vaccines product manager for the U.S. Army.

—Heather Kerrigan

Following is a Department of State press release from September 29, 2009, regarding the testing of an HIV vaccine.

HIV Combo Vaccine Trial Conducted

September 29, 2009

Medical researchers in Thailand have developed an approach to prevent HIV the same way it has been treated, by using a combination vaccine to successfully halt the spread of the disease.

Public health officials announced September 24 in Bangkok that they successfully used two previously unsuccessful HIV vaccines in combination in a large, six-year study to prevent people from getting HIV, which causes AIDS. The vaccines used in the study cannot cause HIV infection because they are not made from and do not contain the whole virus, active or dead, the medical researchers said.

The combination vaccine cut the risk in 16,402 Thai volunteers by 31.2 percent, Thai Health Minister Witthaya Kaewparadai reported at a briefing. "The result of the study is a very important step for developing an AIDS vaccine. It's the first time in the world that we have found a vaccine that can prevent HIV infection," Kaewparadai told reporters.

Researchers say the results are not enough to go ahead immediately with widespread production of the combo vaccine using the "prime-boost" approach developed in Thailand. Normally, vaccine results have to exceed 50 percent before being accepted for general use, medical researchers say. Officials at the two pharmaceutical companies that manufactured the vaccines said it will take many years of testing and further research before the combo vaccine can be used widely.

STUDY BEGAN IN 2003

The study, which began in October 2003, was conducted by the Thai Ministry of Public Health with funding and support from the U.S. Army's Walter Reed Army Institute of Research and the U.S. National Institute of Allergy and Infectious Diseases (NIAID), which is part of the National Institutes of Health based in Washington. The principal investigator was Dr. Supachai Rerks-Ngarm of the Thai Ministry of Public Health's Department of Disease Control.

Thailand was selected for the $105 million study because U.S. Army medical researchers had conducted initial research when the HIV/AIDS epidemic first emerged there in the 1990s, identifying and isolating virus strains and providing the virus's genetic information to vaccine makers. The study was conducted with the full support of the Thai government because the country had an emerging problem with AIDS when the study began.

The World Health Organization (WHO) and the Joint United Nations Programme on HIV/AIDS (UNAIDS) began support work for this trial 18 years ago, in 1991, when Thailand was recommended as one of the WHO-sponsored countries in preparation for HIV vaccine trials.

A study in 2006 by the HIV Vaccine Advisory Committee found that the "trial was being conducted at the highest scientific and ethical standards and with active community participation."

The study, the largest in HIV vaccine history, was conducted in the Rayong and Chonburi provinces with 16,402 men and women ages 18 to 30 who were at various levels of risk for HIV infection, the NIAID said. These provinces were selected because the populations in both are generally stable.

"We thank the trial staff in Thailand and the United States for their years of effort in successfully conducting this study and the study participants and the people of Thailand for their long-standing support of HIV vaccine research," said NIAID Director Dr. Anthony Fauci. "These new findings represent an important step forward in HIV vaccine research."

Thai men and women were given either a placebo or the "prime-boost" combination of the vaccine ALVAC, from Sanofi Pasteur SA, which is the vaccine division of French drug maker Sanofi-Aventis; and the vaccine AIDSVAX, originally developed by VaxGen Inc. and now held by Global Solutions for Infectious Diseases, a nonprofit organization created by former VaxGen employees.

Half of the volunteers received four "priming" doses of ALVAC and two "boost" doses of AIDSVAX over a six-month period. The other half received dummy doses of a placebo. The volunteers were tested for HIV every six months for three years after the vaccinations ended.

NIAID said the vaccines are based on the B and E strains of HIV that commonly circulate in Thailand. Researchers readily acknowledge that they do not know why the combination works to prevent HIV infection, and that it is unlikely the combination would work in the United States, where only the B strain is most common, in Africa or elsewhere in the world.

In previous HIV vaccine trials, neither ALVAC nor AIDSVAX proved effective in preventing HIV infection when used alone, researchers said, but when used in a prime-boost approach they tend to work. The first vaccine, ALVAC, primes the body's immune system to attack HIV, and the second vaccine, AIDSVAX, strengthens the body's immune response, researchers said.

The volunteers were given thorough briefings on the potential risks associated with receiving the experimental vaccine before agreeing to participate. All were given condoms, counseling and treatment for any other sexually transmitted diseases. On each clinic visit, each volunteer was counseled on how to avoid becoming infected with HIV. Any volunteer who became infected with HIV was given free treatment with anti-retroviral therapy based on the guidelines of the Thai Ministry of Public Health.

"For the first time, an investigational HIV vaccine has demonstrated some ability to prevent HIV infection among vaccinated individuals. Additional research is needed to better understand how this vaccine regimen reduced the risk of HIV infection, but certainly this is an encouraging advance for the HIV vaccine field," Fauci said.

NIAID and its partners are working with other scientific experts to determine the next steps, including additional research of the vaccine regimen and the need to consider the impact of these new findings on other HIV vaccine candidates, NIAID said.

ADDITIONAL STUDIES NEEDED

A conference is being held in New York during the week of September 28–October 2 with dozens of researchers, vaccine makers, major research donors and HIV/AIDS groups to determine where to go next. At the conference will be medical researchers from Thailand, the U.S. Army, NIAID and independent researchers.

U.S. Army Colonel Jerome Kim, an infectious disease expert and the Army HIV vaccine product manager at the Walter Reed Army Institute of Research's Division of Retrovirology, said researchers now will try to understand why the vaccine worked in some people and how the combo vaccine blocks infections.

"Additional studies are clearly needed to better understand how this vaccine regimen reduced the risk of HIV infection," Kim said.

"The Thai study demonstrates why the HIV vaccine field must take a balanced approach to conducting both the basic research needed to discover and design new HIV vaccines and, when appropriate, testing candidate vaccines in people," said Margaret Johnston, director of NIAID's Vaccine Research Program within the Division of AIDS. "Both avenues provide critical information that will continue to help us better understand what is needed to develop a fully protective HIV vaccine."

Lieutenant General Eric Schoomaker, the Army surgeon general and commander of the U.S. Army Medical Command, said the Thai study results are important, but modest.

"I'm pleased and proud to announce the results of the trial, which for the first time ever have shown that it is possible for a vaccine to reduce the risk of HIV infection in humans," Schoomaker said September 24 in Washington. "Although the level of protection is modest, at 31 percent efficacy, the study represents a major scientific achievement."

"Military medicine is interested in research that improves global health and makes the world safer for everyone," he added.

WHO and UNAIDS said in a joint statement that the study results, representing a significant scientific advance, are the first demonstration that a vaccine can prevent HIV infection in a general adult population, and characterized the results as modestly protective.

"However, these results have instilled new hope in the HIV vaccine research field and promise that a safe and highly effective HIV vaccine may become available for populations throughout the world who are most in need of such a vaccine," the statement said.

SOURCE: U.S. Department of State. Press release. "Successful HIV Vaccine Study Will Lead to Further Research." September 29, 2009. www.america.gov/st/scitech-english/2009/September/20090929113245d mslahrellek0.7651789.html.

OTHER HISTORIC DOCUMENTS OF INTEREST

FROM PREVIOUS *HISTORIC DOCUMENTS*

October

DOCUMENT IN CONTEXT

Swine Flu in the United States

OCTOBER 1, 7, AND 9 AND NOVEMBER 13, 2009

In 2009, an outbreak of influenza H1N1, or swine flu, hit the United States, causing millions of infections and killing more than 10,000 people. Federal health officials scrambled to respond to the panic that swept the nation, which led to school closures and fear of travel or contact with others in a confined space. While hospitals and health clinics filled with patients worried that they had contracted the disease, drug producers worked to create a vaccine that would effectively combat H1N1 and send it into mass production as quickly as possible. By late 2009, the first vaccines for H1N1 were available, and those people most at risk—pregnant women, children, young adults, older Americans, and those with certain preexisting conditions—were encouraged to see their doctors immediately for vaccination. The federal government worked to educate the public on the dangers of swine flu but also help people understand that, in many cases, it was no more serious than seasonal flu.

The first global outbreak of swine flu in 2009 took place in Mexico, where widespread panic led to school, church, and store closures. As the virus spread to other parts of the world, hospitals and health clinics were flooded with people concerned about their risk of contracting H1N1. On June 11, the World Health Organization (WHO) declared a swine flu pandemic, meaning the disease was widespread and continuing to grow—at that point, having reached seventy-four countries. In the United States, federal health officials were able to react quickly to contain the disease by putting into use the lessons learned from combating avian flu years earlier. However, at the end of 2009, Thomas Frieden, director of the Centers for Disease Control and Prevention (CDC), warned that the virus had entered its second wave and was still affecting thousands across the country, killing five times more children and young adults—those most susceptible to the H1N1 virus—than seasonal flu does in an average year in the United States.

EARLY SWINE FLU CASES

The first U.S. cases of swine flu in 2009 were reported in early spring in California. It was believed that the disease had spread from Mexico, where the first outbreak had occurred earlier in the year. By mid-April, states across the country were beginning to see people with flu symptoms, and by May the disease had reached all fifty states. By late June 2009, more than 25,000 cases had been reported by the CDC. Although the number of reported cases remained near 25,000, the CDC announced that it estimated one million people had contracted swine flu.

U.S. health officials first declared the virus a public health emergency in April 2009, the same month the first death from the disease was recorded. The WHO had not yet classified the disease a pandemic, as it found it did not have enough information to justify such an announcement. Because only two labs in the world were equipped to test for the disease, it would be some time before the WHO would be able to make a more accurate determination about the threat and spread of the disease.

U.S. officials cautioned that declaring a public health emergency was in no way related to a significant increase in cases or an indication that the disease had become more dangerous, but rather that the declaration allowed the federal government to release more funds as needed. "It's like declaring one for a hurricane," said Secretary of Homeland Security Janet Napolitano. "It means we can release funds and take other measures. The hurricane may not actually hit," she continued. With the declaration, the federal government would be able to spend additional money on vaccines and other antiviral drugs, and release one quarter of the nation's stockpile of antiflu drugs, which at that time stood at 50 million doses.

In response to the announcement of a public health emergency, the Transportation Security Administration (TSA) and Customs and Border Patrol increased efforts to watch for travelers who appeared ill when attempting to enter the United States. Both organizations began asking travelers if they had recently had a fever, and if it was determined that the person may have contracted some form of the virus, he or she would be taken to a safe location until medical testing could be conducted. To contain the spread of the virus people, the Department of Health and Human Services and the CDC advised people to stay home when ill, wash their hands frequently, and cover their nose and mouth in the crook of their elbow when coughing and sneezing. U.S. officials did not, however, issue any bans on travel or public gathering, as had been done in Mexico.

EMERGENCY DECLARED

President Barack Obama officially declared swine flu a national emergency on October 24, 2009. Obama said during his announcement that "rapid increase in illness" has the ability to "overburden health-care resources." The White House was quick to deny that there was any new information available on swine flu or that the disease had suddenly become more severe; White House spokespersons reiterated that the president had made his assessment based on information already publicly available from the CDC.

This announcement would give federal health officials increased ability to help patients and hospitals seeing an increase in the number of cases of H1N1. Secretary of Health and Human Services Kathleen Sebelius was given authority to allow hospitals to set up separate locations in an effort to treat the growing number of patients, a move typically disallowed by federal regulation. In addition, Sebelius could waive requirements of Medicare and Medicaid patients seeking flu treatment and loosen some privacy restrictions in an effort to ensure that appropriate swine flu reporting was being conducted.

White House spokesperson Reid Cherlin said the lifting of restrictions and regulations was made in an attempt to ensure that each person was able to receive care as quickly as possible. "Adding a potential delay while waiting for a National Emergency Declaration is not in the best interest of the public, particularly if this step can be done proactively as we are doing here," said Cherlin.

Health experts said the Obama announcement was a necessary step in ensuring that hospitals and health clinics were able to properly and quickly care for their patients. Jennifer Nuzzo, with the University of Pittsburgh's Center for Biosecurity, said, "We know a number of hospitals are already experiencing high but manageable loads." She said the administration's decision was "just a precautionary move, so if need be we can focus on the care of patients rather than focus on administrative hurdles. In disasters, you often don't have the time or luxury to keep the paperwork in order. You want hospitals focusing on patients."

Other health experts were concerned that the Obama announcement would create more panic. When the WHO had declared swine flu a pandemic in June, many areas around the world experienced chaos as citizens flooded hospitals and health clinics, stretching health care services to their breaking point. There was also concern that the demand for the H1N1 vaccine would rise, which would pose a serious problem to vaccine makers, who were already behind in production.

RESPONSE

After the outbreak in Mexico City had led to the closure of all schools, universities, and churches in the country, state and federal government entities in the United States began issuing warnings to the population to protect themselves against contracting the virus. The CDC recommended citizens regularly wash hands and cover their mouths when they sneeze or cough. In addition, once the vaccine was available, the CDC recommended all people, especially those at high risk, receive the vaccine. It also noted that swine flu symptoms—fever, cough, and sore throat—were basically the same as those of seasonal flu. The biggest difference between seasonal flu and swine flu, they said, was vomiting or diarrhea, but those symptoms appeared in only about one in four cases.

While panic spread, and school districts in California and Texas ordered closures, the CDC reminded the public that this disease had not yet shown itself to be as strong as the seasonal flu, which in 2008 killed approximately 36,000 adults in the United States. According to Dr. Nancy Cox, the CDC's director of influenza, the new swine flu virus did not appear to be as virulent as a different strain of H1N1 that had infected the U.S. population in 1918. That virus killed between 30 million and 50 million people worldwide, and Cox believed the strain of H1N1 circulating around the world would not be as deadly. "What we have found by looking very carefully at the sequence of the new H1N1 virus is that we're not seeing the markers for virulence that we saw in the 1918 virus," she said. It was largely believed that had antiviral drugs been available in 1918, the virus would not have been as deadly. Evidence of this has been shown with each flu pandemic since 1918, as the number of those affected and killed has decreased.

The U.S. government noted that despite its name, the swine flu had not been detected in pigs. Regardless, six countries banned the import of pork products from the United States, but according to the U.S. trade representative's office, the import bans did "not appear to be based on scientific evidence." The White House announced that it would work with the U.S. Treasury to determine any ramifications caused by the import ban.

VACCINE AVAILABILITY

U.S. health officials had hoped to have between 80 and 120 million doses of vaccine available by mid-October. To meet this goal, the Obama administration authorized the use of $2 billion in federal funds to purchase 250 million doses and claimed that it would be able to give everyone the vaccine. Come mid-October, however, that goal was far from being achieved. Only 16.5 million doses had been made available by that time, drawing ire directed at health officials. According to Health and Human Services Deputy Director Nicole Lurie, the companies producing the vaccines "hit some stumbling blocks; they sometimes thought the fix was around the corner and didn't always feel the need to tell us, and then sometimes it turned out that the fix wasn't around the corner."

Vaccine manufacturers said government statements that the manufacturers had not kept officials informed of problems was incorrect. "We have a formal call with them once a week and [were] in touch with them probably on a daily basis," said Donna Cary, a spokesperson for Sanofi Pasteur, one of the vaccine manufacturers.

Local government officials and individuals hoping to get themselves or their children vaccinated were dissatisfied with the government's response. In Fairfax County, Virginia, for example, the government had undertaken a vaccine campaign, encouraging parents to bring students to school during a weekend of vaccinations. That had to be canceled when the county did not receive enough vaccinations to inoculate all the students. The county then switched its focus to vaccinating pregnant women.

—Heather Kerrigan

Following is a press briefing by the Centers for Disease Control and Prevention (CDC) on October 1, 2009, detailing the status of H1N1 across the country and the availability of a vaccine; a press release from the CDC on October 7, 2009, on unfounded reports that receiving the seasonal flu vaccine would leave citizens susceptible to contracting H1N1; a CDC Morbidity and Mortality Weekly Report (MMWR) *from October 9, 2009, on the availability of the H1N1 vaccine; and a November 13, 2009,* MMWR *report updating influenza activity in the United States.*

CDC Press Briefing by Anne Schuchat on Swine Flu in the United States

October 1, 2009

In terms of the disease activity right now, we expect tomorrow in our weekly update of FluView that we'll be reporting substantial flu illness in most of the country, significant flu activity in virtually all states. Most states do have quite a lot of disease right now, and that's unusual for this time of year. We're able to give a little bit of an update about the H1N1 influenza disease in pregnant women. I know that's been an interest to a lot of people. We've updated our numbers, and through late August, we can report that about 100 pregnant women in the United States have required intensive care unit hospitalization for H1N1 flu. Sadly, 28 pregnant women in the U.S. have died so far from the H1N1 influenza. These are really upsetting numbers, I know. And I just want to remind women and doctors and nurse midwives that antiviral medicine can be a very important treatment for pregnant women who have respiratory illness. . . .

I want to mention briefly an MMWR report issued a couple of days ago, it's on fatalities from the H1N1 influenza, and the important role bacteria have in some of these fatal cases. Our scientists reviewed autopsy material from 77 fatal H1N1 influenza patients and found that bacteria were present in terms of bacterial pneumonia in about a third of those fatalities. The good news is the leading bacteria was streptococcus pneumonia, and we have a vaccine for that. Adults are recommended to receive the pneumococcal vaccine if they have chronic medical conditions, like asthma, diabetes, chronic heart disease, chronic lung disease, immunodepression and so forth. Sadly, only about one in five non-elderly adults take advantage of that vaccine. So when people are going in for their seasonal flu vaccines right now, those very same people, we urge them to consider the pneumococcal vaccine which is available right now.

I want to catch people up with the antiviral situation. That's been something we've been hearing a lot about recently. Secretary Sebelius released about 300,000 courses of liquid Tamiflu for children to be made available to the states who may need this. So far, basically each state that needs their proportion of that supply will receive this Tamiflu over the next week. Based on requests we've already received. Texas and Colorado received their proportions today. The amounts, there are about 22,000 pediatric liquid Tamiflu courses for Texas, and about 4,600 of those courses for Colorado. Now, some of the liquid formulations of Tamiflu will have an expiration date that may have passed, but we want people to know that the FDA has extended the expiration date of those courses, after careful testing. Everything that is being released has gone through that sort of testing. I do want to remind people about our guidance on antiviral medicine used. Because this is such an important tool we have to reduce illness complications of influenza, whether it's the H1N1 or regular flu. People who have severe illness, who are hospitalized or who have other warning signs can greatly benefit from antiviral medicine. People who have the influenza-like symptoms and have conditions that make it possible they would have a worse time with flu should also receive antiviral medicine. That includes pregnant women, people with asthma, diabetes, immunosuppression, and the very old and the very young. There are important warning signs that people should know about, in particular parents. These include fast breathing, or difficulty breathing, trouble taking fluids, difficulty being woken up or if our child [sic] looking a little blue or a little gray. And importantly, getting better and then getting worse. Those are warning signs that really it's time to seek care. And we know that parents are concerned about the flu, and we want them to know about those signs. . . .

Lastly, I want to briefly describe where we are with the H1N1 vaccination effort. We are transitioning from the planning phase to the implementation phase. States and the large cities that are part of our program began placing orders yesterday. I can report to you that 25 of these areas placed orders yesterday, and they placed orders for about 600,000 doses of H1N1 vaccine. I want to describe to you the process going forward about how we'll catch you up about where we are with the ordering, and the shipments and all of that. Every Friday we will be updating through either the media press conference or definitely always with our website a couple facts and figures for you. We're going to let you know how much vaccine was available for ordering, and then we're going to let you know how much was shipped to each of the states or large cities by that day. And it will basically be information gathered through Wednesday, and it will be coming out on every Friday. Important to say, we're at the beginning, and we'll be getting more vaccine regularly, and the states and large cities will be ordering regularly. So this is really just the beginning. We expect the vaccine that was ordered yesterday should be arriving out to the sites by Tuesday. And we're really pleased that this is starting. Of course, this is a little bit earlier than we were planning to get started. And as we said last week, we're starting a little bit slow, but we wanted to start as soon as possible. More and more doses will be becoming available out to the sites, and this is the beginning. The first doses that are going to be available out there on Tuesday will be the nasal spray for inhalation. It's a good vaccine, but it's one that it can't be used in absolutely everyone. It's indicated for people 2 years of age through 49 who do not have conditions like pregnancy or chronic medical conditions. It's safe and effective. And we think it's important to get that vaccine out as soon as we've—as soon as it has become available. The state and large cities have been making plans about how to use the vaccines as they come available in the communities. And they—with the doses that we have right now, what they're doing is making practical targeted plans for the best use of the doses that we have. We believe that a lot of the states will be directing these early doses to health care workers. There's a bit of a myth out there that the workers shouldn't get the live vaccine, but that's a myth. Most health care workers who are under 50 and don't have those chronic conditions can receive the nasal spray. I want to make sure that you know that this is just the beginning. We're all in this together. We do expect some bumps in the road over the course as we begin this process together. We're working really closely with the states and large cities to make things go as smoothly and as effectively as possible. . . .

[The Q&A portion of the press briefing has been omitted.]

Source: Centers for Disease Control and Prevention. Press briefing transcripts. "Weekly 2009 H1N1 Flu Media Briefing." October 1, 2009. www.cdc.gov/media/transcripts/2009/t091001.htm.

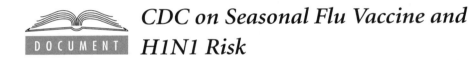

CDC on Seasonal Flu Vaccine and H1N1 Risk

October 7, 2009

BACKGROUND

Recently there have been several media reports describing unpublished findings from seasonal influenza vaccine studies conducted in Canada. The findings from these studies suggest that receiving the 2008–09 seasonal influenza vaccine (given last influenza season) was a risk factor for developing influenza caused by the 2009 H1N1 virus. In the studies done in Canada, the increase in risk among persons vaccinated with a seasonal influenza vaccine was approximately double the risk for those who were not vaccinated with seasonal influenza vaccine. However, the risk for severe influenza was not increased. The results of these studies have been presented by the Canadian investigators to CDC scientists. However, the research findings from Canada have not been published in the medical literature or presented at any public scientific meetings. There has not yet been an opportunity to fully review the studies in detail.

There is no indication that the type of seasonal influenza vaccine received is an important factor. The Canadian study investigators are not able to determine which vaccines study participants received. The influenza virus strains used to make the Canadian seasonal influenza vaccine were the same as those used in the United States and many other countries. However, some seasonal influenza vaccines used in Canada are made by manufacturers not licensed in the United States and vice versa.

CDC Response

Preliminary results of studies conducted in the United States using methods similar to the Canadian studies did not indicate that receiving a seasonal influenza vaccine increased the risk of developing influenza caused by the 2009 H1N1 influenza virus. In addition, no other country has reported that seasonal influenza vaccine increases the risk of developing influenza caused by the 2009 H1N1 influenza virus. Only one study has been published on this issue, which reported data collected in Australia. The Australian study did not find any association between receipt of seasonal influenza vaccine and risk of developing influenza caused by the 2009 H1N1 influenza virus. . . . In addition, seasonal influenza vaccination leading to increased susceptibility to other influenza viruses has never been reported before.

CDC is working with scientists in Canada, the World Health Organization (WHO) and other countries to further investigate the findings from Canada and other countries. Studies in the United States also are continuing. Thus far, no explanation has been found for the differences between results from studies in Canada compared to results of studies conducted in other countries.

CDC continues to recommend seasonal influenza vaccination for the 2009–10 influenza season. Currently the vast majority of influenza being reported to CDC is 2009 influenza A (H1N1). However, influenza is very unpredictable and seasonal influenza viruses might circulate at any point in the season. CDC does not recommend halting or deferring seasonal influenza immunization efforts.

The recommendations for who should receive seasonal influenza vaccine have not changed.

CDC recommends seasonal influenza vaccination for anyone who wants to reduce their chances of getting seasonal flu. Yearly vaccination is particularly important for certain groups of people, including those who are at high risk of having serious seasonal influenza-related complications or people who live with or care for those at high risk for serious seasonal influenza-related complications, including:

- Children aged 6 months up to their 19th birthday

- Pregnant women

- People 50 years of age and older

- People of any age with certain chronic medical conditions

- People who live in nursing homes and other long-term care facilities

- People who live with or care for those at high risk for complications from flu, including:

   o Health care workers

   o Household contacts of persons at high risk for complications from the flu

   o Household contacts and out of home caregivers of children less than 6 months of age (these children are too young to be vaccinated)

Source: Centers for Disease Control and Prevention. Press statement. "Seasonal Influenza Vaccine and Risk of 2009 H1N1 Influenza." October 7, 2009. www.cdc.gov/media/pressrel/2009/s091007.htm.

CDC *Update on Availability of H1N1 Vaccines*

October 9, 2009

On September 15, 2009, four influenza vaccine manufacturers received approval from the Food and Drug Administration for use of influenza A (H1N1) 2009 monovalent influenza vaccines in the prevention of influenza caused by the 2009 pandemic influenza A (H1N1) virus. Both live, attenuated and inactivated influenza A (H1N1) 2009 monovalent vaccine formulations are available; each contains the strain A/California/7/2009(H1N1)pdm. None of the approved influenza A 2009 (H1N1) monovalent vaccines or seasonal influenza vaccines contains adjuvants. CDC's Advisory Committee on Immunization Practices has made recommendations previously for which persons should be the initial targets for immunization with influenza A (H1N1) 2009 monovalent vaccines and has issued guidelines on decisions for expansion of vaccination efforts to other population groups. Children aged 6 months–9 years receiving influenza A (H1N1) 2009 monovalent vaccines should receive 2 doses, with doses separated by approximately 4 weeks; persons aged ≥10 years should receive 1 dose.

The approved age groups for use of inactivated influenza A (H1N1) monovalent influenza vaccines differ by manufacturer....

Influenza A (H1N1) 2009 monovalent vaccine approvals were made on the basis of standards developed for vaccine strain changes for seasonal influenza vaccines, adherence to manufacturing processes, product quality testing, and lot release procedures developed for seasonal vaccines. The age groups, precautions, and contraindications approved for the influenza A (H1N1) 2009 monovalent vaccine are identical to those approved for seasonal vaccines. All influenza vaccines available in the United States for the 2009–10 influenza season are produced using embryonated hen's eggs and contain residual egg protein.

Preliminary data indicate that the immunogenicity and safety of these vaccines are similar to those of seasonal influenza vaccines.... In studies of other seasonal inactivated influenza vaccines, rates of adverse events were not significantly different from placebo injections except for arm soreness and redness at the injection site. The National Institute of Allergy and Infectious Diseases (NIAID) reported preliminary results of a study among children aged 6 months–18 years. Among children aged 6–35 months, 3–9 years, and 10–17 years immunized with a 15 μg inactivated influenza A 2009 (H1N1) monovalent vaccine, 25%, 36% and 76%, respectively, developed antibody titers of 1:40 or more (hemagglutination-inhibition assay) after a single dose of vaccine. Immunogenicity and safety study results similar to those observed for seasonal vaccines also have been reported by the other manufacturers....

Influenza activity attributed to 2009 H1N1 viruses has increased during September 2009 and is expected to continue through the fall and winter influenza season....

[Footnotes and figures have been omitted.]

Source: Centers for Disease Control and Prevention. "Update on Influenza A (H1N1) 2009 Monovalent Vaccines." *Morbidity and Mortality Weekly Report, 58*, no. 39 (October 9, 2009). www.cdc.gov/mmwr/preview/mmwrhtml/mm5839a3.htm.

CDC Update on Influenza Activity in the United States

November 13, 2009

The 2009 pandemic influenza A (H1N1) virus emerged in the United States in April 2009 and has since spread worldwide. Influenza activity resulting from this virus occurred throughout the summer and, by late August, activity had begun to increase in the southeastern United States. Since August, activity has increased in all regions of the United States. As of the week ending October 31, nearly all states were reporting widespread disease. Since April 2009, pandemic H1N1 has remained the dominant circulating influenza strain. This report summarizes U.S. influenza activity from August 30, 2009, defined as the beginning of the 2009–10 influenza season, through October 31, 2009.

VIRAL SURVEILLANCE

During August 30–October 31, World Health Organization (WHO) and National Respiratory and Enteric Virus Surveillance System (NREVSS) collaborating laboratories in the United States tested 163,123 respiratory specimens for influenza viruses, 48,585 (30%) of which were positive. Of the 48,483 (99.8%) specimens positive for influenza A, 32,867 (68%) were subtyped by real-time reverse transcription–polymerase chain reaction (rRT-PCR) or by virus culture. A total of 32,814 (99.8%) of these were 2009 pandemic influenza A (H1N1) viruses, 18 (0.1%) were seasonal influenza A (H1), and 35 (0.1%) were influenza A (H3) viruses. . . .

ANTIVIRAL RESISTANCE OF INFLUENZA VIRUS ISOLATES

CDC conducts surveillance for resistance of circulating influenza viruses to influenza antiviral medications: adamantanes (amantadine and rimantadine) and neuraminidase inhibitors (zanamivir and oseltamivir). Since September 1, a total of 256 pandemic influenza A (H1N1) virus isolates collected in the United States have been tested for resistance to the neuraminidase inhibitors. All but four were susceptible to oseltamivir, bringing the total number of such resistant isolates to 14 since April 2009. Twelve of the 14 patients from whom the resistant isolates were collected had documented exposure to oseltamivir through treatment or chemoprophylaxis. Exposure to oseltamivir has yet to be determined for one patient, and another patient had no documented oseltamivir exposure. All 256 tested viruses were sensitive to the neuraminidase inhibitor zanamivir. Since September 1, one influenza A (H3N2) virus isolate and 152 pandemic influenza A (H1N1) virus isolates also have been tested for resistance to adamantanes (amantadine and rimantadine); all of these virus isolates were resistant to the adamantanes.

STATE-SPECIFIC ACTIVITY LEVELS

During the first week of the influenza season (August 30–September 5), 11 states, clustered mainly in the South, reported widespread activity. By the following week, that number had more than doubled to 26 states. In subsequent weeks, more states reported increased activity. As of the week ending October 31, widespread influenza activity was reported by all but two states (Mississippi and Hawaii). In contrast, during the 2008–09 influenza season, no state reported widespread influenza activity before the week ending January 10, 2009.

Outpatient Illness Surveillance

The weekly percentage of outpatient visits for influenza-like illness (ILI) reported by the U.S. Outpatient ILI Surveillance Network (ILINet) increased from 3.5% in the week ending September 5 to 7.7% in the week ending October 31. ILI activity has remained above the national baseline of 2.3% during this entire period. . . . These percentages are all substantially elevated compared with data recorded in previous years over the same period.

Influenza-Associated Hospitalizations

Laboratory-confirmed influenza-associated hospitalizations are monitored using a population-based surveillance network that includes the 10 Emerging Infections Program (EIP) sites and six new sites. During September–October, cumulative influenza hospitalization rates for persons aged <65 years were substantially elevated for this time of year and exceeded or were approaching the end-of-season cumulative rates for the last three seasons. Preliminary cumulative rates of laboratory-confirmed, influenza-associated hospitalizations reported for children aged 0–4 years were 3.1 per 10,000 population by EIP and 7.3 per 10,000 population by the new sites. Rates for other age groups were as follows: 5–17 years, 1.5 by EIP and 2.9 by the new sites; 18–49 years, 1.2 by EIP and 1.2 by the new sites; 50–64 years, 1.3 by EIP and 1.2 by the new sites; and >65 years, 1.0 by EIP and 1.1 by the new sites.

On August 30, CDC and the Council of State and Territorial Epidemiologists (CSTE) instituted modified case definitions for aggregate reporting of influenza-associated hospitalizations and deaths. This cumulative state-level reporting is referred to as the Aggregate Hospitalization and Death Reporting Activity (AHDRA). During August 30–October 31, a total of 17,838 hospitalizations associated with laboratory-confirmed influenza virus infections were reported to CDC through AHDRA. On average, 31 states each week reported laboratory-confirmed hospitalizations during that period.

Pneumonia- and Influenza-Related Mortality

Influenza-associated deaths are monitored by the 122 Cities Mortality Reporting System and AHDRA. For the week ending October 31, pneumonia or influenza was reported as an underlying or contributing cause of death for 7.4% of all deaths reported through the 122 Cities Mortality Reporting System, above the week-specific epidemic threshold of 6.7% and the fifth consecutive week above the epidemic threshold.

During August 30–October 31, 672 deaths associated with laboratory-confirmed influenza virus infections were reported to CDC through AHDRA. On average, 29 states reported laboratory-confirmed deaths each week during that period. The 672 laboratory-confirmed deaths are in addition to the 593 laboratory-confirmed deaths from 2009 pandemic influenza A (H1N1) that were reported to CDC from April through August 30, 2009.

INFLUENZA-ASSOCIATED PEDIATRIC MORTALITY

During August 30–October 31, CDC received 85 reports of pediatric deaths associated with influenza infection. Seventy-three of these cases were associated with laboratory-confirmed 2009 pandemic influenza A (H1N1) virus. The remaining 12 pediatric deaths were associated with an influenza A infection for which the subtype was undetermined.

Of the 85 pediatric deaths reported since August 30, a total of 12 (14%) were among children aged <2 years, nine (11%) were among children aged 2–4 years, 30 (35%) were among children aged 5–11 years, and 34 (40%) were among children aged 12–17 years. Seventy-eight (92%) of the 85 decedents had a medical history reported. Of the 78, 56 (72%) had one or more medical conditions associated with an increased risk for influenza-related complications.

Since April 26, CDC has received 145 reports of pediatric deaths associated with influenza infection. Of these, 129 (89%) cases were associated with laboratory-confirmed 2009 pandemic influenza A (H1N1) virus. The remaining 16 pediatric deaths were associated with seasonal influenza or an influenza A virus for which the subtype was undetermined. In comparison, during the preceding five influenza seasons, the total number of reported pediatric influenza deaths ranged from 46 to 153, with an average of 82 deaths each year. . . .

[The editorial note, figures, and footnotes have been omitted.]

SOURCE: Centers for Disease Control and Prevention. "Update: Influenza Activity—United States, August 30–October 31, 2009." *Morbidity and Mortality Weekly Report, 58,* no. 44 (November 13, 2009). www.cdc.gov/mmwr/preview/mmwrhtml/mm5844a4.htm?s_cid=mm5844a4_e.

OTHER HISTORIC DOCUMENTS OF INTEREST

FROM THIS VOLUME

FROM PREVIOUS *HISTORIC DOCUMENTS*

Rio de Janeiro Selected as 2016 Olympic Host City

OCTOBER 2 AND NOVEMBER 3, 2009

In a historic first for South America, Rio de Janeiro, Brazil, won the honor of hosting the 2016 Summer Olympic Games. Following a long, expensive, and highly competitive bidding process, on October 2, 2009, the International Olympic Committee (IOC) voted to award Rio the coveted honor. The city must overcome significant financial and logistical challenges in the coming years to deliver the "beautiful game" it promised.

THE CONTENDERS

On June 4, 2008, the IOC announced the four candidate cities to host the 2016 Olympic Games: Chicago, Illinois; Rio de Janeiro, Brazil; Madrid, Spain; and Tokyo, Japan. The four cities had made it through the first stage of the IOC's bidding process. As part of a broader group of applicant cities, they had undergone an assessment by an IOC working group of their "potential to stage high-level, international, multi-sports events and their potential to organize" the games successfully, in addition to an evaluation of their ability to meet a set of eleven technical criteria. The IOC executive board consulted these assessments and determined that Rio, Chicago, Madrid, and Tokyo were the most capable applicants to be considered candidate cities.

Following the announcement, each city hosted the IOC Evaluation Commission for a visit. The commission presented its findings to the full IOC, and a final vote to determine the host city for the 2016 games was scheduled for October 2, 2009, in Copenhagen, Denmark. Each candidate city was given an opportunity to make a final hour-long presentation the day of the selection. Voting took place in several rounds, eliminating the city with the lowest number of votes each round, and continuing until one city received a majority of votes.

AN UNPRECEDENTED U.S. BID

Chicago's bid marked an unprecedented effort on the part of the United States to secure the honor of hosting the games, with an all-time high in spending and involvement by U.S. officials. Traveling to Copenhagen for the final vote, Barack Obama became the first U.S. president to appeal to the IOC in person. First lady Michelle Obama and media mogul (and Chicago resident) Oprah Winfrey also lent their celebrity status to winning support for Chicago's bid. The women spent two full days in Copenhagen—the president only five hours—to attend the IOC's gala and other social events.

Chicago's presentation included personal anecdotes from the first lady, who spoke of her love for her hometown as well as her fond memories of growing up with sports and watching the Olympics with her father as a child. President Obama urged IOC members to "choose Chicago," saying, "if you do—if we walk this path together—then I promise you this: The city of Chicago and the United State of America will make the world proud."

The Obamas's personal participation was, however, ineffective. Surprisingly, Chicago was eliminated in the first round of voting, receiving a mere 18 of 94 votes. ESPN News called it "one of the most shocking defeats ever in International Olympic Committee voting." Rene Fasel, an IOC member from Switzerland, said, "Everybody was shocked at that result. Everybody expected Chicago and Rio, everybody." Reacting to the news, the president said he believed Chicago had made the "strongest bid possible" despite the outcome. "You can play a great game and still not win," he said. "Although I wish we had come back with better news, I could not be prouder of my hometown." In the highly charged partisan atmosphere of Washington, D.C., Chicago's loss instantly became politicized. Democrats worried that Obama had wasted precious political capital, while Republicans assailed the president for jet-setting to Copenhagen while the country faced pressing domestic problems.

Most observers saw apolitical considerations as the root of Chicago's loss. Some speculated that Chicago lost because of the unimpressive presentations made by the city's mayor, Richard Daley, and the leader of Chicago 2016, Pat Ryan, who spoke primarily about the new local sports programs the Olympics would help start and nearby universities that wanted to participate in the effort—a narrow focus that sharply contrasted with the global aspirations of other bids. Others pointed to concerns about potential cost overruns, outdated city infrastructure, and a lack of public support among Chicagoans as reasons for the defeat. Chicago was also the only candidate city that did not have full financial support from government for the games. A number of IOC session members claimed Chicago's loss could be attributed to a testy relationship between the IOC and the U.S. Olympic Committee (USOC). The USOC had recently experienced a year-long period of internal upheaval, resulting in a sudden change of leadership and had also caused a stir by announcing it would start its own cable network without seeking the approval of prominent IOC members.

TOKYO'S TECHNICAL APPEAL

Shortly after Chicago's defeat, Tokyo was eliminated in the second round of voting. Tokyo's bid had received high marks from the IOC Evaluation Commission for its solid financial backing, having already set aside $4 billion, and for its technical vision. The city planned to renovate and reuse several of the Olympic venues that had been constructed for the 1964 games, as well as build the first Olympic stadium powered by solar energy. It also put forth a unique concept for highly compact games, proposing to hold all but one event within five miles of the city center.

However, Tokyo had the lowest public backing of all candidate cities in polls conducted by the IOC. The city had also received several low marks for the quality of its existing venues, operations management, and land area available for the athletes' village. Some in attendance for Tokyo's presentation also noted a lack of emotion or enthusiasm among members of the bid team, thereby failing to convince IOC members that they really wanted the Games.

Tokyo's elimination marked Japan's third consecutive failed bid to host the summer games. The Japanese Olympic Committee (JOC) seemed to take the news in stride. "It's a pity. We united as a team and did everything we could," said Tsunekazu Takeda, chief executive of the JOC. "There is a winner and a loser and this time we couldn't win, but we have also gained something. We have to figure out how to go for the 2020 Olympics."

Madrid Makes Emotional Plea, Rio Makes History

The elimination of Chicago and Tokyo left only Madrid and Rio. Juan Antonio Samaranch Sr., a former IOC president who had retained considerable influence among its members, made a "deathbed appeal" as part of Madrid's presentation. "Dear colleagues, I know I am very near the end of my time. I am, as you know, 89 years old," he said. "May I ask you to consider granting my country the honor and also the duty to organize the Games and Paralympic Games in 2016."

Samaranch's appeal was not enough. In a landslide vote of 66 to 32, Rio de Janeiro was declared the official host city of the 2016 Olympic Games, making Brazil the first South American country to win the honor. The news sparked a massive party on Rio's Copacabana Beach, where nearly 50,000 people celebrated well into the evening. Brazilian president Luiz Inácio Lula da Silva, in Copenhagen with soccer legend Pelé for Rio's bid presentation, began to sob. "From the bottom of my heart, I should say this is the most emotional day in my life," the president said. "Rio deserves it, and Brazil deserves it."

Rio's bid for the 2016 games was strengthened by Brazil's designation as the tenth largest economy in the world and the country's relative financial stability during the global economic downturn. The bid also enjoyed significant public backing, with 85 percent of those living in Rio and 69 percent of Brazilians supporting the city's candidacy. In addition, the bid proposed a budget of more than $14 billion, and governments at the federal, state, and local level guaranteed the financing. Rio also promised that nearly a third of all tickets for the games would be priced at less than $20 and that the city, in an effort to produce a carbon-neutral Olympics, would plant 24 million trees in the years leading up to the event.

Rio plans to create four separate "venue zones," each located in a different part of the city and each hosting different sporting events. The Olympic village will be located in an area called Barra, as will venues for gymnastics, tennis, swimming, and diving. Rio's world-famous Copacabana Beach will host such temporary sports as beach volleyball and marathon swimming. The city's Deodoro neighborhood will have venues for mountain biking, BMX cycling, equestrian, and shooting events. Finally, the Marcana Stadium, primarily used for track and field events, will be renovated to host the opening and closing ceremonies, as well as soccer games. In addition, Rio promised to spend nearly $430 million to build an athletes' village that replicates "the outdoor lifestyle of Rio's beachside neighborhoods."

Perhaps of greatest concern to IOC members was Rio's ongoing struggle with high, drug-related crime rates. Although the committee acknowledged the city had improved public safety, the homicide rate had been rising and had increased nearly 10 percent by the time of the vote. In an attempt to overcome these fears, city officials highlighted a $3.35 billion homicide prevention program being implemented across Brazil, as well as laws passed in 2003 that tightened restrictions on the private ownership of firearms. They also noted that since hosting the 2007 Pan American Games, Rio has adopted new policing policies, implementing a more efficient, single line of authority and emphasizing engagement with the public rather than enforcement. The bid also included promises to improve training and structure within the city's police force, an expansion of closed-circuit television systems within the metropolitan area, and an increased military police presence during the games.

Rio faces significant challenges in addition to curbing the crime rate in preparing for the summer games. The city will need to build eleven new, permanent venues and must renovate eight existing structures built for the 2007 Pan American Games to meet the IOC's minimum seating requirements. In addition, Rio has a limited metro system that does not link the city center to the city's outer limits where the majority of event venues will be located. Although the city has proposed spending $5 billion to develop rapid-transit bus lines, fans could still be stuck in traffic for up to an hour. City officials must also clean Rio's polluted waterways, which would be used for sailing and other water sports. Furthermore, although the city intends to build a number of new complexes to provide the 48,000 hotel rooms needed for the games, it will have to rely on cruise ships docked in the port areas of Rio to ensure sufficient accommodations.

Yet Brazilian officials remain confident the 2016 Olympic Games will be successful and will provide a firsthand measure of the country's growth and future potential. Indeed, they have already hosted a Rio 2016 Orientation Seminar to discuss management and development of the games, held just twenty-eight days after winning the vote. "For us, it will hardly be our last Olympics. For us, it will be an opportunity to be equal," President Lula said. "It will increase self-esteem for Brazilians, will consolidate recent conquests and stimulate new advances."

—Linda Fecteau

Following is a press release from October 2, 2009, from the International Olympic Committee announcing the choice of Rio de Janiero to host the 2016 Olympic Games, and a press release from November 3, 2009, from the Rio 2016 committee explaining ongoing preparations for the 2016 Olympic games.

DOCUMENT

IOC Announces Rio Chosen to Host 2016 Olympic Games

October 2, 2009

The International Olympic Committee (IOC) has elected Rio de Janeiro (Brazil) as the host city of the Games of the XXXI Olympiad in 2016 during its 121st Session in Copenhagen, Denmark. Rio de Janeiro received 66 votes compared to Madrid's 32 in the final round of voting.

IOC President Jacques Rogge congratulated Rio de Janeiro on its election and praised the high quality of the bid: "I would like to congratulate the city of Rio de Janeiro on its election as the host of the 2016 Olympic Games. Rio de Janeiro presented the IOC with a very strong technical bid, built upon a vision of the Games being a celebration of the athletes and sport, as well as providing the opportunity for the city, region and country to deliver their broader long-term aspirations for the future. This call to "live your passion" clearly struck a chord with my fellow members and we now look forward to seeing Rio de Janeiro stage the first Olympic Games on the continent of South America. Well done, Rio!"

Rogge also thanked the other competing cities of Chicago (USA), Tokyo (Japan) and Madrid (Spain): "Unfortunately, there can only be one victor in this competition and I'd like to thank the cities of Chicago, Tokyo and Madrid for participating. Their projects and dedication to spreading the Olympic values throughout their countries and beyond has been outstanding. Despite not being elected today, these cities have all seen the benefit of being candidates for the Games. I would like to congratulate them all for their efforts and for their commitment to the Olympic Movement."

Results:

ROUND 1:

MADRID:	28
RIO DE JANEIRO:	26
TOKYO:	22
CHICAGO:	18

ROUND 2:

RIO DE JANEIRO:	46
MADRID:	29
TOKYO:	20

ROUND 3:

| RIO DE JANEIRO: | 66 |
| MADRID: | 32 |

SOURCE: International Olympic Committee. Press release. "Rio de Janeiro Elected as the 2016 Host City." October 2, 2009. www.olympic.org/en/content/Media/?MediaNewsTab=0&articleNewsGroup=-1& articleId=73322.

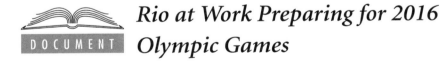

Rio at Work Preparing for 2016 Olympic Games

November 3, 2009

Rio 2016 Sets Record in Early Start to Work on the Organization of the Olympic and Paralympic Games

IOC Director Praise at Close of Orientation Seminar

Rio de Janeiro is the host city to begin work most quickly on the organization of the Olympic Games and Paralympic Games. The fact was praised by the Swiss Olympic

Games executive director, Gilbert Felli, at the closure of the Rio 2016 Orientation Seminar organized by the IOC. Only 28 days after the election of Rio de Janeiro to host the 2016 Games, the event marked the official start of the work of the Rio 2016 Organizing Committee.

Topics for the Orientation Seminar included the structure, management and development planning of the Games over the next seven years. No specific technical data of Rio de Janeiro's project was analyzed. The event, held at the Copacabana Palace Hotel, brought together 200 people, including representatives of three levels of government—Federal, State and Municipal—as well as the Rio 2016 Committee, the Brazilian Olympic Committee and the Brazilian Paralympic Committee. "I would like to congratulate everyone. Brazil can be proud of what was achieved in Copenhagen. The two days of this seminar have been very important because we know that there is no time to lose over the next seven years. At this meeting we met people who understand perfectly the importance of the Olympics. Rio de Janeiro is the host city that began work on organizing the Games most quickly," Felli said.

In addition to the Olympic Games executive director, the IOC delegation included six other members: Timo Lumme, director of television and marketing services; Christophe Dubi, sports director; Antony Scanlon, head of Games services and coordination of the Olympic Games; Jennifer O'Brien, Olympic Games coordination project manager; Robert Roxburgh, director of media relations, and Toshio Tsurunaga, manager of IOC services for National Olympic Committees. "The objective of this seminar was to build partnerships between the different levels of organization of the Games. We are responsible for a special event, and we have to provide the best for all clients. We explained what kind of support the IOC can give to the Organizing Committee. We are feeling confident, because we believe that everything was very well understood and that Rio 2016 will do an excellent job," added Felli.

For Rio 2016 president, Carlos Arthur Nuzman, the presence of Sports Minister Orlando Silva, state governor, Sergio Cabral and Mayor Eduardo Paes shows the commitment of the three levels of government to the project. "The seminar was very helpful. The day after Rio de Janeiro's election as host city, we had meetings with the IOC, and then we met with many other sectors, but this event actually marks the beginning of the Committee's work. In February, during the IOC session we will present the first Rio 2016 progress report," he said.

SOURCE: Rio 2016. Press release. "Rio 2016 Sets Record in Early Start to Work on the Organization of the Olympic and Paralympic Games." November 3, 2009. www.rio2016.org/en/Imprensa/Releases/Release .aspx?idConteudo=1087.

OTHER HISTORIC DOCUMENTS OF INTEREST

FROM PREVIOUS HISTORIC DOCUMENTS

- Concerns over the 2008 Beijing Summer Olympic Games, *2008*, p. 286

Educational Assessment Shows States Lagging

OCTOBER 14 AND 29, 2009

President George W. Bush's No Child Left Behind (NCLB) program hit another wall on October 29, 2009, when a National Assessment of Educational Progress (NAEP) report showed no growth in math scores between 2007 and 2009. The lack of growth meant that fewer than 40 percent of fourth- and eighth-grade students were at a proficient level in math, a subject often considered most important to the United States' ability to continue to compete in the international marketplace. The test, mandated by NCLB, is given to randomly selected students in grades four and eight every other year to assess how the nation's students as a whole are performing.

The program had been under considerable fire from states during the Bush administration, with critics arguing that the federal government was forcing educational standards on them without providing funding to help them meet these standards. NCLB faced increasing criticism from President Barack Obama, who made it a campaign promise to improve the program and provide states the appropriate funding to ensure each student achieves at least the minimum proficiency standards required by NCLB.

Proposed in 2002 by President Bush and passed with bipartisan support in Congress, NCLB requires that states give students math and reading tests every year from grades three through eight and again once they enter high school. If a school fails to meet an Adequate Yearly Progress (AYP) standard on these tests for two years in a row, that school must implement improvement measures, including additional tutoring or offering school choice. The scores of these tests have to be published and broken down into groups by race and sex. Previously, only averages were required to be published. These new rules were targeted at recognizing and closing the achievement gap between white students and their Hispanic and African American counterparts.

OCTOBER REPORT

The October 29, release of the NAEP, or "nation's report card," found that fewer than four out of every ten fourth and eighth graders tested at a proficient level in math. These scores were compared to 2007 results, the last time the math portion of the test was given. They revealed that there were no significant gains made in the number of students who tested at the proficient level. Before 2007, fourth graders had been gaining in proficiency on every national math assessment test since 1990. Eighth-grade math students showed a small increase in scores over 2007, but according to David Driscoll, chair in charge of the group that oversees the NAEP, "the improvement is so modest that it just isn't going to do what our kids need."

The NAEP is administered by the Department of Education on various subjects, including math and reading. The tests are given to a sampling of fourth- and eighth-grade students across the country every other year and are considered to be more advanced than state achievement tests, which are given annually. The math test scores in this case were derived from an assessment given in January, February, and March 2009 to 330,000 students. On average, fourth-grade students scored at a "basic" proficiency, getting 240 out of 500 points; and eighth-grade students scored an average of 283 points (also out of 500), once again at the "basic" level. Secretary of Education Arne Duncan called these results "unacceptable" and said they indicate the need for "reforms that will accelerate student achievement."

This wasn't the first test to show that students were unable to meet basic math requirements. In early 2009, ACT (originally known as American College Testing), an independent organization that offers an array of standardized tests, said that only 42 percent of high school graduates taking its assessment test were proficient enough for college-level math. Similarly, the SAT Reasoning Test, a college admissions exam administered by the College Board, showed no improvement in math skills among high school graduates over the previous year.

In addition, the results of the NAEP math test showed no decrease in the proficiency gap between white students and their Hispanic and African American classmates. On the fourth-grade math test, whereas white students scored an average of 248, Hispanics scored an average of 227, and African American students scored an average of 222. On the eighth-grade test, the results were similar. White eighth graders scored an average of 293, Hispanics scored an average of 266, and African Americans scored an average of 261. Although the thirty-two-point gap between African American and white eighth-grade students seems small, it represents the knowledge gained in approximately three years of math classes.

Math is considered an essential skill for students, given the increasing number of jobs in the global economy that require such skills. Economists and labor experts worry that without better math skills, the United States will continue to fall behind other nations in job growth and creation in a number of sectors that depend on math. Scores from trends in International Mathematics and Science Study, a test given in the United States and other nations, were released in September 2009 and showed that although U.S. students were making gains in math, their scores still lagged behind those of students in a number of places, including Hong Kong, Singapore, Taiwan, England, and the Russian Federation.

CURRENT STATUS OF NO CHILD LEFT BEHIND

When President Bush signed NCLB into law in 2002, it was touted as the greatest educational reform since the 1950s, when desegregation went into effect. In 2007, when the program came up for congressional reauthorization, however, it ran into a road block. As of the end of 2009, Congress had been unable to muster enough support from either Democrats or Republicans to reauthorize the program, which had been funded only by extensions since 2007.

NCLB mandates that all students from kindergarten through high school meet required state proficiency standards in math and reading. This goal, according to the program, must be reached by 2014. Any school that falls short of proficient could face penalties, including takeover or restructuring of the administration and staff by a state's department of education.

Although the law has been criticized heavily since its inception, mainly by states that object to it as an unfunded mandate, some observers point to positive aspects of it. Some teachers say that the education gap between their white students and minority counterparts was exposed because of NCLB, leading some to believe that the problem will finally be addressed. In addition, historically low-performing schools have been identified, giving some hope that additional funding might be considered for these schools to bring them up to higher standards. On the other hand, critics argue that because there are no stipulations in the law about *what* students have to learn at each grade level, states are able to reduce the difficulty level of their standardized tests to help all students meet minimum proficiency levels. This, they say, leaves students even further behind. Duncan agrees. "The biggest problem with NCLB is that it doesn't encourage high learning standards," Duncan said. "The net effect is that we are lying to children and parents by telling kids they are succeeding when they are not," he continued.

Recognizing that the United States cannot compete in a global marketplace without higher education standards and outcomes, during his campaign for president, Obama promised to "improve NCLB's accountability system so that we are supporting schools that need improvement, rather than punishing them." To achieve this goal, Duncan said the administration would work through the Elementary and Secondary Education Act of 1965, under which NCLB was created. After completing a "listening and learning tour" around the country to gather feedback on educational programs, Duncan announced that he would consider tests that better track student progress in various educational areas from year to year and would also work on a program to help schools that consistently fall below proficiency levels.

On July 24, 2009, President Obama and Secretary Duncan announced a new federal education program, Race to the Top, which would give states competitive grants—funded by $4.35 billion in stimulus funds allocated to education—if they set higher achievement standards and worked to better measure student progress through regular testing.

Education experts and some legislators believe the Race to the Top program will be used as a test for a revised NCLB program. According to Rep. George Miller, D-Calif., chair of the House education committee, the Race to the Top program could be the push that finally breaks the NCLB reauthorization logjam in Congress.

STATE REACTION

The promise of education funds through Race to the Top led states to begin making revisions to their education policies to qualify for as much federal funding as possible. In California, the legislature rewrote a law that had once prohibited schools from using student performance when evaluating teachers. California was left with little choice but to change its educational standards after Duncan said that in a state with 300,000 teachers, no one could tell which teachers were among the "best in the world" and which "should probably find another profession."

Other states, including Illinois, Indiana, Louisiana, and Tennessee, also moved to rewrite policies to ensure they were in compliance with Race to the Top regulations. In each case, states were trying to come into compliance with the provision requiring that a state have no "barriers to linking data on student achievement or student growth to teachers and principals for the purpose of teacher and principal evaluation."

The New Teacher Project, a nonprofit organization, released a report rating states on whether they would be eligible to receive federal stimulus funds. While states such as Florida and Louisiana were considered among those most likely to receive funds, New York and Wisconsin were among those that the organization believed would not be able to fund because of state policies limiting how schools are able to use student performance to evaluate teachers. New York is fighting back, indicating that it only bans the use of student data when determining whether a teacher is eligible for tenure.

While some states and school districts scrambled to get policies in order, others filed complaints with the Department of Education. In Orange County, Virginia, the school superintendent called the regulations "overly burdensome," saying "[t]hey give the impression that stimulus funds provide the federal government with unbridled capacity to impose bureaucratic demands." Other educators around the country, many of whom said they had voted for Obama in 2008 in hopes that he would change NCLB standards, said the policies required to receive funding under the stimulus program could increase student testing more than NCLB had.

—Heather Kerrigan

Following is a press release from the National Assessment Governing Board on October 14, 2009, on the results of the "nation's report card"; a press release from Secretary of Education Arne Duncan issued October 29, 2009, on the results of the National Assessment of Educational Progress; and exerpted text of the National Assessment of Educational Progress, released October 29, 2009.

Press Release on the 2009 Nation's Report Card

October 14, 2009

There has been no significant change in the performance of the nation's 4th-graders in mathematics from 2007 to 2009, a contrast to the progress seen from 1990 to 2007 at that grade level and subject, according to the 2009 National Assessment of Educational Progress (NAEP) in mathematics. But the 8th-grade mathematics score on the NAEP, which is also called The Nation's Report Card, continued to improve nationwide and reached its highest level since 1990.

The Nation's Report Card: Mathematics 2009, released today, details the achievement of 4th- and 8th-graders on the NAEP, administered by the U.S. Department of Education earlier this year. The report compares national results in 2009 with each prior assessment year going back to 1990, and state results going back to 1990 at grade 8 and 1992 at grade 4.

At the state level, scores improved at 4th-grade in eight states, while four states saw decreases from 2007. At the 8th-grade, scores increased from 2007 to 2009 in 15 states, and no states showed declines. Overall, four states and the District of Columbia saw increases at both 4th- and 8th-grades.

None of the gaps in either grade narrowed from 2007 to 2009. The gaps between Black and White students and between private and public school students narrowed from 1990 to 2009 for 4th-graders and remained unchanged for 8th-graders.

"While the scores for 8th-graders in math continue to be encouraging, the failure of our 4th-graders to make progress nationally is a cause for concern," said David P. Driscoll, chair of the National Assessment Governing Board, which sets policy for NAEP. "With a lack of progress at 4th-grade and large achievement gaps that are relatively unchanged, we need to re-examine our efforts to improve student achievement in math."

While average scores for 4th-graders in all racial/ethnic groups reported in NAEP did not change significantly since 2007, they were higher than in 1990 for those groups with reportable results. Scores for 8th-graders were higher in 2009 than in both 2007 and 1990 for all racial/ethnic groups except American Indian/Alaska Native students, who showed no significant change since 2007.

The trends at different achievement levels mirrored the overall trends in scores. For example, the percentages of 4th-graders performing at or above *Basic* (82 percent) and at or above *Proficient* (39 percent) in 2009 were the same as those in 2007 but still higher than they were from 1990 to 2005. Improvements in national 8th-grade scores since 2007 and all previous assessment years were consistent with increases in the percentages of 8th-graders performing at or above *Basic* (73 percent) and at or above *Proficient* (34 percent) in 2009.

Results across NAEP performance levels were also consistent with national trends. In grade 4, there were no significant changes in scores from 2007 to 2009 for lower-performing students (at the 10th and 25th percentiles), middle-performing students (at the 50th percentile), or higher-performing students (at the 75th and 90th percentiles). The scores at grade 8 improved at all performance levels, except for the lowest-performing students (10th percentile), who saw no significant change since 2007.

Male students continue to score two points higher than female students in mathematics at both grades 4 and 8. The gaps have not widened, however, since 2007. . . .

SOURCE: National Assessment Governing Board. Press release. "2009 Nation's Report Card in Mathematics Reveals No Change at 4th-Grade, But New High for 8th-Grade Score." October 14, 2009. http://nationsreportcard.gov/math_2009/media/pdf/math_board_news_release.pdf.

Secretary of Education Arne Duncan on NAEP Report

October 29, 2009

Today's study confirms what we've known for a long time: States are setting the bar too low. In all but a few cases, states aren't expecting students to meet NAEP's standard of proficiency. Far too many states are telling students that they are proficient when they actually are performing below NAEP's basic level. At a time when we should be raising standards to compete in the global economy, more states are lowering the bar than raising it. We're lying to our children when we tell them they're proficient but they're not achieving at a level that will prepare them for success once they graduate.

I am grateful that leaders from 48 states are working together to set standards that will determine whether students are college- and career-ready. Their work will set a common standard that all states will be able to use to measure the success of their students.

But it will take more than college- and career-ready standards to succeed in school reform. We'll need tests that fairly and accurately measure students' performance on those standards. We'll need data systems that help teachers know whether students are on track for success in college and the workplace. We'll need effective teachers in every classroom, especially in ones serving students that need the most help. We'll also need strategies to turn around our lowest-performing schools.

The Obama administration is providing unprecedented resources to states and districts to drive reform through these policies, and we're working with state and district leaders to put these policies into action.

SOURCE: U.S. Department of Education. Press release. "U.S. Education Secretary Releases Statement on National Center for Education Statistics NAEP Report Released Today." October 29, 2009. www2.ed.gov/news/pressreleases/2009/10/10292009.html.

NAEP Report on State Proficiency Standards

DOCUMENT

October 29, 2009

EXECUTIVE SUMMARY

Since 2003, the National Center for Education Statistics (NCES) has sponsored the development of a method for mapping each state's standard for proficient performance onto a common scale—the achievement scale of the National Assessment of Educational Progress (NAEP). When states' standards are placed onto the NAEP reading or mathematics scales, the level of achievement required for proficient performance in one state can then be compared with the level of achievement required in another state. This allows one to compare the standards for proficiency across states. . . .

This report presents mapping results using the 2005 and 2007 NAEP assessments in mathematics and reading for grades 4 and 8. The analyses conducted for this study addressed the following questions:

- How do states' 2007 standards for proficient performance compare with each other when mapped on the NAEP scale?

- How do the 2007 NAEP scale equivalents for state standards compare with those estimated for 2005?

- Using the 2005 NAEP scale equivalent for state standards to define a state's *proficient* level of performance on NAEP, do NAEP and that state's assessment agree on the changes in the proportion of students meeting that state's standard for proficiency from 2005 to 2007?

To address the first question, the 2007 *NAEP scale equivalent* of each state reading and mathematics proficiency standard for each grade was identified. The mapping procedure was applied to the test data of 48 states. Key findings of the analysis presented in Section 3 of the report are:

- In 2007, as in 2003 and 2005, state standards for *proficient* performance in reading and mathematics (as measured on the NAEP scale) vary across states in terms of the levels of achievement required. For example, the *distance* separating the five states with the highest standards and the five states with the lowest standards in grade 4 reading was comparable to the difference between *Basic* and *Proficient* performance on NAEP. The distance was as large in reading at grade 8 and as large in mathematics in both grades.

- In both reading and mathematics, the 29- to 30-point distance separating the five highest and the five lowest NAEP scale equivalent of state standards for *proficient* performance was nearly as large as the 35 points that represent approximately one standard deviation in student achievement on the NAEP scale.

- In grade 4 reading, 31 states set grade 4 standards for proficiency (as measured on the NAEP scale) that were lower than the cut point for *Basic* performance on NAEP (208). In grade 8 reading, 15 states set standards that were lower than the *Basic* performance on NAEP (243).

- In grade 4 mathematics, seven states set standards for proficiency (as measured on the NAEP scale) that were lower than the *Basic* performance on NAEP (214). In grade 8 mathematics, eight states set standards that were lower than the *Basic* performance on NAEP (262).

- Most of the variation (approximately 70 percent) from state to state in the percentage of students scoring proficient or above on state tests can be explained by the variation in the level of difficulty of state standards for proficient performance. States with higher standards (as measured on the NAEP scale) had *fewer* students scoring proficient on state tests.

- The rigor of the state standards is not consistently associated with higher performance on NAEP. This association is measured by the squared correlation between the NAEP scale equivalent of the state standards and the percentages of students who scored at or above the NAEP *Proficient* level. In grade 4 reading and mathematics, the squared correlations are around .10 and statistically significant. In grade 8 reading and mathematics, the squared correlations are less than .07 and are not statistically significant.

To address the second question, the analyses focused on the consistency of mapping outcomes over time using both 2005 and 2007 assessments. Although NAEP did not change between 2005 and 2007, some states made changes in their state assessments in the same period, changes substantial enough that states indicated that their 2005 scores were not comparable to their 2007 scores. Other states indicated that their scores for those years are comparable. Comparisons between the 2005 and 2007 mappings in reading and mathematics at grades 4 and 8 were made separately for states that made changes in their testing systems and for those that made no such changes. Key findings of the analysis presented in Section 4 are:

- In grade 4 reading, 12 of the 34 states with available data in both years indicated substantive changes in their assessments. Of those, eight showed significant differences between the 2005 and 2007 estimates of the NAEP scale equivalent of their state standards, half of which showed an increase and half a decrease.

- In grade 8 reading, 14 of the 38 states with available data in both years indicated substantive changes in their assessments. Of those, seven showed significant differences between the 2005 and 2007 estimates of the NAEP scale equivalent of their state standards, all seven showed lower 2007 estimates of the NAEP scale equivalents.

- In grade 4 mathematics, 14 of the 35 states with available data in both years indicated substantive changes in their assessments. Of those, 11 showed significant differences between the 2005 and 2007 estimates of the NAEP scale equivalent of their state standards: 6 states showed a decrease and 5 showed an increase.

- In grade 8 mathematics, 18 of the 39 states with available data in both years indicated substantive changes in their assessments. Of those, 12 showed significant differences between the 2005 and 2007 estimates of the NAEP scale equivalent of their state standards: 9 showed a decrease and 3 showed an increase.

For the states with no substantive changes in their state assessments in the same period, the analyses presented in Section 4 indicate that for the majority of states in the comparison sample (14 of 22 in grade 4 reading, 13 of 24 in grade 8 reading, 15 of 21 in grade 4 mathematics and 14 of 21 in grade 8 mathematics), the differences in the estimates of NAEP scale equivalents of their state standards were not statistically significant.

To address the third question, NAEP and state changes in achievement from 2005 to 2007 were compared. The percentage of students reported to be meeting the state standard in 2007 is compared with the percentage of the NAEP students in 2007 that is above the NAEP scale equivalent of the same state standard in 2005. The analysis was limited to states with (a) available data in both years and (b) no substantive changes in their state tests. The number of states included in the analyses ranged from 21 to 24, depending on the subject and grade. The expectation was that both the state assessments and NAEP would show the same changes in achievement between the two years. Statistically significant differences between NAEP and state measures of changes in achievement indicate that more progress is made on either the NAEP skill domain or the state-specific skill domain between 2005 and 2007. A more positive change on the state test indicates students gained more on the state-specific skill domain. For example, a focus in instruction on state-specific content might lead a state assessment to show more progress in achievement than NAEP. Similarly, a less positive change on the state test indicates students gained more on the NAEP skill domain. For example, focus in instruction on NAEP content that is not a part of the state assessment might lead the state assessment to show progress in achievement that is less than that of NAEP. Key findings from Section 5 are:

- In grade 4 reading, 11 of 22 states showed no statistically significant difference between NAEP and state assessment measures of changes in achievement; 5 states showed changes that are more positive than the changes measured by

NAEP, and 6 states showed changes that are less positive than those measured by NAEP.

- In grade 8 reading, 9 of 24 states showed no statistically significant difference between NAEP and state assessment measures of achievement changes; 10 states showed changes that are more positive than the changes measured by NAEP, and 5 states showed changes that are less positive than those measured by NAEP.

- In grade 4 mathematics, 13 of 21 states showed no statistically significant difference between NAEP and state assessment measures of achievement changes; 5 states showed changes that are more positive than the changes measured by NAEP, and 3 states showed changes that are less positive than those measured by NAEP.

- In grade 8 mathematics, 9 of 21 states showed no statistically significant difference between NAEP and state assessment measures of achievement changes, 7 states showed changes that are more positive than the changes measured by NAEP, and 5 states showed changes that are less positive than those measured by NAEP. . . .

In conclusion, these mapping analyses offer several important contributions. First, they allow each state to compare the stringency of its criteria for proficiency with that of other states. Second, mapping analyses inform states whether the rigor of their proficiency standards as represented by NAEP scale equivalents changed from 2005 to 2007. Significant differences in NAEP scale equivalents might reflect changes in state assessments and standards and/or other changes such as changes in policies or practices that occurred between the years. Finally, when key aspects of a state's assessment or standards remained the same, these mapping analyses allow NAEP to corroborate state-reported changes in student achievement and provide states with an indicator of the construct validity and generalizability of their test results. . . .

[Parts 1 through 5 of the report, containing information on the National Assessment of Educational Progress performance standards, estimation methods, and complete state education data and charts have been omitted.]

6 CONCLUSIONS

The purpose of state-to-NAEP comparisons is to aid in the interpretation of state assessment results by providing a benchmark. Despite the limitations of state-to-NAEP comparisons, there is a need for reliable information that compares state standards to one another. What does it mean to say that a student is proficient in reading in grade 4 in Massachusetts? Would a fourth-grader who is proficient in reading in Wyoming also be proficient in Massachusetts? The analyses presented in this study provide a basis for answering such questions.

Mapping state standards for proficient performance on the NAEP scales showed wide variation among states in the rigor of their standards. The implication is that students of similar academic skills, but residing in different states, are being evaluated against different standards for proficiency in reading and mathematics. All NAEP scale equivalents of states' reading standards were below NAEP's *Proficient* range; and in mathematics, only two states' NAEP scale equivalent were in the NAEP *Proficient* range (Massachusetts in grades 4 and 8, and South Carolina in grade 8). In many cases, the NAEP scale equivalent for a state's standard, especially in grade 4 reading, mapped below the NAEP achievement level for *Basic* performance. There may well be valid reasons for state standards to fall below NAEP's *Proficient* range. The comparisons simply provide a context for describing the rigor of performance standards that states across the country have adopted.

Almost one-half of the states changed aspects of their assessment policies or the assessment itself between 2005 and 2007 in ways that prevented their reading or mathematics test results from being comparable across these two years. Either explicitly or implicitly, such states have adopted new performance standards. By mapping the state standards in both years to the same NAEP scale, the changes in rigor of the standards can be measured. For states with both years of data, the mapping results showed that the NAEP equivalents representing state standards for proficiency were lower in 2007 in one-third to one-half of the states that made such changes (depending on subject and grade). A decrease in the stringency of the NAEP equivalent of state standards was more likely to occur for grade 8 than for grade 4.

In the remaining states in which no changes were made or the changes in assessment policies were minor enough that their test results remained comparable, it was possible to check the extent to which NAEP corroborates the changes in achievement measured in the states' assessments. In two-fifths to three-fifths of the states (depending on subject and grade), NAEP's measurements of student progress agreed with the progress measured by state assessments. In cases in which NAEP and the state disagreed on their measurement of student progress, the findings could both be accurate, as the underlying domains of the two tests may not involve the same skills or the same skills in equal weights. Similarly, there may have been a methodological change between 2005 and 2007 in the state tests, in such areas as exclusions, time of administrations, or scaling.

In all three sets of analyses, assessing the relative rigor of state standards, describing changes in relative rigor of standards when states establish new policies or testing systems, and corroborating state progress in student performance, the results of this study show that NAEP, as a common yardstick, is an essential benchmark for states in evaluating their standards. . . .

SOURCE: U.S. Department of Education. National Center for Educational Statistics. "Mapping State Proficiency Standards onto NAEP Scales: 2005–2007." October 29, 2009. http://nces.ed.gov/nations reportcard/pdf/studies/2010456.pdf.

OTHER HISTORIC DOCUMENTS OF INTEREST

FROM THIS VOLUME

- President Obama Signs the American Recovery and Reinvestment Act of 2009, p. 41

FROM PREVIOUS *HISTORIC DOCUMENTS*

- GAO on Education Department Propaganda, *2005,* p. 644

Justice Department Announces Medical Marijuana Policy

OCTOBER 19, 2009

On October 19, 2009, the U.S. Department of Justice declared that it would not seek federal prosecution against those who distribute, use, or prescribe marijuana for medical use in the fourteen states that have laws allowing it. As long as a person is in compliance with all local laws, the department announced, he or she will be allowed to use or distribute marijuana for medical purposes. In a statement accompanying the decision, Attorney General Eric Holder said, "It will not be a priority to use federal resources to prosecute patients with serious illnesses or their caregivers who are complying with state laws on medical marijuana." However, Holder cautioned that this decision did not constitute a complete reversal in the way the federal government would combat marijuana use. According to Holder, "we will not tolerate drug traffickers who hide behind claims of compliance with state law to mask activities that are clearly illegal." The distribution of marijuana, for medical purposes or otherwise, still "remains the single largest source of revenue for Mexican drug cartels," and given the recent rise in violence along the United States–Mexico border, law enforcement officials will continue to crack down on the growers and distributors of the drug, Holder said.

In March 2009, Holder had stated that the federal government would no longer prosecute medical marijuana use as long as it was allowed by state law. The October 19 guidelines made the earlier announcement official. Holder encouraged law enforcement officials to shift their focus to high-volume traffickers and drug smuggling rings.

The Controlled Substances Act, passed more than thirty years earlier, remains intact, keeping marijuana on a list of drugs heavily restricted by the federal government. The official memorandum announcing the decision, issued by Deputy Attorney General David Ogden, said the decision "does not 'legalize' marijuana." However, "prosecution of individuals with cancer or other serious illnesses who use marijuana as part of a recommended treatment regimen consistent with applicable state law" are unlikely to be prosecuted because it would be an inefficient use of federal resources, which are already stretched thin.

Alaska, California, Colorado, Hawaii, Michigan, Montana, Nevada, New Jersey, New Mexico, New York, Oregon, Rhode Island, Vermont, and Washington had all decriminalized the use of marijuana for medicinal purposes during the past decade. Each state instituted a different set of policies for obtaining marijuana for medical purposes. In Washington, for example, a patient must have a qualifying condition and obtain a written recommendation from a licensed doctor to be able to legally use the substance. The law maintains that buying or selling marijuana is illegal, as are dispensaries, but a patient may either grow the marijuana at home or receive it from a provider that has been licensed by the state.

Although the October announcement marked a reversal of the federal government's long-running policy of targeting all marijuana use, distribution, and prescription, in states with legalized policies, state law was unclear in some cases, leaving questions unanswered about when state law prevailed over local law. As a result, many cities and counties continued cracking down on marijuana use.

Medical Marijuana Use in the States

States with legalized medical marijuana policies, and their citizens who use marijuana in line with state law, have always been at odds with the federal government. The Controlled Substances Act of 1970, which categorizes legal and illegal drugs into "schedules," lists marijuana as a Schedule I drug, meaning it cannot be prescribed by doctors or sold in stores because of the high likelihood of abuse and lack of evidence of medical benefit. Since California first legalized the substance for medical use in 1996, the federal government has tried to overturn state medical marijuana policies. President Bill Clinton's administration took a medical marijuana case to the U.S. Supreme Court and won, forcing nonprofit organizations in California that distributed the substance for medical purposes to be shut down. President George W. Bush's administration also won a U.S. Supreme Court case on the issue and used federal drug laws to target those growing, using, or distributing marijuana for medical purposes. President Bush said at the time, "If you removed the obstacles to research, in 10 to 15 years, marijuana will be available in pharmacies." The Obama administration took a different stance on the issue.

Although some states made medical marijuana use legal, many issues remained about their policies. In California, there are few standard state laws on the distribution or use of medical marijuana, and the policy can differ depending on which county or city a person resides in. In Los Angeles County, for example, the district attorney is working to find and close all illegal distributors of medicinal marijuana. In Rhode Island and New Mexico, state law enforcement officials have been working to ensure that all medical marijuana providers are formally licensed by the state, an attempt at not only controlling the practice but also making the law clearer by defining which authorities are responsible for enforcement and who may or may not distribute and use medical marijuana.

Although some states will now create a legal distribution system for those prescribed marijuana for medicinal purposes without fear of federal prosecution, the federal government is still cracking down on research institutions that want to look into the different uses of medical marijuana. A request to open a lab to do so was denied by the Drug Enforcement Administration (DEA) in early 2009. However, at the University of Mississippi, the Marijuana Project, a lab growing and studying marijuana's practical uses, has been running for more than four decades.

After the federal government's decision in October, a number of states moved to legalize the use of medical marijuana. More than two dozen were actively considering bills for decriminalizing the use or possession of marijuana for medicinal purposes at the end of 2009. According to Ethan Nadelmann, executive director of the Drug Policy Alliance Network, a New York–based group that promotes alternative policy based on science and human rights to the ongoing drug debate, "In terms of state legislatures, this is far and away the most active year that we've ever seen." He acknowledged, however, that it is unlikely that states will be quick to pass legislation to legalize use, but, he said, "[W]e are close to the tipping point." He saw the increase in the number of states seeking decriminalization as a positive turn of events. The increase in legislative activity "is elevating the level of public discourse on this issue and legitimizing it," said Nadelmann.

ADVOCATES OF THE FEDERAL GOVERNMENT'S DECISION

Over the years, as an increasing number of states have passed laws decriminalizing the use of marijuana for medical purposes, polls have shown that U.S. citizens generally support making the drug available to those who are suffering from serious medical conditions. Despite public support, Congress and the DEA have worked to continue to block any attempt to stop the prosecution of those using or distributing marijuana for medicinal purposes.

Medical marijuana advocates naturally celebrated the federal government's decision. Graham Boyd, the director of the Drug Law Reform Project at the American Civil Liberties Union, said the decision was "an enormous step in the right direction and, no doubt, a great relief to the thousands of Americans who benefit from the medical use of marijuana."

Advocates, including Boyd, agreed that the Justice Department's decision would push cities, counties, and states to "create regulated, safe and sensible means of getting marijuana to patients who need it."

Although medical marijuana advocates saw the move as a step in the right direction for patient's rights, they also pointed to the government resources that could be aided because of the decision, including already overburdened police units. Americans for Safe Access, a group supporting the legalization of medical marijuana programs in the states, said that during President George W. Bush's administration 200 raids were conducted in California by federal authorities combating marijuana use. While the government will still go after drug rings that remain illegal under state law, it is expected that fewer raids will be conducted.

Others noted the decision was not just a win for marijuana advocates but also for patients suffering from long-term illness. "It's obvious that if they're not going to be prosecuted by the feds, and they're not going to be prosecuted by the states, they now are free of a huge legal threat," said Randy Barnett, a professor of legal theory at Georgetown University. This, he said, will make life easier for those who are suffering. Donald Abrams, a professor of medicine at the University of California, San Francisco, agreed. The announcement "certainly gives the nation sort of new hope that there's beginning to be some recognition that there is some medical value to this ancient medicine," he said.

The Justice Department's decision raised the ire of some who saw the department as exceeding its powers. In 2005, the U.S. Supreme Court ruled that even though states had legally enacted policies allowing for the legal use of medical marijuana, the federal government still had the right to enforce a zero-tolerance policy on users, distributors, and prescribers. Rep. Lamar Smith, R-Texas, a ranking member of the House Judiciary Committee, said the guidelines "fly in the face of Supreme Court precedent and undermine federal laws that prohibit the distribution and use of marijuana." He continued, "[W]e cannot hope to eradicate the drug trade if we do not first address the cash cow for most drug-trafficking organizations—marijuana." Smith said that by ignoring federal drug laws, the Obama administration was simply supporting the use of marijuana, which would harm the work done in the so-called war on drugs. He called on federal prosecutors to investigate and prosecute all marijuana dispensaries.

DOES MEDICAL MARIJUANA WORK?

Debate continues about marijuana's effectiveness in treating medical conditions. Doctors say the drug lessens chronic pain, nausea, and side effects from cancer treatment and glaucoma and can help HIV patients improve appetite and combat the side effects of HIV drugs. Some health professionals claim that the drug can be used to reduce spasms in those with multiple sclerosis or Lou Gehrig's disease. Others hail the drug for its benefits in treating psychological disorders, such as depression, anxiety, and bipolar disorder; however, there is less evidence to support the claims that marijuana helps in treating mental health–related conditions than the others noted here.

The risks of long-term marijuana use are also in doubt, but because research has often been limited by the federal government, there is little data available. Some studies claim that there is no harm done to the lungs and other body systems by using marijuana. However, Jeannette Tetrault, an assistant professor of medicine at Yale University, says after looking at thirty-four studies conducted on the effects of marijuana use, she finds evidence that the drug can be linked to chronic obstructive pulmonary disease, which can lead to constant coughing or wheezing. "I don't think we know enough to really be in a place where we can say that it's something that we should be allowing. I think the jury's still out in terms of what it may do in terms of long-term complications," said Tetrault. However, she continued, compared to the use of tobacco or alcohol, the use of marijuana is "relatively benign." The American Medical Association has opposed the use of medical marijuana since 2001 and continued to do so after the Justice Department's announcement.

—Heather Kerrigan

Following is a press release from October 19, 2009, announcing the Justice Department's new policies on medical marijuana, and a memorandum from October 19, 2009, detailing the formal guidelines the federal government will abide by when dealing with medical marijuana cases in states that have legalized its use.

DOCUMENT

Justice Department Announcement of New Medical Marijuana Policies

October 19, 2009

Attorney General Eric Holder today announced formal guidelines for federal prosecutors in states that have enacted laws authorizing the use of marijuana for medical purposes. The guidelines make clear that the focus of federal resources should not be on individuals whose actions are in compliance with existing state laws, while underscoring that the

Department will continue to prosecute people whose claims of compliance with state and local law conceal operations inconsistent with the terms, conditions, or purposes of those laws.

"It will not be a priority to use federal resources to prosecute patients with serious illnesses or their caregivers who are complying with state laws on medical marijuana, but we will not tolerate drug traffickers who hide behind claims of compliance with state law to mask activities that are clearly illegal," Holder said. "This balanced policy formalizes a sensible approach that the Department has been following since January: effectively focus our resources on serious drug traffickers while taking into account state and local laws."

The guidelines set forth examples of conduct that would show when individuals are not in clear and unambiguous compliance with applicable state law and may indicate illegal drug trafficking activity of potential federal interest, including unlawful use of firearms, violence, sales to minors, money laundering, amounts of marijuana inconsistent with purported compliance with state or local law, marketing or excessive financial gains similarly inconsistent with state or local law, illegal possession or sale of other controlled substances, and ties to criminal enterprises.

Fourteen states have enacted laws in some form addressing the use of marijuana for medical purposes. . . .

Source: U.S. Department of Justice. Press release. "Attorney General Announces Formal Medical Marijuana Guidelines." October 19, 2009. www.justice.gov/opa/pr/2009/October/09-ag-1119.html.

Justice Department Memorandum on the Use of Medical Marijuana

October 19, 2009

FROM: David W. Ogden, Deputy Attorney General
SUBJECT: Investigations and Prosecutions in States *Authorizing the Medical Use of Marijuana*

This memorandum provides clarification and guidance to federal prosecutors in States that have enacted laws authorizing the medical use of marijuana. These laws vary in their substantive provisions and in the extent of state regulatory oversight, both among the enacting States and among local jurisdictions within those States. Rather than developing different guidelines for every possible variant of state and local law, this memorandum provides uniform guidance to focus federal investigations and prosecutions in these States on core federal enforcement priorities.

The Department of Justice is committed to the enforcement of the Controlled Substances Act in all States. Congress has determined that marijuana is a dangerous drug, and the illegal distribution and sale of marijuana is a serious crime and provides a significant source of revenue to large-scale criminal enterprises, gangs, and cartels. One timely example underscores the importance of our efforts to prosecute significant marijuana traffickers: marijuana distribution in the United States remains the single largest source of revenue for the Mexican cartels.

The Department is also committed to making efficient and rational use of its limited investigative and prosecutorial resources. In general, United States Attorneys are vested with "plenary authority with regard to federal criminal matters" within their districts. USAM 9–2.001. In exercising this authority, United States Attorneys are "invested by statute and delegation from the Attorney General with the broadest discretion in the exercise of such authority." *Id.* This authority should, of course, be exercised consistent with Department priorities and guidance.

The prosecution of significant traffickers of illegal drugs, including marijuana, and the disruption of illegal drug manufacturing and trafficking networks continues to be a core priority in the Department's efforts against narcotics and dangerous drugs, and the Department's investigative and prosecutorial resources should be directed towards these objectives. As a general matter, pursuit of these priorities should not focus federal resources in your States on individuals whose actions are in clear and unambiguous compliance with existing state laws providing for the medical use of marijuana. For example, prosecution of individuals with cancer or other serious illnesses who use marijuana as part of a recommended treatment regimen consistent with applicable state law, or those caregivers in clear and unambiguous compliance with existing state law who provide such individuals with marijuana, is unlikely to be an efficient use of limited federal resources. On the other hand, prosecution of commercial enterprises that unlawfully market and sell marijuana for profit continues to be an enforcement priority of the Department. To be sure, claims of compliance with state or local law may mask operations inconsistent with the terms, conditions, or purposes of those laws, and federal law enforcement should not be deterred by such assertions when otherwise pursuing the Department's core enforcement priorities.

Typically, when any of the following characteristics is present, the conduct will not be in clear and unambiguous compliance with applicable state law and may indicate illegal drug trafficking activity of potential federal interest:

- unlawful possession or unlawful use of firearms;
- violence;
- sales to minors;
- financial and marketing activities inconsistent with the terms, conditions, or purposes of state law, including evidence of money laundering activity and/or financial gains or excessive amounts of cash inconsistent with purported compliance with state or local law;
- amounts of marijuana inconsistent with purported compliance with state or local law;
- illegal possession or sale of other controlled substances; or
- ties to other criminal enterprises.

Of course, no State can authorize violations of federal law, and the list of factors above is not intended to describe exhaustively when a federal prosecution may be warranted. Accordingly, in prosecutions under the Controlled Substances Act, federal prosecutors are not expected to charge, prove, or otherwise establish any state law violations. Indeed, this memorandum does not alter in any way the Department's authority to enforce federal law, including laws prohibiting the manufacture, production, distribution, possession, or use of marijuana on federal property. This guidance regarding resource allocation does not "legalize" marijuana or provide a legal defense to a violation of federal law, nor is it intended to create any privileges, benefits, or rights, substantive or procedural, enforceable by any individual, party or witness in any administrative, civil, or criminal matter. Nor does clear and unambiguous compliance with state law or the absence of one or all of the above factors create a legal defense to a violation of the Controlled Substances Act. Rather, this memorandum is intended solely as a guide to the exercise of investigative and prosecutorial discretion.

Finally, nothing herein precludes investigation or prosecution where there is a reasonable basis to believe that compliance with state law is being invoked as a pretext for the production or distribution of marijuana for purposes not authorized by state law. Nor does this guidance preclude investigation or prosecution, even when there is clear and unambiguous compliance with existing state law, in particular circumstances where investigation or prosecution otherwise serves important federal interests.

Your offices should continue to review marijuana cases for prosecution on a case-by-case basis, consistent with the guidance on resource allocation and federal priorities set forth herein, the consideration of requests for federal assistance from state and local law enforcement authorities, and the Principles of Federal Prosecution.

cc: All United States Attorneys

Lanny A. Breuer
Assistant Attorney General
Criminal Division

B. Todd Jones
United States Attorney
District of Minnesota
Chair, Attorney General's Advisory Committee

Michele M. Leonhart
Acting Administrator
Drug Enforcement Administration

H. Marshall Jarrett
Director
Executive Office for United States Attorneys

Kevin L. Perkins
Assistant Director
Criminal Investigative Division
Federal Bureau of Investigation

SOURCE: U.S. Department of Justice. "Memorandum for Selected United States Attorneys on Investigations and Prosecutions in States Authorizing the Medical Use of Marijuana." October 19, 2009. www.justice.gov/opa/documents/medical-marijuana.pdf.

OTHER HISTORIC DOCUMENTS OF INTEREST

DOCUMENT IN CONTEXT

Hate Crimes Bill Becomes Law

OCTOBER 28, 2009

On October 28, 2009, U.S. president Barack Obama signed into law the Matthew Shepard and James Byrd, Jr., Hate Crimes Prevention Act. The legislation was named after Matthew Shepard, a twenty-one-year-old college student who was tortured and murdered in 1998. The crime allegedly was motivated by the fact that he was homosexual. The act was also named for James Byrd, Jr., an African American man who died after a racially motivated attack in Texas in 1998. The act, passed more than ten years after it was first proposed, was hailed as a significant step in acknowledging the importance of extending protection to lesbians, gay, transgendered, minority, and disabled individuals.

The bill updates previous hate crime legislation to include violent crime motivated by bias based on the "actual or perceived sexual orientation, gender identity, or disability of the victim." The 1969 Federal Hate Crimes law covered crimes motivated by race, color, religion, or national origin that were committed while the victim is undertaking a federally protected activity. The new act eliminates the provision in the earlier legislation that the victim must be participating in a federally protected activity, such as voting or acting as a juror, to be covered by the act. The new legislation also gives federal authorities the ability to extend grants of up to $100,000 per year to local authorities to help cover the cost of investigating and prosecuting hate crimes. According to the Federal Bureau of Investigation, there were more than 77,000 hate crimes committed in the United States between 1998 and 2007.

MANY YEARS IN THE MAKING

The expanded legislation was first introduced in the U.S. House of Representatives by Rep. John Conyers, D-Mich., in 2001, but failed to advance past the committee stage. Conyers introduced the bill again in 2004 and 2005, but both attempts were unsuccessful. Sen. Gordon Smith, R-Ore., attached similar legislation to a defense authorization bill in 2004, which was eventually passed in the Senate. However, the hate crimes amendment was ultimately removed by a conference committee. In 2007 Conyers tried yet again to get the legislation passed, but this time had more success. The House passed the bill in May of that year by a vote of 237-80, but the bill failed to make it out of the Senate Judiciary Committee. Shortly thereafter, Sen. Ted Kennedy, D-Mass., re-introduced the legislation as an amendment to a defense re-authorization bill, and in late September 2007, the bill was passed by the Senate. However, then-President George W. Bush threatened to veto the re-authorization bill if the hate crimes amendment was attached, saying that state and local law already covered enforcement of these crimes, therefore negating the need for the federal government to set its own standards. As a result, the amendment was discarded by its supporters.

Before assuming office in January 2009, President Barack Obama stated his support for expanding hate crimes laws by passing the Matthew Shepard and James Byrd, Jr., Hate Crimes Prevention Act. The president's backing was a boon to Conyers, who introduced the legislation again on April 2, 2009. The act was passed by the House as an amendment to the National Defense Authorization Bill for Fiscal Year 2010 on October 8, 2009, by a vote of 281-146, and was later passed by the Senate by a vote of 64-35.

PROVISIONS OF THE ACT

The act states that violent crime motivated by bias "disrupts the tranquillity and safety of communities and is deeply divisive" and goes on to note that such crimes are "sufficiently serious, widespread" to deserve federal assistance in investigations and prosecutions. House majority leader Steny Hoyer, D-Md., stated that hate crimes "terrorize entire segments of our population and tear at our nation's social fabric." Although largely seen as a symbolic rather than harsher punishment structure, the act also states that individuals who are convicted of willfully causing bodily harm or attempting to cause bodily harm in a crime motivated by bias can be imprisoned for up to ten years and/or fined. However, if the victim dies or the offense involves kidnapping or attempted kidnapping, aggravated sexual abuse (or an attempt to commit such abuse), or an attempt to kill, the act allows the offender to be sentenced up to life.

The 1994 Violent Crime Control and Law Enforcement Act required the U.S. Sentencing Commission to increase the penalties for hate crimes. The 2009 hate crimes prevention act does not lay out new penalties for those convicted of perpetrating a hate crime, but it requires the U.S. Sentencing Commission to complete a study on mandatory minimum sentencing no later than October 28, 2010.

The most important facets of the expanded legislation are the inclusion of violent acts motivated by actual or perceived sexual orientation, gender identity, or disability; the provision that federal authorities can support investigations and prosecutions; and the removal of the provision that the crime must be committed while the victim is engaging in a federally protected activity. The act also allows the federal government to prosecute hate crimes even if the alleged perpetrator has already been acquitted in a state or local court.

Under this legislation, for the first time federal authorities will be able to provide monetary resources to local authorities for the investigation and prosecution of hate crimes. A local jurisdiction may receive up to $100,000 per year to help with provisions of the act. In total, the government has appropriated $5 million per annum in fiscal years 2010, 2011, and 2012 for grants of this nature. The provision in the act also allows the Department of Justice to grant local authorities funds to train law enforcement officers in "identifying, investigating, prosecuting and preventing hate crimes." Federal authorities insist that grants are necessary to ensure that local jurisdictions have the means to undertake often lengthy, complicated, and expensive investigations and prosecutions of hate crimes. The federal government will also be able to provide local authorities with federal investigators and forensic tools that may otherwise have been unavailable to them.

SUPPORT FOR AND OPPOSITION TO THE ACT

Some opponents of the act criticized its sponsors for attaching it to the defense authorization bill, which approved $681 billion in military spending, arguing that it was tantamount to legislative blackmail. Indeed, some members of the House Armed Services Committee who supported the defense bill later voted against the legislation because it contained the hate crimes act. The divide was largely along party lines. Although Democratic support for the act was stronger than that of their Republican counterparts, in the end the bill was passed with support from 237 Democrats and 44 Republicans in the House. The Senate approved the bill with a vote of 63-28, with ten Republican senators voting in favor of the legislation.

Supporters of the legislation hailed its passage with the inclusion of crimes motivated by sexual orientation, gender identity, or disability as a significant step toward increased protection for these groups. However, detractors argued that hate crimes legislation is unnecessary given that violent acts against individuals are already illegal and that singling out groups for protection undermines equal justice under the law. Many opponents also argued that the act would make it a crime to express an antihomosexual religious belief. This argument, however, was unfounded given that the legislation specifically protects freedom of expression, stating, "Nothing in this division shall be construed to allow prosecution based solely upon an individual's expression of racial, religious, political, or other beliefs or solely upon an individual's membership in a group advocating or espousing such beliefs." Moreover, the act states, "Nothing in this division shall be construed to prohibit any constitutionally protected speech, expressive conduct or activities (regardless of whether compelled by, or central to, a system of religious belief), including the exercise of religion protected by the first amendment to the Constitution of the United States and peaceful picketing or demonstration." Thus even speech that could be considered by some to be discriminatory or offensive cannot be criminalized. However, in language not unique to hate crimes legislation, the act states that the Constitution does not protect "speech, conduct or activities consisting of planning for, conspiring to commit, or committing an act of violence."

Opponents also expressed dismay at the inclusion of the provision for federal prosecution of hate crimes. The act states that prosecutions may be undertaken by federal authorities if at least one of four conditions is met: "[T]he state does not have jurisdiction; the state has requested that the federal government assume jurisdiction; the verdict or sentence obtained pursuant to state charges left demonstratively unvindicated the federal interest in eradicating bias-motivated violence; or a prosecution by the United States is in the public interest and necessary to secure substantial justice." This would allow an individual accused of a hate crime to be retried in federal courts, even if they had already been acquitted in a state court. This is an exception to the double-jeopardy clause known as the dual sovereignty doctrine, which is applicable in other areas of law outside of hate crimes. The doctrine allows certain crimes to be prosecuted by more than one sovereign, such as a state and the federal government, if the crime violates the laws of each sovereign entity.

—Hilary Ewing

Following is the text of the Matthew Shepard and James Byrd, Jr., Hate Crimes Prevention Act, signed into law on October 28, 2009, as an amendment to a defense authorization bill.

Matthew Shepard and James Byrd, Jr., Hate Crimes Prevention Act

October 28, 2009

[Text in the defense authorization bill not pertaining to hate crimes has been omitted.]

[The short title of the act has been omitted.]

SEC. 4702. FINDINGS.

Congress makes the following findings:

(1) The incidence of violence motivated by the actual or perceived race, color, religion, national origin, gender, sexual orientation, gender identity, or disability of the victim poses a serious national problem.

(2) Such violence disrupts the tranquility and safety of communities and is deeply divisive.

(3) State and local authorities are now and will continue to be responsible for prosecuting the overwhelming majority of violent crimes in the United States, including violent crimes motivated by bias. These authorities can carry out their responsibilities more effectively with greater Federal assistance.

(4) Existing Federal law is inadequate to address this problem.

(5) A prominent characteristic of a violent crime motivated by bias is that it devastates not just the actual victim and the family and friends of the victim, but frequently savages the community sharing the traits that caused the victim to be selected.

(6) Such violence substantially affects interstate commerce in many ways, including the following:

    (A) The movement of members of targeted groups is impeded, and members of such groups are forced to move across State lines to escape the incidence or risk of such violence.

    (B) Members of targeted groups are prevented from purchasing goods and services, obtaining or sustaining employment, or participating in other commercial activity.

    (C) Perpetrators cross State lines to commit such violence.

    (D) Channels, facilities, and instrumentalities of interstate commerce are used to facilitate the commission of such violence.

    (E) Such violence is committed using articles that have traveled in interstate commerce.

(7) For generations, the institutions of slavery and involuntary servitude were defined by the race, color, and ancestry of those held in bondage. Slavery and involuntary servitude were enforced, both prior to and after the adoption of the 13th amendment to the Constitution of the United States, through widespread public and private violence directed at persons because of their race, color, or ancestry, or perceived race,

color, or ancestry. Accordingly, eliminating racially motivated violence is an important means of eliminating, to the extent possible, the badges, incidents, and relics of slavery and involuntary servitude.

(8) Both at the time when the 13th, 14th, and 15th amendments to the Constitution of the United States were adopted, and continuing to date, members of certain religious and national origin groups were and are perceived to be distinct "races." Thus, in order to eliminate, to the extent possible, the badges, incidents, and relics of slavery, it is necessary to prohibit assaults on the basis of real or perceived religions or national origins, at least to the extent such religions or national origins were regarded as races at the time of the adoption of the 13th, 14th, and 15th amendments to the Constitution of the United States.

(9) Federal jurisdiction over certain violent crimes motivated by bias enables Federal, State, and local authorities to work together as partners in the investigation and prosecution of such crimes.

(10) The problem of crimes motivated by bias is sufficiently serious, widespread, and interstate in nature as to warrant Federal assistance to States, local jurisdictions, and Indian tribes. . . .

[Definitions for terms used in the act have been omitted.]

SEC. 4704. SUPPORT FOR CRIMINAL INVESTIGATIONS AND PROSECUTIONS BY STATE, LOCAL, AND TRIBAL LAW ENFORCEMENT OFFICIALS.

(a) ASSISTANCE OTHER THAN FINANCIAL ASSISTANCE.—

(1) IN GENERAL.—At the request of a State, local, or tribal law enforcement agency, the Attorney General may provide technical, forensic, prosecutorial, or any other form of assistance in the criminal investigation or prosecution of any crime that—

    (A) constitutes a crime of violence;

    (B) constitutes a felony under the State, local, or tribal laws; and

    (C) is motivated by prejudice based on the actual or perceived race, color, religion, national origin, gender, sexual orientation, gender identity, or disability of the victim, or is a violation of the State, local, or tribal hate crime laws.

(2) PRIORITY.—In providing assistance under paragraph (1), the Attorney General shall give priority to crimes committed by offenders who have committed crimes in more than one State and to rural jurisdictions that have difficulty covering the extraordinary expenses relating to the investigation or prosecution of the crime.

(b) GRANTS.—

(1) IN GENERAL.—The Attorney General may award grants to State, local, and tribal law enforcement agencies for extraordinary expenses associated with the investigation and prosecution of hate crimes.

(2) OFFICE OF JUSTICE PROGRAMS.—In implementing the grant program under this subsection, the Office of Justice Programs shall work closely with grantees to ensure that the concerns and needs of all affected parties, including community groups and schools, colleges, and universities, are addressed through the local infrastructure developed under the grants.

(3) APPLICATION.—

(A) IN GENERAL.—Each State, local, and tribal law enforcement agency that desires a grant under this subsection shall submit an application to the Attorney General at such time, in such manner, and accompanied by or containing such information as the Attorney General shall reasonably require. . . .

(C) REQUIREMENTS.—A State, local, and tribal law enforcement agency applying for a grant under this subsection shall—

    (i) describe the extraordinary purposes for which the grant is needed;

    (ii) certify that the State, local government, or Indian tribe lacks the resources necessary to investigate or prosecute the hate crime;

    (iii) demonstrate that, in developing a plan to implement the grant, the State, local, and tribal law enforcement agency has consulted and coordinated with nonprofit, nongovernmental victim services programs that have experience in providing services to victims of hate crimes; and

    (iv) certify that any Federal funds received under this subsection will be used to supplement, not supplant, non-Federal funds that would otherwise be available for activities funded under this subsection.

(4) DEADLINE.—An application for a grant under this subsection shall be approved or denied by the Attorney General not later than 180 business days after the date on which the Attorney General receives the application.

(5) GRANT AMOUNT.—A grant under this subsection shall not exceed $100,000 for any single jurisdiction in any 1-year period.

(6) REPORT.—Not later than December 31, 2011, the Attorney General shall submit to Congress a report describing the applications submitted for grants under this subsection, the award of such grants, and the purposes for which the grant amounts were expended.

(7) AUTHORIZATION OF APPROPRIATIONS.—There is authorized to be appropriated to carry out this subsection $5,000,000 for each of fiscal years 2010, 2011, and 2012. . . .

[Additional information on grants has been omitted.]

SEC. 4707. PROHIBITION OF CERTAIN HATE CRIME ACTS.

(a) IN GENERAL.—Chapter 13 of title 18, United States Code, is amended by adding at the end the following:

"§ 249. Hate crime acts

"(a) IN GENERAL.—

"(1) OFFENSES INVOLVING ACTUAL OR PERCEIVED RACE, COLOR, RELIGION, OR NATIONAL ORIGIN.—Whoever, whether or not acting under color of law, willfully causes bodily injury to any person or, through the use of fire, a firearm, a dangerous weapon, or an explosive or incendiary device, attempts to cause bodily injury to any person, because of the actual or perceived race, color, religion, or national origin of any person—

"(A) shall be imprisoned not more than 10 years, fined in accordance with this title, or both; and

"(B) shall be imprisoned for any term of years or for life, fined in accordance with this title, or both, if—

"(i) death results from the offense; or

"(ii) the offense includes kidnapping or an attempt to kidnap, aggravated sexual abuse or an attempt to commit aggravated sexual abuse, or an attempt to kill.

"(2) OFFENSES INVOLVING ACTUAL OR PERCEIVED RELIGION, NATIONAL ORIGIN, GENDER, SEXUAL ORIENTATION, GENDER IDENTITY, OR DISABILITY.—

"(A) IN GENERAL.—Whoever, whether or not acting under color of law, in any circumstance described in subparagraph (B) or paragraph (3), willfully causes bodily injury to any person or, through the use of fire, a firearm, a dangerous weapon, or an explosive or incendiary device, attempts to cause bodily injury to any person, because of the actual or perceived religion, national origin, gender, sexual orientation, gender identity, or disability of any person—

"(i) shall be imprisoned not more than 10 years, fined in accordance with this title, or both; and

"(ii) shall be imprisoned for any term of years or for life, fined in accordance with this title, or both, if—

"(I) death results from the offense; or

"(II) the offense includes kidnapping or an attempt to kidnap, aggravated sexual abuse or an attempt to commit aggravated sexual abuse, or an attempt to kill.

"(B) CIRCUMSTANCES DESCRIBED.—For purposes of subparagraph (A), the circumstances described in this subparagraph are that—

"(i) the conduct described in subparagraph (A) occurs during the course of, or as the result of, the travel of the defendant or the victim—

"(I) across a State line or national border; or

"(II) using a channel, facility, or instrumentality of interstate or foreign commerce;

"(ii) the defendant uses a channel, facility, or instrumentality of interstate or foreign commerce in connection with the conduct described in subparagraph (A);

"(iii) in connection with the conduct described in subparagraph (A), the defendant employs a firearm, dangerous weapon, explosive or incendiary device, or other weapon that has traveled in interstate or foreign commerce; or

"(iv) the conduct described in subparagraph (A)—

"(I) interferes with commercial or other economic activity in which the victim is engaged at the time of the conduct; or

"(II) otherwise affects interstate or foreign commerce.

"(3) OFFENSES OCCURRING IN THE SPECIAL MARITIME OR TERRITO-RIAL JURISDICTION OF THE UNITED STATES.—Whoever, within the special maritime or territorial jurisdiction of the United States, engages in conduct described in paragraph (1) or in paragraph (2)(A) (without regard to whether that conduct occurred in a circumstance described in paragraph (2)(B)) shall be subject to the same penalties as prescribed in those paragraphs.

"(b) CERTIFICATION REQUIREMENT.—

"(1) IN GENERAL.—No prosecution of any offense described in this subsection may be undertaken by the United States, except under the certification in writing of the Attorney General, or a designee, that—

"(A) the State does not have jurisdiction;

"(B) the State has requested that the Federal Government assume jurisdiction;

"(C) the verdict or sentence obtained pursuant to State charges left demonstratively unvindicated the Federal interest in eradicating bias-motivated violence; or

"(D) a prosecution by the United States is in the public interest and necessary to secure substantial justice.

"(2) RULE OF CONSTRUCTION.—Nothing in this subsection shall be construed to limit the authority of Federal officers, or a Federal grand jury, to investigate possible violations of this section.

"(c) DEFINITIONS.—In this section—

"(1) the term 'bodily injury' has the meaning given such term in section 1365(h) (4) of this title, but does not include solely emotional or psychological harm to the victim;

"(2) the term 'explosive or incendiary device' has the meaning given such term in section 232 of this title;

"(3) the term 'firearm' has the meaning given such term in section 921(a) of this title;

"(4) the term 'gender identity' means actual or perceived gender-related characteristics; and

"(5) the term 'State' includes the District of Columbia, Puerto Rico, and any other territory or possession of the United States.

"(d) STATUTE OF LIMITATIONS.—

"(1) OFFENSES NOT RESULTING IN DEATH.—Except as provided in paragraph (2), no person shall be prosecuted, tried, or punished for any offense under this section unless the indictment for such offense is found, or the information for such offense is instituted, not later than 7 years after the date on which the offense was committed.

"(2) DEATH RESULTING OFFENSES.—An indictment or information alleging that an offense under this section resulted in death may be found or instituted at any time without limitation".

(b) TECHNICAL AND CONFORMING AMENDMENT.—The table of sections for chapter 13 of title 18, United States Code, is amended by adding at the end the following:

"249. Hate crime acts." . . .

[Information on statistics and severability have been omitted.]

SEC. 4710. RULE OF CONSTRUCTION.

For purposes of construing this division and the amendments made by this division the following shall apply:

(1) IN GENERAL.—Nothing in this division shall be construed to allow a court, in any criminal trial for an offense described under this division or an amendment made by this division, in the absence of a stipulation by the parties, to admit evidence of speech, beliefs, association, group membership, or expressive conduct unless that evidence is relevant and admissible under the Federal Rules of Evidence. Nothing in this division is intended to affect the existing rules of evidence.

(2) VIOLENT ACTS.—This division applies to violent acts motivated by actual or perceived race, color, religion, national origin, gender, sexual orientation, gender identity, or disability of a victim.

(3) CONSTRUCTION AND APPLICATION.—Nothing in this division, or an amendment made by this division, shall be construed or applied in a manner that infringes any rights under the first amendment to the Constitution of the United States. Nor shall anything in this division, or an amendment made by this division, be construed or applied in a manner that substantially burdens a person's exercise of religion (regardless of whether compelled by, or central to, a system of religious belief), speech, expression, or association, unless the Government demonstrates that application of the burden to the person is in furtherance of a compelling governmental interest and is the least restrictive means of furthering that compelling governmental interest, if such exercise of religion, speech, expression, or association was not intended to—

(A) plan or prepare for an act of physical violence; or

(B) incite an imminent act of physical violence against another.

(4) FREE EXPRESSION.—Nothing in this division shall be construed to allow prosecution based solely upon an individual's expression of racial, religious, political, or other beliefs or solely upon an individual's membership in a group advocating or espousing such beliefs.

(5) FIRST AMENDMENT.—Nothing in this division, or an amendment made by this division, shall be construed to diminish any rights under the first amendment to the Constitution of the United States.

(6) CONSTITUTIONAL PROTECTIONS.—Nothing in this division shall be construed to prohibit any constitutionally protected speech, expressive conduct or activities (regardless of whether compelled by, or central to, a system of religious belief), including the exercise of religion protected by the first amendment to the Constitution of the United States and peaceful picketing or demonstration. The Constitution of the United States does not protect speech, conduct or activities consisting of planning for, conspiring to commit, or committing an act of violence. . . .

[Guidelines for hate crimes offenses have been omitted.]

SEC. 4712. ATTACKS ON UNITED STATES SERVICEMEN.

(a) IN GENERAL.—Chapter 67 of title 18, United States Code, is amended by adding at the end the following:

"§ 1389. Prohibition on attacks on United States servicemen on account of service

"(a) IN GENERAL.—Whoever knowingly assaults or batters a United States service-man or an immediate family member of a United States serviceman, or who knowingly destroys or injures the property of such serviceman or immediate family member, on account of the military service of that serviceman or status of that individual as a United States serviceman, or who attempts or conspires to do so, shall—

"(1) in the case of a simple assault, or destruction or injury to property in which the damage or attempted damage to such property is not more than $500, be fined under this title in an amount not less than $500 nor more than $10,000 and imprisoned not more than 2 years;

"(2) in the case of destruction or injury to property in which the damage or attempted damage to such property is more than $500, be fined under this title in an amount not less than $1000 nor more than $100,000 and imprisoned not more than 5 years; and

"(3) in the case of a battery, or an assault resulting in bodily injury, be fined under this title in an amount not less than 10 years.

"(b) EXCEPTION.—This section shall not apply to conduct by a person who is subject to the Uniform Code of Military Justice.

"(c) DEFINITIONS.—In this section—

"(1) the term 'Armed Forces' has the meaning given that term in section 1388;

"(2) the term 'immediate family member' has the meaning given that term in section 115; and

"(3) the term 'United States serviceman'—

"(A) means a member of the Armed Forces; and

"(B) includes a former member of the Armed Forces during the 5-year period beginning on the date of the discharge from the Armed Forces of that member of the Armed Forces.." . . .

Sec. 4713. Report on Mandatory Minimum Sentencing Provisions.

(a) REPORT.—Not later than 1 year after the date of enactment of this Act, the United States Sentencing Commission shall submit to the Committee on the Judiciary of the Senate and the Committee on the Judiciary of the House of Representatives a report on mandatory minimum sentencing provisions under Federal law.

(b) CONTENTS OF REPORT.—The report submitted under subsection (a) shall include—

(1) a compilation of all mandatory minimum sentencing provisions under Federal law;

(2) an assessment of the effect of mandatory minimum sentencing provisions under Federal law on the goal of eliminating unwarranted sentencing disparity and other goals of sentencing;

(3) an assessment of the impact of mandatory minimum sentencing provisions on the Federal prison population;

(4) an assessment of the compatibility of mandatory minimum sentencing provisions under Federal law and the sentencing guidelines system established under the Sentencing Reform Act of 1984 . . . and the sentencing guidelines system in place after Booker v. United States. . . .

(5) a description of the interaction between mandatory minimum sentencing provisions under Federal law and plea agreements;

(6) a detailed empirical research study of the effect of mandatory minimum penalties under Federal law;

(7) a discussion of mechanisms other than mandatory minimum sentencing laws by which Congress can take action with respect to sentencing policy; and

(8) any other information that the Commission determines would contribute to a thorough assessment of mandatory minimum sentencing provisions under Federal law.

SOURCE: U.S. Government Printing Office. Public Law No. 111–84. "National Defense Authorization Act for Fiscal Year 2010." October 28, 2009. www.gpo.gov/fdsys/pkg/PLAW-111publ84/pdf/PLAW-111publ84 .pdf.

OTHER HISTORIC DOCUMENTS OF INTEREST

FROM THIS VOLUME

- FBI Report on Crime in the United States, p. 417

FROM PREVIOUS *HISTORIC DOCUMENTS*

- Court on Hate Crime Sentence, *1993*, p. 385
- Supreme Court on Hate-Crime Law, *1992*, p. 543

Secretary of State Hillary Rodham Clinton Visits Pakistan

OCTOBER 28, 2009

Secretary of State Hillary Rodham Clinton visited Pakistan from October 28 through October 30, 2009, to work on building a stronger relationship between the two nations. It was her fifth visit to the country and her first as an Obama administration official. Her trip took place as the Pakistani military was intensifying operations against the Taliban and other Islamist insurgents based along the Pakistan-Afghanistan border. The al-Qaida network is also ensconced in this remote mountain region. In meetings with Pakistan's president, prime minister, foreign minister, army chief of staff, and Inter-Services Intelligence director, Secretary Clinton sought confirmation that Pakistan and the United States faced a common enemy. She also delivered pledges of economic and energy assistance to the Pakistani government, emphasizing that the relationship between the two nations transcended the mutual need for security. In frank dialogue with journalists, business leaders, women's groups, and other audiences, Secretary Clinton endeavored to allay popular mistrust and antipathy toward the United States.

A FRAGILE DEMOCRACY

Pakistan had recently entered what Foreign Minister Shah Mehmood Qureshi called a "democratic dispensation." General Pervez Musharraf, who originally took power in a bloodless military coup in 1999, resigned the presidency in August 2008 under the threat of imminent impeachment. The following month, Asif Ali Zardari, widower of the slain former prime minister Benazir Bhutto, was elected president. In November 2008, terrorists based in Pakistan killed hundreds in a series of attacks in Mumbai, India.

The Islamist insurgency, which has shadowy ties to Pakistan's military and intelligence agencies, increasingly threatened the state itself as the Taliban gained ground. In February 2009, President Zardari accepted a cease-fire agreement that included the imposition of Islamic law in the Swat valley, northwest of the capital, Islamabad, a city the Taliban was quickly moving toward. The Taliban subsequently took control of the adjoining Buner district, a mere 60 miles from the capital. The Pakistani army, former backers of the Taliban, then went on the offensive in the Swat valley against the Taliban, prompting a mass exodus of more than a million people from the area. In June, the military announced that the offensive would extend to South Waziristan, in the federally administered tribal areas near the Afghan border. The fighting intensified in October, in the days before Secretary Clinton's arrival in the capital, as did the number of suicide attacks coordinated by the militants. Five UN workers were killed in early October in an attack on a UN office in Islamabad.

The U.S. military and its coalition partners in Afghanistan were also battling insurgents in the border region, having failed to eliminate Osama bin Laden and his followers in Afghanistan in 2001. The al-Qaida leadership had escaped through the mountains and established a safe haven in Pakistan's North-West Frontier Province. From this sanctuary, the militants were able to launch attacks into both Afghanistan and Pakistan. The Obama administration stepped up the coalition's presence in the border area and increased the frequency of missile attacks inside Pakistan conducted by drones (unmanned aerial vehicles). These drone attacks, which killed hundreds of civilians in the tribal areas during 2009, were a major factor contributing to popular hostility toward the Americans in Pakistan. The activities of private security forces in Pakistan, supplied by companies such as DynCorp and Blackwater, were also highly controversial.

SENSITIVITIES OVER AID

With the Pakistani military engaging against the Taliban, the Americans responded by increasing military aid, advisors, and equipment, and sharing surveillance and target information. In June, for example, President Barack Obama approved a request from the Pakistani army chief for a shipment of Mi-17 cargo helicopters. Both governments kept the extent of military cooperation quiet, for tactical and political reasons. The Pakistanis wanted to downplay the impression that the Americans were underwriting their military policy and deny the insurgents an opportunity to use U.S. aid as a propaganda and recruitment vehicle. They also feared that public exposure would damage the political position of President Zardari, who had faced fierce criticism for being too close to the Americans. In fact, the Americans were not only providing material support for Pakistani military operations but urging the government to expand the scope of its efforts by going after the key Taliban leadership, such as Mullah Omar.

The Obama administration, for its part, was undertaking a thorough review of its military policy in Afghanistan and Pakistan throughout autumn 2009. Preserving political stability in Pakistan was an important part of those calculations—all the more so because of Pakistan's arsenal of nuclear weapons. The security of Pakistan's weapons and nuclear facilities remained open to question, considering allegations of ongoing ties between the country's military and intelligence agencies and terrorist networks. Al-Qaida had proclaimed interest in acquiring and using a nuclear warhead, so the stakes could hardly be higher.

On October 15, President Obama signed into law the Enhanced Partnership with Pakistan Act of 2009, known as the Kerry-Lugar bill for its two Senate sponsors, John Kerry, D-Mass., and Richard Lugar, R-Ind. This legislation, which passed both houses of Congress unanimously, steeply increased nonmilitary aid to Pakistan to $1.5 billion annually for five years. American officials, including Secretary of State Clinton, said the act was intended to demonstrate that the United States was making a long-term commitment to its partnership with Pakistan and to help strengthen the country's democratic institutions and economic development.

However, the reaction to Kerry-Lugar from Pakistan's military, opposition parties, and much of its media was sharply negative. Several conditions attached to the aid, and accepted by President Zardari, struck Pakistanis as potential violations of the nation's sovereignty. Especially sensitive were provisions meant to ensure civilian control of the military, such as a requirement that military aid be used in the struggle against Islamist insurgents, rather than diverted for other purposes, such as Pakistan's running feud with India over the contested province of Kashmir. Clinton and other U.S. officials countered that these strictures were placed in the bill to ensure accountability to American taxpayers rather than to impose conditions on Pakistan's behavior. Sen. Kerry and Rep. Howard Berman, D-Calif., delivered a note to this effect to Foreign Minister Qureshi.

SECURITY AND BEYOND

Secretary Clinton's diplomatic mission thus took place against a backdrop of complex and sensitive bilateral relations. One of her objectives, as she mentioned to interviewers before her trip, was to establish a tone of trust and mutual respect in her dealings with government officials and citizens from different walks of life. With her characteristic frankness and her penchant for dialogue, she hoped to build confidence by addressing some of the causes, historical and current, of mistrust and misunderstanding between the two societies. Another key goal, she told reporters traveling with her, was to broaden the spectrum of issues on which the two nations based their cooperation. "We are turning the page on what has been for the past several years primarily a security, anti-terrorist agenda," she said.

Because of security concerns, the secretary's itinerary was not announced in advance. On the morning of her arrival, October 28, a suicide bombing in a crowded marketplace killed nearly 100 people in the city of Peshawar. At their joint press conference in Islamabad that day, both Clinton and Qureshi harshly condemned the perpetrators of the attack. "You think by attacking innocent people and lives, you will shake our determination? No, sir, you will not," stated the foreign minister. Clinton called the attacks "cowardly." "If the people behind these attacks were so sure of their beliefs, let them join the political process. . . . Let them make that case in the political arena and see how far they would get. They know they are on the losing side of history, but they are determined to take as many lives with them as their movement is finally exposed for the nihilistic, empty effort that it is," she said. The moment strongly reinforced the emerging understanding that Pakistan and the United States faced a common enemy in the network of Islamic extremists that includes the Taliban and al-Qaida. Secretary Clinton clarified that she sees these two organizations as so closely connected that "they cannot be separated at the leadership level."

In her opening remarks, Clinton emphasized that "our relationship with Pakistan goes far beyond security." In particular, she announced a new program to assist Pakistan's energy sector by repairing underperforming power stations, replacing and upgrading equipment, such as tube well pumps, and improving energy efficiency and output. The United States pledged $125 million for the first phase of this Signature Energy Program. While in Pakistan, the secretary also pledged $56 million in humanitarian assistance to refugees in the tribal regions; $103.5 million to help the government police the border; and $85 million for the Benazir Income Support Program, a welfare program for poor women.

In addition to her press conference with the foreign minister, Clinton gave numerous interviews with Pakistani media, receiving extensive exposure during her three-day stay. Vowing to improve U.S. public diplomacy in the country, the secretary told several broadcast journalists, "Frankly, I think one of the problems is that we did not have a program to reach out to the Pakistani press. That will never happen again."

Her exchanges with journalists were frequently contentious, and some of the secretary's responses were as blunt as the questions. Asked by a newspaper editor on October 29 why the United States has devoted so much attention to Pakistan during the "war on terror," she replied, "Al Qaeda has had safe haven in Pakistan since 2002. I find it hard to believe that nobody in your government knows where they are and couldn't get them if they really wanted to." Although she tried to soften this remark, it received a great deal of play in the press. Pakistani officials replied with a request for additional U.S. intelligence assistance in verifying the precise whereabouts of al-Qaida leaders and other key extremist figures.

—Roger Smith

Following is the transcript from a press briefing on October 28, 2009, given by U.S. secretary of state Hillary Rodham Clinton and Pakistani foreign minister Shah Mehmood Qureshi.

Secretary Clinton's Remarks with Pakistani Foreign Minister

October 28, 2009

FOREIGN MINISTER QURESHI: . . . I think this visit is well timed, and I said this to Secretary Clinton. Because Pakistan, as you know, ladies and gentlemen, has entered a critical phase in its fight against extremism and terrorism. And to visit Pakistan at this stage to express solidarity with the people of Pakistan, I think, is an expression, a loud and clear message from the government, the Administration, and the people of the United States of America.

I think this trip is important because it is taking place when there is a democratic dispensation in Pakistan. And your Administration, Madame, has very clearly felt for the first time, in black and white, that we want to deal with a democracy. We uphold and share common democratic values. And I think for a country which is developing democratic institutions, that message is a powerful message for the people of Pakistan.

There is a policy shift that one sees in your approach, and that's a very welcome shift. And the shift is that you move from individuals to people, and you want a people-centric relationship, and that, I think, is very important. We are democracies. You are a democracy, and you have supported the transition to democracy in Pakistan. And today, we are a democracy as well. . . .

What we need to do is to build a relationship, a relationship based on trust, a relationship based on mutual respect, and a relationship based on shared objectives. And today, in our engagement, we discussed how to reinforce the trust, how to understand and be sensitive to each other's concerns, and how to identify and align our objectives, our strategic interests for the future. Democracies, as you know, ladies and gentlemen, cannot be oblivious of public opinion.

So there are fears and concerns on both sides. Let's acknowledge and admit that. And we need to address them. And I think we have now in place a mechanism, a leadership on both sides, that is willing to address those fears and concerns, have the mindset to address those fears and concerns to our mutual benefit.

We also discussed the situation in Afghanistan. We both have a stake in Afghanistan. We both have an interest in a peaceful, stable Afghanistan. And we discussed the— Afghanistan. We discussed the new review that is taking place in the United States, and I requested the Secretary to share the views with us, take Pakistan's input in that. And in my view, it will be useful.

And finally, we've had a very frank and a very honest discussion, and it started with history—you know, the seesaw in our relationship, the baggage that both of us carry of decades—over the last six decades. And we cannot ignore history. We should not ignore history. Keeping that in view, we have to build a relationship for the future. We have to regain each other's confidence. And I think this Administration, ever since it's come into office, from the trilateral process we've had in Washington and the various engagements— the appointment of the special representatives, the frequent interaction that we've had, is willing to engage and understands the importance of confidence in each other.

We both are of the view that our relationship has to go beyond terrorism. Terrorism and defeating—combating terrorism is a shared objective, but we have to go beyond that. When we need to—when we go beyond that, we have to help build each other's strength. Pakistan is a resource-rich country. We need United States support and help in using our resources, wealth. We need greater market access, and we've talked about the FDA. We talked about how important it is to have trade as opposed to aid. Pakistan's preference is trade.

We also discussed how important it is for Pakistan to resolve the energy crisis and the input that we have shared with each other through the task force that you set up of late. We have also talked about how important it is to build capacity of institutions, institutions that can deliver and improve the quality of life of the ordinary citizen of Pakistan by providing better health, education, you know, sanitation, pulling people out of poverty. And finally, we've discussed how we can be sensitive to each other's core interests.

I think this engagement was very useful. I think, ma'am, your presence and your trip, which—and a comprehensive program that's set forth would be very useful in adding a new chapter to our relations. So thank you for coming.

SECRETARY CLINTON: . . . This is a critical moment. And the United States seeks to turn the page to a new partnership with not only the government, but the people of a democratic Pakistan.

We hope to build a strong relationship based on mutual respect and mutual shared responsibility. I am confident that if we listen to one another, we consult, we work closely together, we will succeed. Because while we may disagree from time to time, as friends and partners do, we are bound together by common interests and common values that are stronger than any of our differences. There are many areas where our nations already work together. Now, we seek to deepen those efforts and find additional opportunities for partnership. Again, not just government to government, but in the private sector, in universities, in nongovernmental organizations, civil society groups, religious institutions, and of course, and most importantly, people to people, which is the kind of diplomacy that I think has the longest benefit.

In this regard, I am delighted that the foreign minister and I have agreed to resume and intensify the U.S.–Pakistan strategic dialogue, which I will personally oversee for my country. We want a comprehensive dialogue that is results-oriented.

Now it's obvious that one important issue facing both of our nations is security. Pakistan is in the midst of an ongoing struggle against tenacious and brutal extremist groups who kill innocent people and terrorize communities. I know that in recent weeks, Pakistan has endured a barrage of attacks, and I would like to convey my sympathy and that of the American people to the people of Pakistan. But I want you to know that this fight is not Pakistan's alone. These extremists are committed to destroying that which is dear to us as much as they are committed to destroying that which is dear to you and to all people. So this is our struggle as well, and we commend the Pakistani military for their courageous fight, and we commit to stand shoulder to shoulder with the Pakistani people in your fight for peace and security. We will give you the help that you need in order to achieve your goal.

But our relationship with Pakistan goes far beyond security. That may be what is in the headlines for obvious reasons. Today, we had more vicious and brutal attacks that killed more innocent people. The terrorists and extremists are very good at destroying, but they cannot build. That is where we have an advantage. Because today, the foreign minister and I discussed the ways in which our two nations can work more closely together on behalf of the people of Pakistan as you continue your journey toward an effective, responsive, and enduring democracy.

In this time of economic challenge, we want to help you to do what you believe is best for your country. In the economic arena, we want to help you with jobs and economic development and the infrastructure that will create investments—access to education, providing more support in healthcare, and in particular, improving the energy supply, something I have heard about in every meeting that I've had with any Pakistani since I became Secretary of State.

Pakistan's energy shortfall poses serious challenges to your economy and to the lives of individual people and businesses. For months, families have endured sweltering heat and evenings spent in the dark without appliances or televisions or computers. And in some places, I'm told that it happened in my own country. Blackouts prompt an increase in crimes. Without power, some factories and small businesses have closed their door, which undermines economic growth. And America wants to help.

Our first initiatives in this field were launched by Ambassador Holbrooke and his team earlier this year. And they've been working closely with Ambassador Patterson and our Embassy here in Islamabad, who have been working closely with your government. We recently completed an extensive energy dialogue with the Pakistani Government, led on our side by our International Energy Coordinator David Goldwyn.

In this collaboration, our experts identified several ways that the United States can help. And today, I am very proud to announce the first phase of a signature energy program for Pakistan which will help repair facilities, improve local energy providers, and promote energy efficiency. These projects, designed in close collaboration with Pakistan's government, will repair and upgrade key power stations across your country which currently operate well below full capacity.

We will help you install new and better equipment at the Tarbela Dam power station on the Indus River. And we will help you repair or replace more than 10,000 tube well pumps nationwide, which will both save energy and increase agricultural productivity. This first phase is only the beginning of our new emphasis on assisting Pakistan in its energy sector. And as we move forward, together, we will, if Congress approves future requests, do far more together.

The foreign minister and I discussed this and many other ways that our nation will strengthen and deepen our relationship. I shared with him, as he shared with me, some of the misperceptions, some of the stereotypes and misinformation that occasionally blocks both of our countries from fully understanding and appreciating each other. Over the course of my visit, I look forward to discussing many issues of concern with business leaders, members of parliament, representatives from civil society, students, women, citizens from the northwest and other parts of the country.

And of course, my time in Pakistan would not be complete without visits to some of Pakistan's extraordinary cultural, religious, and historic sites that make your country so important to Islamic civilization and to the modern Muslim world.

But let me end with this point, the partnership between our countries is not limited to the halls of government. I enjoyed greatly my meeting and the gracious lunch which the foreign minister hosted. But he and I both know that in democracies, there has to be a partnership between the people, and that is what I am aiming to foster. We have a united and shared vision of the kind of future that our children in both countries should be able to enjoy, where each child doesn't have to fear when he or she goes to school or to a market that they may not make it home safely, where the God-given abilities of each child can be nurtured, and then once again, see the fruits of that kind of investment in the benefits to families, communities, and to great nations. Our fates are intertwined in the 21st century. We are interdependent and interconnected. And I'm betting that we can make the kind of future that the children of our two nations deserve. . . .

QUESTION: Madame Secretary, you said you want to turn the page in our relationship and correct some misperceptions. As you increase the amounts of U.S. economic assistance along the lines that you've discussed, how important is it that the Pakistani people themselves actually know that this assistance in very local projects comes from the United States? And how do you propose to tell them that when U.S. officials have so much difficulty traveling around the country?

And if I might, to the foreign minister, on the question of sharing information and your views on the Administration's strategy review, you said that the Secretary is going to carry Pakistan's views back. Do you feel like those views have been adequately represented thus far, and in particular, on the question of the U.S. decision to begin to remove some of its military units from the Afghan border?

SECRETARY CLINTON: Let me answer the question that was addressed to me and then say something about the question addressed to the foreign minister. Well, we're talking right now in front of—I've lost count of how many cameras and how many journalists are in this audience—to convey both the intent of our Administration to turn that page, but also the specifics. I hope that in the coverage of my visit today there will be notice of the work we are doing together to improve the energy sector, to provide more reliable electricity for the people of Pakistan in a very specific proposal that I have just put forth. I will be visiting with many members of the Pakistani press over the next three days. I will be having town halls, both here and in Lahore. So we are going to reach out and make clear as best as I can what our intentions are and what our commitments are. And it is, of course, important that that be communicated not only in English, but in other languages as well, none of which, unfortunately, I can speak. But I know that others can and that we can convey the sincerity of our commitment.

With respect to the part of your question, Karen, about military outposts, it is actually true that we have more military presence on the border, but we have changed some of the outposts' locations. We have consolidated into some bigger outposts. And we are looking to cooperate with the Pakistani military to determine how best we can jointly address the challenges along the border. . . .

QUESTION: Okay. (Inaudible) from CNBC. We know that we are fighting a war against extremism. In particular, in the last operation, there was a marked shift of mood in people towards Taliban, and that was a huge achievement. And now also today, we lost people on the street. We're losing soldiers in the fight against Taliban. But then we hear confusing messages from American think tanks, where they say that the real enemy is al-Qaida and not really Taliban. For instance, recently, the White House press secretary Robert Gibbs also played down the threat from Taliban, saying that their capability is different from that of al-Qaida. And then, these confusing messages could also confuse a normal man in Pakistan, who have now made up their minds that the real enemy is Taliban. So who is the real enemy?

SECRETARY CLINTON: Thank you for asking that. I mean, we view the extremists and the terrorists as part of a syndicate. They are connected. Al-Qaida has played a role in promoting the Taliban in Pakistan to go against the Pakistani Government, to attack the military headquarters. They cannot be separated at the leadership level. And similarly in Afghanistan, there is a very strong connection.

But what we are saying by the comments that you referred to is that in many conflicts, not just here but around the world, not everyone who picks up a gun is a committed terrorist. They might be a young man who is pushed into joining by people in his community or someone who in Afghanistan doesn't have the way of making a livelihood, and therefore joins up because he gets paid for being a member. So we are very determined to root out the leadership and the lieutenants who are behind these kinds of attacks, who fund them, organize them, train people, recruit suicide bombers, that do what has caused such pain to the people of Pakistan and the people of Afghanistan.

But we are also open to those who change their minds, who renounce violence, are not connected with al-Qaida, and are willing to pursue their views in a peaceful, democratic manner. So that's really what that means. Our resolve against the extremists is as strong as ever, and we are going to take measures against them that we believe will be more effective. So that's what we're trying to demonstrate and convey to people. . . .

QUESTION: (Inaudible) from Dawn news. Are you satisfied with the steps Pakistan's military is taking to take on Afghani network, Hekmatyar group and other such militants who are present, according to the U.S. military reports, in Pakistani territory? And do you agree with the definition of good Taliban?

SECRETARY CLINTON: Well, on the second part, what I was saying is really in response to that, that I don't know about good, but I know that there are people who are caught up in the Taliban movement who may well be less than committed to any cause. They may not even be ideologically in line with what the leadership is doing, but find themselves there. And we've actually seen that happening on both sides of the border. I know from reports from your authorities here in Pakistan that in Swat there were people who came forth and said, "I was forced to be a Taliban. I'm not really one." And in Afghanistan, people on the battlefield who say, "I don't want to be part of this, but I had no choice." So that's what we mean. Let's sort out the hard core and make sure we defeat them. But if there are people who wish to renounce violence and begin to get reintegrated back into society, we should at least be open to that and deal with it on a case-by-case, individual-by-individual basis.

Now, you mentioned some of the other networks that we find very troubling. But I think that the Government of Pakistan has been paying a lot of attention to all of these groups because there are connections among all of these groups. But of course, the fight in South Waziristan is of the paramount importance to the government and the people of Pakistan, and we understand that. . . .

SOURCE: U.S. Department of State. "Remarks with Pakistani Foreign Minister Shah Mehmood Qureshi." October 28, 2009. www.state.gov/secretary/rm/2009a/10/131008.htm.

OTHER HISTORIC DOCUMENTS OF INTEREST

FROM THIS VOLUME

FROM PREVIOUS HISTORIC DOCUMENTS

November

Shooting at Fort Hood

On November 5, 2009, a lone gunman opened fire at the Fort Hood army base in Texas, wounding approximately thirty and killing thirteen. Those injured and killed in what turned out to be the nation's most deadly attack on a domestic military installation included soldiers and civilians. President Barack Obama called the shootings "tragic" and "a horrific outburst of violence." He continued, "These are men and women who have made the selfless and courageous decision to risk, and at times give, their lives to protect the rest of us on a daily basis. It's difficult enough when we lose these brave Americans in battles overseas. It is horrifying that they should come under fire at an Army base on American soil."

The lone shooter, Maj. Nidal Malik Hasan, had been treating soldiers on the base with psychological issues, including posttraumatic stress disorder. Hasan was set to be deployed to Iraq himself at the end of November, and he had spoken with friends and family about his hope that President Obama would end troop deployments before then. Before the shootings, Hasan had posted inflammatory remarks on an Internet site, including comments that called suicide bombers no more than soldiers doing their jobs. These remarks, coupled with Hasan's communication with an imam known to have extremist views, sparked an investigation into what exactly the army knew about Hasan and why officials had not acted to prevent the tragedy or investigated to find out if Hasan was a danger to those around him.

SHOOTING AT AN ARMY BASE

Fort Hood is the largest active duty military base in the United States, covering 339 square miles and housing more than 50,000 troops and their families. The day the shooting took place, a graduation ceremony was under way not far from where the first shots were fired, and soldiers from multiple separate units were lined up where the shooting began, waiting for dental and medical exams to be conducted before they were deployed overseas. According to witnesses, Hasan was carrying two weapons, both handguns, and began firing them, apparently at random, beginning at 1:30 p.m. inside the soldier readiness processing center. Army officials said Hasan was able to fire more than 100 rounds of ammunition within and directly nearby the centre before he was stopped.

In the aftermath of the shootings, military personnel scrambled to help the wounded, in some cases ripping off pieces of their own uniforms to use as bandages. Others meanwhile tried to stop the shooter. Eventually, a civilian officer shot and wounded Hasan, stopping his rampage ten minutes after it had begun. Early reports said that Hasan was one of the victims of the attack, but after the chaos subsided, it was learned that Hasan had been taken into custody and was in stable condition. The chaos of the situation caused a delay in how quickly the army was able to identify the shooter. The situation could have been much worse, according to Lt. Gen. Robert Cone, but "[t]hanks to the quick reaction of several soldiers, they were able to close off the doors to that auditorium where there were some 600 people inside." For some time there was a belief among law enforcement that Hasan had not acted alone, given the amount of damage he was able to inflict in such a short period of time, but after interviewing more than 170 witnesses, the army was able to conclude that Hasan had been the only shooter.

Immediately after the shooting, the army locked down the base and all installations on it, calling on the schools and other departments to ensure that all staff, students, and residents were accounted for and safe.

Suspect Charged

Shortly after the shooting rampage, information on Hasan's background began to emerge. Hasan, thirty-nine years old, was born in a suburb of Washington, D.C. He had graduated from Virginia Tech, where he first became involved in the military through a stint in the campus Reserve Officer Training Corps (ROTC). Hasan earned a bachelor's degree in biochemistry from Virginia Tech and went on to receive a medical degree from the Uniformed Services University of Health Sciences. He did his residency in Maryland at Walter Reed Army Medical Center, where he worked for six years. Records indicate that Hasan's performance at Walter Reed was not exceptional, and in fact, he required extra supervision and counseling during his time there. Hasan was licensed in psychiatric care, which led him to a position at Fort Hood's Darnall Army Medical Center. According to Col. Steven Braverman, the hospital commander at Fort Hood, Hasan never displayed any troubling signs while on the job. "I'm not aware of any problems here," he said. "We had no problems with his job performance."

Those investigating the shooting immediately began asking questions about what in Hasan's life had led him to commit such a violent act. The day after the shooting, agents with the Federal Bureau of Investigation (FBI) searched Hasan's apartment for clues. According to the Associated Press, before the shooting Hasan had given his neighbor leftover food from his apartment and a copy of the Quran. He also asked if she would clean out his apartment for $60. Hasan had told his neighbor that he was being deployed to Iraq on Friday and would no longer need his apartment or possessions.

Hasan's attack came as a surprise to some who knew him as a deeply religious person. The imam at the mosque Hasan frequently attended said there was no reason for him to believe that Hasan had extremist beliefs or tendencies; the imam said Hasan wore his military uniform to prayer services. Multiple reports indicate that the FBI had been investigating comments made on Web sites by someone with the screen name "NidalHasan." Some of the remarks, calling suicide bombers soldiers, among other things, led some to believe that Hasan in fact did have extremist beliefs and may have been sympathetic to al-Qaida.

It also came to light that Hasan had been in contact with an imam in Yemen who had previously been involved with two of the suspected September 11, 2001, hijackers. After the shootings, Anwar Aulaqi, the imam in question, praised Hasan's actions on his Web site. According to Aulaqi, any American Muslim who denounced the attacks at Fort

Hood was committing treason against Muslim teachings. He encouraged Muslims to "follow in the footsteps of men like Nidal." According to counterterrorism officials, intelligence agencies knew that Hasan had been in contact with Aulaqi but took no further action because they deemed the contacts to be of no threat to the United States. Investigators also said they had no indication that Aulaqi had told Hasan to conduct the attacks, but were looking into whether Hasan was a member of an extremist or terrorist group. According to some witnesses to the shootings, Hasan had yelled, "Allahu Akbar," an Arabic phrase translated to "God is Great," before he began shooting. Investigators have not been able to confirm whether this allegation is true.

Before the shootings, Hasan told friends and family that he hoped he would not be deployed to Iraq in late November and even hired a lawyer to help him get out of deployment, claiming that it was illegal for President Obama to send troops into the region. According to Hasan's aunt, Noel Hasan, Hasan was uncomfortable with battle and shooting, and she believes he may have turned against the wars in Iraq and Afghanistan while practicing psychiatry at Fort Hood. "He must have snapped," she said. According to Noel, her nephew had been harassed for his Muslim background and beliefs, even called a "camel jockey," according to some reports. She said Hasan could not deal with the harassment he was receiving from those around him. "He had listened to all of that and he wanted out of the military," she said.

Investigators said the scale at which the rampage was carried out indicated that the shootings had been premeditated, and on November 12, 2009, Hasan was charged with the murder of thirteen people at Fort Hood. If it is determined that the murders were planned, Hasan could face the death penalty. At the end of 2009, Hasan was awaiting trial by a military court. The army was also considering additional charges, and according to Chris Grey, a spokesperson for the Criminal Investigation Division of the army, "We are doing everything possible and we are looking at every reason for the shooting."

INTELLIGENCE CALLED INTO QUESTION

The U.S. military was criticized after the shootings. In particular questions were raised about why they had not taken action against Hasan after learning that he had been in contact with an imam sympathetic to al-Qaida. According to Pentagon officials, they had not been informed of the contact until after the November 5 shootings. However, the intelligence agencies that learned of the contact had shared that information with the FBI. President Obama ordered an official review of what information U.S. intelligence agencies had on Hasan before the shooting and how they handled it before November 5. Obama sought to find out whether contacts Hasan made or behavior he displayed should have been perceived as warning signs. "I directed that an immediate inventory be conducted of all intelligence in U.S. Government files that existed prior to November 6, 2009, relevant to the tragic shooting at Fort Hood, Texas, especially anything having to do with the alleged shooter, Major Nidal Malik Hasan, U.S. Army," President Obama said. Although information would be flowing from various federal agencies, Secretary of Defense Robert Gates warned that any leak of information could jeopardize the case. "My view is everybody ought to just shut up," he said.

Recognizing the Hasan case as part of a potentially larger problem, President Obama also ordered a review of how intelligence agencies and government departments share vital information. After the al-Qaida attacks of September 11, 2001, when questions were raised about whether they could have been prevented, intelligence reforms were implemented to ensure that agencies share appropriate data with each other. However, according to counterterrorism expert Evan Kohlmann, this is yet to happen. Kohlmann called the inability of the federal government to devise a method through which critical information can be shared troubling. "It's no secret that there are still the same frustrations, in terms of sharing the information for use in law enforcement cases, as there have always been," Kohlmann said.

—Heather Kerrigan

Following are four press releases from the Department of Defense pertaining to the Fort Hood shooting. The first, from November 5, 2009, identifies the sole suspect in the shooting; the second, also from November 5, 2009, contains President Obama's pledge of support for soldiers and their families; the third, from November 6, 2009, details the army support teams sent to Fort Hood to aid in recovery; and the fourth, from November 6, 2009, discusses the actions of first responders during the episode.

DOCUMENT

Sole Suspect Named in Fort Hood Shooting

November 5, 2009

U.S. Army Maj. Nidal Malik Hasan is believed to be the lone shooter of some 43 people on Fort Hood, Texas, and he survived being shot by a civilian police officer, the base commander said.

In a televised press briefing tonight, Army Lt. Gen. Robert Cone corrected earlier reports that said Hasan and the police officer, who shot him several times, were killed. Rather, he said, both are recovering at a nearby hospital.

All but two of the victims are soldiers, Cone said.

Cone confirmed the identity of Hasan, reportedly a psychiatrist on the base who was scheduled soon to deploy, but would not say more about the suspect. Hasan has been in the company of a Criminal Investigative Division officer since the midday shooting, he said.

In answer to a reporter's question, Cone said of the suspect, "I would say his death is not imminent." Hasan is not yet talking to investigators.

Three other soldiers were initially detained for questioning, but later released. After interviewing more than 100 people at the scene, Cone said, investigators determined there was only one shooter.

While investigators haven't ruled out terrorism in the case, Cone said, the evidence doesn't suggest it.

The shooting began about 1:30 Central Time at Hood's Soldier Family Readiness Center where Cone said soldiers from multiple units were crowded into the center for a scheduled weekly "make up time" for medical and dental appointments.

Casualties were high due to the enclosed location, but would have been much worse were it not for the training and quick reaction of the soldiers, Cone said, adding that he was on the scene quickly after the shooting began.

"Suffice it to say . . . the American soldier did a great job," he said.

From the reports of eyewitnesses, he said, the soldiers—"many of them combat lifesavers"—reacted instantaneously, ripping off parts of their own clothing to treat the wounded.

"I credit the first responders," he said. "God bless these soldiers and Department of Army civilians. As horrible as this was, it could have been much worse."

Some 600 people attending a college graduation of 138 soldiers in an adjacent building were unharmed because first responders secured the building, he said.

The suspect is believed to have used two handguns in the shooting, one a semiautomatic, Cone said. And in responding to a question, "As a matter of practice, we do not carry weapons on Fort Hood," he said. "This is our home."

However, Cone said, "We will increase our security presence here in the coming days."

The FBI is working the investigation, along with military and other law enforcement, he said. The base was on lockdown until 7 P.M., a base spokesman said.

For now, Cone said, Fort Hood officials are focused on caring for the wounded, securing the base, notifying victims' families and providing grief counseling. . . . Cone, who received a call from President Barack Obama soon after the shooting, said he was grateful for an outpouring of support. "It is truly overwhelming the offers of support we have had from around the nation," the general said. "Tomorrow at Fort Hood, we return to normalcy, schools will be open."

The Central Texas base is the military's largest, covering some 340 square miles and is home to 40,000 soldiers. And, according to its Web site, is known as "The Great Place" for its quality of life for soldiers and their families.

SOURCE: U.S. Department of Defense. Press release. "Army Major Declared Sole Suspect in Hood Shooting." November 5, 2009. www.defense.gov/news/newsarticle.aspx?id=56558.

DOCUMENT   *Obama Pledges Support to Fort Hood*

November 5, 2009

President Barack Obama condemned the fatal shooting rampage today on Fort Hood, Texas, that left 11 soldiers and a civilian police officer dead and 31 soldiers wounded.

Obama promised full-scale support to get to the bottom of what happened and help the Fort Hood community recover from the tragedy.

Police detained but later released three soldiers they initially believed were involved in the shooting. The gunman, who had been reported as dead, survived being shot by the civilian police officer and is hospitalized in the company of a Criminal Investigative Division officer, officials said.

The shooting began about 1:30 P.M. Central Time at the post's Soldier Readiness Processing Center and Howze Theater, Fort Hood officials confirmed.

The incident reportedly occurred as soldiers were conducting their final preparations for deployment.

"These are men and women who have made the selfless and courageous decision to risk, and at times, give their lives to protect the rest of us on a daily basis," the president said.

"It's difficult enough when we lose these brave Americans in battles overseas," he said. "It is horrifying that they should come under fire at an Army base on American soil."

Obama said he is in close coordination with Defense Secretary Robert M. Gates and Chairman of the Joint Chiefs of Staff Adm. Mike Mullen in monitoring the situation.

Meanwhile, the White House is working with the Pentagon, FBI and Department of Homeland Security to ensure Fort Hood is secure.

Obama said his thoughts and prayers are with the wounded and families of the fallen, and the Fort Hood community.

"We will continue to support the community with the full resources of the federal government," he said. "We will make sure that we get answers to every single question about this horrible incident."

Obama said he has no greater honor than serving as commander and chief, but also recognizes the responsibility that entails in ensuring servicemembers are properly cared for and that their safety is assured while they are at home.

"So we are going to stay on this," he said. "But I hope in the meantime that all of you recognize the scope of this tragedy, and keep everybody in their thoughts and prayers."

Speaking to reporters at Fort Hood, Army Lt. Gen. Robert W. Cone, commander of 3rd Corps and Fort Hood, credited quick response by police forces with bringing down a gunman after he opened fire at the soldier readiness unit.

"There were several eyewitness accounts that there was more than one shooter," he said, noting that two additional soldiers had been taken into custody.

"The soldiers and family members are absolutely devastated," he said. "It's a terrible tragedy," he said, but offered assurances, "We will work through it."

Source: U.S. Department of Defense. Press release. "Obama Pledges Support for Fort Hood Community." November 5, 2009. http://preview.defenselink.mil/news/newsarticle.aspx?id=56556&456556=20091105.

DOCUMENT *Army Support Teams Sent to Fort Hood*

November 6, 2009

Resources to help those affected by the tragedy at Fort Hood, Texas, are flowing to the post, Army officials said today.

Army Maj. Nidal Malik Hassan [*sic*] killed 13 Fort Hood personnel and wounded another 30 during a shooting spree at the post's Soldier-Family Readiness Center yesterday. Hassan was wounded and is in custody.

Army Secretary John M. McHugh and Army Chief of Staff Gen. George W. Casey Jr. are at the post conferring with officials to determine the best way forward, said Maj. Gen. Kevin Bergner, chief of Army public affairs.

Army Lt. Gen. Robert W. Cone, the commander of 3rd Corps and Fort Hood, has requested additional capabilities to help post personnel get through this tragedy. "We are already generating capabilities to deal with the consequences of the situation at Fort Hood," Bergner told reporters this morning.

The service is sending 13 unit ministry teams to the post. Each team has chaplains and chaplain assistants who can support the spiritual needs of soldiers, families and civilians at Fort Hood, Bergner said.

The Army also is sending 35 family life consultants to the base. "These are folks who specifically are trained and equipped to deal with the stress that military families confront—from the children to the spouses," the general explained.

The service also is sending 13 behavioral health specialists from to Fort Hood from Brooke Army Medical Center in San Antonio to help with grief counseling.

Four Operation Homecoming counselors, 20 more behavioral health specialists and 17 critical-incident stress-management personnel will deploy to Fort Hood soon, Bergner said, and five combat stress teams are moving to the post to augment teams already at the base.

Some of the additional teams will arrive today and tomorrow, and others will flow in later, the general said. "If more is needed, we will provide it," he added.

SOURCE: U.S. Department of Defense. Press release. "Army Sends Support Teams to Aid Fort Hood Soldiers, Families." November 6, 2009. www.defense.gov/news/newsarticle.aspx?id=56567.

Fort Hood First Responders Prevented Additional Causalities

November 6, 2009

. . . Soldiers' excitement and anxiety about an upcoming deployment were tossed aside, replaced by the reality of broken glass, blood and bullets when Army Maj. Nidal Malik Hasan, a psychiatrist at Carl R. Darnall Army Medical Center, allegedly shot and killed 13 soldiers and wounded 43 others.

Army Secretary John McHugh said it was the heroic actions of Fort Hood's first responders that prevented a bad situation from getting worse.

"Their actions saved lives," he said during a press conference here Friday.

Hoping to bring an end to the chaos inside the post deployment readiness center, Sgt. Kimberly Munley, an officer with Fort Hood's Department of Emergency Services, and Senior Sgt. Mark Todd, K-9 Division, DES, moved in to the fight. According to Todd, as soon as officers pulled up to the scene, people were pointing them in the direction of the shooter.

Hasan reportedly started firing on Todd and Munley, who took cover behind a vehicle. Munley left her cover to pursue the shooter and Todd followed around the other side of the building, where the major was hiding. When Todd looked around the corner of the building, he saw Munley on the ground. She had been shot.

Hasan was hiding behind a light post and firing at people who were fleeing the scene. Todd recalls firing five shots at Hasan. The major fell. Todd then confiscated

Hasan's weapons and cuffed him. The entire exchange between Todd and the gunman lasted less than 45 seconds.

"We did just like we were trained to do . . . shouting commands and working as a team," Todd said. "We had no time to feel anything, just to react."

While law enforcement officers drew fire away from the trapped soldiers, medics from the site and the neighboring graduation ceremony at Howze Theater began treating the wounded as best they could. Plastic tables were used as makeshift stretchers to move the wounded from the bloody building and get them evacuated to medical facilities.

Todd then started helping provide lifesaving care to wounded troops who were scattered around the readiness area; both inside and outside. Afterwards, Todd had the time to reflect on all that had happened.

"I felt so much for the wounded and the dead and their families," he said. "I didn't feel guilty about shooting someone while doing my job; the only guilty feeling I had was that we didn't get there sooner."

After ambulances cleared out the wounded and most of the concerned crowd had dispersed, units across Fort Hood began the emotionally exhausting mission of dealing with their losses.

The 36th Engineer Brigade had about 200 soldiers at the site working on deployment preparations after lunch. Less than two hours later, the engineer unit had more soldiers wounded and killed than any other unit on post during the incident.

"Every member of our organization was impacted by this tragic incident in some way," said Lt. Col. Jason E. Kelly, deputy commander, 36th Engineer Brigade.

"Commanders and senior noncommissioned officers were able to visit with these brave young men and women last night and their spirits are extremely high," Kelly said. "These soldiers represent everything that is good about America."

Many of the soldiers visited by the brigade leadership downplayed the severity of their injuries. The wounded showed more concern about the welfare of their fellow troops and families, he said.

The post and local community are making sure those soldiers are taken care of and helping to put those soldiers' minds at ease. A Fort Hood Grieving Center has been established and has both chaplains and counselors available to soldiers and families.

"We take care of our own. We will grieve as a family," said Army Chief of Staff Gen. George W. Casey during a Friday press conference on Sadowski Field. "We will stay focused on our missions around the world."

SOURCE: U.S. Department of Defense. Press release. "Fort Hood First Responders Save Lives." November 6, 2009. www.defense.gov/news/newsarticle.aspx?id=56583.

OTHER HISTORIC DOCUMENTS OF INTEREST

FROM THIS VOLUME

Congressional Debate on Health Care Reform

NOVEMBER 7 AND DECEMBER 21 AND 23, 2009

President Barack Obama's initiative to reform the U.S. health care system dominated the congressional agenda for much of 2009. Five separate committees in the House and Senate prepared versions of a health care bill. While Congress was on its summer recess, the issue heated up in town hall meetings across the country. Public opinion remained generally supportive of health care reform, Obama's signature domestic issue, but some people grew increasingly anxious about the bill's prospective cost and the sizable expansion of government it might entail. The legislative and public debate over health reform produced highly intense and bitter partisanship. Both chambers of Congress had passed broadly similar legislation by the end of the year, but the issue was far from concluded, as the need to reconcile the two bills into one threatened to unravel the compromises that had wrought slender majorities in each house.

Health Reform Objectives

Central goals of the legislation included covering tens of millions of Americans who lacked basic health insurance, regulating insurance companies to prevent abusive activities (such as denying coverage to patients in need of care), and containing the cost of health care, which had risen at a rate much higher than inflation for many years. The reform bills were predicated on requiring American adults to carry an insurance policy, just as automobile owners must insure their vehicles. Those who chose not to purchase insurance, and do not receive it through their employers, would pay a fine. Subsidies would help defray the cost of premiums for those with low and moderate incomes, and the income limit would be raised for those applying for Medicaid. As another means of extending coverage, young adults would be allowed to remain on their parents' policies well into their twenties.

The insurance industry thus stood to gain a large influx of new paying customers, while the country moved a step closer to universal coverage. The idea of achieving universal care in one fell swoop by creating a government-run "single-payer" system, like those in Canada and much of Europe, was dismissed by President Obama and other leading Democrats who deemed it politically unfeasible.

Under the proposed reform, insurance companies would be banned from denying a policy to any applicant because of his or her medical history, or what the industry refers to as a "pre-existing condition." Insurance companies could no longer impose either an annual or a lifetime cap on any individual's claims. The reform effort also sought to open up the marketplace in the health sector through the creation of insurance exchanges, open to self-employed individuals, small businesses, and others without coverage.

This complex proposal with its many moving parts began its arduous journey through Congress soon after President Obama's inauguration. The president urged Congress to put the measure on a fast track to passage, but made clear that he hoped his proposal would win broad bipartisan consensus. Deliberations languished through the spring in the Senate Finance Committee, chaired by Sen. Max Baucus, D-Mont. Baucus, a leading recipient of campaign contributions from the insurance and pharmaceutical industries, spent months negotiating with five fellow senators, three of them Republicans and two of them centrist Democrats, hoping to craft a measure that could attract Republican support. Agreement remained elusive as Congress left Washington for its annual August recess.

A TEA PARTY BREAKS OUT

Reform proponents had hoped to demonstrate the public's demand for change as legislators held town hall meetings during recess to hear from their constituents on health care. Instead, it was the opposition's unexpected furor that created headlines in August. Many citizens lambasted their representatives at the town halls for supporting an alleged "government takeover" of health care that they feared would cause the deficit to balloon. Some critics invoked the word "socialism" to capture their concerns about the reform bill. Others wove references to the Third Reich into their characterizations of President Obama and his "Obamacare" proposal. A movement on the right calling itself the Tea Party (TEA for "taxed enough already") staged a high-profile rally in Washington on September 12 to protest government spending.

Some of the charges of health care reform opponents served to amplify misperceptions about the bill. Former vice presidential candidate Sarah Palin, just days after resigning the governorship of Alaska, was roundly criticized for warning that the reform would result in the rationing of medical services and the creation of bureaucratic "death panels" that would dictate who is worthy of care. President Obama called Palin's statement irresponsible and gave assurances that nothing in his plan would empower government authorities to "pull the plug on Grandma." Throughout the public airing of dissent, opinion polls continued to show majority support for health care reform.

As Congress reconvened in September, key Democratic leaders, including, the president, House speaker Nancy Pelosi, D-Calif., and Senate majority leader Harry Reid, D-Nev., maintained that they could deliver a bill for signing by year's end. Nevertheless, even with a sizable majority, House Democrats had to scramble for votes. In floor debate on November 7, Rep. Henry Waxman, D-Calif., chair of the Energy and Commerce Committee, urged support for the measure, arguing that it would bring the deficit down over twenty years and that "the only thing not affordable is to do nothing." The committee's ranking Republican, Joe Barton, R-Texas, lampooned the Democratic objective of "coverage no matter what." Barton stated that more than a third of uninsured Americans are illegal immigrants—a disputed figure in a category difficult to enumerate—and he said another third prefers to go without coverage—again, a figure difficult to verify. Conservative "Blue Dog" Democrats were also upset about the fiscal impact of the sweeping reform plan. A smaller group on the left, including Dennis Kucinich, D-Ohio, and Eric Massa, D-N.Y., argued that the bill was actually too weak and too industry friendly.

The issue of abortion became a sticking point for a number of socially conservative Democrats. Rep. Bart Stupak, D-Mich., proposed an amendment to the legislation preventing any government-subsidized insurance plan from covering abortions. Liberals protested that the amendment would severely restrict reproductive rights, but the Stupak amendment stayed in the House health bill as it came to a vote on November 7. It passed by 220–215, with thirty-nine Democrats and all but one Republican in opposition.

FIXING FOR SIXTY

Meanwhile in the Senate, the Finance Committee passed its version of the health care bill on October 13 with the support of a single Republican, Maine's Olympia Snowe. However, Snowe made known that her assent to the final bill was by no means assured. As Senator Reid began synthesizing the committee markups into a single package, attention turned to efforts by the two parties to whip their caucuses into unanimity. Because of Senate operating rules, a supermajority of sixty votes is required to start debate, and end debate, on almost all controversial legislation. If all forty Senate Republicans agreed to filibuster the health care bill, the Democrats would have to keep all the remaining sixty—fifty-eight Democrats and two independents, Joe Lieberman of Connecticut and Bernie Sanders of Vermont—in line. This struggle hinged on one of the most contentious provisions in the bill, the so-called public option.

As a candidate, Obama had held out the vision of a government-sponsored health plan to compete with the private sector within the insurance exchange. This public insurance option, he said, would infuse much-needed competition into the health care market, putting downward pressure on the cost of premiums and helping keep the insurance companies honest. Opinion polls showed that the public option was among the most popular pieces of health care reform, even among independents and conservatives. In the face of vociferous opposition from Republican legislators and industry voices, however, the White House gradually weakened the public option and equivocated in its support. Its starting date was pushed back to 2013 at the earliest. To limit eligibility, Democrats declared it would be available only to individuals and small businesses. Although the House bill included the public option, House leaders rejected a "robust" plan with provider reimbursement rates pegged to Medicare.

Numerous alternatives to the public option surfaced in the Senate debate, such as a network of nonprofit insurance cooperatives or an option for adults ages fifty-five to sixty-four to buy into Medicare. No option appeared sure of gaining the approval of sixty senators. Senator Reid announced on October 26 that the legislation he was cobbling together would retain the public option, although states could opt out of participating. However, Senator Lieberman foiled the plan the next day by warning that he would join a Republican filibuster unless this plank was removed. Lieberman's maneuver earned him the wrath of liberal Democrats—not for the first time—but because of the Senate's arithmetic, the party had little choice but to cater to his interest.

By this point, the debate had been overtaken by ferocious partisanship, despite the president's appeal for bipartisan pragmatism. The right was digging in its heels against what it branded a government takeover of the health care system. Meanwhile, progressives on the left worried that a reform bill mandating that all Americans purchase insurance, but providing them no means to do so within the public sector, amounted to little more than a handout to the insurance industry.

A TENUOUS TISSUE OF COMPROMISES

On November 21, the Senate voted 60–39 (with Lieberman in favor and Snowe opposed) to open floor debate on the health care bill. The Obama administration pressed Congress to deliver the bill for the president's signature by Christmas, but Republicans vowed to obstruct this timetable through parliamentary tactics. When Sanders introduced an amendment in favor of a single-payer system, hoping to force a vote, Sen. Tom Coburn, R-Okla., demanded that the 767-page amendment be read aloud in its entirety, forcing Sanders to withdraw it. Reid and the leadership were still negotiating with centrist holdouts, including Senator Lieberman and Sen. Ben Nelson, D-Neb., to preserve their sixty-vote margin. To appease Nelson, new restrictions on the funding of abortion were added to the Senate bill. In addition, Reid agreed to exempt Nebraska from its share of the cost of expanding Medicaid—a compromise that was soon deemed the "Cornhusker kickback."

As the holidays approached, Reid finally abandoned his attempt to preserve a public option or Medicare buy-in, a victory for Republicans and centrist Democrats. The vote for cloture, or ending debate, took place after midnight on December 21, as Washington was blanketed by two feet of snow. The Democrats persevered through several more votes, passing the measure 60–39 on December 24—the first Senate vote to take place on Christmas Eve in more than a century.

Although the core planks of the House and Senate health reform bills were in alignment, the differences were large enough to require a conference committee or other procedure to resolve them. The most publicized gap between the bills concerned the public option, which remained a lightning rod on the left and the right. Just as significant was the difference in how to pay for the costs of reform. The House bill would impose a tax on the wealthy, and the Senate bill included several revenue mechanisms, including a tax on the most expensive health insurance policies, those costing more than $8,500 annually per individual or $23,000 per family. The American Federation of Labor and Congress of Industrial Organizations (AFL-CIO) and other unions opposed taxing health benefits, because some unions had fought hard to win these high-quality policies, sometimes termed "Cadillac plans." Both the House and Senate bills would reduce the federal deficit by more than $130 billion over ten years, according to the Congressional Budget Office.

The continuing battle over health care reform promised to spill over into 2010 and loomed large as an issue for both parties in midterm elections. Merging the two bills while preserving the delicate compromises that had allowed them to pass, amid ongoing attack from Republicans and a public growing weary of the debate, posed a formidable challenge.

—Roger Smith

Following is the text of the floor statement by Rep. Henry Waxman, D-Calif., on November 7, 2009, in support of health care reform legislation; the text of the floor statement by Rep. Joe Barton, R-Texas, on November 7, 2009, opposing health care reform legislation; the text of the floor statement by Sen. George Voinovich, R-Ohio, on December 21, 2009, in opposition to health care reform legislation; and the text of a floor statement by Sen. Carl Levin, D-Mich., on December 23, 2009, in support of health care reform legislation.

Rep. Henry Waxman, D-Calif., on Health Care Reform

November 7, 2009

. . . Today, we have an historic opportunity. Sixty-five years after Franklin Roosevelt and Social Security and 35 years after Medicare, we have an opportunity—under the leadership of President Obama and Speaker Nancy Pelosi—to reform our health care system and, at last, provide coverage to all Americans.

We know that health insurance today is failing our families and our economy. If we do nothing, the system will go bankrupt, premiums will keep skyrocketing, benefits will be slashed, what you get will cost much more, and the deficit will increase by billions of dollars.

Today, Americans with health insurance know that they are just one serious illness away from debt and bankruptcy. And millions of Americans have no insurance at all.

With this legislation, we can fix these problems.

First and foremost, this bill provides health insurance security for all Americans. If you have health insurance today, you can keep it. You keep your doctor and your other health care providers. But if you lose your job, you will not lose your health insurance. If you have a pre-existing medical condition, you cannot be denied health insurance. If you have a serious illness, we remove the cap insurance companies have imposed on paying for treatment over your lifetime. Effective immediately, it will be illegal for insurance companies to put a lifetime cap on your coverage. And children under age 27 can be covered on their parent's policies.

Our bill has historic reforms. It expands coverage and reduces costs. It trains more doctors and supports community health clinics. There is a public health insurance option that will give Americans more choice and competition.

Our legislation strengthens Medicare. We will eliminate co-payments for preventive services. We close and then eliminate the donut hole that makes prescription drugs unaffordable for so many seniors.

And this legislation is affordable. The only thing not affordable is to do nothing. The legislation is fully paid for. It will in fact reduce the deficit over the next two decades.

Today, we have a chance of a lifetime to do something great and momentous for the American people. By passing this bill, we can reform health insurance in America and provide all Americans with the security of knowing that when they get sick, care will be available and affordable.

I urge all my colleagues to support this bill. . . .

SOURCE: Rep. Henry Waxman. "Affordable Health Care for America Act." *Congressional Record* 2009, 155, pt. H12837. www.gpo.gov/fdsys/pkg/CREC-2009-11-07/pdf/CREC-2009-11-07-pt1-PgH12623-3.pdf.

Rep. Joe Barton, R-Texas, on Health Care Reform

November 7, 2009

Mr. Speaker, I asked to go after the distinguished chairman of the Education and Labor Committee because what we have here is a failure to communicate, or perhaps a difference in philosophy.

The Democrats have decided that the bottom line is coverage. By golly, coverage no matter what. Whether you want to be covered or not, you are going to be. We are going to have an employer mandate. We are going to have an employee mandate and an individual mandate. We are going to have a premium mandate.

We are going to have how you cover the insurance, a "comparative research council," to dictate the practice of medicine. We are going to raise Medicaid to 150 percent of poverty, and automatically enroll every individual in this country who is unmarried, whether they want to be or not.

We are going to tell every young American who has decided that they don't want to pay those premiums, they want to save up to get married or to buy a home, that, by golly, they are going to have to take insurance, and they are going to pay three to four times what they would under the current system because there is only a two-to-one ratio. So they are going to get their coverage, at a cost of $1.2 trillion.

Now, we have a different philosophy. We think you need to control costs, but we also agree that you have to provide access to the private insurance market if you can't get it today and you want it.

Congressman MILLER talks about the 40 to 50 million Americans that are not insured, and he is right. But of those 40 to 50 million, 15 to 20 million are in this country illegally. Ten or 15 million are young Americans who don't want insurance.

When you really boil it down, there are 5 to 10 million Americans who have a preexisting condition or work where insurance is not provided and they can't afford it.

Our plan covers them. It gives them the opportunity. That doesn't give them the money, but it gives them the opportunity. So we have a difference in a philosophy.

We don't believe in mandates and make no apology about it, but we do believe in the individual opportunity.

We believe in individual choice. We believe in the American system of free enterprise. We believe in lowered taxes, and we believe in a plan that's going to lower premiums an average of $5,000 per person per year for the next 10 years. That's what CBO says. That's not me. That's the CBO.

So there is a choice. Bigger government, more mandates, more control, less freedom, or lower costs, more opportunity, more freedom, more choice. I vote for more freedom.

Vote "no" on the Big Government plan. Vote "yes" on the individual opportunity plan.

SOURCE: Rep. Joe Barton. "Affordable Health Care for America Act." *Congressional Record* 2009, 155, pt. H12953–H12954. www.gpo.gov/fdsys/pkg/CREC-2009-11-07/pdf/CREC-2009-11-07-pt1-PgH12623-3 .pdf.

DOCUMENT

Sen. George Voinovich, R-Ohio, on Health Care Reform

December 21, 2009

. . . Tragically, for the American people, unlike other important health care-related bills such as the Medicare Modernization Act that garnered wide bipartisan support, this bill is nowhere near bipartisan and did not receive a single Republican vote for cloture at 1 this morning, and only one Republican in the House of Representatives supported it.

In my humble opinion, the way this bill was negotiated behind closed doors, and without the input of Members from both sides, will sour relations and bipartisan discussion on other major issues to come before the Senate . . .

The problems facing our country are too serious for business as usual, each side one-upping the other for political advantage, with the 2010 elections casting shadows on what we should be doing for the benefit of our country, at a time when this Nation is as fragile as I have seen it in my entire life.

Our future and the future of our children and grandchildren is in our hands. Our constituents and the world are watching. Our credibility and credit are on the line, and so is our economic and national security, and, quite frankly, our leadership position in the world. We need fewer partisans in this body and more statesmen. . . .

I ask my colleagues, can our Nation take on new programs and costs when we cannot pay for what we are doing right now? Our Nation's fiscal picture is not pretty. Our obligations to our entitlement programs are exploding. If we keep going the way we are, our debt will double in 5 years and triple in 10. . . .

This brings me back to the health care bill. I have heard all the arguments of why health care reform is needed, and—do you know something—I agree with most of them. Frankly, there are a number of incremental things we could do today to make real improvements in our system in a bipartisan way. In fact, I encourage my colleagues to take a look at some of the proposals contained in the alternatives offered by my colleagues, including Senators WYDEN and BENNETT.

These and other legislative proposals include things we can do on an incremental basis to improve our system, such as making it easier for small business to group together to reduce their health care costs; passing medical liability reform, where we have more tests being taken because doctors are afraid of being sued; increasing flexibility in the private market so people have more options and can choose insurance products that best meet their needs; implementing policies that encourage wellness and prevention; eliminating the fraud and abuse that have and will continue to plague our public health care programs; eliminating the ability of insurance companies to deny people insurance coverage because of preexisting conditions; or eliminating the caps that insurance companies put once an individual reaches a certain amount.

Instead, we are going to pass a massive new spending bill that does little to fix our problems in the long run. What too many of my colleagues do not understand is there are limits to what government can do. There are limits on what government can do. . . .

What people in this country want is to go back to work and have some assurance that their jobs are safe. The best way to give them security and access to health insurance is to get them back to work.

We should not be asking our Nation's businesses to take on new tax burdens in the current recession. Yet this bill before us would impose $28 billion in new taxes on employers—$28 billion. Furthermore, the legislation creates a new Medicare payroll tax that will likely hit approximately one-third of the small businesses in this country, which employ some 30 million Americans. These new taxes are likely to significantly hinder these engines of job growth. . . .

By the way, there is a point of order that lies against this bill as an unfunded mandate in terms of local and State government, and also business. The American people should understand that the new State obligations under the Medicare expansion will mean less funding, OK, less funding for primary and secondary education, higher education programs, roads and bridges, county and local government projects, and safety service programs run by their States. In fact, I used to call Medicaid the Pacman that gobbled up our State budget dollars. . . .

Another legacy I am upset about leaving for our children and grandchildren is the public funding of abortion. The other day, I explained to an individual that since Roe v. Wade, we have had over 40 million abortions—40 million abortions. Yet I have friends of mine who are wanting children, and they are going to China, they are going to Russia, they are going to other places to find those children, but here in the United States over 40 million abortions. Unfortunately, the language that was inserted in the managers' amendment does not protect taxpayer dollars from being used to fund abortion. . . .

SOURCE: Sen. George Voinovich. "Health Care Reform." *Congressional Record* 2009, 155, pt. S13706–S13708. www.gpo.gov/fdsys/pkg/CREC-2009-12-21/pdf/CREC-2009-12-21-pt1-PgS13706-4.pdf.

Sen. Carl Levin, D-Mich., on Health Care Reform

DOCUMENT

December 23, 2009

. . . We can vote, now, to address decades of frustration and anguish over a health care system most Americans know is broken. Or we can destroy the hopes of millions of Americans whose modest ambition is not a perfect system, but an improved one. We cannot vote to end every problem in health care; this bill will not do that. But we can make life safer, more secure, less costly, for most Americans, because we can give them a better health care system.

Briefly, here is some of what this legislation will accomplish:

People with pre-existing conditions who are currently left out of the system will be able to get access to health care in the future. Within six months of enactment, this legislation will allow those not covered at work and who are unable to find insurance in the individual market because of pre-existing conditions to buy a plan that will remain in place if they get sick. And it will offer free preventive services and immunizations.

This bill has provisions to help strengthen Medicare by giving seniors access to important preventive services that they may otherwise not be able to afford. And also for seniors, this bill reduces the Medicare doughnut hole, a gap in prescription drug coverage that I hope we are able to eventually close altogether.

After 2014, new plans will be barred from imposing annual limits on coverage, and sliding tax credits will be available to make insurance more affordable for those earning below $88,000 for a family of four, or earning below $43,000 for an individual. The credits that will be offered to make coverage more affordable will bring millions of Americans under the umbrella of health insurance, an important improvement for those families now without insurance and a step toward reducing burdens and inefficiencies that make health care more expensive for all of us. State-based exchanges will offer those seeking individual coverage both the purchasing power of belonging to a larger group, and a transparent marketplace in which benefits are standardized and costs are clear.

The bill also helps small businesses that are struggling to get a handle on ever increasing health care insurance costs. Beginning in 2010, small businesses will receive a tax credit of up to a 35% of their costs for insuring their employees and their employees' families. In 2014 and beyond, the tax credit can be as much as 50% of an employer's costs for covering employees. These credits will encourage these employers, which are the backbone of our economy, to provide health care insurance coverage.

The bill also includes some major insurance company reforms. Beginning in 2011, plans that do not spend a high percentage of their revenue for patient care—85 percent of revenue for large-group programs, and 80 percent in the individual and small-group market—will have to provide rebates to their enrollees.

One of the benefits of this new requirement on insurance companies is reversing the troublesome trend that has seen more and more of our health care dollars spent on administration. Since 1970, the number of administrative positions in our health care system has increased by nearly 3,000 percent, far outstripping the growth in the number of physicians over the same period. It is long past time to ensure that we are spending precious health care dollars on care and not on paperwork and bureaucracy. Hospitals will become more transparent as well—every hospital in the nation will publish a list of standard charges for the items and services it provides.

The bill includes incentives to boost the availability of primary care, including financial incentives under Medicare to increase the number of primary care physicians. And it also promotes standardizing health information technology in an effort to reduce costly administrative overhead.

This is not everything I hoped for. But it is what we can get done. It is what we should do.

The minority has offered no alternatives, just apocalyptic rhetoric. Some of them stood before rallies, leading chants about socialism. They claimed it's a big government takeover. "Kill the bill" was their slogan. Before television cameras our efforts to produce reform were compared to the activities of financial fraudsters like Bernie Madoff. . . .

The extreme rhetoric of the minority is a repeat of similar rhetoric which was used when Social Security and Medicare were being considered by the Congress.

In 1935, as Social Security was being debated, one Republican warned the program would "enslave workers," and another declared "the lash of the dictator will be felt" if it passed. Three decades later, as the Congress debated the Medicare program, one Republican member of Congress said, "Let me tell you here and now, it is socialized medicine." . . .

Incredibly, the same Republican party that once equated Medicare with socialism would now have the public believe they are defending Medicare from the threat of socialism. The mental gymnastics this requires is breathtaking. If this bill is such a threat to seniors, why does AARP support its passage? If it will destroy our health care system, why do so many of the groups that know health care first-hand, from the American Medical Association to the American Heart Association to the American Cancer Society, and dozens of others support passage of this bill? If this bill will explode the deficit, why does the non-partisan Congressional Budget Office tell us it will reduce the deficit by $132 billion over the first decade after enactment, and up to $1.3 trillion dollars in the second? . . .

Let me ask one final question: What do opponents say to our constituents who speak to us every day of their belief that the time for health reform has come? That today is not the time? The man from Kalamazoo, Michigan, who went bankrupt because his health insurance would not cover $40,000 in costs for a life-saving heart operation—will they tell him this is not the time? The woman from Jackson, Michigan, who spent months fighting to get coverage because insurance companies considered her pregnancy a pre-existing condition—will they tell her this is not the time? The worried mother who wrote my office to say, "We will lose too many bright young people—if something is not done"—will they tell her this is not the time?

No, this is the time. Now is the time to embrace the same call of history that led our predecessors to ignore the apocalyptic rhetoric and establish Social Security and Medicare. We must pass this bill, so that generations after us do not look back on a broken health care system and say, "Here was another lost moment when it could all have changed." We must pass this bill. Now is the time. Just as we are ploughing the roads of record snow to get to work, our work now is to plough through the endless filibusters to get our job done.

SOURCE: Sen. Carl Levin. "Service Members Home Ownership Act of 2009." *Congressional Record* 2009, 155, pt. S13853–S13854. www.gpo.gov/fdsys/pkg/CREC-2009-12-23/pdf/CREC-2009-12-23-PT2-PgS13796-4.pdf.

OTHER HISTORIC DOCUMENTS OF INTEREST

FROM THIS VOLUME

President Obama Visits East Asia

NOVEMBER 13, 2009

President Barack Obama spent a week visiting Japan, Singapore, China, and South Korea in November 2009. The impetus for his travel was the annual Asia Pacific Economic Cooperation (APEC) conference, held in Singapore in tandem with a summit of the Association of Southeast Asian Nations (ASEAN). It was the first time a U.S. president had attended a meeting of the ten-member ASEAN. The agenda for President Obama's week of diplomatic encounters was chock-full of issues—trade and economic policy, negotiations to moderate the effects of global climate change, the war in Afghanistan, and efforts to restrain the nuclear programs of Iran and North Korea—and the administration predicted in advance that the visits would yield few noteworthy agreements. Key aides said the president merely aimed to establish a foundation of diplomatic relationships and deliver the message that the United States remained fully committed to the region and to equal partnerships with Asian powers.

MUTUAL INTERESTS AND MUTUAL RESPECT

In 2009 Asia was coming increasingly to represent the world's locus of economic growth, while the U.S. economy remained mired in its deepest crisis since the 1930s, and much of the rest of the world suffered an economic slump as well. China was by far the largest U.S. creditor, holding nearly $1 trillion in federal debt, and the huge Sino-American trade imbalance had become a source of discomfort for American officials. Asian government ministers, for their part, believed with some justification that the United States had sparked the recent global downturn by inadequately regulating its financial industry. The U.S. share of Asian trade was in danger of dropping further, because of free trade deals that ASEAN had recently struck with China, India, South Korea, Australia, and New Zealand. The Americans had finalized few trade pacts in the region; a deal with South Korea awaited congressional approval.

Representing a nation perceived by some as an empire in decline, President Obama was prepared to persuade Asian leaders that the United States sought to pursue, as he put it in Tokyo, "a new era of engagement with the world based on mutual interests and mutual respect." It was a message Obama had delivered all over the world, signaling that his approach to foreign affairs would differ starkly from his predecessor's. President Obama visited more foreign countries during his first year in office than any previous president.

In addition to the issues of trade and economic cooperation, a host of other important matters of foreign policy were in play as Obama toured Asian capitals in mid–November. The president hoped to obtain pledges of economic and military aid for U.S.-led operations in Afghanistan and Pakistan; the administration was in the midst of an extensive strategy review over whether to send up to 40,000 additional troops to Afghanistan. All parties were looking ahead to the Copenhagen conference on global climate change in early December. The meeting had been expected to result in a binding international agreement on long-term reductions in carbon emissions, but the chances of a breakthrough were becoming remote. Legislation imposing emissions limits had passed the U.S. House in June but was languishing in the Senate, leaving the Obama administration with little apparent credibility to negotiate on the issue with China, which had passed the United States as the world's leading producer of greenhouse gases.

OBAMA ATTENDS APEC, ASEAN SUMMITS

The president's departure was delayed one day so that he could speak at the memorial for the thirteen victims of a mass shooting at the Fort Hood military base in Texas. He arrived in Japan on November 13 and met with the recently elected prime minister, Yukio Hatoyama. In their joint news conference, both leaders paid tribute to the alliance between the two nations, noting the upcoming fiftieth anniversary of the signing of the revised U.S.-Japan Security Treaty. In fact, Hatoyama, whose Democratic party of Japan bested the nation's long-dominant Liberal Democratic party, had promised in his campaign to press for more "equal" relations with the Americans and a reduced U.S. military presence on the island of Okinawa. President Obama vowed that the two nations would confer as equal partners in a high-level working group to address the issue of the relocation of U.S. forces from the Futenma air station. The Japanese pledged $5 billion in civilian aid to Afghanistan over five years, but also announced they would no longer refuel Afghanistan-bound U.S. military vessels in the Indian Ocean. Hatoyama said, "I believe that for Japan, it is more appropriate, desirable, that we provide such civilian assistance."

Before leaving Japan the following day, Obama met the Emperor Akihito and Empress Michiko at the Imperial Palace in Tokyo. The president's deep bow before the figurehead monarch, relayed on television, led some conservative pundits in the United States to criticize him for excessive deference. Obama then flew to Singapore to attend the APEC forum. The United States, Canada, and Mexico are among the twenty-one member economies of this Pacific Rim association, as is Russia. At the summit, the president announced the U.S. intention to join the Trans-Pacific Partnership, a trade initiative currently including Singapore, Brunei, New Zealand, and Chile, all APEC members. The United States intended to increase its share of exports to the Asian Pacific, a strategy that would raise the region's standard of living and promote job growth at home, the president said. Singapore officials welcomed the news as a step toward gradually converting APEC into a regional, free trade zone.

The major news from the APEC meeting concerned climate change. Unable to secure agreement on concrete figures for emission reductions, the leaders pledged only to work for a positive outcome at the upcoming meeting in Copenhagen. Observers concluded that hopes for a meaningful global agreement in Copenhagen were virtually dashed. Meanwhile, on the margins of the APEC forum, President Obama held bilateral meetings with several leaders, including Russian president Dmitry Medvedev. The two discussed the status of their talks on a new strategic arms reduction agreement, intended to update and replace the expiring Strategic Arms Reduction Treaty I (START I), as well as the crisis over Iran's nuclear program.

Obama's presence at an ASEAN summit meeting, the first by a U.S. leader, conveyed the president's overarching message of faithful participation in the region's affairs. Previous administrations had been reluctant to send high-level emissaries to ASEAN because of the presence of Myanmar's military leadership. However, the Obama White House was signaling a new openness to communication with the regime, which had jailed opposition leaders, such as Aung San Suu Kyi. Jeffrey Bader, a senior National Security Council official, told CNN, "The statement we're trying to make here is that we're not going to let the Burmese tail wag the ASEAN dog." Bader made clear, however, that Obama would not hold a bilateral meeting with his counterpart from Myanmar.

LITTLE MOVEMENT IN CHINA

The president's three-day stay in China was tightly scripted. His itinerary included meetings in Beijing with President Hu Jintao, Prime Minister Wen Jiabao, and other leaders; a state dinner; and sightseeing tours of the Great Wall and the Forbidden City. President Obama also held a televised town hall–style meeting in Shanghai, the first of its kind in China by an American leader; the youthful audience had been carefully selected by Chinese authorities. President Obama made no public denunciations of the government's policies on human rights, free speech, Tibet, or other sensitive matters. U.S. officials said the president spoke bluntly in private on issues of concern, in keeping with his public statement in Tokyo that "we can move these discussions forward in a spirit of partnership rather than rancor."

One pressing matter for the Americans was monetary policy. The Chinese had kept their currency, the yuan, pegged at a relatively low value to take advantage of their strength in exports. U.S. officials wanted China to shift to a market-based exchange rate, as part of a broader strategy to address the bilateral trade imbalance. Such a strategy, supported by the Group of 20 leaders at their meeting in Pittsburgh in September, would allow Americans to save more while the Chinese, increased their consumption. However, the talks produced no visible sign that the Chinese leadership was open to a shift in policy. Similarly, Obama seemed to gain no concessions from the Chinese on emissions targets or on the possibility of levying sanctions on Iran if negotiations failed to resolve the nuclear standoff.

South Korea was the president's final Asian stop; he was greeted heartily with a welcoming ceremony in Seoul. The proliferation challenges of North Korea and Iran topped the agenda at Obama's November 19 joint press conference with his South Korean counterpart, Lee Myung-bak. Obama gently chastised the Iranians for refusing an offer to have a third country reprocess uranium produced in Iranian reactors: "[T]hey are unable to get to yes," the president put it. "We have begun a dialogue with our international partners about the importance of having consequences," he added, in his clearest reference to date to the likelihood of imposing sanctions. At the time Obama arrived in South Korea, fears over Iran's nuclear proliferation were growing, as talks with Iranian officials had reached an impasse. Regarding North Korea, Obama revealed that he would be sending special envoy Stephen Bosworth to Pyongyang in December in an effort to restart the six-party talks between North Korea, the U.S., South Korea, China, Japan, and Russia. Lee spoke of a "grand bargain" that could provide North Korea a package of economic aid and security concessions if it agreed to surrender its nuclear weapons capability and adhere to the Nuclear Non-proliferation Treaty. Although the president returned from his intense week of diplomacy with no deliverable victories, his aides maintained that the journey had been a successful one. The president's political advisor, David Axelrod, said the talks had advanced the administration's foreign policy goals in ways that would bear fruit over time. "These things don't change overnight," Axelrod said.

—Roger Smith

Following is the text of a press conference on November 13, 2009, held by U.S. president Barack Obama and Japanese prime minister Yukio Hatoyama.

President Obama and Japanese Prime Minister Hatoyama on U.S.-Japanese Relations

November 13, 2009

Prime Minister Hatoyama. . . . Well, we've come to call each other Barack and Yukio. I think we've quite—I've grown quite accustomed to calling each other by our names. And we did cover a lot of ground today. First, for Japan's diplomacy, the U.S.-Japan alliance is the cornerstone. And this is one thing that I've stressed. But as time changes and as the international environment changes, there is a need for us to further develop and deepen the U.S.-Japan alliance to make it even more constructive and future-oriented alliance. And this was what I proposed today. . . .

Now, the U.S.-Japan alliance, looking at it from the security front, naturally we have to cooperate in proliferation deterrence, on information protection, missile defense, and the use of outer space, amongst others. We need to consider these new systems for issuing security. And this is my thinking.

But the U.S.-Japan alliance is not just focused on security—for example, disaster prevention or health, education. We had many levels—and also environmental issues as well. We need to cooperate in all these areas so as to cooperate in the Asia Pacific and others so that we can further deepen our bilateral alliance. I believe that we have reached an agreement on these points.

Now, turning our eyes to the global situation, again, there are different topics that we've covered. From our side, I've talked about Afghanistan and our support to Afghanistan. Well, to Afghanistan, we will not be taking part in the refueling, but instead, providing civil assistance, and we are planning to mainly provide civil assistance of 5 billion yen in 5 years for agriculture, building of infrastructures, schools. So this is the type of assistance we want to provide. And also to improve security, we want to support the police force in Afghanistan. Furthermore, for the former soldiers, we want to provide vocational training. These are the types of things that we want to conduct.

I have communicated this to the President, and towards this new assistance package, President Obama, in principle, has stated his gratitude, appreciation towards this assistance. And furthermore, when it comes to assistance to Afghanistan, it's important that we try to directly talk with one another as to the assistance to be provided.

Now, in the area of climate change, again, we have talked on this subject. By 2015 [2050]*, I have set out this goal of an 80 percent reduction. And both Japan and U.S. have agreed on this. And we want to make COP 15 a success, and we agreed to cooperate towards this end. And including China and others, there are other issues that needs to be resolved, and therefore, we need to collaborate to address these challenges.

Now, in regards to nuclear disarmament, again, we have agreed to cooperate with one another. Now, in regards to nuclear issues and also climate change, we are going to—we have issued a joint statement. And I do believe that this is quite innovative in itself, and the fact that we can take up these issues as core issues at the summit meeting is something of vital importance.

Now, on the economic front—well, the economy was not a major issue this time, but again, this might reflect the times in which we're living. And over dinner, maybe, we hope to be able to discuss the issue of the economy.

Now, in relation to nuclear issues, North Korea, Iran was also discussed from President Obama. And again, we have agreed to closely cooperate with one another. And Special Representative Bosworth will be visiting North Korea—or may be visiting North Korea shortly. But this is on the premise of the six-party talks. And I do endorse this thinking and have stated so to the President.

And in regards to Iran, again, we have to support—we would like to support the approach to Iran. On the one hand, we want to emphasize our historic relationship, but also, at the same time, I promise to strengthen our alliance vis-à-vis Iran.

And also, again, in Asia, President Obama has stated that we have some—we do have a vital role to play, especially in East Asia. I have set out the concept of East Asian community, and this is because I believe that there is this alliance as the cornerstone on which we can rely.

And in Asia, the fact that the U.S. presence increases is something that have great extension towards at various levels in Asia and East Asia and Asia on the whole [sic]. And both Japan and the United States should deepen, and as a result, in East Asia, we hope to bring about peace, stability, and economic prosperity in this region. And this is something that we have pledged.

I don't want to take up all the time myself, and therefore, I'd like to conclude. But I do think that this summit meeting was extremely meaningful. And on this note, I'd like to once again say that I am very grateful to Barack, President Obama, to take time to join us here at Japan. And also, I'm thankful that he's chosen Japan as his first leg to his visit to Asia. And as Prime Minister, representing the Japanese people, I'd like to express my gratitude. Thank you.

Moderator. And next, President Obama, please.

President Obama. . . . Japan is my first stop as President in Asia. I began my trip here in Tokyo because the alliance between the United States and Japan is a foundation for security and prosperity, not just for our two countries but for the Asia Pacific region. In

*White House correction.

a few months, we'll be marking the 50th anniversary of our alliance, which is founded on shared values and shared interests, that has served our people so well and has provided peace and security for the region in an unprecedented way. . . .

Throughout my trip and throughout my Presidency, I intend to make clear that the United States is a Pacific nation, and we will be deepening our engagement in this part of the world. As I said to Prime Minister Hatoyama, the United States will strengthen our alliances, build new partnerships, and we will be part of multilateral efforts and regional institutions that advance regional security and prosperity.

We have to understand that the future of the United States and Asia is inextricably linked. The issues that matter most to our people, issues of economic growth and job creation, nonproliferation, clean energy, these are all issues that have to be part of a joint agenda. And we had very productive discussions about these issues this evening.

It's true that because of the strength of our economic ties, that was not the first item on our agenda, but we are fortunately going to have the opportunity to spend a lot of time discussing that in Singapore in the coming days. As the world's two leading economies, we have spent a lot of time working together in the G-20 to help bring the world back from the brink of financial crisis, and we're going to continue to work to strengthen our efforts so that we can expand job growth in the future. And we will be discussing with our APEC partners how to rebalance our deep economic cooperation with this region to strengthen our recovery.

The Prime Minister and I discussed our cooperation on Afghanistan and Pakistan. And I did thank the people of Japan and the Prime Minister for the powerful commitment of a—$5 billion over the next 5 years to support our shared civilian efforts in Afghanistan, as well as the commitment of a billion dollars to Pakistan.

This underscores Japan's prominent role within a broad international coalition that is advancing the cause of stability and opportunity in Afghanistan and Pakistan. And I shared with the Prime Minister our efforts in refining our approach to make it more successful in the coming year.

We discussed our shared commitment to stopping the spread of nuclear weapons and, ultimately, seeking a world without them. Since I laid out a comprehensive agenda in Prague to pursue these goals, Japan has been an outstanding partner in those efforts. And together, we passed a historic resolution in the Security Council last September. We are building a new international consensus to secure loose nuclear materials and strengthen the nonproliferation regime.

And to that end, we discussed both North Korea and the situation in Iran, recognizing that it's absolutely vital that both countries meet their international obligations. If they do, then they can open the door to a better future. If not, we will remain united in implementing U.N. resolutions that are in place and continuing to work in an international context to move towards an agenda of nonproliferation.

Finally, we discussed our partnership on energy issues and climate change. The United States and Japan share a commitment to developing the clean energy of the future, and we're focused on combating the threat of climate change. This is an important priority for us; I know it's an important priority for the people of Japan. And we discussed how we can work together to pave the way for a successful outcome in Copenhagen next month.

So I believe that we are off to a very successful start. I'm looking forward to continuing the conversation during dinner, as well as, as we both travel to Singapore. And

I am confident that we will continue to strengthen the U.S.-Japan alliance so that it serves future generations.

Thank you very much.

Moderator. Thank you very much. Now I'd like to proceed to questions. . . .

Q. . . . And to President Obama, you are a proponent of a nuclear-free world, and you've stated, possible, you would like to visit Hiroshima and Nagasaki while in office. Do you have this desire? And what is your understanding of the historical meaning of the A-bombing in Hiroshima and Nagasaki? Do you think that it was the right decision?

And also considering the North Korean situation, how do you think the U.S.-Japan alliance should be strengthened, and how should both countries cooperate in the field of nuclear disarmament?

And also on the Futenma relocation issue, by when do you think the issue needs to be resolved? And—well, if should it be that Japan carry over the discussion—decision to next year or decide on something outside of what is being discussed, how would you respond?

Moderator. Starting with Prime Minister.

Prime Minister Hatoyama. . . . On the issue of the relocation of the Futenma Air Station, in regards to this issue, well, to give you the conclusion, there is the high-level working group. We've set up this group so as to be able to resolve the issue as early as possible. I've stated this, and my commitment was also expressed during our talks.

But before that, I have explained why we have this discussion, and under the previous Government, the U.S.-Japan agreement needs to be regarded seriously. During the election campaign, especially to the Okinawans, I've stated that we would consider relocation outside of Okinawa and outside of the country. It is a fact that we did campaign on this issue, and the Okinawans do have high expectations.

It will be a very difficult issue for sure, but as time goes by, I think it will become even more difficult to resolve the issue. Especially the residents in the Futenma district will find it even more difficult to resolve the issue as time goes by. So we do understand that we need to resolve the issue as soon as possible, and we'll make every effort to resolve the issue as quickly as possible within the working group.

And we hope that this will lead the way to strengthening our alliance, and I sincerely hope that such discussions will take place within the working group. And this is something that I have communicated to the President. . . .

President Obama. Well, first of all, I am impressed that Japanese journalists use the same strategy as American journalists—[*laughter*]—in asking multiple questions. . . .

That's reflected in the Japan-U.S. alliance. It will be reflected in the resolution of the base realignment issues related to Futenma. As the Prime Minister indicated, we discussed this. The United States and Japan have set up a high-level working group that will focus on implementation of the agreement that our two Governments reached with respect to the restructuring of U.S. forces in Okinawa, and we hope to complete this work expeditiously.

Our goal remains the same, and that's to provide for the defense of Japan with minimal intrusion on the lives of the people who share this space. And I have to say that I am extraordinarily proud and grateful for the men and women in uniform from the United States who help us to honor our obligations to the alliance and our treaties.

With respect to nuclear weapons and the issues of nonproliferation, this is an area where Prime Minister Hatoyama and I have discussed repeatedly in our meetings. We share, I think, a vision of a world without nuclear weapons. We recognize, though, that this is a distant goal, and we have to take specific steps in the interim to meet this goal. It will take time. It will not be reached probably even in our own lifetimes. But in seeking this goal, we can stop the spread of nuclear weapons, we can secure loose nuclear weapons, we can strengthen the nonproliferation regime.

As long as nuclear weapons exist, we will retain our deterrent for our people and our allies, but we are already taking steps to bring down our nuclear stockpiles and—in cooperation with the Russian Government—and we want to continue to work on the nonproliferation issues.

Now, obviously, Japan has unique perspective on the issue of nuclear weapons as a consequence of Hiroshima and Nagasaki. And that, I'm sure, helps to motivate the Prime Minister's deep interest in this issue. I certainly would be honored, it would be meaningful for me, to visit those two cities in the future. I don't have immediate travel plans, but it's something that would be meaningful to me. . . .

With respect to North Korea, we had a [*sic*] extensive discussion about how we should proceed with Pyongyang. Obviously, we were disturbed by the testing that took place, some of the belligerent actions that had taken place in an earlier period of this year. We have continued to say that our goal is a non-nuclear Korean Peninsula. That's vital for the security of East Asia.

And the United States and Japan, with the other members of the six-party talks, will continue to work to show North Korea that there is a pathway, a door, for them to rejoin the international community that would serve their people well and, I believe, enhance their security over the long term. They have to walk through that door. In the meantime, we will continue to implement the sanctions that have already been put in place, and we will continue to coordinate closely with Japan and the other six-party members in helping to shape a strategy that meets our security needs and convinces Pyongyang to move in a better direction . . .

Q. . . . And on Afghanistan, if I might, can you explain to people watching and criticizing your deliberations what piece of information you're still lacking to make that call?

And if I could add one to the Prime Minister, please. Can you explain why your country decided not to continue refueling ships going to Afghanistan?

President Obama. . . . With respect to Afghanistan, Jennifer, I don't think this is a matter of some datum of information that I'm waiting on. It's a matter of making certain that when I send young men and women into war and I devote billions of dollars of U.S. taxpayer money, that it's making us safer, and that the strategies that are placed not just on the military side but also on the civilian side are coordinated and effective in our primary goal, which is to make sure that the United States is not subject to attack and its allies are not subject to attack by terrorist networks, and that there is a stability in the region that helps to facilitate that larger goal. . . .

And the decision will be made soon. It will be one that is fully transparent so that the American people understand exactly what we're doing and why we're doing it and what it will entail. It will also, I think, send a clear message that our goal here, ultimately, has to be for the Afghan people to be able to be in a position to provide their own security, and that the United States cannot be engaged in an open-ended commitment. . . .

Prime Minister Hatoyama. I thank you for keeping it to just one question, having come all the way to Japan. Now, your question was about why we ended the refueling in the Indian Ocean. And we believe that Japan's assistance to Afghanistan will, in the larger context—terms should be considered. And—well, as antiterrorism, you know, to eradicate terrorism, there is a need to take certain measures, but we have to consider what Japan should be doing in terms of antiterrorism. I think that it's important that we extend civilian support so as to eliminate terrorism from its roots. And I do believe that this is appropriate for Japan, and this is the first focal point I want to communicate to you.

And also, the refueling support, I've looked at the activities. Compared to the beginning, recently the refueling support is declining. Last month, in 1 month, there was only one—refueling for one ship. And we wonder how much effect we are bringing about. And so I think that we have to consider the meaning of this logistic support, and we've come to think that there is another type of assistance that is more appropriate for Japan. . . .

SOURCE: U.S. Executive Office of the President. "The President's News Conference with Prime Minister Yukio Hatoyama of Japan in Tokyo, Japan." *Daily Compilation of Presidential Documents* 2009, no. 00910 (November 13, 2009). www.gpo.gov/fdsys/pkg/DCPD-200900910/pdf/DCPD-200900910.pdf.

OTHER HISTORIC DOCUMENTS OF INTEREST

FROM THIS VOLUME

Justice Department Announces Khalid Sheikh Mohammed Will Be Tried in New York City

NOVEMBER 13 AND 17, 2009

As the Obama administration sought to close the detention facility at Guantánamo Bay Naval Base in Cuba, officials had to determine whether to release the remaining detainees, bring them to trial before a military tribunal or U.S. courts, or hold them indefinitely. On November 13, 2009, Attorney General Eric Holder announced that five detainees, including alleged September 11, 2001, mastermind Khalid Sheikh Mohammed, would face trial before a federal court in New York. The announcement was immediately controversial, raising security concerns and igniting political debate.

CHARGES OF TERRORISM

Mohammed was reportedly born in Pakistan and had joined the Muslim Brotherhood at the age of sixteen. He spent several years studying in the United States before going to Afghanistan to fight the government following the Soviet invasion. Mohammed remained active in the Afghan mujahidin movement and began cultivating a relationship with al-Qaida, becoming a fully fledged member in the late 1990s. Given Mohammed's background, intelligence officials suspected that he had helped in selecting the September 11 hijackers, coordinating their financing and training and directing the attacks from abroad. They also believed he had served as Osama bin Laden's operations chief following the U.S. invasion of Afghanistan in 2001. Mohammed was captured by U.S. and Pakistani forces in 2003 and had been held in a secret CIA prison before being transferred to the Guantánamo Bay facility.

In March 2007, the Pentagon released a transcript of Mohammed's confession that he had read during a Combatant Status Review Tribunal at Guantánamo. In the confession, Mohammed claimed he "was responsible for the 9/11 operation from A to Z" and took responsibility for thirty-one other terrorist attacks since the early 1990s. Some of the plots he outlined were never carried out or were discovered by international counterterror authorities before they could be executed. Mohammed confessed to planning the 1993 World Trade Center bombing and to personally beheading *Wall Street Journal* correspondent Daniel Pearl in 2002.

On February 11, 2008, the Department of Defense announced sweeping charges against Mohammed and his alleged conspirators: Ramzi bin al-Shibh, Mohammed al-Qahtani, Ali Abd al-Aziz, Mustafa Ahmed al-Hawsawi, and Walid bin Attash. Walid bin Attash had allegedly selected and trained a number of the nineteen hijackers, and Ali Abd al-Aziz and Mustafa Ahmed al-Hawsawi had worked together to coordinate and provide funding for them. Ramzi bin al-Shibh was suspected of having been an intermediary between the hijackers and al-Qaida leaders and also to have secured funding for the operation. Mohammed al-Qahtani was alleged to have been the twentieth hijacker, but he had been unable to enter the United States shortly before September 11, 2001. The charges described a conspiracy dating back to 1996, which is when Mohammed allegedly first proposed the idea of the 9/11 attacks to Osama bin Laden.

Because the detainees were considered enemy combatants, it was determined that they would be tried before a military tribunal under the military commission system established by President George W. Bush in October 2001. The system was considered controversial, because the military commissions required defendants to forgo some of the rights they are entitled to in civilian courts, and the system is also more accepting of evidence gleaned through harsh interrogation tactics. Although preliminary court proceedings against the accused began in the summer of 2008, trial was not set to begin until after the Bush administration.

In January 2009, the status of Mohammed and his alleged conspirators was suddenly called into question. On January 22, newly elected president Obama issued Executive Order 13492, calling for the Guantánamo Bay detention center to be closed within one year and suspending all current and pending proceedings before military commissions until a full review of that system could be completed. Administration officials were charged with determining whether the remaining 245 detainees could be repatriated or transferred to some third country, whether to hold them indefinitely, or whether they should face trial before a modified military commissions system or in federal court. Each detainee's case was evaluated individually by a task force consisting of prosecutors from the Department of Justice and the Pentagon that assessed where the alleged offense took place, the identity of the victims, and the manner in which evidence against the detainee had been gathered. There was considerable internal debate over who would handle the trials, which were certain to be the most high profile trials in the United States in years.

JUSTICE AT GROUND ZERO

On November 13, 2009, Attorney General Holder held a press conference to announce that Mohammed and four conspirators would face trial before the U.S. District Court for the Southern District of New York, approximately one mile from the site of the destroyed World Trade Center in New York City. Holder declared that Mohammed, Ramzi bin al-Shibh, Ali Abd al-Aziz, Mustafa Ahmed al-Hawsawi, and Walid bin Attash would be tried together, and the trial would be open to the public, although he noted some portions that dealt with classified information might be closed. Holder said he had personally reviewed the detainees' cases in the weeks before making his decision. "After eight years of delay, those allegedly responsible for the attacks of September the 11th will finally face justice," Holder said. "I am confident in the ability of our courts to provide these defendants a fair trial, just as they have for over 200 years." President Obama, on a diplomatic trip to Asia at the time, voiced his support for the decision.

"I'm absolutely convinced that Khalid Sheikh Mohammed will be subject to the most exacting demands of justice. The American people insist on it and my administration insists on it," he said.

The U.S. attorney in Manhattan had competed with the U.S. attorney's office in the Eastern District of Virginia, site of the Pentagon and one of the September attacks, for the right to prosecute Mohammed and the others. Holder said a team of prosecutors from both districts would handle the government's case and that they were expected to seek the death penalty for each of the accused. A Department of Defense official later said that even if prosecutors failed to win convictions in the cases, the administration would not release dangerous detainees inside the country. No detainees would be moved to a federal prison in New York for forty-five days, because of a law requiring that advance notice be given to Congress before any prisoner could be transferred from Guantánamo. Holder said he had called New York City mayor Michael Bloomberg and New York governor David Paterson before his announcement to let them know of his decision. "It is fitting that 9/11 suspects face justice near the World Trade Center site where so many New Yorkers were murdered," Bloomberg said. But Governor Paterson did not agree. "This is not a decision that I would have made. . . . It's very painful," he said. "We still have been unable to rebuild that site, and having those terrorists tried so close to the attack is going to be an encumbrance on all New Yorkers."

Controversy Erupts

Paterson's opposition was an early indicator of the controversy that would flow from Holder's announcement. Politicians and officials in the intelligence community raised questions about how the trial would be conducted and what impact it might have on national security. Perhaps the biggest question was whether statements made by the accused while being subjected to harsh interrogation techniques would be allowed in court. According to a 2005 Department of Justice memo released by the Obama administration, Mohammed had been waterboarded 183 times, and it was suspected that at least two of the other men had endured "enhanced interrogation," including periods of sleep deprivation and questioning lasting as long as twenty hours at a time. Many assumed defense lawyers would try to have the charges thrown out based on this information, but Holder rebuffed these concerns, claiming that both the court system and the "untainted evidence" would be strong enough to secure a guilty verdict. Holder also dismissed claims that it would be difficult to impanel an impartial grand jury in a city that had been a target of the September 11 attack. Others said the trial would pose a high security risk for New York, making it a prime target for another attack. "We should not be increasing the danger of another terrorists strike against Americans at home and abroad," said Rep. Peter King, R-N.Y.

The Republican party pounced on the announcement and voiced a series of objections to the trial. Republicans claimed a trial in the federal court system would give Mohammed the same legal rights and benefits of U.S. citizens and questioned what this would mean for future military or intelligence missions. "Will U.S. personnel have to read terrorists their *Miranda* rights on the battlefield?" asked one press release. They also maintained that the government would be forced to reveal all of its intelligence on Mohammed and the others, as well as details of how that evidence had been obtained, arguing that the country's enemies would be able to study its intelligence-gathering techniques and determine how to outmaneuver them. "Classified information can be inadvertently leaked," said Sen. Mitch McConnell, R-Ky. In addition, Republican critics expressed concern that the trial would provide a platform for the accused to voice propaganda and that a guilty verdict and death sentence would give Mohammed the martyr status he said he wanted.

Other lawmakers voiced support for the decision. "New York is not afraid of terrorists," said Rep. Jerrold Nadler, D-N.Y. "Any suggestion that our prosecutors and our law enforcement personnel are not up to the task of safely holding and successfully prosecuting terrorists on American soil is insulting and untrue." Many human rights organizations also lauded the announcement. "The transfer of these cases is a huge victory for restoring due process and the rule of law, as well as repairing America's international standing, an essential part of ensuring our national security," said Anthony Romero, executive director of the American Civil Liberties Union. Reactions from friends and family members of the victims of the September 11 attacks were also mixed, although many were supportive. "It would give many of us access to attend the hearings," Kristen Breitweiser, the widow of one of the victims, told CNN. "This will be our opportunity to see justice served and have our day in court."

The accused had yet to be moved from Guantánamo to New York by the year's end, and formal charges had not been filed. Their trial is expected to occur in 2010, although there was speculation that the Obama administration might reconsider its decision.

—Linda Fecteau

Following is a statement by Attorney General Eric Holder on November 13, 2009, announcing the decision to try Guantánamo detainees in federal court; a statement by New York City mayor Michael Bloomberg on November 13, 2009, in response to Holder's statement; and a press release from November 17, 2009, from the House Republican Conference in response to Holder's decision.

Attorney General Eric Holder Announces Federal Trial for Guantánamo Detainees

November 13, 2009

Good morning. Just over eight years ago, on a morning our nation will never forget, nineteen hijackers working with a network of Al Qaeda conspirators around the world launched the deadliest terrorist attacks our country has ever seen. Nearly 3,000 people lost their lives in those attacks, and in the years since, our nation has had no higher priority than bringing those who planned and plotted the attacks to justice.

One year before, in October 2000, a terrorist attack on the USS *Cole* killed seventeen American sailors.

Today we announce a step forward in bringing those we believe were responsible for the 9/11 attacks and the attack on the USS *Cole* to justice.

Five detainees at Guantánamo have been charged before military commissions with participation in the 9/11 plot: Khalid Sheikh Mohammed, Walid Muhammed Salih Mubarak Bin Attash, Ramzi Bin Al Shibh, Ali Abdul-Aziz Ali, and Mustafa Ahmed Al Hawsawi. Those proceedings have been stayed since February, as have the proceedings pending in military commissions against four other detainees accused of different crimes. A case in military commissions against the alleged mastermind of the *Cole* bombing, Abd al-Rahim al-Nashiri, was withdrawn in February.

For the past several months, prosecutors at the Department of Justice have been working diligently with prosecutors from the Pentagon's Office of Military Commissions to review the case of each detainee at Guantánamo who has been referred for prosecution. Over the past few weeks, I have personally reviewed these cases, and in consultation with the Secretary of Defense, have made determinations about the prosecution of ten detainees now held at Guantánamo, including those charged in the 9/11 plot and the alleged mastermind of the *Cole* bombing.

Today, I am announcing that the Department of Justice will pursue prosecution in federal court of the five individuals accused of conspiring to commit the 9/11 attacks. Further, I have decided to refer back to the Department of Defense five defendants to face military commission trials, including the detainee who was previously charged in the USS *Cole* bombing.

The 9/11 cases that will be pursued in federal court have been jointly assigned to prosecutors from the Southern District of New York and the Eastern District of Virginia and will be brought in Manhattan in the Southern District of New York. After eight years of delay, those allegedly responsible for the attacks of September the 11th will finally face justice. They will be brought to New York to answer for their alleged crimes in a courthouse just blocks from where the twin towers once stood.

I am confident in the ability of our courts to provide these defendants a fair trial, just as they have for over 200 years. The alleged 9/11 conspirators will stand trial in our justice system before an impartial jury under long-established rules and procedures.

I also want to assure the American people that we will prosecute these cases vigorously, and we will pursue the maximum punishment available. These were extraordinary crimes and so we will seek maximum penalties. Federal rules allow us to seek the death penalty for capital offenses, and while we will review the evidence and circumstances following established protocols, I fully expect to direct prosecutors to seek the death penalty against each of the alleged 9/11 conspirators.

In his speech at the National Archives in May, the President called for the reform of military commissions to ensure that they are a lawful, fair, and effective prosecutorial forum. The reforms Congress recently adopted to the Military Commissions Act ensure that military commission trials will be fair and that convictions obtained will be secure.

I know that the Department of Defense is absolutely committed to ensuring that military commission trials will be consistent with our highest standards as a nation, and our civilian prosecutors will continue to work closely with military prosecutors to support them in that effort.

In each case, my decision as to whether to proceed in federal courts or military commissions was based on a protocol that the Departments of Justice and Defense developed and that was announced in July. Because many cases could be prosecuted in either federal courts or military commissions, that protocol sets forth a number of factors—including the nature of the offense, the location in which the offense occurred, the identity of the victims, and the manner in which the case was investigated—that must be considered. In consultation with the Secretary of Defense, I looked at all the relevant factors and made case by case decisions for each detainee.

It is important that we be able to use every forum possible to hold terrorists accountable for their actions. Just as a sustained campaign against terrorism requires a combination of intelligence, law enforcement and military operations, so must our legal efforts to bring terrorists to justice involve both federal courts and reformed military commissions. I want to thank the members of Congress, including Senators Lindsay Graham, Carl Levin and John McCain who worked so hard to strengthen our national security by helping us pass legislation to reform the military commission system.

We will continue to draw on the Pentagon's support as we bring cases against the alleged 9/11 conspirators in federal court. The Justice Department has a long, successful history of prosecuting terrorists for their crimes against our nation, particularly in New York. Although these cases can often be complex and challenging, federal prosecutors have successfully met these challenges and have convicted a number of terrorists who are now serving lengthy sentences in our prisons. And although the security issues presented by terrorism cases should never be minimized, our marshals, court security officers, and prison officials have extensive experience and training dealing with dangerous defendants, and I am confident they can meet the security challenges posed by this case.

These detainees will not be transferred to the United States for prosecution until all legal requirements are satisfied, including those in recent legislation requiring a 45 day notice and report to the Congress. I have already spoken to Governor Paterson and Mayor Bloomberg and am committed to working closely with them to ensure that all security and related concerns are properly addressed. I have every confidence that we can safely hold these trials in New York, as we have so many previous terrorism trials.

For the many Americans who lost friends and relatives in the attacks of September 11, 2001, and on the USS *Cole*, nothing can bring those loved ones back. But they deserve the opportunity to see the alleged plotters of those attacks held accountable in court, an opportunity that has been too long delayed. Today's announcements mark a significant step forward in our efforts to close Guantánamo and to bring to justice those individuals who have conspired to attack our nation and our interests abroad.

For over two hundred years, our nation has relied on a faithful adherence to the rule of law to bring criminals to justice and provide accountability to victims. Once again we will ask our legal system, in two venues, to rise to that challenge. I am confident it will answer the call with fairness and justice.

SOURCE: U.S. Department of Justice. Press release. "Attorney General Announces Forum Decisions for Guantánamo Detainees." November 13, 2009. www.justice.gov/ag/speeches/2009/ag-speech-091113 .html.

Mayor Michael Bloomberg Responds to Holding 9/11 Trial in New York City

November 13, 2009

I support the Obama Administration's decision to prosecute 9/11 terrorists here in New York. It is fitting that 9/11 suspects face justice near the World Trade Center site where so many New Yorkers were murdered. We have hosted terrorism trials before, including the trial of Omar Abdel-Rahman, the mastermind of the 1993 World Trade Center bombing. When I spoke to Attorney General Holder earlier today, I told him New York City stands ready to assist the federal court in the administration of justice in any way necessary. I have great confidence that the NYPD, with federal authorities, will handle security expertly. The NYPD is the best police department in the world and it has experience dealing with high-profile terrorism suspects and any logistical issues that may come up during the trials.

SOURCE: New York City Office of the Mayor. Press release. "Statement of Mayor Michael R. Bloomberg on Federal Prosecution of Terrorism Suspects in New York City." November 13, 2009. www.nyc.gov/portal/site/nycgov/.

House Republican Conference Response to Holder Announcement

November 17, 2009

On November 13, 2009, Attorney General Eric Holder announced that Khalid Sheikh Mohammed (KSM) and four conspirators will face a trial in federal court in New York for masterminding the 9/11 terrorist attacks that claimed nearly 3,000 innocent American lives. This political decision on behalf of the Obama Administration will have serious negative consequences for national security and the justice system.

Khalid Sheikh Mohammed: Khalid Sheikh Mohammed (KSM), 44, was born to a Pakistani family living in Kuwait and was educated in the United States. KSM is the self-identified mastermind of the 9/11 terrorist attacks on the World Trade Center and Pentagon. The 9/11 Commission report identified him as a "terrorist entrepreneur." Along with Osama bin Laden, KSM selected the 9/11 hijackers, coordinated their financing and training, and directed the attack from abroad. KSM became Osama bin Laden's operations chief after the U.S. invasion of Afghanistan. He was captured by U.S. and Pakistani forces on March 1, 2003, in Pakistan. KSM has been held at Guantánamo since September 2006.

Delayed Justice: In New York, KSM will enjoy the legal rights and benefits of U.S. citizens and resident aliens under the Constitution. A criminal trial will force the government to reveal all of its intelligence on KSM and how it obtained it. Additionally, treating the 9/11 attacks as a simple criminal matter rather than an act of war will hinder

U.S. efforts to fight terrorism and sends the wrong signal to U.S. enemies abroad. A costly civilian court trial for KSM will also likely take years. The trial of Zacarias Moussaoui, for example, was tied up in court for more than four years by his lawyers and ended only when Moussaoui pleaded guilty.

Undermining Military Commissions: The terrorist acts plotted by KSM were an act of war against the U.S. and should be prosecuted by a military commission, not a common criminal court. In 2001, President Bush established military commissions, a wartime system of justice used during the Revolutionary War, the Civil War, and World War II. Congress approved procedures for military commissions in 2006 and 2009, and the Supreme Court has upheld their use. Military commissions held at Guantánamo Bay would produce a fair trial while guarding sensitive national security information from exposure. Appropriately, the Administration announced just last week that it would use commissions to try five Guantánamo Bay detainees involved with the 2000 attack on the USS Cole in Yemen.

National Security Liability: At trial, prosecutors will be forced to reveal U.S. intelligence on KSM, along with the methods and sources used in acquiring it. This will enable al Qaeda to better understand our intelligence-gathering techniques and respond accordingly. For example, Osama bin Laden used U.S. government information revealed during the 1993 World Trade Center bombing criminal trial to update and enhance his techniques. KSM's relationships to other al Qaeda figures will also be released, enabling the terrorist group to discard individuals who have been compromised. The KSM trial will also jeopardize future military and intelligence missions. Will U.S. personnel have to read terrorists their Miranda rights on the battlefield? Will they have to collect and secure evidence in a war zone? At what risk to U.S. troops and intelligence professionals?

Unnecessary Cost to New York: The already high security risk to New York will be further increased by locating KSM and his co-conspirators in Manhattan. According to Governor David Paterson (D-NY), "This is not a decision that I would have made . . . It's very painful . . . We still have been unable to rebuild that site, and having those terrorists tried so close to the attack is going to be an encumbrance on all New Yorkers." The Southern District Court House is within walking distance of Ground Zero, City Hall, the Brooklyn Bridge, NYPD Headquarters, Wall Street and the Battery Tunnel. The trial of Zacarias Moussaoui in Alexandria, Virginia, demonstrated the risk posed to trial cities. Alexandria was a scene of rooftop snipers, bomb-sniffing dogs inspecting cars, identification checks, and heavily armed patrols. Replicating this security presence on a larger stage in New York will come at a huge cost to the federal, State, and local governments and enormous inconvenience and risk to residents and taxpayers.

SOURCE: House Republican Conference. Policy news. "Khalid Sheikh Mohammed's Manhattan Show Trial." November 17, 2009. www.gop.gov/policy-news/09/11/17/khalid-sheikh-mohammed-s-manhattan.

OTHER HISTORIC DOCUMENTS OF INTEREST

U.S. Task Force Recommends Changes to Mammography Guidelines

NOVEMBER 16 AND 19, 2009

On November 16, 2009, the United States Preventive Services Task Force (USPSTF), an independent panel appointed by the U.S. Department of Health and Human Services to make recommendations on disease prevention and primary care, presented a controversial decision about women's health screenings, announcing that women should receive mammograms, the screening technique used to detect breast cancer, once every two years upon turning fifty, rather than the previously recommended yearly screenings beginning at age forty. The announcement drew criticism from the American Cancer Society and led women to wonder if their health insurance plans would continue to cover the yearly screenings if they chose to continue in that manner.

New Guidelines

To formulate its new guidelines, the panel looked at studies conducted in England and Sweden and put together statistical models to analyze the data available on the effectiveness of mammograms. These models helped doctors involved in the study decide whether there was enough benefit in annual mammograms to continue to warrant their recommendation. Before the November announcement, the last time new guidelines had been released on mammograms was in 2002, when the USPSTF recommended that women in their forties begin receiving mammograms every one to two years. According to the chair of the panel at that time, Dr. Alfred Berg, the recommendation made clear that "the benefit will be quite small" if women decide to receive mammograms in their forties, as the screening shows the most benefit in older women.

The recommendations announced by the USPSTF were multifaceted. In addition to recommending that women receive fewer mammograms, and begin at a later age, the panel also advised doctors not to teach women how to conduct self breast exams because there is little evidence that they prevent breast cancer deaths and said that it would not recommend regular screenings for breast cancer for those over age seventy-five. According to the group, there was not enough evidence available to support the idea that mammograms were effective at detecting breast cancer in women over seventy-five. The group strongly cautioned that their new recommendations do not apply to women who are at a higher risk of developing breast cancer, such as those with a family history of the disease or those who have undergone gene mutation or chest radiation that makes them increasingly susceptible.

Although the USPSTF recognized that breast cancer screenings were an effective method for decreasing the risk of death caused by the disease, they said that the benefit of receiving the screening did not outweigh the harm that could be caused by the screening in women aged forty to forty-nine. According to the panel, women at that age have a higher probability of getting a false positive during the test, which then leads to biopsies that eventually show no cancer. This, the group said, puts added stress on this part of the population.

The guidelines recommended by the USPSTF differed from the guidelines developed by the American Cancer Society (ACS) and on which many women based the frequency of their mammograms. The ACS had recommended that women begin screening annually for breast cancer at age forty if they were at an average, rather than elevated, risk. Those with a family history of breast cancer, or who displayed other warning signs, were encouraged to undergo screenings at a much earlier age.

CHANGES CAUSED BY THE NEW RECOMMENDATIONS

The immediate concern of many women on hearing the new guidelines was whether insurance companies would continue to cover yearly mammograms. It was not expected, at least in the near term, that any private insurance plans, which by state law are required in all states but Utah to cover mammograms for women, would change the amount of coverage women received; however, the change in guidelines could lessen an insurance company's drive to promote yearly testing as a way to avoid paying the costly expenses incurred if a woman developed breast cancer. Those on government-funded health plans, such as Medicare, would still be able to receive annual screenings. Congress mandates that Medicare offer annual screenings to women, and the only way to change that guideline would be if federal officials decided it was no longer necessary to offer coverage for annual mammograms.

What the new guidelines would change is the National Committee for Quality Assurance's health grades. The independent organization offers grades to health plans and organizations, which hospitals can use to better market their facilities. One of the indicators used in the study is the number of women receiving mammograms annually, or once every other year, beginning at age forty. The group said it would work to change the guideline to the number of women receiving mammograms every other year beginning at age fifty.

THE OBAMA ADMINISTRATION RESPONDS

When the new guidelines were released in 2009, some health experts criticized President Obama and his administration, charging that the recommendations were a politically motivated decision to lower the cost of health care. The administration denied this allegation. Although billions of dollars could be saved if women did not receive annual mammograms until age fifty, according to Dr. Donald Berry, a statistician at the cancer center at the University of Texas, "The economy benefits, but women are the major beneficiaries."

Secretary of Health and Human Services Kathleen Sebelius responded to the new guidelines, saying, "My message to women is simple. Mammograms have always been an important life-saving tool in the fight against breast cancer, and they still are today. Keep doing what you have been doing for years: talk to your doctor about your individual history, ask questions and make the decision that is right for you." Sebelius made it clear that the report was not a direct product of her department but rather that of an independent panel that advises it. She also noted that each woman had to make the decision for herself and that the decision should be based on previous history, not blanket regulations. "There are other groups who have disagreed with this information," Sebelius said. She continued, the task force is simply "making recommendations, not coverage decisions, not payment decisions."

MAMMOGRAM RISKS

According to the USPSTF, when women receive mammograms every other year rather than annually, the risks associated with the test are cut in half, but the benefit derived from screening remains unchanged. Many women do not recognize the risks associated with receiving mammograms. They can lead to further tests because the results are either unclear or show a false positive. Mammograms also detect very small cancers that may grow so slowly that they would never affect the health of a woman. These detections can lead to treatments that are unnecessary given the scope of the cancer found. According to the report, changing the recommendation to dissuade mammograms for women in their forties would cause less harm to the group. The panel said that women between the ages of forty and forty-nine are 60 percent more likely to experience a false positive or other unwanted effect from a mammogram but are far less likely to actually have breast cancer than women in their fifties, sixties, and beyond. And, they reminded women, mammograms only prevent a small number of breast cancer deaths—for every 1,904 women between the ages of forty and forty-nine who are screened for breast cancer, only one death is prevented. Once women are in their fifties, this ratio shifts to 1:1,339, and by the time women are in their sixties, the ratio is 1:377.

Doctors, researchers, and the USPSTF said it would remain up to each woman whether she decided to follow the new guidelines or stick with yearly screening beginning at age forty. According to Berg, "[I]t would be perfectly rational for a woman to decide she didn't want to [follow the new guidelines]."

THE MEDICAL COMMUNITY RESPONDS

After the USPSTF announcement, medical organizations debated whether this suggested change in policy was a matter of rationing care to women. The American College of Radiology Breast Cancer Imaging Commission, in a statement by Dr. Carol Lee, the group's chair, said the recommendations could be used by insurers to cut health costs and the availability of necessary health screenings. According to Lee, women had been receiving regular mammograms since 1990, and since that time, the death rate due to breast cancer had fallen 30 percent. Therefore, Lee said, her organization would continue recommending regular mammograms beginning at age forty.

The American Cancer Society took strong issue with the report. Although recognizing the risks associated with breast cancer screening, Dr. Otis Brawley, the group's chief medical officer, said his organization had looked at "virtually all" the data used by the task force to make its recommendation, as well as other available data, and concluded that there should be no change in the screening guidelines. "The most recent data shows us that approximately 17 percent of breast cancer deaths occurred in women who were diagnosed in their 40s, 22 percent occurred in women diagnosed in their 50s. Breast cancer is a serious health problem facing adult women, and mammography is part of our solution beginning at age 40 for average risk women," Brawley said. The group's deputy chief medical officer, Dr. Len Lichtenfeld, said he worried some women may decide to never seek a mammogram. "Frankly, from our point of view that would be the worst possible outcome," he said.

Others looked at the announcement through the lens of the ongoing debate over health care playing out in Congress. "There were no new data to assess," said Dr. Daniel Kopans, a professor of radiology at Harvard Medical School. "One has to wonder why these new guidelines are being promulgated at a time when healthcare is under discussion and I am afraid their decision is related to saving money rather than saving lives," he said.

The National Cancer Institute announced plans to reevaluate its own guidelines calling for annual mammograms given the USPTF report. The National Cancer Institute was not alone in welcoming new guidelines. "This is our opportunity to look beyond emotions," said Fran Visco, president of the National Breast Cancer Coalition. The panel, she said "are the people we should be listening to when it comes to public health messages."

—Heather Kerrigan

Following is the text of breast cancer screening recommendations, released on November 16, 2009, by the U.S. Preventative Services Task Force, and a press release from the American Cancer Society from November 19, 2009, in reaction to the new guidelines.

Report on Changes to Breast Cancer Screening Guidelines

November 16, 2009

[All footnotes have been omitted.]

[The importance of breast cancer screening and beneficial and harmful effects of testing and early detection have been omitted.]

USPSTF [United States Preventative Services Task Force] Assessment

The USPSTF has reached the following conclusions:

For biennial screening mammography in women aged 40 to 49 years, there is moderate certainty that the net benefit is small. Although the USPSTF recognizes that the benefit of screening seems equivalent for women aged 40 to 49 years and 50 to 59 years, the incidence of breast cancer and the consequences differ. The USPSTF emphasizes the adverse consequences for most women—who will not develop breast cancer—and therefore use the number needed to screen to save 1 life as its metric. By this metric, the USPSTF concludes that there is moderate evidence that the net benefit is small for women aged 40 to 49 years.

For biennial screening mammography in women aged 50 to 74 years, there is moderate certainty that the net benefit is moderate.

For screening mammography in women 75 years or older, evidence is lacking and the balance of benefits and harms cannot be determined.

For the teaching of BSE [breast self-examinations], there is moderate certainty that the harms outweigh the benefits.

For CBE [clinical breast examinations] as a supplement to mammography, evidence is lacking and the balance of benefits and harms cannot be determined.

For digital mammography and MRI as a replacement for mammography, the evidence is lacking and the balance of benefits and harms cannot be determined.

CLINICAL CONSIDERATIONS

Patient Population Under Consideration

This recommendation statement applies to women 40 years or older who are not at increased risk for breast cancer by virtue of a known underlying genetic mutation or a history of chest radiation.

Assessment of Risk

Increasing age is the most important risk factor for breast cancer for most women. Women without known deleterious genetic mutations (such as *BRCA1* or *BRCA2*) may still have other demographic, physical, or historical risk factors for breast cancer, but none conveys a clinically important absolute increased risk for cancer.

Screening Tests

In recent decades, the early detection of breast cancer has been accomplished by physical examination by a clinician (CBE), by a woman herself (BSE), or by mammography. Standardization of mammography practices enacted by the Mammography Quality Standards Act have led to improved mammography quality. Clinicians should refer patients to Mammography Quality Standards Act–certified facilities, a listing of which is available at http://www.fda.gov/cdrh/mammography/certified.html.

Screening Intervals

In trials that demonstrated the effectiveness of mammography in decreasing breast cancer mortality, screening was performed every 12 to 33 months. The evidence reviewed by the USPSTF indicates that a large proportion of the benefit of screening mammography is maintained by biennial screening, and changing from annual to biennial screening is likely to reduce the harms of mammography screening by nearly half. At the same time, benefit may be reduced when extending the interval beyond 24 months; therefore the USPSTF recommends biennial screening.

Treatment

Effective treatments, including radiation, chemotherapy (including hormonal treatment), and surgery, are available for invasive carcinoma. Although the standard treatments women receive for ductal carcinoma in situ (DCIS) include surgical approaches as well as radiation and hormonal therapy, considerable debate exists about the optimal treatment strategy for this condition.

Considerations for Practice Regarding I Statements . . .

[The various forms of breast cancer screening have been omitted.]

Screening Mammography in Women 75 Years or Older

Potential Preventable Burden. No women 75 years or older have been included in the multiple randomized clinical trials of breast cancer screening. Breast cancer is a leading cause of death in older women, which might suggest that the benefits of screening could be important at this age. However, 3 facts suggest that benefits from screening would probably be smaller for this age group than for women aged 60 to 69 years and probably decrease with increasing age: 1) the benefits of screening occur only several years after the actual screening test, whereas the percentage of women who survive long enough to benefit decreases with age; 2) a higher percentage of the type of breast cancer detected in this age group is the more easily treated estrogen receptor-positive type; and 3) women of this age are at much greater risk for dying of other conditions that would not be affected by breast cancer screening.

Potential Harms. Screening detects not only cancer that could lead to a woman's death but also cancer that will not shorten a woman's life. Women cannot benefit from—but can be harmed by—the discovery and treatment of this second type of cancer, which includes both cancer that might some day become clinically apparent and cancer that never will. Detection of cancer that would never have become clinically apparent is called *overdiagnosis,* and it is usually followed by overtreatment. Because of a shortened life span among women 75 years or older, the probability of overdiagnosis and unnecessary earlier treatment increases dramatically after about age 70 or 75 years. Overdiagnosis and unnecessary earlier treatment are important potential harms from screening women in this age group.

Current Practice. Studies show that many women 75 years or older are currently being screened. . . .

OTHER CONSIDERATIONS

Implementation

The Task Force on Community Preventive Services has reviewed the evidence on methods to increase breast cancer screening, including reminder systems and other interventions.

Explanation of Change in Recommendation

The 2002 USPSTF issued a B recommendation for screening mammography for women 40 years or older. However, it went on to say:

The precise age at which the benefits from screening mammography justify the potential harms is a subjective judgment and should take into account patient preferences. Clinicians should inform women about the potential benefits (reduced chance of dying from breast cancer), potential harms (for example, false-positive results, unnecessary biopsies), and limitations of the test that apply to women their age. Clinicians should tell women that the balance of benefits and potential harms of mammography improves with increasing age for women between the ages of 40 and 70.

The updated USPSTF recommendation endorses this approach to deciding when to start screening. However, the current USPSTF is now further informed by a new systematic review, which incorporates a new randomized, controlled trial that estimates the "number needed to invite for screening to extend one woman's life" as 1904 for women aged 40 to 49 years and 1339 for women aged 50 to 59 years. Although the relative risk reduction is nearly identical (15% and 14%) for these 2 age groups, the risk for breast cancer increases steeply with age starting at age 40 years. Thus, the absolute risk reduction from screening (as shown by the number needed to invite to screen) is greater for women aged 50 to 59 years than for those aged 40 to 49 years.

The current USPSTF statement is also informed by the Cancer Intervention and Surveillance Modeling Network (CISNET) modeling studies that accompany this recommendation. The Task Force considered both "mortality" and "life-years gained" outcomes. In this case, given that the age groups (40 to 49 years and 50 to 59 years) are adjacent, the Task Force elected to emphasize the mortality outcomes from the modeling studies. Of the 8 screening strategies found most efficient, 6 start at age 50 years rather than age 40 years. The frontier curves for the mortality outcome show only small gains but larger numbers of mammograms required when screening is started at age 40 years versus age 50 years.

In conclusion, the USPSTF reasoned that the additional benefit gained by starting screening at age 40 years rather than at age 50 years is small, and that moderate harms from screening remain at any age. This leads to the C recommendation. The USPSTF notes that a "C" grade is a recommendation against *routine* screening of women aged 40 to 49 years. The Task Force encourages individualized, informed decision making about when to start mammography screening.

RESEARCH NEEDS AND GAPS

A series of randomized clinical trials that would compare the results of stopping breast cancer screening at different ages (by first comparing stopping screening at age 75 years with continued screening, and then further comparing stopping screening at earlier ages, depending on the results of the first study) would be ethical and informative.

Extended follow-up of this type of study might also provide useful information about overdiagnosis in this age group. In general, more studies of overdiagnosis, including comparisons of lifetime breast cancer incidence among similar screened and unscreened women, would be helpful. Studies on overdiagnosis might also include long-term follow-up of women with probable missed cases of DCIS on the basis of microcalcifications that were missed in an earlier mammogram. Such studies could provide the percentage of these women who develop invasive breast cancer over the next 10 or more years.

Randomized clinical trials of film versus digital mammography among women with dense breast tissue, with sufficient follow-up to detect stage shifts (reductions of late-stage cancer) or decreases in clinical interval cases, would also be ethical and helpful.

Better understanding of certain facets of tumor biology is needed, particularly how age, race, breast density, and other factors may predispose certain women toward tumors with faster growth rates and greater lethality. This would improve the ability to determine at diagnosis which patients can be treated minimally. . . .

[Information on the burden of breast cancer has been omitted.]

Scope of Review

The systematic evidence review undertaken in support of this recommendation addressed the efficacy of 5 breast cancer screening methods for reducing breast cancer mortality— film mammography, CBE, BSE, digital mammography, and MRI—by using published reports of randomized, controlled screening trials and specifically updated information from mammography trials among women in the age groups of 40 to 49 years and 70 years or older. Information on harms of breast cancer screening, such as false-positive test results, pain, anxiety, and biopsy rates, were sought from multiple sources, including systematic reviews, meta-analyses, and recently published literature. To assess the follow-up testing and other outcomes of a mammography screening program, the reviewers included data from the Breast Cancer Surveillance Consortium from 2000 to 2005.

In addition to the systematic review of screening tests, the USPSTF requested a report from the CISNET Breast Cancer Modeling Group to provide data from comparative decision models on optimal starting and stopping ages and intervals for screening mammography. . . .

[The accuracy of screening tests and benefits of screening have been omitted.]

[The potential harms of breast cancer screening have been omitted.]

How Does Evidence Fit with Biological Understanding?

Current knowledge about the development of breast cancer is limited. The effectiveness of screening mammography seen in trials presumably results from the early detection of smaller, earlier-stage tumors, which are more responsive to available treatments. Although the most common breast cancer occurs in the epithelial cells that line the duct system of the gland (ductal carcinoma), the sequence of development of invasive cancer is not entirely known. For example, DCIS does not always represent a precursor to invasive ductal cancer. Studies of women with untreated DCIS showed progression to invasive disease in half or fewer of the cases. Because DCIS is often found only by mammography, its incidence has increased steadily since the advent of widespread screening mammography. In 1983, 4900 cases of DCIS were diagnosed; by 2008, that number was expected to be 67,770. Because the likelihood that DCIS will progress to invasive cancer is unknown, surgical removal—with or without adjuvant treatment—may represent overdiagnosis or overtreatment. Lobular carcinoma in situ, in contrast, is not considered a true precursor lesion but connotes a higher risk for subsequent invasive lobular or ductal cancer in either breast. Lobular carcinoma in situ is often multifocal, appearing in several distinct locations. Knowledge of what determines the rapidity with which invasive cancer can spread (tumor characteristics, host factors, hormonal triggers) is limited. Because of these elements of biological uncertainty, it is clear that lesion sensitivity alone is not a sufficient metric for assessing effectiveness of new screening methods.

Update of Previous USPSTF Recommendation

This recommendation updates the 2002 recommendation by providing specific recommendations for mammography screening by age. The previous recommendation statement recommended screening mammography every 1 to 2 years for all women older than 40 years. The USPSTF now recommends against routine screening of women aged 40 to 49 years (C recommendation), recommends biennial screening mammography for all women aged 50 to 74 years (B recommendation), and provides an I statement regarding screening of women older than 75 years. The USPSTF now recommends against teaching BSE (D recommendation), replacing the previous statement of insufficient evidence. The evidence for CBE continues to be assessed as insufficient. Digital mammography and MRI as screening tools were not addressed in the 2002 recommendation statement; the USPSTF concludes that the evidence is insufficient to assess the harms or benefits of these methods for screening.

Recommendations of Others

Numerous organizations have provided breast cancer screening recommendations. These recommendations are summarized below. All recommendations are for women not at increased risk for breast cancer.

In 2003, the American Cancer Society recommended annual mammography beginning at age 40 years, annual CBE after the age of 40 years. It does not recommend MRI for women at average risk for breast cancer and states that there is insufficient evidence to recommend BSE.

The American Medical Association, in 2002, and the National Comprehensive Cancer Network, in 2009, have made recommendations similar to those of the American Cancer Society, except for the inclusion of a positive recommendation for BSE.

The American Academy of Family Physicians has endorsed the USPSTF recommendation on breast cancer screening in the past. The American College of Physicians recommended in 2007 that screening mammography decisions in women aged 40 to 49 years should be based on individualized assessment of risk for breast cancer; that clinicians should inform women aged 40 to 49 years about the potential benefits and harms of screening mammography; and that clinicians should base screening mammography decisions on benefits and harms of screening, as well as on a woman's preferences and breast cancer risk profile.

In 2001, the Canadian Task Force on Preventive Health Care recommended mammography every 1 to 2 years beginning at the age of 40 years and recommended CBE as part of a periodic evaluation (every 1 to 3 years) for women aged 50 to 69 years. It does not recommend BSE.

In 2003, the American College of Obstetrics and Gynecology recommended mammography every 1 to 2 years for women aged 40 to 49 years and annually after the age of 50 years. It recommended CBE for all women and noted that BSE can be recommended.

In 2009, the World Health Organization recommended mammography every 1 to 2 years for women aged 50 to 69 years, but does not recommend CBE or BSE. . . .

[A list of members of the USPSTF and footnotes have been omitted.]

Source: U.S. Department of Health and Human Services. Agency for Healthcare Research and Quality. U.S. Preventative Services Task Force. "Screening for Breast Cancer: Recommendation Statement." November 16, 2009. www.ahrq.gov/clinic/uspstf09/breastcancer/brcanrs.htm.

The American Cancer Society Responds to New Mammography Guidelines

November 16, 2009

The American Cancer Society continues to recommend annual screening using mammography and clinical breast examination for all women beginning at age 40. Our experts make this recommendation having reviewed virtually all the same data reviewed by the USPSTF [United States Preventative Services Task Force], but also additional data that the USPSTF did not consider. When recommendations are based on judgments about the balance of risks and benefits, reasonable experts can look at the same data and reach different conclusions.

In 2003, an expert panel convened by the American Cancer Society conducted an extensive review of the data available at the time, which was not substantially different from the data included in the current USPSTF review. Like the USPSTF, the Society's panel found convincing evidence that screening with mammography reduces breast cancer mortality in women ages 40–74, with age-specific benefits varying depending on the results of individual trials and which trials were combined in meta-analyses. And like the USPSTF, the American Cancer Society panel also found that mammography has limitations—some women who are screened will have false alarms; some cancers will be missed; and some women will undergo unnecessary treatment. These limitations are somewhat greater in women in their forties compared with women in their fifties, and somewhat greater in women in their fifties compared with women in their sixties. We specifically noted that the overall effectiveness of mammography increases with increasing age. But the limitations do not change the fact that breast cancer screening using mammography starting at age 40 saves lives. As someone who has long been a critic of those overstating the benefits of screening, I [chief medical director Otis W. Brawley] use these words advisedly: this is one screening test I recommend unequivocally, and would recommend to any woman 40 and over, be she a patient, a stranger, or a family member.

The USPSTF says that screening 1,339 women in their 50s to save one life makes screening worthwhile in that age group. Yet USPSTF also says screening 1,904 women ages 40 to 49 in order to save one life is not worthwhile. The American Cancer Society feels that in both cases, the lifesaving benefits of screening outweigh any potential harms. Surveys of women show that they are aware of these limitations, and also place high value on detecting breast cancer early.

With its new recommendations, the USPSTF is essentially telling women that mammography at age 40 to 49 saves lives; just not enough of them. The task force says screening women in their 40s would reduce their risk of death from breast cancer by 15 percent, just as it does for women in their 50s. But because women in their 40s are at lower risk of the disease than women 50 and above, the USPSTF says the actual number of lives saved is not enough to recommend widespread screening. The most recent data show us that approximately 17 percent of breast cancer deaths occurred in women who were diagnosed in their 40s, and 22 percent occurred in women diagnosed in their 50s. Breast cancer is a serious health problem facing adult women, and mammography is part of our solution beginning at age 40 for average risk women.

The American Cancer Society acknowledges the limitations of mammography, and we remain committed to finding better tests, and currently are funding a large study to improve the accuracy of mammography. In fact, data show the technology used today is better than that used in the studies in this review, and more modern studies show that mammography is achieving better results than those achieved in these early experimental studies that go back as far as the mid-60's. And as scientists work to make mammography even more effective, the American Cancer Society's medical staff and volunteer experts overwhelmingly believe the benefits of screening women aged 40 to 49 outweigh its limitations.

SOURCE: American Cancer Society. Press release. "American Cancer Society Responds to Changes to USPSTF Mammography Guidelines." November 16, 2009. www.cancer.org/docroot/MED/content/MED_2_1x_American_Cancer_Society_Responds_to_Changes_to_USPSTF_Mammography_Guidelines.asp.

OTHER HISTORIC DOCUMENTS OF INTEREST

FROM THIS VOLUME

- President Obama Speaks to Congress on Health Care Reform, p. 399
- Congressional Debate on Health Care Reform, p. 533

FROM PREVIOUS *HISTORIC DOCUMENTS*

- Presidential Panel on Health Care for Cancer Patients, *2001*, p. 867
- Report on Mammograms for Women in their Forties, *1997*, p. 142
- Presidential Panel Report on Breast Cancer, *1993*, p. 905

IRS Reveals Details for Targeting Swiss Bank Accounts

NOVEMBER 17, 2009

On November 17, 2009, the Internal Revenue Service (IRS) and the government of Switzerland announced the details of a landmark agreement to expose Americans who were keeping money in secret Swiss bank accounts, thereby avoiding taxes on the funds. The terms of the plan stemmed from a July 2008 summons from the United States to UBS, the Swiss banking giant, to provide information on Americans holding bank accounts with the company in Switzerland, where tax evasion is a civil, not criminal, offense as in the United States. The agreement on providing information ended a legal battle that had stretched over eight months and would eventually cost UBS $780 million in fines.

The deal, originally reached in August but kept secret, was an attempt by the IRS to overcome Switzerland's long-running secrecy on American tax dodgers and collect the money owed to it. Although the Swiss government did not agree to hand over information on all 52,000 accounts the IRS had requested, the agreement was a serious blow to a nation that prides itself on banking secrecy. According to Scott D. Michel, from a law firm that represented UBS clients, the agreement between the U.S. and Swiss governments meant that "Switzerland is no longer a place where Americans can freely think that their account information will be forever protected."

John Doe Summons

On July 21, 2008, the U.S. Department of Justice sent what is known as a "John Doe summons" to UBS. The summons, made out to John Doe because there was no official person to name, demanded the account information and account holder names of 52,000 accounts held at UBS by American citizens. It was suspected by the IRS that these Americans were keeping their accounts secret to dodge federal taxes and could therefore be required to pay all back taxes owed. The summons, delivered to the company's head of compliance read,

> United States taxpayers, who at any time during the years ended December 31, 2002, through December 31, 2007, had signature or other authority (including authority to withdraw funds; to make investment decisions; to receive account statements, trade confirmations, or other account information; or to receive advice or solicitations) with respect to any financial accounts maintained at,

monitored by, or managed through any office in Switzerland of UBS AG or its subsidiaries or affiliates in Switzerland and for whom UBS AG or its subsidiaries or affiliates (1) did not have in its possession Forms W-9 executed by such United States taxpayers, and (2) had not filed timely and accurate Forms 1099 naming such United States taxpayers and reporting to United States taxing authorities all payments made to such United States taxpayers.

The matter was settled on August 19, 2009, at the same time the U.S. and Swiss governments agreed to a deal in which UBS would provide information on a fraction of the 52,000 accounts the IRS had requested. The Swiss Federal Tax Administration (SFTA) would take responsibility for processing information from UBS to determine which account holders were in violation of U.S. tax law, pursuant to the U.S.-Switzerland Double Taxation Treaty, and forward that information to the United States. UBS remained against giving the U.S. government any information about its account holders, but in the August deal, both sides agreed to relent on some points: UBS would pay the $780 million in fines and penalties relating to allegations that it had attempted to defraud the U.S. government by setting up offshore accounts for U.S. clients, thus avoiding criminal prosecution, and process the request from the IRS, and the U.S. government would allow some who were holding Swiss bank accounts to avoid criminal charges.

UBS was given 270 days, beginning on September 1, 2009, to put together all requested information and send it to the SFTA, as well as notify clients that their information had been passed to the agency. Once the SFTA received the information, it would determine which accounts should be disclosed to the IRS and which, based on the client's rights and the double taxation treaty, could remain secret. A forty-person team was set up in Switzerland to help process the account information.

UBS OFFSHORE ACCOUNTS

The IRS had long been pressuring banks in Switzerland to hand over information on account holders who were not disclosing their funds to the U.S. government. The banks held out, but became increasingly concerned over time and made it more difficult for Americans to open accounts, pay mortgages, or do other banking transactions in Switzerland. According to Ellen Wallace, an American living in Switzerland, the Swiss banks had put in place a complicated system "in which [U.S. expatriates] can't make those transactions happen in a straightforward way." Before the UBS-IRS announcement, Migros Bank and Raiffeisen Bank, both based in Switzerland, had made it nearly impossible for an American, whether residing in the United States or in Switzerland, to open an account. While this made the banks feel at ease because they were able to prevent themselves from being targets of a U.S. government probe, it caused serious problems for Americans living in Switzerland. "It's easy to distort the picture and say the 52,000 names that are wanted by the IRS are 52,000 crooks," said Wallace, but she continued, "[t]hey're not all evil people trying to hide their money. It's somewhere in between."

Although some of those holding Swiss bank accounts may have been acting in an innocent and legal fashion, UBS admitted to the IRS that between 2000 and 2007, some private bankers had assisted U.S. residents set up offshore accounts and helped them conceal their existence from the federal government. According to UBS, these bankers had "participated in a scheme to defraud the United States." UBS had its own offshore banking business, which, according to government prosecutors, the company had used to assist U.S. clients with opening secret accounts. According to prosecutors, UBS had encouraged those U.S. citizens who wanted to hide assets to destroy records of the accounts they held in Switzerland, to conceal tangible goods they had purchased with money from these accounts, and to use a credit card from Switzerland that would not be traceable by the U.S. government.

Once it was hit with fines from the U.S. government, UBS began backtracking on earlier policies and offered an apology to the United States. "UBS sincerely regrets the compliance failures in its U.S. cross-border business that have been identified by the various government investigations in Switzerland and the U.S., as well as our own internal review. We accept full responsibility for these improper activities," said UBS chair Peter Kurer. Not all UBS executives settled for being contrite, however. One senior executive, Raoul Weil, went on the lam after being indicted in federal court for helping with the offshore banking activities of UBS and is still at large.

WHAT THE DECISION MEANS FOR AMERICANS

Swiss tax law had historically allowed Americans to keep money secretly in bank accounts in Switzerland, thus shielding those who were hiding their funds from the IRS. According to the Swiss government, to be turned over to the U.S. government before the John Doe summons, a person had to conduct "fraud and the like." The "fraud and the like" threshold included failure to send a W-9 disclosure to the IRS for three years or more in a row, but only if the account had more than $992,802 in it at any point from 2001 through 2008.

According to the agreement between the IRS, Swiss government, and UBS, any American with less than $248,200 dollars in his or her Swiss bank account would be able to keep their account confidential, as would anyone who received less than $99,280 in revenue from the account. However, anyone who did not disclose their funds to the IRS and had more in their account or earned more in interest than those amounts would have their account information sent directly from UBS to the IRS.

Although these details had been agreed to in August, they did not become public until November because the IRS wanted U.S. citizens with Swiss bank accounts to come forward on their own. The government promised to be lenient with anyone who came forward before the details were announced. The IRS gave account holders until mid-October to disclose them, and as the final day to let the government know about secret accounts got closer, nearly 15,000 people filed statements with the IRS. Not all of the people who filed disclosures were UBS clients. Some holding other illegal overseas accounts came forward as well to avoid potential punishment in the future.

Although the U.S. government would not know how much money in taxes it stood to recoup until receiving the final report from UBS, according to IRS commissioner Douglas Shulman, "We are talking about billions of dollars coming into the U.S. Treasury."

On Capitol Hill, Democrats criticized the willingness of the IRS to agree to Switzerland's terms. "The tortured wording and the many limitations in this annex shows the Swiss government trying to preserve as much bank secrecy as it can for the future, while pushing to conceal the names of tens of thousands of suspected U.S. tax cheats," said Sen. Carl Levin, D-Mich. "It is disappointing that the U.S. government went along," he continued.

WHAT THE DECISION MEANS FOR UBS AND SWITZERLAND

The disclosure requirements were far more lax than many had expected. Based on the agreement reached by the IRS and the Swiss government, U.S. citizens would still be able to open Swiss bank accounts, in some cases as freely as they had in the past. The Swiss government agreed to inform the U.S. government about anyone it felt was committing tax evasion, but the company would not allow the IRS to simply get a dump of all information to wade through, such as the original 52,000 names the government had requested. UBS said that it had agreed to provide to date information on "approximately" 4,450 accounts to Swiss tax authorities, who would then determine whether the information was germane to the IRS case. The agreement further stated that no Swiss banking laws would need to be changed. "This agreement helps resolve one of UBS's most pressing issues," said UBS chair Kaspar Villiger, who replaced Kurer in early 2009. "The agreement will allow the bank to continue moving forward to rebuild its reputation through solid performance and client service. UBS welcomes the fact that the information-exchange objectives of the settlement can be achieved in a lawful manner under the existing treaty framework between Switzerland and the United States."

According to Bruce Zagaris, a lawyer representing some UBS clients, the Swiss banking system may never recover the number of international clients it once had. The Swiss, according to Zagaris, place a good deal of pride in their ability to protect clients, a position Swiss banks can no longer take if they're willing to freely give information to the U.S. government. "There are a number of policy issues having to do with the role of different financial service jurisdictions. The Swiss have to balance their policy of confidentiality on the one hand with law enforcement cooperation," said Zagaris.

—Heather Kerrigan

Following is a press release from the government of Switzerland from November 17, 2009, announcing the official agreement regarding assistance between the Internal Revenue Service and UBS on releasing Swiss bank account information.

DOCUMENT

IRS and UBS Agree to Official Terms of Assistance

November 17, 2009

Bern. The official assistance that Switzerland is providing to the US tax authorities in connection with the UBS affair is on track. The tax treaty between Switzerland and the USA provides the corresponding legal framework. Issues relating to implementation, the associated deadlines and the number of cases involved (4,450) were laid down in the agreement of 19 August 2009 between the Swiss Confederation and the USA. The criteria for granting assistance under the treaty request were published today, 90 days after the agreement was signed, in Switzerland's official compilation of legislation.

According to the criteria set out in the annex to the agreement, the US treaty request covers the following persons where there is a reasonable suspicion of "tax fraud or the like":

- US-domiciled clients of UBS who directly held and beneficially owned undisclosed (non-W-9) custody accounts and banking deposit accounts in excess of CHF 1 million at any point in time between 2001 and 2008;

- US persons (irrespective of their domicile) who beneficially owned offshore company accounts established or maintained between 2001 and 2008.

Further investigations are ongoing in both categories to establish whether "tax fraud or the like" has been committed under the terms of the tax treaty. The term "tax fraud or the like" is defined in greater detail in the agreement on the UBS affair. On the one hand, it also extends to fraudulent conduct (e.g. constructing a scheme of lies or submitting incorrect or false documents) that might result in the concealment of assets and the underreporting of income. Where such conduct is proven, the qualifying threshold under the US treaty request is lowered to include holders of accounts containing assets of CHF 250,000 or more. In addition to cases of conventional "fraudulent conduct," Switzerland may also be asked to obtain information on continued and serious tax offenses. According to the annex, this refers to accounts that generated revenues of more than CHF 100,000 on average per year for a period of at least three years, where such revenues were not reported to the IRS.

EFFICIENT HANDLING—RIGHTS SAFEGUARDED

Under the terms of the agreement, the Swiss Federal Tax Administration (SFTA) must evaluate the 4,450 UBS accounts within 360 days of the treaty request being received (31 August 2009). An efficient system was set up to handle the treaty process. It is based on the electronic processing of the client dossiers filtered by UBS. Subject to the usual security precautions, these dossiers are sent to the SFTA, where audit firm PricewaterhouseCoopers (PWC) reviews the facts in accordance with SFTA instructions. The legal qualification lies with the SFTA. It will allow the individuals concerned to inspect their dossiers upon request, and will also give them the opportunity to state their case. The rights of these individuals are therefore safeguarded in full. Finally, the SFTA will decide whether or not assistance will be provided, and will issue a final decision. Upon receipt of this decision, the individuals concerned have 30 days in which to lodge an appeal with the Federal Administrative Court, which will issue a final decision. The Federal Government estimates the costs of the UBS affair at around 40 million Swiss francs.

TASK FORCE FULLY OPERATIONAL

The SFTA set up a dedicated task force to speed up the treaty request process. Hans-Jörg Müllhaupt, who was appointed by the Federal Council as overall project manager in August 2009, is in charge of proceedings. Following set-up work in September, the task force became fully operational in October 2009. The first 500 client dossiers prepared by UBS were received by the end of that month, i.e. within the agreed 60-day period that began when the treaty request was received by the SFTA.

Around 40 people—ten of them from PWC—are currently employed on the project. Where necessary, additional lawyers may be brought in at short notice from other departments, particularly those of the Federal Office of Justice (FOJ).

Final decisions are being issued on an ongoing basis, meaning that the first can be sent out as early as today. Under the terms of the agreement, the SFTA has 90 days from receipt of the treaty request, i.e. until the end of November 2009, to issue the first 500 decisions. The remaining dossiers must be processed by the SFTA within 360 days of receiving the treaty request.

SOURCE: Government of Switzerland. Federal Department of Justice and Police. "UBS: Treaty Process on Track." November 17, 2009. www.ejpd.admin.ch/ejpd/en/home/dokumentation/mi/2009/2009-11-17 .html.

OTHER HISTORIC DOCUMENTS OF INTEREST

FROM PREVIOUS *HISTORIC DOCUMENTS*

■ Report on How "Neutrals Aided Nazi Germany," *1997*, p. 257

Afghan President Elected to Second Term

NOVEMBER 19, 2009

Hamid Karzai, who first came to power in 2002, was elected to a second term as president of Afghanistan in early November 2009. The controversial election was fraught with alleged voter fraud, but Karzai was declared victorious after his opponent dropped out of the runoff contest.

Karzai, a close ally of the United States who had worked with American military forces to expel the Taliban from Afghanistan, is considered a centrist figure in Afghan politics, lending to his popularity and aura as an effective diplomat. Karzai's family history and tribal and ethnic alliances had put him in a position to secure the position of president twice. However, Karzai was not without his critics and had escaped multiple assassination attempts during his time at the helm of Afghanistan's fledgling democratic government.

KARZAI's RISE TO POWER

Some international analysts and experts on Middle Eastern politics saw Karzai as a natural choice for president during both his election campaigns. Karzai was born a member of the Popalzai clan, which had had close ties with Afghanistan's monarchy throughout history. Karzai's father was a well-respected tribal elder in the Popalzai clan and a member of parliament shortly after Karzai's birth.

Karzai spent his early life in Afghanistan and later earned his university education in India. In 1979 Karzai and his family fled to Pakistan to escape the Soviet invasion of their native Afghanistan. During his time in Pakistan, Karzai raised money for the mujahidin fighting the Soviet invaders.

Karzai returned to Afghanistan in 1989, after the Soviets had withdrawn, and began work shortly thereafter with Afghanistan's government, then led by the Northern Alliance. It was not long after that Karzai was appointed to the position of deputy foreign minister. However, these were not peaceful times in Afghanistan, as disagreements among party leaders forced the nation into turmoil. A civil war broke out, and the Taliban was victorious, taking control of the government in 1996.

At first, Karzai supported the new government and was offered the position of UN ambassador in 1995. He turned down the job, however, over concerns that the Taliban was not the right group to lead the government because it was heavily influenced by outside groups. After refusing the position, Karzai fled to Pakistan. His father was then murdered, apparently by members of the Taliban.

After the September 11, 2001, al-Qaida attacks on the United States, Karzai became an outspoken supporter of the U.S. plan to invade Afghanistan and remove the Taliban from power. "These Arabs, together with their foreign supporters and the Taliban, destroyed miles and miles of homes and orchards and vineyards. They have killed Afghans. They have trained their guns on Afghan lives. . . . We want them out," Karzai said.

When the invasion began, Karzai returned to Afghanistan and worked with his ethnic group, the Pashtun, to help them combat the Taliban. Karzai was chosen by Afghan leaders and UN mediators to be the chairman of the interim administration of Afghanistan in December 2001. He would hold this position until a formal government could be set up.

In 2002 Karzai was appointed by Afghan leaders to the position of president of the newly created transitional government, and in 2004 he was selected by the people of Afghanistan to be the first elected president in the nation's history.

Karzai's first five-year term expired in 2009. Although Karzai did not receive the level of support his party had hoped for in the 2009 election, some experts of Middle Eastern politics say that it was both Karzai's personality and his link to the United States that brought people out to vote in his favor. "They did not see in any of the other candidates the possibility, if they were elected, that the United States would continue to provide the kind of material support and political support that Karzai was expected to bring," said Nazif Shahrani, a professor of Middle Eastern studies at Indiana University.

KARZAI'S QUESTIONABLE REELECTION

After its invasion in 2001, the United States worked with Afghan and UN leaders to set up an effective democracy in a nation that had never held a presidential election. Setting up an effective and stable democracy would prove to be challenging.

On August 20, 2009, Karzai was declared the winner of the election. However, an investigation was launched immediately after the votes had been tallied in response to claims that mass voter fraud might have changed the outcome of the election. A panel to investigate the election was created, overseen by the United Nations. The members threw out nearly one-third of all votes for Karzai, determining that they had been cast fraudulently.

After the investigation concluded, it was learned that Karzai had not received the 50 percent of the vote required to be seated, so a runoff election was necessary. The runoff, scheduled for November 2009, would feature Karzai and his next closest opponent, Abdullah Abdullah, a former Afghan foreign minister. Abdullah had called on election officials to resign, citing their appointment by Karzai, which indicated to some that they would not be able to make an impartial decision. Because his request was rejected, Abdullah withdrew his name from the runoff election. "I want this to be an example for the future so that no one again tries to use fraud to abuse the rights of the Afghan people." Following Abdullah's withdrawal, the vote was cancelled, and Karzai was declared the winner by default.

Some in Afghanistan criticized the decision of the country's Independent Electoral Commission, saying it should have held the vote with only one candidate to properly determine the popularity of Karzai. The commission, however, said it did not have the money required to conduct an unnecessary election nor was security adequate.

The international community, however, congratulated the commission on its determination to avoid fraud in elections and welcomed Karzai back on to the world stage. U.S. president Barack Obama called Karzai to congratulate him on his victory and offer the continued support of the American government in rebuilding Afghanistan as a secure, democratic nation. President Obama said "this has to be a point in time in which we begin to write a new chapter based on improved governance, a much more serious effort to eradicate corruption, joint efforts to accelerate the training of Afghan security forces so that the Afghan people can provide for their own security."

Given the events surrounding his election, the issue for Karzai was whether he could set up a government that would be viewed as legitimate. UN secretary-general Ban Ki-moon said in reaction to the election, "This has been a difficult election process for Afghanistan and lessons must be learned. Afghanistan now faces significant challenges and the new president must move swiftly to form a government that is able to command the support of both the Afghan people and the international community."

Karzai's Inaugural Address

Even after what many considered to be a flawed election, Karzai was determined to take the reins of Afghanistan's government. During his inaugural address, Karzai promised to have Afghan security forces trained and fully prepared to take control of the nation from American forces by the end of his second term, five years later. "The role of the international troops will be gradually reduced," he said. "We are determined that in the next five years, the Afghan forces are capable of taking the lead in ensuring security and stability across the country." Karzai also indicated that he would convene a *loya jirga,* or assembly, where those who are interested in restoring the security of Afghanistan would be able to meet and discuss their concerns.

In his address, Karzai struck a conciliatory tone, speaking to the various ethnic groups in Afghanistan, his election competitors, and Western nations that would continue to work with Afghanistan's government. Karzai made a number of promises in his speech, including creating a transparent government and combating corruption. According to those in attendance at the speech, and those watching on television, it was difficult to tell whether Karzai believed in the promises he was making. One critic, Ramazan Bashardost, an opponent from the presidential election who finished third, said, "He believes his power is his warlords. It's not important what is true. What is important is the interest of your family. It's why he cannot fight the warlords and cannot fight the corruption." These loyalties, according to Bashardost, would have to be set aside before true change could be accomplished. Citizens of Afghanistan were also doubtful that anything would change during Karzai's second five years at the head of the nation's government. "We don't have any hope for the future," said Taimoor, an Afghan lawyer. "Rule of law is not something we've seen in eight years, and Karzai is not elected on the basis of law. He can't get rid of corruption, because he came to his position by fraud," he added.

Challenges Ahead for Karzai

In a brutal reminder that many challenges lie ahead for Karzai, extremists in Afghanistan killed eighteen people the day after Karzai's inaugural address. Coupled with earlier attacks, the number of those killed after Karzai was sworn into office reached thirty, leading Karzai's critics to question whether his goal of Afghans being fully in charge of their own security within five years was truly possible.

According to international observers, Karzai's biggest challenge will be combating corruption at the highest levels of Afghanistan's government. Karzai was said to have put his friends into positions of power, many of whom were corrupt and had mismanaged or abused their positions. "He has no vision—absolutely no vision, no quality for leadership," said former Afghan ambassador to the United States Ishaq Shahryar. However, Shahryar said, it is not Karzai himself who is corrupt but rather those he choses to surround himself with.

U.S. secretary of state Hillary Clinton said she would continue to monitor the level of corruption in Afghanistan, saying that although Karzai had worked toward a reduction in corruption, he had not done enough. Secretary Clinton did, however, praise the work done thus far, saying that it "provides an important new starting point, and we intend to build on it." In an indication of how far Karzai has to go to remove corruption at the highest levels, the swearing in of his two vice presidents was questioned. Both have been accused of human rights abuses and have been linked to Afghanistan's lucrative drug trade. Another close supporter of Karzai has been accused of killing thousands of Taliban prisoners in 2001 after American forces invaded.

—Heather Kerrigan

Following is the text of the inaugural speech given by Afghanistan's President Hamid Karzai on November 19, 2009.

Hamid Karzai Delivers Inaugural Address

November 19, 2009

In the name of God, the most merciful, the most compassionate
Your Excellency, Mr. Zardari, President of the Islamic Republic of Pakistan;
Distinguished guests;
Your Excellencies Speakers of both Houses of the Parliament;
Your Excellency Chief Justice;
Members of the National Assembly;
Distinguished Jihadi Leaders, Tribal Elders and Respected Ulemma;
Members of the Diplomatic Corp;
Members of the Press;
Members of the Cabinet;
Ladies and Gentlemen!
May peace be upon you all!
I thank Almighty Allah (SWT) for bestowing upon our nation the ability and success to proudly come out of another major test. The participation of millions of citizens of the Islamic Republic of Afghanistan in presidential and provincial elections

once again demonstrated that the Afghan nation has reached a stage of political maturity of which we can be proud.

I would like to thank and express my heartfelt gratitude to my country's men and women, who despite threats, made sacrifices to take part in this great national process. I also applaud all of the candidates for their participation in the election process; this process has moved our country one step further towards democratic maturity. Let me also commend all the candidates for their peaceful campaigns and rallies. The conduct of the election campaigns in shaping opinions and giving direction to the people's votes were major strides towards stabilizing and ensuring the people's preeminence in our young democracy.

The notable characteristic of the recent elections was that it broke all ethnic boundaries. Widespread participation by our people in the elections showed that they, irrespective of their political affiliation, came out and voted for the president on the basis of national interest. Looking at the combination of votes, one finds that ballots were cast in a more national and Afghan spirit than ever before.

Taking this opportunity, I would like to sincerely thank the Independent Election Commission (IEC). Taking the current difficult situation into consideration, these elections would have been impossible without the great sacrifice and effective management of the IEC. We must learn from our good and bad experiences in these elections and put all our energy to ultimately fully Afghanize the process. The election law has to be ratified and enforced as soon as possible, and Afghan voters must know and be assured that it is only the people's vote that can give legitimacy to the government.

In the same vein, let us remember the services of all the members of the national army, the national police and other security services, as well as the soldiers of our allied countries who put their lives in danger to make possible the participation of our people in the elections. I pray for those who lost their lives and wish a quick recovery for those who suffered injuries.

Distinguished Guests, Sister and Brothers!

Arguing and disputing our political ideas and beliefs are famously embedded in our Afghan character. However, we stand united when it comes to defending our fatherland and our national values. Using this opportunity, I would like to invite all the presidential candidates, including my brother Dr. Abdullah Abdullah, and Ashraf Ghani Ahmadzai, who is here with us today to come together to achieve the important task of national unity, and make our common home, Afghanistan, proud and prosperous. I believe that the obligation of patriotism and loyalty to Afghanistan, its political system, and its state must remain the highest values we believe in.

Honorable Guests, Dear Compatriots

With international support, Afghanistan has had many successes in the past eight years; these successes have been the result of sacrifices made by our people and the peoples of our allied countries.

I do not want [to] go over all of the successes of the last eight years. I do, however, want to state that during the last eight years, we were able to bring Afghanistan out of a situation where it did not have a responsible government and the necessary legal foundations. Today, we have a law-based state along with institutions that are at the service of the people of our country.

We are proud of Afghanistan's achievements in providing its sons and daughters with access to education and health services. Today, Afghanistan enjoys an open and free media, a developing civil society, a rehabilitated economic infrastructure, a set of well-conducted monetary reforms and a budding free-market economy.

Grasping the opportunity of today's august occasion, I would like to talk about Afghanistan's tomorrow. We have to learn from the mistakes and shortcomings of the past eight years. It is through this self evaluation that we can better respond to the aspirations and expectations of our people.

At this point, I would like to set out the priorities that will serve as the basis for our future endeavors:

1. Peace and Reconciliation:

Securing peace and an end to fighting are the most significant demands of our people. For the last thirty years, our people have offered continuous sacrifices to achieve peace.

It is a recognized fact that security and peace cannot be achieved through fighting and violence. This is why the Islamic Republic of Afghanistan has placed national reconciliation at the top of its peace-building policy. We welcome and will provide necessary help to all disenchanted compatriots who are willing to return to their homes, live peacefully and accept the Constitution.

We invite dissatisfied compatriots, who are not directly linked to international terrorism, to return to their homeland. We will utilize all national and international resources to put an end to war and fratricide.

We will call Afghanistan's traditional Loya Jirga and make every possible effort to ensure peace in our country.

At this point, I am compelled to note that His Majesty King Abdullah, Custodian of the Two Holy Mosques, has made many commendable efforts towards peace and national reconciliation in Afghanistan. We thank His Majesty, the Custodians of the Two Holy Mosques, and hope that he will continue his endeavors for this cause.

2. Security:

Defending our country and providing security for our nation is the duty of all Afghans. The state's monopoly over security forces and the leadership and organizational role of our security forces can ensure security for our country.

Based on the state monopoly of the Islamic Republic of Afghanistan over the defense and security forces of our country, and other imperatives of national sovereignty, we want to organize and improve the national army and our other security forces in quantitative and qualitative terms, in consonance with the defensive needs of Afghanistan. Our country, consistent with our financial capabilities, should be able to provide for needs of our national army and security forces.

Within the next three years, Afghanistan, with continued international support and in line with the growth of its defense capacity, wants to lead and conduct military operations in the many insecure areas of the country. As they already have in Kabul, our own security forces should be able to take control of security of other provinces as well, and thus the role of the international troops will be gradually reduced and limited to support and training of Afghan forces. We are determined that by the next five years, the Afghan forces are capable of taking the lead in ensuring security and stability across the country.

The detention and prosecution of suspects is the authority and responsibility of the Afghan government. We have to strengthen the security of our prisons and detention centers, and expedite further the reform process within our justice system. We will continue to discuss this issue with the United States of America to ensure that detention and legal prosecution of suspects will be the responsibility of the government of Afghanistan alone.

Civilian casualties continue to remain an issue of concern to the people and government of Afghanistan. I am pleased to see that our continuing discussions with NATO and ISAF, and our joint operational measures, have resulted in a considerable reduction in the number of civilian casualties. We would like to expand and enhance such measures, so that casualties among our civilian population to be avoided.

The goal of a powerful national government can be realized by the stronger presence of national security forces in all parts of the country. Within the next two years, we want operations by all private national and international security firms to be ended and their duties delegated to Afghan security entities.

3. Good Governance:

A fundamental prerequisite for good governance is to ensure individual and social security of the people. Security and the rule of law can only be effectively ensured when both the government and the citizens are equal before law.

It is noteworthy that our people throughout the long years of conflict never felt safe even in their home out of fear of government security agencies. People have the right to be safe and we are responsible to provide them with the safety.

Good governance can be practiced by good and authoritative executives. We must use full care and foresight in appointing all government officials and members of the administration. The ministers of Afghanistan must possess integrity and be professionals serving the nation. All senior officials, especially the ministers, governors and deputy ministers have the duty to declare and register their moveable and unmovable assets. To prevent corruption, we will adopt a law in consultation with the National Assembly for making it obligatory for senior government officials to identify the sources of their assets and to declare their properties in a transparent manner.

Strengthening administrative reforms and improving the capacity-building of the civil administration from center to the district level, are those future measures that we will pursue with great seriousness. As a first step, in line with these reforms, fifty thousand teachers were asked this week to undergo aptitude tests. Afghanistan's civil administration, its diplomatic corps, national army, national police, and national security forces must be non-political and act as true public servants.

The Government of Afghanistan is committed to end the culture of impunity and violation of law and bring to justice those involved in spreading corruption and abuse of public property. To do this, will require effective and strong measures. Therefore, alongside an intensified judicial reform, all government anti-corruption efforts and agencies have to be strengthened and supported. Particular attention will be given to building the capacity and upgrading the High Office of Oversight for the Implementation of the Anti-Corruption Strategy. Measures for supporting the anti-corruption agencies include: increasing the scope of their authority, improving their capacity and resources for detection and investigation, expanding their organizational structure, as well as reforming the relevant anti-corruption laws and regulations.

Since some time, the media has widely reported on corruption in our country's offices and administration. Whatever the truth may be, these allegations have given the

Afghan administration a very bad reputation. Corruption and bribery constitute a very dangerous problem. We want to follow this issue seriously. To conduct research on this problem, we will soon organize a conference in Kabul so that we can find new and effective ways to combat this problem. We consider combating this difficulty our duty. In the same vein, combating moral corruption has its own place in our programs.

Cultivation and trafficking of illicit drugs is another serious threat that is directly intertwined with terrorism and corruption. The government has the duty to decisively fight against the cultivation, trafficking and consumption of illicit drugs. The Government of Afghanistan considers it to be its responsibility to dismiss all government employees who are connected to the cultivation and trafficking of illicit drugs, and to deliver them to the hands of the law.

We seriously ask for close coordination within the international community, as well as cooperation from the international community with the Government of Afghanistan to fight illicit drugs.

For the purpose of strengthening oversight over government decisions, we want to organize district level elections in addition to the parliamentary elections next year. For the purpose of better city management, mayoral elections will be held soon.

In addition to its previous efforts, the Islamic Republic of Afghanistan considers it to be its duty to secure the rights of women in the three branches of government, so that the condition of women and their rights in our society can be further improved.

4. Economic Development:

We have had numerous economic achievements during the last eight years. Between 1381–1386,* our country experienced an average economic growth rate of 15%. This is good news about the resilience of our expanding economy.

Economic development and growth, as well as the creation of a legitimate national economy, consistent with the realities of the Afghan society, can be achieved only within the framework of a market economy.

For the purpose of achieving economic growth, we will continue our endeavors towards strengthening agriculture, livestock, irrigation, energy, and education. Moreover, we will also build more highways and make further efforts towards the improvement of our infrastructure.

With the goal of developing the rural areas, we support the National Solidarity Program and other similar programs. We will provide our youth with vocational training based on the reconstruction needs in Afghanistan. This will enable us to provide thousands of job opportunities for our citizens.

With the aim of implementing a new operational program during the next five years, we are seeking a new cooperation framework with the international community. This cooperation will be based on Afghan ownership. In light of the principle of Afghan ownership, Afghans will have the central role in prioritizing, designing and implementing development projects.

Currently, only 20% of international funds are spent through the government budget. This percentage should be raised. We ask the donor countries to raise this percentage to 40%, and increase it to 50% over the next two years.

---

*Editorial note: These numbers reflect Gregorian calendar dates; they translate to 2002–2008.

Transparency in spending international aid is another important issue. Lack of transparency and accountability in aid spending reduces people's trust and causes the spread of administrative corruption.

5. REGIONAL COOPERATION:

Ladies and Gentlemen,

Strong regional cooperation is a major contributor to social, economic and cultural growth of countries. With the cooperation of our neighbors and the rest of the world, we intend to expand regional solidarity through practical measures in regional trade and transit, aiming to position Afghanistan as a bridge between the countries of Central Asia, South-East Asia, and the Middle East.

Afghanistan has the potential to become a transit corridor for goods and energy between north and south Asia.

Connecting Afghanistan to the region's railway networks, and linking the countries of the region through Afghanistan to regional roads and sea ports, present some of the real opportunities that can bring the countries of our region together.

6. FOREIGN POLICY AND AFFAIRS:

During the last eight years, the United Nations has had the civilian leadership of the international community in organizing international conferences as well as coordinating the world's efforts in Afghanistan. Afghanistan appreciates the role of the United Nations and asks for a strengthening of the role of this organization in the areas of agreement.

Dear Guests,

We believe that our friendship with the United States of America is not limited to our joint struggle against violent extremists and the forces of division and destruction; rather, it is based on Afghanistan's long-term interests towards the consolidation of stability and tranquility for our people in this region.

America is the largest contributor in the provision of security, economic development, and good governance in our country. I am fully confident that this friendship will further expand. The people of Afghanistan will never forget the sacrifices made by American soldiers to bring peace to Afghanistan. Afghanistan is determined to take all the necessary steps towards strengthening US-Afghan relations through initiation of dialogue and discussions on the provisions of the Joint Declaration of the United States–Afghanistan Strategic Partnership. Afghanistan hopes to acquire the status of a major non-NATO ally of the United States.

We express our thanks to the member countries of the European Union, NATO, Canada, Australia and all the other allies of Afghanistan who, during the past eight years, have participated and made sacrifices in strengthening our state institutions, supporting our reconstruction, and providing security. Following past contributions, the recent $5 billion aid pledge by Japan deserves our heartfelt thanks.

We are fully confident that members of NATO will take effective steps towards accelerating the task of training and equipping the Afghan national army and police. It is only through this process that Afghanistan's hope with regard to a quick return of our friends' soldier to their countries will be realized, enabling us to take full responsibility for our security.

Dear Guests,

Ladies and Gentlemen,

We are always directly affected by positive and negative changes in the Islamic world. For this reason, our relations with the Islamic world are akin to relationships based on values within a single family. We are thankful for the efforts of Islamic countries, Saudi Arabia, the Islamic Republic of Iran, Turkey, the United Arab Emirates, other sisters and brothers of the Islamic Community, and members of the Organization of Islamic Conference (OIC)[.]

Our relations with our neighbors are based on mutual respect and genuine friendship. We will make efforts to expand and strengthen these relations. We are thankful for the assistance of our neighbors in the reconstruction of Afghanistan, particularly Iran and Pakistan.

We enjoy strategic relations with the Republic of India. India has contributed $1.3 billion to Afghanistan's reconstruction. Thousands of Afghan students are educated in Indian universities.

The People's Republic of China is our good neighbor and partner in the development process in Afghanistan.

The Republic of Turkey has been a loyal and historic brother of Afghanistan in the course of history. The presence of Turkey's soldiers in Afghanistan and the efforts made by Turkey's leadership towards peace and security in our country are highly appreciated.

Our relations with the Russian Federation are expanding rapidly and we thank Russia for supporting us in international forums.

The presence of my brother, His Excellency President Zardari, in this gathering is a sign of friendship and brotherhood between the peoples of our countries, and the commitment of the Government of Pakistan in the fight against terrorism as a common threat. I have full confidence that the democratically-elected governments of our two countries will soon overcome the problem of terrorism.

Excellencies,

Dear Guests, Fellow Citizens,

Ladies, Gentlemen

The next five years, while short in the context of the ancient history of this country, confront us with great responsibilities and duties.

Taking advantage of all national and international opportunities and facilities, we will endeavor to implement social and political reforms in our country.

I consider myself responsible to Almighty Allah and to the people of Afghanistan to carry this heavy burden on my shoulders and to truthfully take it to its destination.

Our people have the right to enjoy security and a comfortable life in the light of a democratically-elected system of governance. Recognizing this right of my people, for the next five years, I want Afghanistan to become a country that is capable of defending itself, and where peace reigns across the whole nation. With the help of the Almighty God, Afghanistan will be in the possession of a strong democratic order for the next five years.

Tens of thousands of Afghan youth will be employed in reconstruction of their country and management of its affairs. All cities and some rural areas will have electricity. Road networks will be asphalted and completed, and work on building railroads will begin.

In the next five years, lawlessness will end with the help of our people. The task of establishing security and protection of peoples' lives will be taken over by the state to the full extent, and the state of Afghanistan will be bound by and operate on the basis of law.

To open a new chapter in cooperation and assistance between Afghanistan and the international community, soon an international conference will be organized in Kabul. This conference will reiterate the mutual responsibilities and commitments of Afghanistan and the international community towards each other.

I ask Almighty Allah with great humbleness to bestow upon Afghanistan and the whole world peace and tranquility, and wish my people comfort and pride.

Success belongs to the Almighty God.

Source: Office of the President of Afghanistan. "Un-Official Translation of the Inaugural Speech by H.E. Hamid Karzai President of the Islamic Republic of Afghanistan." November 19, 2009. www .president.gov.af/Contents/72/Documents/960/President_Karzai_s_Inaugural_Speech_Nov.pdf.

Other Historic Documents of Interest

From this volume

From previous *Historic Documents*

University of California Tuition Hikes Meet with Massive Protests

NOVEMBER 19 AND 23, 2009

In mid-November 2009, students from the University of California, considered to be one of the nation's best public university systems, protested a 32 percent increase in the tuition (called student fees). The fee increases were approved by the system's Board of Regents, which insisted that the rise in fees would allow them to offer better services to students and reinstate classes that had previously been cut because of a lack of funds. Protests took place across the state, and many students were arrested and cited for trespassing. By the end of 2009, administrators had refused to reverse the decision; student complaints were unrelenting. The tuition increase for students at the University of California was directly related to the recession and the state of California's serious budget problems. The week the increases were announced, California's budget analyst said that over the next eighteen months, the budget deficit in the state would grow to $21 billion. With less revenue coming in from the state, the university system was forced to rethink how it would provide for students.

University of California students, while experiencing the nation's most drastic tuition increase, were not alone. Public universities across the country, including those in Arizona, Michigan, North Carolina, and Wisconsin, were all cutting budgets and increasing the costs to students to maintain educational standards. In each case, the schools pegged tuition hikes to a decrease in state funds, coupled with the rising cost of providing a quality education.

REGENTS APPROVE TUITION HIKES

University of California students first learned of potential tuition hikes when university officials had proposed them in September. A two-tier tuition hike, with half charged during the first year and the other half during the next, would be coupled with additional charges for those students pursuing professional degrees in business and engineering. The 32 percent rise in tuition would bring tuition up to $10,302 per year by 2011. In addition to tuition, students are required to pay $930 to cover campus costs, which were also expected to increase by 9.3 percent. Those students living on campus could end up paying more than $17,000 per year in tuition, housing, and books. At their September meeting, university officials also proposed cutting the size of enrollment in the freshman class by 7 percent, a move they had previously used to cut costs.

Before the September meeting, university officials had already laid off hundreds of employees and forced most of its labor force to take unpaid furlough days. This, officials said, made it difficult to attract the best and brightest to the University of California system. Various courses and academic programs had also been cut.

On November 19, the Board of Regents met to approve the university system's budget, at which time they voted to instate the two-tier, 32 percent tuition hike. A little more than ten years before the vote, students had been paying one-third of what they would now be expected to pay per year. Recognizing the anger their decision would cause, university officials announced that the tuition hikes would mean they could keep classes and programs that would have otherwise been cut and bring back those that had been previously ended. The regents added that they planned to ask the state for $900 million in additional funding in 2010. Whether the additional funding would be granted was up in the air, given the state's severe budget crisis.

Mark Yudof, president of the University of California system, said the Board of Regents had no choice but to vote to raise tuition, given California's budget and the amount of funds the state allocated to the university. At the time of the vote, the ten-campus system was getting only half of what it had received on a per-student basis from the state in 1990. Yudof's fear, he said, was "an exodus of faculty."

Protests on University of California Campuses

The day before the vote, at the University of California at Los Angeles (UCLA), twelve students had been arrested for disrupting the meeting of the Board of Regents. Determined to be there when the decision was made, some students slept inside a campus building, while others pitched tents outside. Students gathered outside the building where the Board of Regents were voting, waiting on their decision. When the news broke, they began chanting and locking arms, refusing to allow the regents to leave the building. Nearly one hundred students surrounded one regent as he attempted to leave, shouting, "Shame on you." Police intervened to allow the regent to leave safely.

Two thousand students from the university system came to UCLA to protest the Board of Regents decision during their two days of meetings. They encountered riot police while chanting, holding signs, and blocking university officials from leaving the buildings. Campus buildings were seized by students, but the police force kept control of the situation, and according to reports, tasers were used on some students.

At one protest, students blocked vehicles from leaving the campus. Michael Hawley, a UCLA student leader, shouted at the regents through a bullhorn. "We want one regent to come out to speak to us about why the world's richest country will be denying some students higher education next quarter," he yelled. In another area of campus, where students stopped cars from leaving a parking garage, protestors spoke of friends who would not be able to attend the university next quarter because of the increase in tuition. Others looked at larger problems caused by the increase. "It took a long time for minorities to increase their numbers at the University of California. Now those numbers are going to go down," said Veronica Hernandez, a student from the Riverside campus.

As the protests escalated, fifty students were arrested for trespassing after occupying a classroom on the University of California at Berkeley campus. On the university's Santa Cruz campus, student protestors took over an administration building the night of the decision and stayed there through the next day. According to the campus's provost, David Kliger, the students made multiple demands, although he did not release the details. "We cherish the principle of free speech," he said. "Regrettably, these actions go well beyond that," Kliger said in response to the barricades students set up.

As some student leaders had indicated, the tuition hikes called into question what would happen to minority students, who are often economically disadvantaged in greater numbers. Minority students had already been put at a disadvantage in 1996, when state voters passed Proposition 209, banning affirmative action. The status of illegal immigrants was also brought into question. The university system does not require students to disclose their citizenship status, allowing illegal immigrants to attend school, but they are banned from receiving most state and federal financial aid, meaning all tuition costs must be paid for by the student. Officials at the university system said they are unsure how many illegal immigrants were attending school; their goal was to find the best students and educate them, not to enforce immigration laws.

PROTESTS AROUND THE COUNTRY

Across the nation, tuition costs at public and private universities had been on the rise. According to a report by the Delta Project, a nonprofit group that tracks the cost of education, between 2002 and 2006, student tuition covered one-half of the share of education costs at four-year public universities, up from one-third. "Students are paying more and getting less in the classroom," said Jane Wellman, author of the report. While tuition dollars rose, the amount of money being spent on classroom instruction decreased across the board. Public colleges and universities were forced to raise tuition and fees because of a decrease in state funds available for education. According to the Delta Project report, in 2006, taxes paid in each state broke down into $7,078 per student at a public university. In 2002 that number was nearly $1,300 higher. The deepening recession made the situation worse in many areas, with public university funds being used to cover maintenance and other essential services rather than for teacher pay and classroom instruction.

Due to state budget cuts, California's other public university system, California State University, also took action to cut costs and raise revenue, including an increase in tuition, but it was nowhere near the 32 percent at the University of California. The outgoing chair of the system, Jeff Bleich, recognized the potential downfall of increasing tuition. "California is on the verge of destroying the very system that once made this state great." Every year the state government decides to invest less in education, according to Bleich, who maintained that this was a serious mistake. "For every dollar the state invests in a CSU student, it receives $4.41 in return."

Elsewhere, students in the University of Michigan system saw tuition rise 11.6 percent from school year 2007–2008 to 2009–2010. New students at Arizona State University saw their tuition and fees increase by 20 percent from the previous year. Likewise, students protested a plan to raise undergraduate tuition at the University of North Carolina system by 5.2 percent. At the University of Wisconsin, students have seen tuition rise 5.5 percent for the past three years, which the system's president, Kevin Reilly, called "modest and predictable." These increases, Reilly said, have allowed the system of 174,000 students to continue to maintain current enrollment levels, classroom sizes, and student programs. "It is simply not possible to maintain the integrity of our academic programs, the quality of our university experience, without raising tuition—particularly in the face on ongoing declines in state support," said Reilly.

—Heather Kerrigan

Following is a November 19, 2009, press release from the University of California detailing student fee increases, and a November 23, 2009, press release from the University of California on student protests related to the increases.

Board of Regents Approves Fee Increases

November 19, 2009

The University of California Board of Regents today (Nov. 19) approved a systemwide budget plan that seeks an infusion of an additional $913 million in state funding and also incorporates two student fee increases, measures that together are designed to help bridge a severe budget shortfall brought on by the state fiscal crisis.

More than two-thirds of the additional money to be sought in Sacramento represents a restoration of previous state budget cuts enacted in the past two fiscal years. The Regents acted at the recommendation of President Mark G. Yudof, who said the budget "is designed to provide access, maintain quality and stabilize the fiscal health of the university."

The fee increases will be enacted in two stages: a mid-year fee increase for 2009–10, and fee increases for the 2010–11 academic year.

For California residents, the new fee levels include a mid-year fee increase in January 2010 of $585 or 15 percent for undergraduates and graduate professional degree students. The increase will be $111 or 2.6 percent for graduate academic degree students. For the 2010–11 academic year, fees will rise again by $1,334 or 15 percent for both resident undergraduates and graduate students starting in summer 2010.

The Regents also approved increases in professional degree fees for 2010–11 that range from $280 to $5,696. . . .

As has been past practice, a third of the revenue from the fee increases will be set aside to provide need-based financial aid for undergraduates and professional school students, while one half will be set aside to help graduate academic students.

The Regents also approved an expansion of the Blue and Gold Opportunity Plan to ensure that qualified California undergraduates with financial need and family incomes of $70,000 or below will have all systemwide fees covered.

Yudof said it was important to view the increases in the context of the overall budget plan and the ongoing financial downturn that has all but paralyzed the state budget process.

"We can no longer tolerate fiscal uncertainty and continual cutting as we wait for Sacramento to navigate through this crisis," he said. "We will keep working hard with state political leaders to restore the university's funding to an appropriate level. In the meantime, however, we must act now to shore up our own finances if we are to preserve the quality and ensure the access that California expects from the world's premier public research university system.

"I know this is a painful day for university students and their families, but as I stand here today I can assure you this is our one best shot at preventing this recession from pulling down a great system toward mediocrity. In the long term, that would not be good for the students of today or tomorrow. And it would be devastating for California as a whole."

In presenting the budget plan, Yudof traced a long and steady pattern of state disinvestment in the university, a slide which began when many of UC's current students were not yet in kindergarten. As a result, he said, UC now receives from the state half as much in support for each student as it did in 1990.

Yudof said revenue from higher fees will allow UC campuses "to restore cancelled courses that students may need to graduate on time, along with some vital student services, such as more regular library hours. We will also use this revenue to hire more faculty, and to begin to address the issue of larger class sizes."

Taken together, the 2009–10 mid-year fee increase and the 2010–11 increases will generate approximately $505 million, of which $175 million will be set aside for financial aid.

That revenue will address only a portion of UC's budget shortfall, which was created by unprecedented state budget cuts of $814 million in 2008–09 and $637 million in 2009–10. In addition, UC campuses face $368 million in mandatory costs that the state failed to fund in the last two years, and an additional $218 million in mandatory costs for 2010–11. These costs are a result of a variety of factors—enrollments that the state has left unfunded, inflation, rising utility costs, health benefit increases and union pay raises required by collective bargaining agreements.

Beyond fee increases, a variety of other measures have been taken to balance the UC budget, including a one-year emergency furlough/salary reductions plan for faculty and staff that took effect Sept. 1 and is expected to generate $184 million in savings; a systemwide salary freeze for members of the senior management group that has been in place for the past two years; continued downsizing and restructuring of UC Office of the President that, so far, has yielded more than $60 million in savings; as well as debt restructuring, curtailment of freshmen enrollment, and other campuswide initiatives such as energy savings and centralized procurement strategies.

In addition to these systemwide actions, campuses are instituting a wide variety of cost-saving measures, including consolidation and elimination of programs, hiring reductions—despite continuing increases in enrollment—layoffs and significant curtailment of travel and other purchases.

Despite these actions, the severity of the state budget cuts and the rapidity with which UC campuses have been forced to absorb them threaten the basic quality of the education being provided to UC's students.

For example, faculty hiring has slowed dramatically and is not keeping up with enrollment demand; course sections have been eliminated; hours of service are being shortened for many programs of importance to students; staff positions are being eliminated and vacancies frozen.

Specifically, campuses report they are in the process of reducing instructional budgets by $139 million, laying off 1,900 employees, eliminating 3,800 positions and deferring hiring of nearly 1,600 positions, most of them faculty.

"This is not a sustainable pattern going forward," Yudof said. "We and all those who support the UC mission must advocate relentlessly in Sacramento for increased state funding. This funding is critical if the university is to continue serving Californians with superior educational, research and medical facilities."

Yudof said he recognized the fiscal challenges the state government still faces, given a deficit already projected to reach $7 billion to $8 billion for 2010–11, but he felt compelled to submit a UC budget request that truly reflects the needs and priorities of the university.

Accordingly, UC's budget plan for 2010–11 seeks an increase of $913 million in state general funds that includes:

- Unfunded enrollments (14,000)—$155.8 million

For the last two years, 2008–09 and 2009–10, the state has not provided funding for enrollment growth at UC, even as demand for access has grown. As a result, UC is currently overenrolled by approximately 14,000 students for whom it receives no state funding. This request asks the state to provide funding for those students to ensure timely access to classes, to improve the student-to-faculty contact and to re-establish the breadth and depth of UC's course offerings.

As part of the request, the Regents' Committee on Finance approved a plan to further curtail California freshman enrollment if funding for UC's 14,000 unfunded students is not included in the governor's 2010–11 budget proposal to be released in January. In that case, the university would curtail California freshman enrollments by an additional 2,300 students (for a two-year total of 4,600 students) and increase enrollment of community college transfer students by 250 in 2010–11.

- Restoration of one-time cuts—$305 million; re-investment in academic excellence—$332.1 million

The revenue from the restoration of this funding would be used to reinvest in academic excellence by restoring programs to previous levels, including hiring more faculty, restoring course offerings, reinstituting service hours, such as those for libraries and student services, and restoring instructional and academic support.

- State obligation to UCRP and retiree health benefits—$109.8 million

The university is requesting funding of the state's obligations to UC retirees, consistent with the state's treatment of state and CSU employees.

- Health sciences initiatives—$10.4 million

The university is requesting $10 million in funding to help support a new medical school at the Riverside campus. This funding would provide necessary startup and core academic support for the state's first new public medical school in over 30 years. In addition, the university is requesting $444,000 for the first year of enrollments at the new nursing school at the Davis campus.

FINANCIAL AID TO MITIGATE IMPACT OF HIGHER FEES

- Expansion of the Blue and Gold Opportunity Plan

The Regents also approved an expansion of the Blue and Gold Opportunity Plan. In 2010–11 the Blue and Gold Opportunity Plan will be expanded to include eligible resident undergraduates with family incomes up to $70,000. Under the higher income ceiling, California residents with financial need and family incomes of $70,000 or below are assured that they will receive gift assistance that will, at a minimum, cover all their mandatory systemwide fees.

With the expansion, the plan is expected to provide full fee coverage to an additional 800 undergraduates who were not previously eligible, and UC projects that overall 52,000 undergraduates will be covered under the Blue and Gold Opportunity Plan in 2010–11. The plan's expansion is anticipated to cost $2.7 million; UC is currently examining options for funding the added costs. The plan is expected not only to benefit more UC students, but to encourage a greater number of low-income Californians to apply to and enroll at UC.

- $1 billion student fundraising effort

The university has also announced Project You Can, an ambitious effort in which all 10 UC campuses have committed to raise $1 billion in the aggregate over the next four years from private sources. This effort would double the amount of private support the system has raised for scholarships, fellowships and other gift aid in the previous five years. The effort recognizes the need to focus fundraising efforts more sharply on student support.

- Return-to-aid and other assistance

UC intends to maintain its commitment to assisting financially needy low- and middle-income students through its strong institutional financial aid program and the Blue and Gold Opportunity Plan. Furthermore, UC will work with the state to ensure that the Cal Grant Program continues to cover mandatory systemwide fees for eligible UC students.

As UC has historically done, 33 percent of the revenue generated from the approved fee increases will be set aside to mitigate the impact of higher fees and other costs on undergraduate students with financial need. Similarly, 50 and 33 percent of revenue generated by the increases will be set aside to provide financial aid for graduate academic students and professional school students, respectively.

These amounts, combined with 2009–10 increases in Cal Grants, federal Pell Grants and federal tuition tax credits, will provide enough additional resources to cover the full amount of the fee increases already approved for 2009–10, along with the 2009–10 mid-year increase for three-quarters of students with family incomes below $180,000.

For 2010–11, these new resources, along with further expected increases in UC grants and Cal Grants should cover the additional 2010–11 fee increase for the 45 percent of students who receive these awards. Students with family incomes up to $70,000 per year typically qualify for Cal Grants and UC grants.

Other students with financial need will have half of the 2010–11 fee increase covered if their parents' income falls below $120,000—an increase in the cap from $100,000 in prior years. Middle-income families will also continue to benefit from federal higher education tax credits in 2010.

SOURCE: University of California. Press release. "Regents Approve Budget Plan, Student Fee Increases." November 19, 2009. www.universityofcalifornia.edu/news/article/22414.

Students Protest Fee Increases

November 23, 2009

About 60 UC students occupied the lobby of the UC Office of the President headquarters in downtown Oakland Monday to protest the recent fee increases and campus cuts and layoffs.

The students spent two hours sitting on the lobby floor having a dialogue with UC Provost Lawrence Pitts and Nathan Brostrom, interim executive vice president of business operations. Another 70 to 80 students marched outside the building on Franklin Street.

The students descended on the UC headquarters around 3:30 P.M., asking to meet with President Mark Yudof to talk about the increase in fees UC Regents approved at their Nov. 19 meeting. Yudof was not in Oakland at the time. Pitts and Brostrom agreed to meet with the students instead.

The protesters peppered them with questions about the UC budget and asked what they could do to repeal the fee increases.

The increases were a result of a dramatic drop in state funding—an unprecedented 20 percent cut, Pitts said. He urged students to write letters to their legislators and to join in advocating for higher funding from the state to avoid the need for fee increases.

"We do not control the state revenue," Pitts told the students. "There needs to be pressure on the legislators to be willing to give more resources to education."

Other students said that financial aid measures like the Blue and Gold Opportunity Plan, intended for low-income students, didn't address the needs of middle-class students.

"I'm a disadvantaged poor, but I don't want to look across the campus and see another student because they're not as poor as I am to be excluded from a public higher education," said Alejandro Lara-Briseno, a UC Berkeley senior.

Students also complained about the way campus police handled demonstrations at UC Berkeley Friday when students occupied Wheeler Hall. Brostrom, who also serves as vice chancellor of administration at UC Berkeley, told students that all the activities surrounding the building occupation and protests would be investigated.

Marika Goodrich, a UC Berkeley student who acted as protest spokesperson, told the administrators that students wanted to see them supporting their efforts to speak out against higher fees.

"I hope you see how committed we are and how passionate," she said as she presented the two administrators with red arm bands like the students were wearing and asked them to stand with the students.

"You're right to hold all of us accountable," Brostrom said. " . . . We need to have a march on Sacramento where we have tens of thousands of students. I'll march with you."

Pitts and Brostrom tied the bands to their arms, and the students left the building peacefully. They rallied on the street outside for about 15 minutes, and then said they were going back to the Berkeley campus, where most of the protesters had come from.

SOURCE: University of California. Press release. "Students Protest Fees, Budget at UC Headquarters." November 23, 2009. www.universityofcalifornia.edu/news/article/22461.

OTHER HISTORIC DOCUMENTS OF INTEREST

FROM THIS VOLUME

FROM PREVIOUS *HISTORIC DOCUMENTS*

South Carolina Governor Mark Sanford Charged with Ethics Violations

NOVEMBER 19, 2009

On November 19, 2009, charges against Gov. Mark Sanford were announced by the South Carolina Ethics Commission for a number of violations, including use of state planes to travel to private functions. The beleaguered governor, who months earlier had admitted to having an affair with a woman in Argentina after he disappeared for a week, refused to resign his position or to cede any of his gubernatorial power. Although his marriage dissolved and his position at the head of the Republican Governors Association ended, Sanford faced little resistance to keeping his job as governor other than the threat of impeachment from the legislature, which despite initial movement never materialized.

GOVERNOR SANFORD'S DOWNFALL

A former U.S. representative from South Carolina, Governor Sanford was considered a rising star in the Republican party; his name was even floated as a possible candidate for the 2012 presidential election. Sanford had gained national recognition as an outspoken critic of President Barack Obama's stimulus package, saying he would refuse to accept funds for his state, even though South Carolina had the third-highest jobless rate in the nation. The state's legislature passed a budget based on the expectation that the state would receive stimulus money from the federal government regardless of Sanford's unwillingness to accept it, making Sanford the first U.S. governor to defend his position against stimulus funds in court. Sanford, who was ordered by the state's legislature to accept the funds, filed suit in federal district court against the state's attorney general with a claim that the legislature was in violation of federal law. A South Carolina district court judge rejected Sanford's case, which was remanded to the South Carolina supreme court. The state court ruled unanimously that Sanford was required to accept the $700 million in stimulus funds. Sanford continued to use his position as chair of the Republican Governors Association to speak out against what he perceived as government overspending.

Sanford's troubles began in earnest in June, when he went missing for a week, leaving the state without a security detail and no way for his staff to contact him. In addition to the secrecy and suddenness of his trip, Sanford had given no instructions to the state's lieutenant governor for taking control of state matters while he was away. It seemed that while Sanford was out of contact, there was no executive in charge of the state.

Questions were raised about Sanford's whereabouts. His wife, Jenny, was with their four sons at the family's home. She said she was unaware of where he had gone, but that "he was writing something and wanted some space to get away from the kids." Although Sanford had been on previous trips where he did not take security or staff with him, never had he left without providing contact information. Staff claimed that they had been in touch with the governor and that he had informed them that he had been hiking the Appalachian Trail and would return shortly. Jake Knotts, a South Carolina Republican lawmaker, said, "While I believe every person deserves a vacation, our constitution gives only one man authority to act in case of an emergency the governor of South Carolina. Should the governor decide to vacation away from South Carolina again, it is my sincere hope that he will take his security detail and keep his cell phone on so that he can be reached in case of a large-scale emergency."

Upon his return, Sanford was greeted by a staff member at Atlanta's Hartsfield-Jackson International Airport. With the staffer was a member of the press who questioned the governor about his trip. Sanford admitted to the reporter that he had not been hiking but rather driving the coastline in Buenos Aires, Argentina. He would not admit whether he had been alone or with someone else; he only said that he had decided not to hike the Appalachian Trail because he wanted instead to "do something exotic."

Argentina

On June 24, Sanford called a news conference, during which he announced that he had been having an extramarital affair with a woman in Argentina. He did not name her at the time, but later revealed her name to be María Belén Chapur. "I'll lay it out," said Sanford. "It's going to hurt, and let the chips fall where they may. I've been unfaithful to my wife. I've let down a lot of people. That's the bottom line," the two-term governor said. Sanford's wife did not appear at the news conference, and it was later learned that she and her husband had been seeing a counselor for five months, the length of time Jenny had known that her husband was having an affair. Sanford apologized for lying to his family and to the people of South Carolina. Fighting back tears, Sanford delivered his remarks just hours after returning from Argentina.

As the story of Sanford's affair began to spread, one South Carolina newspaper, *The State,* obtained e-mails that had been passed between Sanford and his mistress. In one from July 2008, Sanford wrote that he and Maria were in a "hopelessly impossible situation of love." An e-mail from Maria that month read, "I wasn't aware till we met last week, the strong feelings I had for you. I haven't felt this since I was in my teen ages. I do love you." Apparently, Sanford had met the woman eight years before his fateful secret trip and at one point had counseled her through her failing marriage, which he encouraged her to stay in for the sake of her two young sons. Sanford said that despite the distance, the two grew increasingly close over time, mainly through e-mail. During his press conference, Sanford called himself "committed to trying to get my heart right."

Ethics Charges and Impeachment Considerations

Sanford's secret trip to Argentina drew criticism from state legislators. South Carolina Senate Majority Leader Harvey Peeler said, "He left the country and deliberately made himself unavailable. . . . [H]e misled his staff who unknowingly misled the public." Peeler continued, "We cannot let the Governor's personal life overshadow his public responsibility, or in this case, his negligence of gubernatorial authority."

The South Carolina legislature introduced impeachment proceedings against Sanford for lying and leaving the state without designating anyone to be in charge. According to Sanford's lawyers, the impeachment charges would not stick because the South Carolina constitution requires the reason for impeachment to be "serious crimes or serious misconduct in office" to ensure "only the most egregious offenses would lead to impeachment, and not merely personal moral failings, neglect of duty or a temporary absence from the state." A successful impeachment would first go before a judiciary subcommittee for review, then to the full judiciary committee, which would decide whether to send it to the House for a vote. If the House received the impeachment proceedings, it would need a two-thirds majority to impeach the governor. No governor in South Carolina had been impeached. Because of the ongoing ethics investigation into Sanford's use of state funds and equipment to travel for personal reasons, the subcommittee decided to take those charges into account when considering impeachment.

In the end, the subcommittee found, in accordance with South Carolina law, that an affair would not be reason enough to impeach Sanford. The measure still went to the House Judiciary Committee, but in mid-December, the full committee voted not to send impeachment proceedings to the full House. Speaker Bobby Harrell, although agreeing that Sanford deserved a reprimand, said the decision would allow the House, when it reconvened to refocus on matters most important to the state. "Our Legislature needs to be focused on jobs and education, and not have to deal with this when we return in January," he said.

On November 19, 2009, the South Carolina Ethics Commission announced the result of its three-month-long look into possible ethics charges against Sanford, many of which did not stem from his trip to Argentina or his affair. The commission charged the governor with thirty-seven ethics violations, including using state funds to travel business class rather than coach; using state vehicles, including a plane, to travel to private functions; and reimbursing himself with campaign funds for personal matters, such as a ticket to the inauguration of President Barack Obama. Eighteen of the charges were for improper use of state funds to purchase first- and business-class tickets, including flights to Argentina (which Sanford's office argued had been set up by the Department of Commerce as official overseas business, not as personal trips), a violation of a state law that requires that the lowest-cost transportation method be used; nine were for use of the state's airplane to travel to personal events; and ten were for reimbursement with campaign funds. The charges ranged from September 2005 to April 2009. It was not until Sanford had admitted lying to staffers when he traveled to Argentina to meet his mistress that other trips the governor had taken were called into question. The ethics charges may have stung worse for Sanford than the impeachment proceedings, as he had spent two terms as governor calling for limited government and reduced spending in the state.

If found guilty on all thirty-seven charges, Sanford could owe fines up to $74,000. The ethics panel in charge of determining Sanford's fate was set to meet in early 2010.

—Heather Kerrigan

Following is the text of the ethics charges against South Carolina governor Mark Sanford filed on November 19, 2009, by the state's Ethics Commission.

DOCUMENT

Ethics Complaint Filed Against Governor Mark Sanford

November 19, 2009

Complaint C2010–020
In the Matter of Governor Mark Sanford

November 18, 2009
RE: COMPLAINT C2010–020
In the Matter of Governor Mark Sanford

TO: The Honorable Henry D. McMaster
Attorney General
State of South Carolina

FROM: Herbert R. Hayden, Jr., Executive Director
Donald M. Lundgren, Chief Investigator

LOCATION: Statewide

Pursuant to your letter of August 13, 2009, an investigation was conducted into alleged violations of the State Ethics Act. . . .

The investigation centered on the use of a public office for personal financial gain; use of public equipment for personal use and/or in an election; use of campaign funds for personal expenses; and use of public equipment by family members.

The attached investigative report is submitted for your review and action as you deem appropriate. The investigators shown above will be available at your convenience should you have any questions or need additional information. . . .

[The table of contents has been omitted.]

Summary of Investigation

. . . On August 19, 2009, and subsequent dates through November 12, 2009 an investigation was conducted into the alleged violations. The investigation examined five areas of Governor [Mark] Sanford's activities to include: (1) Overseas Trade Missions; (2) Use of state-owned aircraft; (3) Use of Privately-owned aircraft; (4) Use of campaign funds for personal expenses. . . .

A personal interview was not conducted with Governor Sanford; however, he was given the opportunity to provide any statement he desired and to also answer specific questions through his attorneys. . . .

On September 11, 2009 the Governor's attorneys provided electronic copies via e-mail of telephone records of Governor Sanford and various members of his staff, press briefings, and the Governor's calendar for calendar years 2003 and 2004. On September 15, 2009 the Governor's attorneys provided two compact discs containing the Governor's calendar for calendar years 2003 through 2009, Governor's staff e-mails, Governor's e-mails and cell phone records, and credit card records for various staff members. With the exception of the calendars, copies of which are enclosed in the appropriate sections, none of the information contained on either disc was relevant to this investigation. . . .

OVERSEAS TRADE MISSIONS . . .

[State policies and regulations have been omitted.]

QUESTION: Did Governor Sanford violate Section 8–13–700 (A) by using his official position to approve/authorize first class or business class tickets for himself on overseas trade missions in violation of Budget and Control Board Regulations, thereby gaining an economic benefit for himself?

On August 20, 2009 telephone contact was made with Ms. Karen Manning, Chief Legal Counsel for the South Carolina Department of Commerce and a request was made for copies of all flight information, ticket information, and agendas for all overseas trade missions in which Governor Sanford participated. A meeting was scheduled for August 25, 2009. Ms. Manning also advised that the South Carolina Division of Aeronautics had been transferred from the Department of Commerce to the Budget and Control Board earlier in 2009 and all records of flights on state-owned aircraft had been transferred also.

On August 25, 2009 investigators met with Ms. Manning and Ms. Kara Borie, Marketing and Communications Manager, at the Commerce Department. . . .

They stated that all tickets for overseas travel are charged to a Commerce Department credit card and the bill is paid by the State Comptroller General's office. They indicated that the Comptroller's office has never questioned the purchase of business class tickets. They also noted that the State Auditor's Office has never mentioned the purchase of business class tickets in their annual audit reports. . . .

Ms. Manning provided investigators with copies of ticket invoices and itineraries for five overseas trips: Farnborough Air Show/London/July 2006; Paris Air Show/Paris/Munich/June 2007; China World Economic forum/September 2007; Brazil Trade Mission/Brazil/Argentina/June 2008; and Poland Trade Mission/April 2009. . . .

In the presence of Ms. Manning and Ms. Borie, investigators interviewed Ms. Vickie Wooten, Executive Assistant to the Secretary of Commerce. Ms. Wooten stated that she does the scheduling for Commerce trips and has booked flights for Governor Sanford on occasion; however, his flight arrangements are usually done by someone at the Governor's office, usually Mary Neil Stroud. She stated that when a travel request was presented to her she would contact Mary Watts at Forest Lake Travel to arrange airline tickets. She stated that she does not remember if she ever specifically requested that Forest Lake Travel book business class for the Governor; however, it has always been accepted practice for the Governor and the Secretary of Commerce to fly business class. . . .

On August 26, 2009 Ms. Mary L. Watts was interviewed at Forest Lake Travel Service. . . . She stated that over these many years she has booked numerous airline tickets for the Commerce Department and the Governor. She stated that she would customarily secure airline tickets for Governor Sanford after being contacted by the Department of Commerce. On nearly every occasion when she booked tickets for Governor Sanford she was in contact with Vicki Wooten at the Commerce Department. Sometimes she would be contacted by someone in the Governor's office to change an itinerary. She stated she always had approval to book business class tickets for Governor Sanford and certain

Commerce Department employees. Support staff of the Department of Commerce or other Departments traveling with the Governor would always be booked in coach class. In most situations she was specifically requested to book business class seating for the Governor. After being contacted by Vicki Wooten Ms. Watts would prepare a proposed itinerary and fax it to Ms. Wooten. If the itinerary was approved, Ms. Watts would book the flights and charge the cost on a credit card provided by the Commerce Department. She commented that she also booked airline tickets for former Governor Hodges, who also always had business class seating. She stated she would provide copies of the airline tickets that Forest Lake Travel secured for Governor Sanford.

Upon return to the Commission office, investigators received, via facsimile from Ms. Watts, copies of ticket information for: Mission to Rome/November 2004; Austrian Investment Trip/September 2005; Mission to China/October 2005; Farnborough Air Show/London/July 2006; Paris Air Show/Paris/Munich/June 2007; China World Economic forum/September 2007; Brazil Trade Mission/Brazil/Argentina/June 2008; and Poland Trade Mission/April 2009. . . .

On September 1, 2009 Ms. Karen Manning provided investigators with additional travel information from Department of Commerce records. These documents include itineraries and financial/expense records for: Brazil Trade Mission/Brazil/Argentina/2008; and Poland Trade Mission/2009. . . .

On September 2, 2009 investigators met with Senator David L. Thomas at his law office. . . . Senator Thomas stated that he had undertaken an investigation of Governor Sanford's travel after questions were raised. He stated that he had been in written contact with Ms. Swati Patel, General Counsel for the Governor's Office, and had received several letters from Ms. Patel. He stated also that he had been in contact with Forest Lake Travel Service and had obtained copies of ticket invoices for several overseas trips taken by Governor Sanford. He said he would provide copies to investigators as soon as possible. He indicated that he had spoken with Governor David Beasley and Bob McAllister of Governor Carroll Campbell's staff, and both had confirmed that all overseas travel taken during the respective administrations had been paid for with private funds. He further stated that he had obtained copies of vouchers from the Comptroller General's office which showed that Governor Sanford's travel was paid for with state funds. Senator Thomas indicated that he had provided copies of his findings to Senator Glenn McConnell and Senator Hugh Leatherman, and would provide investigators with copies of those letters also. . . .

Investigators reviewed the twelve overseas trips considered investment or trade missions from October 2003 through April 2009. . . .

No itineraries are available for the November 2004 Rome Mission or the September 2005 Austrian Investment Trip; however, all seven legs were flown business class. . . .

Using the Governor's calendars, flight logs, ticket information and itineraries provided, Investigators conducted an analysis of each overseas trip and return. A brief summary of each trip follows. . . .

[The brief summary of each trip has been omitted.]

In the Governor's October 5, 2009 response it is pointed out that " . . . the practice of purchasing business class flights due to the exigencies surrounding foreign economic development trips has also been approved by the Comptroller General . . ." and mentioned a letter from State Development Board Director, Mr. J. Mac Holladay. The response further indicates "The letter, which requests approval for business class seats, is marked 'approved by Mr. Morris' on June 22, 1987." . . .

In her August 12, 2009 and September 1, 2009 letters to Senator David L. Thomas, Ms. Swati Patel, the Governor's Chief Legal Counsel, refers to the Department of Commerce's interpretation of [the] exigent clause, and quotes Mr. Holladay's letter as justification for blanket purchasing of business class tickets. . . .

On September 2 and 3, 2009 three news articles appeared with comments from Mr. Holladay on his letter to Mr. Morris confirming his statement. . . .

The Governor's October 5, 2009 response includes a letter from Ms. Swati Patel dated September 1, 2009 to Senator Thomas in which she points out that the Legislative Audit Council preformed an audit of the Department of Commerce in 2002. Her letter states, "In conducting its audit, the LAC 'reviewed a sample of travel vouchers (from FY97–FY 01) and found that Commerce generally complied with state travel law and regulations.' Furthermore, a 2004 LAC Follow-Up Report stated that '(i)n 2002, we did not find material noncompliance with state travel regulations . . . ' . . . Accordingly, the LAC likely reviewed Commerce's purchase of business class seats and determined that there was no violation of state travel law and regulations." . . .

Governor Sanford is also quoted on page 2 of a Greenvilleonline.com article on August 29, 2009 as referring to the same Legislative Audit Council report of no irregularities of travel. . . .

During the August 25, 2009 interview with Ms. Karen Manning and Ms. Kara Borie . . . they both stated that the charges for business class tickets had been billed to Department of Commerce credit cards and paid by the Comptroller General's office. They both stated that the Comptrollers office had never questioned the purchase of business class tickets.

On November 3, 2009 investigators interviewed Mr. James H. Holly, Chief of Staff, South Carolina Comptroller General's office (CG). Mr. Holly was interviewed via telephone and stated that the Comptroller General's responsibility is to pay the bills which are submitted by the agencies. The decision on approving a business class ticket rather than a coach ticket lies with the agency based on exigencies per the state travel regulations. He stated that when the CG's office receives a voucher for an airline ticket it is accepted with the understanding that the agency has justification for the purchase of that ticket. Employees of the CG's office do not second guess an agency's decision to purchase a business class ticket. He emphasized that on most ticket information provided with a voucher it is very difficult to determine the class of the ticket, and if the ticket is purchased using a credit card there is sometimes no information as to the class of the ticket; therefore, CG employees rarely know what class of ticket has been purchased.

Mr. Holly provided investigators an electronic copy of current Comptroller General's Travel Regulations.

USE OF STATE-OWNED AIRCRAFT . . .

[State policies and regulations have been omitted.]

QUESTION: Did Governor Sanford violate Sections 8–13–700(A), 8–13–765(A), and/or 8–13–1346(A) by using state-owned aircraft for personal and/or political travel?

On August 25, 2009 investigators contacted Ms. Reve' Richardson with the South Carolina Division of Aeronautics and scheduled an interview with pertinent individuals for later in the day. At the Division of Aeronautics office, Investigators met with Ms. Richardson, Executive Assistant; Mr. Paul G. Werts, Executive Director; and Pilots, Mr. John Young and Mr. Hugh Tuttle.

Mr. Young advised that he has been with the Aeronautics Division since before Governor Sanford became Governor and with various different co-pilots has flown on almost all of the flights transporting the Governor. He stated the manner in which Governor Sanford would secure the aircraft started with a call from Jack Proffitt, a SLED agent who is part of the Governor's security detail. Upon Proffit's call, the aircraft would be reserved. Later Proffitt would call back with the exact times of travel, destination and the identity of all the passengers. Young would then prepare a manifest with the flight details and a list of passengers. At boarding time the passengers are required to sign the manifest. Upon completion of a flight, Young would fax the manifest to Mary Neal Stroud at the Governor's office who would complete the bottom portion of the manifest with the reason for the flight and fax the form back to him usually within twenty-four (24) hours. Young stated that the cost of flying Constitutional Officers and members of the General Assembly is built into the Aeronautics Division's budget. Therefore, the Governor's office is not billed for each trip; however, the cost is recorded and made a part of the flight log. . . . Young stated the agency does not question the purpose of any flight made by Governor Sanford. They assume that if the Governor's office schedules a flight it is official business. He stated that in his memory he did not fly Governor Sanford to any locations where it appeared the trip was solely personal or political. He stated there were some occasions when the Governor would have personal business in conjunction with a state business trip. He indicated that he was unaware of any trip which did not involve official business on at least one leg of the trip. . . .

On August 27, 2009 investigators received copies of thirty-five (35) SLED Aviation Mission Report Forms for DNR aircraft that have flown Governor Sanford and/or his family as passengers from the year 2002 until August 26, 2009. On August 31, 2009 investigators received a response from Ms. Beard regarding flight scheduling. . . .

On September 11, 2009 the Governor's attorneys provided electronic copies via e-mail of telephone records of the Governor's calendar for calendar years 2003 and 2004. On September 15, 2009 the Governor's attorneys provided two compact discs containing the Governor's calendar for calendar years 2003 through 2009.

From September 11, 2009 through October 21, 2009 investigators compared flight logs and flight manifests from the Aeronautics Division and Department of Natural Resources with Governor Sanford's calendars. During this examination investigators reviewed a total of 663 flights on state-owned aircraft by Governor Sanford and/or his family members. These flights are broken down by agency and reveal 628 flight legs on Division of Aeronautics' aircraft between January 13, 2003 and October, 15, 2009, and thirty-five (35) flights on Department of Natural Resources aircraft between April 26, 2004 and August 26, 2009. DNR flight logs do not break down flights into flight legs as does the Aeronautics Division. Of the flights reviewed, investigators questioned fifty-three (53).

On September 9, 2009 investigators contacted Ms. Tina M. Beard at DNR to clarify the date of a flight to Charleston to attend a National Republican Senatorial Committee event. DNR Flight log No. 8684 showed a date of April 30, 2006; however, the Governor's calendar indicated that the flight took place on April 29, 2009. Her response indicates the correct date was April 29, 2009. She provided an amended flight log and a statement from the pilot . . .

On October 22, 2009 a request for information regarding the fifty-three questioned flights was hand delivered to Governor Sanford's attorneys. A copy of the request with accompanying flight logs, flight manifests and related Governor's calendar pages are enclosed as Attachment S.

On November 9, 2009 a response was delivered to the State Ethics Commission office. The response includes a spreadsheet detailing the Governor's response for each of the fifty-three flights. . . .

DISCLOSURE OF PRIVATELY-OWNED AIRCRAFT USE . . .

[State policies and regulations have been omitted.]

QUESTION: Did Governor Sanford violate Section 8–13–1120(A)(9)(a) by failing to disclose flights provided to him on privately-owned aircraft as gifts?

From September 28, 2009 through October 6, 2009, utilizing Governor Sanford's daily calendars as provided by his attorneys, investigators found a total of seventy-eight (78) flights on privately owned aircraft for the five (5) year period January 2004 through December 2008. Investigators also examined Statements of Economic Interests (SEI) filed by Governor Sanford with the State Ethics Commission from January 2005 through January 2009. A total of seventeen (17) flights were disclosed by Governor Sanford on disclosure forms filed with the State Ethics Commission. A Statement of Economic Interests form was not on file for January 2004, therefore, investigators did not examine Governor Sanford's 2003 calendar. Also, 2009 flights would not be disclosed until the January 2010 Statement of Economic Interests is filed. . . .

With this amendment to previous filings, Governor Sanford will have complied, albeit late, with the filing requirements of Section 8–13–1120(A)(9)(a) and Section 8–13–1140 of the 1976 Code of Laws.

USE OF CAMPAIGN FUNDS FOR PERSONAL EXPENSES . . .

[State policies and regulations have been omitted.]

QUESTION: Did Governor Sanford violate Section 8–13–1348(A) & (B) by using campaign funds for personal expenses not related to his campaign or for expenses not incurred in connection with his official duties?

From August 19, 2009 through August 21, 2009 investigators reviewed fifteen (15) Campaign Disclosure reports filed by Governor Sanford for period October 1, 2005 through June 30, 2009, the last filing at the time of the review. Eleven (11) reports revealed [to be] reimbursements to either Governor Sanford or Mrs. Sanford. No reports prior to the January 2006 report were available.

The examination revealed seventeen (17) reimbursements to Governor Sanford totaling $6,724.47, and eight (8) reimbursements to Mrs. Sanford totaling $4,119.87. . . .

[Section 5, including questions about whether the governor's family used state-owned aircraft, has been omitted.]

CONCLUSION

This completes this Investigative Report. All relevant evidence obtained is attached and made a part of this formal report.

A summary of this investigation was presented to the State Ethics Commission on November 18, 2009 to determine if probable cause exists to formally charge Governor Sanford with violations of the above-captioned code sections.

RESPECTFULLY SUBMITTED,

Herbert R. Hayden, Jr.
Executive Director

Donald M. Lundgren
Chief Investigator

HRH/DML

SOURCE: South Carolina State Ethics Commission. "Complaint C2010–020 in the Matter of Governor Mark Sanford." November 18, 2009. http://ethics.sc.gov/NR/rdonlyres/D44BC8C4-FD05-4A46-BE8F-D81382F90BA8/0/InvestigativeReport.pdf.

OTHER HISTORIC DOCUMENTS OF INTEREST

FROM PREVIOUS *HISTORIC DOCUMENTS*

- Resignation of New York Governor and U.S. Political Corruption Probes, *2008*, p. 105
- Conviction of Governor on Ethics Law Violations, *1993*, p. 303

December

Dubai Credit Crisis

DECEMBER 1, 9, 14, AND 21, 2009

In November 2009, the government of Dubai announced that it would restructure the debt payments of Dubai World, an investment corporation made up of smaller companies established by the government of Dubai to oversee projects including global investment and building for the government. This announcement sent global markets into a panic as it was learned that billions of dollars in bonds would not be repaid on time. The news out of Dubai, a nation once known only for its oil but that in recent years had transformed itself into a world financial center and sought-after tourist destination, was another sign that the global economy still had a long way to go before a full recovery from the serious effects of recession.

The news was disappointing to many in the international community who had hoped that the worst of the global economic crisis was behind them. Strategists at Bank of America Merrill Lynch warned investors that "one cannot rule out—as a tail risk—a case where this would escalate into a major sovereign-default problem, which would then resonate across global emerging markets." By the end of 2009, however, that worst-case scenario had not come to fruition. The United Arab Emirates (UAE) central bank agreed to back Dubai's banks with increased liquidity. Regardless, the restructuring announcement was like pouring salt in a wound for investors.

DUBAI WORLD RESTRUCTURING PLAN

The government of Dubai asked Dubai World to stop debt repayments for at least the next six months. Dubai, considered an icon around the world for its seemingly nonstop flow of money, had $80 billion dollars of debt, much of which was owned by Dubai World. Through the chain of events that led to Dubai's request to halt debt repayments, Nakheel, Dubai World's property arm, would be unable to repay a $4 billion Islamic bond, which many had expected would come through on time and in full. Because there was no money from either Dubai World or the government of Dubai to repay the bond, all of Dubai World's other liabilities were put at serious risk. In a statement, Dubai World cautioned those around the globe not to panic as "[i]nitial discussions have commenced with the banks of Dubai World and are proceeding on a constructive basis. It is envisaged the restructuring process will be carried out in an equitable way for the overall benefit of all stakeholders."

Although the global markets went into a tailspin at the news, the person in charge of Dubai's finances, Sheikh Ahmed bin Saeed Al-Maktoum, head of the Supreme Fiscal Committee, said that the restructuring had been "carefully planned." According to

Al-Maktoum, "The Government is spearheading the restructuring of this commercial operation in the full knowledge of how the markets would react. We understand the concerns of the market and the creditors in particular. However, we have had to intervene because of the need to take decisive action to address its particular debt burden." Dubai, like most cities around the world, was experiencing economic challenges, Al-Maktoum admitted. And although it was often seen as otherwise, Al-Maktoum said, "No market is immune from economic issues. This is a sensible business decision."

Dubai's billionaire leader, Sheikh Mohammed bin Rashid Al-Maktoum, added that Dubai would not suffer from this setback, which he considered to be blown out of proportion by international economic experts, and would continue to remain "an attractive regional market." Indeed, during the first trading day after the announcement, Dubai's stocks did not fall as much as had been expected and closed only 7.3 percent down. That did little to calm fears of investors, who worried that Dubai would default. "A lot of people are pretty freaked out," said one American businessperson.

Those in Dubai were standing by Sheikh Mohammed's claim. According to a comment on one of the nation's most popular newspaper Web sites, "Dubai is a victim of media distortion. All the Western countries have ganged up on Dubai. Why? Because it has succeeded." Another reader agreed. "This is all because of jealousy from the Western world," the person wrote. Dubai's citizens seemed to have little concern for the future of the country, pointing to the fact that not long ago, Dubai was nothing but desert, and these people reasoned that if it could rise from nothing, it would take more than a small financial crisis to bring the nation down. Sheikh Mohammed was at the center of this hope. One Emirati businessperson said, "Even if there is a crisis, he can solve it. We have great confidence in him." Abdulrahman al-Saleh, director general of the Dubai Department of Finance, also called worldwide media reports exaggerated. "I think banks are not at a stage where they need any extra liquidity from the central bank," he said. "Creditors need to take part of the responsibility for their decision to lend to the companies. They think Dubai World is part of the government, which is not correct."

The question remained, however, whether Dubai would be able to work its own way out of this financial crisis or whether it would have to get aid from Abu Dhabi, the capital of the UAE and its second largest city. It was widely speculated that Abu Dhabi might inject itself into any decisions about a bailout-type program that had been used in various other nations and require Dubai to give it a stake in its burgeoning companies, such as Emirates Airlines. Officials in Dubai rejected the speculation. When asked about the situation, Sheik Mohammed told a reporter to "shut up." Abu Dhabi, with its oil wealth, more so than Dubai, could easily pay off the $59 billion in debt Dubai World had incurred.

To some economic observers, it came as no surprise that Dubai had suddenly found itself in an uncomfortable financial position. Dubai is the second biggest of the seven emirates that make up the UAE, and to move the nation from desert to booming metropolis and icon on the world stage Dubai borrowed $80 billion. Although this worked for some time, like in many other nations, a serious housing crisis hit, and Dubai World struggled to find new loans to keep the nation from falling into a recession. In the second quarter of 2009, home prices were down 47 percent, the largest decrease anywhere in the world. There was no indication that the housing sector would begin an uptick anytime soon.

Effect on Dubai's Workforce

As a growing, relatively rich Middle Eastern nation, Dubai attracted businesspersons from around the world hoping to benefit from its (formerly) booming economy. The financial crisis also created a serious problem for these laborers who had moved to Dubai during the boom years looking for work and a way to support their families abroad. One nation with a large population receiving an influx of cash from Dubai was the Philippines. After news of the restructuring plan, the Philippines central bank announced that it did not think "there would be a significant adverse impact on flows to the country in the near term," said Amando Tetangco, governor of the central bank.

Ninety percent of Dubai's population is foreign, and the announcement of the restructuring brought to the surface long-simmering tensions between the minority emirate population and immigrants, who had long complained that the growth rate in Dubai was too fast to be able to sustain itself and came at the high cost of distrust in government institutions.

Effect on the Rest of the World

Although government officials in Dubai remained determined in asserting that the crisis was not as serious as it was being made out to be, panic quickly spread through markets in Asia, Europe, the United States, and elsewhere. The markets turned on fear that the world was seeing the beginning of a second financial crisis. At Nomura Securities, based in Tokyo, the question, according to brokers was, "What falls next?"

According to Moody's, although the situation in Dubai was bad, international banks that had invested in Dubai World, or that otherwise had ties to the company, would not see an adverse effect. "The only consequence that we expect to result from this event," according to a report from Moody's Investors Service, "is a change in investors' perceptions of the risks associated to Dubai and the United Arab Emirates, and a re-pricing of risks and opportunities." This was enough for investors, however, whose reactions sent stock prices down around the world; in addition, investors began speculating which banks were tied to Dubai World and might not have their bonds repaid.

The crisis was most strongly felt in India, where developers would not see their bonds repaid on time; the decrease in capital would mean a decline in the volume of exports leaving India for Dubai. The UAE is the nation to which India exports the most goods; Dubai consumes one-third of the products imported from India to the UAE. The announcement out of Dubai would mean that 3 percent of India's total export income was in jeopardy. In addition, Dubai World owned five shipping terminals in India's ports, representing 40 percent of the container ship traffic India sees each year.

—Heather Kerrigan

Following are Dubai World press releases from December 1, 9, 14, and 21 on its restructuring plan.

Dubai World Announces Restructuring Plan

December 1, 2009

Dubai World ("Dubai World") and its subsidiaries (the "Group") would like to update their lenders on recent developments relating to their debt obligations.

Following a detailed review of the Group's liquidity and capital structure, Dubai World has concluded that it should immediately consider alternatives in respect of the debt obligations of certain entities within the Group.

The proposed restructuring process will only relate to Dubai World and certain of its subsidiaries including; Nakheel World and Limitless World. The process will not include Infinity World Holding, Istithmar World and Ports & Free Zone World (which includes DP World, Economic Zones World, P&O Ferries and Jebel Ali Free Zone), all of which are on a stable financial footing.

The total value of debt carried by the companies subject to the restructuring process amounts to approximately US$26 billion, of which approximately US$6 billion relates to the Nakheel sukuk.

It is envisaged the restructuring process will be carried out in an equitable way for the overall benefit of all stakeholders and will comprise several phases including: long term plans and commitment of stakeholders; determination of maintainable profit and cash generation; assessment of deleveraging options, including asset sales; assessment of funding requirements and the formulation of restructuring proposals to financial creditors and their implementation.

Initial discussions have commenced with the banks of Dubai World and are proceeding on a constructive basis. In light of the current operational challenges and the future obligations of the Group, it is anticipated that the process and any related actions to address strategic alternatives will be conducted on an expedited basis. As part of this overall process, Nakheel requests its sukuk holders to appoint an authorised representative with whom discussions can commence.

Moelis & Company have been appointed to advise on the Dubai World restructuring with Rothschild, who will continue their ongoing role as financial advisor.

Dubai World intends to adopt a policy of regular communication and will provide further updates as this process develops.

Source: Dubai World. Press release. "Statement from Dubai World." December 1, 2009. www.dubai worldmedia.net/2009/12/76751502.html.

Dubai World Releases More Details about Its Restructuring Plan

December 9, 2009

Further to the announcement of 30 November 2009, Dubai World would like to announce that following further review, Drydocks World and its subsidiaries will not be included in the proposed restructuring process for Dubai World and its Real Estate related subsidiaries.

Drydocks World has been in constructive dialogue with its lenders for several months and its financial profile does not require it to be included in the more wide-ranging restructuring process envisaged in last week's announcement.

Drydocks World has to date reacted promptly to the challenges of the global economic slowdown which have impacted the shipping sector globally. The company has implemented extensive operational improvements over the past year. Drydocks World continues to have sufficient financial capacity to service its debt and remains well positioned to take advantage of the expected improvements in the ship building and offshore industries in the coming years.

Drydocks World is a leading international player in ship repair, shipbuilding, rig building, ship conversion, offshore fabrication and fleet operations with facilities across the Middle East and Southeast Asia.

SOURCE: Dubai World. Press release. "Statement from Dubai World." December 9, 2009. www.dubai worldmedia.net/2009/12/77271502.html.

Dubai World Announces Financial Support from Government

December 14, 2009

Dubai World ("Dubai World" and/or "the Group") welcomes the announcement today by the Government of Dubai to provide financial support to the Group, including full repayment of the Nakheel 2009 sukuk. This support provides funding and a stable basis for the restructuring process which continues.

Dubai World will continue to work with financial creditors to negotiate a standstill in an orderly way. As long as a standstill is successfully negotiated, Dubai World has assurances that the Government of Dubai, through the DFSF [Dubai Financial Support Fund], will provide financial support to cover working capital and interest expenses to ensure the continuity of key projects.

Dubai World is also pleased to note that the Government of Dubai has moved to address the concerns of trade creditors and contractors.

Dubai World is committed to regular, direct and timely communications which it believes will yield the best outcome for all stakeholders.

DUBAI WORLD ADVISERS

A number of advisers have been appointed to assist the Group with the restructuring process. Aidan Birkett of Deloitte has been appointed as Chief Restructuring Officer by the DFSF.

Rothschild and Clifford Chance continue to act as financial and legal advisers respectively to Dubai World in relation to the restructuring. Alix Partners continue to assist in resolving certain operational issues.

SOURCE: Dubai World. Press release. "Statement from Dubai World." December 14, 2009. www.dubai worldmedia.net/2009/12/77771502.html.

Dubai World Updates Banks on Restructuring Plan

December 21, 2009

Dubai World ("the Group") has announced that it today held a meeting in Dubai with its creditor banks involved in the restructuring of the Group's debt.

The purpose of the meeting was to provide an update to the banks on the development of the Group's restructuring plans as it seeks to reach a standstill agreement with financial creditors. Also in attendance were Dubai World's appointed advisers Deloitte, Rothschild and Clifford Chance.

As was confirmed in its statement of December 14th, Dubai World will continue to work with financial creditors to seek a standstill in an orderly way. As long as a standstill is successfully implemented, Dubai World has assurances that the Government of Dubai, through the DFSF, will provide financial support to cover working capital and interest expenses to ensure the continuity of key projects.

Dubai World is committed to working closely with the banks' appointed Coordinating Committee to work towards a consensual solution for the benefit of all lending banks, trade creditors and other stakeholders affected by the restructuring.

SOURCE: Dubai World. Press release. "Statement from Dubai World." December 21, 2009. www.dubai worldmedia.net/2009/12/78031502.html.

OTHER HISTORIC DOCUMENTS OF INTEREST

FROM THIS VOLUME

- The London Summit on Global Economic Recovery, p. 157

FROM PREVIOUS *HISTORIC DOCUMENTS*

- World Leaders and the IMF on the Global Economic Crisis, *2008,* p. 418

President Obama Announces Troop Increase in Afghanistan

DECEMBER 1, 2009

On December 1, 2009, President Barack Obama called for an increased troop commitment of 30,000 to respond to the worsening situation in Afghanistan. This was the second increase Obama had called for in 2009. The United States had spent much of its resources on Iraq after launching the war there in 2003, allowing the Taliban to regain a foothold in Afghanistan. Since 2001, 900 Americans had lost their lives in Afghanistan, far fewer than in Iraq but still more than many Americans deemed necessary.

The increase in troops drew criticism from Obama's own party, which pointed to the $30 billion price tag for the additional troops that was hitting the nation at the same time that unemployment continued to rise and social services at home were stretched to the limit. Republicans were generally supportive of the troop surge, but encouraged the president not to create a timeline for troop withdrawal.

Additional criticism of the president came not because of his decision to send additional troops but because of how long he took to make it. By the time Obama called for an increase in troops at the end of 2009, he had been in office for nearly one year. According to a CNN/Opinion Research Corporation poll conducted in early November 2009, 49 percent of Americans thought Obama was taking too long to make a decision on how to handle the situation in Afghanistan. In October, Obama had responded to critics, including former vice president Dick Cheney, who accused Obama of being "afraid" to make a decision. In a speech before members of the military and their families in Jacksonville, Florida, Obama said, "I will never rush the solemn decision of sending you into harm's way. I won't risk your lives unless it is absolutely necessary."

GENERALS CALL FOR TROOP INCREASE

As the number of casualties continued to mount in Afghanistan, Gen. Stanley McChrystal, the top military commander in Afghanistan, sent a confidential assessment of U.S. strategy to Defense Secretary Robert Gates. The sixty-six-page report, which was given to President Obama for review, was first disclosed by the *Washington Post* in September amid growing concern over the eight-year U.S. involvement in Afghanistan. In his report, McChrystal noted the inadequacy of the North Atlantic Treaty Organization (NATO) forces and the Afghan government's lack of support. He called the NATO troops unorganized and unprepared to deal with the situation. As for Afghanistan's government, McChrystal said, "[t]he weakness of state institutions, malign actions of power-brokers, widespread corruption and abuse of power by various officials . . . have given Afghans little reason to support their government."

General McChrystal said that without additional troops, the U.S. mission would "likely result in failure." McChrystal continued, "Failure to gain the initiative and reverse insurgent momentum in the near term (next 12 months)—while Afghan security capacity matures—risks an outcome where defeating the insurgency is no longer possible." According to McChrystal, the insurgency was becoming increasingly powerful and was recruiting new members from prisons. "These detainees are currently radicalizing non-insurgent inmates," McChrystal wrote in his report.

However, according to McChrystal, it was not all bad news. "While the situation is serious, success is achievable." However, according to McChrystal, success could only be achieved with an increase in troops, a decision for President Obama. McChrystal's assessment of the situation and call for more troops was backed by other top military officials, including Mike Mullen, chair of the Joint Chiefs of Staff, and Gen. David Petraeus, head of U.S. Central Command.

While the American public became increasingly concerned about the situation as violence in the region rose and the Taliban continued to fight, President Obama was still undecided about how to respond to the situation. "Right now," he said on a CNN talk show, "the first question is, are we doing the right thing? Are we pursuing the right strategy? When we have clarity on that, then the question is, O.K., how do we resource it?" Although Obama remained skeptical about whether sending more troops to Afghanistan was the right thing to do, he asserted that his administration would not delay making a decision to send more troops if they felt that was the necessary course of action and would most certainly not make it based on possible political gains. This "is not going to be driven by the politics of the moment," Obama said.

President Obama said he did not want to make a snap decision to send more troops until he had weighed all sides of the issue. "We're not going to put the cart before the horse and just think by sending more troops we're automatically going to make Americans safe," Obama said.

Obama's top generals gave him options for troop surges of 40,000, 30,000, and 20,000 to 25,000. There were 71,000 troops already in Afghanistan. In making his decision, Obama had to tread lightly, because the issue was delicate on both sides of the political aisle. Even his vice president, Joe Biden, expressed his doubts about whether a troop increase would make the most strategic sense.

Obama's Plan

President Obama announced his decision to send additional troops in a speech at the U.S. Military Academy at West Point on December 1, 2009. He said that he would call on an additional 30,000 troops to be sent to Afghanistan to reinforce those already in the region. According to the president, this increase, which would be filled by forces leaving Iraq and offered a chance to leave Afghans with a stable and secure government. His decision was influenced by his top commanders in Afghanistan. "There is no imminent threat of the government being overthrown," Obama said, "but the Taliban has gained momentum. Al Qaeda has not re-emerged in Afghanistan in the same numbers as before 9/11, but they retain their safe-havens along the border." Because of this new reality, President Obama said, the "status quo is not sustainable."

The president also said that the additional troops would assist in training Afghan forces to be able to take control of the security of the nation. The larger number of troops, coupled with NATO forces in the region, would "allow us to accelerate handing over responsibility to Afghan forces," which would mean a faster withdrawal from the region. It was President Obama's intent to begin sending the additional troops to Afghanistan in early 2010, and he planned to make it a goal of his administration to begin to withdraw troops during the summer of 2011. According to those in Obama's administration, it was the president's goal to have nearly all troops out of Afghanistan by the end of his first term in office.

In the near term, President Obama said the troop surge would help with his major goals in the region: to stop al-Qaida and ensure that it not be allowed to remain in Afghanistan; to stop the momentum of the Taliban and ensure that the Afghan government remained stable and in power; and to bolster the authority and ability of Afghanistan's military and security forces. President Obama called on the Afghan government to work hard to ensure its fledgling democracy would remain stable. Only one month before Obama's speech, Hamid Karzai had been reelected president in an election wrought with voter fraud. Obama encouraged the government in Kabul to stamp out corruption and focus on building a stronger nation and gaining the support and belief of its people.

Obama also said that he would work with Pakistan and encourage Afghanistan's leaders to do the same, to ensure that Taliban leaders would be unable to find safety along the Afghanistan-Pakistan border. "We are in Afghanistan to prevent a cancer from once again spreading through that country. But this same cancer has also taken root in the border region of Pakistan. That is why we need a strategy that works on both sides of the border."

REACTION FROM AFGHANISTAN

In Afghanistan, the reaction to Obama's speech and troop surge decision was mixed. One member of Afghanistan's parliament, Khalid Pashtun, said that he saw the speech as a call to action for Afghan leaders. President Obama, he said, "may not be convincing the normal people or the Taliban, but by saying these things in the speech, this gives to the politicians, scholars, and spiritual leaders a free hand now. We are the ones . . . to win over our people." Although some in the United States criticized Obama's offer as a timeline for eventual withdrawal, Pashtun saw it as encouragement to the government to work as quickly as it could to get the nation into working order.

Others were not as positive. "For the Taliban," said Waliullah Rahmani, director of the Kabul Center for Strategic Studies, "this is good news." According to Rahmani, insurgents will simply wait eighteen months before making their next move toward regaining power. The Afghan government of today, Rahmani said, "cannot remain in power for [even] a month when the U.S. leaves." Even American support would not be enough for some Afghan security forces to continue fighting for their nation, especially given their salary of $165 per month. According to some Middle Eastern scholars, the Taliban offered recruits more benefits, including power and prestige within their clans. The Taliban had also been adept at convincing many in Afghanistan that it is the intent of the United States to remain there indefinitely and take control of the government. "The additional 30,000 troops is going to be a good opportunity for the Taliban to recruit more," said Jabar Waifaie, a security guard working in Kabul.

A NATION DIVIDED

Critics of the war in Afghanistan, and of President Obama's willingness to increase the number of troops there two times during the first year of his presidency, compared the situation to that of the Vietnam War, in which the United States was entrenched in a quagmire and eventually left the region without a victory. President Obama rejected this analogy in his speech at West Point, saying, "Unlike Vietnam, we are joined by a broad coalition of 43 nations that recognize the legitimacy of our action. Unlike Vietnam, we are not facing a broad-based popular insurgency. And most importantly, unlike Vietnam, the American people were viciously attacked from Afghanistan, and remain a target for those same extremists who are plotting along its border." To ensure Americans that he would not allow U.S. troops to languish in the region, he rejected the idea that a timeline should not be set. According to Obama, "the absence of a timeframe for transition would deny us any sense of urgency in working with the Afghan government. It must be clear that Afghans will have to take responsibility for their security, and that America has no interest in fighting an endless war in Afghanistan." He added that his administration had no interest in occupying Afghanistan in the long term. Instead, he said, the United States would offer its support to the people of Afghanistan as they work toward a solid democracy.

Some Democrats in Congress questioned Obama's decision because of the cost. Rep. Dave Obey, D-Wis., said, "The biggest threat to our long-term national security is a stunted economy." Obey's solution to financing the war was to charge a surtax levied on middle-income families on top of their current tax liability. Anyone who is or has fought in Iraq or Afghanistan since September 11, 2001, or anyone who has lost a soldier in service in those two nations would be exempt from the tax. "If this endeavor is to be pursued, we must have a renewed sense of shared sacrifice—because right now only military families are paying the cost for this war. A progressive war surtax is the fairest way to pay for it—fairest to working class families and fairest to military families," said Obey. Sen. Russ Feingold, D-Wis., called the president's decision "an expensive gamble."

Republicans generally supported the president. Michael Steele, chair of the Republican National Committee, criticized the president for having taken so long to make a decision, but congratulated him for sending the additional troops to Afghanistan. "I am glad the president will finally provide General McChrystal with the troops he needs." Steele said President Obama would have the support of the Republican party, as long as he remained committed to the situation in Afghanistan and did not begin a plan to bring the troops out of the nation too soon.

—Heather Kerrigan

Following is the text of a speech given by President Barack Obama on December 1, 2009, addressing the situation in Afghanistan and his decision to send more troops to the region.

President Obama on Afghanistan

December 1, 2009

. . . Just days after 9/11, Congress authorized the use of force against Al Qaida and those who harbored them, an authorization that continues to this day. The vote in the Senate was 98 to nothing; the vote in the House was 420 to 1. For the first time in its history, the North Atlantic Treaty Organization invoked Article 5, the commitment that says an attack on one member nation is an attack on all. And the United Nations Security Council endorsed the use of all necessary steps to respond to the 9/11 attacks. America, our allies, and the world were acting as one to destroy Al Qaida's terrorist network and to protect our common security.

Under the banner of this domestic unity and international legitimacy—and only after the Taliban refused to turn over Usama bin Laden—we sent our troops into Afghanistan. Within a matter of months, Al Qaida was scattered and many of its operatives were killed. The Taliban was driven from power and pushed back on its heels. A place that had known decades of fear now had reason to hope. At a conference convened by the U.N., a Provisional Government was established under President Hamid Karzai, and an International Security Assistance Force was established to help bring a lasting peace to a war-torn country.

Then, in early 2003, the decision was made to wage a second war, in Iraq. The wrenching debate over the Iraq war is well-known and need not be repeated here. It's enough to say that for the next 6 years, the Iraq war drew the dominant share of our troops, our resources, our diplomacy, and our national attention, and that the decision to go into Iraq caused substantial rifts between America and much of the world.

Today, after extraordinary costs, we are bringing the Iraq war to a responsible end. We will remove our combat brigades from Iraq by the end of next summer and all of our troops by the end of 2011. That we are doing so is a testament to the character of the men and women in uniform. Thanks to their courage, grit, and perseverance, we have given Iraqis a chance to shape their future, and we are successfully leaving Iraq to its people.

But while we've achieved hard-earned milestones in Iraq, the situation in Afghanistan has deteriorated. After escaping across the border into Pakistan in 2001 and 2002, Al Qaida's leadership established a safe haven there. Although a legitimate Government was elected by the Afghan people, it's been hampered by corruption, the drug trade, an under-developed economy, and insufficient security forces.

Over the last several years, the Taliban has maintained common cause with Al Qaida, as they both seek an overthrow of the Afghan Government. Gradually, the Taliban has begun to control additional swaths of territory in Afghanistan, while engaging in increasingly brazen and devastating attacks of terrorism against the Pakistani people.

Now, throughout this period, our troop levels in Afghanistan remained a fraction of what they were in Iraq. When I took office, we had just over 32,000 Americans serving in Afghanistan, compared to 160,000 in Iraq at the peak of the war. Commanders in Afghanistan repeatedly asked for support to deal with the reemergence of the Taliban, but these reinforcements did not arrive. And that's why, shortly after taking office, I approved a longstanding request for more troops. After consultations with our allies, I then announced a strategy recognizing the fundamental connection between our war effort in Afghanistan and the extremist safe havens in Pakistan. I set a goal that was narrowly defined as disrupting, dismantling, and defeating Al Qaida and its extremist allies, and pledged to better coordinate our military and civilian efforts.

Since then, we've made progress on some important objectives. High-ranking Al Qaida and Taliban leaders have been killed, and we've stepped up the pressure on Al Qaida worldwide. In Pakistan, that nation's army has gone on its largest offensive in years. In Afghanistan, we and our allies prevented the Taliban from stopping a Presidential election, and although it was marred by fraud, that election produced a Government that is consistent with Afghanistan's laws and Constitution.

Yet huge challenges remain. Afghanistan is not lost, but for several years, it has moved backwards. There's no imminent threat of the Government being overthrown, but the Taliban has gained momentum. Al Qaida has not reemerged in Afghanistan in the same numbers as before 9/11, but they retain their safe havens along the border. And our forces lack the full support they need to effectively train and partner with Afghan security forces and better secure the population. Our new commander in Afghanistan, General McChrystal, has reported that the security situation is more serious than he anticipated. In short, the status quo is not sustainable.

. . . There has never been an option before me that called for troop deployments before 2010, so there has been no delay or denial of resources necessary for the conduct of the war during this review period. Instead, the review has allowed me to ask the hard questions and to explore all the different options, along with my national security team, our military and civilian leadership in Afghanistan, and our key partners. And given the stakes involved, I owed the American people and our troops no less.

. . . I have determined that it is in our vital national interest to send an additional 30,000 U.S. troops to Afghanistan. After 18 months, our troops will begin to come home. These are the resources that we need to seize the initiative, while building the Afghan capacity that can allow for a responsible transition of our forces out of Afghanistan. . . .

So, no, I do not make this decision lightly. I make this decision because I am convinced that our security is at stake in Afghanistan and Pakistan. This is the epicenter of violent extremism practiced by Al Qaida. It is from here that we were attacked on 9/11, and it is from here that new attacks are being plotted as I speak. This is no idle danger, no hypothetical threat. In the last few months alone, we have apprehended extremists within our borders who were sent here from the border region of Afghanistan and Pakistan to commit new acts of terror. And this danger will only grow if the region slides backwards and Al Qaida can operate with impunity. We must keep the pressure on Al Qaida, and to do that, we must increase the stability and capacity of our partners in the region.

Of course, this burden is not ours alone to bear. . . .

To meet that goal, we will pursue the following objectives within Afghanistan. We must deny Al Qaida a safe haven. We must reverse the Taliban's momentum and deny it the ability to overthrow the Government. And we must strengthen the capacity of Afghanistan's security forces and Government so that they can take lead responsibility for Afghanistan's future.

We will meet these objectives in three ways. First, we will pursue a military strategy that will break the Taliban's momentum and increase Afghanistan's capacity over the next 18 months.

The 30,000 additional troops that I'm announcing tonight will deploy in the first part of 2010—the fastest possible pace—so that they can target the insurgency and secure key population centers. They'll increase our ability to train competent Afghan security forces and to partner with them so that more Afghans can get into the fight. And they will help create the conditions for the United States to transfer responsibility to the Afghans.

Because this is an international effort, I've asked that our commitment be joined by contributions from our allies. . . .

Now, taken together, these additional American and international troops will allow us to accelerate handing over responsibility to Afghan forces and allow us to begin the transfer of our forces out of Afghanistan in July of 2011. . . .

Second, we will work with our partners, the United Nations, and the Afghan people to pursue a more effective civilian strategy so that the Government can take advantage of improved security. This effort must be based on performance. The days of providing a blank check are over. President Karzai's inauguration speech sent the right message about moving in a new direction. . . .

Third, we will act with the full recognition that our success in Afghanistan is inextricably linked to our partnership with Pakistan. We're in Afghanistan to prevent a cancer from once again spreading through that country. But this same cancer has also taken root in the border region of Pakistan. And that's why we need a strategy that works on both sides of the border.

In the past, there have been those in Pakistan who've argued that the struggle against extremism is not their fight and that Pakistan is better off doing little or seeking accommodation with those who use violence. But in recent years, as innocents have been killed from Karachi to Islamabad, it has become clear that it is the Pakistani people who are the most endangered by extremism. Public opinion has turned. The Pakistani Army has waged an offensive in Swat and South Waziristan. And there is no doubt that the United States and Pakistan share a common enemy.

In the past, we too often defined our relationship with Pakistan narrowly, and those days are over. Moving forward, we are committed to a partnership with Pakistan that is built on a foundation of mutual interest, mutual respect, and mutual trust. We will strengthen Pakistan's capacity to target those groups that threaten our countries and have made it clear that we cannot tolerate a safe haven for terrorists whose location is known and whose intentions are clear. . . .

These are the three core elements of our strategy: a military effort to create the conditions for a transition; a civilian surge that reinforces positive action; and an effective partnership with Pakistan. . . .

First, there are those who suggest that Afghanistan is another Vietnam. . . . Unlike Vietnam, we are joined by a broad coalition of 43 nations that recognizes the legitimacy of our action. Unlike Vietnam, we are not facing a broad-based popular insurgency. And most importantly, unlike Vietnam, the American people were viciously attacked from Afghanistan and remain a target for those same extremists who are plotting along its border. To abandon this area now and to rely only on efforts against Al Qaida from a distance would significantly hamper our ability to keep the pressure on Al Qaida and create an unacceptable risk of additional attacks on our homeland and our allies.

Second, there are those who acknowledge that we can't leave Afghanistan in its current state, but suggest that we go forward with the troops that we already have. But this would simply maintain a status quo in which we muddle through and permit a slow deterioration of conditions there. It would ultimately prove more costly and prolong our stay in Afghanistan, because we would never be able to generate the conditions needed to train Afghan security forces and give them the space to take over.

Finally, there are those who oppose identifying a timeframe for our transition to Afghan responsibility. . . . I reject this course because it sets goals that are beyond what can be achieved at a reasonable cost and what we need to achieve to secure our interests. Furthermore, the absence of a timeframe for transition would deny us any sense of urgency in working with the Afghan Government. . . .

As President, I refuse to set goals that go beyond our responsibility, our means, or our interests. . . .

Over the past several years, we have lost that balance. We've failed to appreciate the connection between our national security and our economy. In the wake of an economic crisis, too many of our neighbors and friends are out of work and struggle to pay the bills. Too many Americans are worried about the future facing our children. Meanwhile, competition within the global economy has grown more fierce. So we can't simply afford to ignore the price of these wars. . . .

Now, let me be clear: None of this will be easy. The struggle against violent extremism will not be finished quickly, and it extends well beyond Afghanistan and Pakistan. It will be an enduring test of our free society and our leadership in the world. . . .

So as a result, America will have to show our strength in the way that we end wars and prevent conflict, not just how we wage wars. We'll have to be nimble and precise in our use of military power. . . .

And we can't count on military might alone. We have to invest in our homeland security, because we can't capture or kill every violent extremist abroad. We have to improve and better coordinate our intelligence so that we stay one step ahead of shadowy networks.

We will have to take away the tools of mass destruction. And that's why I've made it a central pillar of my foreign policy to secure loose nuclear materials from terrorists, to stop the spread of nuclear weapons, and to pursue the goal of a world without them, because every nation must understand that true security will never come from an endless race for evermore destructive weapons; true security will come for those who reject them.

We'll have to use diplomacy, because no one nation can meet the challenges of an interconnected world acting alone. I've spent this year renewing our alliances and forging new partnerships. And we have forged a new beginning between America and the Muslim world, one that recognizes our mutual interest in breaking a cycle of conflict and that promises a future in which those who kill innocents are isolated by those who stand up for peace and prosperity and human dignity.

And finally, we must draw on the strength of our values, for the challenges that we face may have changed, but the things that we believe in must not. That's why we must promote our values by living them at home, which is why I have prohibited torture and will close the prison at Guantanamo Bay. And we must make it clear to every man, woman, and child around the world who lives under the dark cloud of tyranny that America will speak out on behalf of their human rights and tend to the light of freedom and justice and opportunity and respect for the dignity of all peoples. That is who we are. That is the source, the moral source, of America's authority.

Since the days of Franklin Roosevelt and the service and sacrifice of our grandparents and great-grandparents, our country has borne a special burden in global affairs. We have spilled American blood in many countries on multiple continents. We have spent our revenue to help others rebuild from rubble and develop their own economies. We have joined with others to develop an architecture of institutions—from the United Nations to NATO to the World Bank—that provide for the common security and prosperity of human beings.

We have not always been thanked for these efforts, and we have at times made mistakes. But more than any other nation, the United States of America has underwritten global security for over six decades, a time that, for all its problems, has seen walls come down and markets open and billions lifted from poverty, unparalleled scientific progress and advancing frontiers of human liberty. . . .

As a country, we're not as young, and perhaps not as innocent, as we were when Roosevelt was President. Yet we are still heirs to a noble struggle for freedom. And now we must summon all of our might and moral suasion to meet the challenges of a new age.

In the end, our security and leadership does not come solely from the strength of our arms. It derives from our people: from the workers and businesses who will rebuild our economy; from the entrepreneurs and researchers who will pioneer new industries; from the teachers that will educate our children and the service of those who work in our communities at home; from the diplomats and Peace Corps volunteers who spread hope abroad; and from the men and women in uniform who are part of an unbroken line of sacrifice that has made government of the people, by the people, and for the people a reality on this Earth.

This vast and diverse citizenry will not always agree on every issue, nor should we. But I also know that we, as a country, cannot sustain our leadership, nor navigate the momentous challenges of our time, if we allow ourselves to be split asunder by the same rancor and cynicism and partisanship that has in recent times poisoned our national discourse.

It's easy to forget that when this war began, we were united, bound together by the fresh memory of a horrific attack and by the determination to defend our homeland and the values we hold dear. I refuse to accept the notion that we cannot summon that unity again. I believe with every fiber of my being that we, as Americans, can still come together behind a common purpose. For our values are not simply words written into parchment, they are a creed that calls us together and that has carried us through the darkest of storms as one Nation, as one people.

America, we are passing through a time of great trial. And the message that we send in the midst of these storms must be clear: That our cause is just, our resolve unwavering. We will go forward with the confidence that right makes might and with the commitment to forge an America that is safer, a world that is more secure, and a future that represents not the deepest of fears but the highest of hopes.

Thank you. God bless you, and God bless the United States of America. Thank you very much. Thank you.

Source: U.S. Executive Office of the President. "Remarks at the United States Military Academy at West Point, New York." *Daily Compilation of Presidential Documents* 2009, no. 00962 (December 1, 2009). www.gpo.gov/fdsys/pkg/DCPD-200900962/pdf/DCPD-200900962.pdf.

Other Historic Documents of Interest

Jobs Report Shows Improvement

DECEMBER 4, 2009

Unemployment continued to grow in 2009, despite efforts by the federal government to stem the outflow of jobs overseas, factory closings, and the number of American citizens needing services from government. An investment in job creation, through the American Recovery and Reinvestment Act of 2009 (ARRA), promoted slow growth in many sectors, but economists predicted that it could be well into 2010 before the United States saw even the slightest turnaround. However, when the Bureau of Labor Statistics (BLS), an arm of the U.S. Department of Labor, released its November report on employment and unemployment on December 4, 2009, it revealed the largest one-month decline in the number of unemployed workers in the past three years. Although the Obama administration reminded Americans that there was still work to be done and that there would still be many months of slow growth ahead, the report provided some hope to politicians and economists alike that the economy might make a turnaround sooner than expected.

NOVEMBER JOBS REPORT

According to the report released by the BLS, 11,000 jobs were lost in November, more than 100,000 less than had been lost in previous months, raising some questions about the cause of the steep decline in job loss. In addition to the November numbers, the bureau revised its statistics for September and October job losses, lowering them to 139,000 and 111,000, respectively. Of course, some sectors of the economy were still experiencing significant job loss, and 15.4 million Americans were still without work. The number of construction jobs available fell for the twenty-ninth month in a row, the number of manufacturing jobs fell for the twenty-fourth straight month, and retail sales fell for the twenty-second month in a row. However, in November, 52,000 additional temporary workers were added to the job force, meaning that employers were beginning to test the waters and bring on more staff, indicating an increased demand for employees. The additional 52,000 was the largest growth in temporary workers in five years.

Not only were fewer jobs lost in November, the unemployment rate also fell to 10 percent. Before November, twelve of the previous thirteen months had seen an increase in unemployment, which in October had hit a twenty-six-year-high at 10.2 percent. There was another positive from the report: Employers who had previously cut staff hours were beginning to add working hours again, as evidenced by the slight growth in the average work week from 33 hours to 33.2 hours. This increase in 0.2 hours would lead to slightly larger paychecks for those Americans who had their working hours restored. The additional hours increased the average weekly American paycheck to $622. Longer hours and larger paychecks usually translate into spending, which is essential to an economic turnaround. "Consumer spending is a function of income, not jobs," said Jay Bryson, an economist with Wells Fargo Securities. By working longer hours and gaining more income, consumers would have more money to spend at their leisure. November reports showed that consumer spending had increased by 0.5 percent over October, and there was evidence of an increase in overall consumer confidence as well.

The report caught economists by surprise; they had predicted that 125,000 jobs would be lost and that the unemployment rate would remain at 10.2 percent in November. The Congressional Budget Office (CBO) had predicted unemployment to remain at 10.2 percent throughout most of 2010, on average, with a percentage point decrease in 2011. There was still a note of caution in the excitement over the positive November report, however. "I think it's a little bit premature for champagne, but after enduring two years of really bad news, let's enjoy this one," said Bryson. "You've got to walk before you start running. I don't think we're walking yet, but we're starting to get back up on our feet," he said. President Obama agreed: "There are going to be some months where the reports are going to be a little better, some months where the reports are worse, but the trend line right now is good." Stocks responded positively to the news, posting the largest one-day rally since January.

After the positive jobs report, economists estimated that jobs would begin being added back to the economy in March 2010, as long as the number of jobs lost and percentage of unemployment continued to fall. This would mean that, although this was the most severe recession in recent memory, the workforce turnaround would happen much sooner than had been the case in the two previous recessions, in the early 1990s and 2001.

What It All Means

Fewer jobs lost and lower unemployment meant different things to various sectors of the American public. For economists, the report presented a conundrum. Although the report from the BLS was generally positive, or at least more positive than had recently been seen, other data coming in was not as positive. At the time the BLS released its report, ADP (Automatic Data Processing, Inc.), a provider of business solutions and data, reported the loss of jobs in the private sector at 169,000 in November. In response to the BLS data, Joshua Shapiro, chief U.S. economist at MFR, a research firm, said, "This was a shocking report because the reported payroll data bear little resemblance to any other evidence concerning the labor market, including the ADP survey, which is based on hard data from a much wider sample of payrolls than is the government's survey." Because of the discrepancies in various data available, economists cautioned that the positive BLS report for November might be a product of overcalculating the number of losses in October.

A jobs summit at the White House brought together 130 business leaders proposing ideas for creating more jobs. Passing another stimulus package was not viewed favorably, but an increase in credit available to small businesses and investment in various growing sectors, including green technology, were floated. "My economic team is looking at ideas such as additional investments in our aging roads and bridges, incentives to encourage families and businesses to make buildings more energy-efficient, additional tax cuts for small businesses to create jobs, additional steps to increase the flow of credit to small businesses, and an aggressive agenda to promote exports to help American manufacturers sell their products around the world," said President Obama. While the administration worked to create additional jobs in the public and private sectors, the president also focused on helping those still out of work by signing another extension of the unemployment benefits.

The BLS report further divided the pro- and anti-stimulus camps. According to Secretary of Labor Hilda Solis, the November jobs report made it clear that the stimulus plan was working. "While there has been a lot of rhetoric about the Recovery Act, when you look at today's report and other recent favorable economic trends, it is hard to argue that the Recovery Act is not working." Vice President Joe Biden's chief economist, Jared Bernstein, agreed. "I think you have to give our interventions a lot of credit." After the positive report, the Obama administration briefed reporters on how the stimulus package had improved the American economic outlook thus far, citing 1.6 million jobs that were created. According to the administration, over the nearly two years of recession, without ARRA job loss would have been nearly nine million, rather than seven million.

Republicans were not as quick to agree that ARRA was driving the turnaround. According to Kevin Hassett, the director of economic policy studies at the American Enterprise Institute and the chief economist for Sen. John McCain, R-Ariz., during the 2008 presidential campaign, "Even if you accept their analysis that we are creating jobs this year, when you remove the stimulus you are going to destroy jobs." This, he said, was reason enough to consider less spending by the federal government and more tax cuts for businesses.

STILL MORE WORK TO DO

At all levels of the federal government, and at economic organizations, there was little willingness to celebrate the November jobs report as marking the end of the recession. According to many, there was still work left to be done. In a speech in Allentown, Pennsylvania, President Obama told listeners, "This is good news, just in time for the season of hope. But I want to keep this in perspective. Good trends don't pay the rent. We've got to actually grow jobs and get America back to work as quickly as we can." That more work remained to be done was backed up by the BLS December 2009 jobs report, which showed 85,000 jobs lost that month.

The outlook on long-term employment remained grim as well. According to Jan Hatzius, the chief domestic economist at Goldman Sachs, "Assuming we have a strong recovery, it will take at least five years or more to get the unemployment rate down to a more normal 5 percent." In addition, Hatzius cautioned, when Americans remain out of work for long periods of time, they begin to lose necessary skills to perform their jobs and be active participants in the job market. Given this, said Hatzius, America may be facing unemployment that stands at 6 percent for a long time. In November, the long-term unemployment situation hit its worst point in sixty-one years, the worst point since records have been kept on this statistic. Nearly six million people had been out of work for six months or more, and for the employed actively looking for work, their time without a job hit 28.5 weeks. "The trend of slow healing continues but there is a long way to go before the labor market returns to full health," said Department of the Treasury chief economist Alan Krueger.

—Heather Kerrigan

Following is the Bureau of Labor Statistics November jobs report, released on December 4, 2009, and press releases from December 4, 2009, celebrating the November jobs report from Department of Labor Secretary Hilda Solis, House Speaker Nancy Pelosi, and House Majority Leader Steny Hoyer.

Bureau of Labor Statistics November 2009 Jobs Report

December 4, 2009

[Table references and tables have been omitted.]

The unemployment rate edged down to 10.0 percent in November, and nonfarm payroll employment was essentially unchanged (-11,000), the U.S. Bureau of Labor Statistics reported today. In the prior 3 months, payroll job losses had averaged 135,000 a month. In November, employment fell in construction, manufacturing, and information, while temporary help services and health care added jobs.

Household Survey Data

In November, both the number of unemployed persons, at 15.4 million, and the unemployment rate, at 10.0 percent, edged down. At the start of the recession in December 2007, the number of unemployed persons was 7.5 million, and the jobless rate was 4.9 percent.

Among the major worker groups, unemployment rates for adult men (10.5 percent), adult women (7.9 percent), teenagers (26.7 percent), whites (9.3 percent), blacks (15.6 percent), and Hispanics (12.7 percent) showed little change in November. The unemployment rate for Asians was 7.3 percent, not seasonally adjusted.

Among the unemployed, the number of job losers and persons who completed temporary jobs fell by 463,000 in November. The number of long-term unemployed (those jobless for 27 weeks and over) rose by 293,000 to 5.9 million. The percentage of unemployed persons jobless for 27 weeks or more increased by 2.7 percentage points to 38.3 percent.

The civilian labor force participation rate was little changed in November at 65.0 percent. The employment-population ratio was unchanged at 58.5 percent.

The number of people working part time for economic reasons (sometimes referred to as involuntary part-time workers) was little changed in November at 9.2 million. These individuals were working part time because their hours had been cut back or because they were unable to find a full-time job.

About 2.3 million persons were marginally attached to the labor force in November, an increase of 376,000 from a year earlier. (The data are not seasonally adjusted.) These individuals were not in the labor force, wanted and were available for work, and had looked for a job sometime in the prior 12 months. They were not counted as unemployed because they had not searched for work in the 4 weeks preceding the survey.

Among the marginally attached, there were 861,000 discouraged workers in November, up from 608,000 a year earlier. (The data are not seasonally adjusted.) Discouraged workers are persons not currently looking for work because they believe no jobs are available for them. The remaining 1.5 million persons marginally attached to the labor force had not searched for work in the 4 weeks preceding the survey for reasons such as school attendance or family responsibilities.

ESTABLISHMENT SURVEY DATA

Total nonfarm payroll employment was essentially unchanged in November (-11,000). Job losses in the construction, manufacturing, and information industries were offset by job gains in temporary help services and health care. Since the recession began, payroll employment has decreased by 7.2 million.

Construction employment declined by 27,000 over the month. Job losses had averaged 117,000 per month during the 6 months ending in April and 63,000 per month from May through October. In November, construction job losses were concentrated among nonresidential specialty trade contractors (-29,000).

Manufacturing employment fell by 41,000 in November. The average monthly decline for the past 5 months (-46,000) was much lower than the average monthly job loss for the first half of this year (-171,000). About 2.1 million manufacturing jobs have been lost since December 2007; the majority of this decline has occurred in durable goods manufacturing (-1.6 million).

Employment in the information industry fell by 17,000 in November. About half of the job loss occurred in its telecommunications component (-9,000).

There was little change in wholesale and retail trade employment in November. Within retail trade, department stores added 8,000 jobs over the month.

The number of jobs in transportation and warehousing, financial activities, and leisure and hospitality showed little change over the month.

Employment in professional and business services rose by 86,000 in November. Temporary help services accounted for the majority of the increase, adding 52,000 jobs. Since July, temporary help services employment has risen by 117,000.

Health care employment continued to rise in November (21,000), with notable gains in home health care services (7,000) and hospitals (7,000). The health care industry has added 613,000 jobs since the recession began in December 2007.

In November, the average workweek for production and nonsupervisory workers on private nonfarm payrolls rose by 0.2 hour to 33.2 hours. The manufacturing workweek increased by 0.3 hour to 40.4 hours. Factory overtime rose by 0.1 hour to 3.4 hours. Since May, the manufacturing workweek has increased by 1.0 hour.

In November, average hourly earnings of production and nonsupervisory workers on private nonfarm payrolls edged up by 1 cent, or 0.1 percent, to $18.74. Over the past 12 months, average hourly earnings have risen by 2.2 percent, while average weekly earnings have risen by 1.6 percent.

The change in total nonfarm payroll employment for September was revised from -219,000 to -139,000, and the change for October was revised from -190,000 to -111,000. . . .

SOURCE: U.S. Bureau of Labor Statistics. Press release. "The Employment Situation—November 2009." December 4, 2009. www.bls.gov/news.release/archives/empsit_12042009.htm.

Secretary of Labor Solis on November Jobs Report

December 4, 2009

This past November, the economy lost 11,000 jobs, and the unemployment rate decreased to 10 percent.

I am encouraged by the pattern of moderated job loss; however, I will not be satisfied until there are robust job gains.

This administration is focused on jobs and job creation every day. We are working hard to sustain economic growth and spur renewed hiring for the millions of Americans who need and want work but cannot find it.

Over the past 10 months, the Obama Administration has taken bold steps to break the back of this recession. While there has been a lot of rhetoric about the Recovery Act, when you look at today's report and other recent favorable economic trends, it is hard to argue that the Recovery Act is not working.

Reports from the Council of Economic Advisors, Recovery Act recipients and most recently the non-partisan Congressional Budget Office confirm that the Recovery Act has saved or created more than one million jobs. The economy is now growing again for the first time in more than a year—and faster than at any time in two years.

We already have taken additional steps to boost job creation—from extending business tax breaks and benefits for homebuyers to increasing access to capital for small banks. Yesterday, I participated in the Forum for Jobs and Economic Growth at the White House. This forum was an opportunity to discuss ways to spur job creation with some of the leading voices in the public and private sectors.

The Department of Labor is working to provide opportunities and training for hundreds of thousands of people through our Workforce Investment Act training and other programs. Earlier this month, we awarded $55 million in grants to states and community organizations to support job training and labor market information programs to help workers, many in underserved communities, find jobs in expanding green industries and related occupations.

At the Department of Labor, we are working tirelessly to ensure that we fulfill our responsibility to provide workers with the assistance they need today to help them find good jobs. We still have work to do before we can be sure that all Americans have access to good jobs, but I am confident that we will reach that goal.

SOURCE: U.S. Department of Labor. Press release. "Statement of US Secretary of Labor Hilda L. Solis on November Employment Numbers." December 4, 2009. www.dol.gov/opa/media/press/opa/opa20091508 .htm.

Speaker of the House Pelosi on November Jobs Report

December 4, 2009

Today's jobs report is evidence that our recovery efforts are moving our economy in the right direction. After losing an average of 673,000 jobs per month in the final three months of the Bush Administration, the report for November showed a job loss of 11,000 jobs—the lowest level since the recession began in December 2007.

The economy grew by nearly 3 percent in the third quarter, compared to a decline of 6.4 percent in the first quarter of 2009—in large part because of the Recovery Act, according to the non-partisan Congressional Budget Office. These economic trends are clear signs that our country is on the path back to job growth and illustrate that the economic policies of President Obama and the Democratic Congress are starting to work.

But our work is not over. Too many people have lost their jobs, which is devastating for any household trying to make ends meet, pay the bills, and put food on the table. The Bush Administration policies created a huge jobs deficit, and getting Americans back to work has been and will remain our top priority. In the coming weeks, House Democrats will continue to build on our efforts to grow the economy and create jobs by investing in our infrastructure, helping local governments keep teachers, police officers, and firefighters on the payroll, and assisting small business owners.

SOURCE: Office of Speaker of the U.S. House of Representatives Nancy Pelosi. Press release. "Pelosi Statement on Better-Than Expected November Jobs Report." December 4, 2009. www.speaker.gov/newsroom/pressreleases?id=1463.

House Majority Leader Hoyer on November Jobs Report

December 4, 2009

Today's news that the unemployment rate fell in November is an encouraging sign. While the number of Americans out of work remains unacceptably high, a lower unemployment rate is evidence that Democratic economic policies are meeting success. Nearly a year after President Obama inherited the worst economic crisis since the Great Depression, the nonpartisan Congressional Budget Office reported this week that the Recovery Act has saved or created more than one million jobs, while creating economic growth for the first time in more than a year. So today's news adds to the evidence that the economic growth spurred by the Recovery Act has had a positive impact on jobs.

Those are reasons to be hopeful—but as long as so many Americans remain out of work, the president and Congress will not rest. That's why President Obama held a jobs summit yesterday to hear the best employment ideas from economic leaders and American workers, and why Congress is considering the best way to turn those ideas into jobs legislation. Though there are still challenges ahead, today is further evidence that Democrats' economic policies are making a difference for average working Americans.

SOURCE: Office of Majority Leader Steny Hoyer. Press release. "Hoyer Statement on November Jobs Report." December 4, 2009. www.majorityleader.gov/media/press.cfm?pressReleaseID=3626.

OTHER HISTORIC DOCUMENTS OF INTEREST

FROM THIS VOLUME

- President Obama Signs the American Recovery and Reinvestment Act of 2009, p. 41
- President Obama's Address Before a Joint Session of Congress and Republican Response, p. 81
- Federal Reserve Board Chair Announces End of Recession, p. 430
- Economic Outlook in the States, p. 646

FROM PREVIOUS *HISTORIC DOCUMENTS*

- U.S. Governors on Economic Outlook in the States, *2008*, p. 452
- Federal Reserve and Economists on the U.S. Financial Crisis at Year-End, *2008*, p. 557

DOCUMENT IN CONTEXT

President Obama Wins Nobel Peace Prize

DECEMBER 10, 2009

On the morning of October 9, 2009, the world woke to the startling news that President Barack Obama had been declared the winner of the Nobel Peace Prize. In granting him the award, the Norwegian Nobel Committee cited the president's "extraordinary efforts to strengthen international diplomacy and cooperation between peoples" and his declared intention to work toward the goal of a nuclear-weapon-free world. President Obama said in his remarks that morning that he had not been chosen because of his accomplishments. Instead, he called the award "an affirmation of American leadership on behalf of aspirations held by people in all nations."

Reaction to the announcement in the United States and abroad was mixed. Some questioned the wisdom of granting the Nobel prize to a leader so early in his career. A more complex issue was how the president could reconcile accepting the world's most prestigious peace award while leading a nation fighting two wars. Obama addressed this question head-on in his acceptance speech on December 10 in Oslo, offering a spirited case for military action in pursuit of international peace and security. The president traveled to Norway to deliver it just days after calling for an additional 30,000 U.S. troops to be sent to Afghanistan.

GLOBAL ELATION AT OBAMA'S ELECTION

President Obama became the third sitting U.S. president to receive the Nobel Peace Prize. Earlier recipients were Theodore Roosevelt, recognized in 1906 for helping to end the Russo-Japanese War, and Woodrow Wilson, granted the prize in 1919 for his role in creating the League of Nations after World War I. Former president Jimmy Carter, the 2002 peace laureate, was honored primarily for his contributions to world peace since leaving the White House. President Obama, by contrast, was chosen for the award in the first year of his presidency, long before his policy efforts had had time to bear fruit; in fact, his name had been submitted in nomination less than two weeks after his inauguration.

The phenomenon of Obama's rise to power had captured the attention of the world. More than with any presidential candidate in U.S. history, people abroad shared in the excitement of Obama's 2008 campaign and the elation of his victory. His popularity overseas contrasted the overwhelmingly negative feelings George W. Bush had created in his two terms in office. The election of Obama brought hope for a more constructive U.S.

635

role in areas such as arms control, climate change negotiations, and other issues demanding international cooperation.

Part of Obama's appeal as a presidential candidate lay in his success in presenting himself as a worldly figure. His unusual biography—the son of a black man from Kenya and a white woman from Kansas, a childhood spent in Hawaii and Indonesia—seemed to promise leadership that could ameliorate America's racial divide and its deteriorating image overseas. After winning the Democratic nomination, Obama traveled to the Middle East and Europe. His speech in Berlin before a large, rapturous crowd on July 24, 2008, confirmed his viability as a potential leader.

A New Internationalism

In his first year in office, Obama made global outreach a high priority, seeking to rebuild alliances frayed during the Bush years and open possibilities for diplomatic engagement with adversaries. Speaking in Prague on April 5, the president vowed that "the United States will take concrete steps towards a world without nuclear weapons," including a new round of strategic arms reductions with Russia, a more limited role for those weapons in its national security plans, and promotion of more robust international efforts at nonproliferation. Two months later, President Obama delivered a high-profile speech in Cairo in which he called for a fresh start and a new foundation of mutual respect in relations between the United States and the Muslim world. A third major address followed in Accra, Ghana, on July 11. The president's oratorical skills and the consistently frank and thoughtful substance of his public remarks helped augment his personal popularity and also helped soften the anti–American sentiment that had grown virulent in many parts of the world.

Such efforts in support of international friendship and cooperation coincided with the concept of the Nobel Peace Prize. Thorbjorn Jagland, chair of the Nobel Committee, said in explanation of the committee's unanimous decision: "The question we have to ask is who has done the most in the previous year to enhance peace in the world, and who has done more than Barack Obama?" The committee also emphasized the boost President Obama had given to multilateral institutions, in stark contrast to the previous administration's unilateralism and apparent disdain for treaties and diplomatic instruments. Nothing symbolized this commitment more than Obama's visit to the United Nations as world leaders gathered in September for the annual opening of the General Assembly. On September 24, Obama became the first American president to chair a session of the UN Security Council, introducing a resolution on nuclear nonproliferation and disarmament that passed unanimously.

Nevertheless, it was clear that many skeptical voices were likely to greet the Nobel Committee's announcement. Shortly after receiving word of his selection, President Obama told the gathered reporters, "To be honest, I do not feel that I deserve to be in the company of so many of the transformative figures who've been honored by this prize—men and women who've inspired me and inspired the entire world through their courageous pursuit of peace." On the other hand, he added, "throughout history, the Nobel Peace Prize has not just been used to honor specific achievement; it's also been used as a means to give momentum to a set of causes." For this reason, he was willing to accept the award as "a call for all nations to confront the common challenges of the 21st century."

Inspiration or Embarrassment?

Republicans and conservative commentators in the United States responded to the president's prize with disapproval and even mockery. The chair of the Republican National Committee, Michael Steele, asserted that President Obama had upstaged worthier candidates with his "star power." In the *National Review Online,* conservative Jonah Goldberg maintained that the president had taken few real steps toward peace: "All he's done is offer words the Nobel committee likes to hear and an image of America they like to see." Some suggested that the honor would strengthen the perception, already in common currency on the right, that the president is too interested in currying favor with Europeans. The *Los Angeles Times* editorialized, "Giving the Peace Prize to the president so soon in his term embarrasses him and diminishes the honor." *New York Times* columnist David Brooks advised him to refuse the award.

Even an earlier Nobel laureate joined in the criticism: 1983 winner Lech Walesa, former president of Poland, called the award to President Obama, "Too fast—he hasn't had the time to do anything yet." Others offered gracious, sometimes guarded, words of praise. Mohamed ElBaradei, director of the International Atomic Energy Agency and 2005 peace laureate, said of President Obama, "In less than a year in office, he has transformed the way we look at ourselves and the world we live in and rekindled hope for a world at peace with itself." Archbishop Desmond Tutu of South Africa, 1984 peace laureate, suggested that the award to the youthful president "anticipates an even greater contribution towards making our world a safer place for all." In a similar vein, 2008 honoree Martti Ahtisaari, former president of Finland, told the *New York Times,* "Of course, this puts pressure on Obama. The world expects that he will also achieve something." Other analysts suggested that the Nobel Committee intended to give the president a gentle prod to seek peaceful solutions to ongoing crises, such as the Israeli-Palestinian conflict and the standoff over Iran's nuclear program.

Mairead Maguire, given the Nobel Peace Prize in 1976 for her peace advocacy in Northern Ireland, sounded a discordant note of disappointment in the committee's choice. She pointed out that Obama "continues the policy of militarism and occupation of Afghanistan, instead of dialogue and negotiations with all parties to the conflict" and expressed concern that the peace prize "will be rightly seen by many people around the world as a reward for his country's aggression and domination." This critique, perhaps the most potent of all, was echoed by many on the ground in the war zones of the Middle East. "Please show me which peace?" asked a member of the Afghan parliament in the *Washington Post.* "The Americans are killing 75 Pashtuns a day in Afghanistan. For this they give a prize to Obama?"

War and the Peace Prize

The war in Afghanistan, launched in the wake of the September 2001 al-Qaida attacks on New York and Washington, presented itself as one of the Obama administration's most pressing foreign policy problems. When the peace prize was announced in October, the administration was in the midst of a lengthy and contentious deliberation over its Afghanistan strategy. The military commander in the region, Gen. Stanley McChrystal, was publicly advocating deployment of as many as 40,000 additional troops to implement a counterinsurgency campaign, joining more than 70,000 American soldiers already in

Afghanistan. On December 1, in a nationally televised address, the president announced he would authorize a "surge" of 30,000 troops beginning in early 2010 and that U.S. forces would begin to withdraw from Afghanistan in July 2011.

Thus, President Obama flew to Oslo to accept the Nobel Peace Prize eight days after escalating a war. His acceptance speech was a meditation on this apparent paradox. He introduced the war in Afghanistan as "a conflict that America did not seek; one in which we are joined by 42 other countries—including Norway—in an effort to defend ourselves and all nations from further attacks." The other ongoing American war, in Iraq, was winding down, the president stated. Obama invoked the ancient theory of "just war," noting that most wars throughout history have not met the doctrine's principles. In an era of new threats and means of warfare, he argued, the notion of defining legitimate criteria for the use of force remains relevant.

"We must begin by acknowledging the hard truth," said the president. "We will not eradicate violent conflict in our lifetimes. There will be times when nations—acting individually or in concert—will find the use of force not only necessary but morally justified." Obama paid tribute to the power of nonviolence to bring about change, a power embodied in the lives of Mohandas Gandhi and Martin Luther King Jr., but claimed that a head of state "cannot be guided by their examples alone. . . . For make no mistake: Evil does exist in the world. A non-violent movement could not have halted Hitler's armies. Negotiations cannot convince al Qaeda's leaders to lay down their arms." Despite war's occasional necessity, President Obama concluded, nations must concentrate on building stronger institutions of collective security that discourage the resort to arms while honoring human rights and aspirations.

President Obama's address may have been the most vigorous defense of militarism ever uttered from the rostrum of the Nobel lecture. American politicians and commentators of both parties, including leading Republicans such as Newt Gingrich and Karl Rove, offered praise. A leading speech writer for President George W. Bush, Michael Gerson, noted in the *Washington Post* that "Obama was recognizing that the great commitments and themes of American foreign policy are durably bipartisan." Voices on the antiwar left broke with this consensus; the president's rhetoric struck Rep. Dennis Kucinich, D-Ohio, as a step along "the Orwellian journey to the semantic netherworld where war is peace, where the momentum of war overwhelms hopes for peace."

—Roger Smith

Following is the text of President Barack Obama's Nobel Prize acceptance speech given on December 10, 2009.

President Barack Obama Accepts the Nobel Peace Prize

December 10, 2009

Your Majesties, Your Royal Highnesses, distinguished members of the Norwegian Nobel Committee, citizens of America, and citizens of the world: I receive this honor with deep gratitude and great humility. It is an award that speaks to our highest aspirations, that for all the cruelty and hardship of our world, we are not mere prisoners of fate. Our actions matter, and can bend history in the direction of justice. And yet I would be remiss if I did not acknowledge the considerable controversy that your generous decision has generated. [*Laughter*] In part, this is because I am at the beginning and not the end of my labors on the world stage. Compared to some of the giants of history who've received this prize— Schweitzer and King, Marshall and Mandela—my accomplishments are slight. And then there are the men and women around the world who have been jailed and beaten in the pursuit of justice, those who toil in humanitarian organizations to relieve suffering, the unrecognized millions whose quiet acts of courage and compassion inspire even the most hardened cynics. I cannot argue with those who find these men and women, some known, some obscure to all but those they help, to be far more deserving of this honor than I.

But perhaps the most profound issue surrounding my receipt of this prize is the fact that I am the Commander-in-Chief of the military of a nation in the midst of two wars. One of these wars is winding down. The other is a conflict that America did not seek; one in which we are joined by 42 other countries, including Norway, in an effort to defend ourselves and all nations from further attacks.

Still, we are at war, and I'm responsible for the deployment of thousands of young Americans to battle in a distant land. Some will kill, and some will be killed. And so I come here with an acute sense of the costs of armed conflict, filled with difficult questions about the relationship between war and peace, and our effort to replace one with the other.

Now these questions are not new. War, in one form or another, appeared with the first man. At the dawn of history, its morality was not questioned; it was simply a fact, like drought or disease, the manner in which tribes and then civilizations sought power and settled their differences.

And over time, as codes of law sought to control violence within groups, so did philosophers and clerics and statesmen seek to regulate the destructive power of war. The concept of a "just war" emerged, suggesting that war is justified only when certain conditions were met: if it is waged as a last resort or in self-defense; if the force used is proportional; and if, whenever possible, civilians are spared from violence.

Of course, we know that for most of history, this concept of just war was rarely observed. The capacity of human beings to think of new ways to kill one another proved inexhaustible, as did our capacity to exempt from mercy those who look different or pray to a different God. Wars between armies gave way to wars between nations—total wars, in which the distinction between combatant and civilian became blurred. In the span of 30 years, such carnage would twice engulf this continent. And while it's hard to conceive of a cause more just than the defeat of the Third Reich and the Axis powers, World War II was a conflict in which the total number of civilians who died exceeded the number of soldiers who perished.

In the wake of such destruction and with the advent of the nuclear age, it became clear to victor and vanquished alike that the world needed institutions to prevent another world war. And so a quarter century after the United States Senate rejected the League of Nations—an idea for which Woodrow Wilson received this prize—America led the world in constructing an architecture to keep the peace: a Marshall plan and a United Nations, mechanisms to govern the waging of war, treaties to protect human rights, prevent genocide, restrict the most dangerous weapons.

In many ways, these efforts succeeded. Yes, terrible wars have been fought and atrocities committed. But there has been no third world war. The cold war ended with jubilant crowds dismantling a wall. Commerce has stitched much of the world together. Billions have been lifted from poverty. The ideals of liberty and self-determination, equality and the rule of law have haltingly advanced. We are the heirs of the fortitude and foresight of generations past, and it is a legacy for which my own country is rightfully proud.

And yet, a decade into a new century, this old architecture is buckling under the weight of new threats. The world may no longer shudder at the prospect of war between two nuclear superpowers, but proliferation may increase the risk of catastrophe. Terrorism has long been a tactic, but modern technology allows a few small men with outsized rage to murder innocents on a horrific scale.

Moreover, wars between nations have increasingly given way to wars within nations. The resurgence of ethnic or sectarian conflicts; the growth of secessionist movements, insurgencies, and failed states, all these things have increasingly trapped civilians in unending chaos. In today's wars, many more civilians are killed than soldiers; the seeds of future conflict are sown, economies are wrecked, civil societies torn asunder, refugees amassed, children scarred.

I do not bring with me today a definitive solution to the problems of war. What I do know is that meeting these challenges will require the same vision, hard work, and persistence of those men and women who acted so boldly decades ago. And it will require us to think in new ways about the notions of just war and the imperatives of a just peace.

We must begin by acknowledging the hard truth: We will not eradicate violent conflict in our lifetimes. There will be times when nations, acting individually or in concert, will find the use of force not only necessary but morally justified.

I make this statement mindful of what Martin Luther King Jr. said in this same ceremony years ago: "Violence never brings permanent peace. It solves no social problem: it merely creates new and more complicated ones." As someone who stands here as a direct consequence of Dr. King's life work, I am living testimony to the moral force of non-violence. I know there's nothing weak, nothing passive, nothing naïve, in the creed and lives of Gandhi and King.

But as a head of state sworn to protect and defend my nation, I cannot be guided by their examples alone. I face the world as it is, and cannot stand idle in the face of threats to the American people. For make no mistake: Evil does exist in the world. A non-violent movement could not have halted Hitler's armies. Negotiations cannot convince al Qaeda's leaders to lay down their arms. To say that force may sometimes be necessary is not a call to cynicism; it is a recognition of history; the imperfections of man and the limits of reason.

I raise this point—I begin with this point because in many countries there is a deep ambivalence about military action today, no matter what the cause. And at times, this is joined by a reflexive suspicion of America, the world's sole military superpower.

Yet the world must remember that it was not simply international institutions, not just treaties and declarations, that brought stability to a post–World War II world. Whatever mistakes we have made, the plain fact is this: The United States of America has helped underwrite global security for more than six decades with the blood of our citizens and the strength of our arms. The service and sacrifice of our men and women in uniform has promoted peace and prosperity from Germany to Korea, and enabled democracy to take hold in places like the Balkans. We have borne this burden not because we seek to impose our will. We have done so out of enlightened self-interest, because we seek a better future for our children and grandchildren, and we believe that their lives will be better if others' children and grandchildren can live in freedom and prosperity.

So yes, the instruments of war do have a role to play in preserving the peace. And yet this truth must coexist with another: That no matter how justified, war promises human tragedy. The soldier's courage and sacrifice is full of glory, expressing devotion to country, to cause, to comrades in arms. But war itself is never glorious, and we must never trumpet it as such.

So part of our challenge is reconciling these two seemingly irreconcilable truths— that war is sometimes necessary, and war at some level is an expression of human folly. Concretely, we must direct our effort to the task that President Kennedy called for long ago. "Let us focus," he said, "on a more practical, more attainable peace, based not on a sudden revolution in human nature but on a gradual evolution in human institutions"—a gradual evolution of human institutions. What might this evolution look like? What might these practical steps be?

To begin with, I believe that all nations, strong and weak alike, must adhere to standards that govern the use of force. I, like any head of state, reserve the right to act unilaterally if necessary to defend my nation. Nevertheless, I am convinced that adhering to standards—international standards strengthens those who do, and isolates and weakens those who don't.

The world rallied around America after the 9/11 attacks and continues to support our efforts in Afghanistan because of the horror of those senseless attacks and the recognized principle of self-defense. Likewise, the world recognized the need to confront Saddam Hussein when he invaded Kuwait, a consensus that sent a clear message to all about the cost of aggression.

Furthermore, America—in fact, no nation—can insist that others follow the rules of the road if we refuse to follow them ourselves. For when we don't, our actions appear arbitrary and undercut the legitimacy of future interventions, no matter how justified.

And this becomes particularly important when the purpose of military action extends beyond self-defense or the defense of one nation against an aggressor. More and more, we all confront difficult questions about how to prevent the slaughter of civilians by their own government or to stop a civil war whose violence and suffering can engulf an entire region.

I believe that force can be justified on humanitarian grounds, as it was in the Balkans, or in other places that have been scarred by war. Inaction tears at our conscience and can lead to more costly intervention later. That's why all responsible nations must embrace the role that militaries with a clear mandate can play to keep the peace.

America's commitment to global security will never waver. But in a world in which threats are more diffuse, and missions more complex, America cannot act alone. America alone cannot secure the peace. This is true in Afghanistan. This is true in failed states like Somalia, where terrorism and piracy is joined by famine and human suffering. And sadly, it will continue to be true in unstable regions for years to come.

The leaders and soldiers of NATO countries and other friends and allies demonstrate this truth through the capacity and courage they've shown in Afghanistan. But in many countries, there is a disconnect between the efforts of those who serve and the ambivalence of the broader public. I understand why war is not popular, but I also know this: The belief that peace is desirable is rarely enough to achieve it. Peace requires responsibility;

peace entails sacrifice. That's why NATO continues to be indispensable. That's why we must strengthen U.N. and regional peacekeeping and not leave the task to a few countries. That's why we honor those who return home from peacekeeping and training abroad to Oslo and Rome, to Ottawa and Sydney, to Dhaka and Kigali. We honor them not as makers of war, but of wagers—but as wagers of peace.

Let me make one final point about the use of force. Even as we make difficult decisions about going to war, we must also think clearly about how we fight it. The Nobel Committee recognized this truth in awarding its first prize for peace to Henry Dunant, the founder of the Red Cross, and a driving force behind the Geneva Conventions.

Where force is necessary, we have a moral and strategic interest in binding ourselves to certain rules of conduct. And even as we confront a vicious adversary that abides by no rules, I believe the United States of America must remain a standard bearer in the conduct of war. That is what makes us different from those whom we fight. That is a source of our strength. That is why I prohibited torture. That is why I ordered the prison at Guantanamo Bay closed. And that is why I have reaffirmed America's commitment to abide by the Geneva Conventions. We lose ourselves when we compromise the very ideals that we fight to defend, and we honor those ideals by upholding them not when it's easy, but when it is hard.

I have spoken at some length to the question that must weigh on our minds and our hearts as we choose to wage war. But let me now turn to our effort to avoid such tragic choices, and speak of three ways that we can build a just and lasting peace.

First, in dealing with those nations that break rules and laws, I believe that we must develop alternatives to violence that are tough enough to actually change behavior—for if we want a lasting peace, then the words of the international community must mean something. Those regimes that break the rules must be held accountable. Sanctions must exact a real price. Intransigence must be met with increased pressure, and such pressure exists only when the world stands together as one.

One urgent example is the effort to prevent the spread of nuclear weapons, and to seek a world without them. In the middle of the last century, nations agreed to be bound by a treaty whose bargain is clear: All will have access to peaceful nuclear power; those without nuclear weapons will forsake them; and those with nuclear weapons will work towards disarmament. I am committed to upholding this treaty. It is a centerpiece of my foreign policy. And I'm working with President Medvedev to reduce America and Russia's nuclear stockpiles.

But it is also incumbent upon all of us to insist that nations like Iran and North Korea do not game the system. Those who claim to respect international law cannot avert their eyes when those laws are flouted. Those who care for their own security cannot ignore the danger of an arms race in the Middle East or East Asia. Those who seek peace cannot stand idly by as nations arm themselves for nuclear war.

The same principle applies to those who violate international laws by brutalizing their own people. When there is genocide in Darfur, systematic rape in Congo, repression in Burma, there must be consequences. Yes, there will be engagement; yes, there will be diplomacy. But there must be consequences when those things fail. And the closer we stand together, the less likely we will be faced with the choice between armed intervention and complicity in oppression.

This brings me to a second point: the nature of the peace that we seek. For peace is not merely the absence of visible conflict. Only a just peace based on the inherent rights and dignity of every individual can truly be lasting.

It was this insight that drove drafters of the Universal Declaration of Human Rights after the Second World War. In the wake of devastation, they recognized that if human rights are not protected, peace is a hollow promise.

And yet too often, these words are ignored. For some countries, the failure to uphold human rights is excused by the false suggestion that these are somehow Western principles, foreign to local cultures or stages of a nation's development. And within America, there has long been a tension between those who describe themselves as realists or idealists, a tension that suggests a stark choice between the narrow pursuit of interests or an endless campaign to impose our values around the world.

I reject these choices. I believe that peace is unstable where citizens are denied the right to speak freely or worship as they please, choose their own leaders or assemble without fear. Pent-up grievances fester, and the suppression of tribal and religious identity can lead to violence. We also know that the opposite is true. Only when Europe became free did it finally find peace. America has never fought a war against a democracy, and our closest friends are governments that protect the rights of their citizens. No matter how callously defined, neither America's interests nor the world's are served by the denial of human aspirations.

So even as we respect the unique culture and traditions of different countries, America will always be a voice for those aspirations that are universal. We will bear witness to the quiet dignity of reformers like Aung Sang Suu Kyi; to the bravery of Zimbabweans who cast their ballots in the face of beatings; to the hundreds of thousands who have marched silently through the streets of Iran. It is telling that the leaders of these governments fear the aspirations of their own people more than the power of any other nation. And it is the responsibility of all free people and free nations to make clear that these movements of hope and history, they have us on their side.

Let me also say this: The promotion of human rights cannot be about exhortation alone. At times, it must be coupled with painstaking diplomacy. I know that engagement with repressive regimes lacks the satisfying purity of indignation. But I also know that sanctions without outreach, condemnation without discussion, can carry forward only a crippling status quo. No repressive regime can move down a new path unless it has the choice of an open door. In light of the Cultural Revolution's horrors, Nixon's meeting with Mao appeared inexcusable, and yet it surely helped set China on a path where millions of its citizens have been lifted from poverty and connected to open societies. Pope John Paul's engagement with Poland created space not just for the Catholic Church, but for labor leaders like Lech Walesa. Ronald Reagan's efforts on arms control and embrace of perestroika not only improved relations with the Soviet Union but empowered dissidents throughout Eastern Europe. There's no simple formula here. But we must try as best we can to balance isolation and engagement, pressure and incentives, so that human rights and dignity are advanced over time.

Third, a just peace includes not only civil and political rights—it must encompass economic security and opportunity. For to—true peace is not just freedom from fear, but freedom from want. It is undoubtedly true that development rarely takes root without security; it is also true that security does not exist where human beings do not have access to enough food, or clean water, or the medicine and shelter they need to survive. It does not exist where children can't aspire to a decent education or a job that supports a family. The absence of hope can rot a society from within.

And that's why helping farmers feed their own people or nations educate their children and care for the sick is not mere charity. It's also why the world must come together to confront climate change. There is little scientific dispute that if we do nothing, we will face more drought, more famine, more mass displacement, all of which will fuel more conflict for decades. For this reason—it is not merely scientists and environmental activists who call for swift and forceful action, it's military leaders in my own country and others who understand our common security hangs in the balance.

Agreements among nations, strong institutions, support for human rights, investments in development: All these are vital ingredients in bringing about the evolution that President Kennedy spoke about. And yet, I do not believe that we will have the will, the determination, the staying power, to complete this work without something more, and that's the continued expansion of our moral imagination; an insistence that there's something irreducible that we all share. As the world grows smaller, you might think it would be easier for human beings to recognize how similar we are, to understand that we're all basically seeking the same things: That we all hope for the chance to live out our lives with some measure of happiness and fulfillment for ourselves and our families.

And yet somehow, given the dizzying pace of globalization, the cultural leveling of modernity, it perhaps comes as no surprise that people fear the loss of what they cherish in their particular identities: their race; their tribe; and perhaps most powerfully, their religion. In some places, this fear has led to conflict. At times, it even feels like we're moving backwards. We see it in the Middle East, as the conflict between Arabs and Jews seems to harden. We see it in nations that are torn asunder by tribal lines.

And most dangerously, we see it in the way that religion is used to justify the murder of innocents by those who have distorted and defiled the great religion of Islam, and who attacked my country from Afghanistan. These extremists are not the first to kill in the name of God; the cruelties of the Crusades are amply recorded. But they remind us that no holy war can ever be a just war. For if you truly believe that you are carrying out divine will, then there is no need for restraint, no need to spare the pregnant mother, or the medic, or the Red Cross worker, or even a person of one own's faith. Such a warped view of religion is not just incompatible with the concept of peace, but I believe it's incompatible with the very purpose of faith. For the one rule that lies at the heart of every major religion is that we do unto others as we would have them do unto us.

Adhering to this law of love has always been the core struggle of human nature. For we are fallible; we make mistakes and fall victim to the temptations of pride and power and, sometimes, evil. Even those of us with the best of intentions will at times fail to right the wrongs before us.

But we do not have to think that human nature is perfect for us to still believe that the human condition can be perfected. We do not have to live in an idealized world to still reach for those ideals that will make it a better place. The non-violence practiced by men like Gandhi and King may not have been practical or possible in every circumstance, but the love that they preached, their fundamental faith in human progress, that must always be the North Star that guides us on our journey.

For if we lose that faith, if we dismiss it as silly or naïve; if we divorce it from the decisions that we make on issues of war and peace, then we lose what's best about humanity. We lose our sense of possibility. We lose our moral compass.

Like generations have before us, we must reject that future. As Dr. King said at this occasion so many years ago: "I refuse to accept despair as the final response to the ambiguities of history. I refuse to accept the idea that the 'isness' of man's present condition makes him morally incapable of reaching up for the eternal 'oughtness' that forever confronts him." Let us reach for the world that ought to be, that spark of the divine that still stirs within each of our souls.

Somewhere today, in the here and now, in the world as it is, a soldier sees he's outgunned, but stands firm to keep the peace. Somewhere today, in this world, a young protestor awaits the brutality of her government, but has the courage to march on. Somewhere today, a mother facing punishing poverty still takes the time to teach her child, scrapes together what few coins she has to send that child to school because she believes that a cruel world still has a place for that child's dreams.

Let us live by their example. We can acknowledge that oppression will always be with us, and still strive for justice. We can admit the intractability of depravation, and still strive for dignity. Clear-eyed, we can understand that there will be war, and still strive for peace. We can do that, for that is the story of human progress. That's the hope of all the world; and at this moment of challenge, that must be our work here on Earth. . . .

SOURCE: U.S. Executive Office of the President. "Remarks on Accepting the Nobel Peace Prize in Oslo, Norway." *Daily Compilation of Presidential Documents* 2009, no. 00985 (December 10, 2009). www.gpo .gov/fdsys/pkg/DCPD-200900985/pdf/DCPD-200900985.pdf.

OTHER HISTORIC DOCUMENTS OF INTEREST

FROM THIS VOLUME

FROM PREVIOUS *HISTORIC DOCUMENTS*

Economic Outlook in the States

DECEMBER 18 AND 30, 2009

Although the United States began to see some economic improvement in 2009, individual states, which are responsible for delivering many social services to their citizens, were still feeling the pinch. The American Recovery and Reinvestment Act (ARRA) helped some states balance their budgets and overcome massive budget gaps, but when the realization came that the money would eventually dry up, governors had to come up with creative ways to continue to keep budgets balanced and deliver services to citizens at an increasing rate as more and more people were without work. In states like California and Michigan, experiencing their highest unemployment rates in recent history, rising job losses drained social services that had already suffered severe budget cuts when the governors of both states worked to close massive, multimillion dollar budget gaps.

UNEMPLOYMENT

As unemployment rose throughout 2009, state services were hard hit. Many states saw their unemployment insurance funds nearly dry up and were unable to keep up with increasing demand for various welfare programs.

In August, the nation's most populous state, California, had its highest unemployment rate in 70 years, at 12.2 percent, giving it the fourth highest unemployment rate in the nation. While California faced many of the same recession pressures as the rest of the nation, it was hardest hit by the collapse of the housing and construction markets, the two industries that had fueled growth and job creation in the state for decades. Since 2005, California had seen its building levels drop $40 billion, and new home construction in 2009 was a quarter of what it had been in 2005. In July 2009, the state passed a budget that closed a $24 billion budget gap by cutting social services, education funds, and other government services as well as employees. For some government employees with jobs, closing the budget gap meant being forced to take one day per week as unpaid furlough. Nevada and Rhode Island had the nation's second and third highest unemployment rates in 2009, both climbing above 12 percent. Michigan was hardest hit during this economic downturn, and had already been at a serious disadvantage going into it, having never truly recovered from the 2001 recession. This, coupled with the crumbling auto industry that caused the closure of many manufacturing plants around the country, lead to an unemployment rate in Michigan above 15 percent for most of the year—well above the national average. In June, when the state's unemployment rate topped 15 percent, Michigan became the first state in twenty-five years to witness an unemployment rate of that magnitude. To process unemployment benefits requests Michigan had to hire hundreds of additional staff members. Even then the state still faced a serious backlog of applications; those who attempted to handle their benefits over the phone faced hours of wait time. Michigan had to borrow $2.4 billion from the federal government to keep its unemployment insurance benefits afloat, second only to the amount requested by California.

BUDGET SHORTFALLS

At the end of 2009, thirty-six states were facing budget gaps that collectively totaled $28 billion, according to a report by the National Conference of State Legislatures (NCSL). (The outlook was no better for 2010 and beyond, according to the group, which predicted that thirty-five states would have a total budget shortfall of $69 billion in 2010, and twenty-five states would see a budget shortfall in 2011.) The largest budget shortfalls were in Oklahoma, at 18.5 percent, and Arizona, at 18 percent of the state's budget.

Although many states recognized the problem before it hit and had somewhat prepared to deal with increasing demand on services along with a decreasing budget, some states had not anticipated how bad the situation would be. According to the NCSL, "Even pessimistic forecasts have been missed." In Connecticut, the state estimated that it would receive 9 percent less in tax revenue over the year, and used that figure to balance its budget. In reality, the tax revenue the state took in declined by 16 percent.

Sales taxes declined significantly in a majority of states, where the growing number of unemployed meant less disposable income. In early 2009, the Rockefeller Institute of Government reported that by the end of 2008, state tax collections had fallen by 4 percent, meaning a bad year was in the making. Personal income tax dropped 1.1 percent, and corporate income tax decreased by 15.5 percent. The institute did not foresee an upswing in tax increases in the near future. According to the group, during the first four months of 2009, the overall revenue decline in the states was 12 percent, "a further dramatic worsening of fiscal conditions nationwide."

With few places to make cuts, and more money flowing to citizens most at need, governors got creative with ways to fund state budgets. According to the National Governors Association, states would face a collective budget gap of $230 billion through 2010. To combat this, the most widely used method was to increase taxes—sales taxes, corporate taxes, personal income taxes, and the like—and impose new fees on consumers.

Tax increases, although unpopular with politicians and voters, received the greatest amount of attention in 2009, with Democrats and Republicans alike calling for tax hikes. In Illinois, the governor proposed increasing the state income tax by 50 percent, bringing it to 4.5 percent, which would have pinched citizens, especially those in Cook County (Chicago) who already had some of the nation's highest tax rates; in Arizona, Gov. Jan Brewer called for a $1 billion tax increase; and in Idaho, the gas tax and vehicle registration fees were increased. The recommendations became broader as the year went on. In Nevada, for example, the state recommended a tax on brothels, and in California, some legislators called for a $50-per-ounce tax on marijuana sales. (Medical use of marijuana is legal in the state.) People in California felt a majority of the tax and fee increase pain, seeing a 1 percent state sales tax increase, a personal income tax increase, and a higher fee to license a vehicle. Lower tax revenue also meant that the state's two university systems, the University of California and California State University, saw sharp tuition increases to make up for decreases in state education funding. At the University of California, a 32 percent tuition increase led to student protests across the state. Other states considering sales tax hikes included Arizona, Florida, Illinois, Kentucky, Massachusetts, and Rhode Island. Corporate tax increases were proposed in Delaware, Florida, Illinois, New Jersey, Oregon, and Wisconsin.

The most widely used tax, known as a "sin tax," was on alcohol, gas, and tobacco. States including Arkansas, Kentucky, and Rhode Island imposed or increased such fees, while more than a dozen states considered proposals for the tax. In New York, Gov. David Paterson recommended a so-called fat tax, which he said would be added to soda drinks. Various fees were proposed in half the states in 2010, and the goods and services to which to add fees ranged from divorce to death to the number of pigs and cows slaughtered.

Supplemental Nutrition Assistance Program (SNAP)

One of the first government programs many unemployed workers turn to when they lose their jobs is SNAP, the food stamp program, which allows those under a certain income level to purchase food items at the federal government's expense. When the recession hit, the food stamp program was in serious danger of running out of funds for families in need. In late spring, states put their focus on giving those who needed the money the most a larger amount. According to Mark Zandi, chief economist and cofounder of Moody's Economy.com, investing in the food stamp program was a sure way to quickly boost local economies. "People who receive these benefits are hard-pressed and will spend any financial aid they receive very quickly," said Zandi. For every dollar put into the food stamp program, local economies see a benefit of $1.73.

Beginning in April, states used funds offered by ARRA to increase food stamp benefits by about 13.6 percent per person, or approximately $20. "It's smart for states to promote food stamps," said Sheri Steisel, a poverty expert at the NCSL, "because that and unemployment checks often are enough to delay the need for other types of public assistance—such as welfare and Medicaid—that put pressure on state budgets."

Although the food stamp program benefited recipients and local economies that saw an influx of cash spent on necessities, because of the high number of unemployed, it was hard for many states to keep up with increasing demand. Yet, the benefit far outweighed the cost of processing additional paperwork. In Ohio, where 1.3 million residents were receiving food stamps, Gov. Ted Strickland worked with community leaders on an outreach program to get those who qualified registered to receive the benefit. In Nevada, one of the states hardest hit by the recession, the state set up computers in grocery stores for shoppers to be able to immediately find out whether they would be eligible to receive food stamps.

A Positive Outlook—For Some

Near the end of 2009, a report released by Moody's Economy.com reported that eleven states and the District of Columbia were beginning to climb out of recession. Alaska, Idaho, Indiana, Iowa, Louisiana, Mississippi, Missouri, Montana, Nebraska, North

Dakota, South Dakota, and the nation's capital were all showing signs of recovery based on their unemployment rate, home prices, and growth in the construction and manufacturing sectors of the economy. Thirty-eight other states, while not yet recovering, were beginning to see a slowing of the recession's effects.

The outlook was not rosy for all states. Nevada, the report said, was still deeply entrenched in recession. According to Moody's Economy.com, the state, which relies heavily on tourism and gambling dollars, was seeing its key economic indicators continue to drop as families cut back travel budgets.

Steve Cochrane, Moody's managing director, cautioned that although the outlook for states was beginning to improve, they were not anywhere near out of the water just yet. "We could see unemployment rise right through the first half of next year," he said, pointing to the fact that when companies begin producing more, they do not immediately begin hiring. He also cautioned that the end of federal stimulus dollars could hurt states that had put millions of dollars into infrastructure and social services projects, only to find that they would be left with the long-term cost, without any federal funds to back them up.

States will be slower to recover from the downturn than the nation as a whole, as budget gaps are a persistent problem, and the end of federal stimulus funding will mean deeper cuts to produce balanced budgets each year. Without the federal safety net provided by ARRA, some states, especially California, Kentucky, Nevada, New York, and Washington, which are seeing the largest budget deficits in recent history, will continue to have to make tough decisions for the foreseeable future.

—Heather Kerrigan

> *Following is the monthly state employment and unemployment report released on December 18, 2009, by the Bureau of Labor Statistics, and the text of a radio address given on December 30, 2009, by Michigan governor Jennifer Granholm on her state's economy.*

Bureau of Labor Statistics State Employment and Unemployment Report

December 18, 2009

Regional and state unemployment rates were generally lower in November. Thirty-six states and the District of Columbia recorded over-the-month unemployment rate decreases, 8 states registered rate increases, and 6 states had no rate change, the U.S. Bureau of Labor Statistics reported today. Over the year, jobless rates increased in all 50 states and the District of Columbia. The national unemployment rate edged down in November to 10.0 percent, 0.2 percentage point lower than October, but 3.2 points higher than November 2008.

In November, nonfarm payroll employment increased in 19 states and decreased in 31 states and the District of Columbia. The largest over-the-month increase in employment occurred in Texas (+17,300), followed by Ohio (+5,400), Georgia (+4,800), and Arizona and Iowa (+4,300 each).

Alaska experienced the largest over-the-month percentage increase in employment (+0.5 percent), followed by Iowa (+0.3 percent). The largest over-the-month decrease in employment occurred in Florida (-16,700), followed by Michigan (-14,000), California and Pennsylvania (-10,200 each), and New Jersey (-9,400). Hawaii (-1.0 percent) experienced the largest over-the-month percentage decrease in employment, followed by Nevada (-0.7 percent) and Maine, Mississippi, and Montana (-0.6 percent each). Over the year, nonfarm employment decreased in all 50 states and increased in the District of Columbia. The largest over-the-year percentage decreases occurred in Nevada (-6.1 percent), Wyoming (-6.0 percent), Michigan (-5.9 percent), Arizona (-5.6 percent), and Oregon (-5.2 percent).

REGIONAL UNEMPLOYMENT (SEASONALLY ADJUSTED)

In November, the West reported the highest regional jobless rate, 10.6 percent, while the Northeast recorded the lowest rate, 8.7 percent. These two regions experienced the only statistically significant over-the-month rate changes—the Northeast, -0.3 percentage point, and the West, -0.2 point. Over the year, all four regions registered significant rate increases, the largest of which was in the West (+3.4 percentage points).

Among the nine geographic divisions, the Pacific continued to report the highest jobless rate, 11.6 percent in November. The East North Central recorded the next highest rate, 11.0 percent. The West North Central registered the lowest November jobless rate, 7.2 percent, followed by the West South Central, 7.7 percent. The rate in the South Atlantic (10.0 percent) was the highest in its series. (All region, division, and state series begin in 1976.) Two divisions experienced statistically significant unemployment rate changes from a month earlier, the Mountain and West South Central (-0.3 percentage point each). In contrast, all nine divisions had significant over-the-year rate increases, with the largest of these occurring in the Pacific (+3.7 percentage points), East North Central (+3.6 points), and East South Central (+3.5 points).

STATE UNEMPLOYMENT (SEASONALLY ADJUSTED)

Michigan again recorded the highest unemployment rate among the states, 14.7 percent in November. The states with the next highest rates were Rhode Island, 12.7 percent, and California, Nevada, and South Carolina, 12.3 percent each. North Dakota continued to register the lowest jobless rate, 4.1 percent in November, followed by Nebraska, 4.5 percent, and South Dakota, 5.0 percent. The rate in South Carolina set a new series high, as did the rate in Florida (11.5 percent). In total, 31 states posted jobless rates significantly lower than the U.S. figure of 10.0 percent, 9 states and the District of Columbia had measurably higher rates, and 10 states had rates that were not appreciably different from that of the nation.

Seven states reported statistically significant over-the-month unemployment rate decreases in November. Kentucky and Connecticut experienced the largest of these (-0.7 and -0.6 percentage point, respectively). One state, Florida, posted a significant increase from October (+0.2 percentage point). The remaining 42 states and the District of

Columbia registered jobless rates that were not appreciably different from those of a month earlier, though some had changes that were at least as large numerically as the significant changes.

All states and the District of Columbia recorded statistically significant increases in their jobless rates from November 2008. The largest of these were in Michigan (+5.1 percentage points) and Alabama, Florida, and Nevada (+4.3 points each), while the smallest rate increases occurred in Nebraska and North Dakota (+0.9 point each).

Nonfarm Payroll Employment (Seasonally Adjusted)

In November, four states experienced statistically significant over-the-month changes in employment. Statistically significant job losses occurred in Michigan (-14,000), Nevada (-8,800), Mississippi (-6,100), and Hawaii (-6,000).

Over the year, 45 states experienced statistically significant changes in employment, all of which were decreases. The largest statistically significant job losses occurred in California (-617,600), Florida (-284,800), Texas (-271,700), Illinois (-250,400), Michigan (-240,200), and New York (-210,500). The smallest statistically significant decreases in employment occurred in South Dakota (-6,800) and Vermont (-7,800)....

[All tables and definitions have been omitted.]

Source: U.S. Bureau of Labor Statistics. Press release. "Regional and State Employment and Unemployment—November 2009." December 18, 2009. www.bls.gov/news.release/archives/laus_12182009.htm.

Gov. Jennifer Granholm on Michigan's Economy

December 30, 2009

Hello, this is Governor Jennifer Granholm.

One of the most difficult years in Michigan history is drawing to a close. In 2009, the unimaginable happened with the bankruptcies of General Motors and Chrysler. The subsequent restructuring of the auto industry has made one thing crystal clear: The old Michigan economy is gone, and it's not coming back.

In response, our strategy continues to be to diversify Michigan's economy, educate and train our citizens for 21st century jobs, and protect people during this transition from the old economy to the new.

Our diversification plan focuses on six economic sectors: advanced manufacturing, such as nanotechnology and robotics; clean energy; life sciences; defense and homeland security; tourism; and film. Let me highlight just a few of this year's successes.

Michigan is well on its way to becoming the advanced-battery capital of the world. State tax credit legislation that I signed in January combined with the Department of Energy grants announced in August have laid the foundation for this entire new industry. Battery plants will begin sprouting up across the state, from Holland on the west side to Brownstown Township on the east. An MSU economist projects that up to 40,000 jobs will be created in this industry by the year 2020.

Solar energy manufacturing also is rapidly growing with investments topping $3.5 billion over the last five years. The Saginaw Valley area is emerging as a hub for solar manufacturing, with another two companies recently announcing they're joining Hemlock Semiconductor in the area.

Advanced manufacturing is also on the rise. General Motors announced recently it's investing $700 million to build the Chevrolet Volt in Michigan. Ford will invest $550 million in its Wayne Assembly plant to build its new electric vehicle, and Chrysler is investing $179 million to build a new engine in Dundee.

With more than 540 life sciences companies, Michigan ranks second in the nation for overall industrial research. Defense contracts and jobs have doubled in the state since 2007, and we see continued growth in our tourism and film industries.

For economic diversification to continue to succeed, we need an educated and trained workforce. So more than 105,000 people have enrolled in our No Worker Left Behind program to receive training for jobs in high demand—105,000 people. And the Race to the Top education reforms recently passed by the state Legislature are going to help prepare our children for college and beyond.

While 2009 was a tough year for Michigan, better days lie ahead. Our plan to diversify Michigan's economy, educate and train our citizens, and protect people during this time of economic transition is the right plan for Michigan.

Thank you for listening.

SOURCE: Office of Governor of Michigan Jennifer Granholm. Press release. "Governor Granholm Says While 2009 Was Tough, Better Days Lie Ahead." December 30, 2009. www.michigan.gov/gov/0,1607, 7-168-23442_21974-228774--,00.html.

OTHER HISTORIC DOCUMENTS OF INTEREST

FROM THIS VOLUME

FROM PREVIOUS *HISTORIC DOCUMENTS*

UN Summit on Climate Change

DECEMBER 19, 2009

To address the issue of climate change around the world, international leaders gathered at the request of the United Nations in Copenhagen, Denmark, in December to work together to find solutions to combat this international issue. Various behind-the-scenes meetings and deals took place, and on December 19, 2009, world leaders at the summit announced the Copenhagen Accord, expressing shared ideals of working toward climate change, which many considered to be a complete failure of the meeting—derailed mainly by China, a nation that, since the summer Olympic Games of 2008, had been the target of widespread criticism over its poor air quality. Regardless of the meaningfulness of the resolution, UN secretary-general Ban Ki-moon tried to end the summit on a positive note. "We have sealed the deal. This accord cannot be everything that everyone had hoped for, but it is an essential beginning," he said.

Copenhagen

As a precursor to Copenhagen, Ban had invited world leaders to meet in New York City at the United Nations building in September, to "mobilize political will and strengthen momentum for a fair, effective, and ambitious climate deal in Copenhagen this December." The day-long summit was opened by Ban, who said that "[f]ailure to reach broad agreement in Copenhagen would be morally inexcusable, economically short-sighted and politically unwise. Now is the moment to act in common cause." For U.S. president Barack Obama and Japanese prime minister Yukio Hatoyama, the occasion was their first meeting and first opportunity to speak on this world stage.

When the leaders arrived in Denmark, it quickly became clear that the preliminary meeting in New York would mean little to the negotiations. Some delegates at the conference walked out in protest, and Connie Hedegaard, the Danish minister heading the summit, resigned her conference position. Although some saw the resignation as an indication that talks were not going as well as planned, according to some reports, it was more a formality and an indication that the talks had reached a high enough level that the Danish prime minister would be more appropriate to lead the remainder of the summit.

As the high-level negotiations reached their final days, Ban reminded attendees that this was their chance to make real progress on climate change. By working to reduce carbon emissions, Ban said, "We have a chance—a real chance, here and now—to change the course of our history." He encouraged developing and industrialized nations to work together toward the common goal of stopping climate change, rather than blaming one another as the cause of the problem. "This is a time to stop pointing fingers," said Ban.

"This is a time to start looking in the mirror and offering what they can do more of." In making these remarks, Ban hit on a key issue stalling negotiations—finger pointing between developing and industrialized nations. U.S. secretary of state Hillary Rodham Clinton did little to stop the blame game, contributing an opinion piece to the *International Herald Tribune* in which she wrote, "Nearly all of the growth in emissions in the next 20 years will come from the developing world." She continued, "Without their participation and commitment, a solution is impossible." The environmental policy of the United States, however, was not without criticism at the summit. President Obama made it clear from the beginning that he would not sign any agreement that forced the United States to cut carbon emissions by more than 4 percent by 2020, a blow to nations who wanted a greater commitment from the world's largest economic power. Lumumba Di-Aping, the representative of 130 developing nations at the summit, in reaction to the blame Obama placed on the developing world, said, "Obama has eliminated any difference between himself and Bush."

Although many industrialized nations were working to find cleaner energy alternatives, the developing world was not yet in a position to make that move and saw the finger pointing as a threat to their future growth and prosperity. If restrictions were imposed on carbon emissions in developing nations, their representatives argued, they would not be able to follow in the footsteps of Western nations that had not faced such restrictions as they moved toward prosperity hundreds of years earlier.

PROTESTS IN COPENHAGEN

The meetings in Denmark were not without incident. Danish police arrested hundreds of protestors who had organized demonstrations around the buildings where the summit was taking place. The Climate Justice Action (CJA) group, which organized many of the protests, called on its members to "take over the conference for one day and transform it into a 'People's Assembly.'" This People's Assembly, according to the group, would speak out against the "false solutions and elitism of the UN climate talks." According to the group, as protestors began their march from a train station to the summit site, police used pepper spray and dogs to control the crowd.

Although the CJA claimed that its protests were peaceful, police in Denmark said the group and other protestors, including those from the group Friends of the Earth, had been throwing fireworks and stones at the police, setting vehicles on fire and breaking nearby windows.

A WEAK AGREEMENT

According to Yvo de Boer, the executive secretary of the UN Framework Convention on Climate Change, the conference did not make the amount of headway on the issue of global warming that he had hoped. "There is still an enormous amount of work and ground to be covered if this conference is to deliver what people around the world expect it to deliver," he said during a news conference. Many international observers and leaders who had been in attendance at the summit agreed. The failure to reach a solid agreement meant developing and industrialized nations would have to go back to the drawing board and that it could be months before a strong agreement might be reached. "This progress is not enough," President Obama said. "We have come a long way, but we have much further to go," he said. British prime minister Gordon Brown saw progress in a few different areas and considered the meeting a move in the direction of international cooperation on climate change: "This is the first step we are taking toward a green and low carbon future for the world, steps we are taking together. But like all first steps, the steps are difficult and they are hard."

The accord agreed to by the nations in attendance, which had not been adopted by the end of 2009 by all 192 countries present at the summit, did little more than recognize the need for global action on climate change. According to Di-Aping, the deal had "the lowest level of ambition you can imagine. It's nothing short of climate change skepticism in action. It locks countries into a cycle of poverty forever." Specifics of the deal included a provision for poor, developing nations to receive $30 billion per year to meet climate change standards from 2010 to 2012; the amount would increase to $100 billion per year by 2020. Although the funds would provide many nations the resources necessary to meet the international climate goals, representatives from developing nations were unhappy with the overall outcome of the summit, because they expected an agreement that would help meet the goal of reducing carbon emissions by 80 percent by 2050, a goal discussed early on in the summit but dropped before the accord was written. The accord also called for the end of deforestation and the offer to pay any nation that could significantly reduce the process, another issue that drew the ire of developing nations.

The Problem with China

The summit produced eight drafts of a resolution, but rather than putting in place regulations for slowing climate change, it simply recognized the scientific evidence of global warming and the urgent necessity to ensure average temperatures rise no more than 2° Celsius. In the end, it came down to negotiations with China, whose leaders were resistant to the regulations suggested by Western nations. President Obama met with the leaders of China, South Africa, India, and Brazil late into the night during the last days of the conference to work on an agreement that would provide $30 billion per year to developing nations to help them implement climate change policies. This $30 billion would be made available from 2010 to 2012 and would then increase to $100 billion per year by 2020.

The United States had met in November with Indian and Chinese officials before coming to Copenhagen in hopes that bilateral talks would help secure a better deal in Copenhagen. Some observers had cautioned that the bilateral talks could lessen the chances for a strong agreement at the climate change summit, as India and China were both looking to block limits on greenhouse gases, and their warnings proved true. The United States had moved ahead with the talks, however, viewing the two nations as key to securing a deal in Copenhagen. Sen. Ben Cardin, D-Md., a member of the foreign relations and environmental committees, said, "China and India are critically important to achieving our international goals on carbon reduction. We need them as part of the system."

India's major goal in both the preliminary meetings with the United States and at the summit was to work with the United States and other members of the international community to help develop green technologies for use in its country. The United States had reached a similar agreement with China in the summer of 2009, and India hoped to replicate it. According to Indian environment minister Jairam Ramesh, India would be working on its own plan to limit greenhouse gas emissions. "We are going to introduce a domestic cap-and-trade programme," said Ramesh, "but the cap will be on energy intensity, not carbon." This plan, India argued, would help it continue to grow and develop while still limiting the pollutants it released into the atmosphere.

Some international observers were hopeful that the United States would be able to get the summit started on the right track by formulating agreements with China. "If the US and China can come to some sort of view on this then I think it will unlock a lot of things," said Björn Stigson, the president of the World Business Council for Sustainable Development. "If that is not the case then I think we will not see a very comprehensive agreement in Copenhagen."

In the end, China refused to work on the draft that had been proposed by Danish leaders at the meeting, which would have broken through the indecision at the summit. Kevin Rudd, Denmark's prime minister and leader of the summit, urged the Chinese to reconsider their decision. He continued finger pointing, accusing the developing world of potentially causing future global warming if they were unwilling to negotiate with industrialized nations. "If the developed world became carbon neutral and the developing world continued to grow on current trends, then the truth is that the emerging economies alone would be responsible for more than half of total global emissions by 2050."

Chinese officials announced that they wanted no more than a "political declaration" to be released at this meeting although they offered no indication about what it should include. President Obama indicated that the Chinese had caused the breakdown of the meetings and condemned developing nations for their unwillingness to act. Those countries, the president said, need to recognize "that we all need to move together" on climate change. Although one of President Obama's objectives vis-à-vis China was for their climate reporting to be more transparent, by the end of the summit, he had backed down on this point, agreeing to allow all nations to report progress every two years, and not requiring verification by independent scientists. Some feared President Obama risked further alienation of China on climate change when he suggested that the United States could use spy satellites to ensure that China was meeting international climate goals.

DISAPPOINTMENT IN DEVELOPING NATIONS

China was not alone in its distaste for the agreements brokered at the summit. Although industrialized nations praised a plan presented by Ethiopia to encourage the United Nations to provide $100 billion per year to the developing world by 2020 for efforts to stem climate change, organizations working for the economic security of African nations were frustrated. "If Prime Minister Meles [Zenawi] wants to sell out the lives and hopes of Africans for a pittance, he is welcome to—but that is not Africa's position," said Mithika Mwenda of the Pan-American Climate Justice Alliance.

Developing nations came to the summit with hope that the global temperature increase could be held to 1.5° Celsius. This hope looked to be agreed on until the last minute, when leaders changed the accord language to 2° Celsius.

Developing nations saw the accord as an attempt by industrialized countries to escape blame for climate change. Di-Aping said the agreement was "asking Africa to sign a suicide pact, an incineration pact in order to maintain the economic dependence of a few countries."

—Heather Kerrigan

Following is a press release from December 19, 2009, on the conclusion of the climate change summit in Copenhagen, Denmark, and the text of the Copenhagen Accord, agreed to on December 19, 2009, at the UN conference on climate change.

Press Release on End of Climate Change Summit

December 19, 2009

The United Nations Climate Change Conference in Copenhagen ended today with an agreement by countries to cap the global temperature rise by committing to significant emission reductions, and to raise finance to kickstart action in the developing world to deal with climate change.

At the meeting, world leaders agreed the "Copenhagen Accord", which was supported by a majority of countries, including amongst them the biggest and the richest, and the smallest and most vulnerable.

"We have sealed the deal," said UN Secretary-General Ban Ki-moon said. "This accord cannot be everything that everyone hoped for, but it is an essential beginning," he said.

The Copenhagen Accord recognizes the scientific view that an increase in global temperature below 2 degrees is required to stave off the worst effects of climate change.

In order to achieve this goal, the accord specifies that industrialised countries will commit to implement, individually or jointly, quantified economy-wide emissions targets from 2020, to be listed in the accord before 31 January 2010.

A number of developing countries, including major emerging economies, agreed to communicate their efforts to limit greenhouse gas emissions every two years, also listing their voluntary pledges before the 31 January 2010.

Nationally appropriate mitigation actions seeking international support are to be recorded in a registry along with relevant technology, finance and capacity building support from industrialised nations.

"We must be honest about what we have got," said UNFCCC [United Nations Framework Convention on Climate Change] Executive Secretary Yvo de Boer. "The world walks away from Copenhagen with a deal. But clearly ambitions to reduce emissions must be raised significantly if we are to hold the world to 2 degrees," he added.

Because the pledges listed by developed and developing countries may, according to science, be found insufficient to keep the global temperature rise below 2 degrees or less, leaders called for a review of the accord, to be completed by 2015.

The review would include a consideration of the long-term goal to limit the global average temperature rise to 1.5 degrees.

Heads of state and government also intend to unleash prompt action on mitigation, adaptation, finance, technology, reducing emissions from deforestation in developing countries and capacity-building.

To this effect, they intend to establish the "Copenhagen Green Climate Fund" to support immediate action on climate change. The collective commitment towards the fund by developed countries over the next three years will approach 30 billion US dollars.

For long-term finance, developed countries agreed to support a goal of jointly mobilizing 100 billion dollars a year by 2020 to address the needs of developing countries.

In order to step up action on the development and transfer of technology, governments intend to establish a new technology mechanism to accelerate development and transfer in support of action on adaptation and mitigation.

119 world leaders attended the meeting, the largest gathering of heads of state and government in the history of the UN. "Climate change is the permanent leadership challenge of our time," said UN Secretary-General Ban Ki-moon. "I therefore urge world leaders to remain engaged," he said.

"We now have a package to work with and begin immediate action," said UNFCCC Executive Secretary Yvo de Boer. "However, we need to be clear that it is a letter of intent and is not precise about what needs to be done in legal terms. So the challenge is now to turn what we have agreed politically in Copenhagen into something real, measurable and verifiable," he added.

The next annual UN Climate Change Conference will take place towards the end of 2010 in Mexico City, preceded by a major two week negotiating session in Bonn, Germany, scheduled 31 May to 11 June.

About the UNFCCC

With 194 Parties, the United Nations Framework Convention on Climate Change (UNFCCC) has near universal membership and is the parent treaty of the 1997 Kyoto Protocol. The Kyoto Protocol has been ratified by 190 of the UNFCCC Parties. Under the Protocol, 37 States, consisting of highly industrialized countries and countries undergoing the process of transition to a market economy, have legally binding emission limitation and reduction commitments. The ultimate objective of both treaties is to stabilize greenhouse gas concentrations in the atmosphere at a level that will prevent dangerous human interference with the climate system.

Source: United Nations Framework Convention on Climate Change. "Copenhagen United Nations Climate Change Conference Ends with Political Agreement to Cap Temperature Rise, Reduce Emissions and Raise Finance." December 19, 2009. http://unfccc.int/files/press/news_room/press_releases_and_advisories/application/pdf/pr_cop15_20091219.pdf.

Copenhagen Accord on Climate Change

December 19, 2009

Decision -/CP.15

The Conference of the Parties,
    Takes note of the Copenhagen Accord of 18 December 2009.

Copenhagen Accord

The Heads of State, Heads of Government, Ministers, and other heads of the following delegations present at the United Nations Climate Change Conference 2009 in Copenhagen: [*List of Parties*]
    In pursuit of the ultimate objective of the Convention as stated in its Article 2,
    Being guided by the principles and provisions of the Convention,
    Noting the results of work done by the two Ad hoc Working Groups,
    Endorsing decision x/CP.15 on the Ad hoc Working Group on Long-term Cooperative Action and decision x/CMP.5 that requests the Ad hoc Working Group on Further Commitments of Annex I Parties under the Kyoto Protocol to continue its work,
    Have agreed on this Copenhagen Accord which is operational immediately.

1. We underline that climate change is one of the greatest challenges of our time. We emphasise our strong political will to urgently combat climate change in accordance with the principle of common but differentiated responsibilities and respective capabilities. To achieve the ultimate objective of the Convention to stabilize greenhouse gas concentration in the atmosphere at a level that would prevent dangerous anthropogenic interference with the climate system, we shall, recognizing the scientific view that the increase in global temperature should be below 2 degrees Celsius, on the basis of equity and in the context of sustainable development, enhance our long-term cooperative action to combat climate change. We recognize the critical impacts of climate change and the potential impacts of response measures on countries particularly vulnerable to its adverse effects and stress the need to establish a comprehensive adaptation programme including international support.

2. We agree that deep cuts in global emissions are required according to science, and as documented by the IPCC Fourth Assessment Report with a view to reduce global emissions so as to hold the increase in global temperature below 2 degrees Celsius, and take action to meet this objective consistent with science and on the basis of equity. We should cooperate in achieving the peaking of global and national emissions as soon as possible, recognizing that the time frame for peaking will be longer in developing countries and bearing in mind that social and economic development and poverty eradication are the first and overriding priorities of developing countries and that a low-emission development strategy is indispensable to sustainable development.

3. Adaptation to the adverse effects of climate change and the potential impacts of response measures is a challenge faced by all countries. Enhanced action and international

cooperation on adaptation is urgently required to ensure the implementation of the Convention by enabling and supporting the implementation of adaptation actions aimed at reducing vulnerability and building resilience in developing countries, especially in those that are particularly vulnerable, especially least developed countries, small island developing States and Africa. We agree that developed countries shall provide adequate, predictable and sustainable financial resources, technology and capacity-building to support the implementation of adaptation action in developing countries.

4. Annex I Parties commit to implement individually or jointly the quantified economy-wide emissions targets for 2020, to be submitted in the format given in Appendix I by Annex I Parties to the secretariat by 31 January 2010 for compilation in an INF document. Annex I Parties that are Party to the Kyoto Protocol will thereby further strengthen the emissions reductions initiated by the Kyoto Protocol. Delivery of reductions and financing by developed countries will be measured, reported and verified in accordance with existing and any further guidelines adopted by the Conference of the Parties, and will ensure that accounting of such targets and finance is rigorous, robust and transparent.

5. Non-Annex I Parties to the Convention will implement mitigation actions, including those to be submitted to the secretariat by non-Annex I Parties in the format given in Appendix II by 31 January 2010, for compilation in an INF document, consistent with Article 4.1 and Article 4.7 and in the context of sustainable development. Least developed countries and small island developing States may undertake actions voluntarily and on the basis of support. Mitigation actions subsequently taken and envisaged by Non-Annex I Parties, including national inventory reports, shall be communicated through national communications consistent with Article 12.1(b) every two years on the basis of guidelines to be adopted by the Conference of the Parties. Those mitigation actions in national communications or otherwise communicated to the Secretariat will be added to the list in appendix II. Mitigation actions taken by Non-Annex I Parties will be subject to their domestic measurement, reporting and verification the result of which will be reported through their national communications every two years. Non-Annex I Parties will communicate information on the implementation of their actions through National Communications, with provisions for international consultations and analysis under clearly defined guidelines that will ensure that national sovereignty is respected. Nationally appropriate mitigation actions seeking international support will be recorded in a registry along with relevant technology, finance and capacity building support. Those actions supported will be added to the list in appendix II. These supported nationally appropriate mitigation actions will be subject to international measurement, reporting and verification in accordance with guidelines adopted by the Conference of the Parties.

6. We recognize the crucial role of reducing emission from deforestation and forest degradation and the need to enhance removals of greenhouse gas emission by forests and agree on the need to provide positive incentives to such actions through the immediate establishment of a mechanism including REDD-plus, to enable the mobilization of financial resources from developed countries.

7. We decide to pursue various approaches, including opportunities to use markets, to enhance the cost-effectiveness of, and to promote mitigation actions. Developing countries, especially those with low emitting economies should be provided incentives to continue to develop on a low emission pathway.

8. Scaled up, new and additional, predictable and adequate funding as well as improved access shall be provided to developing countries, in accordance with the relevant provisions of the Convention, to enable and support enhanced action on mitigation, including substantial finance to reduce emissions from deforestation and forest degradation (REDD-plus), adaptation, technology development and transfer and capacity-building, for enhanced implementation of the Convention. The collective commitment by developed countries is to provide new and additional resources, including forestry and investments through international institutions, approaching USD 30 billion for the period 2010–2012 with balanced allocation between adaptation and mitigation. Funding for adaptation will be prioritized for the most vulnerable developing countries, such as the least developed countries, small island developing States and Africa. In the context of meaningful mitigation actions and transparency on implementation, developed countries commit to a goal of mobilizing jointly USD 100 billion dollars a year by 2020 to address the needs of developing countries. This funding will come from a wide variety of sources, public and private, bilateral and multilateral, including alternative sources of finance. New multilateral funding for adaptation will be delivered through effective and efficient fund arrangements, with a governance structure providing for equal representation of developed and developing countries. A significant portion of such funding should flow through the Copenhagen Green Climate Fund.

9. To this end, a High Level Panel will be established under the guidance of and accountable to the Conference of the Parties to study the contribution of the potential sources of revenue, including alternative sources of finance, towards meeting this goal.

10. We decide that the Copenhagen Green Climate Fund shall be established as an operating entity of the financial mechanism of the Convention to support projects, programme, policies and other activities in developing countries related to mitigation including REDD-plus, adaptation, capacity-building, technology development and transfer.

11. In order to enhance action on development and transfer of technology we decide to establish a Technology Mechanism to accelerate technology development and transfer in support of action on adaptation and mitigation that will be guided by a country-driven approach and be based on national circumstances and priorities.

12. We call for an assessment of the implementation of this Accord to be completed by 2015, including in light of the Convention's ultimate objective. This would include consideration of strengthening the long-term goal referencing various matters presented by the science, including in relation to temperature rises of 1.5 degrees Celsius.

SOURCE: United Nations Framework Convention on Climate Change. "Copenhagen Accord." December 19, 2009. http://unfccc.int/files/meetings/cop_15/application/pdf/cop15_cph_auv.pdf.

OTHER HISTORIC DOCUMENTS OF INTEREST

FROM THIS VOLUME

- The Department of Transportation and the Environmental Protection Agency Release New Fuel Economy Standards, p. 442

FROM PREVIOUS *HISTORIC DOCUMENTS*

- Intergovernmental Panel of Scientists on Climate Change, *2007*, p. 657
- EPA Report on Global Warming, *2002*, p. 298
- UN Scientific Panel on Global Warming, *2001*, p. 109
- Committee of Scientists on the Impact of Global Warming, *2000*, p. 337

Attempted Christmas Day Plane Bombing

DECEMBER 26, 28, AND 29, 2009

On December 25, 2009, on a flight from Amsterdam to Detroit, Michigan, a Nigerian man unsuccessfully attempted to ignite a bomb. His actions claimed no victims. The incident was immediately called "an attempted act of terrorism" by the White House. The device the accused bomber was able to transport through security and on to the plane raised questions about whether security procedures needed to be increased to accommodate new and growing threats.

ATTEMPTED BOMBING

Aboard Northwest Airlines Flight 253, which was filled with 278 passengers, twenty-three-year-old Umar Farouk Abdulmutallab spent much of the time in the bathroom, complaining of an upset stomach. When he returned to his seat, Abdulmutallab pulled a blanket over his body and head, telling the person sitting next to him that he was not feeling well. At this point, Abdulmutallab attempted to ignite a mixture of powder and liquid in an effort to blow up the plane. The device, which did not fully ignite, made popping noises, startling passengers and starting a small fire. Syed Jafry, a passenger on the flight, heard "a pop that sounded like a firecracker," and then, "there was a panic. Next thing you know everybody was on him," Jafry said. The quick-thinking crew and passengers were able to extinguish the fire and subdue Abdulmutallab until the plane landed, and federal officials took him into custody. According to federal officials, Abdulmutallab suffered severe burns from the explosive device hidden in his underpants and was taken to the University of Michigan to be treated at the school's hospital.

After the attack, a senior official in the Obama administration said that he was unsure of the exact motive of the man or how he had managed to get through security with substances that could be used to create a bomb. "We're trying to ascertain exactly what he had and what he thought he was doing, but our sense is he wanted to wreak some havoc here and was attempting to do just that," the official said. Rep. Peter King, R-N.Y., called the attack "the real deal." According to King, "This could have been devastating."

Officials could not immediately determine whether Abdulmutallab would have been able to cause a significant amount of damage with the device had he been able to ignite it successfully. According to an official with the Department of Homeland Security, the powder, which Abdulmutallab had taped to his leg, and the chemicals he mixed in a syringe, were "more incendiary than explosive."

Officials refused to speculate about whether Abdulmutallab was associated with a known terrorist organization. "It's too early to say what his association is," a counterterrorism official said after the attack, but "[a]t this point, it seems like he was acting alone, but we don't know for sure."

The attack wrecked havoc on holiday travel, as extra security measures were put in place at airport screening checkpoints and on board planes, where some airlines banned keeping anything on one's lap, including a book to read, within one hour of landing. Bomb-sniffing dogs added an extra level of screening for luggage, and behavioral specialists were assigned to security checkpoints in plain clothes, looking for passengers displaying odd or nervous behavior. Some, including Representative King, a ranking member on the House Homeland Security Committee, called for even higher levels of security for people on flights originating in Nigeria. "For a while now," Representative King said, "we have had real concerns about Al Qaeda or terrorist connections in Nigeria." Coincidentally, the Transportation Security Administration (TSA) had in November asserted that Nigeria's Lagos airport conformed to international security standards. According to security officials, the explosive ingredients were smuggled on during Abdulmutallab's connecting flight at Schiphol airport in the Netherlands. However, the national coordinator for counterterrorism said the checkpoints at the airport displayed no irregularities that would have led to a breach in security. The official added, "It cannot be excluded," however, "that potentially dangerous items were brought on board, especially objects that cannot be read by current technology."

UMAR FAROUK ABDULMUTALLAB

Abdulmutallab came from a privileged background. As the son of a former Nigerian economics minister who still serves on the boards of some of the nation's most prominent banks, Abdulmutallab had the opportunity to study in London, where he lived in a nearly $3 million apartment. Given his background, he did not fit the profile of the typical terrorist suspect. Those who knew Abdulmutallab said he was quiet and unassuming, a practicing Muslim who never showed any signs of extremism during his time at University College London, where he graduated in 2008. Abdulmutallab returned home to Nigeria after graduation and later tried to go back to London but was denied a visa. In an attempt to get a visa, Abdulmutallab had registered for a short academic course, but it was considered "not genuine" by the United Kingdom Border Agency. After being rejected, Abdulmutallab withdrew from family life and was not seen by friends or family for some time.

EARLY WARNINGS AND REACTION

After the bombing, it came to light that Abdulmutallab had been on a security watch list after his father warned the U.S. government about his son's extremist views, "radicalization and associations," according to the U.S. embassy in Nigeria. It came as a surprise to some that the threat Abdulmutallab posed was not noticed earlier. According to Magnus Ranstorp, with the Center for Asymmetric Threat Studies in Sweden, "On the one hand, it seems he's been on the terror watch list but not on the no-fly list. That doesn't square because the American Department for Homeland Security has pretty stringent data-mining capability.

I don't understand how he had a valid visa if he was known on the terror watch list." The United States had indeed known for at least two years that Abdulmutallab had ties to terrorist organizations and was on a list that was kept by the National Counterterrorism Center, which includes 550,000 names. The U.S. State Department failed to revoke Abdulmutallab's visa because his name was misspelled when run through a State Department computer system.

According to U.S. officials, Abdulmutallab's name was never put on a no-fly list because of "insufficient derogatory information available." Although Abdulmutallab had been denied a visa to return to the United Kingdom, he was granted one by the United States in June 2008 and used it to visit at least twice before the attempted bombing. According to federal officials, before the visa was issued, Abdulmutallab had been interviewed "and his name was run against the watch list maintained by [the Department of Homeland Security] and the FBI. There was no indication of any derogatory information. There is every indication that whatever radicalization took place occurred recently," the official said on the condition on anonymity.

CHARGES

On December 26, Abdulmutallab was charged with attempting to destroy an aircraft and bringing a destructive device on board an aircraft. The U.S. District Court for Eastern Michigan, which announced the charges, said if convicted, Abdulmutallab could be sentenced to up to forty years in prison. Because Abdulmutallab was seriously injured during the attempted bombing, the charges against him were read in a hospital conference room.

According to investigators, Abdulmutallab had visited Yemen, where he received training from a terrorist organization with ties to al-Qaida. During his time in Yemen, he was taught how to assemble and ignite explosive devices.

The attempted bombing raised new questions about how federal agencies charged with security share information with each other and whether the Obama counterterrorism program was strong enough to thwart attacks. Republicans in Congress criticized the administration for not instituting tough enough standards on terrorism. "I think the administration is finally recognizing that they got this terrorism thing all wrong," said Rep. Peter Hoekstra, R-Mich., a ranking member of the House intelligence committee.

In response to the attacks, the TSA began requiring that passengers coming to the United States receive a "thorough pat-down" before being allowed to board a flight. Former secretary of the Department of Homeland Security Michael Chertoff encouraged increased use of better imaging systems at airports that would more easily detect explosive devices. "This plot is an example of something we've known could exist in theory, and in order to be able to detect it, you've got to find some way of detecting things in parts of the body that aren't easy to get at," he said. "It's either pat-downs or imaging." Chertoff said many TSA screeners have inhibitions against conducting thorough pat-downs because travelers see it as an infringement on their privacy.

ANOTHER NEAR TRAGEDY

Supporters of tighter airport security called the attempted Christmas Day bombing just another near miss. According to Sally Leivesley, an expert on terrorism, there have been a number of incidents in which passengers tried to ignite chemical substances and failed. The other most notable attempt occurred in 2001, when Richard Reid attempted to detonate a bomb he had hidden in his shoe but was stopped by crew and passengers.

One troubling theme Leivesley noted was an increase in the number of air passengers concealing weapons on their bodies, including some who implant the device. Leivesley said airport screeners need to be on the look out for people who have been trained or sedated to appear calm when boarding a plane. This was considered the case with Abdulmutallab, who may not have been fully prepared or capable of carrying out a terrorist attack, especially given his willingness to be subdued by the crew on the flight.

After the attempted bombing, President Barack Obama ordered a review of security measures for travelers and an additional review of what went wrong in the intelligence community and how information on Abdulmutallab was handled. This review came after Homeland Security Secretary Janet Napolitano suffered serious public backlash after stating that the failure of the bomber showed that the security systems in place were working. According to President Obama, "When our Government has information on a known extremist and that information is not shared and acted upon as it should have been, so that this extremist boards a plane with dangerous explosives that could have cost nearly 300 lives, a systemic failure has occurred."

—Heather Kerrigan

Following is a press release from the Detroit field office of the Federal Bureau of Investigation from December 26, 2009, announcing the charges against Umar Farouk Abdulmutallab for attempting to blow up a plane on December 25; remarks by President Barack Obama on December 28, 2009, about the event; and remarks by President Obama on December 29, 2009, on strengthening homeland security in light of the attempted bombing.

Nigerian National Charged in Attempted Christmas Day Plane Bombing

December 26, 2009

A 23-year-old Nigerian man was charged in a federal criminal complaint today with attempting to destroy a Northwest Airlines aircraft on its final approach to Detroit Metropolitan Airport on Christmas Day and with placing a destructive device on the aircraft.

According to an affidavit filed in support of the criminal complaint, Umar Farouk Abdulmutallab, 23, a Nigerian national, boarded Northwest Flight 253 in Amsterdam, Netherlands on December 24, 2009 and had a device attached to his body. As the flight was approaching Detroit Metropolitan Airport, Abdulmutallab set off the device, which resulted in a fire and what appears to have been an explosion. Abdulmutallab was then subdued and restrained by the passengers and flight crew. The airplane landed shortly thereafter, and he was taken into custody by Customs and Border Patrol officers.

A preliminary FBI analysis found that the device contained PETN, also known as pentaerythritol, a high explosive. Further analysis is ongoing. In addition, FBI agents recovered what appear to be the remnants of the syringe from the vicinity of Abdulmutallab's seat, believed to have been part of the device.

"This alleged attack on a U.S. airplane on Christmas Day shows that we must remain vigilant in the fight against terrorism at all times," Attorney General Eric Holder said. "Had this alleged plot to destroy an airplane been successful, scores of innocent people would have been killed or injured. We will continue to investigate this matter vigorously, and we will use all measures available to our government to ensure that anyone responsible for this attempted attack is brought to justice[.]"

Abdulmutallab required medical treatment and was transported to the University of Michigan Medical Center after the plane landed. He will make his initial court appearance later today.

Interviews of all of the passengers and crew of Flight 253 revealed that prior to the incident, Abdulmutallab went to the bathroom for approximately 20 minutes, according to the affidavit. Upon returning to his seat, Abdulmutallab stated that his stomach was upset, and he pulled a blanket over himself. Passengers then heard popping noises similar to firecrackers, smelled an odor, and some observed Abdulmutallab's pants leg and the wall of the airplane on fire. Passengers and crew then subdued Abdulmutallab and used blankets and fire extinguishers to put out the flames. Passengers reported that Abdulmutallab was calm and lucid throughout. One flight attendant asked him what he had had in his pocket, and he replied "explosive device."

These prosecutions are being handled by the U.S. Attorney's Office for the Eastern District of Michigan, with assistance from the Counterterrorism Section of the Justice Department's National Security Division.

The investigation is being conducted by the Federal Bureau of Investigation, U.S. Customs and Border Protection, and the Joint Terrorism Task Force. The public is reminded that criminal complaints contain mere allegations, and a defendant is presumed innocent until proven guilty.

SOURCE: Federal Bureau of Investigation. Press release. "Nigerian National Charged with Attempting to Destroy Northwest Airlines Aircraft." December 26, 2009. http://detroit.fbi.gov/dojpressrel/pressrel09/de122609.htm.

 **DOCUMENT** *President Obama on the Attempted Christmas Day Plane Bombing*

December 28, 2009

. . . I want to take just a few minutes to update the American people on the attempted terrorist attack that occurred on Christmas Day and the steps we're taking to ensure the safety and security of the country.

The investigation's ongoing, and I spoke again this morning with Attorney General Eric Holder, the Secretary of Homeland Security Janet Napolitano, and my Counterterrorism and Homeland Security Adviser, John Brennan. I asked them to keep—continue monitoring the situation, to keep the American people and Members of Congress informed.

Here's what we know so far. On Christmas Day, Northwest Airlines Flight 253 was en route from Amsterdam, Netherlands, to Detroit. As the plane made its final approach to Detroit Metropolitan Airport, a passenger allegedly tried to ignite an explosive device on his body, setting off a fire.

Thanks to the quick and heroic actions of passengers and crew, the suspect was immediately subdued, the fire was put out, and the plane landed safely. The suspect is now in custody and has been charged with attempting to destroy an aircraft. And a full investigation has been launched into this attempted act of terrorism, and we will not rest until we find all who were involved and hold them accountable.

Now, this was a serious reminder of the dangers that we face and the nature of those who threaten our homeland. Had the suspect succeeded in bringing down that plane, it could have killed nearly 300 passengers and crew, innocent civilians preparing to celebrate the holidays with their families and friends.

The American people should be assured that we are doing everything in our power to keep you and your families safe and secure during this busy holiday season. Since I was first notified of this incident, I've ordered the following actions to be taken to protect the American people and to secure air travel.

First, I directed that we take immediate steps to ensure the safety of the traveling public. We made sure that all flights still in the air were secure and could land safely. We immediately enhanced screening and security procedures for all flights, domestic and international. We added Federal air marshals to flights entering and leaving the United States. And we're working closely in this country—Federal, State, and local law enforcement—with our international partners.

Second, I've ordered two important reviews, because it's absolutely critical that we learn from this incident and take the necessary measures to prevent future acts of terrorism. The first review involves our watch list system, which our Government has had in place for many years to identify known and suspected terrorists so that we can prevent their entry into the United States.

Apparently, the suspect in the Christmas incident was in this system, but not on a watch list such as the so-called no-fly list. So I've ordered a thorough review not only of how information related to the subject was handled but of the overall watch list system and how it can be strengthened.

The second review will examine all screening policies, technologies, and procedures related to air travel. We need to determine just how the suspect was able to bring dangerous explosives aboard an aircraft and what additional steps we can take to thwart future attacks.

Third, I've directed my national security team to keep up the pressure on those who would attack our country. We do not yet have all the answers about this latest attempt, but those who would slaughter innocent men, women, and children must know that the United States will more—do more than simply strengthen our defenses; we will continue to use every element of our national power to disrupt, to dismantle, and defeat the violent extremists who threaten us, whether they are from Afghanistan or Pakistan, Yemen or Somalia, or anywhere where they are plotting attacks against the U.S. homeland.

Finally, the American people should remain vigilant, but also be confident. Those plotting against us seek not only to undermine our security but also the open society and the values that we cherish as Americans. This incident, like several that have preceded it, demonstrates that an alert and courageous citizenry are far more resilient than an isolated extremist. As a nation, we will do everything in our power to protect our country. As Americans, we will never give in to fear or division; we will be guided by our hopes, our unity, and our deeply held values. That's who we are as Americans. That's what our brave men and women in uniform are standing up for as they spend the holidays in harm's way. And we will continue to do everything that we can to keep America safe in the new year and beyond. . . .

[Statements about Iran have been omitted.]

Thank you very much, everybody, and happy New Year.

SOURCE: U.S. Executive Office of the President. "Remarks on Improving Homeland Security in Kaneohe, Hawaii." *Daily Compilation of Presidential Documents* 2009, no. 01017 (December 28, 2009). www.gpo.gov/fdsys/pkg/DCPD-200901017/pdf/DCPD-200901017.pdf.

President Obama on Strengthening Air Security

December 29, 2009

Good morning. Yesterday I updated the American people on the immediate steps we took, the increased screening and security of air travel, to keep our country safe in the wake of the attempted terrorist attack on Christmas Day. And I announced two reviews, a review of our terrorist watch list system and a review of our air travel screening, so we can find out what went wrong, fix it, and prevent future attacks.

Those reviews began on Sunday and are now underway. Earlier today I issued the former [formal]* guidelines for those reviews and directed that preliminary findings be provided to the White House by this Thursday. It's essential that we diagnose the problems quickly and deal with them immediately.

Now, the more comprehensive, formal reviews and recommendations for improvement will be completed in the coming weeks, and I'm committed to working with Congress and our intelligence, law enforcement, and homeland security communities to take all necessary steps to protect the country.

I wanted to speak to the American people again today because some of this preliminary information that has surfaced in the last 24 hours raises some serious concerns. It's been widely reported that the father of the suspect in the Christmas incident

---

*White House correction.

warned U.S. officials in Africa about his son's extremist views. It now appears that weeks ago, this information was passed to a component of our intelligence community, but was not effectively distributed so as to get the suspect's name on a no-fly list.

There appears to be other deficiencies as well. Even without this one report, there were bits of information available within the intelligence community that could have and should have been pieced together. We've achieved much since 9/11 in terms of collecting information that relates to terrorists and potential terrorist attacks, but it's becoming clear that the system that has been in place for years now is not sufficiently up to date to take full advantage of the information we collect and the knowledge we have.

Had this critical information been shared, it could have been compiled with other intelligence and a fuller, clearer picture of the suspect would have emerged. The warning signs would have triggered red flags and the suspect would have never been allowed to board that plane for America.

Now, the professionalism of the men and women in our intelligence, counter-terrorism, and law enforcement and homeland security communities is extraordinary. They are some of the most hard-working, most dedicated Americans that I've ever met. In pursuit of our security here at home, they risk their lives, day in, day out, in this country and around the world.

Few Americans see their work, but all Americans are safer because of their successes. They have targeted and taken out violent extremists; they have disrupted plots and saved countless American lives; they are making real and daily progress in our mission to disrupt, dismantle, and defeat Al Qaida and other extremist networks around the world. And for this, every American owes them a profound and lasting debt of gratitude.

Moreover, as Secretary Napolitano has said, once the suspect attempted to take down Flight 253—after his attempt, it's clear that passengers and crew, our homeland security systems, and our aviation security took all appropriate actions. But what's also clear is this: When our Government has information on a known extremist and that information is not shared and acted upon as it should have been, so that this extremist boards a plane with dangerous explosives that could have cost nearly 300 lives, a systemic failure has occurred. And I consider that totally unacceptable.

The reviews I've ordered will surely tell us more. But what already is apparent is that there was a mix of human and systemic failures that contributed to this potential catastrophic breach of security. We need to learn from this episode and act quickly to fix the flaws in our system, because our security is at stake and lives are at stake.

I fully understand that even when every person charged with ensuring our security does what they are trained to do, even when every system works exactly as intended, there is still no 100 percent guarantee of success. Yet this should only compel us to work even harder, to be even more innovative and relentless in our efforts.

As President, I will do everything in my power to support the men and women in intelligence, law enforcement, and homeland security to make sure they've got the tools and resources they need to keep America safe. But it's also my job to ensure that our intelligence, law enforcement, and homeland security systems and the people in them are working effectively and held accountable. I intend to fulfill that responsibility and insist on accountability at every level.

That's the spirit guiding our reviews into the attempted attack on Christmas Day. That's the spirit that will guide all our efforts in the days and years ahead.

Thank you very much.

SOURCE: U.S. Executive Office of the President. "Remarks on Improving Homeland Security in Kaneohe, Hawaii." *Daily Compilation of Presidential Documents* 2009, no. 01019 (December 29, 2009). www.gpo.gov/fdsys/pkg/DCPD-200901019/html/DCPD-200901019.htm.

OTHER HISTORIC DOCUMENTS OF INTEREST

FROM PREVIOUS *HISTORIC DOCUMENTS*

Credits

Credits are a continuation from page iv.

"American Cancer Society Responds to Changes to USPSTF Mammography Guidelines." November 16, 2009. Reprinted by the permission of the American Cancer Society, Inc. from www.cancer.org. All rights reserved.

"Global Plan for Recovery and Reform." April 2, 2009. Crown Copyright 2009. Used with permission.

"Regents Approve Budget Plan, Student Fee Increases." November 19, 2009; "Students Protest Fees, Budget at UC Headquarters." November 23, 2009. Copyright © 2009 University of California. Reprinted with permission from the University of California Board of Regents.

"Rio de Janeiro Elected as the 2016 Host City." October 2, 2009. Copyright © 2009 International Olympic Committee. Reprinted with permission from the IOC.

"Security Council Condemns Assassinations of Guinea-Bissau's President, Army Chief; Calls on Government to Bring Those Responsible to Justice," March 3, 2009; "World Now at the Start of 2009 Influenza Season," June 11, 2009; "Security Council, Acting Unanimously, Condemns in Strongest Terms Democratic People's Republic of Korea Nuclear Test, Toughens Sanctions," June 12, 2009; "Iran: UN rights chief concerned over arrests, excessive force following polls," June 19, 2009; "General Assembly President Expresses Outrage at Coup D'Etat in Honduras, Says Crucial for World Community to 'Stand as One' in Condemnation," June 29, 2009; "Copenhagen United Nations Climate Change Conference ends with political agreement to cap temperature rise, reduce emissions and raise finance," December 19, 2009; "Decision -/CP.15 (Copenhagen Accord)," December 19, 2009. Copyright © 2009 United Nations. Reprinted with permission from the UN.

"Situation in Darfur, Sudan, in the Case of the Prosecutor v. Omar Hassan Ahmad al Bashir ('Omar al Bashir')." March 4, 2009. Copyright © 2009 ICC-CPI. Reprinted with permission from the ICC.

Cumulative Index, 2005–2009

*The years in **boldface** type in the entries indicate which volume is being cited.*

Nuclear weapons smuggling, radiation detection
technology, **2006** 118, 120–121, 124
Nuclear weapons testing
ban on, Comprehensive Test Ban Treaty, **2006** 94
in India, U.S.-India agreement on, **2006** 94–95
in North Korea, **2006** 583, 584
al-Nur, Abdul Wahid (rebel leader, Sudan), Darfur conflict
peace agreement, **2006** 499
Nutrition. *See also* Diet; Hunger
calorie needs, **2005** 9–10
carbohydrate recommendations, **2005** 12
federal dietary guidelines, **2005** 3–13
food group recommendations, **2005** 11–12
food guide pyramid, **2005** 3–5
trans fatty acids, consumption guidelines, **2005** 4, 12
Nuzzo, Jennifer, **2009** 468–469
NVSS. *See* National Vital Statistics System
NYSTEM. *See* New York State Stem Cell Science

O

Oakland (CA), crime in, **2007** 561
OAS. *See* Organization of American States
Obaidullah, Mullah (insurgent, Afghanistan), **2007** 443
Obama, Barack (U.S. president; D-Ill.). *See also* Elections;
Executive Orders
background issues of, **2008** 498
cabinet of, **2009** 25
closure of Guantánamo, **2008** 335–336; **2009** 31–38, 83,
225, 553
eulogy for Sen. Edward Kennedy, **2009** 378, 381–384
Fort Hood shooting and, **2009** 525, 527, 529–530
international reactions to his election, **2009** 635–636
inauguration and swearing in of, **2009** 23–26
National Security Act and, **2009** 315
Nobel Peace Prize and, **2009** 222, 635–645
speech at Cairo University on Muslim-American
relations, **2009** 219–229
trial of 9/11 masterminds in New York, **2009** 553–554
U.S. bid for 2016 Summer Olympic Games and, **2009**
478, 479
Obama, Barack—appointments and nominations
nomination of Sotomayor as Supreme Court justice,
2009 321
Obama, Barack—campaigns and elections
Democratic Party convention speech, **2006** 673
presidential candidate, **2006** 673; **2007** 297, 298, 306;
2008 8–9, 10–11, 519–522; **2009** 219–220
Obama, Barack—domestic and social policies
American Recovery and Reinvestment Act of 2009, **2009**
41, 49–50, 85–86, 598
bailout of automakers, **2008** 583; **2009** 82
benefits to same-sex partners of federal employees,
2009 143
call for executive pay caps, **2009** 61–66
Cash for Clunkers program of, **2009** 356–363
climate change, **2009** 443–444, 544, 654, 655, 656
credit card reform legislation, **2009** 182, 189–191
education issues, **2009** 90–91, 484, 486
Emergency Economic Stabilization Act of 2008,
2008 445
employment issues, **2009** 628–629
energy policies, **2009** 88–89
gun control, **2008** 266
hate crimes legislation, **2009** 503
lobbying rules of conduct, **2006** 267
fuel economy standards, **2009** 442, 443–444

medical marijuana, **2009** 495
new mammography guidelines, **2009** 562–563
offshore drilling, **2008** 412
stem cell research, **2009** 241
swine flu, **2009** 468–469
tobacco regulation, **2009** 209, 216–218
Obama, Barack—economic policies. *See also* American
Recovery and Reinvestment Act of 2009
Economic Stimulus Act of 2008, **2008** 44
U.S. economy and, **2008** 559; **2009** 81–82, 85–87, 91, 92,
157, 432
trade, **2009** 543
withdrawal from Iraq and, **2009** 105–106
Obama, Barack—educational policies
educational benefits for veterans, **2008** 188
Obama, Barack—foreign policy
Afghanistan, **2008** 394, 395; **2009** 83, 91, 220, 224–225,
544, 580, 618–619, 620, 621–625, 637–638
China, **2009** 545–546
Cuba, *libertad* and, **2008** 78–79
foreign travels of, **2009** 543–551
global outreach of, **2009** 636
Honduras political crisis and, **2009** 283, 285, 290–291
Iran's missile and nuclear programs and, **2009** 221, 227,
366, 369, 409, 410, 411, 545
Iraq, visit with Prime Minister al-Maliki, **2008** 363
Iraq War, **2008** 363, 364; **2009** 83, 91, 220, 225
Israel nuclear program, **2009** 221
Israel-Palestinian conflict, **2009** 221, 222, 225–227
Japan, **2009** 451, 544, 546–551
Middle East, **2009** 219–220, 222
missile defense program, **2009** 364, 365–366, 369–370
North Korea, **2009** 196, 545
nuclear weapons and, **2009** 221, 227, 365
Pakistan, **2009** 225, 513–521
piracy, **2009** 170
Russia
U.S.-Russian relations, **2009** 364–370, 544–545
view of Medvedev, **2008** 171
Six-Party Talks, **2008** 492
speech before a joint session of Congress on, **2009** 82
summit meetings
U.S.-Russia, **2009** 364–368
terrorism, **2009** 513, 665, 666, 667–671
timeline for ending Iraq War, **2009** 104–112, 220–21, 225
women's rights, **2009** 228
Obama, Barack—health care policies
health care reform, **2009** 89–90, 399–408, 533, 534,
535, 536
proposals, **2007** 587
Obama, Barack—presidential speeches, remarks, and
statements
2008 12–17, 523–526
2009 26–30, 64–66, 81–97, 107–112, 216–218, 222–229,
403–408, 621–625, 638–645
on Afghanistan, **2009** 618–619, 621–625
on election night, **2008** 523–526
on executive pay caps, **2009** 64–66
inaugural address, **2009** 26–30
before a joint session of Congress on health care, **2009**
81–97, 399–408
on Muslim-American relations, **2009** 219–229
on race in America, **2008** 12–17
on Iraq withdrawal timeline, **2009** 107–112
on tobacco regulation, **2009** 216–218
on winning the Nobel Peace Prize, **2009** 638–645

Wood, Robert (spokesperson, State Dept.), **2009** 374
Wood, Susan F. (assistant commissioner, FDA), **2005** 816–817
Woodrow Wilson International Center for Scholars, AIDS in Russia study, **2005** 54
Woodward, Robert ("Bob"; journalist), CIA leak case, **2005** 702, 704; **2007** 331
Woolsey, Lynn (D-Calif.), Iraq War troop withdrawal, calling for, **2005** 836
Wootan, Margo, on federal dietary guidelines, **2005** 5
Workplace, controlling secondhand smoke exposure, **2006** 363–364
World Anti-Doping Agency, **2005** 213; **2007** 718
World Bank. *See also* Wolfensohn, James D.; Wolfowitz, Paul D.; Zoellick, Robert B.
    Afghanistan narcotics trade, **2006** 51
    agriculture programs in Africa, **2007** 592–602
    Bosnia economic situation, **2005** 852
    creation and goals of, **2007** 247, 253–255
    development reports, **2007** 593–594
    Georgia (country) economic situation, **2008** 348
    global food crisis, **2008** 114, 116
    Honduras political crisis and, **2009** 283
    Iraq reconstruction, **2005** 717–718
    Latin America economic growth, **2005** 765
    London Summit on Global Economic Recovery, **2009** 164
    Multilateral Debt Relief Initiative, **2005** 407
    naming new presidents for, **2007** 249–250
    Palestinian economic aid, **2005** 34–35
    problems of, **2007** 250
    trade barriers and subsidies study, **2005** 411–412
World Court. *See* International Court of Justice
World Economic Forum (Davos), **2007** 606
"World Economic Outlook" (IMF report), **2007** 605, **2008** 418
World Food Programme. *See* United Nations World Food Programme (WFP)
World Health Organization (WHO)
    AIDS drug treatment, antiretroviral drugs (ARVs), **2005** 51
    avian flu outbreaks, **2005** 747
    childhood vaccine immunization program, **2006** 259
    flu pandemic
        global action plan conference, **2005** 750
        preparing for, **2005** 750
        swine flu and, **2009** 175, 176, 177, 179–181, 467, 468, 469
    HIV, **2007** 130, 133–135
    HIV vaccine study in Thailand, **2009** 459, 462, 463
    male circumcision, **2007** 130, 133–135
    new mammography guidelines, **2009** 569
    Tobacco Free Initiative, **2006** 350
World Meteorological Organization (WMO), global warming reports, **2005** 926; **2006** 619; **2007** 691
World Stem Cell Hub, **2005** 321
World Trade Center. *See also* September 11 attacks
    bombing in 1993, **2009** 552
    rebuilding and victims memorial, **2006** 182
World Trade Organization (WTO)
    Cancún trade talks collapse, **2005** 409
    customs blocs and, **2009** 365
    Doha Round (Development Agenda), **2005** 410, 411
        London Summitt on Global Economic Recovery and, **2009** 165
        resumption of talks, **2006** 587
        suspension of talks, **2006** 424–429

Hong Kong talks, **2005** 411
membership requests
    for Iran, U.S. objections, **2005** 593; **2006** 214
    for Russia, **2006** 202, 205
Seattle meeting (Millennium Round), **2005** 409
suspension of trade talks, **2006** 424–429
World Vision Australia, **2008** 175
World War II, Japanese Yasukuni Shrine war criminal memorial, **2006** 583
World wide web. *See* Internet
WorldCom
    fraud investigation, **2006** 239
    retirement fund losses, **2005** 201
Wright, Jeremiah, Jr. (former church pastor, U.S.), **2008** 10–11, 14–16
WTO. *See* World Trade Organization
Wurzelbacher, Joe ("Joe, the Plumber"), **2008** 499, 521
Wyatt, Watson, retirement plans study, **2005** 202
Wyden, Ron (D-Ore.), on Negroponte national intelligence director nomination, **2005** 253
Wyoming. *See also* Yellowstone National Park
    primaries (2008), **2007** 298

X

Xi Jinping (Politburo member, China), **2007** 287
Xu Guangyu (researcher), **2009** 196

Y

Yakovlev, Alexander, UN oil-for-food program scandal, **2005** 235
Yanukovich, Viktor F. (presidential candidate, Ukraine), **2005** 65
Yar'Adua, Alhaji Umaru Musa (chairman, ECOWAS), **2009** 124
Yar'Adua, Umaru (president, Nigeria), **2007** 266–272
Yassin, Ali Mohamed Osman (minister of justice, Sunda), Darfur human rights violations, **2005** 516
al-Yawar, Ghazi, Iraq interim government, **2005** 944–945
Yazid (terror suspect), linked to al-Qaida anthrax program, **2006** 519–520
Yekhanurov, Yuri (acting prime minister, Ukraine), **2005** 68–69
Yellowstone National Park, snowmobile regulation, **2006** 483–484
Yeltsin, Boris N. (president, Russia), **2007** 62, 63
Yemen, terrorism and, **2009** 665
Yingling, Edward L. (head, American Bankers Association), **2009** 184
Yom Kippur War (1973), **2008** 182
Yongyuth Tiyapairat (politician, Thailand), **2008** 550
Yonhap News Agency (South Korea), **2009** 196
Yoon Deok-min, **2009** 196–197
York, Jerome B., General Motors management, **2006** 296
Young, C. W. ("Bill") (R-Fla.), American Recovery and Reinvestment Act of 2009, **2009** 41–42, 44, 48–49
Young, Don (R-Alaska), punitive damages for the *Exxon Valdez* oil spill and, **2008** 258
Youth, Helping America's Youth Initiative, **2006** 34. *See also* Children; Teenagers
Yudof, Mark (president, University of California system), **2009** 590, 592, 593
Yugoslavia (former). *See also* Bosnia; Bosnia and Herzegovina; Croatia; Macedonia; Montenegro; Serbia; Slovenia
    background and history of, **2008** 69
    political protests, **2005** 43
    political situation, **2005** 64

Miami Dade College
Kendall Campus Library
11011 Southwest 104th Street
Miami, FL 33176